A Nature Guide to Ontario

Winifred (Cairns) Wake

John Cartwright, Anne Ch̶ ̶Martin
Parker, *Associate Editors*

From Hudson Bay to Pelee Island, from Rainy River to the Quebec border, Ontario offers a rich variety of experiences for nature-lovers of all ages and interests. *A Nature Guide to Ontario* showcases more than six hundred of the best sites for viewing the many forms of plant and animal life found across the province. All sites are open to the general public, most are easily accessible, and a surprising number are located in or near the province's biggest cities.

The book is divided into seven regions, and sites are listed under county, district, or municipality. Entries contain instructions on how to reach sites, descriptions of the major landscape and habitat features, information about typical as well as important or unusual animals and plants to be found at the site, and an address to contact for more information. Introductory chapters give an overview of Ontario's natural history and its rich and diverse plant and animal life. The book also discusses environmental concerns, offers tips on how to get the most out of an outing, and lists the 'top ten' nature sites in Ontario. There are lists of useful addresses and references, a site index, and an extensive glossary.

This volume is a project of the Federation of Ontario Naturalists, whose affiliates and individual members have contributed to the book. *A Nature Guide to Ontario* is an invaluable reference for all who want to experience and enjoy the best of Ontario's natural areas and wildernesses.

WINIFRED (CAIRNS) WAKE lives in London, Ontario, and is a member of the Federation of Ontario Naturalists. She writes a nature column for the *London Free Press* and a column on endangered species for *Nature Canada*.

FEDERATION OF ONTARIO NATURALISTS

The Federation of Ontario Naturalists (FON), established in 1931, is a provincially based, non-governmental charitable organization which protects and increases awareness of Ontario's natural areas and wildlife.

The FON currently represents 15,000 members and a network of 80 local groups – 63 community-based naturalists' clubs and 17 associated groups. The FON is governed by a Board of Directors that represents the individual members, naturalists' clubs, and associated groups.

The FON is Ontario's leading voice in promoting the preservation of wetland habitats, the creation and management of parks, protection for Ontario's rare, threatened, and endangered species, and responsible forest management. The FON publishes *Seasons* magazine, produces a range of environmental education resources for schools and youth groups, and has an extensive program of trips, tours, and summer camps. As well, over the past 30 years, the FON has assembled the province's largest private nature-reserve system.

For more information on the FON, and to inquire about membership, please contact us at: 355 Lesmill Road, Don Mills, Ont M3B 2W8, or call 416-444-8419 or 1-800-440-2366, or FAX 416-444-9866.

A Nature Guide to Ontario

FEDERATION OF ONTARIO NATURALISTS

edited by

Winifred (Cairns) Wake

associate editors:
John Cartwright, Anne Champagne,
Kathy Parker, and Martin Parker

UNIVERSITY OF TORONTO PRESS
Toronto Buffalo London

© University of Toronto Press Incorporated 1997
Toronto Buffalo London
Printed in Canada

ISBN 0-8020-2755-5 (cloth)
ISBN 0-8020-6802-2 (paper)

Printed on acid-free paper

Canadian Cataloguing in Publication Data

Main entry under title:

A nature guide to Ontario

Rev. ed. of: A naturalist's guide to Ontario.
Includes bibliographical references and index.
ISBN 0-8020-2755-5 (bound)   ISBN 0-8020-6802-2 (pbk.)

1. Natural History – Ontario – Guidebooks.
I. Wake, Winifred Cairns.   II. Federation of Ontario
Naturalists.   III. Title: A naturalist's guide to Ontario.

QH106.2.05N39 1996   508.713   C96-931728-X

University of Toronto Press acknowledges the financial assistance to
its publishing program of the Canada Council and the Ontario Arts
Council.

Contents

Foreword

In March 1956 Drs Carl and Aileen Cline, members of the McIlwraith Ornithological Club of London, went on a trip to Florida and took with them a copy of Olin Sewall Pettingill's *Guide to Bird Finding* and found it a great help in locating birds in that state. On return to London, they attended one of the Audubon Screen Tours sponsored by the McIlwraith Club on April 16, 1956. The subject of the film was 'Penguin Summer,' with commentary by Dr Pettingill.

After the meeting a coffee party was held in the YMCA in London attended by Dr and Mrs Pettingill and the executive of the McIlwraith Club. In the course of the conversation, the idea was bandied about that it would be a good idea to have a naturalist's guide to Ontario. The Pettingills were most cooperative and declared that they would be glad to see Pettingill's guide used as a model. Thus we can say that the idea for a naturalist's guide to Ontario originated over cups of coffee in London in 1956.

The proposal for production of the guide was put before the executive of the Federation of Ontario Naturalists and was thoroughly discussed over the next two years. At its meeting of April 19, 1958, the FON executive appointed a committee composed of Aileen Cline, Bruce Falls, Fred Helleiner, W.W. Judd (chairman), Miss A.E. LeWarne, Frank Pammett, James Soper, and Walter Tovell to oversee the production.

After six years of work by the committee the first edition of *A Naturalist's Guide to Ontario* was produced in 1964.

Thirty years have now gone by since the first appearance of the guide and great changes have taken place in the natural landscape of Ontario. Many of the natural areas alluded to in the guide have been transformed by development or have had their points of access much revised. The federal, provincial, and municipal governments, private organizations, and even individuals have been active in adding new parks, conservation areas, and other protected lands.

In view of these changes it is appropriate that the Federation of Ontario Naturalists has seen fit to produce a revision of its guide. The inclusion of the sites of interest in seven groups draws attention to the great diversity of landscapes to be explored in Ontario from the south shores of Hudson and James bays to the northerly limits of the Great Lakes.

With this guide in hand or available in the glove compartment of the car the practised naturalist in Ontario and visitors from elsewhere will be well equipped to explore what the world of nature has to offer in the province.

W.W. Judd

Acknowledgments

The Federation of Ontario Naturalists gratefully acknowledges the financial contribution of the Ontario Ministry of Natural Resources, Wildlife Policy Branch, to the production of this book.

A Nature Guide to Ontario is the successor to *A Naturalist's Guide to Ontario*, published in 1964 and edited by W.W. Judd and J.M. Speirs. Thanks are extended to all contributors to the earlier work.

This book represents a collective effort by naturalists from across the province. In 1990, Anne Champagne undertook the monumental task of assembling background information and drafts. In 1993, one year after Anne had left the province, a committee consisting of Winifred Wake, Kathy Parker, Martin Parker, and John Cartwright set about reworking the material into its final form. Help came from a multitude of volunteers, who have been active in all stages of the book's development. They represent the ranks of individual naturalists, organized naturalist and other groups, FON affiliates and activists, and staff from Canadian Museum of Nature, Canadian Geoscience Information Centre, Parks Canada, Ontario Ministry of Natural Resources, conservation authorities, and allied agencies. These people have been involved in everything from visiting sites, checking directions, and verifying information to researching, writing, revising, and reviewing. Some played small roles while others contributed huge amounts of time and expertise, as well as out-of-pocket expenses. To all the knowledgeable and enthusiastic naturalists who laboured so diligently to put this book together, the Federation of Ontario Naturalists expresses deep appreciation. This book is indeed yours.

Every effort has been made to make the following list of individuals who contributed as complete as possible but, with the lapse of time between editors, some names may have been missed. If so, the Federation of Ontario Naturalists apologizes. Although you are unnamed, your contributions are just as appreciated.

Dave Aikenhead, Bob Alexander, Allan Anderson, Muriel Andreae, Andrew Armitage, Faith Avis, Brenda Axon, Danny Bacon, Margaret Bain, Diana Banville, Rick Battson, Tony Beck, Tom Beechey, Gerry Bennett, Hazel Bird, Ted Bodfish, Mireille Boudreau, Bob Bowles, Jane Bowles, Irene Bowman, Roger Boyd, Bob Bracken, Michael Bradstreet, Dave Brewer, Don Britton, Lorraine Brown, Dan Brunton, Graham Bryan, Barbara Burkhardt, Michael Cadman, Gordon Cameron, Molly Campbell, Bonnie Carey, Margaret Carney, Geoff Carpentier, Barbara Cavin, Susan Chapman-Bossence, Elvira Chelchowski, Ted Cheskey, Gerry Clements, Scott Connop, Terry Crabe, Donald Craig, Mark Cressman, Bill Crins, Sharon Critchley, Don Cuddy, Ed Czerwinski, Stephen Darbyshire, Bob Davidson, Eva Davis, Peter Davis, Mike Dawdy, Sue D'Eon, Barbara Dillon, Dave Dillon, Joanne Doucette, Bruce Duncan, Brian Durell, Paul Eagles, Gord Eason, Dave Elder, Ken Elliott, Joel Ellis, Nicholas Escott, Diane Fahselt, Jim Fairchild, John Fallis, Karin Fawthrop, Donald Fraser, Mary Gartshore, Carol German, Joanne Girvan, Clive Goodwin, Bob Gray, Bob Gummer, Paul Harpley, Al Harris, John Harvey, Audrey Heagy, Mary Ellen Hebb, Fred Helleiner, Leo Heyens, Theo Hofmann, Margo Holt, Dale Hoy, Helen Inch, Spencer Inch, Olive Ireland, Beth Jefferson, Joe Johnson, Vicky Johnston, Scott Jones, W.W. Judd, James Kamstra, Rosemary Kelley, Harry Kerr, Will Kershaw, Lisa King, Donald Kirk, Malcolm Kirk, Richard Knapton, Philip Kor, Ken Koski, Erica Kraayenbrink, Steve LaForest, Larry Lamb, Cathie Lauzon, Betty Learmouth, Dan Lebedyk, Chris Lemieux, Dave Lemkay, Paul Lennox, Dena Lewis, Kathy Lindsay, Tom Lobb, Chris Lompart, John Lounds, Jean MacDonald, Nelson Maher,

Garth Mailman, Frank Mariotti, Dan Martin, Dave Martin, Virgil Martin, Viki Mather, Paul Maycock, Ted McDonald, Steve McGovern, Irene McIlveen, Suzanne McInnis, Barbara McKean, John McKeeman, Eunice McKishnie, John McKishnie, Margaret McLaren, Ariel McLean, Dave McLeod, Greg Meredith, Diane Mew, George Meyers, Chris Michener, Peter Middleton, Gavin Miller, Victor Miller, Ian Montagnes, David Moore, Bob Morris, David Moseley, Ted Mosquin, Gail Muir, Sylfest Muldal, Kathy Munk, Trish Murphy, Jeff Nadir, Lisa Nevar, Terry Noble, Lionel Normand, Todd Norris, Joan O'Donnell, Steve O'Donnell, Michael Oldham, Susan O'Neill, Dan Paleczny, Cheryl Pearce, Andy Penikett, Shirley Peruniak, Dean Phoenix, Ron Pittaway, Ed Poropat, Paul Pratt, Paul Prevett, Cathy Quinlan, Gary Rahn, Suzanne Rancourt, Ron Reid, Brad Reive, Jim Richards, John Riley, Anne Robertson, Louise Robillard, Sam Rosa, Kayo Roy, Jim Rule, Mike Runtz, Dennis Rupert, Sarah Rupert, Maureen Ryan, Doug Sadler, Vicky Sahanatien, Cobina Sauder, Steve Sauder, Don Scallen, Nancy Scott, Ron Scovell, Judie Shore, Helen Smith, Norman Smith, Patricia Smith, Rob Snetsinger, Terry Sprague, Mark Stabb, Bob Stewart, William Stewart, Midge Strickland, Donald Sutherland, Ric Symmes, Sandy Symmes, Chris Tanglis, Brian Taylor, Kim Taylor, Bill Thompson, John Thompson, Adam Thomson, Sheila Thomson, Dorothy Tiedje, Ron Tozer, Pat Tripp, Tim Tully, Jan Vandermeer, Peter van Dijken, Doug van Hemessen, Steve Varga, David Wake, Tony Walker, Mike Walters, Gladys Walwork, Beverly Wannick, Jocelyn Webber, Peter Weilandt, Charles Wheable, Bob Whittam, Mark Wiercinski, Gary Wilkins, Michael Williams, Jean Williamson, Audrey Wilson, Bruce Winterbon, Allen Woodliffe, Maureen Wraight, Liz Yerex, Mary Young, Bob Yukich, Craig Zimmerman.

Photographs appear thanks to the generosity of nature photographers Bill Caulfeild-Browne, Mary E. Gartshore, Dr H.G. Hedges, Michael Patrikeev, Joseph Pearce, Jim Richards, Ric Symmes, Doug van Hemessen, and P. Allen Woodliffe, the Richmond Hill Naturalists, and the FON library.

Preface

In the three decades since the publication of *A Naturalist's Guide to Ontario*, Ontario's wilderness and natural areas have been steadily shrinking. Those that remain are under increasing pressure. Yet the need for contact with wild places is greater than ever. Urbanites, weary of life in a totally human environment, are reaching beyond fabricated cities and carefully controlled farmland to seek a connection with a more natural world.

This book, a complete revision of the earlier work, is a directory to natural areas in Ontario where there are significant natural features or concentrations of wildlife. The change in title to *A Nature Guide to Ontario* reflects a shift to include all who enjoy wild spaces, not just serious naturalists. Those who have contributed to this volume hope that the introductions offered in its pages to places of natural beauty and abundance will elicit in readers an interest in protecting these pockets of wild nature.

This guidebook is not intended to be a comprehensive directory of every natural area in the province; there simply isn't space. Nor is there space to go into a great deal of depth on each area. Some of your favourite spots may not be here. Perhaps they are too fragile to bear the pressure of too many visitors. Or access may be too difficult. Or they might be on private land.

The more than 600 sites described present a sampling of the more interesting and, for the most part, easily accessible natural areas across the province. Each site has its own set of reasons for being included. Some provide small oases of wildlife habitat

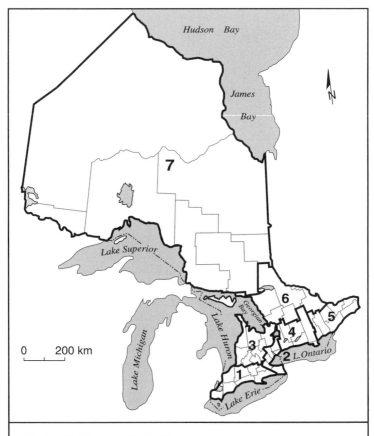

1. North Shore of Lake Erie
2. Golden Horseshoe
3. Lake Huron to Georgian Bay Lobe
4. North Shore of Lake Ontario
5. St Lawrence and Lower Ottawa River valleys
6. Manitoulin to Upper Ottawa River
7. Northern Ontario

Figure 1.   Counties, regional municipalities, and districts in Ontario, grouped according to the geographic regions described in this book.

within large urban centres, while others protect features that are significant on a provincial scale. Many will offer trails and other facilities but some will require greater effort to enjoy. Quite often, the less developed the site, the more significant its natural features are. For example, within the provincial parks system, nature reserves offer few or no amenities, whereas natural environment and recreation parks routinely provide a variety of facilities.

Regular users of this book will soon identify certain sites as personal favourites, to be revisited frequently throughout the seasons. Check 'The Top Ten' list for a sampling of the all-time best places to enjoy nature in Ontario, as selected by contributors to *A Nature Guide to Ontario*.

Entries provide a brief overview of each site and its special features, often pointing out some of the typical or unusual species found there. Where possible, readers are directed to additional sources of information. It is recommended that these be consulted; they can generally provide much more detailed information about the natural features, as well as the hours and seasons of operation. Also, information that was up-to-date at press time may not remain so. Addresses are normally given at the end of an entry, but one that applies to several sites may be listed at the end or beginning of a group of entries, or even at the back of the book, where those for all conservation authorities have been placed.

Entries have been organized by county, regional municipality, or district and grouped by geographic region (see Figure 1). The written directions and a provincial highway map should serve to locate most sites. It is recommended that the local Ministry of Natural Resources office (check blue pages in the phone book) be contacted before travelling the canoe routes or to remote locales. Place-names used in this book largely conform to the listings in the *Gazetteer of Canada* (1988).

Keep in mind that provincial and national parks and conservation areas frequently have user fees. It is illegal to remove plants, animals, fossils, or other natural or historical objects from provincial and national parks. Similar respect for the natural environment should also be practised elsewhere, including at all sites described in this volume. Some areas listed in the book are hunted in season. To avoid run-ins with hunters or trappers, check with the Ministry of Natural Resources for hunting and trapping seasons, especially in provincial wildlife areas.

Common species names are used throughout the book. For the most part, these have been derived from the following sources: wildflowers, Newcomb (1977); trees, Hosie (1979); shrubs, Soper and Heimburger (1982); ferns, Cobb (1963); mammals, Dobbyn (1994); birds, FON checklist (1994) and James (1991); reptiles and amphibians, FON checklist (1988); fish, Mandrak and Crossman (1992); and butterflies, Holmes et al (1991). A list of common and scientific name equivalents appears at the back of the book. Scientific names come from the same sources, with the exception of plants, which largely follow Morton and Venn (1990).

Much of the material in this book was submitted by members of naturalist groups across the province. Anyone interested in going beyond simple enjoyment of the natural world can tap into a wealth of natural history knowledge in these groups. To learn more about wildflowers, birds, or the subtleties of Cecropia Moth mating rituals, contact a local group or the Federation of Ontario Naturalists. Further information and addresses are available from the FON (see address at back of book).

Another important source of information about Ontario's natural areas and wildlife is the Ministry of Natural Resources, Wildlife Policy Branch, also a major contributor to this volume. MNR staff may be able to suggest additional sites of interest not listed here. Naturalist staff at municipal, provincial, and national parks, conservation authorities, and nature centres can provide further insight. Lists of useful resources and addresses are found at the back of the book.

In addition, residents of rural Ontario often have insights into the natural features of the local landscape that they are willing to share with visitors. A stop at a rural store, restaurant, or gas station, and a few questions asked, may lead to more suggestions of good places for enjoying nature. Patronizing local businesses also helps to garner support for the protection of natural landscapes by the people who live in these areas. Topographical maps (1:250,000) are useful for exploring areas that are off the beaten track, especially in regions of sparse population.

The Federation of Ontario Naturalists sincerely hopes this nature guide will be the beginning of many wonderful excursions to wetlands, woodlands, and other wild places. May these pages introduce you to the pleasures of experiencing the lyrical song of a Pine Warbler from a few metres away. And may you come to know how much richer the planet is for its patches of brilliant blue gentians and Great Spangled Fritillary butterflies.

Postscript

FON is eager to hear how you enjoyed this book. Write and tell us about your experiences. Maybe you had a tactile encounter with mud while exploring a swamp! Or overheard the hoots of courting owls in a wintery woodland. Perhaps you were overwhelmed by the perfume of an opening flower. Or dazzled by the brilliant colours of *Xanthoria* lichens on a rainy day.

Maybe you have suggestions for spots you'd like to see included in future editions. If so, tell us about them. And (heaven forbid) we'd even like to know if we've made any errors.

Ontario's Species at Risk

Ontario has a rich variety of species and habitats. In this volume every effort has been made to identify sites of interest, drawing on the knowledge of naturalists and experts from across the province. Some sites, however, contain species or habitats that are particularly susceptible to human disturbance. The intentional and unintentional actions of people can have a serious impact. Yet, the Federation of Ontario Naturalists recognizes that there is a need to make people aware of significant natural areas and species in order to ensure that these sites are appreciated and protected.

In editing the nature guide, an attempt has been made to balance the desire to inform readers of the most significant features or species present at a given site and their need for protection. In preparing site accounts, particular attention has been devoted to determining the appropriateness of naming species designated as 'endangered,' 'threatened,' or 'rare/vulnerable' by the Ontario Ministry of Natural Resources and the Committee on the Status of Endangered Wildlife in Canada (COSEWIC). Likewise, consideration has been given to species noted as rare on a global or provincial basis by the Ontario Natural Heritage Information Centre, and to those species that may be particularly at risk from a whole range of consumptive wildlife users, some of whom follow no code of conduct. (Examples could come from the ranks of the unethical among butterfly collectors, practitioners of alternative medicine, herbalists, wildflower gardeners, bonsai enthusiasts, and dealers in exotic pets.) Some species have increased vulnerability to disturbance at certain seasons or stages of their life cycle or when using certain portions of their habitat (for example, hibernating snakes and bats and colonial nesting birds), and rare and attractive wildflowers and fragile habitats are particularly susceptible to the impact of trampling feet (photographers and curious naturalists, please tread carefully!).

Thus, in selecting information to include in each site account, species have been considered individually by site, and care has been taken to avoid mentioning those that have a high degree of sensitivity at that site. In general, at-risk species are noted only at large sites (usually a minimum of 100 ha, sometimes much more). Exceptions are sometimes made; for example, the Eastern Massasauga rattlesnake is mentioned in the upper Bruce Peninsula, where there is a locally healthy population. And Prickly-pear Cactus is included in the account of Point Pelee National Park, where it has already been well publicized and has some level of protection. So that readers may realize that a particular site harbours significant species, the text frequently indicates that rare or uncommon species are present.

As funding for provincial parks and other protected areas is reduced, it will become increasingly important for those visiting natural areas to assume the role of guardians of these sites. This may be accomplished by education – by speaking to other visitors to increase their awareness of the significance of natural areas, or by gently advising small children why they should not be picking bouquets of trilliums. At times, guardians may also need to report illegal activities to appropriate authorities. Only through vigilance and persistence on the part of *all* those who care will Ontario's rich legacy of natural habitats and their countless wild residents be preserved.

To obtain up-to-date lists of those species of plants, birds, mammals, reptiles, amphibians, fish, and insects that are considered to be 'endangered,' 'threatened,' and 'rare/vulnerable' in Ontario, contact: Ontario Ministry of Natural Resources (provincial list); Canadian Wildlife Service (national list); World Wildlife Fund Canada (national list). Addresses are given at the back of the book.

The Environmental Backdrop

Thirty-one years have passed since this guide was first issued – a full generation of naturalists and ramblers have garnered inspiration for their explorations from its pages. It has been a busy generation; a time of travel into space, of acid rain and global warming, of dwindling rainforest and species extinction. Looking back over the pages of a generation ago, I wonder how many of those natural areas so lovingly described are now gone, and how many more face an uncertain future.

One thing is certain – we know a great deal more now than we did 31 years ago about the state of our natural environment, and the threats facing it. A host of natural area surveys at both the provincial and municipal levels, atlases of breeding birds and herpetofauna and mammals, environmental assessments of a range of projects – all have added to an impressive knowledge base of our ecosystem and how it works.

We have made great strides in other areas as well, from a system of provincial parks to the concept of sustainable development to a massive growth in public support for environmental causes. Increasingly, we have come to accept that our tiny blue planet functions as a system, and that our future existence is inexorably tied to the health of that system.

And yet, the warning signs of system malfunction are clear and urgent. As I write, fully 236 species of wild plants and animals are designated 'at risk' in Canada. At least a dozen songbirds are showing substantial population declines, related to loss of both winter habitats in the tropics and summer habitats here. Great Lakes fish with cancerous tumours have become commonplace; Loggerhead Shrikes and Spotted Turtles increasingly rare.

The underlying causes are far from clear, but without question habitat loss, the effects of synthetic chemicals, and the pressures of human overpopulation loom large in the equation. For the most part, these pressures result not from big decisions on megaprojects, but from the cumulative toll of the millions of little decisions made by all of us. The overall effect may be staggering, but we still lose natural habitats one hectare at a time.

To be effective in conserving nature, then, we must act to influence those millions of little decisions, one at a time. That is where you come in. Put simply, all those who value nature also have a responsibility to work towards its protection. On this crowded planet, natural history is no longer a spectator sport. For our own sake, and the sake of the species that share the living ecosystem, your involvement is vital.

Such involvement does not mean that you must spend your time climbing smokestacks or defying bulldozers, necessary though those roles may be. You can be involved as a landowner, as a far-sighted steward of natural habitats. Or as a consumer, weighing the environmental costs of products before you buy. Or as a recreationist, making sure that your activities do not lead to destruction of habitat or wildlife. Or even as an FON member, by something as simple as a regular donation to support advocacy programs.

Influencing the little decisions means also that naturalists have a responsibility to speak out on behalf of natural environments, especially at the local level, where decisions are often made. Today, your message is likely to meet a sympathetic response; build on that response to look for positive solutions, and to cultivate alliances. Go beyond just reacting to brush fires; work with your community to develop strategies for green corridors and more natural parks.

Every one of us can be involved too as an educator, especially in an informal sense. People cannot miss what they have never experienced. How can we expect a city child, or a city adult, to understand the value of wildlife and wild places they have never seen? If you do nothing else, share some of the wonderful spots outlined in this guide with others, for such sharing nurtures commitment to a more responsible future.

If the past quarter-century is any guide, our generation and the next will be pivotal in determining humankind's relationship to our shared global environment. We face either a massive decline in our legacy of wild species and habitats, or a massive effort to avert that decline. Ontario will be no exception; here, too, we will face difficult choices if our diverse family of wild creatures and places is to be maintained.

E.O. Wilson, the editor of *Biodiversity*, has written that 'the loss of genetic and species diversity by the destruction of natural habitats ... is the folly our descendants are least likely to forgive us.' Avoiding that folly begins with people like you, the people who buy and use this book. Its pages document the best of Ontario's natural heritage; please help ensure that a generation hence, it does not merely chronicle what used to be.

Ron Reid
environmental consultant and writer and
former staff environmentalist at FON
February 1995

Editor's Note
As this book goes to press, natural areas in Ontario are facing difficult times. Provincial funding cuts initiated following the 1995 election will cause some parks and conservation areas to be closed. Conservation authorities and municipalities may sell some of their lands, including natural areas that were formerly protected.

The full effects of these cuts could not be anticipated at the time of the publisher's deadline in December 1995. Thus, as you explore the areas described in this volume, you may find gates that are closed, interpretive centres without staff, or activities and developments taking place that are inconsistent with traditional park values.

Areas that were assumed to be protected 'forever' are at risk once again. Now, as never before, naturalists and all others who care about our province's wildlife and natural areas are being challenged to take action to protect our natural heritage.

The Top Ten

From a survey of some of the province's most travelled and seasoned naturalists, we bring you a purely subjective view of the province's top ten hotspots for naturalist pursuits. For more details, see the relevant write-ups. These are listed in order from northern to southern Ontario, not according to which is the 'best.' Here are their picks, and their comments.

1 Hudson Bay Lowland. The arctic tundra at Cape Henrietta Maria is 'the ultimate wilderness in Ontario.' Where else in the province can you see whales, seals, Polar Bears, saltwater species ...? It retains a sense of mystery. Moosonee is great for fall shorebirds.

2 Rainy River and Lake of the Woods. For prairie species not found (in abundance) anywhere else in the province ... Marbled Godwit, Yellow Rail, Piping Plover ...

3 North Shore of Lake Superior. For the sheer scale and beauty of it all. The Goulais River beach ridge and swale complex west of Sault Ste Marie is one interesting spot; another is the Pic River sand dunes at the mouth of the Pic River. And, of course, there's the brooding grandeur of the Sleeping Giant.

4 Bruce Peninsula. It is 'botanically incredible,' with many good birding locales: Sandhill Crane, northern-breeding warblers ...; Cabot Head for fantastic scenery.

5 Luther Marsh. Southern Ontario 'wilderness.' An oasis within farmland. Great for water birds.

6 Presqu'ile. For the birds, of course. Scores of migrants flock here; colonies of terns and herons; excellent shorebird habitat; interesting wildflowers; boreal nesting species; extensive marsh.

7 Niagara River. Fort Erie to Niagara-on-the-Lake, late October to March, has more species of gulls than any other place in the world, plus shorebirds and waterfowl.

8 Long Point. Landbird and waterfowl migration; reptile and amphibian hotspot. Internationally recognized wetland.

9 Walpole Island. Internationally significant wetlands, perhaps the most significant left on the Great Lakes. Finest remaining tallgrass prairie on the continent. (**Permission must be sought** from the Walpole Island First Nation to enter on their land.)

10 Point Pelee. Point Pelee is one of the finest places in North America for watching bird migration. A chorus of spring migrants gathers here in May, cerulean blue, vibrant yellow, and chestnut coloured warblers – a painter's palate of colours awash among the sprouting trees.

Let it be said that there were many more areas mentioned as favourites than show in this list. They ranged from Rondeau to Algonquin, from Temagami to the north channel of Lake Huron.

Getting the Most out of Your Excursion

An interaction with nature can take many forms. How much you allow your senses to experience determines how much you will get out of your contact with the natural world. Smelling, listening, and watching can all lead to unforgettable discoveries. Anyone who has heard a loon calling on a calm moonlit night can attest to that. It is sometimes surprising how close to home you can experience such things. A clump of grass beside a park bench might reveal a butterfly emerging from its chrysalis, if only one's senses are tuned to notice the event. In the long run, nature always rewards patience and determination.

What to Take

When setting off on an outdoor excursion, a small backpack is useful for carrying items such as extra clothing, lunch, and a water bottle. If your purpose is to experience and enjoy the outdoors as is, that may be sufficient. But many people soon become curious and want to learn the name of the pretty yellow wildflower or to know who is making that peculiar call from the thicket.

If your wish is to understand more about the natural world, you may choose to carry one or more field guides to identification or behaviour. Many people begin with a bird or flower book. Some of the most popular field guides are listed at the back of this book. To help you select which one is best for you, discuss your needs with someone from a naturalist group in your area.

Equipment, though not necessary for enjoying nature, can nevertheless contribute to the pleasure of the experience. In addition to their usefulness for observing birds, binoculars can be reversed and used as hand lenses for looking at pistils and stamens of flowers and beetle antennae segments. Because binoculars and telescopes are costly items, it is wise to consult widely before deciding on a purchase. Again, members of naturalist groups are a good source of advice.

A notebook and pencil tucked into your pack will allow you to jot down pleasant memories to savour later.

Finally, it is wise to become knowledgeable about health and safety in regard to outdoor activities. Local health agencies and Ministry of Natural Resources officials can provide information on issues of concern within a local area. For information on Lyme disease contact Lyme-Borreliosis Support Group of Ontario, 365 St David St S, Fergus, Ont, N1M 2L7 (send a stamped, self-addressed envelope for a free brochure or $5.00 for more detailed information).

A Wildlife Watching Ethic

Visitors to Ontario's natural areas are encouraged to develop a respectful relationship with nature. Wherever possible, avoid damage to vegetation by staying on designated trails. The best method of observing wildlife is to watch from a distance, then approach slowly and quietly. It places a great deal of stress on birds and animals if you approach their eggs or young, and scaring a bird off the nest leaves the eggs exposed to cold, rain, heat, and predators.

It is illegal to keep native animals as pets. In most cases, birds that fall out of their nests and baby animals that appear to be abandoned are still being cared for and fed by their parents. Caring for orphaned wildlife is an intensive, 24-hour-per-day job and, if the animal survives, it is unlikely that it can be reintroduced back into the wild. Most native wildlife species do not make suitable pets.

Handling of frogs, salamanders, and fish removes the protective mucous and puts salt and the chemicals from your sunscreen and insect repellent directly onto their skin or scales. These chemicals are harmful to insects and spiders too. Try watching butterflies through your binoculars. If you peek under a rock or log, be sure to put it back exactly where you found it.

Avoid touching wildflowers and mushrooms since the salt from your hands will transfer to the plant, making it a tasty treat for rodents, rabbits, and deer. Leave the surrounding vegetation intact when photographing flowers.

Experiencing the Seasons

Of the four seasons that visit Ontario annually, the natural features of some are better known and appreciated than others. Winter, in particular, is often neglected, but so too are late fall and early spring, by reputation times of chilly drabness. These so-called off-seasons have much of interest and beauty to offer to anyone prepared to explore (and no biting insects!). Many of the areas listed in this book can be visited year-round, whether by foot or on cross-country skis or snowshoes, including even parks and conservation areas when the gates are closed. Check with local authorities for current policies. Readers are encouraged to become acquainted with the natural world in all its seasons.

What follows is a short journey into the seasons, drawing on the predictable patterns of an unpredictable nature. It is intended to stir the imagination with a few typical settings, and suggest ways to experience each season to its fullest.

Fall, the season for red sumacs, yellow Tamaracks, spiralling Broad-winged Hawks, and confusing warblers on their way south, is regarded as a time of preparation for the winter ahead. It is also a time when many organisms attain peaks of activity. Goldenrods and asters bloom in the fall, Common Snapping Turtles hatch, deer mate, and mushrooms emerge. Through the rain, a muggy day turns into an explosion of fragrances, songs, and patterns of droplets on leaves. Under the leaves hide dainty spiders and lacewings. Even late fall brings happy surprises – the discovery of lingering birds of summer or Witch-hazel in flower.

Winter landscapes and icy abstracts challenge the photographer. Expansive vistas are revealed through leafless woodlands; snow crystals dance in the sunshine. Colourful buds swell tips of twigs, and springtails loll on sun-warmed snowbanks. Birds of the north – Snowy Owls, redpolls, and others – come south to enliven the winter landscape. On days when little stirs, you may

wonder how a weasel protects itself from the cold. Surely hypo-
thermia threatens it too. The weasel has its own secrets for sur-
vival which are told by tracks and trails meandering among
flower seedstocks that stand above the powdered snow. These
can be examined at your leisure, perhaps sitting on snowshoes,
with a field guide in one hand and a hot drink in the other.

One could easily be tricked into putting away the layers of
clothing in the early spring when numerous rafts of ducks
appear once again in open bays rimmed with ice. Sunny days
may still be cool but before long they will burst with the energy
of migration, awakening, and courtship. Wood Frogs quack
early from puddles; then toads trill and woodcocks 'peent'; tree-
frogs gurgle from their poplar perches. By then trilliums are the
talk of the town and you can discard your sweaters. Clear
streams with rubble and riffles are the breeding places of Rainbow Trout, which can be seen by day on their journey upstream
from the lakes where they spend their winters. Where there is
water there are water birds; and shorebirds and marsh birds
make their appearance at mud puddles and cattail islands when
the midges dance in swarms. Walk with your back to the sun
then because it will not be long before warblers, tanagers, and
meadowlarks come, and the sun's rays will bounce from their
plumages back to you in full splendour. Butterflies – blues,
swallowtails, and painted ladies – can be found in the open
fields, near early flowers, such as Dame's Rocket. The shaded
places will have lady's-slippers among grasses and horsetails,
but only for a short while.

Most mammals and birds are more easily seen and heard at
dawn than at any other time (in summer, between 5 and 8 a.m.
is best). A few days before a dawn visit, why not scout an area
for tracks in the mud, or flip through a field guide. Try edges of
forests, fields, marshes, and streams. Places where two habitats
mix accommodate residents of both habitats as well as some
that dwell only in edges. Once you are there – at the break of
dawn – stand or walk slowly but be very quiet and alert. Look
up more than down, and you could find yourself a few metres
away from a doe drinking or from an Indigo Bunting clinging to
grape tangles.

Butterflies pick up where deer leave off. Unable to regulate
their own body temperature, they feed mostly between 10 a.m.

and noon, when the sun's rays are just right. Chicory ends its summons to pollinators by actually closing up by noon. You too may decide to retire in the heat of the day or move to the coolness of a forest, where turning over a new log may interrupt the affairs of a red eft or a yellow-legged millipede. Or, equipped with a hat and water bottle, venture out to fields of net-winged grasshoppers and Common Mullein; into northern bogs of cranberries, dragonflies, and old wooden cabins; or out to bays framed in granite outcrops decorated with small bits of canoe paint and lots of yellow lichen.

If this array of sights and sounds of the seasons has stirred your imagination and awakened a desire to experience the natural world for yourself, then you will enjoy Ontario and will get the most out of your excursions.

Abbreviations and Terms

General

adj	adjacent
hbr	harbour
opp	opposite
RR	railroad
eastern Ontario	generally that portion of southern Ontario that lies between the St Lawrence and Ottawa rivers
northern Ontario	generally the portion of the province north of North Bay
southern Ontario	generally the portion of the province south of North Bay
southwestern Ontario	generally that portion of southern Ontario that lies between Lakes Huron and Erie

Agencies

CA	Conservation Area
CNR	Canadian National Railway
CPR	Canadian Pacific Railway
CWS	Canadian Wildlife Service (agency of federal government)
FON	Federation of Ontario Naturalists
MNR	Ontario Ministry of Natural Resources
Nat'l Park	National Park
NCC	National Capital Commission (Ottawa)

ONR	Ontario Northland Railway
PNR	Provincial Nature Reserve (a category of park owned by the provincial government)
Prov Park	Provincial Park
PWA	Provincial Wildlife Area
RBG	Royal Botanical Gardens in Hamilton (Burlington)

Roadways

co rd*	county road (a road maintained by a county)
conc rd*	concession road (a category of rural road maintained by a township; concession roads are 1.25 miles or 2 km apart and usually parallel to one another)
dist rd*	district road (a road maintained by a district)
drwy	driveway
hwy*	highway (a major road maintained by the province of Ontario)
jct	intersection
pkwy	parkway
QEW	Queen Elizabeth Way (highway)
reg rd*	regional road (a road maintained by a regional municipality)
sdrd*	sideroad (a category of rural road maintained by a township, perpendicular to concession roads)
T-jct	T intersection
twp rd*	township road (any road maintained by a township)

*In some parts of Ontario, especially in the large built-up areas of the south, counties have been replaced by regional municipalities. In the north, districts replace counties. Within the same area, highways, county/regional/district roads, and township roads (usually concession roads or sideroads) are numbered by independent systems. Thus, it is possible for Co Rd 14 to be located in the same general area as Hwy 14. Care should be taken to avoid confusion. At press time many townships, counties, and regional municipalities are renaming and/or renumbering many of their roadways; be alert for changes.

Background

The World beneath Our Feet: Ontario's Earth History

The rocks of the Earth's crust contain the remarkable story of our planet – how it came to be, how solid land developed, and eventually how life, and finally human life, came to occupy it. When we look at the crust today, we see two kinds of rocky materials – hard and soft. The hard rocks are called *bedrock*, while the softer, broken-up material is referred to as *overburden*. Wherever bedrock is visible at the surface, it is called an out-crop. Most of the overburden found in Ontario was deposited by the glaciers and, especially in large lowland regions away from the Canadian Shield, it usually completely covers the bed-rock so that outcrops are very scarce.

Rocks are made of minerals. Although there are several thou-sand minerals known, only about 20 of them are common, and these make up most of the rocks. The rocks of the Earth's crust are formed in four different ways. According to how they are formed, they are said to be igneous, volcanic, sedimentary, or metamorphic. All of them can be changed from one type to another, through a very slow but never-ending process called the *rock cycle*.

Igneous rocks originate in a molten 'soup' called magma. This cools slowly deep within the Earth to create hard rocks with large crystals. Granite is the most common type of igneous rock. Sometimes the liquid magma forces its way between existing layers of rocks before it hardens. Rocks formed by this means

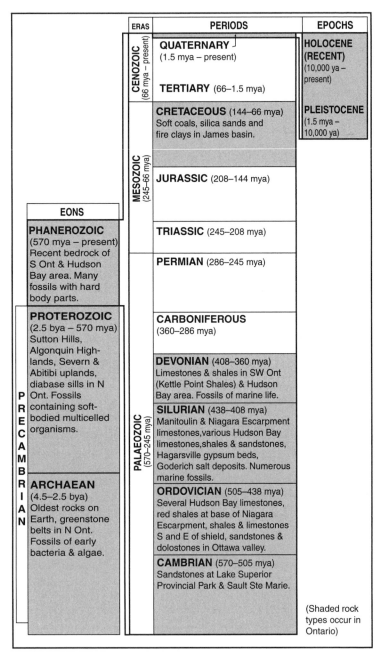

EONS	ERAS	PERIODS	EPOCHS
PHANEROZOIC (570 mya – present) Recent bedrock of S Ont & Hudson Bay area. Many fossils with hard body parts.	**CENOZOIC** (66 mya – present)	**QUATERNARY** (1.5 mya – present)	**HOLOCENE (RECENT)** (10,000 ya – present)
		TERTIARY (66–1.5 mya)	**PLEISTOCENE** (1.5 mya – 10,000 ya)
	MESOZOIC (245–66 mya)	**CRETACEOUS** (144–66 mya) Soft coals, silica sands and fire clays in James basin.	
		JURASSIC (208–144 mya)	
		TRIASSIC (245–208 mya)	
PROTEROZOIC (2.5 bya – 570 mya) Sutton Hills, Algonquin Highlands, Severn & Abitibi uplands, diabase sills in N Ont. Fossils containing soft-bodied multicelled organisms.	**PALAEOZOIC** (570–245 mya)	**PERMIAN** (286–245 mya)	
		CARBONIFEROUS (360–286 mya)	
		DEVONIAN (408–360 mya) Limestones & shales in SW Ont (Kettle Point Shales) & Hudson Bay area. Fossils of marine life.	
		SILURIAN (438–408 mya) Manitoulin & Niagara Escarpment limestones, various Hudson Bay limestones, shales & sandstones, Hagarsville gypsum beds, Goderich salt deposits. Numerous marine fossils.	
		ORDOVICIAN (505–438 mya) Several Hudson Bay limestones, red shales at base of Niagara Escarpment, shales & limestones S and E of shield, sandstones & dolostones in Ottawa valley.	
ARCHAEAN (4.5–2.5 bya) Oldest rocks on Earth, greenstone belts in N Ont. Fossils of early bacteria & algae.		**CAMBRIAN** (570–505 mya) Sandstones at Lake Superior Provincial Park & Sault Ste Marie.	

PRECAMBRIAN

(Shaded rock types occur in Ontario)

Figure 2. Geological Column showing selected bedrock deposits in Ontario (mya = million years ago; bya = billion years ago).

take on the shape of the cracks they flow through and are said to be *intrusive*. Diabase is an example. Igneous rocks may later become exposed to view at the surface after movements occur in the Earth's crust or when overlying materials are removed through erosion.

Volcanic rocks are also formed from fiery-hot liquid magma, but reach the surface of the Earth before hardening. Here, lava seeping from an oceanic ridge or spewed from a volcano cools quickly to form small crystals. Basalt is the most common type of volcanic rock.

Sedimentary rocks result from the deposition of fragments of rock and minerals. For example, coral reefs might develop on the sea floor, mud accumulate on the bottom of a lake, or sand pile up on a beach or desert. With time and the weight of accumulated layers, the particles become cemented into soft rocks such as limestone, shale, and sandstone.

Igneous, volcanic, and sedimentary rocks, with time and changing physical conditions, may experience tremendous heat and pressure, but not enough to melt them. Through this process they become altered (or metamorphosed) to form *metamorphic rocks*. Thus a shale may be transformed into a slate or schist, and sometimes into a rock that looks something like a granite but is called gneiss.

Later, these same rocks may be eroded by weathering and their particles reduced to sediments. Or they could be melted to eventually solidify as igneous or volcanic rock. Or they might remain relatively unchanged for billions of years. Whatever the route, through the rock cycle, all rocky particles are slowly and continuously recycled from one type of rock to another.

Once the type and origin of a rock have been identified, and the age determined through scientific techniques, it begins to tell its part of the story of the Earth's past. An important tool in interpreting events is the Geological Column (Figure 2). It divides the history of the Earth into a series of time blocks, something like chapters of a book. The chapters, subchapters, sub-subchapters, etc. are called eons, eras, periods, and epochs. In each, the fossil record is correlated with the sequence of geological events. For some of the time blocks, there are no rocks (or fossils) of that age present in Ontario today.

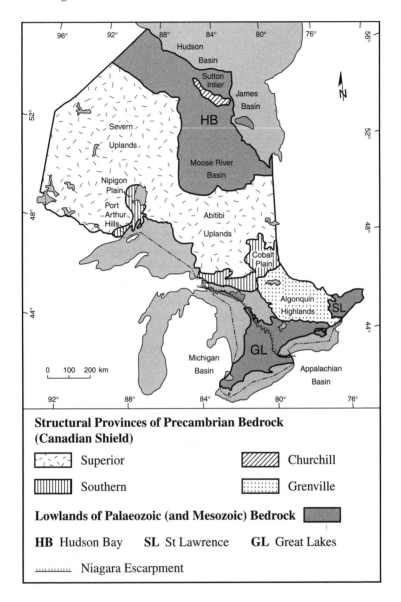

Figure 3. The bedrock regions of Ontario. The four structural provinces of the Precambrian Shield contain the oldest rocks, and the largely Palaeozoic rocks of the lowlands contain the youngest.

THE MARCH OF TIME

Our Sun was born about five billion years ago when a swirling cloud of gas and dust shrank into a fiery ball. By 4.5 billion years ago, bits of matter began to collect around the slowly cooling Sun. These eventually became the planets of the Solar System. The history of the Earth has been divided into three eons. The first two, together known as the Precambrian, cover 85% of the planet's history. It was during this time that the rocks underlying the Canadian Shield were laid down. The bedrock beneath the rest of Ontario was deposited during the third, or Phanerozoic Eon.

ARCHAEAN EON (early Precambrian; 4.5–2.5 billion years ago)

During the earliest part of its history the young Earth developed a dense core, overlain by a mantle of lighter materials. With gradual cooling, fragments of crust began to form on the molten surface. The primitive crust underwent numerous transformations. At times it was uplifted into mountain ranges, remnants of which are now exposed at scattered sites in northwestern Ontario. The 3.25-billion-year-old rocks of the Red Lake area are some of the oldest formations known in the world today.

During the late Archaean, geological upheavals concentrated metal ores in bands of volcanic rocks known as greenstone belts. Such deposits form the backbone of northern Ontario's mining industry. These belts alternate with sedimentary rocks containing some of the Earth's oldest fossils, 2.7-billion-year-old algae and bacteria. By the end of the Archaean, the land mass that was to become northern Ontario had been consolidated into the continent of Laurentia. The ancient rock formation, now known as the Superior structural province, formed the nucleus around which North America grew (Figure 3).

Superior Structural Province. The Superior province, the oldest part of the Canadian Shield, today covers most of northern Ontario. It has been divided into 12 subprovinces that generally run across the region in east–west bands, separated by faults in the Earth's crust. Nine of the subprovinces are granite-greenstones. These long, narrow belts are dominated by metamorphosed volcanic rocks, but among the volcanic greenstones there are broad domes of granite called batholiths. Some of the greenstone subprovinces are separated by two slightly younger bands of metamorphosed sedimentary rocks. The twelfth subprovince contains an assemblage of granitic rocks that have been metamorphosed into gneiss.

PROTEROZOIC EON (late Precambrian; 2.5 billion to 570 million years ago)

During the early Proterozoic, rivers and glaciers eroded the mountains of Laurentia and deposited sediments along its coasts, providing materials from which new rocks could be created. Left behind was a plain of bedrock, now visible in the Severn and Abitibi uplands.

Southern Structural Province. On the southern and eastern margins of the continent, rocks of the Southern structural province were deposited along what are now the north shores of Lakes Huron and Superior around Thunder Bay, Lake Nipigon, Blind River, and Kirkland Lake.

The oldest shoreline rock deposits, developed along the southeastern coast, consist of conglomerates of sand and gravel, and include the uranium deposits of Elliot Lake. Later intrusions of igneous rock into sedimentary layers created slabs of harder rock known as Nipissing diabase sills. These formations can be seen today in Mississagi Provincial Park, the La Cloche Mountains around Killarney Provincial Park, and the Ishpatina Ridge in Lady Evelyn–Smoothwater Provincial Park.

Rock deposits laid down along the southwestern shores of Laurentia included conglomerates, cherts, shales, sandstones, and limestones, today visible southwest of Thunder Bay from Laverendrye Provincial Nature Reserve to Kakabeka Falls Provincial Park and on the north shore of Lake Superior. These sedimentary rocks also contain diabase sills, which now cap the flat-topped mesas of Sleeping Giant Provincial Park and the Nor'Westers near Thunder Bay. The north shore of Lake Superior is also noted for other spectacular geological features, such as 2-billion-year-old fossil stromatolites, Red Rock Cuesta south of Nipigon, and the bright orange Sibley shales near Schreiber.

The mysterious Sudbury structure, an oval-shaped basin

measuring 27 km by 60 km, probably originated through the impact of a meteorite. Sediments subsequently collected in the basin, and nickel-bearing igneous rock was later forced to the surface along the crater's rim.

Churchill Structural Province (Trans-Hudson Orogen). Mountains arose along Laurentia's northern edge, and erosion filled offshore basins with sediments. Intrusions of igneous rock created table-like sills which, in the Sutton Hills, today stand high above the surrounding Hudson Bay Lowland.

Grenville Structural Province. When continental drift brought Laurentia into collision with the offshore seabed, a high mountain range developed along the continent's eastern margin. This and subsequent upheavals created the rock of the Grenville structural province, which extends eastward from a fault running between Killarney Provincial Park and Lake Timiskaming. The northern portion consists largely of gneiss, with intrusions of granite, including the massive Algonquin batholith. At one time buried beneath ancient mountains, it is now exposed as outcrops in the Algonquin Highlands. To the southeast, remnants of highly metamorphosed Grenville rocks are present in the Frontenac Arch, mainly as gneisses and schists, but marble and rocks of volcanic origin also occur. A diversity of high-quality mineral specimens makes this area popular with rockhounds.

PHANEROZOIC EON (570 million years ago to present)

The Phanerozoic Eon, comprising the most recent 15% of the Earth's history, is divided into three eras.

Palaeozoic Era (570–245 million years ago)

During much of the Palaeozoic, the worn-down Precambrian rocks of the Canadian Shield were submersed under seawater, where they became buried beneath a thick blanket of sedimentary rocks. These rocks, made from the sands, muds, and coral reefs that covered the sea floor, formed sandstones, shales, limestones, and dolostones. They contain an abundance of fossils, the remains of the marine life that flourished in the shallow tropical seas. The Palaeozoic Era has been divided into six peri-

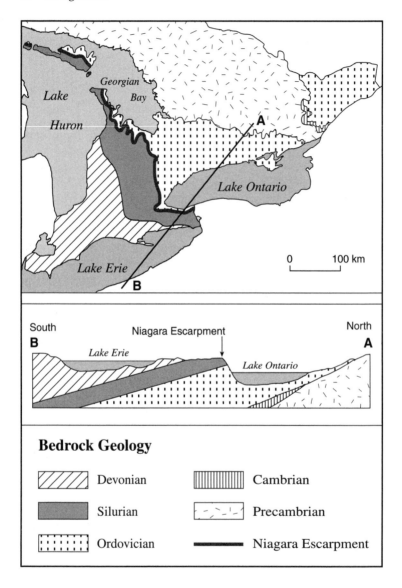

Figure 4. Cross-sectional view of the bedrock geology of southern Ontario. Except on the Canadian Shield, the bedrock is now largely buried beneath glacial deposits.

ods. Rocks from the four earliest Palaeozoic periods have been found in Ontario (Figure 4).

Cambrian Period (570–505 million years ago). Evidence of Ontario's oldest Palaeozoic rocks is found in Lake Superior Provincial Park and at Sault Ste Marie. These sandstones were formed of materials eroded from the surface of Laurentia and deposited in nearby coastal seas.

Ordovician Period (505–438 million years ago). Ontario's oldest Palaeozoic fossils are contained in sedimentary deposits laid down when seawater began to invade the continent. Found near Ottawa, these sandstones were used in the construction of the Parliament Buildings. When shallow water covered Laurentia, limestones and shales were formed. Hudson Bay Lowland limestones and red shales visible along the base of the Niagara Escarpment date from this time.

Silurian Period (438–408 million years ago). Seawater covered Ontario during the Silurian, adding layers of sediments hundreds of metres thick, especially in the lowland basins. Attawapiskat limestone, Cabot Head shales and dolostones, gypsum beds near Hagarsville, and numerous fossils of marine life all originated during this period. A time of rapid evaporation temporarily created Dead Sea conditions and resulted in salt deposits at Goderich and Windsor.

Devonian Period (408–360 million years ago). For a time, much of the Ontario land mass rose above sea level, to be later re-immersed. Coral reefs and other marine life thrived and were incorporated into the accumulating layers of limestones, dolostones, and shales. The shales at Kettle Point date from the Devonian.

During the Palaeozoic, the Precambrian bedrock that lay beneath Ontario developed slight uprisings called arches. These divided the lowlands flanking the shield into basins. Thus, the Hudson Bay Lowland is separated into the Hudson Bay and Moose River basins by the Cape Henrietta Maria Arch; the Ottawa–St Lawrence Lowland is isolated from the Great Lakes Lowland by the Frontenac Arch; and the Algonquin Arch separates the Appalachian basin of the lower Great Lakes from the Michigan basin of the upper Great Lakes. The layers of sedimentary rock that came to occupy the basins are arranged somewhat like a stack of wide, very shallow bowls of decreasing diameter and varying thickness, with the youngest layers on top. When the waters that covered the Canadian Shield during much of the Palaeozoic finally receded, erosion, which continued through subsequent eras, set to work on the soft sedimentary rocks.

In Ontario today, the layers of Palaeozoic bedrock that have not been erased by erosion are largely buried under later glacial deposits, but because the layers slope gently away from the shield, outcrops of the various layers sometimes occur at the surface.

Mesozoic Era (245–66 million years ago)

The Mesozoic, the era of the dinosaurs, saw the development of a much larger continental land mass, the forerunner of present-day North America. Most of Ontario lay above sea level during this era and was thus exposed to the forces of weathering. Steadily, over time, erosion stripped away much of the Palaeozoic sedimentary rock. On the Canadian Shield, Palaeozoic rocks were almost completely removed from the surface to reveal the ancient Precambrian foundations of the continent of Laurentia. In the lowlands bordering the shield, where deposits had been much thicker, only the uppermost layers of Palaeozoic rock were lost to erosion. Relatively little rock-building occurred in Ontario during the Mesozoic, and most of what did occur has since been erased by weathering. The only evidence remaining is found in the James basin: Mattagami soft coals, silica sands, and fire clays. These deposits were laid down during the Cretaceous Period, the last of three periods that make up the Mesozoic Era.

Cenozoic Era (66 million years ago to present)

This era has been divided into two periods.

Tertiary Period (66–1.5 million years ago). As weathering continued, the younger rock covering the Canadian Shield was converted into great quantities of gravel, silt, sand, and clay. Extensive river systems carved valleys and carried the products of erosion downstream. The largest of the rivers, the Laurentian, drained much of the Great Lakes area eastward through the St Lawrence. Escarpments such as the Niagara, Onondaga (in Haldimand), and Red Rock (near Nipigon) developed. In previous eras, eroded materials had become buried and, under pressure, transformed into new rocks. This time the debris remained on the Earth's surface, where the forces of gravity, ice, wind, and water were free to rearrange the landscape above the bedrock.

Quaternary Period (1.5 million years ago to present). This period has been divided into two epochs, the Pleistocene and the Holocene.

During the *Pleistocene Epoch* (1.5 million to 10,000 years ago) or Ice Age, ice sheets covered northern North America, reshaping the landscape each time they advanced and retreated. Reaching thicknesses of 2–3 km, the masses of glacial ice crept southward, scouring, gouging, crushing, and transporting the rocky materials beneath them. Moving ice rounded and smoothed the surface of the Precambrian bedrock and, with the rock fragments embedded in its undersurface, added scratches and grooves.

When an advancing glacier proceeded southward from the hard rocks of the shield, it encountered the softer limestones of southern Ontario, which were more easily broken up and transported. Glacially carried materials might later be deposited as deep layers of drift, or as more defined structures, such as moraines, eskers, drumlins, or kames.

Between each glacial advance there was a lengthy interglacial period when the ice sheets withdrew entirely and temperatures warmed to at least those of the present. During the peak of glaciation, temperatures were probably about 9°C cooler than they are now. As succeeding ice sheets spread southward, they overrode and obliterated landscape features created by earlier glaciations.

Although very few traces remain, the oldest glacial deposits known in Ontario were laid down during the Illinoian Glaciation (190,000–135,000 years ago). Examples of these tills can be seen in Missinaibi River Provincial Park and in the Don Valley Brickyard in East York. After the Illinoian glacier withdrew, the climate warmed and the land remained free of ice for a long period. During this time sediments of non-glacial origin were laid down on top of the glacial tills. In the Don Valley Brickyard, the fossil record documents giant beaver, bison, and bear, as well as numerous Carolinian species, including ones now found only considerably farther south. Fossils in the Moose River

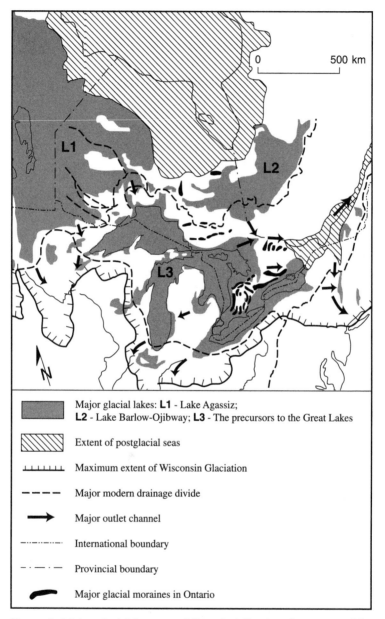

Figure 5. Major glacial features of Ontario following the retreat of the glaciers.

basin record an invasion of seawater and the development of boreal forest after the land rebounded.

The last great Ice Age, known as the Wisconsin Glaciation (115,000–10,000 years ago), was marked by regular advances and retreats – some small and some major, and often with pauses in between. As the ice front spread southward across Ontario, lobes along the forward edge acted somewhat independently, some sweeping ahead while others receded or stagnated. On a number of occasions the climate grew warmer and the ice sheets partially withdrew northward.

During the Early Wisconsin, the last great ice sheet began moving into Ontario from the northeast. With it came a cooling climate and an increase in boreal species. When temperatures warmed slightly, muskoxen, bison, and elk, along with pine, oak, and spruce, occupied the landscape bordering western Lake Ontario. During the Middle Wisconsin, southern Ontario remained largely ice-free.

The Late Wisconsin saw the continental ice sheet spread across southern Ontario several times. During the relatively brief intervals of warmer climate between advances, the ice withdrew from parts of southern Ontario, allowing woolly mammoths and grizzly bears to roam the countryside. About 20,000 years ago, a major thrust carried the Wisconsin ice to its most southerly extent (Figure 5). All of Ontario was covered and much of the north-central United States.

Another significant southward surge occurred around 15,000 years ago. Ice masses in the basins of Georgian Bay and Lakes Erie, Ontario, and Huron expanded towards each other to converge in central southwestern Ontario. When the lobes split and pulled apart, they exposed a broad dome of land completely surrounded by ice and water. Extending from Dundalk to London, this area is referred to as the Ontario Island. About this time a network of large valleys was created in the vicinity of Lake Simcoe by the sudden massive release of stored meltwater that had been trapped beneath the glacier.

The northward retreat of the ice sheet was accompanied by a succession of meltwater lakes impounded along the southern margins of the ice mass; some examples are Lake Iroquois in the Ontario basin, Lake Algonquin in the Huron and Michigan basins, Lake Keweenaw in the western Superior basin, Lake

Agassiz near the Manitoba border, and Lake Barlow-Ojibway in the Abitibi basin. Lakes Maumee, Arkona, Whittlesey, and Warren occupied parts of the Erie basin in sequence.

As the ice mass disintegrated, drainage patterns were repeatedly altered. Water levels in the glacial lakes rose and fell dramatically, often in relatively short periods of time as old outlets were blocked or new ones opened. Initially, meltwater flowed south through the Mississippi system, and later via the Mohawk to the Hudson. Finally, the continuing northward shrinkage of the ice reopened the St Lawrence valley. At various times the upper Great Lakes drained across the Kawarthas to the Trent River, via spillways in the Algonquin Highlands, and through Lake Nipissing and the Mattawa to the Ottawa valley. Isostatic rebound also modified the drainage patterns of the Great Lakes, eventually diverting the outlet of the upper lakes from the Ottawa valley to Lake Ontario via the St Clair River.

During glaciation, the tremendous weight of ice depressed the surface of the Earth's crust. As the ice melted, the land began to rebound, but not as rapidly as sea level rose after huge quantities of glacial meltwater were added to the oceans. As a result, as soon as receding ice opened outlets into the St Lawrence River (11,600 years ago) and Hudson Bay (8,000 years ago), marine waters flooded inland to create the Champlain Sea in eastern Ontario and the Tyrrell Sea in the Hudson Bay Lowland. About 11,500 years ago glacial Lake Agassiz arose in the Rainy River area. Over the next 3,000 years, it grew to enormous proportions to become part of a continuous meltwater lake that lay along the southern margin of the shrinking ice sheet. This vast body of ponded water stretched from Saskatchewan, across Manitoba and northern Ontario, to glacial Lake Ojibway in Quebec. A last, small glacial advance laid down the clay tills that characterize northern Ontario's Claybelt. By 8,000 years ago the remaining ice was rapidly disintegrating. Since then the land surface has continued to rise. The Champlain Sea disappeared more than 8,000 years ago, but new land is still being added along the shores of Hudson Bay.

The *Holocene Epoch* (10,000 years ago to present) followed the Pleistocene. When the glaciers departed from Ontario, they left behind a varied but barren landscape of sand, clay, silt, gravel, till, boulders, and scoured bedrock. Scattered across this surface, especially in the southern part of the province, lay numerous features sculpted by the glaciers. Over the years wind, rain, frost, snow, and ice have been at work modifying the landscape. Primitive plants, bacteria, nematodes, and other small organisms soon arrived and began the work of transforming the parent materials into soils. The fruits of their labours, and those of generations of successors from many species, are evident across Ontario today, showcased in an incredible variety of complex communities of living things.

THE LAY OF THE LAND: MAJOR PHYSIOGRAPHIC FEATURES

Precambrian Shield. The ancient rocks of the shield rise to the surface across much of Ontario. This saddle of often exposed bedrock contains the highest land in the province and forms the watershed divide between the Hudson Bay drainage system and that of the upper Great Lakes. The bedrock consists largely of granite or granite-gneiss but there are also metamorphosed sedimentary and volcanic rocks, including greenstone belts.

Extensive and often spectacular highlands dominate the shield. South of the Hudson Bay Lowland, the Severn Uplands rise in the west and the Abitibi Uplands in the east. Countless small, isolated wetlands are scattered among barren rock outcrops and innumerable interconnected lakes. In some areas, the shield lies buried beneath glacial features such as moraines, eskers, kames, and kettles. The Algonquin Highlands are dominated by numerous lakes and linking waterways, interspersed with glacial features such as eskers, kames, kame terraces, inland dunes, and spillways.

The Port Arthur Hills near Thunder Bay feature flat layers of sedimentary rock containing diabase sills. Erosion has sculpted these rock formations into the spectacular landscape displayed in the Nor'Westers and the provincial parks of Kakabeka Falls, Sleeping Giant, and Ouimet Canyon. To the northeast, the Nipigon Plain is covered with a thick blanket of volcanic basalts.

Lying north of Lake Huron, the La Cloche Mountains near Killarney are the exposed roots of an ancient mountain range. Farther north an area of relatively flat sedimentary rock known as the Cobalt Plain overlies the Abitibi Uplands in the vicinity of Lady Evelyn–Smoothwater Provincial Park.

Lowlands. Flanking the Canadian Shield are three lowlands: Hudson Bay, Ottawa–St Lawrence, and Great Lakes. Here the shield dips below the surface to be buried beneath marine-deposited sedimentary rocks, now overlain by a mantle of glacial deposits. Within the lowlands, domes of Precambrian rock create the Sutton Hills in the Hudson Bay Lowland and the Grey County (Dundalk) Highlands in the Great Lakes Lowland.

Ottawa-Bonnechere Graben. The Ottawa valley and the Nipissing Lowlands lie within a fault in the Earth's crust. Beneath the valley, large blocks of rocks have slipped downward between the Gatineau Highlands to the north and the Algonquin Highlands to the south.

Karst Features. These occur where water percolates through soluble limestone to create underground caves and sinkholes. Examples are found along the Niagara Escarpment, at Warsaw, and at Eganville near Ottawa.

Niagara Escarpment. The Niagara Escarpment winds across southern Ontario from Queenston to Manitoulin Island and beyond. Underlain by Ordovician shales and capped by durable Silurian dolostones, it forms one of the most dramatic landscape features in the province. Sheer cliffs of spectacular beauty often occur along the northeastern face whereas, from the cuesta, the land slopes away gently to the southwest. (See the account under the Regional Municipality of Niagara.)

Glacial Features. Many features in Ontario's landscape owe their origin to the earth-moving activities of the glaciers or their meltwaters. The unsorted mixture of sand, silt, clay, coarse pebbles, and boulders that is carried and later deposited by glaciers is known as *glacial till* or *glacial drift*. Various glacial features can be created from this basic construction material. When a glacier melts, the rocky debris left behind settles onto the ground below to form a hummocky blanket of till known as a *ground moraine*. Ground moraine covers much of Ontario to a depth of several metres; this till layer is thinnest on the Canadian Shield.

Drumlins consist of glacial till deposited as oval-shaped hills. They originate when till carried beneath slow-moving ice is dumped, then moulded into a streamlined shape by the ice passing over it. The Peterborough area is renowned for its extensive drumlin fields.

The most prominent moraines form along the edges of ice sheets. Some attain depths of a hundred metres or more and may form broad ridges that stretch across the landscape for many tens of kilometres. Rocky materials that accumulate along the edges of a glacier flowing through a valley produce ridges of till called *lateral moraines*. When two lobes of ice converge, their lateral moraines merge to build a single *interlobate moraine*. A particularly spectacular example is the Oak Ridges moraine, which stretches for 150 km from the Niagara Escarpment to the Trent River.

An *end moraine* develops when the leading edge of a glacier remains in one position for some time. Rubble released by the melting ice accumulates as a prominent ridge along the forward edge of the ice mass. If the glacier recedes, then becomes stalled at a new location, a new end moraine develops. Members of a series of end moraines formed in this way are called *recessional moraines*. The moraine marking the point of greatest advance of the glacier is the *terminal moraine*. *DeGeer moraines,* common in northwestern Ontario, consist of a series of narrow, evenly spaced ridges that form along ice sheets that are hemmed in by glacial lakes.

Sometimes large boulders hitch rides on glaciers and are transported long distances. When the ice melts, these *erratics* are deposited on top of the till, rather than buried within it.

Eskers appear on the surface of the landscape as long, twisting railway-like embankments. They are formed from deposits of gravel and sand carried by flowing streams within or under the ice mass. They are major sources of such materials for building or highway construction purposes.

Kame terraces occur along valley slopes where streams once ran along margins of glaciers.

Conical hills called *kames* form from debris dropped by a glacial waterfall. A *kame delta* results when the waterfall splashes down into a pond of meltwater at the base of the glacier.

Sometimes huge chunks of ice become buried within moraines. When the ice melts, the till above collapses to form a deep, rounded hole or *kettle*. If water fills the depression, a *kettle lake* results.

An *outwash plain* develops just downstream of most glaciers. Here sorted sands and gravels criss-crossed by braided rivers spread across a broad plain.

When glacial meltwaters seek a drainage route, they carve broad valleys called *glacial spillways* to carry the immense volume of water. Well-worn boulders often occur at the head of such valleys.

Glacial lakes form along the margins of melting glaciers where drainage is temporarily blocked. If water levels in these lakes remain relatively constant for an extended period, features such as beaches, boulder beaches, shoreline bluffs, and lakebed plains sometimes form. Good examples of *raised beach ridges* can be seen today in the Hudson Bay Lowland and around Georgian Bay.

Forests, Fens, and Farms: Ontario's Rich Diversity of Life

The province of Ontario, because of its large size (over 1 million km², great range of habitats, and variety of climatic conditions, is rich in species diversity. Approximately 2,900 species of vascular plants, 458 species of birds (of which 287 are breeding species), 57 species and subspecies of herpetofauna, 86 species of wild mammals, 158 species of fish, 137 species of butterflies, and many other species of plants and animals live in Ontario. These numbers constantly change, as naturalists and professional biologists continue to gather field observations that enhance our understanding of the province's wildlife. The main cause for changes to the species lists – both additions and deletions – is the activities of humans.

PHYSIOGRAPHIC REGIONS

Major differences in underlying bedrock and the surface deposits covering the bedrock divide Ontario into three physiographic regions (Figure 6).

The *Great Lakes–St Lawrence Lowland* flanks the Canadian Shield in southern and eastern Ontario. The southern portion, known as the Great Lakes Lowland, underlies all of southern Ontario to the south of a line that more or less stretches between Orillia and Kingston. The St Lawrence Lowland (also referred to as the Ottawa–St Lawrence Lowland) is east of a line that runs between Gananoque and Arnprior and also extends somewhat

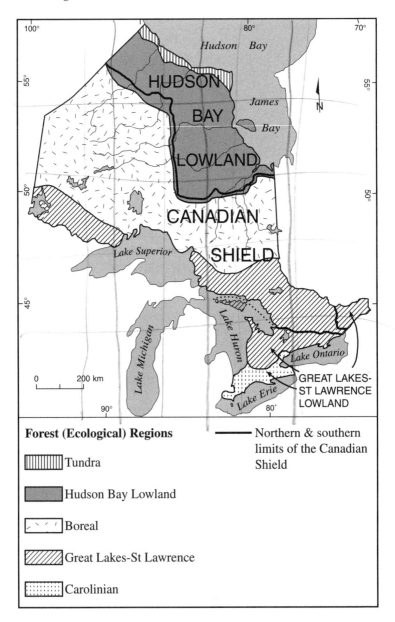

Figure 6. Ontario's five forest (ecological) regions and three physiographic regions.

farther up the Ottawa valley. The underlying sedimentary rocks of these lowlands are generally covered with relatively deep, fertile soils and level topography, the basis of an important agricultural industry.

The *Canadian Shield*, the largest of Ontario's physiographic regions, bridges the vast area between the Hudson Bay Lowland and southern Ontario. The igneous and metamorphic rocks of the Precambrian bedrock are covered by thin soils and countless lakes. The eastern extension of the shield in southern Ontario – the Frontenac Axis – crosses the St Lawrence River east of Kingston.

The *Hudson Bay Lowland* is underlain by sedimentary bedrock. It consists of a flat, poorly drained landscape with numerous small, shallow lakes and ponds. It extends about 200 km inland from the shores of James and Hudson bays to the edge of the Canadian Shield.

For more information on the physiographic regions and their underlying bedrock, consult the section on geology.

FOREST REGIONS

In Ontario the main pattern of natural vegetation consists of broad belts of forest running in an east–west direction. From south to north these are Carolinian Forest, Great Lakes–St Lawrence Forest, Boreal Forest, Hudson Bay Lowland Forest, and Tundra. The boundaries between forest regions are not sharply delineated, and the transition from one to the next is gradual. Most species have ranges that overlap two or more forest regions.

Carolinian Forest Region

Carolinian Forest occupies the southern portion of the Great Lakes Lowland in Ontario, where it forms the northern section of the Deciduous Forest that characterizes much of the eastern United States. In Canada, this forest region extends northward from Lake Erie to a line stretching between Grand Bend on Lake Huron and the Rouge River valley east of Toronto. Some experts consider that it also continues eastward in a relatively narrow band along the north shore of Lake Ontario to Hastings County.

Because of the comparatively warm climate, the extreme south-western part of the province has been called Ontario's 'banana belt.' Throughout much of the Carolinian zone, the natural vegetation has been removed and the landscape converted to agricultural, industrial, commercial, or urban uses.

The Carolinian Forest Region, with its wide range of habitats from wetlands to upland woods, including pockets of prairie and savanna, is home to one-third of Canada's 'vulnerable,' 'threatened,' and 'endangered' species (as defined by the Committee on the Status of Endangered Wildlife in Canada). A few examples of the unique species of the Carolinian zone are the Prickly-pear Cactus; the delicate purple-flowered Miami-mist; the Tulip-tree with its tulip-shaped flowers and leaves; the towering Kentucky Coffee Tree with its enormous seed pods; the spectacular Giant Swallowtail butterfly; the elusive Hooded Warbler; the golden-headed Prothonotary Warbler; the Eastern Mole, which lives a subterranean life; the Spiny Softshell turtle with its pancake-like shell; and the Blue Racer, a beautiful turquoise-blue serpent that is one of the fastest snakes in North America.

Carolinian woodlands consist almost entirely of deciduous trees. The dominant species, American Beech and Sugar Maple, are often associated with Basswood, Red Maple, and Red, White, and Bur Oaks. What distinguishes a Carolinian beech-maple forest from the beech-maple woods of the adjacent Great Lakes–St Lawrence Forest Region to the north is the presence of a number of additional tree species that are typical of more southerly regions, such as Black Gum, Black Walnut, and Sassafras with its mitten-shaped leaves. Conifers such as Red Cedar and Eastern Hemlock grow very sparingly in the Carolinian zone, restricted to specialized habitats. Many Carolinian species reach the northern limits of their ranges in this zone and are found nowhere else in Canada.

In addition to over 70 species of trees, the forests are home to many species of shrubs, vines, and herbaceous plants. Carolinian woodlands are particularly noted for their fine displays of ephemeral spring wildflowers. Some of the most abundant species of shrubs are Maple-leaved Viburnum, Fly Honeysuckle, Red-berried Elder, and Spicebush, whose leaves produce an aromatic odour when crushed. Some Carolinian specialties are

Burning Bush, Dwarf Chinquapin Oak, Dwarf Hackberry, and Rough-leaved Dogwood. Vines such as Bristly Greenbrier, Trumpet Creeper, Summer Grape, Moonseed, and Bur Cucumber proliferate in Carolinian forests, giving them an exotic, southern atmosphere. Many people are surprised to find that Poison-ivy grows here as a bush or a climbing vine, and sometimes even resembles a herbaceous plant.

Another surprise is that over 50,000 hectares, and perhaps up to 200,000 hectares, of tallgrass prairie, savanna, and open woodland greeted the first European settlers in southwestern Ontario. These prairie grasses were so tall that they tickled the noses of the horses that the pioneers rode. Today the province's largest and best pockets of remnant tallgrass prairie are found at Walpole Island and Ojibway Prairie in Windsor. These grassy habitats are dependent on early spring fires to burn successional woody species that would otherwise quickly crowd out prairie plants. Plants with prairie affinities also occur elsewhere, with fine examples at Stone Road alvar on Pelee Island and the rail trail between Brantford and Cambridge. Prairie vegetation sometimes grows on sites where thin soils and drought inhibit the growth of trees, or along riverbanks where ice scours shorelines and removes competing species. Remnant prairie plants include Big Bluestem, Switch Grass, Tall Cord Grass, Spiked Blazing-star, Gray-headed Coneflower, Sneezeweed, Nodding Wild Onion, and towering Prairie Dock with its half-metre-long leaves.

Approximately 200 species of birds breed in the Carolinian Forest Region of southwestern Ontario. Specialties include Northern Bobwhite, Chuck-will's-widow, Tufted Titmouse, Yellow-breasted Chat, and Orchard Oriole. Mammals are generally nocturnal and more difficult to find than the brightly coloured birds that mark their territories by singing. More than 50 species of mammals have been recorded in this southern region. Species reaching the northern limits of their Ontario ranges here include Eastern Mole and Woodland Vole.

In the 'banana belt,' cold-blooded fish and herpetofauna are more abundant than in the rest of the province. Over 125 species of fish live in the waters of this forest zone. Many species, such as Spotted Gar, Pugnose Minnow, Black Redhorse, and Brindled Madtom, reach the northern limits of their ranges in Carolinian

Canada. Approximately 21 species and subspecies of amphibians, including Carolinian specialties such as Blanchard's Cricket Frog and Fowler's Toad, have been recorded in the Carolinian zone. Species and subspecies of reptiles number about 25, among them the Lake Erie Water Snake and species with a typically more southerly distribution, such as Butler's Garter Snake, Queen Snake, and the extirpated Timber Rattlesnake.

Butterflies are abundant in the Carolinian zone. The large colourful Swallowtails – Pipe Vine, Black, Giant, Spicebush, and Tiger – have flights throughout the summer. Common, well-known species such as Monarch, Red Admiral, and Common Sulphur, as well as the rarer Wild Indigo Dusky Wing, Fiery Skipper, Little Glassy Wing, Hackberry Butterfly, and Karner Blue, are among the approximately 110 species of flying jewels that inhabit this area.

Great Lakes–St Lawrence Forest Region

In Ontario, this forest region covers the northern section of the Great Lakes Lowland, all of the St Lawrence Lowland, and the southern part of the Canadian Shield. Sometimes also called Northern Hardwood Forest or Mixed Forest, the Great Lakes–St Lawrence Forest Region is situated between the Carolinian Forest to the south and the Boreal Forest to the north. Forests of the region contain a mixture of coniferous and deciduous trees.

Where Great Lakes–St Lawrence forests lie on the Canadian Shield, they have been extensively logged. Off the shield, much of the land has been cleared for agriculture and other purposes. Because this forest type forms a broad transition belt between regions dominated by coniferous and deciduous forest, many species of plants and animals reach either the northern or southern limits of their ranges here.

Among the primary deciduous tree species are Sugar Maple, Yellow Birch, and, in the southern part of the region, American Beech. Eastern Hemlock and White and Red Pines grow abundantly among the hardwoods. The Canadian Shield underlies the northern part of this forest region and harbours a greater representation of boreal species, such as Balsam Fir and White and Black Spruces. Prairie and western influences are evident near the Manitoba border in mixedgrass prairie, Bur Oak savannas, and an increased presence of species such as Trembling Aspen.

The understorey is well developed, with species such as Striped Maple, Beaked Hazel, Bush and Fly Honeysuckles, and Red-berried Elder growing in abundance. The forest floor is carpeted with clubmosses, Rattlesnake Fern, Goldthread, Wild Sarsaparilla, Sweet-fern, Bunchberry, Starflower, Large-leaved Aster, and many other species.

The typical, commonly occurring birds of the Great Lakes–St Lawrence Forest Region are the same as those of the Carolinian zone. The Common Loon of northern lakes breeds from the Canadian Shield north to the treeline. Indicator species of birds in this forest region include White-throated Sparrow, Northern Waterthrush, Mourning and Black-throated Blue Warblers, and Yellow-bellied Sapsucker. Among species that reach the northern limits of their breeding ranges in this forest zone are Green Heron, Red-shouldered Hawk, Yellow-billed Cuckoo, Eastern Screech-Owl, and Red-headed Woodpecker. Those reaching their southern limits include Spruce Grouse, Gray Jay, and Pine Grosbeak. About 225 species breed in the region.

Of the approximately 58 species of mammals recorded for this forest region, many reach the southern limits of their Ontario ranges near the edge of the Canadian Shield. Examples are Least Chipmunk, Marten, Fisher, Canada Lynx, Bobcat, and Moose. Others reach their northern limits in the region. These include White-footed Mouse, Southern Flying Squirrel, Gray Squirrel, Eastern Small-footed Bat, and Hairy-tailed Mole. The presence of Franklin's Ground Squirrel and White-tailed Jackrabbit is indicative of prairie influences in the Lake of the Woods area.

Twenty species and subspecies of amphibians inhabit the Great Lakes–St Lawrence Forest Region. Two-lined Salamanders occur under rocks along rivers and streams that have moderate- to fast-flowing water; within Ontario they are generally encountered in the southern portion of the Canadian Shield. Most sightings of Mink Frog are from this forest zone. The Central Newt is found west of Lake Superior.

With few exceptions, Ontario's reptile species do not extend northward beyond this forest zone. Approximately 24 species and subspecies have been recorded here. The province's only lizard, the Five-lined Skink, inhabits the southern edge of the

Canadian Shield east of Georgian Bay. The Eastern Massasauga is found on the shores of Georgian Bay, most frequently on the upper Bruce Peninsula and in the Parry Sound area. Black Rat Snakes occur in the vicinity of Kingston. Eastern Fox Snakes have a northern population on the eastern shores of Georgian Bay. Stinkpot turtles are most commonly reported from the southern edge of the Canadian Shield east of Lake Huron, and Wood Turtles have their largest population on the eastern edge of Algonquin Park. Only two turtles, Common Snapping Turtle and Western Painted Turtle, inhabit the portion of the Great Lakes–St Lawrence Forest that lies west of Lake Superior.

Of the 125 or so species of fish that have been recorded here, none is limited to this forest region. Many species of shiners, dace, minnows, trout, and bass, as well such species as Pumpkinseed and Yellow Perch, are very commonly found in the lakes and streams.

Few of the approximately 125 species of butterflies recorded are confined to this forest zone. Some species that are generally found in this region are Olympia Marblewing, Pink Edged Sulphur, and Pepper and Salt Skipper.

Boreal Forest Region

The Boreal Forest Region, which arcs across Canada from Newfoundland to the Yukon, is the largest forest region in North America. In Ontario this is the characteristic forest of the Canadian Shield, especially the northern portion. Black and White Spruces dominate, but Balsam Fir, Jack Pine, and Tamarack are also important. Broad-leaved trees, such as White Birch, Trembling Aspen, and Balsam Poplar, occur as well. Boreal woodlands near the Manitoba border reflect a drier climate and prairie influences. Fire is an important agent of renewal in the Boreal Forest Region. Forest products, Ontario's largest resource-based industry, has driven roads into many woodlands. Compared with more southerly forest regions, there are fewer species of plants, birds, and animals. Severe winters cause the fauna to change markedly with the seasons.

A boreal woodland is a forest of lichen-covered evergreens, having a limited understorey owing to the intense shade caused by a year-round canopy of green branches. This type of forest is sometimes known as the 'spruce-moose' forest because of the presence of large tracts of White Spruce in association with Balsam Fir. The world's largest hoofed mammal, the majestic Moose, roams the Boreal Forest and its bogs. Mosses and low, spreading bushes such as Bearberry and Low Sweet Blueberry are found on the forest floor, along with herbs such as Bunchberry, Nodding Trillium, Wild Lily-of-the-valley, and Northern White Violet.

Lakes, rivers, and bogs are abundant in this vast region. Bogs are acidic, nutrient-poor, stagnant, waterlogged wetlands underlain by peat and dominated by a thick layer of *Sphagnum* mosses. They are found in basins where water collects and the outflow is restricted. The lack of oxygen in waterlogged soils prevents dead plant material from decaying and allows it to accumulate as peat, thereby locking up most of the nutrients in the bog. Closely related to bogs are fens; conditions here are slightly more favourable for plant growth because water slowly seeping through these wetlands carries in nutrients. A few indicator species of northern bogs and fens are Black Spruce, Tamarack, Labrador Tea, Leatherleaf, *Sphagnum* mosses, Pitcher-plant, sundews, cranberries, various orchids and sedges, and Creeping Snowberry (known by native Canadians as the tic-tac plant because the berries resemble these mints in size, colour, and taste).

Indicator species of birds in this forest zone include Great Gray Owl, Northern Hawk Owl, Boreal Chickadee, Black-backed Woodpecker, Three-toed Woodpecker (a species that is almost exclusively found in the Boreal Forest Region), and many species of northern-breeding warblers, including the colourful Cape May and Bay-breasted Warblers, both of which specialize in Spruce Budworm. About 175 species of birds nest in this forest region. The majority of the breeding birds migrate southward for the winter, leaving behind mainly seed-eaters and predators.

Representative of the northern woodlands are the large fur-bearing mammals that grow luxuriant coats as a protection against winter's cold – species such as Beaver, Snowshoe Hare, Canada Lynx, River Otter, Fisher, and Ermine. Other ubiquitous mammalian inhabitants of the needle-leaved forests include Heath Vole and several species of tiny carnivorous shrews that eat at least their own weight in food every 12 hours. In winter a number of boreal mammals hibernate or remain inactive and a few turn white. Over 50 species of mammals make their homes in this forest region.

Relatively few species of herpetofauna are hardy enough to survive the winters of the north. Many of the 14 species of amphibians recorded in the Boreal Forest occur only in the southern part of the region. A western subspecies, the Boreal Chorus Frog, inhabits northwestern Ontario's boreal region eastward to western Algoma. Reptiles are even less well adapted than amphibians to boreal conditions. A notable exception is the Eastern Garter Snake, which ranges widely across boreal habitats, joined near the Manitoba border by the closely related Red-sided Garter Snake.

Approximately 85 species of fish have been reported from the Boreal Forest zone, including common species such as Golden and Emerald Shiners and Northern Pike, and species uncommon in Ontario, such as Goldeye, Blackfin Cisco, and River Darter.

Butterflies typifying this area include Old World Swallowtail, Saepiolus Blue, and Bog Fritillary, as well as many other species that have broad ranges throughout Ontario. About 85 species of butterflies have been recorded from this region. Biting insects such as mosquitoes, wood ticks, and blackflies, and insect species that feed on the foliage and bark of trees, are abundant. Species such as the Spruce Budworm, a Tortricid moth larva that dines on spruce and fir needles, can be damaging to the forest when present in large numbers. Many species of warblers, thrushes, and sparrows exploit the rich supply of insects to feed their young.

Hudson Bay Lowland Forest Region

The Hudson Bay Lowland Forest, also known as the Northern Boreal Forest, stretches from the northern edge of the Canadian Shield northward to the treeline at the southern edge of the tundra. Flat topography and poor drainage have created a vast watery plain of fens and bogs – one of the largest continuous wetlands in the world. The landscape is dominated by open fens and bogs, interspersed with treed fens and bogs in which low stands of Black Spruce and Tamarack grow. *Sphagnum* blankets the wetlands, while lichens form the ground cover on drier sites. A denser forest cover of White Spruce, Balsam Fir, Trembling Aspen, Balsam Poplar, and White Birch occurs nearer the shield and along riverbanks and in other well-drained locations. The proportion of open wetland increases towards the northern and western portions of the region, where Black Spruce and Tamarack become more stunted and widely spaced.

The lowland is an important migratory staging area for millions of geese of several species. Greater and Lesser Yellowlegs nest almost exclusively in the open, sparsely wooded wetlands of the region. Unlike most gull species, Bonaparte's Gulls nest in trees that grow among the muskeg; small colonies occur throughout the lowland. Northern Hawk Owl, Northern Shrike, and Common Redpoll also prefer this habitat. Approximately 165 species of birds nest in this forest region.

Many species of small mammals inhabit the Hudson Bay Lowland, including Black-backed Shrew, Northern Bog Lemming, and Meadow Jumping Mouse. Among the large mammals are Gray Wolf, Arctic Fox, Polar Bear, Wolverine, Canada Lynx, and Woodland Caribou. Bearded Seals lounge on the boat docks at Moosonee. More than 35 species of mammals have been recorded in the lowland.

The cold, harsh climate and long winters are not hospitable to most species of herpetofauna. Only four species are widely distributed in the region. These hardy amphibians are American Toad, Boreal Chorus Frog, Northern Leopard Frog, and Wood Frog.

Fish are in conspicuously short supply in the lowland, probably also because of the climate as well as the inhospitable environment of the countless bogs. There are about 35 species of fish living in this northern habitat. Among these hardy residents are Ninespine Stickleback, Cisco, and White Sucker.

Fifty-four of the common, widespread species of Ontario butterflies have been recorded from Moosonee and a few other coastal communities along James Bay. None has been recorded from any other part of the lowland, probably owing to lack of coverage rather than absence of butterflies.

Tundra Region

A narrow strip of arctic tundra occurs along the coasts of Hudson Bay and the adjacent northwest corner of James Bay. The area is underlain by permafrost and sedimentary rock. It consists of numerous ponds and lakes, uplifted beach ridges, dry uplands with lichens and heath plants, and low-lying swales with their dominant grasses and sedges. Ground-hugging willows and birches, such as Arctic and Labrador Willows and Dwarf Birch, grow on the barrens and beach ridges. Other shrubs include Northern Dwarf Raspberry, Cloudberry, Soapberry, Alpine Bearberry, Alpine Bilberry, and several species of currants. Stunted spruces, which occur singly or in patches along riverbanks, are found with increasing frequency inland towards the transition to the Hudson Bay Lowland Forest in the vicinity of the treeline. Herbaceous plants present include Alpine Bistort, Arctic Pyrola, Marsh Ragwort, Alpine Goldenrod, and the tiny fern called Moonwort. Along the saltwater coast, species such as American Dune Grass, Seabeach Sandwort, Oysterleaf, and Thrift grow.

Breeding birds of the tundra include Red-throated and Pacific Loons, Common and King Eiders, Willow Ptarmigan, Parasitic Jaeger, Arctic Tern, Smith's Longspur, and Common Redpoll. Black Guillemot, an alcid, may be seen offshore. More than 100 species are known to breed in this area.

The fauna of the tundra is made distinctive from that of the rest of Ontario by the presence of marine mammals. Bearded and Ringed Seals, Polar Bear, and Beluga can be found along the entire coast during the ice-free season. Walrus are found in one place in Ontario – a shoal near Cape Henrietta Maria. Approximately 35 species of mammals have been recorded from Ontario's Tundra Region and its shores.

There are about 25 species of fish found in the waters of the Tundra Region. These include Arctic Char, Finescale Dace, and Shorthead Redhorse.

Butterflies which occur in the tundra zone in Ontario, and do not extend inland or farther south than the James Bay coast, include Giant Sulphur, Pelidne Sulphur, Arctic Blue, and Melissa Arctic. Some species commonly found in fields and open spaces elsewhere in Ontario also inhabit the coast of Hudson Bay, to make up a total of 27 species.

CHANGES IN ONTARIO'S FLORA AND FAUNA

Native Species

As the glaciers retreated from various parts of Ontario between

14,000 and 8,000 years ago, plants and animals from the west, south, and east invaded the newly uncovered landscape. Since then, fluctuations in climate have periodically caused changes in the distribution of many species of plants and animals. Coinciding with a warming trend that began during the last century, a number of southern species have extended their distribution northward while several northern species have withdrawn from the southern portions of their ranges.

The greatest agent, however, in bringing about changes in species composition has been mankind. In the last few hundred years, human activities such as logging, agriculture, drainage of wetlands, and farm abandonment have helped to reshape the distribution patterns of many species. Loss or alteration of natural landscape has greatly diminished many habitats and caused large-scale decreases in the species dependent upon them. The creation of urban centres, garbage dumps, sewage lagoons, pasture, cropland, and clear-cut woodlands has produced new habitats attractive to species adapted to conditions at these sites.

With the opening up of the landscape, species associated with second-growth woods, open country, and forest edge have proliferated. White-tailed Deer and Turkey Vulture, a wide-ranging New World scavenger, have moved northward and greatly expanded their numbers. In the late 1980s the Virginia Opossum, in response to a series of mild winters, suitable habitat, and other favourable factors, was sighted as far north as Massey. The Northern Cardinal, first recorded in the province in Chatham in 1849, is now a common breeding species south of the Canadian Shield. Western species such as Brown-headed Cowbird, Brewer's Blackbird (a colonial nester of prairie grasslands), and Coyote, which, prior to 1900, was restricted in Ontario to the Rainy River region, have invaded the farmlands of southern Ontario. Species once confined to natural gaps in a largely forested landscape have multiplied enormously: Killdeer, Red-winged Blackbird, Savannah Sparrow, Eastern Cottontail, and Common Milkweed and the Monarch butterfly that feeds on it.

Simultaneously, destruction or fragmentation of forests and wetlands has led to declines or reduced nesting success in bird species requiring large areas of undisturbed habitat, such as Red-shouldered Hawk, Least Bittern, Wood Thrush, and Ovenbird. Faced with hunting pressure and habitat change, Black

Bear, Gray Wolf, Spruce Grouse, and Woodland Caribou have retreated northward. The Timber Rattlesnake and the Cougar have been extirpated from Ontario, and the Passenger Pigeon, once so numerous that flocks darkened the skies, is now extinct.

Introduced Species

Many present-day Ontario species have been introduced by man, either accidentally or intentionally. Most are native to Europe, but some originate in Asia or other parts of North America. Often arriving without the complement of natural enemies they encountered in their native haunts, they frequently behave in unexpected ways in their new habitat. Some become highly invasive, taking over natural habitats and out-competing native species. The Common Dandelion, a traditional European salad green, quickly jumped the garden fence in the New World, and the European Starling expanded its horizons beyond Central Park in New York City. A fungal blight native to Asia has devastated the American Chestnut.

Most introduced plants thrive on roadsides and other open sites; fewer aliens are found in forests. Especially in southern Ontario and near urbanized centres, up to 30% of flowering plants may be non-native. Examples of naturalized plants are Bladder Campion, Viper's Bugloss, Wild Carrot, Orange Hawkweed, and Helleborine, the last an adaptable orchid equally at home in backyards and woodlands. Purple Loosestrife grows in profusion in wet areas, where it accelerates succession and eventually fills in the wetlands. Garlic Mustard carpets forest floors, leaving no space for native flora.

Norway Rat, House Mouse, Sea Lamprey, and Zebra Mussel took advantage of commercial shipping systems to penetrate the province. The Gypsy Moth extends its range by building cocoons on vehicles and hitching rides to new locations. Weed seeds travel long distances by train. The European Hare escaped from a Cambridge area farm to spread across southern Ontario.

Games species, especially fish, have been purposely introduced, with varying degrees of success. Carp, initially brought in as a food fish, is now widely distributed, much to the detriment of the wetland habitats it occupies. Gray Partridge populations are established in areas of less-intensive agricultural activity. Ring-necked Pheasant, a game bird that originated in Eurasia, does not survive harsh winters, especially if there are ice storms. Thus, every fall, sport hunters supplement wild-bred populations with additional releases.

As a result of these numerous changes, several trends can be noted. In general, the numbers of open-country (often introduced) species, and their abundance, have increased. At the same time, the numbers of many native woodland and wetland species and the amount of habitat available to them have decreased. Over the past two centuries, Ontario has lost elements of some of the distinctive combinations of living things that make the province's natural communities unique. Today the assemblages of plants and animals that occupy Ontario's landscape are increasingly similar to those found in other parts of the world.

Regional Accounts

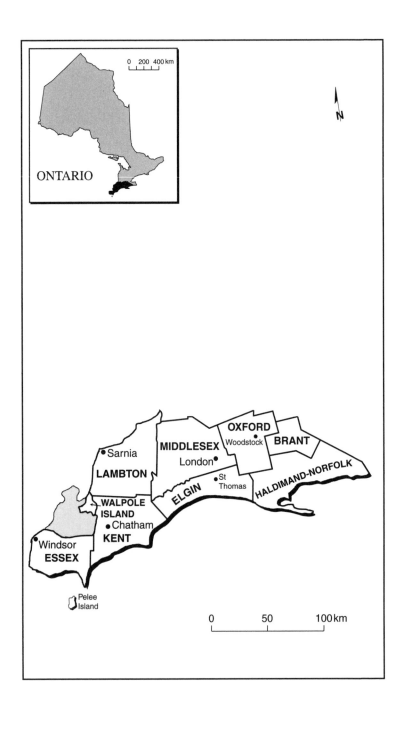

1 North Shore of Lake Erie

Essex   Elgin
Kent   Oxford
Walpole Island   Brant
Lambton   Haldimand-Norfolk
Middlesex

The Carolinian Forest Region in Canada lies more or less south of a line extending from Grand Bend on Lake Huron eastward to just south of Kitchener and along the northern edge of Metropolitan Toronto to the Rouge River. The area marks the northern limit of the Deciduous Forest, a region that continues southward into the United States. The relatively warm climate and rich soils in this area support a great diversity of wildlife and natural habitats. The Carolinian zone in Canada is noted for its numerous rare species, many with southern affinities. Spiny Softshell, Spotted Turtle, King Rail, and Least Bittern are species of marshes and waterways, and among the many rare plants are Smaller Whorled Pogonia, Prairie White Fringed Orchid, Wood Poppy, Pink Milkwort, and Cucumber-tree.

This chapter covers the western portion of Canada's Carolinian zone. Although much of the original landscape of the area consisted of upland deciduous forests, there also were prairies, savannas, and wetlands such as swamp forests and marshes. The topography is flat to gently rolling, formed by glacial deposits over limestones and shales. For the most part, the region has been extensively developed for agricultural, urban, and industrial purposes. Within this highly fragmented landscape few large natural areas remain. Of these, Long Point, Point Pelee, Rondeau, Springwater, and Backus Woods typify some of the best features of the region.

ESSEX COUNTY

> This diminutive little bird [Ruby-throated Hummingbird] showed
> a strange mixture of bravery and caution [during fall migration] ...
> [It] comes sailing down the Point over the tops of the last shrub-
> bery and then dropping down to within a few feet of the sand fol-
> lows its curves and windings out to its most extreme tip when,
> squaring away at an angle to its flight of a moment ago, it makes
> straight for Pelee Island ... Nor did they once hesitate or pause
> from the time when they first hove in sight over the bush tops
> until they faded away in the field of our glasses over the waters of
> the lake. (Point Pelee, fall 1905/6, Percy Taverner [1875–1947] and
> B.H. Swales [1875–1928], ornithologists)

Once the bottom of glacial Lake Warren, Essex County consists
of a low-lying clay plain. The overlying till forms a thick mantle
above the limestone bedrock, which surfaces briefly near
Amherstburg and on Pelee Island. Much of the county originally lay under a swamp forest of American Elm, Black and
White Ashes, and Silver Maple. Natural drainage for the most
part flows northward to Lake St Clair, now aided by an extensive network of ditches.

When travelling through the county, one is struck by the
land's flatness, and the expanse of fields stretching into the distance. Here and there tiny green islands of remaining natural
area contain a rich diversity of flora and fauna and relieve the
landscape of its monocultural croplands. About 3% of the
county remains in a natural state.

Ojibway Prairie Complex

The sandy soils of southwestern Windsor and adjacent LaSalle
were once dominated by prairie and oak savanna. Ojibway Prairie Provincial Nature Reserve and the city of Windsor's Ojibway
Park, Tallgrass Prairie Heritage Park, and Black Oak Woods
Heritage Park are the most accessible parts of the 300-ha complex of remnant prairie-related vegetation. The main vegetation
communities of the Ojibway prairie complex consist of tallgrass
prairie, old field, oak savanna, Black Oak–Pignut Hickory forest, oak woodland, and thickets. The site is now managed by

deliberately set, controlled burns. After a spring fire, everything appears dismally charred, but new greenery shoots up almost immediately. Some species may be 3–4 m high by mid August. The major attraction is the prairie flora, which comes into its own in late July when meadows of wildflowers – waist high and taller – ripple in the midsummer breezes, while grasses such as Big Bluestem, Indian Grass, and Tall Cord Grass tower high overhead. Intermingled among them in various colourful combinations can be found the orange of Butterfly-weed, the purples of Spiked Blazing-star and Tall Ironweed, and the yellows of Tall Coreopsis, Stiff-leaved Goldenrod, and Tall Sunflower. As the weeks go by, other species add whites, pinks, blues, greens, and browns to the constantly changing display of colour. More than 600 plant species have been documented at Ojibway prairie complex. Over one-sixth of these, many of them of prairie origin, are considered rare in Ontario. Among the numerous significant species are American Chestnut, Large Twayblade, Prairie Dock, Culver's-root, Colicroot, Sullivant's Milkweed, Purple Three-awned Grass, Ohio Spiderwort, Two-flowered Rush, White Blue-eyed Grass, Wild Indigo, Winged Loosestrife, and Gray-headed Coneflower.

A wide variety of birds can be found in the area. Many are migrants, but some residents are seldom found much farther north in Ontario. Yellow-breasted Chat is a notable nesting species. Although rarely encountered, Meadow Jumping Mouse, Baird's Deer Mouse, Eastern Fox Snake, Butler's Garter Snake, and Eastern Massasauga are residents. The complex is also noted for its great diversity of butterflies.

– **Ojibway Prairie Provincial Nature Reserve.** The reserve includes trails and an observation platform overlooking a fine example of tallgrass prairie.

– **Ojibway Park.** The park supports wet Pin Oak and dry Black Oak forests. It is an excellent migrant trap for birds. Tufted Titmouse, Red-bellied Woodpecker, and Carolina Wren are common residents. Trails and a nature centre are open year-round. Nearby sites contain drier phases of tallgrass prairie and oak savanna, and small ponds noted for their diversity of dragonflies.

DIRECTIONS. OPPNR is on E side of road; OP is on W. 1) From Hwy 401 at Windsor, exit W onto Hwy 3 (becomes Huron Church Rd); go 4.5 km to Todd Lane & turn left. Drive 2.5 km & turn left on Malden Rd; go 0.5 km & turn right at Sprucewood Ave. Drive 1.5 km & turn right on Matchette Rd; go 1.5 km N. 2) From W-bound E.C. Row Expressway go 1 km S on Matchette Rd. Ask at OP nature centre for directions to other prairie sites.

INFORMATION. For OP: Windsor Dept of Parks & Recreation, 2450 McDougall St, Windsor, Ont, N8X 3N6, 519-966-5852. For OPPNR: c/o Wheatley Provincial Park, Box 640, Wheatley, Ont, N0P 2P0, 519-825-4659.

Ruscom Shores Conservation Area

Trails and a boardwalk provide access to a stretch of Lake St Clair shoreline and adjacent 50-ha remnant wetland, home to several rare species. Shorebirds, marsh birds, and waterfowl use the area during migration. A significant flight of Blue Jays passes through in late April. Marsh Wrens breed in the cattail marsh, and Great Egrets and Black-crowned Night-Herons feed in the area. Map Turtles can be seen offshore.

DIRECTIONS. From Co Rd 35 in Stoney Point go 5 km W on Co Rd 2; just before RR tracks turn right on Surfside Dr; continue to parking lot adj to housing along lakeshore.

INFORMATION. Essex Region Conservation Authority.

Tremblay Beach Conservation Area

Located on Lake St Clair just east of Stoney Point, the seasonally flooded wetlands at Tremblay Beach attract a variety of migrating waterfowl in spring. Nesting birds include Pied-billed Grebe, Marsh Wren, and Yellow-headed Blackbird. Great Egret, Black and Forster's Terns, and Black-crowned Night-Heron visit the area to feed. Nearby lagoons attract migrating shorebirds and waterfowl.

DIRECTIONS. From jct of Co Rds 35 & 2 in Stoney Point, go N to lakeshore road; turn right & go to parking lot at end of road.

INFORMATION. Essex Region Conservation Authority.

Big 'O' Conservation Area

During migration, trails through a swampy woodlot produce a wide range of warblers, including rarities.

DIRECTIONS. From jct of Hwy 77 & Co Rd 46 in Comber, go S on Hwy 77; turn E on 1st side street (Elizabeth St). Enter via wet, poorly marked path between house numbers 7009 & 7011, or continue to end of street & request directions & permission from Big 'O' Inc.

NOTE. Crossroads Restaurant at jct of Hwy 77 & Co Rd 46 maintains sightings book.

INFORMATION. Lower Thames Valley Conservation Authority.

Town of Essex Crow Roost

The town of Essex hosts Canada's largest winter roost of American Crows. Visit the woodlot just before dusk from December to February to watch up to 80,000 crows arrive for the night.

DIRECTIONS. Go to S edge of town near jct of Hwy 3 & Co Rd 23. If roost site changes, follow direction of flying crows to relocate.

Holiday Beach Conservation Area
(including Big Creek Marsh)

From mid August to December, Holiday Beach is one of the best locations in North America for recording high concentrations of migrating raptors passing overhead. Many of the eastern accipiters, falcons, and buteos go through in good numbers. Large passages of migrating Ruby-throated Hummingbird, Blue Jay, American Goldfinch, Cedar Waxwing, and American Crow have also been observed. A 10-m-high tower overlooks the adjacent 800-ha Big Creek Marsh, a major waterfowl migratory stopover site. Expanses of shallow, open water interspersed with cattail stands attract waders such as Great Egret, Green and Great Blue Herons, and Black-crowned Night-Heron.

The area harbours a number of rare species. In August parts of the marsh become a haze of pink when Swamp Rose-mallow flowers. Other significant plants include Prairie Dock, Tall Ironweed, Big Shellbark and Pignut Hickories, Hop-tree, and American Lotus. Eastern Fox Snake, Northern Water Snake, and Blanding's Turtle all occur.

DIRECTIONS. Located on Co Rd 50, about 10 km SE of Amherst-burg off Hwy 18.

INFORMATION. Essex Region Conservation Authority; Holiday Beach Migration Observatory, 313-665-4407 (Michigan).

Cedar Creek Conservation Area

This 48-ha property is part of a much larger natural area that encompasses over 500 ha, much of it floodplain, along the lower reaches of Cedar Creek. The wooded wetlands and adjacent upland forests are noted for their high numbers of Carolinian species. Rare woody species include Black Walnut, Sassafras, Flowering Dogwood, Shagbark and Big Shellbark Hickories, and Pin, Black, and Swamp White Oaks. Among the unusual fauna present in the valley are Eastern Mole and Orange-spotted Sunfish. Bald Eagles are regularly seen in the area.

DIRECTIONS. To reach most accessible portion of CA, from Kingsville go 6.7 km W on Hwy 18; at Arner go 0.5 km S on Co Rd 23 to entrance on W side of road.

INFORMATION. Essex Region Conservation Authority.

Kopegaron Woods Conservation Area

This 20-ha wooded site contains an unusual diversity of swampy and upland Carolinian vegetation, including Black Gum, Sassafras, and Flowering Dogwood. An excellent display of spring wildflowers and ferns can be seen from the trails and boardwalks. Starflower and Red and White Trilliums grow among carpets of Mayapple, Wild Geranium, Yellow Trout-lily, and Narrow-leaved Spring-beauty. Songbirds pass through during spring migration.

DIRECTIONS. On Hwy 3 just W of Wheatley.

INFORMATION. Essex Region Conservation Authority.

Hillman Marsh Conservation Area

Hillman Marsh provides excellent birding during spring and fall migration, but note that hunting is permitted in fall. Rarities show up regularly. The area is used by gulls; terns, including Forster's and Black Terns; several species of herons, such as Great Egret; rails; and songbirds, including Orchard Oriole. Bald

Eagles routinely fly overhead. Many species of shorebirds and a large variety of waterfowl, including Northern Shoveler and Ruddy Duck, visit during migration. Raised dykes bordering the marsh provide ideal locations for viewing and photography. Most of the 400-ha marsh consists of extensive stands of cattails interspersed with open water. Among uncommon plants are Scarlet Ammannia, Strange Cinquefoil, and Yellow Pond-lily. The Eastern Fox Snake is found here. There are trails, interpretive displays, a marsh viewing platform, and a boardwalk.

DIRECTIONS. Located 5 km N of Point Pelee Nat'l Park & 8 km E of Leamington. 1) Follow Co Rd 37 S from Hwy 3. 2) Take Co Rd 20 E from Leamington.

INFORMATION. Essex Region Conservation Authority.

Onion Fields Adjacent to Point Pelee National Park

Watch for shorebirds in migration, especially American Golden-Plover, Black-bellied Plover, Red Knot, Ruddy Turnstone, and Buff-breasted Sandpiper.

DIRECTIONS. Drive roadways just N of Point Pelee Nat'l Park boundary adj to Pelee Marsh.

Point Pelee National Park

Point Pelee National Park is one of the finest places in North America for the study and observation of bird migration. It also has a wide variety of plants and other wildlife, some with restricted ranges in Canada. The point is a narrow, triangular peninsula of sand that separates the central and western basins of Lake Erie. There is an incredible variety of habitats squeezed into the park's 1,600-ha area. Major habitats include beach, Red Cedar savanna, upland forest, swamp forest, and the large freshwater marsh that covers two-thirds of the park. Point Pelee is characterized by plants and animals of the Carolinian zone, some of which are at or near the northern edge of their ranges. The park also hosts flora and fauna that have prairie affinities, but almost totally lacks species typical of the coniferous or mixed forests of the north.

The park offers trails, a bookstore, interpretive programs, camping (groups only), motor train trips to the tip of the point, and a visitor centre that is open year-round.

Flora. Over 750 plant species have been reported from Point Pelee. Many, such as Prickly-pear Cactus, are of special interest because they are rare in Canada or grow more profusely here than in other parts of the country. Trees of note are Black Walnut, Common and Dwarf Hackberries, Red Mulberry, Sycamore, Red Cedar, and Sassafras. Interesting shrubs and herbs include Spicebush, Hop-tree, Wild Potato-vine, Swamp Rose-mallow, Appendaged Waterleaf, and Tall Bellflower.

Birds. Point Pelee is most famous for its spectacular spring and fall bird migrations, when 350 species of birds have been recorded. It is considered one of the top 10 birding spots in North America and, in the month of May, attracts birdwatchers from around the world. By jutting into the lake, the point shortens the over-water flight path for migrating birds and is therefore a natural channel for migrants. Rarities turn up every year. Some southern species, such as Carolina Wren, Blue-gray Gnatcatcher, Orchard Oriole, and Yellow-breasted Chat, nest in the park.

Spring migration begins as early as January or February and continues into the first part of June. First to come are the Horned Larks, followed by waterfowl (whose timing coincides with the melting of the ice), and then blackbirds. A Pelee spring is highlighted by the annual passage of brightly coloured songbirds; on a good day in May an observer may tally over 100 species. The park is especially known for its outstanding warbler migration, over 40 species having been recorded. The peak occurs during the first to third weeks of May.

Southward migration, though less concentrated than the northward passage of birds in spring, also provides good viewing opportunities. By the middle of June shorebirds begin to arrive from farther north. By late July and into August songbirds and swallows move through the park. In September and October, hawks are migrating in good numbers and large flocks of Blue Jays and blackbirds pass through. Regular fall rarities include Golden Eagle, Peregrine Falcon, Merlin, Northern Saw-whet Owl, and Red-necked Phalarope.

Mammals and Herpetofauna. Among the more unusual species are Eastern Mole, Five-lined Skink, Blanding's Turtle, and Eastern Fox Snake. Frogs, such as Spring Peeper and Midland Chorus Frog, call from early March to July. After an absence of many years, Southern Flying Squirrels have recently been reintroduced to the park.

Insects. Point Pelee is one of the best places in Canada to see Hackberry Butterfly and Giant and Spicebush Swallowtails. Autumn is notable for the migration of Monarch butterflies and several species of dragonflies and wasps. Under the right weather conditions, thousands of Monarchs can congregate at the tip of the park before launching themselves across the lake en route to Mexico. The migration generally runs from August 25 to October 5 and is best in mid to late September.

DIRECTIONS. Located 10 km S of Leamington; see prov hwy map.

INFORMATION. Point Pelee National Park, RR 1, Leamington, Ont, N8H 3V4, 519-322-2365.

Pelee Island

Pelee Island, Canada's most southerly inhabited land mass, originally consisted of five small limestone islands connected by marshes and barrier beaches. A system of dykes and drainage ditches built a century ago created a single island of 4,000 ha. Gouges and scratch marks left by retreating glaciers are visible on the limestone bedrock. Because of its southerly location and the moderating influence of Lake Erie, Pelee Island enjoys a milder climate than anywhere else in the province. This, along with drought-prone conditions created by shallow soils over bedrock, has encouraged oak savanna and prairie-like vegetation in some portions of the island.

Pelee Island's savannas support a number of interesting plants, such as Pale Yellow Corydalis, Miami-mist, and Wild Hyacinth. Open-grown Chinquapin Oak, Blue Ash, Red Cedar, Hop-tree, and Burning Bush provide vertical components to these sites. Alvar conditions attract various plants with prairie affinities, among them Big Bluestem, Nodding Wild Onion, and Gray-headed Coneflower. Additional species typical of such habitats are Prairie Rose, Purple Milkweed, Wandlike Bush-clover, and Winged Loosestrife.

Pelee Island is well known for its many rare species with southern affinities – in particular, a number of plants that occur natively in Canada only on Pelee Island and the surrounding small Canadian islands in Lake Erie. Uncommon birds and animals are present also, from the Angular-winged Katydid to the Yellow-breasted Chat and the elusive Gray Fox. Endangered amphibians and reptiles are especially prominent here, including Blue Racer, at present found in Canada only on Pelee Island. The Lake Erie Water Snake, also endangered, is endemic to the islands in western Lake Erie. Other resident herpetofauna include Blanding's Turtle and Eastern Fox Snake. Several outstanding natural areas have been protected on Pelee Island. DIRECTIONS (to island). Take ferry (1-800-661-2220) from Kingsville, Leamington, or Sandusky (Ohio). INFORMATION. MNR; Pelee Island's Heritage Centre (519-724-2291) has sightings book & museum of local natural & human history.

– Fish Point Provincial Nature Reserve. This most southerly tip of Pelee Island consists of a 1 km-long sandspit and wetland complex jutting southward into Lake Erie. In many ways it resembles a miniature version of Point Pelee and, in spring, compares with it as a trap for migrating birds. Fish Point also acts as a funnel for autumn migrants, such as birds, butterflies, and dragonflies. The mature upland woods, Silver Maple swamp, old fields, dogwood-hawthorn scrub, rich lagoon, lakeshore beaches, and open water of Lake Erie make this a very diverse site, and probably the best birding spot on the island, particularly during migration. In spring, wildflowers abound. Dutchman's Breeches, False Mermaid, Appendaged Waterleaf, and Creeping Chervil all grow here. Along the eastern shore, outcroppings of Middle Devonian limestone create a shingle beach.

– Stone Road Alvar. Located in the southeast portion of Pelee Island along both sides of Stone Road, this site is one of the most significant natural areas in the entire province. Most of it is protected under ownership by the Federation of Ontario Naturalists and the Essex Region Conservation Authority. Flat limestone bedrock overlain by thin soils makes the site prone to frequent drought, conditions to which the flora characteristically found on alvars are suitably adapted. Prairie, savanna, alvar, shrub thicket, and woodland communities all occur here. The influence of factors such as variations in the depth of the soil and past farming, grazing, and burning practices has resulted in the present-day mosaic. Late summer is the best time to see many of the site's most unusual plants, including a spectacular display of Gray-headed Coneflower. The open, scrubby nature of the alvar makes it excellent habitat for breeding White-eyed Vireo and Blue-gray Gnatcatcher.

– **Lighthouse Point Provincial Nature Reserve.** Built in 1834, the oldest standing lighthouse on the Canadian side of the lower Great Lakes marks the northern tip of Pelee Island. The peninsula on which it stands juts north into Lake Erie and acts as a channel for migrant birds. The trail leading to the old lighthouse offers first-class birding, especially during spring and fall. At the base of the point a large, shallow lagoon permits excellent viewing of herons, egrets, cormorants, and other water birds. Semi-open woods along the dune ridges are dominated by large, vine-draped Cottonwoods. A savanna community of Blue Ash, Chinquapin Oak, and Common Hackberry is located at the southern end of the reserve.

KENT COUNTY

> No part of the Canadian scenery is more lovely than what is presented, on leaving Chatham, by the windings of the narrow and picturesque Thames. For about twelve miles [downstream] this river runs between ... sloping and verdant banks, until these ... recede, leaving nothing visible ... but a forest of tall rushes, affording shelter and nutriment, at the proper season ... to myriads of wild ducks of every description and quality ... For miles around, as you at length issue into the lake [St Clair], the surface of the latter is seen darkened, at short intervals of space, with huge flocks of these migratory birds. (April 1840, Major John Richardson [1796–1852], soldier and writer)

An extensive sand plain in the northeastern portion of the county marks the delta of the Thames River in glacial Lake Warren. The modern Thames bisects the plain and the county on its way to Lake St Clair. East of the lake, a large tract of very low, flat ground, once a wooded swamp bordered by marshy meadows along the shore, has been drained and dyked. This area is prone to spring flooding by the Thames. A level, poorly drained clay plain spreads across the southwestern part of the county.

Originally covered by swampy forest, this land has also been drained. The Blenheim moraine, a long, bulky ridge of sand and gravel left by retreating glaciers, roughly parallels Lake Erie both east and west of the town of Blenheim. In places it spreads to a width of 10 km and rises nearly 10 m above the surrounding countryside. Most of Kent County is used for agriculture, only 4% still being in a natural state.

Wheatley Provincial Park

A system of broad creeks is a main feature of this largely wooded 240-ha park on Lake Erie. Forest types vary from upland oak and hickory stands, to wet woods of Red Maple and Swamp White Oak, to a pine and spruce plantation. Significant trees include Black Gum, American Chestnut, Tulip-tree, and Black Oak. Open-field communities support several tallgrass prairie species, such as Little Bluestem and American Hazel. The fine showing of spring wildflowers includes extensive displays of Purple Spring Cress. Fall colour is best between September 15 and October 15. There is an excellent bird migration through Wheatley, and a few southern species, such as Acadian Flycatcher and Red-bellied Woodpecker, are known to nest in the mature forest. Black-crowned Night-Heron and Great Egret are frequently observed along the creeks. Eastern Fox Snake and Midland Painted Turtle are seen regularly.

DIRECTIONS. Located off Hwy 3 just E of Wheatley; see prov hwy map.

INFORMATION. Wheatley Provincial Park, Box 640, Wheatley, Ont, N0P 2P0, 519-825-4659.

Two Creeks Conservation Area

This 33-ha conservation area consists of old field, early successional scrub, a pine plantation, and a small creek. Significant vegetation species are few but, because of the proximity to Point Pelee, Wheatley Provincial Park, and Lake Erie, a good number of migrating birds can be found. Watch for breeding Eastern Meadowlark, Bobolink, and Field Sparrow in the old fields.

DIRECTIONS. From Hwy 3 in Wheatley, go 2 km N on Co Rd 1 (Erie St).

INFORMATION. Lower Thames Valley Conservation Authority.

St Clair National Wildlife Area

Extensive wet prairies and marshlands once dominated the landscape along the eastern edge of Lake St Clair. Most have been drained for agriculture, but some of the most important wetlands in the Great Lakes area still survive. Of the 800 ha remaining, the Canadian Wildlife Service owns and manages the 240-ha St Clair National Wildlife Area, a rehabilitated wetland that contains features characteristic of adjacent marshlands, including a number of rare species. In addition to typical marsh vegetation, some wet prairie species, such as Tall Cord Grass, Yellow Stargrass, and Tall Ironweed, can be found. American Lotus and Swamp Rose-mallow grow along the dyke edges and cattail stands.

Waterfowl are the most obvious birds, particularly during the spring and fall migrations. Redhead and Canvasback nest, as do numerous other water birds, such as Least Bittern, Common Moorhen, Yellow-headed Blackbird, and Forster's Tern. Herons and egrets are a common sight, and migrating shorebirds are often seen on mudflats and nearby freshly ploughed fields. Tundra Swans may be observed from mid to late March, ducks from early March to mid April and from early October to December, and geese from late October to early April. There are good populations of reptiles and amphibians, including Eastern Fox Snake, Northern Water Snake, and Blanding's Turtle. Bullfrog, Spring Peeper, and Midland Chorus Frog call from early March to July.

DIRECTIONS. From Chatham go W on Co Rd 34, turning N to Paincourt; go 8 km W on Co Rd 35 to W Townline. Turn N & go 2.5 km to wildlife area on left. Trail along dyke to observation tower is 1 km past entrance.

INFORMATION. Marsh Manager, St Clair National Wildlife Area, RR 1, Paincourt, Ont, N0P 1Z0, 519-354-1418.

Chatham Crow Roosts

Kent County is one of the most productive corn-growing areas in Canada. Because modern harvesting equipment can leave up to 10% of the grain scattered in the fields, there is an ample food supply to attract crows. The relatively mild, snow-free winters contribute to the ease of gleaning the fields by crows. From late

November through February, up to 45,000 American Crows can be found using various roost sites in Chatham. The birds can be seen arriving at dusk or leaving just before sunrise.

DIRECTIONS. The most frequently used sites are along Thames River just E or W of Keil Dr bridge.

C.M. Wilson Conservation Area

Primarily used for recreation, this 30-ha site contains a small pond surrounded by an old-field community. About one-third of the area is wooded, with forest communities consisting of Bur Oak–Red Maple, Sugar Maple–American Beech, and Cotton-wood–Red Ash. Most of the vegetation is typical of a somewhat disturbed, fragmented forest, but there is a good representation of spring wildflowers. Carolinian species include Spicebush, Running Strawberry-bush, Bladdernut, and Sycamore. A good variety of migrating passerines has been noted.

DIRECTIONS. From Hwy 401 SE of Chatham, go 0.5 km S on Hwy 40; turn right on Horton Rd; cross RR tracks; turn right & go 1 km.

INFORMATION. Lower Thames Valley Conservation Authority.

McGeachy Pond Management Area

This 15-ha property is a pond and wetland complex along the shores of Lake Erie. Water levels are controlled and often provide habitat for a wide variety of shorebirds, waterfowl, and wading birds, including rarities. Buff-breasted Sandpiper is occasionally seen in adjacent onion fields. Black and Common Terns have nested here. Whimbrel are sometimes found resting in spring on the gravel shoreline. Common Moorhen, American Coot, Great Egret, and Black-crowned Night-Heron are frequently observed. An observation tower provides good views of the area and Lake Erie.

DIRECTIONS. From Blenheim, go 4.5 km SW on Hwy 3; turn SE on Co Rd 12 (Erieau Rd) & go 8 km.

INFORMATION. Lower Thames Valley Conservation Authority.

Erieau Harbour

The fishing village of Erieau is on a short peninsula that separates Rondeau Bay from Lake Erie. From the main pier at the end of the road, one can see numerous gulls and waterfowl in season. Double-crested Cormorants are often observed, particularly in spring and fall. Bald Eagles, resident in Rondeau across the bay, are occasionally seen. Autumn is often an excellent time to find good numbers of birds, especially after a storm. Purple Sandpiper and Red Phalarope can be present along the pier, rocks, or shoreline. In autumn and early winter, Snowy Owls usually appear on posts or gravel piles.

DIRECTIONS. Follow Co Rd 12 through village to harbour.

Sinclair's Bush

This fine hardwood bush is dominated by American Beech and Sugar Maple, but Black Cherry, Basswood, and Tulip-tree are also present. There is an excellent profusion of spring wildflowers, along with Carolinian indicator species such as Running Strawberry-bush, Clearweed, and Virginia Knotweed. Rare species include Pawpaw, Winged Monkey-flower, and Appendaged Waterleaf. Typical southern and upland woodland bird species occur within the 46-ha tract.

DIRECTIONS. From Chatham, take Hwy 40 SE to Blenheim; follow Hwy 3 SE for 5 km, turning S on 1st unpaved road E of golf course bend. Woods are about 1 km S of hwy. The small publicly owned portion of woodlot is located just NE of bend in main road.

INFORMATION. Lower Thames Valley Conservation Authority.

Rondeau Provincial Park

Proclaimed in 1894, Rondeau is Ontario's second-oldest provincial park and, at 3,250 ha, the largest park in southwestern Ontario. Rondeau consists of a series of ridges and sloughs, formed as a result of local water currents depositing sand eroded from bluffs east and west of the park. A classic example of forest succession is visible, ranging from the grassy beach dunes along the east side of the park, melding into a narrow strip of pine-oak forest, and then beech-maple forest – the major forest type in the park. Wetlands are a predominant feature of Rondeau, from the narrow woodland sloughs to the almost 1,000-ha semi-open cattail marsh. A sizable portion of the shallow waters of Rondeau Bay rounds out the array of major park habitats. The waters in and around the park serve as significant fish-spawning beds. Numerous rare species make their homes within the park.

Rondeau contains the largest protected area of southern deciduous vegetation in Canada. Over 800 species of plants have been noted, including many Carolinian species, which give much of the Rondeau forest a rich, lush appearance. Tulip-tree, Sassafras, and Shagbark Hickory are widely scattered, while Sycamore and Red Mulberry are less frequent. Various southern herbaceous species grow here, and a number of plants with western or tallgrass prairie affinities may also be found. Many rare plants, such as Three-birds Orchid, occur in the park.

The park has a visitor centre, an interpretive program, and trails that are open year-round.

Flora. Specialties include Wild Yam, Yellow Mandarin, Tall Bellflower, False Mermaid, Oswego Tea, Clearweed, Late Coral-root, Cylindric Blazing-star, Wingstem, Wild Bergamot, Green Milkweed, Riddell's Goldenrod, Indian Grass, Clammyweed, Swamp Rose-mallow, and Little Bluestem.

Birds. With the highest species diversity of breeding birds in the province, Rondeau is one of the best locations for birding any time of the year. Of the more than 330 species recorded, 134 have been confirmed as breeding in the area, including the rare Prothonotary Warbler, which has its largest Canadian breeding ground at Rondeau. Bald Eagles are nesting residents, and southern species such as Acadian Flycatcher, Yellow-breasted Chat, Red-bellied Woodpecker, Northern Mockingbird, White-eyed Vireo, Louisiana Waterthrush, Tufted Titmouse, and Chuck-will's-widow nest frequently or are regular summer residents. Rarities show up often. Peaks of songbird migration occur in mid May and from mid August to early September. Rondeau's wetlands serve as a major waterfowl staging area.

Mammals and Herpetofauna. To date, 33 mammal species have been recorded, including Virginia Opossum, Southern Flying Squirrel, and Gray Fox. Raccoon and White-tailed Deer are by far the most obvious species. An impressive 30 species of reptiles and amphibians are known from Rondeau. Residents include Five-lined Skink, Eastern Hognose Snake, and Eastern Fox Snake. Listen for calling frogs from early March to July.

DIRECTIONS. Located 15 km E of Blenheim off Hwy 51.
INFORMATION. Rondeau Provincial Park, RR 1, Morpeth, Ont, N0P 1X0, 519-674-5405.

Bates Marsh

Just north of Rondeau Provincial Park, a causeway crosses a wetland complex of mudflats, cattail marsh, open shallow water, and a small remnant swamp. Numerous turtles can be seen here sunning in season. Swamp Rose-mallow brightens one corner of the marsh in midsummer. Shorebirds are often attracted to the mudflats, and waterfowl are frequent, especially during spring and fall.
DIRECTIONS. Located along Hwy 51 (Kent Bridge Rd), 1.5 km N of Rondeau Prov Park. Park on roadside S of causeway.

Morpeth Cliffs

Rising 20–30 m above Lake Erie, these cliffs provide eroded material to form the base for the Rondeau sandspit. Waterfowl, including large rafts of scaup and mergansers, can be seen both spring and fall. Black, Surf, and White-winged Scoters are regularly observed. In September and October thousands of hawks, Blue Jays, Ruby-throated Hummingbirds, and Monarch butterflies migrate along the shoreline, especially on days with northwest to northeast winds.
DIRECTIONS. From Rondeau Prov Park gate, go 1 km N on Hwy 51; continue straight on Co Rd 17 for 5 km till road turns N. En route, park along road for waterfowl viewing over lake. View hawks from cliffs or along 1st E-W conc rd (New Scotland Line) after co rd veers N.

WALPOLE ISLAND

Our first surveying operations lay among the many mouths of the River St. Clair. They form a number of large, marshy islands, of course partly in Lake St. Clair ... When we arrived we found the scenery here very pretty, the borders of the lake, for miles inland, being a savannah of long, bright green grass, with woods in the rear disposed in capes, islands, and devious avenues. I was delighted, and landed for a run; but to my surprise, I stepped into

water ankle-deep, and forthwith returned. (1821, John J. Bigsby
[1792–1881], medical doctor and geologist)

The Walpole Island First Nation occupies about two-thirds of
the bird's-foot delta complex at the mouth of the St Clair River.
These six islands, covering about 24,000 ha, comprise that portion of the delta which lies on the Canadian side of the international boundary. As unsurrendered Indian territory, Walpole
Island is under the authority of the elected Chief and Council.
Native traditions and philosophies have resulted in the preservation of a wide variety of significant natural areas that are dispersed throughout the territory. About one-sixth of the land
mass, located at the north end of the delta complex, is occupied
by forest, savanna, and prairie communities. Another sixth is
devoted to agriculture, and the remainder consists of wetlands –
sloughs, lakes, channels, the adjacent shallow waters of Lake St
Clair, and vast marshes. This rich mosaic supports a remarkably
diverse assemblage of living organisms. There is a wealth of life
here that is hard to find anywhere else. Of international significance are the oak savanna and tallgrass prairie, and the rare
flora and fauna that occupy these habitats.

Flora. The Walpole Island First Nation is one of the finest
tallgrass prairie sites in North America. Over 800 vascular plant
species have been recorded, of which about 100 are rare in
Ontario and several are not found elsewhere in Canada. Southern Slender Ladies'-tresses, Prairie Rose, and Colicroot are just a
few of the significant plants that occur on Walpole. Other plants
of interest include Spiked Blazing-star, Prairie Dock, and Showy
Goldenrod. Pin Oak, Black Gum, Hop-tree, Sassafras, Ohio
Buckeye, and Kentucky Coffee Tree are among the Carolinian
tree species found on the island.

Birds. A total of 139 species of birds, 37 of which are considered rare in Ontario, have shown evidence of breeding on Walpole Island. Tufted Titmouse, Red-bellied and Red-headed
Woodpeckers, Orchard Oriole, and White-eyed and Yellow-
throated Vireos are distinctive denizens of the woodlands. This
is Ontario's best place for observing Northern Bobwhite.

Mammals and Herpetofauna. The 24 species of mammals
reported include the Southern Flying Squirrel. Among the 26
species of amphibians and reptiles are uncommon species

such as Queen Snake, Eastern Fox Snake, and Butler's Garter Snake.

Butterflies. The uncommon Giant Swallowtail drifts noiselessly above the tallgrass prairies and open oak savannas. Four Dusky Wing species – Wild Indigo, Horace's, Mottled and Persius – are all considered rare. In all, 59 species of butterflies have been found on Walpole Island.

DIRECTIONS. Take Hwy 40 W from Wallaceburg; when Hwy 40 jogs N, continue W on Co Rd 32 to island.

NOTE. **Because of its status as Indian territory, groups or individuals wishing to come to Walpole Island must receive approval from the Chief and Council prior to their visit.** This can be arranged by contacting the Walpole Island Heritage Centre (519-627-1475) or the Walpole Island Band Office (519-627-1481). The best way to see Walpole's wildlife and plants is on an escorted hike, such as those run by the Federation of Ontario Naturalists and sanctioned by the Heritage Centre. The island is large, and many of the species are scattered enough that it would take someone without a knowledgeable guide a great deal of time before a fraction of them could be found.

LAMBTON COUNTY

> In a low cliff on the west side of ... Kettle Point, there is displayed a vertical amount of about twelve to fourteen feet of black bituminous shale ... Many nodules and crystals of iron pyrites are enclosed in the shales, and many peculiar spherical concretions ... They are of all sizes from three inches to three feet in diameter, and while many of them are nearly perfect spheres, others are flattened a little, generally on the under side; sometimes they present one sub-spherical mass on the top of another, the upper of which is smaller than the under, giving a rude resemblance to a huge acorn. (1848/9, Alexander Murray [1810–84], geologist and explorer)

Most of Lambton County is covered by a large, relatively level clay plain. The Lake Huron shoreline and the northeastern part of the county exhibit evidence of ancient glacial lakes: sand deposits, beach terraces, shorecliffs, and moraines. Close proximity to Lake Huron, the St Clair River, and the northern edge of the Carolinian Forest zone give the area an unusual degree of biological diversity. The carving of the Sydenham and Ausable rivers into the topography has created a funnel for the establishment of bird and plant communities that are characteristic of more southerly climates. These two large rivers also provide habitat for two uncommon reptiles, the Queen Snake in the Ausable and the Spiny Softshell turtle in the Sydenham. Much of the county is used for agricultural proposes; about 7% remains in a natural state.

Sarnia and Area

– St Clair River (Sarnia to Port Lambton). Drive this route in January to watch for wintering gulls and ducks in the St Clair River.

DIRECTIONS. From Exit 1 on Hwy 402 in Sarnia, go 2.6 km S on Hwy 40B, following Front St to end. Turn left on Johnston St & go 1 block; turn right on Christina St & go 1.7 km. Go left on Clifford St; go right on Vidal St (Hwy 40B) & go past chemical companies to river, about 4 km. Follow St Clair Pkwy.

– Point Edward Lighthouse. The lighthouse offers great views of water birds in autumn, particularly during the passage of cold fronts, when Parasitic and Pomarine Jaegers, King Eider, Red-throated Loon, Brant, and Black-legged Kittiwake are driven close onshore by northerly winds. Sometimes the migrants stop to rest, either here or on nearby Sarnia Bay (south of the bridge). Hawks and passerines also stream by, crossing the mouth of the St Clair River after following the Lake Huron shoreline.

DIRECTIONS. From Exit 1 on Hwy 402 in Sarnia, go 1 km N on Front St to its end; turn left on Victoria Ave & go 1.1 km; turn N on Fort St & go 0.4 km to lake & lighthouse (actually range marker).

– Canatara Park. This 70-ha city-of-Sarnia park includes a stretch of Lake Huron beach, Lake Chipican (4 ha), and a 9-ha tract of deciduous forest. The woodland contains more than 30 species of native trees, including Tulip-tree and Swamp White Oak, as well as over a dozen species of native shrubs and vines. Information and bird checklists are available at the log cabin near the south end of Lake Chipican.

DIRECTIONS. From Exit 2 on Hwy 402 in Sarnia, go 1.4 km N on Christina St to park gate on Lake Chipican Dr (off Cathcart Blvd W).

– Blackwell Prairie. This site consists of 2 km of the 17-km-long Howard Watson Nature Trail between Modeland Road and Blackwell Sideroad in Sarnia. On the entire trail over 180 species of native plants have been identified. Since its construction in 1859 the 30-m-wide former railway right-of-way has become an important refugium for prairie plants, including Big and Little Bluestems, Indian Grass, Butterfly-weed, Puccoon, Flowering Spurge, Showy Tick-trefoil, Round-headed Bush-clover, and Wild Yam. Among the rarer prairie plants are Stiff-leaved Gold-enrod, Porcupine Grass, and Incised Puccoon.
DIRECTIONS. From Exit 6 on Hwy 402 in Sarnia, go 2.5 km N on Modeland Rd to trail entrance marked by sign set back from road; walk E.

– Wawanosh Wetlands Conservation Area. This conservation area includes a memorial forest on former farmland, and shallow ponds and naturally regenerating vegetation on old borrow pits. Shorebirds are best seen in May and from early August to mid September, ducks in spring and fall, and Green and Great Blue Herons from spring to late fall. There is a viewing tower and a nature trail on the 47-ha property.
DIRECTIONS. From Exit 6 on Hwy 402 in Sarnia, go 1 km N on Modeland Rd; turn right on Michigan Ave & go 2.2 km E to Blackwell Sdrd; turn right & go 1.3 km S to entrance.
INFORMATION. St Clair Region Conservation Authority.

Mandaumin Woods

This 10-ha tract owned by Lambton Wildlife Incorporated is a level wet woods, typical of much of the forest cover that once existed in the county. There is a good showing of wildflowers in the spring. About 15 different species of *Carex* sedges grow here. Trees include Sugar Maple; Basswood; American Beech; White, Red, and Black Ashes; Shagbark and Bitternut Hickories; Bur Oak; Hop-hornbeam; and Blue-beech.
DIRECTIONS. From Exit 15 on Hwy 402, go 4.3 km S on Co Rd 26 to gate & trail on right.

Lake Huron Shore (Kettle Point to Port Franks and Pinery Provincial Park)

This shoreline area represents a fairly continuous 10-km stretch of pine-oak forest, sand dune vegetation, and Carolinian-influenced woodland. A significant number of rare species have been recorded. A good place for observing lichens and fungi, the area also features unusual vascular plants, including Pink Lady's-slipper, Goldthread, and Yellow Stargrass. Wet meadows in the dune sections harbour stunning floral displays, among which are orchids such as Grass-pink, Rose Pogonia, and Great Plains Ladies'-tresses. Spiked, Rough, and Cylindric Blazing-stars dot the landscape in fall, while in summer Blue-hearts grow in their only Canadian stronghold. The shoreline offers excellent opportunities for observing birds in migration. Gulls and waterfowl accumulate in large numbers in spring. During autumn storms jaegers, loons, and scoters sail in. The potential for rarities always exists. Nesting species include Whip-poor-will, Pileated Woodpecker, and Cerulean, Pine, and Hooded Warblers.

– **Kettle Point.** The marshy shale flats of the Kettle Point First Nation are actually a shelf of uncovered bedrock, the only place in southern Ontario where Upper Devonian Kettle Point shales are exposed. Large limestone concretions within the sedimentary shales resemble stone cannonballs. Known as kettles, these are visible along the shore, where Lake Huron erodes the point. This is an excellent spot for watching migrating gulls and waterfowl during fall, early winter, and spring.
DIRECTIONS. From Forest go 9 km N on Hwy 21; when Hwy 21 veers E, turn W onto Co Rd 7, then right almost immediately onto Rawlings Rd (W Ipperwash Rd). Continue 3.3 km N to London Rd; turn left & go 3.4 km to William St; turn right & go 1.7 km to lake. Turn left & go 2.2 km to navigation marker (1st point); continue 2.9 km to 2nd point, marked by large kettle. Park & examine shoreline. Go S to reach Co Rd 7 again.

– **'L' Lake.** Sand dunes, wet meadow, and bog are found here, with a large section of bog and wooded dunes in public ownership. The area is significant as a migratory stopover for songbirds. Sedge Wrens occur, as do Bushy Aster, Tall Ironweed, Tulip-tree, Pitcher-plant, Buckbean, and Twinflower.

DIRECTIONS. From Hwy 79 at Northville go 2.4 km W on Hwy 21 (Lakeshore Rd) to Outer Dr; go 2.2 km N to sign for 'L' Lake Management Area on right. Explore via old woods roads. For views of lake continue N & E along Outer Dr.
INFORMATION. Ausable-Bayfield Conservation Authority.

– **Lambton County Heritage Forest.** Now situated well inland from Lake Huron's present-day shoreline, high sandy dunes support an unusual type of forest known as an oak savanna.
DIRECTIONS. Forest stretches between Outer Dr & Port Franks Rd. From Hwy 79 at Northville go 0.7 km W on Hwy 21 (Lakeshore Rd); turn N onto Port Franks Rd & watch for trails entering woods on left 0.1, 0.8, & 1.5 km N of Hwy 21.

– **Karner Blue Sanctuary.** The Karner Blue, an endangered butterfly subspecies in Ontario, lives in association with Wild Lupines. The butterfly was formerly found at this 14-ha site of forested dunes, and it is hoped that it will someday be present once again.
DIRECTIONS. From Hwy 79 at Northville go 0.7 km W on Hwy 21 (Lakeshore Rd); go 1.1 km N on Port Franks Rd; turn right on Whatham St & go 0.2 km to sign.
INFORMATION. Lambton Wildlife Incorporated, Box 681, Sarnia, Ont, N7T 7J7.

– **Pinery Provincial Park.** Situated on a series of sand ridges parallel to the Lake Huron shoreline this 2,400-ha park contains one of North America's largest remaining oak savannas. Here, dry, poor soils and a regime of infrequent fire attract a number of species more typically encountered west of Lake Michigan, where prairie soils are rich and burns are more frequent. Among the stands of White, Red, and Black Oaks and Red and White Pines at Pinery are found wet and dry meadows and the former channel of the Ausable River. The park's diverse assemblage of prairie and Carolinian species includes Dwarf Chinquapin Oak, Dwarf Hackberry, Tulip-tree, Wild Lupine, and Fringed and Stiff Gentians. Nearly 800 species of plants and 300 species of birds have been recorded. Eastern Hognose Snakes live in the dunes, and good numbers of amphibians are found near the old channel. Dusted, Delaware, and Leonardus Skippers and Olympia Marblewing are among the numerous butterflies. An interpretive program, a visitor centre, and hiking and cross-country ski trails are provided.

DIRECTIONS. Located 5 km SW of Grand Bend on Hwy 21; see prov hwy map.

INFORMATION. Pinery Provincial Park, RR 2, Grand Bend, Ont, N0M 1T0, 519-243-2220.

– **Thedford Marsh.** The peak time for Tundra Swans here is mid to late March. Ducks are best seen from early March to mid April and from early October to December.

DIRECTIONS. Go 1 km NE from Pinery Park gate on Hwy 21; turn right onto Greenway Rd & go 2 km.

Rock Glen Conservation Area and Ausable River Corridor

Access to the Ausable River can be gained by way of Rock Glen Conservation Area. The wooded slopes of the valley harbour outstanding displays of ephemeral spring wildflowers, including Twinleaf, and southern trees such as Flowering Dogwood, Common Hackberry, and Chinquapin Oak. There is a fine show of fall colour in late September and early October. Since the last glaciation, the Ausable River has been eroding its way through 25 m of sedimentary deposits laid down 400 million years ago in the shallow waters of a salty sea. The exposed cross-section reveals layers of glacial till, limestone, and shale. The 28-ha glen property has an attractive 11-m-high waterfall, whose waters flow through a gorge for several hundred metres before emptying into the Ausable. The site's geological features are best seen from the trails and stairways bordering this gorge. Fossils of brachiopods, cephalopods, corals, and other ancient marine creatures can be found at Rock Glen.

DIRECTIONS. To reach Rock Glen CA, from Co Rd 12 at Arkona go 1 km N on Hwy 7; go right on unpaved road for 1 km.

INFORMATION. Ausable-Bayfield Conservation Authority.

A.W. Campbell Conservation Area and Sydenham River Corridor

Along the Sydenham River and its tributaries are a number of wooded sections that provide habitat for Carolinian plant communities and their associated wildlife. In A.W. Campbell Conservation Area, Morrogh Creek meanders through lowland hardwood bush dominated by American Beech, Sugar Maple, and White Oak. The wooded floodplain, uplands, and numerous ravines also support Sycamore, Green and Blue Ashes, Hop-hornbeam, Bitternut and Shagbark Hickories, and Blue-beech. The excellent variety of wildflowers includes Wild Leek, Cut-leaved Toothwort, White Trout-lily, Virginia Waterleaf, and Squirrel-corn. Trails through the 125-ha property can be hiked year-around.

DIRECTIONS. To reach Campbell CA, take Exit 44 from Hwy 402; go 18 km S on Hwy 79 almost to Alvinston; go 2.5 km E on 1st conc rd N of Alvinston (Brooke Conc Rd 6/7).

INFORMATION. St Clair Region Conservation Authority.

MIDDLESEX COUNTY

The banks in general are high, with intervals here and there of fine flats, originally used by the Indians as planting grounds, particularly on the north side of the river adjoining the fork. On the east side of the fork, between the two main branches of the river Thames, on a regular eminence, about forty feet above the water, is a natural plain, interspersed with small groves of wood, affording in its present state the appearance of a beautiful park, cultivated with great cost and taste; the pines which skirt the river shew their tops above the banks, and make a fine termination to the whole. (Site of London, mid 1890s, Sir David Smyth [1764–1837], English gentleman)

Shaped by glacial activity, the level to gently rolling topography of Middlesex County is marked by a mix of morainic ridges and sand, clay, and till plains. The Thames, the major river system, flows west to Lake St Clair, as does the secondary river, the Sydenham. The northwestern part of Middlesex drains northward via the Ausable River to Lake Huron. The county consists largely of farmland, with urban development centred around London. Scattered natural areas support Carolinian zone species that reach their northern limits in Middlesex. The Thames River harbours a significant population of the rare Spiny Softshell turtle.

Parkhill Conservation Area

A large reservoir, open fields, reforested areas, and numerous trails are prominent features of the 800-ha property. Mature hardwoods on the uplands, river bottomlands, and ravine slopes support an excellent display of 25 species of spring wildflowers, including Carolina Spring-beauty. Fall colour is best from mid September to mid October. The area is open for cross-country skiing in winter.

DIRECTIONS. From jct of Hwys 7 & 81 (2 km E of Parkhill), go N on Centre Rd.

INFORMATION. Ausable-Bayfield Conservation Authority.

Strathroy Conservation Area

This 40-ha site, primarily a significant wetland complex along the Sydenham River, includes a reservoir, swamp, pine plantation, and a floodplain dominated by mature Red Maple, Black Ash, American Elm, and Tamarack. Several rare species occur. Large willows and Sycamore form the canopy along the river, while Alternate-leaved Dogwood and Tartarian and Morrow's Honeysuckles are common shrubs. In low areas, Marsh-marigold and Spotted and Pale Touch-me-nots are abundant. Plants of interest include Green Dragon, Wild Yam, Poison Sumac, and Hairy-fruited Sedge. Watch for Red-bellied Woodpecker, Belted Kingfisher, and migrating waterfowl. Trails are open year-round for hiking and cross-country skiing.

DIRECTIONS. From Exit 65 on Hwy 402, go 3 km S on Hwy 81; turn left on Second St. Go 0.5 km; turn right on Head St; go 1 km.

INFORMATION. St Clair Region Conservation Authority.

Coldstream Conservation Area

Trails and a boardwalk here explore a floodplain and nearby uplands on the upper reaches of the Sydenham River. Springs bubbling up from gravel deposits supply cool water for a swampy woodland of White Cedar, Black Ash, and dogwoods. Marsh-marigolds and Skunk-cabbage blanket the wetland in spring; Green Dragon and Golden Alexanders also occur. The site includes a reservoir, rehabilitated gravel pit, and mature woodlot of Sugar Maple, American Beech, elm, ash, and hickory. Chinquapin Oak, Common Hackberry, Black Maple, and Black Cherry are also present. There is an excellent display of spring wildflowers, including a number of uncommon species, and a fine show of fall colour. During migration, waterfowl stop over on the reservoir and a good diversity of songbirds passes through the woodlands.

DIRECTIONS. From Hwy 22 at Poplar Hill go 2 km NE on Co Rd 16 (Ilderton Rd); turn left on Quaker Lane & go 1 km.

INFORMATION. St Clair Region Conservation Authority.

Skunk's Misery

Lying on a flat sandy plain, this lush 1,200-ha tract contains deciduous forest, deciduous swamp, interconnected woodlots, and small coniferous plantations. Much of the area is dominated by upland oak-hickory, wetland Silver Maple, and related communities. The site is significant for its large size, relatively undisturbed character, and numerous rare species, many with southern affinities. Among southern tree species are Tulip-tree, Black Oak, Flowering Dogwood, American Chestnut, Black Gum, and Sassafras. The rich understorey mixture of Carolinian forest and prairie plants includes Horsebalm, Wild Yam, and Poke Milkweed. A good diversity of orchids is present, such as Yellow Lady's-slipper, Nodding Ladies'-tresses, Loesel's Twayblade, Ragged Fringed Orchid, and Northern Green Orchid.

This is a good place for observing breeding warblers, including Cerulean, Golden-winged, Hooded, and Mourning Warblers. Also found are Pileated, Red-headed, and Red-bellied Woodpeckers and Broad-winged Hawk. The most unusual mammal is the rarely seen Badger. Among uncommon reptiles are Butler's Garter Snake, Black Rat Snake, Eastern Hognose Snake, and Eastern Milk Snake. Look for Giant and Spicebush Swallowtail butterflies. Wood ticks and mosquitoes are notable.

DIRECTIONS. From Hwy 2 at Wardsville go N on Co Rd 1 (Hagerty Rd); turn left onto 2nd crossroad N of village (Centreville Dr/Range Rd II N). For next 5 km much of woodland on both sides of road is publicly owned. For good areas to visit, continue W on Centreville Dr for 1.5 km past 1st crossroad (Dogwood Rd); watch for trails leading N & S into woods from here to next crossroad (Sassafras Rd). Trails are informal & largely unmarked; take care to avoid getting lost.

INFORMATION (and additional access points). MNR; Lower Thames Valley Conservation Authority.

Big Bend Conservation Area

The 37-ha property provides public access to the Thames River. Deciduous woodlands bordering the river harbour some interesting and uncommon Carolinian flora, such as False Gromwell and the tall, fall-blooming Cup-plant. Map and Midland Painted Turtles can be seen basking on logs or rocks in the river. This stretch of the Thames is a good spot to look for uncommon winter birds.

DIRECTIONS. From Co Rd 1 in Wardsville, go 2.5 km E on Hwy 2; turn S on Big Bend Rd (Mosa Twp Rd 12) & drive 4 km to river.

INFORMATION. Lower Thames Valley Conservation Authority.

Longwoods Road Conservation Area

Best known for its re-created Indian village, this 63-ha site features varied terrain and habitats, ranging from mature deciduous forests to meadows and stream valleys. American Beech, White Ash, Black Cherry, White Cedar, Red-osier Dogwood, and Staghorn Sumac grow on the sandy soils. There is a good display of all the common spring wildflowers, among which are Wild Ginger, Wild Columbine, and Mayapple. Also present are several uncommon plants, such as Early Saxifrage. Red-bellied Woodpeckers are resident, and Eastern Bluebirds nest in the area. Trails can be used year-round.

DIRECTIONS. Drive 6.5 km W of Delaware on Hwy 2.

INFORMATION. Lower Thames Valley Conservation Authority.

Komoka Provincial Park

Consisting of a mixed hardwood and Eastern Hemlock forest cut by numerous ravines, this 200-ha undeveloped provincial park runs for 4 km along the south side of the Thames River. The vegetation is diverse, containing no fewer than 24 different plant communities, including small prairie-like grasslands and a number of unusual species, such as Blue Ash and Purple-flowering Raspberry. A stand of Tamarack near the Gideon Drive entrance is a good place to look for birds in winter. Relatively uncommon species such as Red-bellied and Pileated Woodpeckers and Louisiana Waterthrush occur in the park. There is a colony of Golden-winged and Blue-winged Warblers and their hybrids. Migrating birds often follow the river corridor. The nearby Komoka gravel pits (junction of County Road 14 [Glendon Drive] and County Road 16 [Komoka Road]) offer excellent waterfowl viewing in spring and fall.

DIRECTIONS. Drive W from London on Commissioners Rd (later becomes Co Rd 14/Glendon Dr). 1) Turn left onto Gideon Dr (Co Rd 3) & drive 2.8 km; turn right onto dead-end spur opp Brigham Rd; park & walk trails through scrubby hills N towards river. 2) From jct with Gideon Dr continue 1.3 km W on Commissioners Rd; park at former MNR field office on left side of road; enter trails into woods.

London

Along the Thames River, which runs through the city, a number of wooded riverbanks and flats have survived in a more or less natural state.

INFORMATION (for first 5 sites). Upper Thames River Conservation Authority; London Parks & Recreation Dept, 111 Horton St, London, Ont, N6B 3N9, 519-661-5391.

– **Warbler Woods.** Located on rolling hills and steep ravines, this 24-ha deciduous woodland is a good place for finding forest birds, especially during migration. A mixture of Carolinian and northern plants grows here: Bloodroot, Sharp-lobed Hepatica, and Mayapple are found on the higher ground, while ferns, horsetails, and clubmosses favour the damp valleys.

DIRECTIONS. Park on old roadway on S side of Commissioners Rd W between Chestnut Hill W & Kains Rd. Follow rough trail into woods.

– **Sifton (Byron) Bog.** This 28-ha relict bog is the only Black Spruce–Tamarack–*Sphagnum* floating bog in the vicinity of London. It contains heath plants such as Leatherleaf, Bog Rosemary, Pale Laurel, Highbush Blueberry, Black Huckleberry, and both Large and Small Cranberries. Insectivorous plants include

Pitcher-plant and Round-leaved and Spatulate-leaved Sundews. Among the several orchids are Rose Pogonia and Grasspink. Water birds, warblers, and finches are particularly evident in spring and fall migration. The Southern Bog Lemming and numerous reptiles and amphibians are found. Low-lying trails and boardwalks are provided.

DIRECTIONS. Located on S side of Oxford St, just W of Hyde Park Rd, across from W end of Oakridge Mall. Enter via pedestrian gate on E side of fence.

– Medway Valley Heritage Forest. Rich bottomland woods and some upland areas contain a number of uncommon flowers, trees, and shrubs, as well as a good range of nesting and migrant birds. In places, high, steep slopes have been eroded to expose the geological history of this ancient glacial spillway.

DIRECTIONS. 1) From University of Western Ontario on Western Rd, follow trail at SW corner of parking lot next Commissariat Bldg near Saugeen-Maitland Residence. 2) Enter through Elsie Perrin Williams Estate at end of Windermere Rd, 1 km W of Western Rd. 3) Enter by Museum of Archaeology on E side of Wonderland Rd 0.5 km S of Hwy 22.

– Westminster Ponds–Pond Mills. Varying topography and drainage conditions create a variety of habitats around several kettle ponds within a 300-ha complex. The woodlands contain an interesting blend of northern and southern species, such as Flowering Dogwood, Shagbark Hickory, Leatherleaf, and Pink Lady's-slipper. The area is an important migration stopover site for both land and water birds.

DIRECTIONS. Enter behind tourist info booth on E side of Wellington Rd 0.5 km N of Southdale Rd.

– Meadowlily Woods. Relatively undisturbed, this 135-ha mature hardwood forest includes terraces, ravines, and floodplain. Birdlife is abundant and diverse; Scarlet Tanager and Wood Thrush breed here. The spring wildflower display is exceptional. Good numbers of orchids are found, as well as several rare Carolinian plants.

DIRECTIONS. From Commissioners Rd E turn N on 1st road (Meadowlily Rd) E of Highbury Ave (Hwy 126). Park along road & walk through stone gates on trail heading E.

– Kirk-Cousins Management Area. Located on the West-minster moraine at the headwaters of Kettle Creek, this 40-ha wetland complex includes a pond, hawthorn scrub, a pine plantation, and an open maple-oak-hickory woodlot. Common Yel-lowthroat, Willow Flycatcher, Spring Peeper, Gray Treefrog, Common Snapping Turtle, and Midland Painted Turtle all frequent the area.

DIRECTIONS. From London, follow Wellington Rd S of Hwy 401. Just S of Regina Mundi College turn E onto Scotland Dr. Pass radio antennae; park in small lot on left.

INFORMATION. Kettle Creek Conservation Authority.

Fanshawe Conservation Area

Fanshawe Lake, a deep reservoir on the northeast edge of London on the North Thames, is a good place for observing water birds in spring and in fall until freeze-up. Extensive pine and spruce plantations attract winter finches. Several rare species, including the Spiny Softshell turtle, are present in the conservation area. Flora of interest include Black Maple, White Trout-lily, and Common Hackberry. Trails through the 1,250-ha site are open year-round.

DIRECTIONS. 1) Water birds are best seen from bluffs just N of Sunningdale Rd (1st road N of Fanshawe Park Rd [Hwy 22]); drive E to end of road, then follow trail N along lakeshore. 2) Entry to Fanshawe Park is E off Clarke Rd 2 km S of Fan-shawe Park Rd.

INFORMATION. Upper Thames River Conservation Authority.

Thames Valley Trail

This 75-km hiking trail follows the Thames River from Komoka Provincial Park (west of London) through the city of London, then north along the North Thames River to St Marys. Numerous rapids, steep wild riverbanks, and level farmland characterize the northern section. Floodplains, greenbelt, and city parks are found in the London area. Specialties of the valley are Black Maple, Common Hackberry, and White Trout-lily. Besides Komoka Park and Fanshawe Lake (see descriptions elsewhere), the trail gives access to the bottomlands between Highbury Avenue and Adelaide Street within the city of London and, to the north, the woods west of the river north of Plover Mills. A 31-km link from Komoka Park south to the boundary of Middlesex County connects the Thames Valley Trail to the Elgin Hiking Trail.

DIRECTIONS. Access from Hwy 7, Co Rd 16, & at various bridges.

INFORMATION. Thames Valley Trail Association, 1017 Western Rd, London, Ont, N6G 1G5, 519-645-2845 (guidebook available).

Dorchester Swamp

Thirteen kilometres east of London, a 550-ha wooded wetland is bisected by Highway 401. Particularly noted for its northern features, Dorchester Swamp harbours a variety of plant communities and a large number of uncommon species, including Yellow Lady's-slipper, Small Purple Fringed Orchid, and Long Manna Grass. White Pine and Tamarack grow here, as do American Beech, Black Cherry, and Shagbark Hickory. Golden-crowned Kinglet, Northern Waterthrush, Canada Warbler, and White-throated Sparrow breed. Because the area remains wet throughout the year and there are no formal trails, the best time to visit is after freeze-up in late fall or winter (on skis or snowshoes).

DIRECTIONS. Located N & S of Hwy 401, E & W of Hwy 73. Access is difficult; contact UTRCA for public entry points.

INFORMATION. Upper Thames River Conservation Authority.

Lake Whittaker Conservation Area

This site contains a diversity of habitats, including a significant wetland area, a kettle lake, coniferous and deciduous woodlands, old fields, and undulating terrain. American Woodcock and Ruffed Grouse are common, and Red-headed Woodpeckers nest in the swamp. During migration, large numbers of Rusty Blackbirds roost around the lake. Trails through the 142-ha property are open all year.

DIRECTIONS. From Hwy 401 go S on Hwy 73. Turn left onto Co Rd 37; go 5 km & turn left.

INFORMATION. Kettle Creek Conservation Authority.

ELGIN COUNTY

> Foggy open weather, thermometer 48[°F]; snow nearly all gone,
> and ice breaking up along the lake [Erie] shore. The noise caused
> by its breaking, when driven by a south wind on the shore, is like
> the various noises arising from the rattling of carriages, and the
> bustle of a large town on approaching it. In the depth of winter, in
> the sharpest weather, the trees, on the sun arising on them, snap
> and crack like the report of pistols in all directions, though there
> are no cracks to be seen. (Talbot Settlement, March 5, 1826, Joseph
> Pickering, farm foreman)

Stretching for almost 100 km along the central north shore of
Lake Erie, the flat to rolling landscape of Elgin County is overlain by glacial till, clay, and outwash sand. The terrain is interrupted by the broad, meandering valleys of several large creeks
and numerous streams. Where these drainage systems empty
into Lake Erie, they have cut steep-sided gullies into the 20–40-
m-high shoreline bluffs. Much of the county is used for agriculture, but scattered examples of Carolinian forest remain and
even a few pockets of prairie habitat persist.

Beattie Access

Located at the mouth of Sixteen Mile Creek, this 8-ha park
incorporates steep shoreline bluffs, very high hills, and areas of
sandy and stony beach. Several interesting plant species grow
along the shoreline. Water birds can be observed offshore and,
during migration, Whimbrel and other shorebirds pass through.
DIRECTIONS. From Rodney go S on Co Rd 3 (Furnival Rd) almost
to Port Glasgow. Turn right on Conc Rd 14, then immediately
left on Havens Lake Rd. At T-jct turn right & go past marina
facilities to parking area by creek.

E.M. Warwick Conservation Area

Open meadowland, steep wooded valleys, a narrow shoreline
beach, and Lake Erie bluffs characterize this 14-ha site. An
observation tower provides views of offshore water birds and
warblers in migration. Carolinian trees and plants are found
here.

DIRECTIONS. From Eagle go 2 km E on Hwy 3; turn right on McKillop Sdrd & drive 1.6 km towards lake.
INFORMATION. Lower Thames Valley Conservation Authority.

John E. Pearce Provincial Park

This small park protects a 68-ha tract of old-growth deciduous forest on the shoreline cliffs overlooking Lake Erie. Steep, 30-m-high clay bluffs provide fine viewing for gulls, diving ducks, and other water birds as well as for Bank Swallows. This is an excellent site for warblers and other forest birds, including nesting Pileated Woodpeckers. Several species of rare Carolinian trees and plants grow here, and fungi thrive. The spectacular display of spring wildflowers includes Red and White Trilliums, Blue Cohosh, Bloodroot, Sharp-lobed Hepatica, Dutchman's Breeches, Cut-leaved Toothwort, and Wild Ginger. Fall foliage peaks between mid September and mid October. Trails can be walked year-round.
DIRECTIONS. Exit Hwy 401 at Dutton; go 10 km S on Co Rd 8 through Wallacetown to T-jct near lake; turn left & go 400 m; see prov hwy map.
INFORMATION. MNR

Fingal Wildlife Agreement Area

This 300-ha reclaimed wartime air station contains agricultural land, open meadows, hedgerows, a 40-ha mixed deciduous woodlot, plantations, and a number of small ponds. Breeding and migratory waterfowl are present in season. A trail system through a wet woods provides opportunities for observing wildflowers and woodland birds. The area is hunted in fall.
DIRECTIONS. From Fingal go 3 km W on Co Rd 16 to entrance & parking lot on S side of road. To reach hardwood trails, continue 1 km W on Co Rd 16; turn left on Scotch Rd & drive 2.4 km to parking area on left; walk right then left around edge of field to woods.

Patterson and Dalewood Conservation Areas

The 75-ha Patterson Conservation Area includes open meadows and successional farmland, as well as Carolinian bottomlands and forested slopes. A trail through mature woodlands and along the Kettle Creek valley provides good habitat for birds, and connects the area to the 285-ha Dalewood Conservation Area. Dalewood features a large pond, interesting shoreline lagoons, mature mixed forest, and Red Pine plantations. Trails can be used in the off-season.

DIRECTIONS. For Dalewood: from Talbot St in St Thomas, go N on Balaclava St to end; turn right onto S Edgeware Rd, then take 1st left (Dalewood Dr) & drive to small parking lot on right just before bridge, or continue 0.5 km further N to main entrance. For Patterson: from Dalewood CA continue N on Dalewood Dr (Twp Rd 18/Co Rd 31) to Co Rd 52 & turn right; at Highbury Ave (Co Rd 30) turn left & go about 1.2 km.

INFORMATION. Kettle Creek Conservation Authority.

Elgin Hiking Trail

From Paynes Mills on Highway 3 to Port Stanley, 42 km of trail follow the course of Kettle Creek and Dodd Creek through bottomlands, ravines, and along wooded hillsides. This is an excellent place for observing spring bird migration and Carolinian trees, wildflowers, and fauna. Plants of note are Twinleaf, Early Saxifrage, Virginia Cowslip, and Harbinger-of-spring. A 13-km link from Paynes Mills north to the edge of Elgin County connects to the Thames Valley Trail.

DIRECTIONS. Enter trail where roads intersect creeks.

INFORMATION. Elgin Hiking Trail Club, Box 250, St Thomas, Ont, N5P 3T9, 519-633-3064 (guidebook available).

Port Stanley Harbour

Sand beach, berms, and piers east and west of the mouth of Kettle Creek provide habitat and viewing opportunities for shorebirds, gulls, water birds, and shoreline flora. In late May, Whimbrel, Red Knot, and other shorebirds can often be found on the piers.

DIRECTIONS. Take Hwy 4 S to Port Stanley; from traffic lights continue S on Main St to E side of hbr. To reach W side, from lights go W across lift-bridge & immediately turn left.

Hawk Cliff

The end of a township road allowance provides an overview of Lake Erie and its 40-m-high shoreline bluffs. Broad-winged Hawks by the thousands (mid September), as well as Peregrine Falcons (end of September), Red-shouldered Hawks, Northern Goshawks, Golden Eagles (end of October), and many other species of raptors, flood by Hawk Cliff during fall migration (late August to November). Many hawks drift by in small groups called kettles, using the lift from successive thermals (rising masses of sun-warmed daytime air) to save energy. Numbers of hawks are highest when warm weather, northwest winds, and light, fluffy cloud cover follow a period of heavy rains. Spring warbler migration and the fall migration of Ruby-throated Hummingbirds, Eastern Bluebirds, dragonflies, and Monarch butterflies can also be observed.

DIRECTIONS. From Hwy 4 at Union (about 5 km N of Port Stanley) go E on Co Rd 27; turn S on Co Rd 22 & follow its southern extension (Hawkescliff Rd) to lake.

INFORMATION. MNR.

Archie Coulter Conservation Area

Located along the main branch of Catfish Creek, the conservation area contains a small pond, conifer plantations, and open bottomland meadows flanked by wooded hillsides. The 54-ha site is a good place for observing spring wildflowers and warbler migration. A number of unusual plants grow here, including Green Dragon, Horsebalm, Wild Yam, Cut-leaved Avens, Broad-leaved Waterleaf, and Black Walnut.

DIRECTIONS. From Aylmer go 5 km W on Hwy 3 to Orwell; turn S on Co Rd 35; turn right on 1st sdrd & go 5 km.

INFORMATION. Catfish Creek Conservation Authority.

Springwater Conservation Area and Agreement Forest (White's Bush)

This 140-ha stand of mixed deciduous and coniferous trees contains a significant assemblage of rare Carolinian plants and trees. Among the interesting plants are Yellow Clintonia, Indian-pipe, Stout Wood Reedgrass, Running Strawberry-bush,

Yellow Mandarin, and Downy Rattlesnake-plantain. Large mature specimens of American Beech, Red and White Oaks, Tulip-tree, and White Pine are present, some of which may pre-date European settlement of the area. Red and Sugar Maples, White Ash, and Black Cherry are also frequently encountered. The varied list of nesting birds includes Scarlet Tanager, Eastern Wood-Pewee, Pileated Woodpecker, Rose-breasted Grosbeak, Pine Warbler, and Wood Duck. A spring-fed pond and stream provide habitat for Smallmouth and Largemouth Bass and Rainbow Trout. Fall foliage is best in late September and early October. Trails can be toured year-round.

DIRECTIONS. Go 5 km W from Aylmer on Hwy 3 to Orwell, then 3 km S on Co Rd 35.

INFORMATION. Catfish Creek Conservation Authority; MNR.

Aylmer Wildlife Agreement Area

Here observation stands overlooking open meadows and ponds permit close-up views of waterfowl during migration. Up to 5,000 Tundra Swans pass through in March. Ducks are present from March to May and September to November, and shorebirds, including occasional rarities, from April to September.

DIRECTIONS. From Aylmer, go N on Hwy 73 to Co Rd 32; follow Co Rd 32 E, then N to viewing area at SE corner of police college grounds.

INFORMATION. MNR.

Calton Swamp

This 24-ha wetland complex of open ponds, marsh, connecting waterways, wet woodlands, and adjacent mixed-forest uplands supports a rich diversity of habitats and species, including rarities. Look for Stout Wood Reedgrass, Flowering Dogwood, and Broad-leaved Waterleaf. Songbirds, marsh birds, and dragonflies are present during the warmer months, whereas migrating ducks pass through in spring and fall.

DIRECTIONS. From Calton, take Co Rd 45 W; turn N on 1st sdrd & go 1 km; watch for parking lot on right.

INFORMATION. MNR.

Port Burwell Provincial Park

The upper portion of this 260-ha park contains open areas and patches of deciduous woodland. From it, deep ravines cut through steep clay bluffs to a marshy area below, which is protected from Lake Erie by a dune system and sand beach. The wet meadows, ponds, and sloughs support a variety of interesting plants, including horsetails and mosses. Swamp Lousewort is found on the beach, and Northern Adder's-tongue Fern grows on the upper hill. During migration, woodland birds pass through, shorebirds frequent the beach, and water birds can be seen offshore. This is a good spot for observing the fall migration of the Monarch butterfly. Trails can be hiked year-round.
DIRECTIONS. At W edge of Port Burwell off Co Rds 42 & 39; see prov hwy map.
INFORMATION. Port Burwell Provincial Park, Box 9, Port Burwell, Ont, N0J 1T0, 519-874-4691.

OXFORD COUNTY

> A cedar swamp is a strange chaos of wood. The cedars lean in all directions, some grey, dead and bleached with the weather, others green and dark. The branches of the dead ones stream off the mother trunk like snakes from Medusa's head ... Here and there the moisture gathers into a clear little pool or small stream which soaks its way through the rotten bed of leaves, winding, though almost imperceptibly, round the twisted and mossy trunks of the old slanting cedars. Young trees are springing up all around you, sometimes from the rotten prostrate trunks, not yet converted into soil. (Ingersoll area, mid November 1833, Alfred Domett [1811–77], English poet and traveller)

Oxford County is intensively farmed, over 90% of the land having been cleared for agriculture. Most farms have woodlots, and there are a few larger wooded areas as well. The land generally is flat to gently rolling. At the extreme south there is tobacco land on the Norfolk sand plain. Proceeding north, a succession of end moraines crosses the county from west to east. Most of the remainder is till plain, with many drumlins in the vicinity of Woodstock. The northeast has some poorly drained land with a number of small wetlands and kettle lakes, while, to the northwest, a few kame hills add variety to the landscape. At Beachville, where an ancient glacial river cut through the overburden to the bedrock, limestone is actively quarried.

Most of the county is drained by branches of the Thames and Grand rivers, which occupy old glacial valleys much larger than these waterways require today. Dams in two of these have created lakes: Wildwood Lake at the extreme northwest and Pittock Lake at Woodstock. These lakes attract large numbers of migrating waterfowl and provide nesting habitat for others.

Wildwood Conservation Area

See entry under Perth County.

Trillium Woods Provincial Nature Reserve

Situated on the side of a drumlin, this 10-ha woodlot is dominated by Sugar Maple, White Ash, and Black Cherry. American Beech, Bitternut Hickory, and Butternut are also present. Red and White Trilliums and Variegated Trillium (the unusual green and white striped form of the White Trillium) flower in early May.

DIRECTIONS. Take Hwy 19 S from Ingersoll & turn E on Co Rd 12; at 4th crossroad turn left. Watch for sign across from Jakeman's Sugar Bush.

INFORMATION. MNR.

Pittock Conservation Area

Encompassing more than 800 ha, this conservation area stretches for about 8 km along both sides of Pittock Lake, which has been created by a large dam at the western end. Along the south shore close to the lake an old railway right-of-way is maintained as a walking trail. Considerable reforestation with pine and spruce has been carried out in patches along this trail. Large numbers of ducks, geese, and swans stop here on migration in both spring and fall.

DIRECTIONS. 1) In Woodstock follow Huron St N from Hwy 2 to parking lot at Harry Roth Park by lake. 2) From Hwy 59 just N of Woodstock, follow CA signs to entrance on N side of lake.

INFORMATION. Upper Thames River Conservation Authority.

Vansittart Woods Provincial Wildlife Area

This woods is outstanding for its diversity; part is low and swampy, while much has a rolling topography with swampy depressions and small ponds. There is mixed upland hardwood forest, conifer plantation, open hawthorn and Staghorn Sumac scrub, and an extensive Silver Maple swamp. Wood Ducks nest in the area. In spring there is a good variety of wildflowers in the woodlands, while the ponds harbour frogs. Resident sala-manders include Yellow-spotted Salamander and Red-spotted Newt. No hunting is permitted on the 80-ha property.

DIRECTIONS. From Woodstock go E on Hwy 2; at 1 km past Hwy 53 turnoff, go 2.8 km N on Blandford Rd; just past Hwy 401 overpass, enter parking lot on left beside outdoor education school.

INFORMATION. MNR.

Chesney Conservation Area

The most significant feature of this 75-ha conservation area is a *Sphagnum* bog located in a kettle depression amidst low kame hills. The very wet floating mat, which supports hum-mocks of Leatherleaf and Water-willow with Marsh Fern in between, is surrounded by a dense fringe forest of Black Spruce, Tamarack, White Cedar, and Black Ash. The bog is encircled by a deep lagg that makes it inaccessible. Nine spe-cies of orchids grow here.

A boardwalk crosses an extensive swamp forest where a lush mixture of northern and southern elements occurs: Red Maple, Yellow Birch, White Cedar, and various boreal species on the raised hummocks and Red Maple, Black Ash, and American Elm on the wet muck between. A fine mixed woodland of mature Sugar Maple, American Beech, and Eastern Hemlock dominates the uplands and steep slopes. Other sections of the property feature successional old fields and young pine planta-tions.

Chesney Conservation Area is rich in spring wildflowers and ferns. Bog Goldenrod, Harbinger-of-spring, and Dewdrop are among uncommon plants present. Watch for Yellow-bellied

Sapsucker, Nashville and Canada Warblers, and White-throated Sparrow. A number of rare species are found on site.

DIRECTIONS. Take Exit 250 from Hwy 401 at Drumbo Rd (Co Rd 29); go 3 km W to gate on N side of road 0.2 km past jct with Co Rd 22.

INFORMATION. Grand River Conservation Authority.

Lockhart Pond Provincial Wildlife Area (Fowler's Pond)

Paths and a dock provide access to a small kettle lake surrounded by a floating mat of *Sphagnum* mosses. Among typical bog flora are Labrador Tea, Rose Pogonia, Poison Sumac, Mountain Holly, and Tamarack. The 35-ha site also contains Highbush Blueberry, willows, dogwoods, an upland maple woods, and a plantation of Scots and White Pines.

DIRECTIONS. At Exit 250 from Hwy 401 go E on Drumbo Rd (Co Rd 29); take 1st right turn & go 4 km S. Turn right on Conc Rd 4; go 5 km W to dead-end; park & walk in.

INFORMATION. MNR.

Black River Swamp

This significant wetland is the largest forested tract in Oxford County. It includes extensive stands of Silver and Red Maples, Black Ash, and Yellow Birch in the river valley, and American Beech–Sugar Maple stands along the edges. Black Spruce, Balsam Fir, and other northern species are also present. Additional wetland communities occur, such as willow scrub, cattail marshes, and open ponds. The large expanse of standing dead trees provides habitat for woodpeckers and flycatchers. Broad-winged Hawk, Yellow-bellied Sapsucker, Nashville Warbler, Purple Finch, Northern Harrier, and White-throated Sparrow are all found in the swamp. Northern mammals such as Porcupine and Southern Bog Lemming are resident, and White-tailed Deer converge on the area in winter. Four-toed Salamander, Blanding's Turtle, and Redbelly Snake are among herpetofauna of note. Many species of fungi are evident in autumn.

DIRECTIONS. Take Exit 250 from Hwy 401 at Drumbo Rd (Co Rd 29); go 1 km W to Hubbard Rd. Turn right & go to T-jct at Conc Rd 8; turn right. Go 1 km & turn left onto King Rd towards Conc Rd 9. View swamp from any of these last 3 named twp rds only, as Black River Swamp, Drumbo Swamp (on S), & abandoned RR bed between them are all privately owned.

BRANT COUNTY

> The foliage had begun to assume its variegated appearance, before the falling of the leaf – and the beautiful tints and mellow hues ... often blended harmoniously in the same tree, or contrasted with the deepest green of a kindred branch ... The bright yellow of the walnut, the scarlet of the maple, the fresh green of the fir, and the sombre brown of the cedar, were often the most prominent colours; but these were mingled with a variety of others more soft and delicate, melting imperceptibly into each other, and throwing a rich and luxuriant beauty over the gorgeous forest. (Along the Grand River, October 1835, Thomas Rolph [1801/2–58], immigration promoter)

Brant County is well represented with southern plants and animals. The Haldimand clay plain, a relatively flat area with heavy soils, large farms, and many swamps, covers the southeastern region of the county. The central portion is part of the large Norfolk sand plain, a gently rolling, sandy landscape. The western and northern sections contain rolling countryside and include moraines, many wetlands, and a good number of forests. Cutting through the centre of the county, the Grand River valley accommodates numerous rich natural history features.

Grand River

The watershed of the Grand River, which covers 6,734 km^2, is not only the largest inland drainage system in southern Ontario but also one of the oldest. The present river had its beginnings during the retreat of the Wisconsin ice sheet 12,000 years ago. Rising (in part) in Luther Marsh in the Great Lakes–St Lawrence Forest Region, the Grand flows southward through the Carolinian zone before emptying into Lake Erie at Port Maitland. During its 290-km course the river crosses five counties and regional municipalities: Dufferin, Wellington, Waterloo, Brant, and Haldimand-Norfolk. A wooded corridor between Cambridge and Paris that contains many significant plants is one of the best remaining Carolinian forests in Ontario. On the lower reaches of the river, a series of 10 marshes provides nesting habitat for several uncommon species of birds. A number of interesting geological features are found along the Grand River and within its drainage basin. The Grand has been designated a 'Canadian Heritage River.' Hiking tails, canoe routes, and conservation areas provide opportunities for exploring the natural features of the watershed. Fall colour is best between September 15 and October 10. See additional entries under Brant County and other jurisdictions through which the river flows.

INFORMATION. *Canoeing on the Grand River* is available from Grand River Conservation Authority.

Grand River Forests

The 20-km stretch along the Grand River between Cambridge in the Regional Municipality of Waterloo and Paris in Brant County contains approximately 750 ha of relatively undisturbed wooded valleyland. The forests clothe a series of terraces that rise up to 40 m above the river. The woodlands are noted for their numerous rare plants and diversity of habitats. These features are made possible by the variations in sun exposure and moisture caused by the winding valley slopes. Habitats include floodplain, mixed swamp, savanna, perched fens, seepage slopes, and gravelly spring-fed lagoons. Oak-hickory forests occur in dry, sunny locales. The river bottoms vary from White Cedar swamp to willow stands to Sycamore groves. Common Hackberry grows in the north end of the forest. Numbered among the plants of interest are Wild Licorice, Water-hemp, Oswego Tea, American Columbo, White Trout-lily, Twinleaf, Moss-pink, and Perfoliate Bellwort, as well as trees such as Wild Crabapple and Chinquapin, Black, and Hill's Oaks. Bird life is also rich in diversity; be alert for Red-bellied Woodpecker, Yellow-throated Vireo, Wild Turkey, Blue-gray Gnatcatcher, and Blue-winged Warbler. The rare fish Greater Redhorse is a resident of the river, an indication of good water quality. Queen Snake and Pickerel Frog make their homes here, and numerous species of diving and dabbling ducks winter on the river.

DIRECTIONS. *Driving:* Follow Hwy 24 & Glen Morris Rd (Co Rd 14) on E side of river, or Hwy 24A & twp rds near river on W side. For good view from Glen Morris bridge (Co Rd 28) park at nearby general store. *Walking:* 1) Grand Valley Trail winds through forests on W bank from Cambridge to Paris. 2) Grand River Rail Trail from Cambridge to Brantford follows E side of valley; enter via Hwy 24 S of Cambridge or at Glen Morris. *Canoeing:* A good run (best in late April & May) goes from S Cambridge to mill pond in Paris.

INFORMATION. Grand Valley Trails Association (address under Regional Municipality of Waterloo); Grand River Conservation Authority.

Grand Valley Trail

See entry under Regional Municipality of Waterloo.

Pinehurst Lake Conservation Area and Spottiswood Lake

This ridge, forest, and lake complex contains a wide diversity of habitats, from prairies to wetlands (including *Sphagnum* bogs) to a variety of woodland communities. Many rare species of both northern and southern affinity thrive in the area. Among the Carolinian plants are Wild Yam, Sassafras, Perfoliate Bellwort, Pignut Hickory, Rue-anemone, Horsebalm, and Black Walnut. Species showing prairie-savanna affinities include Butterfly-weed, New Jersey Tea, Fragrant Sumac, Large-bracted Tick-trefoil, Yellow Stargrass, and Wandlike Bush-clover. Among numerous additional plant species of note are Sickle-pod, Nodding Thistle, Twinleaf, Buttonbush, Swamp Loose-strife, Squawroot, Virginia Water-horehound, Swamp White Oak, Marsh Skullcap, Bristly Greenbrier, White Vervain, and Trailing Arbutus. The area also harbours a diverse community of birds, ranging from Long-eared Owl to Blue-gray Gnat-catcher, and from Acadian Flycatcher to Cerulean Warbler. Some of the significant herpetofauna found on the site are Blue-spotted Salamander, Northern Ribbon Snake, and Eastern Smooth Green Snake.

   Within the varied terrain is a series of moraine ridges, kettle lakes, and high, steep-sided sandhills. Trails in the 100-ha conservation area can be toured year-round, but the larger tract that surrounds Spottiswood Lake is not accessible to the public.

DIRECTIONS. Pinehurst CA entrance is on Hwy 24A, 6.4 km N of

Paris & 12.9 km S of Cambridge; avoid privately owned eastern portion of site.
INFORMATION. Grand River Conservation Authority.

Whitemans Creek and Valley

The creek flows through oak forests and empties into the Grand River south of Paris. A number of rare species thrive in the valley. Among the more interesting plants are Wood Anemone, Pignut Hickory, Black Walnut, Sycamore, Canada Plum, Swamp White Oak, and Hispid Buttercup. Birds of note include Long-eared Owl, Cliff Swallow, and Blue-gray Gnatcatcher. River Chub and Fantail Darter are found in the creek.

– Five Oaks. This United Church retreat is located on the hills overlooking the confluence of the creek and the Grand River. The native non-parasitic American Brook Lamprey inhabits the river. Watch for gypsum tailings, evidence of old mine sites in the vicinity.
DIRECTIONS. From Hwy 403 at Paris, go 1 km S on Rest Acres Rd (Simcoe-Paris Exit); turn left on Bethel Rd & go to end. To visit Five Oaks, request permission at main bldg; a small donation to help with upkeep would be appreciated.

– App's Mills Conservation Area. The site includes Carolinian forest, pine plantation, and open field. This is a good spot for wildflowers in both spring and summer.
DIRECTIONS. From Hwy 403 at Paris, go S on Rest Acres Rd (Simcoe-Paris Exit) to Robinson Rd (2nd sdrd); turn right & follow signs.
INFORMATION. Grand River Conservation Authority.

Six Nations Indian Reserve

The Six Nations and New Credit Indian Reserves comprise one of the largest tracts of Carolinian forest remaining in Canada. Over 80% of the 9,200-ha block is woodland. The uplands are dominated by various species of oak and hickory, while Red and Silver Maples grow on the lowlands. Although much of the area is a wet, relatively flat clay plain, there are local variations in terrain and soils. Some of the most interesting plants are found along McKenzie Creek. Significant flora include Green

Dragon, Twinleaf, Flowering Dogwood, Green Violet, Sweet Joe-Pye-weed, Oswego Tea, Southern Arrow-wood, and Yellow Mandarin. Among the diversity of birds are Blue-gray Gnat-catcher, Blue-winged and Golden-winged Warblers, and Sedge Wren. The Black Rat Snake occurs here near the northern limit of its range in this part of the province. Wood ticks are abundant, and precautions should be taken.

DIRECTIONS. Take Co Rd 4 S from Brantford; go left on Co Rd 6 & continue to village of Ohsweken. To visit excellent example of oak-hickory woods NE of Ohsweken, park at Band Council hdqts (519-445-2201) or at hospital & walk into woods N of road.

NOTE: **To access reserve lands, permission must be obtained from Band Council and individual landowners.**

REGIONAL MUNICIPALITY OF HALDIMAND-NORFOLK

There are some few meadows in the highest and driest portions of [the marshes], but the principal parts are generally overflowed with water. Various descriptions of rushes grow here and flourish luxuriantly, and towards the lake where the water deepens grow vast quantities of the wild rice. These marshes at certain seasons of the year are inhabited by immense flocks of wild fowl which resort here during the Autumn to feed on the plentiful and nutritious seed of the wild rice. There are swans, geese and such prodigious quantities of ducks as to blacken the water when they settle down. (Long Point Bay, 1834, William Pope [1811–1902], farmer and wildlife artist)

The western part of the municipality, the former Norfolk County, is dominated by the relatively flat Norfolk sand plain, originally a delta deposited under glacial lakewaters. Today the area is drained by several creeks, which have cut deep valleys across the plain as it slopes gradually towards Lake Erie. The light sandy soils, easily eroded by wind and water, have, in some areas, been reforested. About 25% of Norfolk is wooded; most of the rest is used for farming, frequently tobacco.

The gently rolling terrain of the former Haldimand County occupies the eastern portion of the region. Here the variably drained soils of a clay plain support a rural agricultural land-scape. Only 12% of the countryside is under forest cover. Formed beneath the waters of glacial Lake Warren, the region is now bisected by the Grand River, which, along with its tributaries, has created numerous deep valleys.

Long Point

Long Point is one of Canada's most significant ecological reserves. Owned by the Long Point Company since 1866, about half of the area was donated to the people of Canada as a 'National Wildlife Area' in 1978–9 and is now managed by the Canadian Wildlife Service. Other parts of the point are owned by the Ontario Ministry of Natural Resources (Long Point Provincial Park and various additional pieces of crown land), Long Point Region Conservation Authority (Lee Brown Waterfowl Management Area), Canadian Coast Guard, and private interests.

The Ramsar Convention on Wetlands of International Importance has declared Long Point's wetlands to be internationally significant, and Long Point and its surrounding waters have been designated as a 'World Biosphere Reserve' by UNESCO (United Nations Educational, Scientific, and Cultural Organization). Long Point's most significant features are rich and healthy wetlands and a pristine erosion-deposit sandspit, the longest such freshwater spit in the world.

The 32-km-long sandspit protrudes eastward into the deepest part of Lake Erie, forming the south shore of Long Point Bay. The north shore of the bay is formed by the mainland shore of Lake Erie. The inner bay is protected at its eastern end by Turkey Point jutting southward form the mainland and by Ryersons Island extending northward from Long Point. The outer bay opens into Lake Erie.

The Long Point area includes an incredibly rich diversity of habitats, among them open lake, shallow bays, sandbars, beaches, dunes, forest and savanna, ponds, sloughs, and marshes. With its lake-moderated temperatures and its position at the southern edge of the Carolinian Forest Region in Canada, the point provides prime habitat for a number of rare or endangered species of plants and animals not found elsewhere in Canada.

Long Point Bird Observatory (LPBO) has a visitor centre on Old Cut Boulevard just outside Long Point Provincial Park; Backus Heritage Conservation Area (just north of Port Rowan on Regional Road 42) has displays.

Flora. Long Point contains one of the few significant remnants of coastal dune and swale habitat in Ontario. About 700 species of vascular plants are found here, including a number of grass-like rarities, such as Broad-winged and Black-edged Sedges; Four-angled, Horsetail, and Capitate Spike-rushes; and Yellow Cyperus. Of particular interest are the wet meadows within Long Point Provincial Park. Here, from late August through September, can be seen a wide assortment of plants characteristic of the prairie-like wet meadows found along the length of the point. Look for Grass-of-Parnassus, Fringed and Closed Gentians, Kalm's Lobelia, Kalm's St John's-wort, Small-flowered Gerardia, Ohio Goldenrod, Sneezeweed, Bushy Aster, Nodding Ladies'-tresses, Low Nut-rush, Indian Grass, and Little Bluestem.

Birds. The marshes and dunes provide ideal habitat for numerous bird species. From 1960 to 1995, over half a million birds of approximately 255 species were banded in the area, and over 350 species have been observed, including many rarities. The marshes are a continentally important staging area for migratory waterfowl. More than 170,000 waterfowl may be in the region at any one time in the fall, and 110,000 may be present in the spring. Large proportions of the global populations of both Canvasback and Redhead appear in Long Point Bay during migration. Thousands of Tundra Swans rest here during spring and fall migration. In spring (late February to March) many can be seen along the Long Point causeway or farther west in cornfields. Look for migrating Sandhill Cranes at the Big Creek dyke.

Mammals and Herpetofauna. Long Point has large numbers and a diverse assemblage of reptiles and amphibians. It probably contains the world's largest concentration of Eastern Fox Snake and Ontario's healthiest populations of melanistic Eastern Garter Snake, as well as rare turtles, including Blanding's Turtle. In late June, the dyke through the Big Creek National Wildlife Area along the causeway is a good place for seeing Green Frogs, Bullfrogs, and Northern Leopard Frogs. Fowler's

Toads are very common on Long Point; their sheep-like baaing can be heard on warm nights from mid May to mid June. Mammals of note include Coyote and Least Shrew.

Fish. The inner bay is home to one of Ontario's best fisheries, including one of the continent's outstanding Smallmouth Bass fisheries. Lake Erie, the most productive of the Great Lakes in terms of fish harvest, supports 65% of the 177 freshwater fish species found in Canada. Rare fish occurring at Long Point are Grass Pickerel, Lake Sturgeon, Pugnose Shiner, Lake Chubsucker, Brindled Madtom, Eastern Sand Darter, and Silver Chub.

Invertebrates. Long Point and Big Creek National Wildlife Area are good places for seeing Monarch butterfly migration in late August and early September. Also look for signs of Meadow Crayfish.

DIRECTIONS. To reach base of Long Point go S on Hwy 59 to end; see prov hwy map.

NOTE. *To protect the fragile ecology, access is restricted on much of Long Point.* Check with LPBO to participate in organized trips to restricted zones.

INFORMATION. Long Point Bird Observatory, Box 160, Port Rowan, Ont, N0E 1M0, 519-586-3531; Long Point Provincial Park, Box 89, Port Rowan, Ont, N0E 1M0, 519-586-2133; Long Point Region Conservation Authority; Canadian Wildlife Service, RR 3, Port Rowan, Ont, N0E 1M0, 519-586-2703.

South Walsingham Sand Ridges Agreement Forest (Wilson and Coppens Tracts)

This is a rewarding area for birding in summer. As many as 18 species of warblers breed here, including Louisiana Waterthrush and Golden-winged, Blue-winged, Pine, Cerulean, and Hooded Warblers. Among northern species are Northern Waterthrush and Blackburnian, and occasionally Magnolia and Yellow-rumped, Warblers. Solitary and Yellow-throated Vireos, Acadian Flycatcher, and Wild Turkey are regular. Butterflies of interest are Spicebush Swallowtail and, in August, Harvesters (collecting not permitted). The woodland has typically Carolinian trees, such as Sassafras, Tulip-tree, Black Gum, Flowering Dogwood, and American Chestnut. Plants of interest include

Yellow Mandarin, Round-leaved Tick-trefoil, and Southern Beech Fern. Eastern Hognose Snake, Eastern Fox Snake, and Black Rat Snake are all present. Careful observers may be rewarded by a glimpse of an Eastern Smooth Green Snake. Jefferson complex Salamanders are frequent, as are Blanding's Turtles in wetter sites.

Nearby, Rowanwood Sanctuary of the Norfolk Field Naturalists is a good place for seeing Wild Turkey, Alder and Willow Flycatchers together, as well as Eastern Bluebirds and other species of more open habitats.

DIRECTIONS. From jct of Hwys 24 & 59 go W on Reg Rd 60 for just under 4 km; turn left onto gravel road & go 1.5 km to T-jct; turn right & proceed to forested section. Coppens Tract lies to S & Wilson Tract to N. To reach Rowanwood Sanctuary turn left at T-jct & proceed to bend; Rowanwood lies to E of road from bend to S extent of road.

INFORMATION. Long Point Region Conservation Authority.

St Williams Forestry Station

Much of the station is accessible on foot via fire roads. The station property is planted in conifers but large tracts remain as natural dry oak forest. This area has a distinctly northern flavour, with bird species such as Barred Owl, Winter Wren, Hermit Thrush, Solitary Vireo, Yellow-rumped Warbler, Red Crossbill, and Dark-eyed Junco. St Williams is a good place for seeing diurnal woodland raptors, including Broad-winged, Red-shouldered, and Sharp-shinned Hawks. Dry, open habitat attracts Prairie Warblers. Several species of snakes are resident, among which are Eastern Hognose, Eastern Fox, and Eastern Smooth Green Snakes.

A spectacular display of several thousand Pink Lady's-slippers can be found in the pines on the fire road immediately west of the sand field and north of the main road. Wild Lupines are common along the roadside. The third week in May is the best time for these showy species. Other plants of interest are Dwarf Chinquapin Oak (along the edges of the sand road), Waxy Meadow-rue, Pasture Rose, Puccoon, and Butterfly-weed. This is an excellent area for watching butterflies (collecting prohibited).

DIRECTIONS. From Reg Rd 16 drive W on Hwy 24 about 3 km past hdqts of forestry station; turn right on East 1/4 Line; go 1.5 km N & turn E on sand road.

INFORMATION. St Williams Forestry Station, St Williams, Ont, N0E 1P0, 519-586-3576.

Backus Woods Agreement Forest

Backus Woods is one of the finest remaining examples of a Carolinian woodland in Canada. Its large size (about 500 ha), maturity, healthy state, and relative lack of disturbance enable it to support a remarkable diversity of flora and fauna. Among the species of interest are Southern Beech Fern, American Chestnut, Flowering Dogwood, Yellow-billed Cuckoo, Yellow-throated Vireo, Eastern Hognose Snake, and Black Rat Snake.

Perhaps the best way to gain access to Backus Woods is through the Charles Sauriol Forest. Here, trails lead into a lush, old-growth woodland of swampy hollows and undulating, sandy ridges. Yellow Birch, ash, and Red and Silver Maples flourish in the swales, while stately oaks, Sugar Maples, and American Beech tower above the drier ridges. Specimens of Sassafras and Shagbark Hickory are among the largest known in Canada. Keep your eyes and ears alert for the wealth of significant Carolinian species that occur here.

The Backus Woods trail system, which can be used year-round, is also accessible through the Backus Heritage Conservation Area. For those willing to venture onto an unmaintained roadway (Concession Road 4), the following additional entry points are described.

On Highway 24 drive 3 km west of St Williams Forestry Station, turn left on East 1/4 Line, proceed 1.5 km to sand road (Concession Road 4), and turn right. Go along the sand road over a bridge to the base of the largest rise. Park and enter a well-hidden trail on the left. (Concession Road 4 can also be reached by going 1.5 km south on Highway 59 from its junction with Highway 24 and turning left.) You are now entering a mature mixed hardwood forest dominated by large Tulip-trees. Watch for Barred Owl, Pileated Woodpecker, Louisiana Waterthrush, and Black-throated Green Warbler. Across the road Golden-winged and Blue-winged Warblers are often found.

After leaving this site, continue west on the sand road to a well-marked track entering the forest on the right. Park and enter a gated track on the left. Proceed a short distance until the path bends left and enter the woods on the right. This low, wet area supports some very large Black Gums, some of which are estimated to be over 400 years old. Note the sucker growth and many seedlings. In August the logs are awash with the rare plant Stalked Water-horehound.

Return to the sand road and walk or drive north on a well-marked track to an excellent area for birding and viewing wildflowers and big trees. The swamp supports Wood Duck, Hooded Merganser, Prothonotary Warbler, and Northern and Louisiana Waterthrushes. Cerulean Warbler and Acadian Fly-catcher may be found in the woods. Small dead snags that contain woodpecker holes may harbour Southern Flying Squirrel. The duff layer of the forest floor has been raised by the activity of Woodland Vole, Hairy-tailed Mole, and Northern Short-tailed Shrew. If you are very lucky you may catch a glimpse of a Woodland Jumping Mouse with its long, white-tipped tail. A visit by night in August will reward the observer with the raucous calls of Northern True Katydid competing with Eastern Screech-Owl, Great Horned Owl, Barred Owl, and the high-pitched alarm squeaks of flying squirrels.

DIRECTIONS. For Charles Sauriol Forest: from jct of Hwys 24 & 59, go 3 km S on Hwy 59; turn left on Conc Rd 3 & go about 2 km to sign on left. For Backus Heritage CA: from Port Rowan go 2 km N on Reg Rd 42; watch for signs.

INFORMATION. Backus Conservation Education Centre, c/o Long Point Region Conservation Authority.

Walsh Carolinian Agreement Forests (Smith, Earl, King, Sloick, and Danylevich Tracts)

At the Smith Tract, enter the forest along the path and go past Red Pines before looking for Cucumber-trees on the right. This area offers excellent birding; watch for Chestnut-sided Warbler, Yellow-throated and Solitary Vireos, Winter Wren, Brown Creeper, and Yellow-bellied Sapsucker. King Tract has some of the largest Black Gums in the region.

DIRECTIONS. Drive S & W from Simcoe on Hwy 24; turn right on

Forestville Rd one road W of Reg Rd 10; travel N about 4 km to LPRCA sign for Smith Tract. Cross road to reach King Tract. INFORMATION. Long Point Region Conservation Authority.

Turkey Point Provincial Park

The old Black Oak savanna barrens have special appeal to botanists. Plants of interest in and near this 300-ha park include Goat's-rue, Birdfoot Violet, Moss-pink, Whorled and Green Milkweeds, Fern-leaved False Foxglove, Cylindric Blazing-star, and Bayberry. Check the Turkey Point overlook for gulls, waterfowl, Bald Eagle, Snowy Owl, and Sandhill Crane in season. The bird community in the park is similar to that found in St Williams Forestry Station. Campers are serenaded by Whip-poor-wills at night and the ethereal strains of Hermit Thrush in the evening. Turkey Point Beach, especially the west end, is often a good place for observing shorebirds. Forster's Terns frequent the pilings. Watch for Great Blue Heron, Wild Turkey, and Virginia Opossum. Trails can be hiked year-round.
DIRECTIONS. Off Reg Rd 10, W of Normandale; see prov hwy map.
INFORMATION. Turkey Point Provincial Park, Box 5, Turkey Point, Ont, N0E 1T0, 519-426-3239.

Waterford Ponds Conservation Area

Dunes and sloughs here harbour an interesting sedge fen community. The dunes are dominated by Shrubby Cinquefoil and Little Bluestem, whereas the sloughs support Winged Loosestrife, orchids, and various sedges. The ponds serve as a spawning area for fish and provide nesting habitat for such waterfowl as Wood Duck and Canada Goose. The site contains 148 ha.
DIRECTIONS. Drive N on Hwy 24 from Simcoe; turn right on Reg Rd 9 & go 1.5 km to gate; park in lot; walk W along shore & enter what appears to be old campground.
INFORMATION. Long Point Region Conservation Authority.

Selkirk Provincial Park

This little park (73 ha) is dominated by Red and White Oaks and Shagbark Hickory. Unusual plants include Early Blue Violet,

Pale Vetchling, and Cooper's Milk-vetch. The birding is good in spring, when Red-bellied and Red-headed Woodpeckers, Carolina Wren, and Tufted Titmouse are most likely to be seen. In winter look for hawks and owls in the open grasslands north of the park.

DIRECTIONS. Off Reg Rd 3, W of Selkirk; see prov hwy map.

INFORMATION. Selkirk Provincial Park, RR 1, Selkirk, Ont, N0A 1P0, 905-776-2600.

Taquanyah Conservation Area

From March to October the area is good for observing American Bittern, Green and Great Blue Herons, and other wetland species. The rare Virginia Mallow is found along the creek below the dam. The 141-ha property has trails, interpretive programs, and a nature centre.

DIRECTIONS. From Hwy 3 in Decewsville go 1 km N.

INFORMATION. Grand River Conservation Authority.

Caistor-Canborough Slough Agreement Forest (Ruigrok Tract)

This 76-ha tract is typical of the patterned ground of the Haldimand clay plain, with low, dry oak ridges surrounding sloughs. The plants are particularly interesting, including a number of rare sedges. Woody plants of note are Black Gum and Southern Arrow-wood. The sloughs are well vegetated with shrubs, and support several rare plants. The birds are diverse for the clay plain and include Carolina Wren, Red-bellied Woodpecker, and Golden-winged, Blue-winged, and Nashville Warblers.

DIRECTIONS. From Caistorville (in Regional Municipality of Niagara) go 2.5 km S on Reg Rd 2 to Ruigrok Tract; watch for signs & trails into woods.

INFORMATION. Niagara Peninsula Conservation Authority.

Rock Point Provincial Park

Located on a stubby peninsula, this park is one of the best all-round birding spots in the region. Songbirds, waterfowl, and shorebirds pass through in migration. Each September, Monarch butterflies gather to await favourable winds to carry them southward on their way to Mexico. In early to mid June Carp can be seen spawning in the shallows. Fossils embedded in the exposed limestone shelves along the shore were formed 350 million years ago in a tropical coral reef. The park contains 188 ha.

DIRECTIONS. E of Port Maitland off Reg Rd 3 & Niece Rd; see prov hwy map.

INFORMATION. Rock Point Provincial Park, Box 158, Dunnville, Ont, N0P 1X0, 905-774-6642.

Grand River Marshes at Dunnville

The large area of marsh upstream and downstream of Dunnville is best reached by canoe. Much of the floodplain is filled with weedy plant communities but the forested section is more natural. Plants of interest include Black Cohosh and Virginia Cowslip. The marsh community has typical marsh birds, including several species of nesting ducks. Watch for Black-crowned Night-Heron, Red-shouldered Hawk, Black Tern, and Marsh Wren. The area is an important one for fish spawning and as a stopover for migratory waterfowl.

DIRECTIONS. Access where Reg Rd 3 crosses river at Dunnville.

Grand River

See entry under Brant County.

Grand Valley Trail

See entry under Regional Municipality of Waterloo.

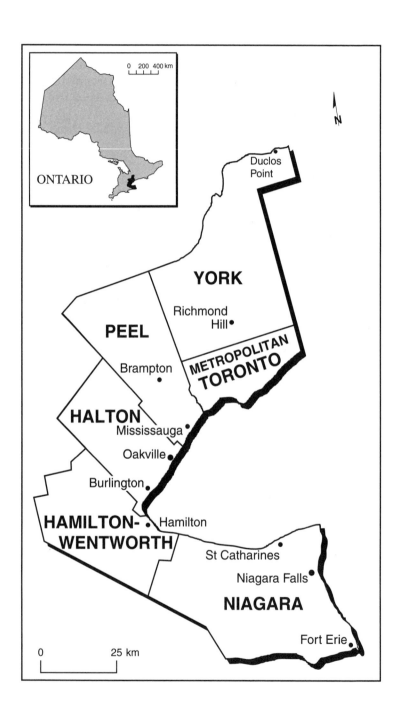

ONTARIO

0   200 400 km

Duclos
Point

N

YORK

Richmond
Hill

PEEL

Brampton

METROPOLITAN
TORONTO

HALTON
Mississauga

Oakville

Burlington

HAMILTON-
WENTWORTH

Hamilton

St Catharines

Niagara Falls

NIAGARA

Fort Erie

0   25 km

2 Golden Horseshoe

York

Metro Toronto

Peel

Halton

Hamilton-Wentworth

Niagara

The intensely developed Golden Horseshoe extends in an arc from the eastern edge of Toronto around the head of Lake Ontario to the Niagara River. Topographically the region is dominated by the Niagara Escarpment. Most of the Golden Horseshoe lies within the Carolinian Forest Region, although elements of the Great Lakes–St Lawrence Forest Region are found within the northern and northeastern portions.

REGIONAL MUNICIPALITY OF YORK

> The cold and snow which we have had has given way today to weather so warm that I have been obliged in walking to throw off shawl after shawl and at last find myself over-clad ... The weather of today is what they call 'Indian summer'. There is a thick dry haze through which we cannot see the length of a field and through which the sun shines like a bright red moon and the trees look like shadows. (Thornhill, October 23, 1828, Mary O'Brien [1798–1876], English settler)

Stretching from the heavily urbanized northern edge of Metropolitan Toronto to the shores of Lake Simcoe, this area includes three major physiographic features: the Lake Simcoe Lowlands, the Oak Ridges moraine, and the Toronto plains. The municipality lies at the southern edge of the Great Lakes–St Lawrence Forest Region. York contains a remarkable diversity of habitats. Among these are deciduous and mixed woodlands, tallgrass prairie, marshes, kettle lakes, Black Spruce bogs, Tamarack swamps, and fens.

LAKE SIMCOE LOWLANDS

The lowlands situated between Lake Simcoe and the Oak Ridges moraine are characterized by a sandy outwash plain with extensive swamps and other wetlands. These occur in association with several river systems, such as the Holland River, Black River, Zephyr Creek, and Pefferlaw Brook. An area of dry sand plains north of Holland Landing supports a remnant tallgrass prairie dominated by two grasses, Big Bluestem and Little Bluestem, and shrub thickets of Saskatoon-berry and American Hazel.

Duclos Point

This excellent example of a wetland on the shores of Lake Simcoe supports Tamarack swamps, Silver Maple and Black Ash swamps, and thicket swamps of Sweet Gale, Swamp Loosestrife, and Speckled Alder. Thirteen species of ferns and eight species of orchids grow here, including Northern Beech, Royal and Cinnamon Ferns, Showy Lady's-slipper, White Adder's-mouth, and Ragged Fringed and Small Purple Fringed Orchids. Conifer swamps provide breeding habitat for such northern birds as White-throated Sparrow, Ruby-crowned Kinglet, and Yellow-rumped Warbler. Marshes of sedges, cattails, rushes, and Northern Wild Rice are found on the Lake Simcoe shores and embayments. In open water there are large beds of Pickerel-weed, Tapegrass, Bushy Naiad, Mare's-tail, Northern Water-milfoil, and six species of pondweeds. This area forms one of the richest submersed aquatic communities in the Regional Municipality of York. The open wetlands are frequented by Caspian Terns, Ospreys, Great Blue Herons, and breeding Marsh Wrens. Great Crested Flycatcher, Coyote, Beaver, White-tailed Deer, Porcupine, Common Snapping Turtle, and Bullfrog may also be seen. This is an excellent area for viewing waterfowl during spring and fall migration.

DIRECTIONS. Take sdrds N of Hwy 48 to Duclos Point or Holmes Point & walk along beach to publicly owned portion of wetland.

Sibbald Point Provincial Park

Northern Pike can be seen spawning at night in late March or early April. Large numbers of migratory waterfowl can be observed offshore in Lake Simcoe during spring and autumn.

DIRECTIONS. On S side of Lake Simcoe off Reg Rd 18; see prov hwy map. For spawning, within park take main road to 4-way stop, then go straight ahead 100 m to creek.

INFORMATION. Sibbald Point Provincial Park, RR 2, Sutton West, Ont, L0E 1R0, 905-722-8061.

Holland Marsh and Pottageville Swamp

Although this once vast marsh has been mostly converted to market gardens, remnant portions of natural habitat still occur.

– **Holland Marsh** (north of Highway 11 to Lake Simcoe). This area supports hardwood swamps and thicket swamps on its periphery, and extensive grass and cattail marshes towards the Holland River. Common birds include Marsh Wren, American and Least Bitterns, and Virginia Rail in the marshes. In the swamps are found such noteworthy southern species as Blue-gray Gnatcatcher and Golden-winged Warbler. Tamarack swamps and fens occur near the Holland River mouth. The fens are home to Small Purple Fringed Orchid, Bog Aster, Rose Pogonia, Grass-pink, Bog Rosemary, Kalm's Lobelia, and nesting populations of Sedge Wren. Migrating Yellow Rails have occasionally been recorded in wet sedge meadows located at the end of the concession road on the west side of the marsh.

DIRECTIONS. For publicly owned land, go to N ends of York Reg Rds 51 & 34, N of Holland Landing.

– **Pottageville Swamp** (south side of Highway 9). This large wetland tract contains extensive Silver Maple swamps that harbour such southern species as Moonseed, as well as Tamarack swamps and thicket swamps with strong boreal elements. Birds of note that can be found nesting in the conifer swamps include White-throated and Lincoln's Sparrows; Black-and-white,

Nashville, Canada, and Yellow-rumped Warblers; Golden-crowned Kinglet; Winter Wren; Veery; and Northern Water-thrush. The conifer swamps also support Creeping Snowberry, Pitcher-plant, and Pink Lady's-slipper.

DIRECTIONS. Drive along Hwy 9, 5 km W of Hwy 400; view this privately owned area from road only. There are several areas where one can pull off hwy; swamp is separated from Hwy 9 by deep canal.

Holland Landing Pine Forest and Seepage Slope

A dry hilltop supports an unusual forest of White and Red Pines, while extensive seepage areas on the slope sustain Tamarack swamps, thicket swamps, and a low shrub fen of Shrubby Cinquefoil and Swamp Birch. Noteworthy plants on these wet slopes include Bog Aster, Kalm's Lobelia, Tall White Bog Orchid, Hudsonian Bulrush, and Small Bladderwort.

DIRECTIONS. Located along York Reg Rd 51 (Yonge St), 3 km N of Holland Landing & S of River Drive Park bridge over Holland River (Reg Rd 77 or Queensville Sdrd); walk W along hydro line to river.

OAK RIDGES MORAINE

This huge terminal moraine rises almost 400 m above sea level, within the Regional Municipality of York encompassing Richmond Hill, Musselman Lake, Ballantrae, and Pottageville. The vigorously rolling terrain is composed of sandy or gravelly materials. The region's most extensive forests and pine plantations are found on these uplands. Kettle lakes are common. About a dozen bogs (all privately owned) support a noteworthy assemblage of boreal species, such as Tamarack, Black Spruce, Bog Rosemary, Leatherleaf, Pitcher-plant, Round-leaved Sundew, cotton-grass, and such showy orchids as Arethusa, Rose Pogonia, and Grass-pink.

Oak Ridges Trail

The 150-km-long Oak Ridges moraine is a unique formation of sand and gravel deposits pushed up into a high ridge by the actions of two glacial lobes during the last Ice Age. Stretching along the moraine, the 200-km trail (parts still under construction) extends from the Niagara Escarpment in the west to the Northumberland Forest in the east. The route passes through rolling upland hills featuring hardwood forests, pine plantations, and scenic agricultural landscapes. Brook Trout thrive in numerous coldwater streams that flow north or south from the height of land. Many interesting plants grow on the moraine, including prairie species such as Big Bluestem, Hoary Vervain, and Showy Tick-trefoil in areas of successional upland meadow. Northern species such as Pitcher-plant and a variety of orchids can be found around some of the kettle lakes.

INFORMATION. Oak Ridges Trail Association, Box 28544, Aurora, Ont, L4G 6S6.

York Regional Forest (Holborn Tract)

Check for Cooper's and Sharp-shinned Hawks, Stilt Sandpiper, Sedge Wren, Coyote, White-tailed Deer, Common Snapping Turtle, and Bullfrog.

DIRECTIONS. Take Hwy 48 N to Holborn Rd E (NW of Mount Albert).

Vivian Forest

This extensive tract of mixed woodlands, mature deciduous forests, and coniferous plantations stretches for 10 km from Vandorf to Vivian. Large pine plantations support a number of northern birds, including Pine, Magnolia, and Black-throated Green Warblers; Hermit Thrush; Solitary Vireo; and Red-breasted Nuthatch. The isolated patches of Sugar Maple–American Beech forest sustain the region's largest population of Red-shouldered Hawks, as well as other forest interior nesting species, such as Pileated Woodpecker and Barred Owl. Successional forests, mixed woodlands, and conifer swamps are common.

DIRECTIONS. To access Vivian Forest: 1) park on W side of Hwy 48 just N of jct of Reg Rd 74 at Vivian; or 2) park on Aurora Sdrd (Reg Rd 15) at Whitchurch CA 5 km W of Ballantrae. Avoid trespassing onto privately owned sections.

INFORMATION. Lake Simcoe Region Conservation Authority.

Glenville Hills

This large forested tract on the northern flanks of the Oak Ridges moraine rises sharply to 112 m above the surrounding lowlands. On the height of land, the former Thornton Bales Conservation Area provides beautiful vistas. Dry hilltops support successional forests of Red Oak, White Birch, aspen, and White Pine. Old-growth forests of Sugar Maple–American Beech occur on the mid slopes, Sugar Maple–Eastern Hemlock on the cooler slopes, and White Cedar–Eastern Hemlock–Yellow Birch on extensive seepage areas near the slope bases. Watch for Cooper's Hawk and such uncommon plants as Hobblebush, Rock Polypody, Black Walnut, and Hairy Honeysuckle. The spring floral display is outstanding on the maple-beech slopes.

DIRECTIONS. 1) Park at former Thornton Bales CA (SW of Newmarket) on N side of Mulock Dr (Reg Rd 74 becomes Sdrd 19) just E of Dufferin St (Reg Rd 53). 2) From Hwy 400 Exit 52 (Lloydtown-Aurora) go E through Kettleby on Sdrd 19; stay on Sdrd 19 & go 3 km E to CA.

NOTE. Area is not maintained; use at own risk.

Lake Wilcox Fish and Wildlife Park

In March Northern Pike spawn in a marsh that has been created at the west end of Lake Wilcox. Some common marsh birds and amphibians, including Bullfrogs, can be found. A good variety of submersed aquatic plants grows in the shallow waters of the lake.

DIRECTIONS. Take Hwy 11 N to Oak Ridges; take 1st right N of King Sdrd (Reg Rd 11) & 1st right to park.

THE TORONTO PLAINS

The southern portion of York is overlain by till and lake-bottom sediments deposited during the retreat of the glaciers. These gently sloping plains are dissected by various rivers and creeks that flow south to Lake Ontario.

Humber Trails Forest and Wildlife Conservation Area

Humber Trails preserves a small pocket of wildlife habitat in the picturesque Humber valley. A stream meanders through a mixed coniferous forest of pine, spruce, White Cedar, and Tamarack; there is a beautiful patch of Wintergreen on the west side. Small land birds pass through during migration. Breeding species include Ruffed Grouse, Sharp-shinned Hawk, Hairy Woodpecker, Eastern Phoebe (nesting under the Mill Road bridge), Great Crested Flycatcher, Northern Rough-winged Swallow, Mourning Warbler, Northern Cardinal, Rose-breasted Grosbeak, Indigo Bunting, and Northern Oriole. Humber Trails is also noted for its nocturnal Coyote choruses.

DIRECTIONS. 1) Exit Hwy 400 at King/Nobleton (Reg Rd 11); proceed 7 km W on King Sdrd; turn S (left) on Mill Rd & drive 1 km. 2) From Nobleton on Hwy 27, turn E at lights & proceed 3.1 km to Mill Rd.

Kortright Centre for Conservation

Located in the Humber River watershed, Kortright's major habitats include mature upland and floodplain forests, ponds, marsh, and open fields. The 162-ha site is a good year-round birding area. Feeders and fruit trees attract an excellent variety of winter birds, including waxwings. Waves of migrant passerines stop in spring and fall. Among resident birds are Ring-necked Pheasant, Ruffed Grouse, Eastern Screech-Owl, Great Horned Owl, Pileated Woodpecker, Blue Jay, Northern Cardinal, and House Finch. Summering birds include Green Heron, Wood Duck, American Woodcock, Least Flycatcher, White-breasted Nuthatch, Blue-gray Gnatcatcher, Veery, Wood Thrush, Ovenbird, Mourning Warbler, Indigo Bunting, and Field Sparrow. Kortright features all-season trails, an interpretive program, a nature centre, and other facilities.

DIRECTIONS. 1) Exit Hwy 400 at Major Mackenzie (Reg Rd 25) in Vaughan; go 3.3 km W to Pine Valley Dr; turn left & drive 1 km. 2) On Hwy 27 go 6 km N of Hwy 7 & turn right on Major Mac.

INFORMATION. Metro Toronto and Region Conservation Authority.

Woodcock Woods

Experience a rousing dawn chorus in Vaughan from 4:30 to 6:30 a.m. from mid May to late June. By 4:30 a.m. (unless it's below

6°C), there should be American Woodcock displaying. As daylight approaches, songs of Rufous-sided Towhee, Field Sparrow, American Robin, Brown Thrasher, and Song Sparrow will fill the air. By the time the sun has been up half an hour, the whole valley will be ringing, with additional melodies provided by Ovenbird, Wood Thrush, Veery, Rose-breasted Grosbeak, and a half-dozen other species.

DIRECTIONS. Exit Hwy 400 at Major Mackenzie (Reg Rd 25) & go 4.7 km E through Maple to Dufferin St (Reg Rd 53). Turn N (left); at exactly 4.0 km from Major Mac, stop at Kirby Sdrd allowance. Park & listen.

Thornhill Area

– Oakbank Pond. Located in a residential area, the pond is bordered by large Weeping Willows and narrow strips of cattails. Ducks, shorebirds, and warblers stop during migration, and there are resident Canada Geese and Mallards.

DIRECTIONS. Go 0.7 km W of Yonge St (Hwy 11) on Centre St.

– Uplands Golf Course and Ski Area. This small natural area along the Little Don River is good for woodland birds. Fall and winter visits can be quite productive.

DIRECTIONS. Go 0.8 km W from Yonge St (Hwy 11) on Uplands Ave (3 blocks S of Hwy 7) to golf course.

METROPOLITAN TORONTO

> Ontario means 'the beautiful,' and the word is worthy of its signification, and the lake of its beautiful name ... Sometimes the sunset converts its surface into a sea of molten gold, and sometimes the young moon walks trembling in a path of silver; sometimes a purple haze floats over its bosom like a veil; sometimes the wind blows strong, and the wild turbid waves come rolling in like breakers, flinging themselves over the pier in wrath and foam, or dancing like spirits in their glee. (Toronto, June 8, 1837, Anna Jameson [1794–1860], English traveller)

Stretching inland from the shores of Lake Ontario, this area lies on a physiographic feature known as the Toronto plains, which not only encompasses Metropolitan Toronto but also extends northward to Markham, Thornhill, and Woodbridge. The basic topography consists of gradually sloping till plains and plains composed of materials deposited beneath glacial lakewaters. The plains are deeply cut by major ravines, such as those of the Rouge River, Highland Creek, Don River, Humber River, Mimico Creek, and Etobicoke Creek. A number of Toronto's major rivers rise beyond the city's boundaries in the Oak Ridges moraine in the Regional Municipality of York. Metropolitan Toronto lies at the very northern and eastern extremity of the Carolinian Forest Region in Canada, the Rouge River often being regarded as the eastern boundary.

Although it is Ontario's most heavily urbanized region, this area has a remarkable diversity of habitats. Among these are deciduous and mixed woodlands, Black Oak savanna, marshes, sand beaches, cool Eastern Hemlock slopes, Tamarack swamps, fens, and wet meadows.

INFORMATION (for most Toronto parklands). Metro Toronto Parks and Culture Dept, 24th floor, Metro Hall, 55 John St, Station 1240, Toronto, Ont, M5V 3C6, 416-392-8186; Metro Toronto and Region Conservation Authority.

Colonel Sam Smith Waterfront Park

A wildlife rehabilitation project is being created on this man-made landfill site. A wetland has been designed with suitable habitat for fish, turtles, and amphibians. Native aquatic plants will be introduced, and trees and shrubs are to be planted in the drier areas. The existing mudflats will be expanded for shorebirds such as Whimbrel, which are regular visitors in late May. In late fall and winter flocks of diving ducks, loons, and grebes can be seen offshore. In winter the open landfill area attracts falcons, Snow Buntings, and Lapland Longspurs, as well as Snowy Owls when there is a southward migration. The mature trees on the adjacent former hospital grounds offer food and shelter for migrating songbirds in spring and fall.

DIRECTIONS. Located S of Lake Shore Blvd (Hwy 2) at Kipling. *Transit:* Kipling bus or Long Branch streetcar. *Car:* Parking available on spit.

Humber Bay Park

– **Humber Bay Park East.** Migrating ducks can be seen on

Toronto waterfront at Mimico Creek in spring (peak April 1–15). Wintering dabbling ducks are present from mid October to March, with the largest numbers in November.

DIRECTIONS. Located on Lake Shore Blvd (Hwy 2) just W of jct with QEW. *Transit:* Long Branch 507 streetcar. *Car:* Exit S from QEW onto Park Lawn Rd; cross Lake Shore Blvd onto park road.

– Humber Bay Park West. The construction of Humber Bay West has created a large sheltered bay between the landfill and the lakeshore that has become a major wintering grounds for diving ducks. Scan the rafts of scaups, goldeneyes, Bufflehead, and mergansers for concentrations of Redheads and the occasional Harlequin Duck.

DIRECTIONS. To reach best viewing area, go W on Lake Shore Blvd from Humber Bay Park E. After crossing Mimico Creek, turn S at sign for W marina & park. When entering, keep right & drive to park at very end of road. Park there & walk N across grass.

Lower Humber River Valley

– Humber River Marshes. South of Bloor Street, several lakeshore marshes support dense beds of yellow and white pond- and water-lilies on ponds ringed by cattails, Purple Loosestrife, and Canada Blue-joint. Hooded Mergansers come in spring, Black-crowned Night-Herons in summer, and Rusty Blackbirds in fall. The mudflats in the southernmost marshes attract migrating shorebirds. Huge Cottonwoods tower above the Manitoba Maple bottomlands, home to an impressive spring display of Yellow Trout-lilies and Golden Alexanders. On the surrounding slopes Sugar Maple and Red Oak forests sustain such southern species as Yellow Pimpernel, White Trout-lily, and Sassafras.

DIRECTIONS. *Transit:* From Old Mill subway station walk E across Bloor St bridge; steep paths lead down to marshes. For W side marshes at sewage treatment plant, take Queen St streetcar to Kingsway; walk W on N side of Queensway across Humber bridge; follow sign to bike path & go N.

– Magwood Park. Red Oak bottomlands and seepage slopes of

Yellow Birch and Manitoba Maple support an abundance of Skunk-cabbage here.
DIRECTIONS. On E side of Humber River, N of Bloor & S of Dundas. *Transit:* From Old Mill Rd, walk N. *Car:* Park at Lambton Park at Dundas St W or parking lot at NE side of Old Mill bridge.

– **Lambton Woods.** The Humber's largest seepage slopes support Tamarack and Yellow and White Birches scattered among sedge meadows, alder thickets, and dense carpets of Skunk-cabbage. Noteworthy plants include Purple Spring Cress, Turtle-head, Great Lobelia, Rough-leaved Goldenrod, and Water Avens. Great Horned Owls are regularly observed and conifers attract winter birds. Fruiting shrubs encourage fall migrants to linger. In spring and fall this is a great area for migrating warblers.
DIRECTIONS. Located N of Dundas St W. *Transit:* Take Royal York bus & walk E on Edenbridge Dr to James Gardens; follow trail S. *Car:* Park at James Gardens or Lambton Park (E side of Humber River at Dundas St W); take bike path N & cross on bike bridge.

High Park

The sandy soils in the southwest corner of Toronto once supported extensive, open Black Oak woodlands known as savannas and noted for their prairie flora and fauna. The remnant savannas on the drier uplands and the northwest slopes of High Park are being restored. In June, the ground under a rich Black Oak remnant is carpeted with the blue spikes of Wild Lupines. In late summer, other prairie species are in bloom, such as the grasses Big Bluestem, Little Bluestem, and Indian Grass and the herbs Pale-leaved Sunflower, Hairy Bush-clover, Cylindric Blazing-star, and Frostweed. Cool, wooded ravines in the eastern half of the park support such northern species as Yellow Clintonia, Bunchberry, Goldthread, and Trailing Arbutus. Grenadier Pond on the park's western side is an excellent place for observing dabbling ducks, grebes, and swallows during migration, and Northern Shovelers in winter. The open areas around the Grenadier Restaurant serve as an official hawk monitoring site from September 1 to November 30.
DIRECTIONS. Located at SW corner of Parkside Dr & Bloor St. *Transit:* From High Park or Keele subway stops, walk S, or take

College or Queen St W streetcars to Parkside Dr. *Car:* Park inside park, except Sundays & holidays from May 1 to Oct 1.

INFORMATION. Toronto Parks and Recreation Information, main floor, E tower, City Hall, 100 Queen St W, Toronto, Ont, M5H 2N2, 416-392-1111.

Don River Valley

Two branches of the Don River and their major tributaries form an extensive ravine valley system.

– West Don. Serena Gundy, Sunnybrook, and Wilket Creek parks have valley forests of Sugar Maple, American Beech, and Red Oak and of Eastern Hemlock, White Pine, and White Cedar. Noteworthy plants to be found here are Silvery Glade Fern, Leatherwood, Feverwort, and New York Fern. The spring display of trilliums, hepaticas, and trout-lilies is spectacular. Rose-breasted Grosbeak, Wood Thrush, Eastern Wood-Pewee, Great Crested Flycatcher, White-breasted Nuthatch, and Pileated Woodpecker are common in these woodlands. Park bottomlands and seepage slopes have grassy meadows, cattail marshes, and several ponds. These wetlands support Great St John's-wort, Water-pennywort, and colonies of Turtlehead. Elsewhere on the bottomlands are fields, thickets, and forests of Manitoba Maple, White Cedar, and White Ash.

DIRECTIONS. Located in block bounded by Bayview, Lawrence, Leslie, & Eglinton. Park NW of Leslie St & Eglinton Ave (walk N), at Edwards Gardens (walk S), or at Glendon Campus of York University (walk into valley & head S).

– East Don. An excellent natural area south of Finch Avenue includes a sizable cattail and bur-reed marsh and a variety of northern wetlands, such as alder thicket swamps, a sedge fen with scattered Tamaracks, and a White Cedar swamp. One can hear Least, Willow, and Alder Flycatchers calling. Interesting plants of damp habitats include Pale Sedge, Stout Wood Reedgrass, Great Water Dock, Naked Miterwort, Alder-leaved Buckthorn, and Rough-leaved Goldenrod.

DIRECTIONS. Located between Leslie & Bayview. *Transit:* Get off Finch E bus at shopping centre gas station on W side of river. Trails lead down into valley from Page Ave.

Toronto Islands

Created over the centuries by sands eroded from the Scarborough bluffs, the Toronto Islands today support the region's best examples of shoreline dunes, beach strands, wet meadows, sand prairies, and Cottonwood woodlands. Although the islands have been largely converted to formal parkland, accessible natural areas are found at Hanlan's Point and the eastern corner of Ward's Island.

In late summer, wet meadows sustain showy displays of False Dragonhead, Purple Gerardia, Fringed Gentian, Kalm's Lobelia, and such orchids as Nodding Ladies'-tresses. Sand dunes are covered by American Beach Grass and Cottonwoods. On the beaches Strange Cinquefoil, Seaside Spurge, and Sea Rocket grow. Inland, openings support Pringle's Aster, Virginia Mountain-mint, and such prairie grasses as Big Bluestem and Switch Grass. The Cottonwood forests, with their dense shrub layer of willows and Red-osier Dogwood, are one of the best places in North America for seeing Northern Saw-whet Owls during migration in late October and early November. Spring migration can be a wondrous time. In winter, watch for wintering waterfowl, such as Oldsquaw, Common Merganser, Greater Scaup, and Bufflehead, from the ferry.

DIRECTIONS. Take ferry from foot of Bay St to Ward's & Centre islands & Hanlan's Point. From Oct 15 to Apr 15 ferry goes to Ward's Island & Hanlan's Point on weekdays, & on weekends to Ward's only.

Leslie Street Spit

This 5-km-long peninsula of construction fill and dredged sand has become one of the most significant wildlife areas on the Toronto waterfront, colonized by over 300 plant species. Developing meadows, Cottonwood woodlands, beach strands, and marshes support such plant rarities as Strange Cinquefoil, Seaside Spurge, Sea Rocket, Nodding Ladies'-tresses, and Slender Gerardia. The spit is home to nesting Double-crested Cormorant, Common Tern, Herring and Great Black-backed Gulls, and one of the largest Ring-billed Gull colonies on the Great Lakes. Keep an eye out for Black-crowned Night-Herons feeding in the lagoons. Colonial nesting birds are highly sensitive to disturbance during the breeding season; it is therefore very important to obey signs restricting access. The spit and the outer harbour are renowned for migratory and wintering waterfowl and other birds, including scoters, mergansers, Horned Grebe, Oldsquaw, Ruddy Duck, Whimbrel, Bufflehead, scaup, Gadwall, and American Wigeon.

DIRECTIONS. Year-round access on weekends & public holidays only. Mid Apr to Thanksgiving free shuttle van goes from main gate to pedestrian bridge halfway down spit. Walk rest of year. No pets on spit. *Transit:* Take Queen St E streetcar or Jones Ave bus to Leslie St; walk S. *Car:* Park at foot of Leslie St.

Scarborough Bluffs

These spectacular 100-m-high bluffs are known internationally for their unique geological features. The bluffs consist of tills deposited over the past 120,000 years by glacial advances and retreats. A secondary bluff well exposed at Cudia and Sylvan parks (and along Davenport Road) is the former shoreline of glacial Lake Iroquois, which was once 60 m above the present Lake Ontario shoreline. The best views of the bluffs are from Lake Ontario at Bluffers Park. A lagoon behind this landfill park is often a good spot for observing shorebirds, ducks, and gulls. At intervals along the bluffs, short, deep ravines sustain White Birch woods and mature Sugar Maple–American Beech forests. These sheltered ravines are attractive for migrant land birds. Uplands above the bluffs at Guildwood Inn are Silver Maple swamps and forests of Sugar Maple and Eastern Hemlock. At East Point, the uplands sustain fields, thickets, and young forests with scattered wet meadows where Closed (white form) and Fringed Gentians and such orchids as Nodding Ladies'-tresses are found. To the north on a CN railway line (1 km west of Highland Creek) grow prairie grasses such as Little Bluestem, Switch Grass, and Ensheathed Dropseed.

DIRECTIONS. *Transit:* Take Kingston Rd bus. To reach foot of bluffs, walk S on Brimley Rd to Bluffers Park. From W to E, parks & access points on top of bluffs include Scarborough Heights Park (walk S on Cliffside Dr; trail goes E to Brimley Rd), Cathedral Bluffs Park (Brooklawn Ave), Cudia Park (Fenwood Heights), Gates Gully (Bellamy Rd), Sylvan Park (S on Bethune Blvd, then W on Sylvan Ave or E to Rogate Place & follow trail E along bluffs to Guildwood Inn). For Guildwood Park take Morningside bus from Kennedy station. For East Point Park, take Lawrence Ave E bus; walk S on Beechgrove Dr. *Car:* Parking is available at most parks.

Morningside Park

Within Morningside Park Metropolitan Toronto's only large boreal swamp supports White Cedar and Tamarack with an understorey of Skunk-cabbage and thousands of Marsh-marigolds in spring. Noteworthy northern plants include Naked Miterwort and Twinflower. Surrounding lands sustain Eastern Hemlock–White Cedar terraces and wooded slopes of Sugar Maple, Red Oak, or American Beech with a large number of White Pines. The rich maple slopes have a spectacular display of spring flowers. Ten species of ferns occur. Blue-gray Gnatcatcher, Pileated Woodpecker, and Great Horned Owl nest in the park. Sharp-shinned Hawk, Carolina Wren, and warblers are seen during spring and fall migration.

DIRECTIONS. *Transit:* Take Morningside bus from Kennedy station. *Car:* Park entrance is on W side of Morningside Ave just S of Ellesmere Rd.

Rouge Park

This large park in the eastern portion of Metropolitan Toronto protects the region's best river valley system. At the mouth of the river along Lake Ontario are found a large marsh and beaches and meadows that are home to Sea Rocket and Seaside Spurge. Elsewhere, there are dry woodlands of Red and White Oaks, prairie-like openings with Big Bluestem and Azure Aster, and spectacular 30-m-high bluffs. Horsetail meadows support Fringed and Closed Gentians, Slender Gerardia, and Shining Ladies'-tresses, while rich Eastern Hemlock, White Cedar, American Beech, Black Maple, and Sugar Maple forests are home to Goldie's Wood Fern and Broad-leaved Waterleaf. A high ridge with a large stand of White Pine is located near Twyn Rivers Drive. There are also deciduous and coniferous swamps, ephemeral ponds frequented by Wood Ducks, successional forests, thickets, and fields. White-tailed Deer are among the 27 species of mammals recorded.

Some of the Rouge's breeding birds are Yellow Warbler;

Pileated Woodpecker; southern species such as Cooper's Hawk, Yellow-throated Vireo, Carolina Wren, and Scarlet Tanager; and northern breeders such as White-throated Sparrow and Canada, Black-throated Blue, Chestnut-sided, and Mourning Warblers. Migrating songbirds are abundant in the valley from mid April to mid May and migrating raptors in April, May, September, and October.

The Rouge also supports the region's largest concentration of rare plants, many with southern affinities, such as Shy Bulrush, Sassafras, Sycamore, Black Walnut, Poke Milkweed, American Hazel, Dryland Blueberry, and Sharp-leaved Goldenrod.

DIRECTIONS. Pearse House Interpretive Centre is on Meadowvale Rd, opposite Metro Zoo entrance. *Transit:* Take Sheppard Ave E bus or Scarborough 86 zoo bus from Kennedy subway station to zoo & walk 0.5 km E to valley. For Rouge Marshes take Rouge Hill bus. *Car:* Take Meadowvale Exit from Hwy 401; go E on Sheppard Ave to Twyn Rivers Dr; trails here go into wooded valleys & uplands of Little Rouge Creek & Rouge River. For Rouge Marshes take Island Rd or Lawrence Ave from Port Union Rd Exit on Hwy 401.

REGIONAL MUNICIPALITY OF PEEL

> We trotted merrily through the pine woods ... After several hours' ride we exchanged the pines for beech and oak, from which the leaves fell in rustling showers around us, and the squirrels bounded across the path, and blithely chirping, nimbly mounted the grey stems ... A wild whoop in the woods ... told us that we were near the Credit Creek, and shortly we found ourselves on an elevated plateau, cleared of wood, and with three rows of detached cottages, among fields surrounded with rail fences; below, a clear stream, abounding in fish, rushed over its rocky bed to join the waters of Lake Ontario. (1831, Captain James Alexander [1803–85], Scottish military officer)

From its northern boundary along Dufferin and Simcoe counties, the wedge-shaped region of Peel tapers towards the southeast to the city of Mississauga and Lake Ontario. The region is bordered on the east by York and Metropolitan Toronto, and on the west by Wellington and Halton. The land slopes gently towards Lake Ontario from the Albion Hills in the northeast and the Caledon Hills in the northwest, both part of the western extension of the Oak Ridges moraine. The Credit River, Etobicoke Creek, and tributaries of the Humber River form the major drainage systems.

Glacial features such as spillways, moraines, and drumlins are prominent in the northern third of the region. Here, among the dry, exposed hillsides, pockets of boreal vegetation can be found in the cool valleys. Sandy soils are common in the Albion Hills, and gravel deposits occur in the Caledon Hills. The Niagara Escarpment extends into Peel from the northwest. Its crest meanders more or less diagonally across the regional municipality from Terra Cotta to Mono Mills, although the northern portion is buried beneath the glacial tills of the Oak Ridges moraine.

The central part of Peel, a relatively level area known as the Peel plain, consists of clay soils laid down by glacial lakes. To the south, the narrow strip of land between the old shoreline of glacial Lake Iroquois and present-day Lake Ontario is characterized by a sand plain.

The northern two-thirds of Peel lie within the Great Lakes–St Lawrence Forest Region, while the southern portion is part of the Carolinian (Deciduous) Forest Region. Southern Peel is heavily developed, and the agricultural lands of the central section are rapidly becoming urbanized. The most extensive tracts of woodland are found among the rolling hills and farms of northern Peel, an area becoming increasingly popular for country estates.

Caledon Lake Forest

More than 160 ha of forest border Caledon Lake and its surrounding wetlands. The property is located on a large glacial meltwater channel that overlies extensive marl deposits. Marl, a fine granular material covering the lake bottom, is composed of layers of crushed crustaceans that lived long ago in a shallow, warmwater sea. These deposits produce an alkaline environment that supports calcium-loving plants, such as Shrubby Cinquefoil, Grass-of-Parnassus, Kalm's Lobelia, and Rush Aster. In close proximity to the series of alkaline marl lakes are acidic bogs, an uncommon feature in southern Ontario. Unusual bog species found here include Pitcher-plant, sundew, Small Cranberry, Creeping Snowberry, Leatherleaf, Sweet Gale, and Swamp Birch. Also found in the area are Mountain Fly Honeysuckle, Green Adder's-mouth, and Bristly Black Currant.

DIRECTIONS. From Hwy 9 in Orangeville go 5 km S on Hwy 136 (Porterfield Rd); turn right onto Highpoint Sdrd; at 2nd crossroad turn right on Mississauga Rd & go N to end. Park outside Gord Finlayson Outdoor Education Centre (Peel Board of Education).

INFORMATION. Credit Valley Conservation Authority.

Niagara Escarpment–Bruce Trail

Throughout Peel, the Bruce Trail (look for white blazes) provides numerous access points to spectacular scenery along the face of the Niagara Escarpment and through the Caledon and Albion hills. Carpets of spring wildflowers, limestone-loving ferns, and migrating birds can be found along the route. See entry under Regional Municipality of Niagara.

INFORMATION. Bruce Trail Association; Niagara Escarpment Commission.

Glen Haffy Forest and Wildlife Area

This 385-ha conservation area is located on the Niagara Escarpment where it encounters the western extension of the Oak Ridges moraine. The Bruce Trail crosses the property and links up with shorter trails that explore mature hardwoods and open, grassy meadows. Ongoing reforestation projects have extended the mixed coniferous-deciduous vegetation. Several species of grape ferns, quite common on the sandy, open sites of the moraine, grow here. Streams surfacing in the area are important water sources for the Humber River. Fall colour peaks between late September and mid October. Wild Turkeys are found just east of the conservation area.

DIRECTIONS. Located on E side of Airport Rd (Reg Rd 7) 2 km S of Hwy 9, between Caledon East & Mono Mills.

INFORMATION. Metro Toronto and Region Conservation Authority.

Palgrave Forest and Wildlife Area

Located on the Oak Ridges moraine, this 444-ha area contains the valley of the main branch of the Humber River. Long ago, a glacial river originating high on the Niagara Escarpment meandered through the Palgrave district, depositing sandy loam in huge hummocks; these knobby knolls can be seen today throughout the area. Upland sections of the property consist of mixed hardwoods, with Sugar Maple as a predominant species. Old fields, low-lying hardwood and conifer swamps, the Humber River, ponds, and lakes create a diversity of habitats. Beaver and White-tailed Deer inhabit the area. There are myriad equestrian trails within the Palgrave Forest, and cross-country skiing is popular.

DIRECTIONS. Located N of Albion Hills CA on W side of Hwy 50, just S of Hwy 9.

INFORMATION. Metro Toronto and Region Conservation Authority.

Albion Hills Conservation Area

Blanketed with glacial till, Albion Hills Conservation Area is situated on the Oak Ridges moraine complex. Tiny kettle lakes formed during the last glacial period are found throughout the 517-ha site. One-sixth of the land is covered in mature upland hardwood stands of Sugar Maple, American Beech, ash, and Basswood. Low-lying swampy sections contain White Cedar. A portion of the property is maintained in agricultural fields and operated as part of a farm demonstration program. The fish population in the streams is diverse: Brook Trout, White Sucker, Pumpkinseed, Largemouth Bass, Brown Bullhead, and Yellow Perch. A wide range of outdoor recreation opportunities is offered, including hiking and cross-country skiing.

DIRECTIONS. On W side of Hwy 50, 8 km N of Bolton.

INFORMATION. Metro Toronto and Region Conservation Authority.

Oak Ridges Trail

See entry under Regional Municipality of York.

Willoughby Nature Reserve

The Federation of Ontario Naturalists' Willoughby Reserve protects 48 ha in the scenic Caledon Hills. The property has mature mixed forests and coniferous plantations set in a river valley. Spring wildflowers are abundant. Common species found here are White-tailed Deer, Coyote, Great Horned Owl, Pileated Woodpecker, Eastern Bluebird, Brook Trout, and Brown Trout.

DIRECTIONS. From Hwy 10, 6.5 km S of Caledon Village (jct Hwys 10 & 24), go 1.4 km E on Grange Sdrd (Caledon Sdrd 5). Go 1 km N on Kennedy Rd (1st Line E) to just past top of large hill. Gate & fence on W side mark road allowance along S edge of reserve. Property extends SW nearly to Hwy 10.

NOTE. This parcel of land is different from the Willoughby estate property within Belfountain CA.

Belfountain Conservation Area

Significant natural features are found in this 13-ha recreation park. The Credit River slices through the site, creating a flood-plain and steep valley slopes; good examples of Niagara Escarpment talus slopes are visible. The maple woodland, part of one of the most extensive forest tracts in the Regional Municipality of Peel, provides breeding habitat for numerous species of birds. Among the rare plants present are Cooper's Milk-vetch and Goldie's Wood Fern.

In 1995, the 38-ha Willoughby estate was added to the east side of the conservation area. The property is bound on the north and east by the meandering Forks of the Credit Road and on the south by the West Credit River valley wall. The newly acquired land contains excellent examples of escarpment talus slopes and uncommon ferns, such as Rock Polypody, Maidenhair Spleenwort, and Daisy-leaved Grape Fern.

DIRECTIONS. From Exit 336 of Hwy 401, go N on Mississauga Rd (Reg Rd 1) to village of Belfountain. Entrance is 0.5 km N & E of main jct in Belfountain, off Forks of Credit Rd (Reg Rd 11). Access Willoughby estate via footpath heading E across CA.

INFORMATION. Credit Valley Conservation Authority.

Forks of the Credit Provincial Park and Area

Lands belonging to the park lie along both sides of the north branch of the Credit River between the villages of Cataract and Belfountain; in this 4-km stretch the river drops 68 m. Notable features in the 261-ha natural environment park include preglacial river valleys, a kettle lake, escarpment rim, cliff, talus slope, clay slope, and vegetation typical of such sites. Just east of the village of Belfountain at the southern edge of the park, the two branches of the Credit River that drain the upper parts of the Regional Municipality of Peel converge in a spectacular gorge at what is called the Forks of the Credit. The river then flows along the bottom of a cliff known as the Devils Pulpit. This Amabel dolostone cliff is the most pronounced promontory of the Niagara Escarpment in the vicinity of the park. A rare orange variety of the mineral celestite is found in the area. Upstream 4 km along the north fork of the Credit River is the Cataract, the only significant waterfall in Peel. Viewing platforms have been built here. The whole area is noted for its magnificent display of fall colour.

There are large, relatively undisturbed tracts of woodland above and below the exposed limestone cliffs of the escarpment. On top, the prevalent forest cover is Sugar Maple, occurring both in pure stands and in association with American Beech and White Ash. Below, mixed stands of White Birch, White Cedar, Sugar Maple, Eastern Hemlock, and Butternut are interspersed with wet, low-lying areas of Red Maple, Black Ash, and American Elm. As is the case along much of the Niagara Escarpment, the cliff face supports deformed, shrub-like White Cedar. Ferns, some of them rare, thrive: Hart's-tongue Fern, Green and Maidenhair Spleenworts, Goldie's Wood Fern, Rock Polypody, Slender and Smooth Cliffbrakes, Walking Fern, and Daisy-leaved Grape Fern. Cooper's Milk-vetch also grows here.

During migration seasons, the area is noted for the large number of bird species that travel along the wooded riverbanks. Air currents rising over the cliffs attract large numbers of Turkey Vultures from early spring through summer.

DIRECTIONS. 1) From Caledon Village on Hwy 10, go W on Hwy 24; turn S on McLaren Rd (2nd Line) & go 1.5 km to main entrance. 2) From Forks of Credit Rd (Reg Rd 11) 3 km W of

Hwy 10 & 2.5 km E of Belfountain, turn N on McLaren Rd & go
1 km. Side trail to Bruce Trail provides walk-in access. No public
parking in villages of Brimstone & Cataract.
INFORMATION. MNR.

Inglewood Slope

Just west of the village of Inglewood, the Niagara Escarpment
takes the form of two steep slopes separated by a flat bench of
land on which are situated a number of quarries. The total
height of the escarpment in the area is 30–45 m. Three small
streams emerging from the escarpment face have eroded deeply
into the clay till and Queenston shale on their way to the Credit
River. Disturbed areas support scrub vegetation, while small,
wet sites below the escarpment are dominated by White Cedar
forests. Extensive Sugar Maple woodlands of mixed age occur
above and below the escarpment, including on the steep talus
slope, where a number of uncommon plants occur. Among
these are Pale Touch-me-not and limestone-loving ferns such as
Rock Polypody.
DIRECTIONS. From Hwy 10 at Inglewood, go 2.5 km W on Base
Line Rd (Reg Rd 12); turn right onto Chinguacousy Rd (Caledon
2nd Line W). Walk 0.7 km to end of road; hike 3 km along Bruce
Trail to Grange Sdrd or continue 2 km more to Forks of Credit
Rd (Reg Rd 11). Stay on trail & avoid trespassing.

Cheltenham Badlands

In the southwest corner of the Inglewood Slope, this site is an
example of severe soil erosion. The property presents a picture
of raw, red and grey striated soil reminiscent of the Alberta Badlands. The area serves as a grim reminder of what can happen if
we abuse our environment. When farming was attempted on
the thin soil overlying the Queenston shale, the topsoil eroded,
leaving the barren landscape that remains today. Good views
are possible from Base Line Road. The Bruce Trail traverses the
badlands as it crosses from Creditview Road to Base Line Road.
DIRECTIONS. Located SW of Inglewood village. Go 2.5 km W
from Hwy 10 on Base Line Rd (Reg Rd 12). Property is on S side
of Base Line between Chinguacousy & Creditview Rds (Caledon 2nd & 3rd Lines W).

Ken Whillans Resource Management Area

A complex of five wetlands dominates this tract of mixed forest and old field on the lower slopes of the Niagara Escarpment. The 88-ha property is significant as a wintering area for wildlife and as a protected fish spawning and rearing site.

DIRECTIONS. From Base Line Rd (Reg Rd 12) at Inglewood, go 1.8 km N on Hwy 10 (Hurontario St). Entrance is on W side of road; watch for sign.

INFORMATION. Credit Valley Conservation Authority.

Caledon Mountain Slope Forest

A combination of public and private property, this significant 383-ha site contains numerous features associated with the Niagara Escarpment. Main and side trails of the Bruce Trail enable hikers to view the rich bedrock forests, talus forests, and cliff and crevice communities. About one-quarter of the site is composed of rich wetlands, including a peatland conifer swamp and the southernmost fen along the escarpment. The wetlands provide breeding habitat for large numbers of amphibians of various species. The most widespread vegetation community consists of broad-leaved forests of Sugar Maple associated with American Beech, White Ash, Hop-hornbeam, White Birch, Trembling Aspen, and Balsam Poplar. White Cedar and Eastern Hemlock woodlands are present, and Black Maple grows in the moist, deciduous bedrock forests on the escarpment plain.

Among the many rare plants are Lake Cress, Beaked Sedge, Downy Willow-herb, Satin Grass, Spring Clearweed, Tubercled Orchid, and Tall White Cinquefoil. Eastern Bluebird and Broad-winged Hawk use the area, and 13 species of wood warbler (Blue-winged, Black-throated Green, and Blackburnian, to name a few) have been recorded. Northern Flying Squirrel and Porcupine have also been sighted.

DIRECTIONS. Access via Bruce Trial (watch for white blazes): 1) from E side of Winston Churchill Blvd (Reg Rd 19) 2 km N of King St (Reg Rd 9, main street of Terra Cotta); or 2) from W or E sides of Heritage Rd, about 1.5 km N of King St in Terra Cotta. Stay on trails & avoid trespassing.

INFORMATION. Credit Valley Conservation Authority.

Terra Cotta Conservation Area

See entry under Regional Municipality of Halton.

Heart Lake Conservation Area

The 169-ha property is located on the north end of an esker that projects above the flat Peel plain. This gravelly ridge is a glacial formation with the typical steep, irregular, and hummocky surface of an esker. Heart Lake is a 17-ha kettle lake that was formed by melting ice at the edge of the Ontario lobe of the Wisconsin glacier. The lake is a source area for East Etobicoke Creek. The typical soil type here is Chinguacousy clay loam; this soil is poorly drained and resistant to erosion. The hilly property supports a mature Sugar Maple–American Beech community; sections of swampy lowland are located at the north end of the lake. There has been some reforestation, cleared areas being reserved for recreation. Cross-country skiing is available in winter.

DIRECTIONS. Follow Heart Lake Rd (Hwy 7 in part) N through Brampton; continue N for 3 km past Bovaird Dr.

INFORMATION. Metro Toronto and Region Conservation Authority.

Meadowvale Conservation Park

This significant natural site encompasses 75 ha of Credit River floodplain and associated upland. Among the lush and diverse ground flora are uncommon species such as White Trout-lily. The area provides habitat for a large number of bird species and, during migration, becomes a local hotspot where Mourning, Chestnut-sided, and Black-throated Blue Warblers and many other species can be seen. Winter birds include Long-eared Owl and Rough-legged and Sharp-shinned Hawks. Coho and Chinook Salmon and Rainbow Trout frequent the Credit River during spawning runs.

DIRECTIONS. From Mississauga Rd (Reg Rd 1) just N of Exit 336 from Hwy 401, go 500 m E on Derry Rd W; turn right on Meadowvale Blvd & go 150 m to Old Derry Rd, turn left, & travel 2 km to 2nd Line. Turn left & go 500 m N to entrance.

INFORMATION. City of Mississauga (905-896-5384).

Erindale Park and Area

A city of Mississauga park, Erindale consists of Credit River floodplain, valley wall, rim, and adjacent forest. Differences in microclimate account for different types of vegetation along the river. The east-facing slopes are cooler than normal and forested by Eastern Hemlock and White Cedar. The warmer, west-facing slopes found along the east side of the Credit are occupied by deciduous woodlands containing a number of southern species. Open sites along the valley rim support some interesting and uncommon plants, such as New Jersey Tea, Harebell, Northern Bedstraw, Soapberry, Yellow Pimpernel, Snowberry, and Dryland Blueberry. Hay-scented Fern grows in the woodlands. The area is noted for its good birding, and has yielded nesting Cliff Swallows (under Highway 403 bridge) and Great Horned Owls, calling American Woodcock, Rose-breasted Grosbeaks, and Northern Orioles, plus Great Blue Heron, White-tailed Deer, Red Fox, and Beaver.

DIRECTIONS. Main entrance (with parking lot) at jct of Mississauga Rd & Dundas St (Hwy 5). Or park in lot on N side of Burnhamthorpe Rd, W of Creditview & E of Mississauga Rd.

INFORMATION. City of Mississauga (905-896-5384).

Sawmill Creek Valley

The rolling terrain of the valley system supports one of the largest continuous tracts of woods in Mississauga. Sugar Maple, White Ash, Hop-hornbeam, and White Cedar are scattered throughout. Black Walnut and Witch-hazel are present, and large numbers of mature White Pines grow on the upland slopes. The valley lands and forested slopes are used by nesting and wintering birds. In summer, watch at dusk as hundreds of fireflies light up the woods with their mating rituals.

DIRECTIONS. Ravine runs 1.5 km W from S end of Erindale College in Mississauga. Enter trails from NW corner of Mississauga Rd (0.7 km N of Dundas St) & Collegeway. Park at Springbank Visual Arts Bldg.

INFORMATION. City of Mississauga (905-896-5384).

Mouth of the Credit River

The extensive cattail marsh that dominates the floodplain at the mouth of the Credit River is one of the few marshes remaining in the lower reaches of the river. The area is best seen by canoe as the adjacent steep, wooded, valley walls are privately owned. Watch for Great Blue Heron, Belted Kingfisher, rails, and nesting Northern Oriole. Purple Loosestrife is gradually invading the wetlands. In late March and April, Northern Pike spawn in the shallow mouth area and Rainbow Trout swim through to spawn upstream. Largemouth Bass use the marsh area for spawning from April through June. The native Atlantic Salmon, now slowly returning to spawning areas upriver, along with the introduced Chinook Salmon, can be seen in September and October.

DIRECTIONS. Park on Front St, N of Lake Shore Rd (Hwy 2), just W of Credit River in Mississauga.

Rattray Marsh

Rattray Marsh, the last remaining large shoreline marsh between Burlington and Toronto, is situated at the confluence of Sheridan Creek and Lake Ontario. The marsh is surrounded by valley walls up to 12 m in height and separated from the lake by a shingle bar. The wetland contains a high diversity of flora and fauna in close proximity to an urban area. Species with southern affinities found here include Witch-hazel, Sassafras, Cottonwood, Black Oak, Skunk-cabbage, and Long-spined Sandbur. Among the uncommon plants are Dryland Blueberry, Swamp Loosestrife, Swamp Candles, and Meadow Horsetail. Migrating and breeding wetland birds are abundant: American Bittern, Wood Duck, Virginia Rail, Sora, Black Tern, and Marsh Wren. A raised boardwalk has viewing towers.

DIRECTIONS. From jct of Southdown Rd & Lake Shore Rd (Hwy 2) in Mississauga, go 3.5 km E on Lake Shore to Jack Darling Municipal Park. Enter marsh via Lake Ontario Waterfront Trail in SE corner of park.

INFORMATION. Credit Valley Conservation Authority.

REGIONAL MUNICIPALITY OF HALTON

> Not long after we had got settled in our new home, one evening about sundown we were treated to an impromptu chorus by some of the denizens of the forest ... *the howling of a pack of wolves* ... To one who never heard the sound before, the impression would likely be that the noise came out of the ground. At first he hears a plaintive tone ... Then it seems to ascend step by step until the highest major notes are reached ... The lower tones do not cease as the higher are produced; but they continue right on until the listeners hear sounds that represent every note on the musical scale. (Esquesing Township, reminiscing about 1822, Rev. Joseph Hilts [1819–1903], Methodist circuit rider)

The Regional Municipality of Halton contains a variety of rich natural areas, several of them associated with the Niagara Escarpment. The escarpment's rugged nature here has historically discouraged agriculture and development, and permitted some very large blocks of ecologically diverse forested land to remain. In its current, largely unbroken state, the escarpment serves as a valuable wildlife corridor, even though extensive quarrying operations are active and its natural beauty makes it attractive for housing.

Elements of two forest regions are present in Halton. Carolinian species such as Flowering Dogwood, Sassafras, and American Chestnut grow in the southern part towards Lake Ontario. Farther north, the mixed deciduous and coniferous forest typical of much of southern Ontario occurs.

The valleys of Bronte and Sixteen Mile creeks and the Credit River provide important wildlife habitat. Water quality in the upper reaches of these streams is excellent, and Brook Trout thrive.

The region harbours numerous butterfly species, including some rarities. Look for Mulberry Wing and Two Spotted Skipper in marshy areas and damp meadows with long grasses and sedges; larvae of both species feed on sedges and, in the case of the Mulberry Wing, especially on Tussock Sedge. Sandy, open sites may support Purplish Copper, whose food plants include docks and knotweeds. The Satyr Angle Wing is a woodland species whose larvae feed on nettles.

Niagara Escarpment–Bruce Trail

The Niagara Escarpment runs diagonally across the Regional Municipality of Halton from Waterdown in the south to Terra Cotta in the north. In many sections the terrain is steep and rugged, and the scenery magnificent. Conservation areas, other public parklands, and the Bruce Trail (marked by white blazes) provide access at a number of points. See entry under Regional Municipality of Niagara.

INFORMATION. Bruce Trail Association; Niagara Escarpment Commission.

Terra Cotta Conservation Area

This 165-ha conservation area comprises about half of a large forested block known as Terra Cotta Woods. Above the Niagara Escarpment, the conservation area lands consist of rocky outcrops and shallow soils, mainly Lockport clays. Streams dissecting the property have created very steep slopes. Groundwater seeps from bedrock outcroppings to discharge into the numerous streams and small lakes that serve as a source area for the Credit River.

The greater part of the woodlands is covered by Red Oak, Sugar Maple, and White Birch. Valleys have slope forests of White Pine, Eastern Hemlock, and Sugar Maple. The deeply entrenched Silver Creek valley runs through the western end of the property, and a lowland swamp complex of elm–White Cedar forest and marshy meadows lies along the northeastern boundary. Significant flora are Ebony and Maidenhair Spleenworts, Smooth Solomon's-seal, and Pale Touch-me-not. A few Carolinian species approach their northern limits of distribution at this site; examples are Shagbark Hickory and Running Strawberry-bush. Other plants of note are One-flowered Pyrola and Fringed Polygala. Most of southern Ontario's typical woodland birds can be found here, including several rarities.

The conservation area offers an interpretive centre and an extensive system of trails, including the Bruce Trail. Cross-country skiing is available in winter.

DIRECTIONS. From Exit 333 on Hwy 401 go 17 km N on Winston Churchill Blvd (Reg Rd 19) to Terra Cotta village (where WC

Blvd becomes King St). Go 0.5 km on King St; turn left & go 1.6 km N on Winston Churchill Blvd to CA on left.
INFORMATION. Credit Valley Conservation Authority.

Silver Creek Valley

This deep, forested valley, an outlier of the Niagara Escarpment, is actually a glacial spillway formed during the retreat of the glaciers during the last Ice Age. Scenic, pristine, and alive with natural diversity, the 166-ha site is 2.5 km long and 75 m deep. The valley bottom, erosion-prone slopes, and surrounding uplands support meadow marshes, extensive seepage zones, White Cedar and Silver Maple swamps, post-fire successional forests, and mature Sugar Maple and mixed deciduous-coniferous forests.

Straddling the Carolinian and Great Lakes–St Lawrence forest regions, the valley harbours both northern and southern species, including some rarities. Turkey Vulture, Hermit Thrush, Blue-winged and Golden-winged Warblers, and Porcupine use the area. Brook Stickleback and Central Mudminnow are found in the marsh, while Brook Trout and Redside Dace occur in the cold waters of Silver Creek. The diversity of plants is outstanding: Canada Milk-vetch, Spicebush, Running Strawberry-bush, Yellow Water Buttercup, Bitternut Hickory, Walking Fern, Leatherwood, Butternut, Christmas Fern, and American Yew.
DIRECTIONS. From Exit 328 on Hwy 401 take Trafalgar Rd (Reg Rd 3) N to Hwy 7; turn left towards Acton & go 4 km N. Where Hwy 7 veers left, turn onto Trafalgar Rd N; turn at 1st right onto Sdrd 27; go to Falbrook (9th Line); turn left & take 1st driveway on left. There are also several access points via Bruce Trail (look for white blazes) between Trafalgar Rd (Reg Rd 3) & Winston Churchill Blvd (Reg Rd 19).
INFORMATION. Credit Valley Conservation Authority.

Wilfrid G. Crozier Nature Reserve

This tiny 4-ha reserve owned by the Federation of Ontario Naturalists protects a fragment of the Niagara Escarpment. The site includes cliff-edge habitat and upland meadows recently rehabilitated by local naturalists. Among plants of interest are Spikenard, Early Saxifrage, Shinleaf, Feverwort, and Great-spurred

Violet – a northern species found only very locally in southern Ontario.

DIRECTIONS. From Hwy 401 at Milton (Exit 320), go 6.5 km N on Hwy 25; turn W on St Helena Rd. Site is difficult to access.

Hilton Falls Conservation Area and Halton Regional Forest Complex

Located on the Niagara Escarpment, this relatively undisturbed upland woods contains 1,100 ha of mature hardwoods. The tract is actually a series of adjacent forested blocks, which together form an impressive system of ravines, tablelands, and lowlands. Wetlands are occupied by Silver Maple–White Cedar swamps, woodland ponds, wet sedge meadows, cattail marshes, and clear streams inhabited by Brook Trout and Water Shrew. Gorges and waterfalls occur where streams flow over the edge of the escarpment.

The area's rich diversity of habitats and species is no accident; size is the key ingredient. Flora and fauna typical of both northern and southern woodland habitats, and those requiring large areas of forest cover, thrive here. Nesting birds include 14 species of warblers, such as Nashville, Cerulean, and Canada Warblers, Louisiana Waterthrush, and Golden-winged and Blue-winged Warblers and their hybrids. Among other birds that use the area during the breeding season are Cooper's and Broad-winged Hawks, Yellow-billed Cuckoo, Blue-gray Gnatcatcher, and Yellow-throated Vireo. Escarpment outcrops provide nest sites for Turkey Vultures. Beaver ponds supply habitat for Mink, woodland ducks, and a wealth of reptile and amphibian life. Porcupines are common; Northern Flying Squirrel, Snowshoe Hare, Pickerel Frog, Jefferson complex Salamanders, and Northern Water Snake all occur. The long list of significant plant species found in the area includes Broad-leaved Waterleaf, Yellow Lady's-slipper, Showy Orchis, Maidenhair Spleenwort, Spicebush, Groundnut, Moonseed, Green Violet, Rose Twisted-stalk, Leatherwood, and Walking Fern. An extensive trail system permits all-season access.

DIRECTIONS. For Hilton Falls CA: from Hwy 401, take Exit 312 (Guelph Line or Reg Rd 1) N to Campbellville Rd (Reg Rd 9); turn right & travel 3 km E to CA entrance (1.5 km W of 6th

Line). For Halton Regional Forest: from Milton (Exit 320 from Hwy 401) go N on Hwy 25 to Campbellville Rd (Reg Rd 9); turn W & go 3.5 km to 6th Line; turn N & go 3.2 or 3.6 km to small parking lots.

INFORMATION. Halton Region Conservation Authority.

Calcium Pits

As glacial ice pushed across the escarpment in this area, it cut a deep trench now occupied by the headwaters of Bronte Creek. An ancient glacial waterfall (long since abandoned) and the escarpment bluff are the most distinctive landform features visible today; other geological features include meltwater channels and marl deposits. The re-entrant valley supports upland deciduous woodlands, as well as wetlands on the valley floor, where there is a large conifer swamp. Orchids and other uncommon plants, such as Variegated Scouring-rush, Marsh Bellflower, Green Violet, Long-fruited Snakeroot, Fringed Gentian, Showy Lady's-slipper, and Rush Aster, are found. Porcupine, Red-headed Woodpecker, and Winter Wren occur.

DIRECTIONS. Located S & W of Crawford Lake CA. From Guelph Line (Reg Rd 1) 4 km S of Hwy 401, go 1.5 km W on Steeles Ave to Twiss Rd; turn left & go 2.5 km to entrance on W side of road (just past Camp Manitou entrance).

INFORMATION. Halton Region Conservation Authority.

Crawford Lake Conservation Area

Extensive woodlands, rich undisturbed wetlands, and rugged limestone cliffs are the major features of the 154-ha site. Cool temperatures and an abundance of coniferous trees provide habitat for a number of northern species. Crawford Lake, which fills a collapsed underground cavern, is one of relatively few meromictic lakes in the province. Relative to its small surface area, the lake is too deep to enable wind-driven waves to turn its waters over and mix them from top to bottom. Lack of circulation between warm, oxygen-rich upper layers and cold, deep, oxygen-poor lower layers has resulted in over 5,000 years of well-preserved bottom sediments, a boon to those studying the biological history of the region through pollen analysis.

Bird life is diverse; breeding season records include Black-throated Blue and Canada Warblers, Yellow-bellied Sapsucker, Red-breasted Nuthatch, Hermit Thrush, Blue-gray Gnatcatcher, and Yellow-throated Vireo. Resident mammals are an interesting mix of northern and southern species, such as Woodland Vole, Water Shrew, Porcupine, and Ermine. The small and secretive Stinkpot turtle occurs. Trails can be used throughout the year.

Uncommon plants are well represented at Crawford Lake Conservation Area. These range from orchids, such as Showy Orchis and Downy Rattlesnake-plantain, to vines, such as Groundnut and Climbing Fumitory, to plants that thrive in wet places, including Round-leaved Sundew, Blunt-leaved Pondweed, Buckbean, and Small Bladderwort. Among other species of note are Spicebush, Green Violet, Goldie's Wood Fern, Indian Cucumber-root, and Small-flowered Leafcup.

DIRECTIONS. From Hwy 401, take Exit 312 (Guelph Line or Reg Rd 1); go 4 km S to Steeles Ave; turn left for entrance.

INFORMATION. Halton Region Conservation Authority.

Rattlesnake Point Conservation Area

Dominated by a sheer escarpment cliff face with talus slope below, Rattlesnake Point contains 260 ha of diverse terrain, vegetation, and wildlife. Its location in the transition zone between the Carolinian and Great Lakes–St Lawrence forest regions enhances its floral diversity. Thus Spicebush, Climbing Fumitory, and Burning Bush – species with southern affinities – exist here, as does Bearberry, a species more common farther north. Other interesting flora are Goldie's Wood Fern, Purple Virgin's-bower, Horsebalm, and Squawroot. There is a fine stand of Common Hackberry. The variety of habitats supports many bird species during the breeding season, including Turkey Vulture, Black-throated Green Warbler, Orchard Oriole, and Scarlet Tanager. Among mammals, Southern Bog Lemming is notable. Trails can be toured all year.

DIRECTIONS. From Hwy 401 at Milton (Exit 320), take Hwy 25 S 1 km to Steeles Ave. Turn right on Reg Rd 8 & drive 5 km W to Appleby Line; turn left & go 2.5 km S. To access Nassagaweya Canyon (a valley that is extremely rich botanically): from Derry Rd (Reg Rd 25) between Guelph Line (Reg Rd 1) and Appleby

Line, go N on Walker's Line to parking lot at dead-end past quarry; follow trail.

INFORMATION. Halton Region Conservation Authority.

Mount Nemo Conservation Area

Beyond the rugged beauty of Mount Nemo's sheer escarpment cliff face lie other interesting physical features, such as well-developed fissure or chimney caves. Scree skirts the foot of the cliffs, while hardwood forests dominate the top. Cool, damp crevices in the rock provide habitat for the limestone-loving Hart's-tongue Fern and Maidenhair Spleenwort. Additional noteworthy plants include American Chestnut, Poke Milkweed, Yellow Mandarin, Rock Sandwort, the parasitic pinecone-shaped Squawroot, and the vines Moonseed and Climbing Fumitory. Winter Wrens occur in the area.

DIRECTIONS. From Hwy 401, take Exit 312 (Guelph Line or Reg Rd 1) & go 13 km S to Colling Rd; entrance is on left.

INFORMATION. Halton Region Conservation Authority.

Clappison Escarpment Woods

See entry under Regional Municipality of Hamilton-Wentworth.

Waterdown Escarpment Woods

See entry under Regional Municipality of Hamilton-Wentworth.

Grindstone Creek Valley (including Hendrie Valley, Royal Botanical Gardens)

Grindstone Creek is known for its numerous rare species. The stream has cut deeply through the Queenston shales of the Niagara Escarpment to flow along a narrow, sheltered valley where dense stands of Shagbark Hickory, Sugar Maple, and American Beech grow. The combination of wooded floodplain bordered by forested ravines forms a natural corridor linking the escarpment with the Lake Ontario waterfront. Here a large sand and gravel bar protects the cattail marshes along the valley's lower reaches. The valley is the most important stopover site for migratory birds in the area. Among nesting species are Barred Owl and Blue-gray Gnatcatcher. Varied habitats also support a rich diversity of other species, such as Northern Ribbon Snake, Long-tailed Weasel, and Star-nosed Mole. Rainbow Trout and Northern Pike spawn in the creek. The valley harbours a number of noteworthy plants; watch for Yellow Mandarin, Twinleaf, Southern Arrow-wood, Silverrod, and Low Sweet Blueberry.

DIRECTIONS. Take trail at Cherry Hill gate across from RBG Centre on Hwy 2 (Plains Rd) in W Burlington.

INFORMATION. Royal Botanical Gardens (address under Regional Municipality of Hamilton-Wentworth).

LaSalle Park

This waterfront municipal park on the north shore of Hamilton Harbour is good for viewing waterfowl during migration and through the winter. The forests of Sugar Maple, Red Oak, White Pine, and Eastern Hemlock also contain Black Oak, Sassafras, Skunk-cabbage, and Forked Panic Grass. A major fish and wildlife habitat restoration project is under way at the park.

DIRECTIONS. From Hwy 2 (Plains Rd) in W Burlington, take Waterdown Rd S to harbour.

Burlington Beach

There is good viewing of hawk, falcon, and eagle migration from March to June and September to October. Although the site has had considerable disturbance, it represents the only dune habitat in Halton. Adjacent to the canal, on the north side of the lift-bridge that connects to the Hamilton side of the beach strip, are planted colonies of American Beach Grass, which may have been native to the site before development. Several interesting native dune grasses and sedges occur here as well, including Schweinitz's Cyperus and Purple Sand Grass.

DIRECTIONS. For birding, from Hwy 2 just E of jct with QEW, go S on Lake Shore Rd; park on E side of road.

Bronte Creek Provincial Park

The forested valley of Bronte Creek cuts through Queenston shales to form a deep, narrow, gorge. Unusual plants, including prairie species, find sanctuary in the varied habitats in and near the winding ravine. Eastern Hemlock grows on the cool, damp north-facing slopes while the hot, dry southwest-facing slopes provide sites for Shagbark Hickory and Chinquapin Oak. Some of the uncommon plant species are Wandlike Bush-clover, Large-bracted Tick-trefoil, Virginia Yellow Flax, White Trout-lily, Butterfly-weed, Sassafras, Black Walnut, and Sycamore.

The valley is used as a wintering site by Long-eared Owls and provides an important spring migration route for songbirds. Cooper's Hawk and Bald Eagle also pass through during migration. Watch for Black-backed Woodpecker, White-eyed Vireo, Orchard Oriole, and Mourning Warbler. The area shelters a number of animals, including Red Fox, Coyote, Ermine, Northern Water Snake, and Northern Ringneck Snake. There is an abundance of moths and butterflies. Rainbow Trout and Coho and Chinook Salmon can be seen moving upstream to spawn in spring and fall. A number of significant species have been recorded within the 684-ha park. Hiking trails are open for cross-country skiing in winter.

DIRECTIONS. From QEW between Burlington & Oakville take Exit 109; go N on Burloak Dr to entrance on E side of road; see prov hwy map.

INFORMATION. Bronte Creek Provincial Park, 1219 Burloak Dr, Burlington, Ont, L7R 3X5, 905-827-6911.

Iroquois Shoreline Woods

Situated on the former shoreline of glacial Lake Iroquois, this 40-ha municipal park contains features such as a bluff and a wave-cut terrace. The site is dominated by an upland forest of Sugar Maple, but White and Red Oaks, White Pine, Shagbark Hickory, American Beech, and Basswood also occur. Warblers pass through during migration; notable breeding birds are Nashville Warbler, Wood Duck, and Eastern Screech-Owl. Plants of interest include Sharp-leaved Goldenrod, Pilewort, and Southern Arrow-wood. Porcupines are found here.

DIRECTIONS. From Hwy 403 just N of QEW in Oakville, go W on Upper Middle Rd (Reg Rd 38); or from Trafalgar Rd (Reg Rd 3) go E on Upper Middle Rd; go S on 9th Line to parking lot on W side.

REGIONAL MUNICIPALITY OF HAMILTON-WENTWORTH

M. [Robert] de la Salle, having gone hunting, brought back a high
fever which pulled him down a great deal in a few days. Some say
it was at the sight of three large rattlesnakes he found in his path
whilst climbing a rock that the fever seized him ... There are a
great many of them at this place, as thick as one's arm, six or
seven feet long, entirely black. The rattle that they carry at the end
of the tail, and shake very rapidly, makes a noise like that which a
number of melon or squash seeds would make, if shut up in a box.
(A native village in the Beverly Swamp, September 1669, René
Bréhant de Galinée (?–1678), Sulpician priest and explorer)

The dominant physical feature of the Regional Municipality of
Hamilton-Wentworth is the 90-m-high Niagara Escarpment,
which curves sharply around the western tip of Lake Ontario.
The green ribbon of the escarpment passes through the city of
Hamilton and adjacent suburban and agricultural areas. Despite
the intensive development, White Cedars over 700 years old
occur on the cliff faces here, as they do in many places elsewhere along the escarpment. Several waterfalls are present,
each formed by a small creek as it cascades down the escarpment face.

Just west of Hamilton in the Dundas valley, a prominent gap
occurs in the familiar rocky cliffs. This break marks a buried,
bedrock gorge that extends eastward from Copetown, through
Dundas and Hamilton Harbour, and out under the western end
of Lake Ontario. The bottom of this gorge is below the level of
Lake Ontario; the valley, however, is almost completely filled in
with glacial deposits. The buried valley and flanking escarpment walls constitute a varied landscape that supports a great
diversity of upland, wetland, and aquatic habitats. Many of
these are now protected within nature sanctuaries or conservation areas.

An extensive network of natural areas is also present on the
shallow, stony, poorly drained soils found throughout Flambor-
ough Township, north of Dundas and east of Cambridge. Most
of these areas, however, are privately owned. Elsewhere in the
regional municipality, few natural areas remain.

Hamilton-Wentworth is located near the northern margin of

the Carolinian Forest zone, with both Carolinian and northern species present. In some locales, unusual plants typical of alvar, bog, or prairie communities can be found. The western end of Lake Ontario is an important staging and wintering area for waterfowl. In the fall, migrating hawks flying westward along the north shore of Lake Ontario funnel around the western end of Hamilton Harbour before heading overland towards Lake Erie.

Mountsberg Wildlife Centre and Conservation Area

See entry under Wellington County.

Beverly Swamp

At almost 2,000 ha, this is one of the largest relatively intact swamps in southwestern Ontario. The dense woods support many northern species that are near their southern limits here. Grass-pink, Showy Lady's-slipper, Sweet Gale, and Labrador Tea represent a plant diversity that reflects both northern and southern influences. The area features many uncommon nesting birds, such as Winter Wren, Brown Creeper, Veery, Northern Waterthrush, Black-and-white Warbler, and Golden-crowned Kinglet. A number of mammals, including Snowshoe Hare, Woodland Jumping Mouse, and Porcupine, occur here near the southern edge of their distribution. Pickerel Frog and Northern Water Snake inhabit the waterways. Much of the swamp is in private ownership, and hunting is allowed in some areas. The Hamilton Region Conservation Authority has acquired several tracts in the central section of this elongate swamp. Trails may be wet, especially in spring.
DIRECTIONS. From jct of Hwys 5 & 8, go W on Hwy 8 to Reg Rd 552; turn N. Either: 1) go 4 km to Reg Rd 501 (Safari Rd, Conc Rd 7) & 3.4 km E to small parking lot on N side; or 2) go 6 km to Conc Rd 8 & 4 km E to small parking lot on N side.

Rockton Area (Westfield Alvar and Hyde Forestry Tract)

The Westfield Heritage Centre property (managed by the Hamilton Region Conservation Authority) and nearby Hyde Forestry Tract (managed by the Ministry of Natural Resources) encompass a mixture of pine plantations, second-growth thickets, and small open meadows. Most of this area was formerly farmland but was abandoned because of the shallow, drought-prone soils and numerous rocks and dolostone bedrock outcroppings. Several rare and unusual species are present, including typical alvar plants. Among the interesting plants are Chinquapin Oak, Rock Elm, Fragrant Sumac, Prickly-ash, Swamp Fly Honeysuckle, False Pennyroyal, and Foxglove Beardtongue. Because of the varied habitats, many different birds (over 70 breeding species) and butterflies (over 50 species) occur in close proximity. Watch for specialties such as Grasshopper Sparrow and the hard-to-see Hairy-tailed Mole.

DIRECTIONS. From jct of Hwys 5 & 8, go W on Hwy 8 to Reg Rd 552. For Westfield Heritage Centre: turn N & go 1.7 km; access is through pioneer village. For Hyde Tract: go 1 conc rd N on E side of Reg Rd 552; park by trailhead located 0.6 km N of Conc Rd 6 or continue N to Reg Rd 501 (Safari Rd, Conc Rd 7) & go 0.6 km E to trailhead on S side of road. See also directions to Beverly Swamp.

Niagara Escarpment–Bruce Trail

In the Regional Municipality of Hamilton-Wentworth the Niagara Escarpment roughly parallels the Lake Ontario shoreline, presenting panoramic vistas of the lowland plain and lake that lie below it. The Bruce Trail follows the escarpment through the region and can be accessed at numerous points (look for white blazes), including conservation areas and other public parklands. See entry under Regional Municipality of Niagara.

INFORMATION. Bruce Trail Association; Niagara Escarpment Commission.

Spencer Gorge Wilderness Area (Websters and Tews Falls)

This 54-ha conservation area encompasses a spectacular Y-shaped gorge with two scenic waterfalls. Lookouts, trails, and stairways provide access to features such as Dundas Peak lookout and the gorge below Websters Falls. Among plants of interest are Early Saxifrage, Black Huckleberry, Poke Milkweed, Small-flowered Leafcup, and Fern-leaved False Foxglove. This is a good place to observe warblers.

DIRECTIONS. Take Hwy 8 NW from Dundas; at sharp bend in hwy above escarpment by Greensville, keep right on Reg Rd 504 (Brock Rd); go 0.8 km. Turn right on Harvest Rd & go 0.8 km to parking lot.

Conservation Areas in Dundas Valley

About 1,000 ha of conservation lands owned by Hamilton Region Conservation Authority within the Dundas valley contain numerous trails that can be used all year. The combination of rolling mixed hardwood bush and open fields supports a rich and diverse flora and fauna, including several Carolinian species. Some of the more interesting plants are Yellow Mandarin, Green Violet, Twinleaf, Witch-hazel, Flowering Dogwood, Spicebush, Tulip-tree, and American Chestnut.

Up to 100 species of birds may nest in this area, including Blue-winged, Golden-winged, and Hooded Warblers, Cooper's and Broad-winged Hawks, and Louisiana Waterthrush. Among the more than 20 species of herpetofauna are Wood Frog, Pickerel Frog, Red-spotted Newt, Yellow-spotted Salamander, Jefferson complex Salamanders, Redbelly Snake, Northern Ribbon Snake, and Northern Ringneck Snake. Starting in April, listen for the spring chorus. Later, watch for basking turtles.

INFORMATION (for all CAs in Dundas valley): 1) Hamilton Region Conservation Authority hdqts (weekdays): from Hwy 2 in Ancaster, at lights turn N on Sulphur Springs Rd; go 1 km to stop sign; go right on Mineral Springs Rd; go 2 km to bldg on left. 2) Dundas Valley Trail Centre (weekends); see below.

– Dundas Valley Conservation Area. Wooded hills and stream valleys are good places for enjoying spring wildflowers and forest songbirds.

DIRECTIONS. Proceed to Dundas Valley Trail Centre: from Hwy 8 in Dundas go 4.5 km W on Governors Rd (Reg Rd 399); or from Copetown go 5.2 km E on Governors Rd (Reg Rd 299).

– Governors Road Conservation Area (McCormack's Pond). Rolling fields are particularly good for butterflies, Bobolink, and Field Sparrow. Pond life is abundant.

DIRECTIONS. Trailhead is on N side of Governors Rd, 0.3 km W of entrance to Dundas Valley Trail Centre (see above).

– Martin's Road. Open fields and thickets are especially good for migrating and breeding warblers and other songbirds.
DIRECTIONS. From Hwy 2 in Ancaster, turn N at fire station on Meadowbrook Dr; go 1.2 km to T-jct. Turn left (W) on Jerseyville Rd, then immediately right on Martin's Rd, by Ancaster sports complex. Depending on road conditions, drive or walk 0.5 km downhill to Wilderness Trail.

Clappison Escarpment Woods

The 200-ha segment of greenbelt that extends along the Niagara Escarpment in this region straddles the border between Halton and Hamilton-Wentworth. The habitat includes a wooded talus slope, broad-leaved upland woods, mixed upland coniferous and deciduous forest, successional meadow, and an abandoned quarry. The flora has a southern affinity and includes many Carolinian species as well as some prairie and savanna species. Panicled Hawkweed, Perfoliate Bellwort, Drooping Sedge, Yellow Mandarin, Pignut Hickory, American Chestnut, Red Mulberry, Meadow Sundrops, American Columbo, and Downy False Foxglove reflect the rich diversity of plants present.
DIRECTIONS. From Hwy 5 in Waterdown, go about 2.3 km S on Main St & Snake Rd; follow white blazes of Bruce Trail W.

Waterdown Escarpment Woods

Extending along the top of the escarpment, this 3.5-km-long portion of the continuous escarpment greenbelt supports a high diversity of vegetation. The White Cedar–Red Oak community along the escarpment rim is particularly significant. Some of the unusual plants found here are Yellow Mandarin, Gracilescens Sedge, Sassafras, Small-flowered Leafcup, Drooping Sedge, Pignut Hickory, Red Mulberry, Green Violet, Walking Fern, and Honey Locust.
DIRECTIONS. From Hwy 5 at Waterdown, go S on Mill St & Waterdown Rd to jct with Mountain Brow Rd; turn E; access via Bruce Trail (white blazes) at brow of escarpment.

Royal Botanical Gardens Nature Sanctuaries

Most of the 1,100 ha of land managed by the Royal Botanical

Gardens lies within nature sanctuaries. Trail maps are available at the Royal Botanical Gardens Centre on Highway 2 (Plains Rd) between Burlington and Hamilton and at the RBG arboretum (follow signs off Highways 2, 6, and 403). Varied nature programs are offered.

INFORMATION (for all sites). Royal Botanical Gardens, Box 399, Hamilton, Ont, L8N 3H8, 905-527-1158 or 1-800-668-9449.

– Cootes Paradise (Dundas) Marsh. At present this large and significant wetland consists of open water less than 1 m deep. A major project has been initiated to restore the marsh vegetation. Trails and boardwalks through the sanctuary cross a variety of habitats, from marsh to open parkland, and fallow farmland to mature maple-hickory-oak woodland. Over 800 vascular plant species have been noted on the property. Among these are uncommon species such as Flowering Dogwood, Sassafras, Spicebush, Clinton's Wood Fern, Rue-anemone, Winged Loosestrife, and Stiff-leaved Goldenrod. During migration, up to 100 species of birds can be found per day. In breeding season, over 80 species have been observed using the area, including Wood Duck, Black-crowned Night-Heron, Green Heron, Double-crested Cormorant, Common Moorhen, Marsh Wren, Blue-gray Gnatcatcher, Orchard Oriole, and Northern Mockingbird. In late summer and fall, a great diversity of migrating shorebirds feeds on the mudflats at the west end of the marsh by Willow Point. Resident herpetofauna features species such as Blanding's, Map, Midland Painted, and Common Snapping Turtles.

DIRECTIONS. For North Shore Trails: 1) from Hwy 403 at Hwy 6 follow RBG signs N to arboretum on Old Guelph Rd; 2) enter from small parking lot on York Rd (Reg Rd 344) between Hwy 6 & Dundas, immediately S of CNR overpass. For South Shore Trails: from Hwys 2 & 8 at McMaster University, turn N on Cootes Dr towards Dundas; trail access is on E side of road at bridge over Spencer Creek. For hawkwatching, choose any spot with a good view, such as: 1) Thomas McQuesten Bridge between Cootes Paradise & Hamilton Hbr on York Blvd (Hwy 2); or 2) car pool parking lot on Hwy 6 just N of Hwy 403.

– Rock Chapel. Situated on the Niagara Escarpment, this area features the 25-m-high Borer's Falls. Open fields above the cliff provide habitat for a variety of butterflies, particularly in early to mid July. Other species of interest include Chinquapin Oak, Green Violet, Bobolink, Northern Mockingbird, and Orchard Oriole.

DIRECTIONS. From Clappison's Corners (jct of Hwys 5 & 6), proceed 2 km W on Hwy 5; turn S on Rock Chapel Rd & go 1 km.

– Hendrie Valley. See entry for Grindstone Creek under Regional Municipality of Halton.

East Hamilton Harbour

Despite being in the shadow of Hamilton's steel mills, this area supports a huge concentration of birds; even the Burlington Skyway Bridge is a major roosting site for European Starlings. The waters of the harbour attract many water birds, including most species of waterfowl that occur in Ontario. Berms along the eastern side of the bay provide nest sites for thousands of Ring-billed Gulls, as well as Black-crowned Night-Heron, Caspian and Common Terns, Double-crested Cormorant, and Herring Gull. During the winter, an open channel through Windermere basin at the southeast corner of Hamilton Harbour attracts large numbers of waterfowl; Northern Shoveler, Northern Pintail, and scaup are regulars. Also, watch for Snowy Owls.

DIRECTIONS. 1) From QEW S-bound take Eastport Dr Exit (km 97). 2) From QEW N-bound take North Shore Blvd Exit (km 97); at lights at end of ramp turn left onto North Shore Blvd; proceed 250 m, then exit right to Eastport Dr; follow Eastport Dr under Skyway Bridge & park along road shoulder. Nesting colonies & migrants are easily viewed from vehicles. Continue S on Eastport Dr & return to QEW N or S, or turn left on Beach Rd, then right on Van Wagners Beach Rd to Van Wagners Ponds & Beach (see below).

Western Lake Ontario Shoreline

The western end of Lake Ontario can yield some exciting pelagic birds during fall migration. In recent years, large rafts of diving ducks have overwintered in this area, feeding on Zebra Mussels. Bring a telescope. Road access under the Burlington Skyway Bridge means that birding trips to these areas can be readily combined with visits to the East Hamilton Harbour area (see above). See also Regional Municipality of Halton section for additional access and viewing points.

– Van Wagners Beach and Confederation Park. From September to November, look for jaegers, eiders, scoters, loons, phalaropes, and Black-legged Kittiwakes. Easterly winds are most favourable.

DIRECTIONS. From QEW, take Centennial Pkwy (Hwy 20) Exit (km 88) (5 km SE of Skyway Bridge). Follow signs to Confederation Park (on Lake Ontario shore). Turn left on Confederation Dr, which jogs at Nash Rd, then becomes Van Wagners Beach Rd. Parking lots along road give access to beach-front park.

– Van Wagners Ponds. These small ponds are a favourite summer feeding location for the Common and Caspian Terns that nest at Hamilton Harbour. A small population of Black Terns also feeds here.

DIRECTIONS. Follow directions for Van Wagners Beach. Access to ponds is from Beach Blvd opposite Hutch's Restaurant.

REGIONAL MUNICIPALITY OF NIAGARA

> Betwixt the Lake *Ontario* and *Erie*, there is a vast and prodigious Cadence of Water which falls down after a surprizing and astonishing manner, insomuch that the Universe does not afford its Parallel ... At the foot of this horrible Precipice, we meet the River *Niagara* ... The Waters which fall from this vast height, do foam and boil after the most hideous manner imaginable, making an outrageous Noise, more terrible than that of Thunder; for when the Wind blows from off the South, their dismal roaring may be heard above fifteen Leagues off. (December 6, 1678, Louis Hennepin [1626–1705], Récollet missionary and explorer)

The Niagara Peninsula is bordered on the east by the Niagara River, and is sandwiched between Lake Ontario on the north and Lake Erie on the south. The most striking feature of the region is the Niagara Escarpment, which runs from Queenston westward and then northwestward to the Bruce Peninsula and beyond. In the Regional Municipality of Niagara, a 60-m-high face of exposed rock strata separates the lower plains along

Lake Ontario from the more elevated part of the peninsula extending south to Lake Erie.

The large water bodies provide habitat for water birds throughout the year. Upland areas support a diversity of habitats occupied by numerous Carolinian species. The Virginia Opossum, a nocturnal marsupial which is expanding its range throughout southern Ontario, first established a toehold in the province in the Niagara region.

IROQUOIS PLAIN

The narrow, sandy plain between Lake Ontario and the base of the Niagara Escarpment once lay beneath the waters of glacial Lake Iroquois. The lowland is crossed by a number of small streams, whose lower reaches are often characterized by lagoons, marshes, and barrier beaches.

Port Weller (St Catharines)

The Welland Canal enters Lake Ontario at Port Weller. Both east and west piers, which hug the canal, are extremely attractive to migrant birds. The east pier, in particular, has hosted about 300 species. The pier is about 1.5 km long and has a variety of habitats to explore. Mary Malcolmson Park is located along the west pier.

DIRECTIONS. To reach E pier from Lakeshore Rd (Reg Rd 87), turn N on Broadway Ave, just E of canal. Go 0.5 km; turn left on 1st unpaved road & drive to barrier; park well to one side & walk.

NIAGARA ESCARPMENT

Niagara Escarpment–Bruce Trail

The Niagara Escarpment, a 'World Biosphere Reserve,' stretches across southern Ontario for 725 km from Queenston on the Niagara River, through Niagara, Hamilton-Wentworth, Halton, Peel, Dufferin, Simcoe, Grey, and along the east side of the Bruce Peninsula to Manitoulin and St Josephs islands.

The escarpment began to form 450 million years ago, when the area lay under an inland sea centred in Michigan and whose shoreline in part approximated today's escarpment. Over time, accumulations of sand, silt, and clay washed into the warm, shallow waters and later became compressed into sedimentary rocks, mostly soft shales and sandstones. Meanwhile marine organisms rich in lime were creating reefs that eventually turned into dolostone, a rock similar to limestone. Today the escarpment is noted for the quality of its rocks and fossils from the Palaeozoic Era.

Following the retreat of the sea 300 million years ago, the rim of the escarpment began to emerge as a visible feature. Erosion gradually wore away the softer shales, leaving behind chunks of the harder dolostone. The vertical face of the escarpment was created when easily erodable layers underneath broke down, allowing the harder caprock above to become undercut and fall. Today, along the top edges of the escarpment cliffs dolostone is visible, while lower down the slope reddish-coloured shales can be seen.

The successive advances of the glaciers during the Pleistocene drastically altered the topography of the escarpment. In some places the brow was scraped clear of soil, while in others stretches of the escarpment were buried under glacial moraines. Erosion continues to change the face of the Niagara Escarpment. Streams carve their way into cliffs, frost action promotes undercutting and rock falls, and waves eat away at vertical shorelines. Chemical weathering is also at work, dissolving the porous dolostone to create caves and sinkholes. During the past two centuries, when much of southern Ontario was being cleared for agriculture, the inaccessible or undesirable portions of the escarpment often became refugia for native flora and fauna. Today the Niagara Escarpment Commission seeks to control environmental degradation along the escarpment corridor.

The Bruce Trail provides hikers with the opportunity to traverse the escarpment from Queenston to Tobermory or for shorter portions in between. The trail is noted for its rugged hikes, spectacular scenery, and the abundance and diversity of its flora, particularly ferns and orchids. There are numerous access points, and accounts of many sites along the trail appear elsewhere in this book. The main trail is marked by white blazes and side trails are indicated by blue or yellow blazes.

INFORMATION. Bruce Trail Association; Niagara Escarpment Commission.

Beamer Memorial Conservation Area

This is the focal point of spring hawkwatching in Ontario (best between March and May), when tens of thousands of north-ward-migrating hawks follow the shorelines of Lakes Erie and Ontario. Viewing is best on warm days with a southeast wind. Peak numbers of adult Red-shouldered Hawks pass through the last week of March. April brings the greatest number of species. The 53-ha conservation area also protects a portion of the Niagara Escarpment and a number of rare plants. Floral specialties include Yellow Giant Hyssop, Sicklepod, Stout Wood Reedgrass, Squawroot, Wild Plum, Canada Snakeroot, Ensheathed Dropseed, and Summer Grape.

DIRECTIONS. From QEW near Grimsby, take Exit 71 S at Christie St (Mountain Rd or Reg Rd 12). At top of escarpment, turn right on Ridge Rd (Reg Rd 79); go 1.6 km to Quarry Rd. Turn right & go 100 m to CA parking lot on right.

INFORMATION. Niagara Peninsula Conservation Authority; Niagara Peninsula Hawkwatch, 1365 Bayview Ave, Unit 3, Toronto, Ont, M4G 3A5.

Waterfalls on the Niagara Escarpment

Several creeks that tumble over the Niagara Escarpment on their way to Lake Ontario create a series of small picturesque waterfalls. Below the falls, the creeks pass through deep ravines, which, because of their relative inaccessibility, retain many of their original features, such as rock-stewn walls, forested banks, and vegetation of moss, ferns, and wildflowers. Interesting ferns growing in the crevices in the rocks are Purple-stemmed Cliffbrake, Northern Maidenhair Fern, Walking Fern, and Maidenhair Spleenwort. Flowering plants in the ravines include Wild Ginger, Poke Milkweed, and Variegated Trillium.

INFORMATION. Niagara Peninsula Conservation Authority.

– **Balls Falls.** Twenty Mile Creek plunges over the escarpment here in a spectacular drop that is two-thirds the height of Nia-

gara Falls. Uncommon plants found include Tall Bellflower, Horsebalm, Shining Wedge Grass, and Dryland Blueberry.
DIRECTIONS. From QEW Exit 57 at Vineland Station go 6 km S on Reg Rd 24 (Victoria Ave). Watch for signs to Balls Falls CA.

– Rockway Falls. Here Fifteen Mile Creek falls 40 m over layers of limestone and shale.
DIRECTIONS. Located just W of St Catharines on Reg Rd 69 (Pelham Rd), 2.5 km W of its jct with Reg Rd 28. Rockway CA lies to N.

– DeCew Falls. Water tumbling over the falls here joins Twelve Mile Creek in the valley below.
DIRECTIONS. Follow Hwy 20 for 5 km W from Welland Canal at Allanburg to Reg Rd 50 (Merrittville Pkwy). Go 6.5 km N to Lake Gibson. Cross lake; immediately turn left & follow DeCew Rd along N shore of lake for 1.5 km.

Short Hills Provincial Park

Steep, sensitive slopes, floodplains, and wooded ravines and uplands are features of the wetland and forest communities at Short Hills. Fossils are found embedded in the exposed limestone of Dry Falls. Rare species include Pawpaw and Cucumbertree. Watch for Wild Turkeys in winter. Twelve Mile Creek, one of the few coldwater streams in the area, runs through the park.
DIRECTIONS. From Fonthill, travel W on Hwy 20 to Effingham Rd (Reg Rd 32, becomes Reg Rd 28). Turn N & go 6.2 km to Roland Rd. Turn E & drive 0.5 km to small parking lot.
INFORMATION. MNR.

St Johns Conservation Area

This 30-ha-site protects a high-quality mature forest with an exceptional richness of flora and fauna, including many rare plants. Watch for Hairy Agrimony, Purple Spring Cress, American Chestnut, Panicled Hawkweed, and Rough-leaved and Elm-leaved Goldenrods. Peak fall colour occurs from late September to mid October.
DIRECTIONS. From main jct (traffic lights) in Fonthill, turn N off Hwy 20 onto Pelham St (becomes Hollow Rd) & follow signs to CA.

INFORMATION. Niagara Peninsula Conservation Authority.

UPLAND CLAY PLAIN

An unevenly drained clay plain, broken by sand and gravel deposits in the Fonthill area, extends from the escarpment southward towards Lake Erie. A low, north-facing limestone ridge formed by the Onondaga Escarpment near Lake Erie sends drainage north and east to Lake Ontario.

Harold Mitchell Nature Reserve

This Federation of Ontario Naturalists' reserve protects 13 ha of ponds, wet woodland, rolling sloughs, and low ridges. Swamp White Oak, American Beech, Yellow Birch, Red, White, and Black Ashes, and Red and Sugar Maples grow on the property. Watch for Indian Cucumber-root, Spicebush, Southern Arrow-wood, and a stand of mature Eastern Hemlock, as well as Great Horned Owl and many species of songbirds. High rubber boots are recommended.
DIRECTIONS. Take Hwy 3 W from Port Colborne, then Reg Rd 3 S, then W along Lake Erie shoreline, following signs to Long Beach CA. Go N on road just W of CA.

Wainfleet Marsh

This vast, poorly drained tract includes one of Ontario's few southern acid bogs, which occupies several hundred hectares at the east end of a 1,500-ha forested swamp. Located between the Niagara and Onondaga escarpments, the site is known to har-bour a number of rare species. The open wetland contains an assemblage of plants characteristic of treeless bogs, such as Labrador Tea, Pitcher-plant, Leatherleaf, and Gray Birch. North-ern species such as Nashville Warbler and Lincoln's Sparrow occur here along with scarcer southern species, such as White-eyed Vireo and Yellow-breasted Chat.
DIRECTIONS. Go 6.5 km W from Port Colborne on Hwy 3 to Wil-son Rd; turn N & go 1 km.
INFORMATION. Niagara Peninsula Conservation Authority; MNR.

Mud Lake Wildlife Management Area

This is an excellent area for both land and water birds, especially during migration season. Watch for Green Heron, Virginia Rail, and Sora, along with other wetland species, from March to October.

DIRECTIONS. From Hwy 3 at Port Colborne, turn N onto Elm St (Reg Rd 80) just W of canal; go 1.5 km (just past Barrick St) & park in small lot on right.

Point Abino

Point Abino is a 3-km-long sandbar jutting between the north shore of Lake Erie and a limestone shelf offshore. The peninsula contains a complex of high, forested sand ridges, extensive wetlands, and sand and limestone pavement beaches. The abundance of significant native species found here includes Halberd-leaved Tearthumb, Hop-tree, Prothonotary Warbler, Acadian Flycatcher, Southern Flying Squirrel, and Eastern Hognose Snake. The point is a good place for seeing songbird migration, especially warblers during May. Unfortunately much of the peninsula is privately owned and inaccessible to the public.

DIRECTIONS. Take Hwy 3 W of Fort Erie to Point Abino Rd or Holloway Bay Rd; go S about 6 km to publicly accessible area at base of point. Avoid trespassing.

Eastern Lake Erie Shoreline

Look for water birds between Dunnville and Fort Erie.

NIAGARA RIVER AND GORGE

Niagara River

The Niagara River is one of the best places in Canada for seeing migratory gulls and waterfowl. Terns, cormorants, herons, wetland and shore birds, and sometimes jaegers can also be seen. Fall and winter and, to a lesser extent, early spring are the best viewing times. Migrating and wintering ducks are present from November to March and migrating gulls from September to December. Birds are attracted to the river's plentiful stock of small fish and other edible aquatic creatures that flourish in waters kept clear of ice by the force of rushing water.

DIRECTIONS. Approaching river from W via Queen Elizabeth Way (ends at Fort Erie), take Hwy 55 to Niagara-on-the-Lake, Hwy 405 to Queenston or Hwy 420 to Niagara Falls. Follow signs to Niagara River Pkwy along river (numerous stopping places provided).

– Niagara-on-the-Lake. Here, at the mouth of the Niagara River, ducks and other water birds occur in abundance in spring and fall. In fall and early winter, a main attraction visible from the marina is the fly-by of thousands of Bonaparte's Gulls (with the occasional Little, Common Black-headed, or Franklin's Gull) heading off at dusk to roost on Lake Ontario. Also watch here for Oldsquaw and Common Loon. In the west end of town (e.g., Wilberforce off Lakeshore Road [Regional Road 87]), winter bird feeders attract an excellent variety of birds, including Northern Mockingbird, Red-bellied Woodpecker, Tufted Titmouse, and Carolina Wren. South of town, the parkway passes through the magnificent Paradise Grove Park, where rare prairie and savanna plants, such as Fern-leaved False Foxglove, can be seen in season. Continue south 13 km to Queenston.

– Queenston. In fall and early winter, check below Queenston for Little, Sabine's, and Common Black-headed Gulls among the thousands of Bonaparte's Gulls foraging along the river. South of town, stop at the lookout for the Adam Beck generating station. Among the thousands of Herring and Ring-billed Gulls, look for Glaucous, Iceland, and Lesser Black-backed Gulls, from September through December. Continue 11 km south to the Rainbow Bridge at Niagara Falls. Along the way several footpaths descend into the Niagara Gorge, especially at Niagara Glen.

– Niagara Falls. Common Terns nest above the falls, and Forster's Terns occur in late summer. In fall look for Red-necked and Red Phalaropes above the falls opposite Dufferin Islands Park, and Purple Sandpiper on rock ledges in the rapids above the falls. The waters by the pier near the water control system should have hundreds of Canvasback, scaup, and Redhead. Scan the islands, rapids, and ledges above the falls for a good variety of diving and dabbling ducks, including the occasional

Eurasian Wigeon, Harlequin Duck, and Barrow's Goldeneye. Among the hundreds of gulls that occur in fall and early winter you may see Glaucous and Iceland Gulls and occasionally Lesser Black-backed, Little, and Thayer's Gulls.

– Niagara Parkway South of Niagara Falls. Continue 14.5 km south, en route looking for waterfowl, gulls, and Bald Eagles during the cooler months, to the mouth of Boyer's Creek, where stands of Flowering-rush grow. Continue south 16 km to the Peace Bridge at Fort Erie. Waterfowl gather in flocks in spring and fall around Navy Island south of Chippewa and along the river off the Niagara Parkway to Fort Erie. Little, Sabine's, and Franklin's Gulls and Black-legged Kittiwake have occurred among Bonaparte's Gull flocks near the Peace Bridge.

– Fort Erie. About 1.5 km south of Fort Erie, the beaches at the restored Old Fort Erie afford an opportunity to see wading birds, gulls, and shorebirds. Stop often along the next few kilometres to look for migrant shorebirds in late summer and fall.

Niagara River Geology

About 32 km downstream from Lake Erie, the Niagara River tumbles over Niagara Falls. Above, the river is broad and swift; below, it flows 11 km through the steep-sided Niagara Gorge with its rock walls, jumbled rock slides, and wooded ravines. The river emerges from the gorge and the escarpment at Queenston Heights, and continues northward another 12 km before emptying into Lake Ontario.

– Bedrock. The major rock formations exposed along the Niagara Escarpment and Gorge are all sedimentary in origin, deposited in an inland sea about 400 million years ago during the Ordovician and Silurian periods of the Palaeozoic Era. Rocks of Ordovician origin are the Queenston shales. These are the red shales that can be seen at various localities along the base of the escarpment. They are also visible in the lower part of the gorge walls from the mouth of the Niagara River almost to Niagara Glen. Rocks of Silurian origin can be seen along the entire length of the gorge. They consist of sandstones, shales, limestones, and dolostones. The formation over which the falls cascade is Lockport dolostone, a hard calcium-magnesium-carbonate rock. It can be traced along the rim of the gorge in its entirety as well as along the rim of the Niagara Escarpment.

– Why a Falls? The arrangement of hard dolostone overlying softer shales and sandstones controls the kind of erosion produced by the running waters of the Niagara River. At the lip of the falls, the hard dolostone at the surface becomes undermined, owing to the ease with which the softer rocks beneath it can be worn away by spray and frost. Cracks develop and rock falls occur. Continued undercutting allows the river to erode its way upstream while still maintaining a vertical waterfall rather than a gradually sloping waterway.

– Gorge Development. Over thousands of years, water flowing from Lake Erie to Lake Ontario has cut an 11-km-long gorge between Niagara Falls and the Niagara Escarpment at Queenston. During that time the volume of water carried by the Niagara River has varied considerably. When water flow was heaviest, the river carved a wide gorge; when water volume decreased, the gorge narrowed. Other factors have also helped to influence the shape and character of the gorge.

Rock Glen. The rubble at Rock Glen (4 km upriver from Queenston) is the remains of an island that at one time split the river into two channels, of which the eastern channel carried the bulk of the flow. On the Canadian side of the gorge, the shoreline of the old river is visible as a small bluff, and the flat area at its base is a former channel bed.

The Whirlpool. At the Whirlpool (best viewed from a cable-car or Whirlpool House), the developing Niagara Gorge encountered a buried gorge from an earlier time. Known as St David Gorge, it had been filled with sands, clays, and tills by the glaciers. These glacial deposits, instead of bedrock, are visible in the walls of the embayment around the Whirlpool. Immediately upstream, the narrow Whirlpool Gorge is also considered to be part of the old buried gorge.

Upper Great Gorge. This is located just below the 54-m-high Horseshoe (Canadian) Falls and the 64-m-high American Falls. In the past few centuries the natural rate of erosion has averaged a little more than 1 m annually at Horseshoe Falls, over which 94% of the river's flow passes. The rate has slowed considerably in recent years because much of the water is now diverted for hydroelectric purposes.

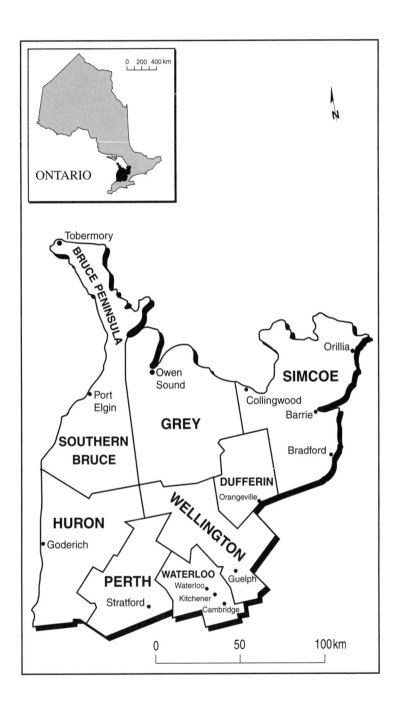

0   200   400 km

ONTARIO

Tobermory

BRUCE PENINSULA

Owen Sound

Port Elgin

SOUTHERN BRUCE

GREY

Orillia

SIMCOE

Collingwood

Barrie

Bradford

DUFFERIN

Orangeville

WELLINGTON

HURON

Goderich

PERTH

WATERLOO

Waterloo

Kitchener

Cambridge

Guelph

Stratford

0   50   100km

3 Lake Huron to Georgian Bay Lobe

Bruce Peninsula	Waterloo
Southern Bruce	Wellington
Grey	Dufferin
Huron	Simcoe
Perth	

This area lies in the Great Lakes–St Lawrence Forest Region. It extends southward from the shores of Lake Huron and Georgian Bay to the northernmost edge of the Carolinian Forest zone in Canada. Within the region described in this chapter, a prominent topographic feature, the Niagara Escarpment, runs north from Orangeville to Collingwood and thence northwest, approximately following the Georgian Bay shoreline, to the tip of the Bruce Peninsula. From the crest of the escarpment the land slopes to the west and south through highlands, rolling hills, and level sand, clay, or till plains. Numerous glacial features are visible, such as gravel terraces, moraines, drumlins, glacial spillways, and former lake bottoms. Except in rocky or swampy areas and the limestone plains of the Bruce Peninsula, much of the land is used for pasture or cropland.

BRUCE PENINSULA

Next morning, the waters of [Georgian Bay] were unmolested by the wind, and we sailed towards [Cape Hurd], deviating a little from our direct course to view the islands of the Flower Pots, lofty rocks which rise from the lake, shaped like such utensils, and bearing a gigantic bouquet of trees. We then bore away for [Cape Hurd], with the sight of which I was agreeably disappointed ...; we saw only a woody stretch of land not very lofty, lying calm in the sunshine of a still afternoon, and instead of dark clouds and lurid lightnings, beheld only beauty and calm. (Aboard the gunboat *Bee*, early summer 1827, John Galt [1779–1839], writer and Canada Company official)

The dominant landform feature of the peninsula is the Niagara Escarpment, which forms a backbone along the eastern shore. Here steep, white dolostone cliffs up to 60 m high rise from the blue-green waters of Georgian Bay to create spectacular scenery. From the top of the escarpment, the peninsula gradually slopes westward and eventually disappears under the waters of Lake Huron. Variations in the dip have resulted in the series of offshore islands known as the Fishing Islands.

Along the west shore, evidence of the passage of continental ice sheets is visible as glacial grooves carved in the bedrock. Changing lake levels periodically flood the shoreline fens that support many of the significant plants for which the peninsula is renowned. Elsewhere along the west coast are sand dunes built up during times of high water. Among the plants associated with the dunes are species endemic to the upper Great Lakes. The Sky, Boat, and Isaac lakes system forms an extensive wetland complex that abounds with wildlife and aquatic species.

Flora

The amazing diversity of plant life on the Bruce Peninsula has led to the nickname 'the garden of North America.' Most of the peninsula's plants are typical of the Great Lakes–St Lawrence Forest Region, but specialized conditions, particularly along the shoreline, have also allowed plants that are characteristic of other parts of the continent to prosper here. Such plants migrated through the Bruce following the last continental glaciation as habitats were re-establishing across North America. Arctic plants arrived shortly after the ice departed and now persist in sites where cool lake breezes, groundwater flow, and soil and bedrock conditions restrict the growth of trees. Prairie plants survive in fens and other open habitats unable to support forest communities. Maritime plants reached the region when the sea extended inland to the Ottawa valley.

A unique forest community of lichens, herbaceous plants, and stunted trees occupies the vertical cliffs of the Niagara Escarpment. The small White Cedars growing out of the rock face are up to 1,000 or more years old – the oldest trees in eastern North America. Few plant communities in the province have changed so little since European settlement.

The floral regions represented in the peninsula, together with some of their indicator plant species, are:

Great Lakes–St Lawrence (Mixed) Forest: Sugar Maple, White Birch, Yellow Birch, Red Pine, White Pine, Striped Maple, Choke Cherry, Leatherwood, and Wild Sarsaparilla

Boreal Forest: White Spruce, Yellow Clintonia, Wild Lily-of-the-valley, Goldthread, Bearberry, Heart-leaved Twayblade, and Tamarack

Carolinian (Eastern Deciduous) Forest: Canada Violet, Squirrel-corn, and Puttyroot

Prairie: Little Bluestem, Wood Lily, Indian Paintbrush, and White Camass

Western: Alaska Orchid, Northern Holly Fern, and Green-leaved Rattlesnake-plantain

Maritime: Seaside Arrow-grass and Beach Pea

Arctic: Butterwort, Fen Spikemoss, and Bird's-eye Primrose

Mississippi: Tuberous Indian-plantain

A number of shoreline plants that are endemic to the Great Lakes basin grow in abundance on the Lake Huron shoreline. These include Dwarf Lake Iris, Hill's Thistle, Kalm's St John's-wort, Smaller Fringed Gentian, Ohio Goldenrod, Low Calamint, and Sand Cherry.

Orchids. Excluding Florida, the Bruce Peninsula is regarded as the finest location for observing wild orchids in North America. The abundance and diversity of species are unsurpassed. Varied habitats and soil conditions, ranging from acid sands to alkaline fens, permit high diversity. Cold water slowly seeping through the soil creates 'cold-bottom' conditions that contribute to abundance. At least 44 species of orchids have been recorded on the peninsula; all but 4 occur within 3.2 km of Lake Huron. The orchids bloom through the growing season, with a progression of different species from early May to early October. At times, the roadsides are lined with Yellow Lady's-slippers.

Insectivorous Plants. The fen communities along the Lake Huron shore contain 10 species of insectivorous plants: Pitcher-plant, 3 species of sundews, Butterwort, and 5 species of bladderworts.

Ferns. The escarpment cliffs of the eastern shore provide prime habitat for a variety of fern species. The lower Bruce Peninsula and Grey County are the centre of abundance for Hart's-tongue Fern in North America. Wall-rue is known from only a few sites in Canada, all of them on the Bruce Peninsula or Manitoulin Island.

Fauna

Birds. The Bruce Peninsula provides a corridor northward for land birds migrating through southwestern Ontario. In both spring and fall, loons, grebes, and waterfowl concentrate from Dyer's Bay to Cabot Head. The spring passage of hawks moves along the eastern shore, then across Manitoulin Island to northern Ontario. The Lake Huron shoreline is prime nesting habitat for warblers and other land birds. The list of birds breeding in the upper Bruce Peninsula shows similarities to that of central Algonquin Park. Open farmlands around Ferndale attract western breeders. Over 175 species have been recorded breeding on the peninsula.

Mammals. Black Bear, River Otter, and Southern Red-backed Vole reach the southern limits of their Ontario ranges here. Fishers have been successfully reintroduced. Mild winters in the late 1980s and early 1990s enabled the Virginia Opossum to push its range northward into the peninsula. Seven of Ontario's eight resident species of bats are found on the upper Bruce.

Herpetofauna. The Bruce harbours a great diversity of reptiles and amphibians. The Eastern Massasauga rattlesnake is locally common, particularly in the area of the Bruce Peninsula National Park.

Butterflies. Of the more than 54 species reported from the upper Bruce Peninsula, most are typical of southwestern Ontario. The Silvery Checkerspot, a more northerly species, inhabits meadows, grassy areas, and wood edges.

Niagara Escarpment–Bruce Trail

Both the escarpment and the trail approximately follow the

Georgian Bay shoreline along the east side of the peninsula. The land is rugged, and the scenery wild and spectacular. Access to the Bruce Peninsula section of the escarpment is available at various locations, including the Bruce Trail (marked by white blazes), national parks, conservation areas, provincial nature reserves, and other properties. See entry under Regional Municipality of Niagara.

INFORMATION. Bruce Trail Association; Niagara Escarpment Commission.

Fathom Five National Marine Park

Canada's first national marine park protects a submerged section of the Niagara Escarpment north of Tobermory. There are good representations of both the warmwater habitat of Lake Huron and the coldwater habitat of Georgian Bay, as well as 21 shipwrecks, many from the late 1800s. Dissolved limestone gives a sparkling turquoise colour to the waters surrounding the 19 islands that form the above-water portion of the park. Fathom Five's waters reach to a depth of 200 m and include spectacular underwater scenery. An ancient spillway similar to the re-entrant valleys found above water elsewhere along the Niagara Escarpment and a 5-m-high pop-up ridge that runs for a kilometre along the lake floor are significant features. The park is popular with scuba divers. Offshore islands offer a variety of geological features and plant communities of note.

DIRECTIONS. Boat tours leave from Tobermory wharf.

INFORMATION. Canadian Parks Service, Box 189, Tobermory, Ont, N0H 2R0, 519-596-2233.

– **Flowerpot Island.** This mecca for fern and orchid lovers is the best known of the Tobermory Islands. Flowerpots and caves were formed when wave and frost action eroded soft layers of limestone from under the thick layers of rock that cap the surface. Beneath a shallow pond lies a marl bed, the result of dissolved limestone settling to the bottom as a murky precipitate. Numerous rare species occur on Flowerpot. Ferns such as Bulblet Fern, Northern Holly Fern, and Wall-rue flourish. Among the 20 species of orchids are Calypso, Spotted (including yellow form) Coralroot, Striped Coralroot, Northern Green Orchid, Green-leaved Rattlesnake-plantain, and Round-leaved Orchid.

A White Cedar that attained a height of only 1.5 m in 1,650 years is thought to be one of the longest-lived trees in Canada. Common Ravens nest on cliffs; American Redstart, Black-throated Green Warbler, and the harmless Eastern Garter Snake are abundant.

Birding Tobermory

Bald Eagle, Osprey, and other raptors can be seen from Cape Hurd to Dunks Point from mid April to May. Open fields around Tobermory are good for observing fall hawk migration. Numerous bird feeders attract many wintering birds, including species that normally migrate south.

Bruce Peninsula National Park

Established in 1987, the park occupies lands on both sides of Highway 6 near the northern end of the Bruce Peninsula. Along the park's Georgian Bay boundary the Niagara Escarpment creates spectacular coastal scenery: vertical cliffs, sea caves, overhanging rock ledges, raised pebble beaches, boulder barrier bars, and talus slopes. The shoreline is paralleled by the Bruce Trail and can be accessed by trails from Little Cove Road, Cyprus Lake campground, and Emmett Lake Road.

Features of the unusual underground drainage system characteristic of the Bruce are illustrated by several inland lakes near the Georgian Bay shoreline in the vicinity of Cyprus Lake. In the absence of surface outflow streams, water moves between lakes by seeping through terraced cobblestone beaches or through joints or cracks in the dolostone bedrock. A sinkhole in the bottom of Horse Lake enables water to flow by way of underground passages to re-emerge as springs on the shores of Marr Lake.

Much of the park's interior is covered by mixed and often dense forests of White Cedar, Balsam Fir, White Spruce, White Birch, and Trembling Aspen. There is an abundance of wetlands. The diversity of habitats supports numerous significant species. Highlights of the park's flora are the numerous species of orchids, ferns, and insectivorous plants. Ferns such as Wallrue, Purple-stemmed Cliffbrake, and Maidenhair Spleenwort grow along the cliffs. Woodlands, including the campground, support Downy Rattlesnake-plantain and major colonies of

Alaska Orchids. The Eastern Massasauga is locally abundant in the vicinity of the park.

The park is open in winter for camping, snowshoeing, and cross-country skiing.

DIRECTIONS. Located 10 km S of Tobermory on Hwy 6; see prov hwy map.

INFORMATION. Canadian Parks Service, Box 189, Tobermory, Ont, N0H 2R0, 519-596-2233.

– Dorcas Bay. A recent significant addition to Bruce Peninsula National Park is the 134-ha Dorcas Bay Nature Reserve, previously owned by the Federation of Ontario Naturalists. The property preserves a fine section of Lake Huron shoreline and numerous rare species. The principal features of the site are a wet, sandy fen extending inland from Singing Sands Beach and a sand dune complex along the north shore of the bay. There are also open alvar clearings, extensive coniferous woodlands, a small White Cedar swamp, and a glacier-sculpted shoreline of dolostone pavement. The diversity of habitats contains a remarkable assemblage of plants, including an abundance of orchids and insectivorous fen plants. Among orchids are Green-leaved Rattlesnake-plantain, Northern Green Orchid, Small Purple Fringed Orchid, and Showy, Yellow, and Ram's-head Lady's-slippers. Dwarf Lake Iris forms mats of blue in May. The reserve has a relatively high density of Eastern Massasauga rattlesnakes.

DIRECTIONS. Enter via Singing Sands day-use area of Bruce Peninsula Nat'l Park; cross footbridge at N end of beach.

'Rubberweed' Nature Reserve

This as-yet-unnamed 67-ha property is a recent addition to the Federation of Ontario Naturalists' system of nature reserves. For now, it is informally called the Rubberweed Reserve, in honour of the large colony of Lakeside Daisy (also known as Rubberweed) that it protects. Lakeside Daisy, a plant endemic to the Great Lakes region, is known from approximately 20 stations in the world, most of them on Manitoulin Island or the Bruce Peninsula. In late May and June the yellow daisy-like flowers combine with Indian Paintbrush and Balsam Ragwort to blanket the bedrock in yellows and reds.

The reserve lies just south of Bruce Peninsula National Park and consists largely of open Jack Pine forest interspersed with areas of exposed dolostone bedrock. The dolostone pavement is a harsh environment, cold and windy in winter and dry in summer. The alvar community that has developed here is home to an unusual assemblage of mosses, algae, and herbaceous plants featuring many rare and unusual species.

Despite its beauty and botanical wealth, little is known about this unique bedrock environment. What is known is that mosses and algae coat the rock surfaces and play a vital role in the ecology of the site. Lying exposed on the dolostone pavement, all members of the plant community are vulnerable to damage, including Lakeside Daisy and other plants that are virtually indistinguishable once they have flowered.

At press time, no signs identify the site, and the planned trails and boardwalks have not yet been completed. *Until trails and signs are in place, the property is not open to visitors. When the site opens, all visitors, including guided groups, must stay on designated trails.* Please help preserve the 'Rubberweed' Reserve so we may learn its secrets.

DIRECTIONS. Entrance is on W side of Hwy 6, 0.4 km N of Dyer's Bay Rd.

Birding Dyer's Bay to Cabot Head

The shoreline road from Dyer's Bay to Cabot Head lighthouse is bordered by the Niagara Escarpment's spectacular cliffs. In spring, offshore waters host hundreds of water birds, including concentrations of Red-necked and Horned Grebes in April and May. A raptor migration corridor also passes over this area in spring. The northeastern corner of Cabot Head acts as a migration concentration area where rare species are regularly observed.

DIRECTIONS. Choose locations with extensive open sky: 1) small wetland 1 km S of lighthouse; 2) open field 3 km W of Dyer's Bay.

Gillies Lake Outflow

Gillies Lake is a deep lake perched on the top of the escarpment north of Dyer's Bay. The lake drains eastward through an underground system to Georgian Bay. Check the small stream that flows under the road through a culvert. Walk the trail up the cliff on the south side of the stream; note the spot where it emerges from the talus slope and, at the top, locate where it disappears into the bedrock.

DIRECTIONS. From Dyer's Bay go 5 km N along shore road towards Cabot Head lighthouse.

Devil's Monument (Devil's Pulpit)

Located on the mainland between Cape Chin and Dyer's Bay, this flowerpot is actually an ancient sea stack from glacial Lake Nipissing. A small display area on site explains how the rocky pillar was formed by wave action when lake levels were higher. A stairway gives access to Georgian Bay. At the top of the cliff northwest of the stairs one can hear water running in a small cave. At several locations, an underground stream emerges and disappears in the cliff face and talus slope. This is one of many underground or karst stream systems that flow from west to east on the Bruce. Surface water systems flow from east to west.

DIRECTIONS. From T-jct 0.5 km W of Dyer's Bay village, follow Bruce Trail 3 km S.

Birding Stokes Bay Area

The shallow bays and islands around Stokes Bay provide resting and feeding areas for water birds. On days with westerly winds, large rafts of birds gather behind the islands.

Fishing Islands and Adjacent Shoals and Shallows

This chain of islands and exposed shoals off the Lake Huron shore stretches from Sauble Beach to Stokes Bay. Located in a prime spawning area for Lake Whitefish and other fish, the islands support numerous nesting water birds, including colonial species. Three gull, one tern, and two heron species are represented. Many waterfowl nest here and also use the area for migratory stopovers. To avoid trespassing and disturbance of breeding colonies during the nesting season, view from water only.

Black Creek Provincial Park

The headland between Stokes Bay and Myles Bay is an undeveloped provincial park. Old roads and trails lead from the sand beach, low, vegetated dunes, and rocky Lake Huron shoreline into the wooded interior. A swamp and a Beaver pond form part of a wetland complex. The park is a prime area for nesting Olive-sided Flycatcher and warblers, including Northern Parula and Canada, Black-throated Green, and Magnolia Warblers.
DIRECTIONS. From Hwy 6 at Ferndale, go 4 km W; turn N on Stokes Bay Rd & go 1.5 km. Turn W & go 1 km to lake at Myles Bay; turn N & follow road to parking lot. Walk N on beach & watch for trails through dunes before reaching creek.

Ferndale Flats

Several nesting colonies of Brewer's Blackbirds can be seen in the open pasturelands around Ferndale. Western Meadowlarks also nest here on the flat bottom of a former glacial lake. Watch for Snowy Owls and Rough-legged Hawks in winter.

Smokey Head–White Bluff Provincial Nature Reserve

A spectacular stretch of shoreline cliffs borders Georgian Bay here. The 90-m-high vertical rock faces have a rich hardwood forest on the top and a talus debris slope at the base.
DIRECTIONS. From Lion's Head village go 5 km N on Co Rd 9 until it veers left; park & walk 5–12 km N along Bruce Trail.

Lions Head Provincial Nature Reserve

A portion of rocky headland south of the village of Lion's Head is protected in the reserve. Glacial features on the site include outwash deposits and eroded potholes. Vegetation is second-growth maple-dominated woodland. There are wonderful views of the Georgian Bay shoreline.
DIRECTIONS. Take Bruce Trail 2–12 km S from Lion's Head village.

Hope Bay Forest Provincial Nature Reserve

This natural area on the shores of Georgian Bay encompasses

extensive lands on the north side of Hope Bay, including Georgian Bay shoreline, the brow of the Niagara Escarpment, and a significant area of upland forest. The site is notable for its showy spring flora. Glacial potholes occur within the mature forest dominated by Sugar Maple. On rocky outcrops, among the many ferns are uncommon species such as Northern Maidenhair Fern. More rare ferns are found west of the reserve in Cathedral Woods, also known for its wild jumble of fissures and fractured rock, formed by the collapse of ancient underground caverns. The 90-m-high cliffs that border the north shore of Hope Bay open into wave-cut and solution caves, sculpted when lake levels were much higher.

DIRECTIONS. Take Co Rd 9 to Hope Bay; go 1–5 km N on Bruce Trail.

St Jean Point Nature Preserve and Sucker Creek

The tiny St Jean Point Nature Preserve contains a good representation of the Great Lakes coastal meadow marsh and rocky shoreline plant communities found on the Bruce Peninsula. Thin soils over dolostone pavement support a woodland dominated by White Cedar. Pale-spiked Lobelia and various sedges and other grass-like plants grow along the shore.

East of where the road crosses Sucker Creek, a significant wetland contains a shallow pond surrounded by cattails, Sweet Gale, Swamp Rose, and other shrubs. A number of outstanding natural features, including rare species, lie inland from the marsh. Alvar and fen communities occur on calcareous sites, while an area of rich, mixed Sugar Maple forest is underlain by sandy, acidic soil. Among breeding birds of note are Barred Owl, Red-shouldered Hawk, and Solitary Vireo. Orchids and other species that characterize the flora of the Bruce, such as Tuberous Indian-plantain and Low Nut-rush, grow in the area. Because much of the 1,000-ha natural area upstream from the bridge is privately owned and not readily accessible, viewing should be done from the road.

DIRECTIONS. From Howdenvale take shore road 2.4 km N to St Jean Point Nature Preserve parking area. Sucker Creek crosses road just N of preserve.

INFORMATION. Grey Sauble Conservation Authority; MNR.

Petrel Point Nature Reserve

This Federation of Ontario Naturalists' reserve, one of the best and most intact fen communities in the lower Bruce, harbours an abundance of significant plant species. The 21-ha tract is a rich mosaic of open shoreline fen interspersed with swampy fingers of Black Spruce, White Cedar, Tamarack, shrubs, and hardwoods. Calcareous groundwater results in an alkaline environment and an accumulation of marl precipitate, a white muck visible below shallow pools of standing water. The plant display along the boardwalks includes Seaside Arrow-grass, Prairie Loosestrife, Smaller Fringed Gentian, Sticky Tofieldia, Ohio Goldenrod, and Grass-of-Parnassus. Among the many orchid species are Showy Lady's-slipper, Rose Pogonia, Grass-pink, and Small Purple Fringed Orchid.

DIRECTIONS. Drive 1.5 km S from Howdenvale; turn W on Petrel Pt Rd; watch for signs on both sides.

Red Bay Conservation Area

This property protects a small section of Lake Huron shoreline, including parallel sand dune ridges, upland hardwoods, and a densely wooded raised *Sphagnum* bog. Numerous orchids grow here.

DIRECTIONS. Go S from Howdenvale; turn right to Reid Pt on S shore of Red Bay; take 1st road right.

INFORMATION. Grey Sauble Conservation Authority.

Oliphant Fens

Wet, open calcareous fens with sections of exposed marl flats flank the shoreline along Lake Huron north and south of Oliphant. Orchids and other rare plants for which the Bruce Peninsula is known are prominent here. Among the highlights are Grass-pink, Rose Pogonia, Showy Lady's-slipper, and Tuberous Indian-plantain. At one area purchased by local naturalists, a boardwalk with interpretive signs permits access to the fen while preventing trampling of the vegetation.

DIRECTIONS. For site with boardwalk: from dock at Oliphant, go 1.5 km N on shore road.

Birding Oliphant Shoreline

The extensive shoreline here attracts migrating shorebirds and waterfowl. Migrants move along the west side of the Bruce Peninsula in May and from mid August to September. The bordering woodlands harbour a wide variety of nesting songbirds.

Sky, Isaac, and Boat Lake Complex
(Rankin Resources Management Area)

A low, fossil-rich escarpment inland from Lake Huron diverts drainage southward. Immediately to the east shallow lakes, marshes, reed swamps, wet thickets, and an interconnecting river form this complex, which is rich with aquatic life of all types. Extensive breeding populations of wetland birds include Black Tern, Least and American Bitterns, Marsh Wren, Osprey, Sora, Virginia Rail, loons, and waterfowl. There is a colony of Sedge Wrens in the wet meadows east of Isaac Lake fire station (Sideroad 25). The wetland serves as a major staging area for waterfowl during migration. Listen for Coyotes at night in February and March. Rainbow and Brown Trout, Northern Pike, Yellow Perch, and Bowfin are found within the complex. A fine drumlin field is located east of Sky Lake.

DIRECTIONS. Canoe access & observation points are 7.5 km W of Wiarton on Co Rd 21 & 5 km W of Hwy 6 on Sky Lake Rd (go W at Mar). Canoe route from Sky Lake via Rankin River to Sauble Falls Prov Park is 18 km long.

INFORMATION. Canoe route map available from MNR; Bruce Peninsula Tourism, Box 269, Wiarton, Ont, N0H 2T0.

Walker's Woods Nature Preserve

Tucked amid the cottage development at Sauble Beach is a 14-ha plot of old-growth forest of White Cedar (up to 350 years old), Eastern Hemlock, and White Pine. The hummocky woodland floor also contains low dunes and boggy swales. The woods is noted for its orchids and northern species, including Pink Lady's-slipper and Round-leaved Sundew.

DIRECTIONS. 1) Go 1.0 km N of main traffic light at Sauble Beach on Co Rd 21; well-concealed path into woods on W side of road leads to trail map. 2) Go 1.2 km N of main traffic light on Co Rd

21; turn left onto 4th St N; watch for well-concealed paths into woods on left.

INFORMATION. Grey Sauble Conservation Authority.

SOUTHERN BRUCE COUNTY (south of Highway 21)

> The river Penetangore is exceedingly serpentine in its course and runs through a broad valley composed of rich flats, dry for the most part, and which lie at a depth of 50 to 60 feet below the natural surface of the adjoining table land. There are numerous springs of pure water issuing from the high banks over the valley ... The mouth [of the river] is very narrow and generally contains only one foot of water, and when strong westerly winds blow, the shifting of the sands causes it to fill up and the water seeks some other outlet into the lake. (Site of Kincardine, 1849, Allan Park Brough, provincial land surveyor)

HURON FRINGE

The Huron Fringe is a narrow strip of land paralleling the current shoreline of Lake Huron. It consists of wave-cut terraces of ancient glacial Lakes Algonquin and Nipissing, plus the associated shoreline features of boulder pavements, gravel bars, and sand dunes. Lake Algonquin's shoreline bluff is most noticeable between Port Elgin and the Bruce nuclear power development. The Huron Fringe complex can be traced south to Sarnia. The land between the Lake Algonquin shoreline and the current lake has been greatly modified by the actions of the former lakes. Disrupted drainage patterns in some sections have resulted in the creation of extensive series of wetlands. At the base of the shoreline terraces, groundwater emerges through an abundance of springs.

The wooded fringe of Lake Huron has much more diverse flora and fauna than locations to the east of the old Lake Algonquin shoreline terraces. Migrating birds travel along this coastal corridor, and nesting species are far more numerous than farther inland. Vegetation communities along the current lake are similar to those of the dunes and fens on the Bruce Peninsula, although the characteristic species gradually disappear as one travels southward.

Chantry Island and Area

Chantry Island Migratory Bird Sanctuary protects colonies of nesting birds: Great Blue Heron, Black-crowned Night-Heron, Great Egret, Double-crested Cormorant, Ring-billed and Herring Gulls, plus many species of waterfowl. The island is located offshore from Southampton, but access is restricted. Birds travelling to and from the sanctuary can be observed readily from the mainland shore. Check the mouth of the Saugeen River in Southampton for rafts of ducks and gulls, and the mudflats in Miramichi Bay (3 km south along the shore road) for shorebirds and other water birds.

INFORMATION. Canadian Wildlife Service.

MacGregor Point Provincial Park

Low sand dunes and beach ridges edge this large 1,200-ha woodland park. Various components of ancient lakes are evident, the shoreline bluff of glacial Lake Nipissing being especially prominent. Drainage patterns have created an extensive and highly significant complex of wetlands ranging from Lake Huron shoreline fens and cattail marshes to *Sphagnum* bogs, open ponds, and Silver Maple swamps. There is a good representation of rare species. Fen and dune communities are major features, and Dwarf Lake Iris grows abundantly along the lakeshore. A good diversity of breeding birds is supplemented by migrants in season. Watch for Caspian Tern, Black-crowned Night-Heron, Cooper's and Red-shouldered Hawks, and Great Egret; Bald Eagle and Northern Shrike in winter; and nesting Blue-gray Gnatcatcher. The moist forests and wetlands support species such as Banded Killifish, Yellow-spotted and Four-toed Salamanders, Northern Ringneck Snake, and Wood Frog (listen for duck-like calls for two weeks in mid April). There are numerous trails, and cross-country skiing is available in winter.

DIRECTIONS. Located 3 km S of Port Elgin off Hwy 21; see prov hwy map.

INFORMATION. MacGregor Point Provincial Park, RR 1, Port Elgin, Ont, N0H 2C5, 519-389-9056.

Baie Du Doré

This small bay draws migrating water birds. In winter, outflows of warm water attract large numbers of Glaucous and Great Black-backed Gulls, as well as one of the largest wintering concentrations of Bald Eagles (up to 16 at once) in the province. Local naturalists have built a viewing tower on the north shore of the bay. The Baie Du Doré wetland provides habitat for a number of uncommon species, such as Horned Grebe, Great Egret, Canvasback, Redhead, Caspian Tern, Beaked Spike-rush, and Stiff Yellow Flax.

DIRECTIONS. On Hwy 21, drive 18 km S from Port Elgin; turn right at jct of Co Rd 20. Bay is on N side of nuclear power station.

Inverhuron Provincial Park

Extensive sand dunes and gravel ridges are evidence of the actions of former glacial lakes. Numerous uncommon species of plants have been recorded in the 290-ha park, including some species of Lake Huron shoreline flora that are unusual this far south. The diversity of breeding birds is good, and Inverhuron Bay serves as a migration concentration area for water birds. Mammals are present in the area in high densities, making the park a good location for observing tracks of many species in winter.

DIRECTIONS. Located NW of Tiverton off Co Rd 15; see prov hwy map.

INFORMATION. Inverhuron Provincial Park, RR 1, Port Elgin, Ont, N0H 2C0, 519-389-9056.

Kincardine Shoreline

During spring migration check the shoreline south of town for grebes and patches of loons, including Red-throated Loons.

Lurgan Beach

This site is one of the most significant natural areas in the southern part of the county. A remnant Red Oak savanna occurs here, and three species of rare grasses are associated with the dune system.

DIRECTIONS. From Hwy 21, go W on 2nd sdrd N of Amberley, or W on 2nd sdrd S of Pine River, to sign on N side near lake.

Point Clark

Point Clark is the southern headland for the large, sweeping bay that starts in the north at Cape Hurd, west of Tobermory. In fall it is a viewing location for waterfowl and rare gulls moving southward through the Lake Huron corridor. During migration, birds that would normally be offshore can be seen here, such as jaegers, Red-throated Loon, phalaropes, and Brant. To the north of the point, the vegetation on the dune system varies from mature Sugar Maple–White Birch communities to oaks (on the open dunes).

DIRECTIONS. Go W from jct of Hwys 21 & 86 at S end of county. Follow signs to lighthouse.

Farmlands East of Glacial Lake Algonquin Bluff

Open farmlands, especially the pasturelands that border Highway 21 between Port Elgin and Amberley, host concentrations of hawks and owls in winter, including Rough-legged Hawk, Snowy Owl, Short-eared Owl, and other raptors. Watch for Northern Shrikes and flocks of Snow Buntings.

INLAND FROM LAKE HURON

Inland from the ravine-notched bluffs of the ancient glacial lakes, the land slopes gently upward across a broad plain of clay and scattered sand pockets. Beyond the plain, drumlins and morainic ridges add relief to the agricultural landscape.

Lower Saugeen River

The Saugeen River and its tributaries run diagonally across southern Bruce County. In contrast to the open farmlands above its bluffs, the river runs through a deep, wooded corridor. Steep, eroded sand bluffs lining the Saugeen have become nesting sites for Bank and Northern Rough-winged Swallows and Belted Kingfishers. Woodlands along the river are flooded each spring and harbour a rich growth of herbaceous plants, dominated by American Ostrich Fern. Within these bottomlands significant plant species include Wild Garlic, Michigan Lily, Hog Peanut, Great St John's-wort, Tuberous Indian-plantain, Common Hackberry, and Sycamore. The Saugeen River offers excellent canoeing during high-water periods. Avoid trespassing, and respect private property bordering the river.

DIRECTIONS. Access river from twp & co rd bridges & public parks between Walkerton & Southampton.

Glammis Bog

This wetland community north of Greenock Swamp contains a kettle lake in which a bog has developed. Plants include Pink Lady's-slipper, Mountain Holly, Bog Rosemary, and Pale Laurel. The open swamp south of the bog is a good place for observing water birds, among them Pied-billed Grebe, bitterns, and herons. Bordering the bog, stands of Sugar Maple clothe the knobby hills, while White Cedar–Red Maple swamps occupy the depressions.

DIRECTIONS. From Glammis go N on Co Rd 1; turn W at 1st conc rd & go 1.2 km; bog lies to N.

INFORMATION. Saugeen Valley Conservation Authority.

Greenock Swamp

At 8,000 ha, Greenock Swamp is one of the largest wooded wetlands in southwestern Ontario. The swamp's communities include pure stands of White Pine, relatively pure stands of oak, fen with Labrador Tea and Pitcher-plant, Eastern Hemlock forest, Red Maple–Blue-beech forest, and elm swamp. Greenock's large size allows for considerable diversity of plants and animals. Some of its plant specialties are Michigan Lily, Round-leaved Orchid, and Great Lobelia. The diversity of breeding birds approaches that of the Huron Fringe, and includes Barred Owl, Red-shouldered Hawk, Pied-billed Grebe, Pileated Woodpecker, and Cerulean Warbler. Bullfrogs occur.

DIRECTIONS. 1) From Hwy 9 go N on gravel road E of Kinloss & W of Riverdale. 2) From Chepstow go W on Conc Rd 6 to transect swamp. 3) For Schmidt & Bester Lakes: from Chepstow go 1 conc rd N, turn W at radio tower & go to sign for lake. 4) Teeswater River through SE section of swamp is navigable by canoe.

INFORMATION. Saugeen Valley Conservation Authority.

Kinloss Township Area

A rolling terrain formed by kame moraines encompasses the headwaters of the Nine Mile (Lucknow) River system. The area is extensively wooded and contains numerous significant natural sites. Although largely privately owned, many of these border municipal roads, from which they can be viewed. The Nine Mile River uplands include a large and diverse Eastern Hemlock–mixed forest community. Purvis Lake is an example of a glacial kettle lake associated with kame moraines.

DIRECTIONS. Area is W of Teeswater & E of Lucknow. For Purvis Lake: on Hwy 86 go SE from Lucknow & take 2nd conc rd NE; go 0.5 km to lake on left. For Nine Mile (Lucknow) River uplands: continue past Purvis Lake on same road.

GREY COUNTY

> Our tall, tall forest trees are now all alive, and the ocean of mingled blossoms and leaves waves and curls and rises in rounded swells farther and farther away, like the thick smoke from a factory chimney. Freshness and beauty are everywhere; flowers are born every hour; living sunlight is poured over all and every thing and creature is glad. (Trout's Mills near Meaford, May 23, 1865, John Muir [1838–1914], American naturalist and conservationist)

Grey County is bordered on the north by the fiords and beaches of Georgian Bay. The southern boundary runs east from Bruce County through the marshlands and fields of the Dundalk plateau to Dufferin County. Southeastern Grey County contains the headwaters of major river systems that flow into Georgian Bay, Lake Huron, and Lake Erie.

The combined influences of the Georgian Bay shoreline and the winding Niagara Escarpment have created breathtaking scenery and outstanding pastoral beauty. The escarpment extends west from the Blue Mountains, then curves northward at Owen Sound to form the backbone of the Bruce Peninsula. The forested crest of the escarpment is intersected by four re-entrant valleys: Beaver, Bighead, Sydenham (Owen Sound), and Colpoy's Bay. The last, submerged in Georgian Bay, forms the northern boundary of the western portion of the county. These valleys were formed when preglacial rivers eroded gouges into the soluble limestone cliff slopes. The Wisconsin ice sheet subsequently broadened and deepened these notches, and they were flooded by glacial Lake Algonquin. This lake retreated 10,000 years ago and remains as Georgian Bay.

Rugged topography prevented the complete conversion of the original forests to agriculture. Today, farmlands are interspersed with corridors of cliffs, wooded talus slopes, moraines, and pockets of wetlands where the original fauna and Great Lakes–St Lawrence flora survive. Many groundwater sources characteristic of limestone topography help to maintain cool, clear streams.

A remarkable profusion of orchids and ferns flourishes here. With over 40 species of ferns, some of them rare, the county is considered the fern capital of Ontario and possibly North America. Both Walking Fern and Hart's-tongue Fern are found along the escarpment.

Over 170 species of birds breed in Grey County. Yellow-bellied Flycatcher, Dark-eyed Junco, Swainson's Thrush, and Common Raven reach the southern periphery of their breeding ranges in the county, while Blue-gray Gnatcatcher nesting in the swamps of southern Grey is near its northern limit.

Mammals, reptiles, amphibians, and fish are generally typical of those found in southern Ontario. The Virginia Opossum has recently spread northward into the county. Black Bear, Southern Red-backed Vole, and Mink Frog approach the southern periphery of their ranges here. The Eastern Massasauga has been virtually extirpated from the county. Among fish, Blackside and Least Darters reach their eastern limits, while Finescale Dace is at the western edge of its range.

Butterflies of interest include Silvery Blue, near its southern limit here, and Mulberry Wing, a resident of marshes and wet areas that feeds on Tussock Sedge.

Niagara Escarpment–Bruce Trail

The Niagara Escarpment wanders across the northern portion of Grey County, creating deep, lush valleys and stunning scenery. The Bruce Trail (look for white blazes) and a number of provincial nature reserves and publicly held conservation and management areas provide access within Grey County. See entry under Regional Municipality of Niagara.

INFORMATION. Bruce Trail Association; Niagara Escarpment Commission.

Keppel Township Escarpment Sites

– **Bruce's Caves Conservation Area.** Here a 97-ha stand of mature hardwood forest harbours unique cave formations along the Niagara Escarpment. The large, open limestone caves were formed in the cliff face by wave action of glacial Lake Algonquin, and are an excellent example of dissolution cave formation and differential weathering. The talus slopes beneath the caves provide a cool, moist home for mosses and ferns such as Slender Cliffbrake, Rock Polypody, and Northern Holly Fern. Trails can be used year-round.

DIRECTIONS. Located just E of Oxenden. From Wiarton go 5.6 km NE on Co Rd 26 (Frank St).

INFORMATION. Grey Sauble Conservation Authority.

– **Skinner's Bluff.** The hike along the bluff leads to a magnificent overhanging projection with a view that on a clear day includes Christian Island and the Awenda Park highlands 80 km to the east across Georgian Bay. The view over the Slough of Despond is spectacular. Overlooking Colpoy's Bay, this high promontory of escarpment outcrop also offers a panoramic view of the Algonquin plain below as well as Griffith, White Cloud, and Hay islands. Large, isolated boulders known as erratics are found along this section of the escarpment. Extensive deciduous forests cover the bedrock uplands, while talus slopes lie below the cliffs. The general area supports numerous plant species of interest, including 8 species of orchids and 17 of ferns.

DIRECTIONS. From Wiarton go 5 km NE on Co Rd 26 (Frank St); turn S at Oxenden; take 1st road E to Lake Charles; at T-jct at Lake Charles turn N & go 2.0 km; at jct past Skinner's Bluff Farm go 2.5 km E to edge of escarpment. Park & hike 2.4 km N along Bruce Trail. Watch for viewing points.

– **Slough of Despond Management Area.** This romantically named wetland is a remnant of glacial Lake Algonquin, created when a baymouth bar prevented the slough from draining into nearby Georgian Bay. Bounded on three sides by escarpment, the site contains two main habitats: a wetland swamp forest dominated by mature Silver Maple, and an upland portion supporting a younger deciduous woodland. Spicebush and Water-willow, both typically southern plants, grow here, and Cerulean Warblers nest.

DIRECTIONS. Take Co Rd 26 (Frank St) NE from Wiarton for 14 km to Big Bay (North Keppel); turn right (S), then right again at 1st road; go to T-jct at end of road. Slough is straight ahead.

INFORMATION. Grey Sauble Conservation Authority.

– Kemble Mountain Management Area. This 140-ha tract of deciduous forest grows on a dry limestone plain above an extensive stretch of escarpment cliffs. The high promontory separates Colpoy's Bay and Owen Sound, two major re-entrant valleys carved by the glaciers. A variety of wetland habitats is found at the base of the slopes. Among the 28 species of ferns are Male Fern and Northern Holly Fern. The abundance of orchids includes Round-leaved Orchid. Near the crest of the mountain a roadside lookout provides a fine view of the escarpment, farm fields, and Owen Sound Bay. From April to October, Turkey Vultures and Red-tailed Hawks soar on the thermals below.

DIRECTIONS. From Co Rd 1 in Kemble, go 2.6 km N on twp rd up escarpment; park on W side at old road allowance; follow trails E & W into woods.

Malcolm Kirk Nature Reserve (The Long Swamp)

This 43-ha Federation of Ontario Naturalists' nature reserve protects an open fen, a *Sphagnum*–Black Spruce bog, and a White Cedar swamp forest. Pink Lady's-slipper and Ragged Fringed Orchid grow in the coniferous swamp. In the fen, cotton-grass, Pitcher-plant, and Seaside Arrow-grass can be seen, as well as typical bog plants, such as Sheep Laurel, Pale Laurel, Leatherleaf, and Small Cranberry.

DIRECTIONS. Located 5 km W of Owen Sound, site is accessible only with a guide.

INFORMATION. Federation of Ontario Naturalists; Owen Sound Field Naturalists, Box 401, Owen Sound, Ont, N4K 5P7.

Owen Sound and Area

INFORMATION (all sites). Grey Sauble Conservation Authority.

– Pottawatomi Conservation Area. This forested section of the Niagara Escarpment is noted for its spring wildflowers and fine autumn colours. The Pottawatomi River, which harbours spawning Rainbow Trout and Chinook Salmon and feeding Brook Trout, plunges over the escarpment at Jones Falls.
DIRECTIONS. From Owen Sound, go 3 km W on Hwy 6/21; turn N on Hwy 70; walk from parking lot of Tourist Information Bureau.

– Black's Park Conservation Area. This tiny park in the heart of Owen Sound harbours 28 species of ferns, including Green and Maidenhair Spleenworts, Christmas Fern, Goldie's Wood Fern, Male Fern, and Slender Cliffbrake. Above the escarpment there is a woodlot and a fine view. Springs emerging from the cliff face feed a damp area and a creek below.
DIRECTIONS. Take Hwy 6/21 (10th St) W through town to 6th Ave W; go S to end of street. Park & follow trail leading above escarpment.

– Inglis Falls Conservation Area. The Bruce Trail winds through the area's mature mixed woodlands bordering the Niagara Escarpment. Warblers, Scarlet Tanager, Indigo Bunting, and other forest birds are regularly seen. There is a spectacular waterfalls and a wide variety of spring flowers, including Showy Orchis. Among the 20 species of ferns are Green Spleenwort, Goldie's Wood Fern, Male Fern, Slender Cliffbrake, and Northern Holly Fern. In fall, the forest is rich in mushroom species. Brook, Rainbow, and Brown Trout all occur here. Round potholes in the limestone are found about 250 m east of the falls. The 384-ha park is accessible year-round.
DIRECTIONS. Located 5 km S of downtown Owen Sound. Go S through town on 2nd Ave (Co Rd 5); watch for signs.

Bognor Marsh Forest Agreement Area

This headwater area of the Bighead River contains 620 ha of wetlands, uplands, and Niagara Escarpment. There is a boardwalk and a viewing tower for water birds and other aquatic wildlife, and a trail through swampy wetlands up through the hardwood forest at the crest of the escarpment. The area supports a wide variety of flowering plants, shrubs, and ferns. Nesting species include Pied-billed Grebe, Green and Great Blue Herons, Black-crowned Night-Heron, American and Least Bitterns, and Black Tern. Snow and Canada Geese pass through in autumn.

DIRECTIONS. From Owen Sound go S on Hwy 10 to Rockford; turn left onto Co Rd 18. Go 10 km to entrance at jct with Conc Rd 4.

INFORMATION. Grey Sauble Conservation Authority.

Lily Oak Forest

This large, diverse tract of upland and lowland habitats is the headwater area of Hamilton Creek, which feeds into the North Saugeen River. Significant species include Walking Fern, Fly Honeysuckle, Marsh Horsetail, Gracilescens Sedge (a rare southern species), Smith's Melic Grass, and Pickerel Frog.

DIRECTIONS. From Hwy 10 in Berkeley go 6 km E on Holland Twp Rd 60; turn left & access from road allowance.

INFORMATION. Grey Sauble Conservation Authority; Saugeen Valley Conservation Authority.

Bighead River

By Canoe. Canoeing is best in early spring. The lower few kilometres offer some good whitewater, but farther upstream the river is slow and easy. Mature woodlots come right down to the water, making the birdwatching good. Great Blue Heron, Belted Kingfisher, plus Common Merganser and other duck species frequent the river. (Access upper river from bridges on concession roads.)

By Road. The Bighead River cuts through an excellent drumlin field. (From Meaford, go 7 km south on County Road 7; turn west on road just north of Griersville. Along next 3 km, hilltops provide good views of drumlins and Bighead River valley.)

Boyne River Valley

A narrow township road follows the Boyne River (and then the Beaver River) downstream through rich woodlands steeply sloped towards the road. View and listen from the road, as adjacent land is privately owned.

DIRECTIONS. At Flesherton go 1.7 km E on Hwy 4 to 1st conc rd. Turn N; go 0.9 km & take road to right (Lower Valley Rd). This road (after 7 km becomes Co Rd 30) follows Boyne River (then Beaver River) 11 km to Kimberley.

INFORMATION. MNR.

– **Hogg's Falls.** Here the Boyne River cascades over the Niagara Escarpment in a symmetrical 4-m-high waterfall set in a steep-sided valley.

DIRECTIONS. From start of Lower Valley Rd go 0.8 km & look for parking area on W side. Follow path to falls.

– **Confluence of Boyne and Beaver Rivers.** The Boyne joins the Beaver in a forested recess of the escarpment, which is well worth exploring for birds and plants. During the summer months the flow of the Beaver may be reduced to a mere trickle.

DIRECTIONS. From start of Lower Valley Rd go 4.5 km & watch for double culvert crossing road.

– **Old Power Plant.** Surrounded by maturing pine plantations now blending into the natural forest, the wet meadows along the Beaver River here are a riot of flowers from August to October.

DIRECTIONS. Plant is on E side of road, 8 km from start of Lower Valley Rd.

Beaver River Valley

The largest glacial re-entrant valley on the Niagara Escarpment, this wooded valley is noted for its scenic views, fine fall colour display (best between September 20 and October 10), and diversity of plant life.

– **Eugenia Falls Conservation Area.** Here the water of the Beaver River takes a 30-m plunge over the Niagara Escarpment face to form one of the most prominent features of the area. The 23-ha site offers a wide variety of habitats for birds, wildlife, and cliff-loving ferns.

DIRECTIONS. From Flesherton go 3.5 km NE on Hwy 4; turn left on Co Rd 13 & go 3.5 km to Eugenia. Follow signs.

INFORMATION. Grey Sauble Conservation Authority.

– Old Baldy Conservation Area (Kimberley Rock). Above and
to the east of the village of Kimberley, this venerable landmark
with the majestic rock face stands 152 m above the Beaver valley. The rock ferns on the scarp, added to the woodland ferns in
the adjoining forest, total 23 species. At the summit, Old Baldy
offers a magnificent view, and one can watch soaring Turkey
Vultures and Red-tailed Hawks from above.

DIRECTIONS. From Kimberley, go NE on Co Rd 13 to 1st sdrd (6–
7) on E. Follow this steep, rough road 1.5 km to T-jct at top of
hill; turn right & go to parking area. Follow trail (15 min).

INFORMATION. Grey Sauble Conservation Authority.

– Beaver River (Kimberley to Heathcote) by Canoe. A leisurely
4-hr (20-km) paddle in a silently moving canoe offers opportunities to see scenic views, as well as Green Herons, Wood Ducks,
and, in the overhanging branches, passerines. Nettles thrive in
the annually flooded swampy Silver Maple woodlands. Go in
early May when the water is high and before deer fly season.

DIRECTIONS. Use public canoe launch site just N of Kimberley off
Co Rd 13.

Craigleith Provincial Park

Located at the base of Blue Mountain, Craigleith is an ideal
place for discovering relics from prehistoric life. Fossils embedded in outcrops of shale bedrock along the Georgian Bay shoreline originated 450 million years ago during the Ordovician
Period. In the warm, shallow, saltwater sea that covered this
area at that time, the most common sea creatures were trilobites.
Today their fossils are easily found in shales formed from muds
rich in the organic materials on which these creatures fed.

DIRECTIONS. Located on Hwy 26 just W of Craigleith; see prov
hwy map.

INFORMATION. MNR.

Georgian Bay Fish Runs

Chinook Salmon can be seen in the fall, and Rainbow Trout can
be seen about mid April and sometimes in the fall (late October)
in several rivers flowing into Georgian Bay. These include the

Bighead River near Meaford, the Beaver River in Thornbury, and the Pottawatomi River and the mill dam on the Sydenham River in Owen Sound.

Kolapore Uplands

The uplands, a tract of publicly owned rugged semi-wilderness on the eastern edge of the Beaver valley, sit on an outlier of the Niagara Escarpment. Significant caves, cliffs, gorges, and bedrock features occur. Criss-crossed by a complex network of hiking and cross-country ski trails, the area encompasses a large section of unbroken hardwoods, including a swamp forest where Common Raven, Black Spruce, Loesel's Twayblade, and ancient White Cedars are found.

DIRECTIONS. From Feversham go 8 km N on Co Rd 2; go 2 km W on Collingwood-Osprey Townline. Park at Blue Mountain springwater bottling plant; hike N.

INFORMATION. University of Toronto Outing Club, Box 6674, Sta A, Toronto, M4W 1X5 (trail map available).

Pretty River Valley Provincial Park

Situated along the Niagara Escarpment, this large, 800-ha park is outstanding for its extensive unbroken slope of Great Lakes–St Lawrence hardwoods. The landscape is dominated by moraine and meltwater channels. The park contains numerous hiking trails, most of the likely spring wildflowers for the area, almost all of Ontario's ferns, and a panoramic view of the Nottawasaga River valley.

DIRECTIONS. 1) Enter from Co Rd 31 near Simcoe Co Line. 2) Take Co Rd 2 S from Ravenna; turn E on Co Rd 19; at 2nd jct, go S to Gibraltar, then E to 1st sdrd; turn right to access park & trails.

INFORMATION. MNR.

Feversham Gorge

Resembling a miniature Elora Gorge, Feversham Gorge on the upper Beaver River is a rare geological feature in Ontario. Seepage down the marly slopes creates a lush garden of mosses and ferns. Ancient trees partially obscure the view of the river below, home to Brook Trout, an indicator of cool, clean, high-quality water. With its many species of rare ferns, mosses, and liverworts, and White Cedar, White Spruce, and Eastern Hemlock, the gorge is a botanist's paradise. The extensive fern list includes Northern Holly Fern, Male Fern, Green and Maidenhair Spleenworts, Bulblet Fern, Rock Polypody, Fragile Fern, Northeastern Lady Fern, Slender Cliffbrake, and Marginal, Spinulose, and Goldie's Wood Ferns. Among the mosses are *Fissidens grandifrons*, *Gymnostomum aeruginosum*, *Gymnostomum recurvirostrum*, and *Tortella tortuosa*. The liverworts sport equally exotic names, such as *Cololejeunea biddlecomiae*, *Conocephalum conicum*, *Lejeunea cavifolia*, and *Plagiochila asplenioides*. While revelling in the abundance of bryophytes, don't forget to listen for Winter Wren and Pileated Woodpecker.

DIRECTIONS. On Co Rd 2 at Feversham, park in Madeleine Graydon CA; follow marked trail to gorge.

INFORMATION. Grey Sauble Conservation Authority.

Moss Lake Conservation Area

The kame and kettle complex at Moss Lake consists of a small kettle lake surrounded by lowland and upland forest. Vegetation communities include an open-water lake; a floating mat of Leatherleaf, *Sphagnum* mosses, and Labrador Tea; a treed bog of Black Spruce and Tamarack; and a variety of upland associations. The diversity of habitats supports a rich assortment of colourful wildflowers, such as Pitcher-plant, One-flowered and Pink Pyrolas, Round-leaved and Spatulate-leaved Sundews, Pale Laurel, and an abundance of orchids: Pink Lady's-slipper, Grass-pink, Spotted Coralroot, Large and Small Yellow Lady's-slippers, Loesel's Twayblade, and Small Purple Fringed Orchid.

DIRECTIONS. Watch for sign 1 km W of Priceville on Hwy 4. Walk 1 km S.

INFORMATION. Saugeen Valley Conservation Authority.

Upper Saugeen River

The Saugeen River is in relatively pristine condition, as evidenced by healthy populations of Brook Trout. While woodlands border much of the main river system, smaller streams often lack buffers. The river drops over 200 m between Priceville and Hanover, producing excellent whitewater sections. Canoeing is best in spring when water is high.

DIRECTIONS. Stop at numerous bridges & public parks along river.

Allan Park Conservation Area

This 160-ha tract of upland forest contains many plant species that are not normally found this far north; for example, Shagbark and Bitternut Hickories, Blue-beech, Smooth Sumac, and Smooth Rock-cress. A kame moraine is visible. Trails can be used throughout the year.

DIRECTIONS. Drive 8 km W from Durham on Hwy 4; turn S on conc rd & go 2 km.

INFORMATION. Saugeen Valley Conservation Authority.

HURON COUNTY

> We encamped close to a breeding-place of these birds [passenger pigeons], when we were kept awake all night by the noise they made. Sometimes, too, a limb of a tree would break with the weight of the birds which had alighted on it, when there would be [much loud] fluttering and flapping of wings ... Towards morning, the sound of their departure to their feeding-grounds resembled thunder. For nearly two hours there was one incessant roar, as flock after flock took its departure eastward. The ground under the trees was whitened with their excrement, and strewn with broken branches of trees. (Huron Tract, ca 1829/30, Samuel Strickland [1804–67], land agent and settler)

The landscape of Huron County has been said to be a compromise between the level lands around Lake Erie in the south and the hillier areas which surround Georgian Bay. A south to north pattern can also be seen in the soil, climate, and vegetation.

The southern part of Huron is exceptionally level country with a very rich, organic soil underlain by heavy clay. The flora here represents a transition from Carolinian to Great Lakes–St Lawrence Forest. Southern hardwoods such as Bitternut Hickory, Cottonwood, Sycamore, Blue-beech, Common Hackberry, Slippery Elm, and various oak species can be found. Agriculture dominates the area, natural habitat mainly being restricted to scattered woodlots, stream valleys, and a few wetlands.

The northern part of the county is characterized by a gently rolling to rolling terrain of glacially deposited materials that deeply cover the bedrock. Dominant landforms here include spillways, till plains, and kame moraines. Vegetation patterns include Sugar Maple–American Beech–Eastern Hemlock communities and, on wetter sites, Eastern Hemlock, Yellow Birch, White Pine, and White Cedar. With forest cover averaging about 18%, natural habitat tends to consist of larger woodlots and swamps, which, in some areas, are interconnected to form fairly large tracts.

There are virtually no lakes in Huron County. The land is drained by four major river systems: Nine Mile (Lucknow), Maitland, Bayfield, and Ausable.

When in Exeter watch for the unusual white-coloured form of the Gray Squirrel.

Point Farms Provincial Park

The park's prior use as farmland has resulted in a distinctive plant community. Flat, open fields broken by hedgerows and orchards predominate. Various stages of plant succession can be seen, from open, grassy fields to a dense covering of dogwood, hawthorn, Ninebark, and Choke Cherry interspersed with saplings of American Elm, Basswood, White Ash, and Sugar Maple. On the west side of the park, a steep bluff dominated by White Cedar, White Pine, White Ash, and birch overlooks the sandy beach. A small Sugar Maple–American Beech–White Birch forest and four wooded ravines provide an important refuge for wildlife. There is good viewing of spring and fall migrating birds, particularly waterfowl, loons, warblers, owls, and most hawk species. White-throated Sparrow, Northern Harrier, Rufous-sided Towhee, and Bobolink have been recorded nesting. Trails can be toured in winter.

DIRECTIONS. Located on Lake Huron, 6 km N of Goderich on Hwy 21; see prov hwy map.

INFORMATION. Point Farms Provincial Park, RR 3, Goderich, Ont, N7A 3X9, 519-524-7124; MNR.

Saratoga Swamp

The 500-ha Saratoga Swamp is the largest wetland remaining in the Maitland River watershed. This significant site contains lowland swamp forest, mixed and deciduous slope forests, creek lowlands, successional communities, thickets, and some upland forests. The rich diversity of habitats supports nearly 500 species of vascular plants. Some of the specialties are Silvery Glade Fern, Goldie's Wood Fern, Virginia Chain Fern, Smith's Melic Grass, Ragged Fringed and Small Purple Fringed Orchids, Pink Lady's-slipper, and Swamp Dewberry. There is a wide range of songbirds, raptors, and waterfowl, including about 100 species of breeding birds, such as Cooper's Hawk, American Coot, Red-headed and Pileated Woodpeckers, Brown Creeper, and Canada and Blue-winged Warblers. Among the mammals are Coyote, Porcupine, Beaver, and Snowshoe Hare. A White-tailed Deer wintering yard is located within the tract. Redbelly and Eastern Milk Snakes, Bullfrog, and Gray Treefrog are all resident. There are several informal nature trails.

DIRECTIONS. Located 10 km NE of Goderich in S end of West Wawanosh Twp. Swamp extends N from W Wawanosh–Colborne Townline between Auburn & Nile to W Wawanosh Conc Rd 4–5. Park along road.

INFORMATION. Maitland Valley Conservation Authority.

Wawanosh Valley Conservation Area

The Maitland River and Belgrave Creek flow through this 167-ha tract of upland hardwoods, conifer plantations, and lowland Eastern Hemlock forests. Springs provide habitat for ferns and marsh grasses, and constant water flow draws wildlife year-round. The Maitland River, which cuts a 30-m-deep valley in the forests, is a good place for seeing waterfowl, as well as the migration of Rainbow Trout and Chinook and Coho Salmon in spring and fall. Typical species include Ruffed Grouse, song-birds, herons, Snowshoe Hare, White-tailed Deer, and various amphibians and reptiles.

DIRECTIONS. Enter at: 1) Wawanosh Nature Centre on Nature Centre Rd off Hwy 4, 2 km S of Belgrave; or 2) Wawanosh Park off Co Rd 22 on Conc Rd 6–7.

INFORMATION. Maitland Valley Conservation Authority.

George G. Newton Nature Reserve

This 40-ha Federation of Ontario Naturalists' reserve (managed by the Huron Fringe Field Naturalists) shows how farmland can be returned to native vegetation. The rolling uplands of former farm fields have been largely replanted in White Pine. A ravine valley bordering a small stream supports a natural stand of White Cedar and a mature forest of Sugar Maple, American Beech, Eastern Hemlock, Bitternut Hickory, White and Red Ashes, and Butternut. Ephemeral spring wildflowers such as Red and White Trilliums and Sharp-lobed Hepatica thrive here. The forests and old fields are home to American Goldfinch, Field Sparrow, Cedar Waxwing, Red-eyed Vireo, Rufous-sided Towhee, Ruffed Grouse, Northern Cardinal, and Eastern Wood-Pewee.

DIRECTIONS. Located SE of Goderich between Hwys 8 & 21. Take Co Rd 18 from Holmesville W to Porter's Hill. Turn N on Conc Rd 6; at next jct turn E & park by road; enter on S, 60 m E of jct.

Naftel's Creek Conservation Area

Hardwood forest and wetland habitats make this a good place for seeing songbirds, including many warblers, on spring migration. Showy Orchis, Sweet White Violet, Michigan Lily, Mayapple, and Indian-pipe are among plants of interest.

DIRECTIONS. Go 7 km S of Goderich on Hwy 21 to parking lot on left.

INFORMATION. Maitland Valley Conservation Authority.

Hullett Provincial Wildlife Area

This is a major wetland complex containing 2,200 ha of marshes, pools, swamps, river valley, forests, and fields. Its location along the South Maitland River on the path of two major migratory flyways makes it an excellent staging and breeding ground for waterfowl. Several rare birds breed here and, when water levels are low, shorebirds stop during migration. Watch for Least Bittern, Great Egret, Sandhill Crane, Bald Eagle, Black Tern, Grasshopper Sparrow, Black-crowned Night-Heron, Redhead, American Coot, Ruddy Duck, Great Blue Heron, and spring displays of Common Snipe and American Woodcock. The fauna also includes Eastern Fox Snake, Mink, Muskrat, and Red Fox. Some of the more interesting plants are Green Dragon, Biennial Gaura, Cardinal-flower, and Small Purple Fringed Orchid. Viewing stands and nature trails are provided. Canoe access is permitted before May 15 and after August 15.

DIRECTIONS. Main office is just NE of Clinton (off Hwy 4 or 8) on Hullett Conc Rd 2–3, E of Sdrd 20.

INFORMATION. Call 519-482-7011, or MNR.

Bannockburn Wildlife Management Area

Located on the Bannockburn River northeast of Varna, this wild-life management area supports a diversity of wildlife in its six natural communities: wet meadow, White Cedar, river, decidu-ous forest, old field and mixed scrub, and marsh. Spring flowers and ferns grow in the Sugar Maple–American Beech forest, and Turtlehead blooms in the wet meadow. Follow the trails to look for resident species, including herpetofauna, White-tailed Deer, Beaver, Ruffed Grouse, and an abundance of songbirds. Ameri-can Woodcock display in the spring, and Belted Kingfishers and herons frequent the river and Walden Creek. Listen for the songs of Indigo Buntings and wrens, and watch for Eastern Bluebirds nesting in the area. There is a superb display of fall colour.

DIRECTIONS. From Brucefield go 4 km W on Co Rd 3 to Stanley Conc Rd 4–5; turn right & go 1.5 km. Look for sign & parking lot on left.

INFORMATION. Ausable-Bayfield Conservation Authority.

Hay Swamp

The 2,150-ha Hay Swamp is an important wetland complex con-sisting of forested swamp, scrub, plantations, and farmland. The area harbours a number of rare species and is a good spot for observing migration and seeing wetland birds. Least Bittern and Red-headed Woodpecker nest here, and Tundra Swans pass through during migration. Purple Meadow-rue, Sycamore, and Small Purple Fringed Orchid are among plants of note. Trails follow logging roads and concession roads. The area is hunted in season.

DIRECTIONS. Trails can be accessed at several points along Conc Rd 4–5 & Conc Rd 6–7, N of Hwy 83 between Dashwood &

Exeter. To ensure access to public land only, obtain brochure from ABCA.

INFORMATION. Ausable-Bayfield Conservation Authority.

Morrison Dam Conservation Area

This 35-ha site features trails, a large reservoir, a stream, upland and lowland hardwood forest, and several small plantations. This is a good area for seeing Great Horned Owl, hawks, a variety of songbirds, and migrating waterfowl in spring and fall. Wood Duck, American Bittern, Great Blue Heron, and Common Snapping Turtle share the reservoir with canoeists.

DIRECTIONS. From Hwy 4 at Exeter, go 2 km E on Hwy 83 (Thames Rd); turn right on Usborne Twp Rd 2–3 & drive 1 km.

INFORMATION. Ausable-Bayfield Conservation Authority.

PERTH COUNTY

I was out in a piece of swampy woods south of the town, when my attention was arrested by the actions of a small bird which was constructing a nest among some leafy twigs growing on the small horizontal branch of a little water-elm, about three feet out from the trunk and ten feet off the ground. Some days after I viewed this nest again ... When this bird flew off her nest and took a position on a branch near by, uttering a few chip-like notes, I identified her as a female bay-breasted warbler. (Listowel, June 1879, William L. Kells, oologist)

The flat to gently rolling land of Perth County is almost entirely devoted to agriculture. Small patches of woods and wetlands are interspersed among farm fields and along creeks and rivers feeding the main river systems: the North Thames flowing southward and the Maitland draining west to Lake Huron. The area is part of the Great Lakes–St Lawrence Forest Region. Lying in the lee of Lake Huron, the region receives heavy winter snowfall.

Ellice Swamp (Ellice Huckleberry Marsh)

Covering approximately 856 ha, Ellice Swamp represents the

largest woodlot in Perth County. The area serves as an important natural water storage and recharge area in the Thames
River watershed. The centre of the swamp is covered with
Sphagnum mosses and Leatherleaf underlain with peat. Altered
drainage patterns have enabled woody vegetation such as
Swamp Birch and Black Ash to rapidly invade the now drier
soils at the expense of wet bog species. The variety of swamp
communities present here offers exceptional species richness
and diversity, including a number of rarities. Among the abundance of birds are Golden-winged Warbler, Blue-gray Gnatcatcher, and Red-headed Woodpecker. The swamp hosts many
plant species of interest, such as Northern Slender Ladies'-
tresses, Yellow Lady's-slipper, and Mountain Fly Honeysuckle.
DIRECTIONS. From Stratford go NE on Hwy 19 through Gads
Hill; turn left on Ellice Conc Rd 10–11. Watch for signs along
road indicating entry point; no definite trail system exists.
INFORMATION. Upper Thames River Conservation Authority.

Gads Hill Agreement Forest

This 535-ha forest contains a great diversity of community
types. A fine Eastern Hemlock–White Cedar swamp and a
White Cedar bog host a variety of northern disjunct plant and
bird species, including Magnolia Warbler, Balsam Fir, and Twinflower. On higher ground, at the southeast edge of the woods, is
a high-quality upland Sugar Maple–American Beech forest.
Northern Harriers feed and breed in the forest. Dense, wet conditions support White-tailed Deer and smaller mammals. The
site serves as an important water storage and discharge area.
DIRECTIONS. From Stratford, go NE on Hwy 19; turn right on N
Easthope Conc Rd 7–8. Forest is on both sides of road; no definite trail exists.
INFORMATION. Upper Thames River Conservation Authority.

T.J. Dolan Natural Area

This natural area features a mature Sugar Maple and Blue-beech
forest, as well as groves of Tamarack, spruce, and pine. Trails
traverse the 4.5-ha site on the Avon River.
DIRECTIONS. From Huron St (Hwy 8) in Stratford, turn S on John
St. Access at S end of John St bridge.

INFORMATION. Parks & Recreation Dept, Stratford, 519-271-0250.

Avon Hiking Trail

Stretching for 100 km from Conestoga in the Regional Municipality of Waterloo via Stratford to St Marys in Perth County, this
hiking trail offers opportunities for exploring the rolling kames
of the Waterloo moraine. The route traverses agricultural landscape, Sugar Maple woodlots, the Avon River valley, and some
scenic natural areas, including a portion of Wildwood Conservation Area. The hilly countryside makes woodland sections
especially interesting for birders and botanists. The trail connects to the Grand Valley Trail at Conestoga and to the Thames
Valley Trail at St Marys.

DIRECTIONS. To hike one attractive segment, from Amulree go E
on Co Rd 15; watch for white flashes where trail joins road from
S & leaves by nearby lane to N.

INFORMATION. Avon Trail Association, Box 20018, Stratford, Ont,
N5A 7V3, 519-625-8097 (guidebook available).

Thames Valley Trail

See entry under Middlesex County.

Wildwood Conservation Area

This property covers approximately 1,200 ha. The shallow
waters and mudflats of Wildwood Lake reservoir provide habitat for thousands of ducks, geese, swans, and shorebirds during
spring and fall migration. In summer, look for Great Blue
Heron, Double-crested Cormorant, Great Egret, and Eastern
Bluebird in the Ducks Unlimited site, where signs and a trail
lead to a viewing tower. The 30-ha Dr R.S. Murray Forest contains an extensive trail system through rolling White Spruce and
White Pine plantations and a Sugar Maple–American Beech forest. This wooded upland hosts many spring wildflowers,
including White and Red Trilliums and Jack-in-the-pulpit. A
wetland area harbours the beautiful Showy Lady's-slipper.
Trails can be used in all seasons.

DIRECTIONS. Located 5.6 km E of St Marys on Hwy 7. Access
Murray Forest from campground. For water birds (Ducks

Unlimited site), from Oxford Co Rd 28 (Road 96) just W of Har-
rington CA go 1 km N on 1st sdrd (W Zorra Conc Rd 1/31st
Line); follow trail on right to viewing tower.
INFORMATION. Wildwood Conservation Area, RR 2, St Marys,
Ont, N4X 1C5, 519-284-2829; Upper Thames River Conservation
Authority.

REGIONAL MUNICIPALITY OF WATERLOO

> One day ... I strayed into the woods ... and came to a tree, the most
> stupendous I had ever seen ... I measured its girth ... at the height
> of a man from the ground, and it was thirty-three feet, above
> which the trunk rose, without a branch, to the height of at least
> eighty feet, crowned with vast branches. This was an oak, proba-
> bly the greatest known, and it lifted its head far above the rest of
> the forest. The trees around, myrmidons of inferior growth were
> large, massy, and vigorous, but possessed none of the patriarchal
> antiquity with which that magnificent 'monarch of the woods'
> was invested. (Corner of Beverly Township now in North Dum-
> fries, late 1820s, John Galt [1779–1839], writer and Canada Com-
> pany official)

Waterloo, Kitchener, and Cambridge form a nearly continuous
urban corridor along the Grand River in the heart of the municipality. The Regional Municipality of Waterloo is characterized
by some of the richest farmland in the province. Most of the area
lies within the Great Lakes–St Lawrence Forest Region, Carolinian woodlands extending into only the southernmost portion in
North Dumfries Township. The municipality's Great Lakes–St
Lawrence forests are dominated by Sugar Maple, American
Beech, and White Ash in the uplands and Black Ash, soft
maples, and White Cedar in the lowlands. The Carolinian
woodlands have Shagbark and Bitternut Hickories, Red Maple,
and Black and White Oaks on higher ground, while lower sites
are characterized by soft maples, American Elm, and White
Cedar. The Carolinian areas also have interesting dry openings
in the forests, with many herbaceous plants, including New Jersey Tea, Yellow Pimpernel, and Black-eyed Susan.
    The region has a very complex geological history, because of

the meeting of three separate ice lobes during the last glaciation. Noteworthy features include eskers east of Elmira; prominent sandy kames north of Elmira, near Hawkesville, Baden, and Chicopee; and massive glacial outwash channels now occupied by the Grand River and its tributaries the Conestoga, Nith, and Speed.

Avon Hiking Trail

See entry under Perth County.

Grand River

See entry under Brant County.

Grand Valley Trail

This 255-km-long hiking trail follows the Grand River from Lake Erie northward through urban and rural landscapes, via Brantford, Paris, Cambridge, Kitchener, and Fergus, to Alton in northern Peel; a side trail connects to the Bruce Trail. Highlights include rolling gravelly glacially deposited hills; remnants of oak, hickory, and maple forests; rich river bottomlands; and the spectacular Elora Gorge in Wellington County. Watch for butterflies in Roseville Swamp and Coyote, White-tailed Deer, and Red-shouldered Hawk in Natchez Hills.

DIRECTIONS. Frequent access points are denoted by roadside markers.

INFORMATION. Grand Valley Trails Association, 75 King St S, Box 40068, RPO Waterloo Square, Waterloo, Ont, N2J 4V1, 519-753-1028 (guidebook available).

Woolwich Conservation Area

This artificial reservoir on Canagagigue Creek is a good spot for seeing migrating waterfowl, especially in early spring. By late summer water levels drop, exposing extensive, algae-covered mudflats that attract hundreds of shorebirds (peaking around the first of September), herons, and ducks.

DIRECTIONS. From Elmira, follow Arthur St (Reg Rd 21) 1 km N; turn left on 1st twp rd (12). For waterfowl viewing (telescope advised) go 1 km to main gate (usually closed) on right; walk in.

For best views of shorebirds continue N on Reg Rd 21 to next twp rd (2), which goes to Floradale. With lake on left, park along road. Follow muddy shoreline to right. In Floradale, check pond for ducks. Also approach reservoir from behind Mennonite church & feed mill.

INFORMATION. Grand River Conservation Authority.

St Jacobs Millrace

A pleasant 2-km trail along the bank of the race to a dam on the Conestoga River provides good year-round birding.

DIRECTIONS. In St Jacobs, trail starts at corner of Front & Isabella, behind old flour mill.

Townline Tract Regional Forest

This rich woodland is part of an extensive complex of provincially significant wetlands and upland hardwoods with a northern flavour. Clubmoss, grape fern, coralroot, rattlesnake-plantain, and Pinesap are among the interesting plants to be found.

DIRECTIONS. From Heidelberg, go 4.5 km S (following Reg Rd 16 but continuing straight when it veers left) to jct at townline. Go 200 m W on dead-end road to small parking lot on left.

INFORMATION. MNR.

Schneider's Woods

Although privately owned, this area is open to the public for passive recreational uses, such as hiking and cross-country skiing. It contains a diversity of habitats, including old fields, pine plantations, Eastern Hemlock stands, and steep upland forests. Ferns and clubmosses are particularly plentiful. It is also a great place to enjoy the spring frog chorus, with as many as six species calling at once.

DIRECTIONS. Take Erb St W (Reg Rd 9) to Waterloo city boundary & turn right; 2nd road to left leads to laneway on right just W of jct. Park on shoulder; 2nd entrance is on townline, opp Wideman Rd.

Kitchener

– **Bingeman Park.** A White Cedar swamp and an interesting

section of the Grand River combine to make an attractive stop here, especially in winter.

DIRECTIONS. Enter at 1380 Victoria St N (Hwy 7).

– Stanley Park. A long, narrow ribbon of woodland near the centre of the city contains the headwaters for two creeks. The main feature is an extensive Silver Maple swamp, but there is also a tract of White Cedar and Yellow Birch and an upland area of Sugar Maple and American Beech. Familiar woodland wildflowers occur, as well as several species of orchids and a variety of breeding birds. Trails are open for cross-country skiing in winter.

DIRECTIONS. 1) Enter from Ottawa St N, off Conestoga Pkwy (Hwy 7/86). 2) Turn N from Ottawa St N to River Rd.

– Idylewood Park. Here wooded wetlands are bisected by a road, with a Silver Maple swamp on the south and, to the north, a bog forest with associated northern species, such as *Sphagnum*, Leatherleaf, Labrador Tea, and sundews. Of particular significance is a stand of Gray Birch, a rarity west of Kingston. The park is known for its rich diversity of plants and butterflies.

DIRECTIONS. From Ottawa St N, turn S onto River Rd; watch for trails into woodlands on both sides.

– Homer Watson Park. This fine example of Carolinian forest contains a great variety of large trees, including impressive old-growth Eastern Hemlocks. High bluffs, especially beautiful in autumn, provide a scenic overlook of the Grand River.

DIRECTIONS. 1) Take Wilson Ave S to end. 2) Enter near Heritage Crossroads Pioneer Village.

– Steckle's Woods. Watch for towering White Pines and other large old-growth trees. In early May a profusion of wildflowers, highlighted by a spectacular display of White Trilliums beneath Red Oaks, carpets the woodland floor.

DIRECTIONS. Located at SW corner of Bleams and Westmount Rds.

F.H. Montgomery Wildlife Sanctuary

This Kitchener-Waterloo Field Naturalists' reserve protects a section of rich deciduous bottomlands along the Nith River. Silt deposits laid down by annual spring floods support a lush growth of wildflowers. Many species uncommon in the area, including ones more typical of the Carolinian woodlands to the south, thrive here. Some examples are Twinleaf, Wild Garlic, False Gromwell, Black Maple, and Bladdernut.

DIRECTIONS. Go 9 km W from New Dundee to sign on left before bridge. Park on S side of road; marked trail is at base of slope.

Cambridge

The Grand and Speed rivers join in Cambridge, and the city marks a recognized northern boundary of the Carolinian zone.

– Riverside Municipal Park. Trails and a boardwalk lead through a variety of vegetation communities along the Speed River.

DIRECTIONS. Take Hwy 8 S from Hwy 401 to Fountain St & turn left; turn right onto King St, then left on Rogers Dr.

– Confluence of Grand and Speed Rivers. Here the riverside parkland consisting of thickets and clumps of vegetation attracts good numbers of migrant land birds, plus vagrant water birds. In winter, this is the best waterfowl viewing site in the Regional Municipality of Waterloo.

DIRECTIONS. Access is gained off Riverside Dr.

– Grand River. Watch for unusual gulls and waterfowl in spring, fall, and winter. Glaucous, Iceland, and Great Black-backed Gulls are winter regulars. Mergansers and goldeneyes winter in open water below the dam and at the rapids near Fountain St. This section of the river is lined with steep, 20-m-high limestone bluffs, the only significant outcroppings along the Grand south of Elora. Calcium-loving ferns grow on the cliffs, and trails along the top provide fine vantage points for birdwatching.

DIRECTIONS. Access from Fountain St, George St Extension just S of Blair Rd, or Galt Dam off Parkhill Rd W.

– Victoria Municipal Park. A deciduous woodland and adjacent cemetery provide good birding in fall, winter, and spring.

DIRECTIONS. Enter from Blenheim Rd or Wentworth Ave.

Speed River Trail

See entry under Wellington County.

Grand River South of Cambridge

See Grand River Forests entry in Brant County.

Dryden Tract Forest (Alps Hills)

Here rugged trails and logging roads meander through rolling hardwood hills owned by the Regional Municipality of Waterloo. Situated on a kame moraine, the forest has a distinctly Carolinian flavour. Black Cherry, Pignut Hickory, and White Pine grow among the dominant oaks and maples. Sassafras and Bitternut and Shagbark Hickories are also present. Some of the other unusual plants to be found are Sicklepod, Squawroot, Ebony Spleenwort, and Witch-hazel. An excellent scenic lookout and raptor viewing site at the edge of the terminal moraine can be reached by following the Grand Valley Trail past an old field undergoing succession. In fall, the hills put on an impressive show of colour. An extensive trail network through the short, steep hills and intervening depressions makes the woodland a favourite of those who enjoy challenging cross-country skiing.

DIRECTIONS. Take Reg Rd 75 SW from Cambridge; turn right on N Dumfries Twp Rd 2 (Alps Rd); go 4.0 km to parking lot on left.

INFORMATION. Grand River Conservation Authority.

Drynan Tract Forest

Here an easy walking trail on logging roads through dense plantations of Red Pine and Black Walnut leads to a small lake. Later, the terrain becomes hillier and clothed in a forest of oaks and hickories. Among the hills are several swampy lowlands and small kettle lakes. The tract offers good possibilities for viewing wildlife, including birds, mammals, and turtles – walk quietly and keep your eyes open when following the paths near the wetlands or through areas of dense cover. Watch too for Poison Sumac, Hill's Oak, and a variety of saprophytic plants.

DIRECTIONS. Take Reg Rd 75 SW from Cambridge; turn right on

N Dumfries Twp Rd 3 (Greenfield Rd); at 2nd jct turn left on
Reg Rd 47 (Dumfries Rd); go 0.8 km to parking lot on right.
INFORMATION. Grand River Conservation Authority.

Sudden Tract

This rich 150-ha tract, one of the larger natural areas in Waterloo, contains an abundance of wildlife, including plants and animals typical of the Carolinian zone as well as some that occur
more commonly farther north. A series of gravelly moraine
ridges supports some excellent oak-hickory and Sugar Maple–
American Beech stands. Interspersed with these are wetlands
varying from Silver Maple swamps to bogs dominated by Tamarack. Among the plant specialties occurring in the tract are
New Jersey Tea, Sassafras, Buckbean, Poison Sumac, Interrupted Fern, and several oak species. Breeding birds of note are
Scarlet Tanager, Blue-gray Gnatcatcher, Red-bellied Woodpecker, Blue-winged Warbler, and Northern Waterthrush. Frogs
and snakes are plentiful and can be easily viewed from the logging roads and hiking trails that provide access. Herpetofauna
include Eastern Smooth Green Snake and Four-toed, Jefferson
complex, and Yellow-spotted Salamanders. The hilly terrain
makes the area popular with cross-country skiers. The Vascan
Trail connects to Bannister Lake and beyond.
DIRECTIONS. Take Reg Rd 75 SW from Cambridge; continue on
Reg Rd 75 for 1.7 km past jct with N Dumfries Twp Rd 3 (Greenfield Rd) to large forest & public parking on left. Or continue S
on Reg Rd 75; turn left on N Dumfries Twp Rd 4 & watch for
parking lot on left.

Bannister and Wrigley Lakes

Bannister Lake and its marshy verges attract spectacular numbers of waterfowl each spring and fall. Migrating Tundra Swans
are a highlight in mid March. An observation tower overlooks
the lake on the south, and the Vascan Trail leads along the east
side to an extensive wetland at the north end. Here a boardwalk
traverses a Silver Maple swamp with fine old trees and lush
undergrowth of ferns and wildflowers. The trail continues eastward through a meadow noted for its midsummer wildflower
display before reaching the Sudden Tract.

Wrigley Lake, south of and across the road from Bannister Lake, draws fewer waterfowl, but its eastern perimeter is good for observing migrating land birds. Abundant Riverbank Grape provides food for large numbers of Cedar Waxwings, American Robins, and Rusty Blackbirds in the fall. Yellow-throated Vireo regularly nests in the deciduous forest nearby. The Vascan Trail along Wrigley Lake connects southward through a fine oak-hickory stand to the Dickson Wilderness Area.

DIRECTIONS. Take Reg Rd 75 SW from Cambridge; turn right on Reg Rd 49 (Ayr Rd); go 0.2 km to parking lot on right just before Bannister Lake & roughly opp Wrigley Lake trail. Or access trail (with boardwalks) from Reg Rd 75, 1.6 km N of its jct with Reg Rd 49; look for well-concealed parking lot on W side of road.

INFORMATION. Grand River Conservation Authority.

F.W.R. Dickson Wilderness Area

An unusual diversity of habitats is found within this 30-ha property. Highlights include a small remnant of tallgrass prairie, a Carolinian oak-hickory forest with Sassafras, and a long boardwalk across a swamp where Tamarack can be found. In mid to late winter the boardwalk is an ideal place to watch for the first signs of Skunk-cabbage blooms melting their way through the snow. The Vascan Trail connects the wilderness area to Wrigley Lake and beyond.

DIRECTIONS. Take Reg Rd 75 SW from Cambridge to county line; turn right (W) on N Dumfries Twp Rd 5 & drive 1 km to parking lot on right.

INFORMATION. Grand River Conservation Authority.

Grass Lake (Cranberry Bog)

This 40-ha kettle pond wetland contains both open-water marsh and a floating bog mat. Among the vegetation communities are bulrush marsh, Leatherleaf and bog grasses, and thickets of willows and Buttonbush. Raptors hunt over the bog, which provides habitat for wildlife and a rich diversity of bog flora. Some of the more interesting plants found here are Ohio Goldenrod, Linear-leaved Sundew, Rose Pogonia, Poison Sumac, Watershield, White Beak-rush, Buckbean, Labrador Tea, Pale Laurel, Bog Rosemary, and Pitcher-plant. Look for Grasshopper Sparrow near the transmission towers. American Bittern, Black Tern, Pied-billed Grebe, Northern Harrier, Common Snipe, and waterfowl also use the area.

DIRECTIONS. Take Reg Rd 75 SW from Cambridge; turn left on N Dumfries Twp Rd 4 & go 2 km; turn right on N Dumfries Twp Rd 14 & go 0.1 km or 0.9 km. There is no access onto bog but its habitats can be well seen from roadside.

WELLINGTON COUNTY

> In a short space the clouds seemed to converge to a point, which approached very near the earth, still whirling with great rapidity ...; apparently from the midst of the woods arose a ... vast column of smoke of inky blackness reaching from earth to heaven, gyrating with fearful velocity; bright lightnings issuing from the vortex – the roar of the thunder – the rushing of the blast – the crashing of timber – the limbs of trees, leaves and rubbish, mingled with clouds of dust, whirling through the air ... As the tornado approached, the trees seemed to fall like a pack of cards before its irresistible current. (Guelph Township, May 1829, Samuel Strickland [1804–67], land agent and settler)

Wellington County is an elongated, sprawling land mass that stretches for 100 km from the Regional Municipality of Hamilton-Wentworth in the south to Grey County in the north. The northern part of Wellington lies within the Dundalk till plain, a high, cool region marked by relatively level, often poorly drained, farmland. The south is characterized by numerous drumlins and moraines flanked by gravel terraces and interspersed with broad low-lying valleys that were once glacial spillways. Most of Wellington drains southward via the Grand River system. Wooded areas in the county are typical of the mixed forests of the Great Lakes–St Lawrence Forest Region. The rolling farmland and woodlots in the southern portion of the county create colourful autumn vistas.

Luther Marsh

See entry under Dufferin County.

Elora Gorge Conservation Area

Stretching for 1.6 km along the Grand River, the scenic Elora Gorge is one of the deepest and narrowest gorges in southern Ontario. Here beds of dolostone have been exposed by thousands of years of erosion by flowing water. Cool, damp microhabitats in the 25-m-high cliff faces are home to a number of unusual plants, notably an excellent assemblage of rock ferns. Huge White Cedars, White Pines, and White Birches grow along the river bottom, while smaller specimens of the same species top the heights. Blunt-lobed Grape Fern, Hay-scented Fern, White Camass, Bird's-eye Primrose, and Prickly-ash are among plants of interest. Cliff and Northern Rough-winged Swallows nest on the sheer rock walls. Each May good concentrations of migrating songbirds pass through the gorge and adjacent woodlands. River Otter and Mink have been seen along the river. Trails through the 145-ha conservation area are open all year.
DIRECTIONS. Take Co Rd 21 SW from Elora.
INFORMATION. Grand River Conservation Authority.

Grand River

See entry under Brant County.

Grand Valley Trail

See entry under Regional Municipality of Waterloo.

Guelph Lake Conservation Area

Situated between the northeastern side of Guelph and Eramosa, this area contains a large, man-made impoundment of water that provides good birding habitat. Showy Orchis grows in woodlots on the west side of the lake.

1) From Guelph go north on Highway 6; turn east and go 2.6 km on Guelph Township Road 6 to a good overview of the dam, lake, and nature centre. A little farther on is the main entrance to the conservation area, from which internal roads give access to other good viewing points.

2) Take Highway 24 (Eramosa Road) northeast from Guelph. Distances are given from the junction of Victoria Road and Highway 24. *Km 3.7:* There is a good overview of the lake to the

north. In spring watch for migrating ducks and in fall, if mud-flats are present, migrating shorebirds. A few hundred metres farther east, there is a good overview on both sides (but parking is difficult); a left turn up a sideroad also gives a good view. *Km 6.1:* Turn right (south) on County Road 29 and go 0.9 km to a good overview of a shallow lake to the east and swamp to the west. Osprey, Virginia Rail, and Hooded Merganser breed here. About 200 m beyond this point a dirt road (Eramosa Concession Road 10) goes right (west); about 400 m along, a trail leads north to a blind erected by the Guelph Field Naturalists, which gives another good viewing point.
INFORMATION. Grand River Conservation Authority.

Guelph Radial Trail

This 30-km hiking trail goes through semi-rural landscape northeast from Guelph, following a former railway right-of-way to Limehouse in the Regional Municipality of Halton, where it connects with the Bruce Trail. Passing mostly through wet White Cedar woodlands, the route offers unusual concentrations of glacial landforms. Among breeding birds are Nashville Warbler, Winter Wren, Brown Creeper, and Red-breasted Nuthatch.
INFORMATION. Guelph Hiking Trail Club, Box 1, Guelph, Ont, N1H 6J6, 519-763-4273 (guidebook available).

Speed River Trail

Running along the Speed River for 30 km between Guelph and the Grand River in Cambridge, this hiking trail passes through a semi-rural landscape of eskers, moraines, drumlins, and glacial outwash plains. Watch for interesting plants, such as One-flowered Pyrola.
INFORMATION. Guelph Hiking Trail Club (address above).

Rockwood Conservation Area

The most striking feature of this 80-ha conservation area is the carved limestone landscape. Notable are white rock cliffs above the Eramosa River, solution caves dissolved by centuries of moving water, and potholes worn by rocks whirled around small pockmarks in the limestone by melting glaciers. This diverse landscape is home to many unusual species of animals and plants, including Green and Maidenhair Spleenworts and Climbing Fumitory.

DIRECTIONS. On Hwy 7 from downtown Guelph, go 11 km NE to Rockwood; turn right at CA sign.

INFORMATION. Grand River Conservation Authority.

Eramosa River Valley

This 30-km stretch of forested river valley between Rockwood and Brisbane contains a high diversity of vegetation communities, including meadow, American Beech–Sugar Maple upland forest, and swampy wooded floodplain supporting White Cedar, alder, Black Ash, and elm. Rapids, gravel terraces, and braided streams can be seen in the river. Much of the land is privately owned and should be viewed only from roadsides or where bridges cross the river. One good access point is on publicly owned land at Everton, where the river rushes through potholes and narrow rock channels. Smooth Cliffbrake, White Adder's-mouth, Hooded Ladies'-tresses, Blunt-leaved Orchid, Sweet Gale, Round-leaved Sundew, Small Cranberry, and Twinflower are some of the more notable plants that occur in the valley. Brown Creeper, Winter Wren, and Nashville, Black-throated Green, Mourning, and Canada Warblers breed in the area. White-tailed Deer winter here.

DIRECTIONS. From downtown Guelph go 15 km NE on Hwy 24; turn right at Conc Rd 6–7 (stone restaurant building) & go 1 km to Everton.

INFORMATION. Grand River Conservation Authority.

Cranberry Bog

Species of interest found here include Buttonbush, Redbelly Snake, and Red-spotted Newt.

DIRECTIONS. From Exit 295 on Hwy 401, go 1 km N on Hwy 6; turn left on Co Rd 34; turn N on Co Rd 35 (Downey Rd); turn right at 1st conc rd & go 0.8 km; follow well-developed bush tracks.

INFORMATION. MNR.

Oil Well Bog–Little Tract

This forested area harbours breeding Pine Warblers and Golden-crowned Kinglets. Plants of interest include Showy Orchis, Pink Lady's-slipper, and Ragged Fringed Orchid.

DIRECTIONS. 1) From Exit 295 on Hwy 401, go 1 km N on Hwy 6; turn left on Co Rd 34 & go 4.9 km (about 250 m past historic plaque). Park & follow trails 2 km N through Little Tract to E edge of bog. 2) From Co Rd 34, turn N on Co Rd 35; turn left on 1st conc rd & go 2.5 km. Remains of oil well are just N of W edge of bog.

INFORMATION. MNR.

Puslinch Lake Wetlands

Located just west of the Paris moraine, Puslinch Lake is the largest and best example of the numerous kettle formations in the area. Associated with it are a rich diversity of habitats, including upland forest dominated by Sugar Maple, American Beech, and Eastern Hemlock. Other plant communities of note are a Tamarack–Black Spruce–Leatherleaf bog; a scrub association of White Cedar, Tamarack, and White Birch; and a fine swamp forest of Yellow Birch and Red and Silver Maples. Among unusual species are Hay-scented Fern and Northern Ribbon Snake.

DIRECTIONS. Located NE of Cambridge on N side of Puslinch Twp Rd 1 (Crieff Rd) just E of Townline Rd. Access is difficult; consult GRCA.

INFORMATION. Grand River Conservation Authority.

Mountsberg Wildlife Centre and Conservation Area

The 445-ha conservation area includes forest, fields, and an extensive reservoir with two viewing towers. During migration, waterfowl, Bald Eagles, Tundra Swans, and a good variety and number of shorebirds can be seen. Hooded Mergansers nest here, Osprey visit regularly, and Ring-necked Pheasants frequent the fields. The forests provide habitat for a large variety of woodland birds, including Pileated Woodpecker. There are a number of interesting plants, such as Walking Fern, Royal Fern, Indian Cucumber-root, Pinesap, Cardinal-flower, Great Lobelia, and Water Avens. A birds of prey centre features rehabilitation facilities and enclosures housing non-releasable hawks and owls.

DIRECTIONS. From Hwy 401, take Exit 312 (Guelph Line or Halton Rd 1) S for 0.7 km to Reg Rd 9 (Campbellville Rd 5). Turn right & drive 5 km W to Milborough Line. Turn right; go 1 km N to CA entrance. Trails lead mostly N from this point.
INFORMATION. Halton Region Conservation Authority.

DUFFERIN COUNTY

> I regret having to say that it is impossible ever to effect a settlement here; for the whole township appears to be one continual swamp, out of which the principal streams of the Grand River take their rise ... The [surveying] work has gone on slowly, on account of the badness of the swamps, as in every place they are almost impossible [impassable] from the great quantity of fallen timber and the young growth of cedar, spruce, fir, and alder being very thick, and the swamps being deep and mirey at the same time (Luther Swamp, September 1, 1831, Lewis Burwell, surveyor)

While the eastern portion of Dufferin County is dominated by the Niagara Escarpment, much of the remainder is occupied by the relatively flat plain of the Dundalk Highlands, where agriculture is an important industry. The county is regarded as the roof of southern Ontario since it contains the headwaters of major river systems flowing into Georgian Bay and Lakes Huron, Erie, and Ontario. Rolling hills, waterfalls, and spectacular fall colours all contribute to Dufferin's scenic beauty. The area lies within the Great Lakes–St Lawrence Forest Region.

Grand River

See entry under Brant County.

Luther Marsh Wildlife Management Area

Straddling the border of Wellington and Dufferin counties, this 6,500-ha wetland is one of the largest and most significant inland marshes in southern Ontario. The site is dominated by Luther Lake, a huge (4,000-ha), shallow, marshy lake containing several islands and surrounded by an extensive, low shrub bog. Along the north shore lies a large area of woodland where some northern bird species may be found. To the southeast is Wylde Lake, noted for a nearby raised bog with boreal characteristics. Associated with the wildlife management area are an esker and till plain, which support deciduous woodland, coniferous plantation, and successional old fields. Among other features are coniferous swamp forests, fen, and sedge meadows.

Luther Marsh lies within the first section of Ontario to re-emerge after the retreat of the last glacial ice sheet. Today's marsh and lake were created by artificially flooding a lowland area in the headwaters of the Grand River. The varied habitats provide for an amazingly rich diversity and abundance of wildlife, including many rare species. The marsh is particularly noted for large populations of breeding and migrating waterfowl. Fifteen species of ducks have nested here, mostly on islands and in the bog along the north side of the lake. These include Hooded Merganser, Northern Pintail, Northern Shoveler, Canvasback, Redhead, Ring-necked Duck, Lesser Scaup, Ruddy Duck, and American Wigeon. All the expected species of marsh birds also nest. Look for Osprey, Least Bittern, Common Loon, Red-necked Grebe, Wilson's Phalarope, Great Blue Heron, Black-crowned Night-Heron, Sedge Wren, and LeConte's and Lincoln's Sparrows. In fall, when the lake is drawn down, mudflats along the shore draw numerous shorebirds.

The wetlands and adjacent uplands support a good variety of mammals, such as Ermine, Long-tailed Weasel, Mink, Red Fox, Coyote, and White-tailed Deer (including a wintering yard). Butler's Garter Snake, Northern Ribbon Snake, Northern Brown Snake, Mink Frog, Blanding's Turtle, and Yellow Perch also make their homes in Luther Marsh. There is an abundance of unusual plants, among them One-Flowered Pyrola, Watershield, Swamp Birch, Broad-lipped Twayblade, Water Stargrass, Swamp Valerian, Leatherleaf, Pale Laurel, Showy Lady's-slipper, and Round-leaved Sundew. There are established trails and viewing towers.

DIRECTIONS. 1) To reach dam, good views of lake, observation towers, trails, & N shore woods: from Grand Valley on Hwy 25, go 8.5 km N to E Luther Conc Rd 8–9; turn W & drive 5.5 km to parking lot; hike. 2) For views of W side of lake: from Arthur, go 5.8 km E on Hwy 9; go 8.2 km N on Co Rd 16; go 2.7 km E on Bootlegger's Rd to lake. To reach concealed slough: 100 m from end of road, follow track S for 600 m. 3) To reach Wylde Lake: from Hwy 9 (7.3 km W of Hwy 25 or 11.5 km E of Arthur), go 5.3 km N along county line; where road turns left, walk 1.5 km E (compass advised). Watch for Lincoln's Sparrow, Tamarack, wet *Sphagnum* bog, and unusual flora. 4) Canoeing is one of best ways to explore lake; access at dam & Bootlegger's Rd. Check re permit, routes, & restricted areas. Unpredictable winds on lake can be hazardous.

NOTE. Floating bogs are bottomless & should not be walked upon. Hunting occurs in fall.

INFORMATION. Grand River Conservation Authority.

Dufferin County Forest

This high, sandy, dry 604-ha property is almost entirely wooded. Large natural stands of White Pine, American Beech, Butternut, Sugar Maple, and Red Oak are mixed with tracts of reforested Red and White Pines. The area provides excellent habitat for Wild Turkey, Ruffed Grouse, and White-tailed Deer.

DIRECTIONS. From Shelburne, go 15 km E on Hwy 89; turn N on Co Rd 18 (Airport Rd) & drive 11.5 km to entrance on E side of road.

INFORMATION. County of Dufferin, 51 Zina St, Orangeville, Ont, L9W 1E5, 519-941-2338.

Niagara Escarpment–Bruce Trail

The Niagara Escarpment traverses eastern Dufferin County from north to south. Within the county extensive sections of the escarpment are buried beneath glacial tills. There are numerous access points to the Bruce Trail (indicated by white blazes), including several provincial nature reserves. See entry under Regional Municipality of Niagara.

INFORMATION. Bruce Trail Association; Niagara Escarpment Commission.

Boyne Valley Provincial Park

A complex glacial landscape is protected within this undeveloped 500-ha park characterized by open field, deciduous slopes, and dense coniferous wetlands. The spring-fed Boyne River flows cool and clear through the park, providing excellent habitat for Brown and Rainbow Trout. Fine examples of the Orangeville moraine and its associated features can be observed from many scenic vantage points. Views are especially nice in fall.

DIRECTIONS. From Hwy 10 at Primrose, go 1.5 km E on Hwy 89 to road allowance on N side of hwy. Follow Bruce Trail into park.

INFORMATION. C/o Earl Rowe Provincial Park, Box 966, Alliston, Ont, L0M 1A0, 705-435-4331.

Mono Cliffs Provincial Park

Known for its two dolostone outliers and beautiful views (particularly in autumn), this undeveloped park is traversed by the Bruce Trail. The park contains the only major exposure of the Niagara Escarpment between Lavender Falls (25 km north) and Credit Forks (25 km south).

Most of the park consists of old field and Sugar Maple–American Beech forests, where Dutchman's Breeches and Spotted Coralroot are found. Mixed stands of Sugar Maple, White Birch, and Large-toothed Aspen harbour spring wildflowers such as Squirrel-corn and Red Trillium. Lopseed, Soft Sweet Cicely, and Smith's Melic Grass thrive in maple-aspen-Butternut stands. The White Cedar forests clinging to the fissures and cliff faces here and elsewhere along the escarpment are among eastern North America's oldest and least disturbed old-growth forests. The diverse escarpment habitats support Hairy Rock-cress and a profusion of ferns and fern allies, including Walking Fern, Smooth Cliffbrake, Northeastern Lady Fern, Oak Fern, Rock Polypody, Maidenhair Spleenwort, and fine stands of clubmosses. Among the fauna of interest are Great Horned Owl, Whip-poor-will, Horned Lark, Vesper Sparrow, Eastern Bluebird, Jefferson complex Salamanders, and Brook Trout. The park contains significant wetlands, including an isolated lake noted for its rare species.

DIRECTIONS. From Orangeville, take Hwy 10/24 N to Co Rd 8 at Camilla. Turn right & continue to park entrance just N of Mono Centre.

INFORMATION. C/o Earl Rowe Provincial Park, Box 966, Alliston, Ont, L0M 1A0, 705-435-4331.

Hockley Valley Provincial Nature Reserve

Within the 400-ha undeveloped park are fine examples of till moraine and other deposits left by glacial meltwaters. The rolling landscape is covered with woodlands and wet meadows. Areas of upland deciduous forest are dominated by intermediate-aged Sugar Maple, White Ash, American Beech, Eastern Hemlock, and Black Cherry. Mixed coniferous-deciduous wetlands support White Spruce, Balsam Fir, Tamarack, White Birch, Trembling Aspen, and Basswood. Flora of interest include Silvery Glade Fern, Walking Fern, and Broad-leaved Waterleaf. Eastern Bluebirds can often be sighted near the grassy hills. The area is noted for its fall colour display.

DIRECTIONS. Just N of Orangeville on Hwy 10, turn E on Hockley Valley Rd (Co Rd 7). Park in lot at Line 2 EHS Mono. Explore park via Bruce Trail & side trails.

INFORMATION. C/o Earl Rowe Provincial Park, Box 966, Alliston, Ont, L0M 1A0, 705-435-4331.

SIMCOE COUNTY

> [Among the majestic pines] it is singular to observe the effect of an occasional gust of wind ... It may not even fan your cheek; but you hear a low surging sound, like the moaning of breakers in a calm sea, which gradually increases to a loud boisterous roar, still seemingly at a great distance; the branches remain in perfect repose, you can discover no evidence of a stirring breeze, till, looking perpendicularly upwards, you are astonished to see some patriarchal giant close at hand – six yards round and sixty high ... – waving its huge fantastic arms wildly at a dizzy height above your head. (Sunnidale Township, fall 1833, Samuel Thompson [1819–86], English settler)

Simcoe County abuts the Niagara Escarpment in the west, and runs east to the alvar plains of Victoria County, north to the southern edge of the Precambrian Shield along the Severn River, and south to the sand plains and market-gardening area in the Holland Marsh. Much of the county consists of low-lying sand and clay plains which at one time lay beneath the waters of glacial Lake Algonquin. Mixed farming exists on the uplands, while the lowland sand plains support cash crops. The Georgian Bay shoreline, Trent-Severn Waterway, and Lake Simcoe sustain intense summer recreational use. The landscape of the west side of the county is dominated by a series of high sand and till islands, beaches, and sand dunes. The north portion is marked by a series of broad rock ridges separated by valleys, and drumlins are numerous to the east.

Nottawasaga Lookout (including Singhampton Caves)

Noted for its significant earth science features, Nottawasaga Lookout contains one of the most important examples of accessible crevice caves in the province. Known locally as the Singhampton Caves, these are perched under the Niagara Escarpment on the southern rim of the Pretty River valley. Actually deep, narrow fissures in the cliffs, the caves are open to the sky, with one green-coated chamber leading to another. Mosses and liverworts abound. The area offers magnificent views of the Niagara Escarpment and surrounding countryside. The Sugar Maple–American Beech woodland puts on a spectacular display of fall colour. Several species of rare and uncommon plants grow at the site, including Ebony and Green Spleenworts. In all, 27 species of ferns are found.

DIRECTIONS. Go N on Hwy 24; where it swings E at Singhampton, continue straight N to end of road; park & follow trails. For caves, go 0.4 km N on Bruce Trail to edge of escarpment; use care to descend slippery ladder & rocks of blue-blazed side trail.

Niagara Escarpment–Bruce Trail

The Niagara Escarpment and the Bruce Trail (look for white blazes) run along a section of the northwestern corner of Simcoe County from Lavender north through Devil's Glen to Singhampton and over the Nottawasaga Lookout. Views along the escarpment are especially spectacular during the fall colour season. See entry under Regional Municipality of Niagara.

INFORMATION. Bruce Trail Association; Niagara Escarpment Commission.

Silver Creek Wetlands and Nottawasaga Island

Here interior swales and marshy shores nourish colourful plants endemic to the Great Lakes. Showy and Yellow Lady's-slippers and Fringed Gentian grow in the wetlands. There is a sporadic abundance of waterfowl, shorebirds, and wading birds. A specialty is foraging Great Egrets from a small colony on Nottawasaga Island offshore. Herons and ducks nesting on the island (a nature sanctuary with restricted access) include Green and Great Blue Herons, Black-crowned Night-Heron, Common and Red-breasted Mergansers, and Northern Pintail.
DIRECTIONS. Drive 3 km W of Collingwood on Hwy 26; watch on N side of road.

Wasaga Beach Provincial Park

Few visitors realize that this park harbours the largest and least disturbed parabolic (crescent-shaped) dunes in Ontario. Inland from the recreational beach, the extensive dunefield and wetland complex acts as a refugium for a number of unusual western and southern plants. Here calcareous fen-like meadows, peaty meadows, and treed fens support species such as Beaked Spike-rush. The huge dunes are forested with Red Oak, White Pine, and Red Maple on their lower slopes, and Red and White Pines higher up. Rare plants of the hot, dry, prairie-like barrens include Hill's Thistle, Houghton's Cyperus, Frostweed, Hairy Hawkweed, Narrow-leaved New Jersey Tea, and Oakes' Evening-primrose. In addition to being an exceptionally rich location for flora, the park is also a great place for observing butterflies. The extensive trail system is open in winter for cross-country skiing.
DIRECTIONS. Off Hwy 92 at Wasaga Beach; see prov hwy map.
INFORMATION. Wasaga Beach Provincial Park, Box 183, Wasaga Beach, Ont, L0L 2P0, 705-429-2516.

Tiny Marsh Provincial Wildlife Area

Originally a lake rimmed with forests, this wetland is now intensively managed to provide habitat for waterfowl during breeding and migration. The area consists of 600 ha of marsh and 300 ha of forest and fields. Among species of interest are

Black Tern, Least Bittern, Osprey, Virginia Rail, and Sora. There are trails and a seasonally operated interpretive centre.

DIRECTIONS. From jct of Hwys 92 & 27 in Elmvale go 3.5 km N on Hwy 27; turn left on Tiny-Floss Townline; go 3.7 km to entrance.

INFORMATION. MNR.

Awenda Provincial Park

This extensive woodland enclave at the northern tip of the Penetanguishene Peninsula includes Giants Tomb Island (3 km offshore) and adjacent waters. The mainland portion of the park contains 1,900 ha, and provides habitat for a number of rare species. Shaped by lakewaters that originated from melting glaciers, the landscape contains glacial features such as boulder fields, cobble beaches, kettle lakes, and sand dunes, as well as a well-preserved sequence of glacial Lake Algonquin shorelines. The most significant feature is the Nipissing bluff, a raised beach rising 60 m above the damp lowlands bordering Georgian Bay. On top of the bluff is a mixed deciduous forest of Red Oak, White Pine, Sugar Maple, American Beech, and White Birch. The display of Red, White, and Painted Trilliums and other spring wildflowers here is noteworthy. Lowland woods are dominated by Eastern Hemlock and Yellow Birch with numerous White Cedar–Red Maple–Speckled Alder–Balsam Fir associations. Other wetland communities are shoreline fens, Beaver ponds, Black Spruce–Tamarack bogs, and swamps of Red Maple, White Cedar, and Black Ash.

Breeding birds show unusual diversity, with southern species such as Hooded and Cerulean Warblers and Yellow-throated Vireo found near Swainson's Thrush and Black-throated Blue Warbler from the north. Among the numerous reptile and amphibian species are Mink Frog and Pickerel Frog. Fall colours are spectacular at Awenda. The extensive trail network is open for hiking, cross-country skiing, and snowshoeing.

DIRECTIONS. Located 11 km N of Penetanguishene; see prov hwy map.

INFORMATION. MNR; Awenda Provincial Park, Box 973, Penetanguishene, Ont, L0K 1P0, 705-549-2231.

Wye Marsh Wildlife Area

This significant wetland is located near the mouth of the Wye River. The 1,200-ha marsh supports both shallow open-water and cattail communities, accessible by boardwalk and canoe. Spring-fed tributaries flow into the marsh from the surrounding Red and Sugar Maple woodlands. The geology and history of the Wye valley have resulted in a diversity of flora and fauna, including rarities. A breeding program for Trumpeter Swans has recently been established. The Wye Marsh Wildlife Centre offers trails, cross-country skiing, and year-round interpretive activities.
DIRECTIONS. Drive to E edge of Midland on Hwy 12.
INFORMATION. Friends of Wye Marsh, Box 100, Midland, Ont, L4R 4K6, 705-526-7809.

Copeland Forest Resources Management Area

Mixed coniferous and deciduous forest predominates in this 1,750-ha tract, which also contains swamp and meadows. The rolling uplands are interspersed with valleys and wetlands from which originate the headwater streams of three rivers. In spring, wildflowers and songbirds are abundant. Specialties include Goldie's Wood Fern and Squawroot. The area has a large winter deer yard where White-tailed Deer gather. Multi-use trails are open year-round.
DIRECTIONS. Located N of Barrie between Medonte Twp Conc Rds 1 & 5. Enter from Ingram Rd off Hwy 93 (S of Hwy 400) or from Conc Rd 4.
INFORMATION. MNR.

Matchedash Lake (Long Lake)

More than a dozen species of Atlantic coastal plain flora have been found growing around Long Lake, the most significant coastal plain lake in Ontario. Examples are Ridged Yellow Flax, Lesser Waterwort, Carey's Knotweed, Virginia Meadow-beauty, and Southern Yellow-eyed Grass. Other rarities recorded here include Small Beggar's-ticks and Four-toed Salamander. Water levels in the lake are regulated by an MNR control dam.
DIRECTIONS. Go N from Orillia on road to Swift Rapids on Severn River (Conc Rd 6 [1st road E of Co Rd 18] & its extension).

Uhthoff Trail

The 11-km-long Uhthoff Trail, a former CPR line, runs from the northern edge of Orillia to the North River just south of Uhthoff quarry. Habitats along the way range from open, dry areas to wetland. Plants of note are Water Speedwell, Torrey's Rush, and Ox-eye. Over 50 species of butterflies, including the trail mascot the Baltimore, and 30 species of dragonflies and damselflies have been recorded on the trail. Watch for warblers in May. The trail is open for hiking, cycling, cross-country skiing, and snow-shoeing.

DIRECTIONS. Enter at Wilson Point Rd in Orillia or Division Rd at Conc Rd 6 in Orillia Twp.

INFORMATION. Orillia Naturalists, Box 2381, Orillia, Ont, L3V 6V7.

Ganaraska Trail

This 450-km-long hiking trail extends from Port Hope to Glen Huron, where it connects with the Bruce Trail. The Ganaraska Trail passes through a tremendous variety of country – from Lake Ontario north through the sandhills of the Ganaraska Forest, past the lakes and drumlin fields of the Kawarthas to the rugged wilderness of the Canadian Shield, then west through the rolling hills of Simcoe County to the edge of the Niagara Escarpment. The route is a mixture of everything from easy walks along quiet country roads to strenuous hikes in rugged wilderness. The trail is open for cross-country skiing and snow-shoeing in winter.

INFORMATION. Ganaraska Trail Association, 12 King St, Box 19, Orillia, Ont, L3V 1R1, 705-325-6470 (guidebook available).

Minesing Swamp

One of the most interesting and important wildlife sites in the county, this 5,000-ha wooded wetland is situated in a natural basin created by the former beach terraces of three ancient glacial lakes. The swamp is flooded annually by the silt-laden waters of the Nottawasaga River and its tributaries. The area's large size and isolation enable it to support a rich assemblage of habitats and uncommon species. Some plants of note are Beaked Spike-rush, Oswego Tea, and Swamp Valerian.

Lush deciduous swampland of Silver Maple and Black Ash covers the largest portion of the wetland. A section of bottomland and levee along the Nottawasaga River harbours numerous Carolinian species, among them Common Hackberry, Moonseed, Bladdernut, Cerulean Warbler, and Blue-gray Gnatcatcher. Wet willow thickets support a multitude of grasses and sedges. There are also large tracts of cool coniferous swamps with northern components such as Golden-crowned Kinglet, Brown Creeper, Balsam Fir, and northern sedges and willows. Other vegetation communities include cattail and sedge marshes, and open fens dotted with teardrop-shaped islands of White Cedar and Tamarack.

DIRECTIONS. From Barrie, drive W on Hwy 90. 1) To visit edges of swamp, go 7.5 km N on Co Rd 28. 2) To find warblers & Black Spruce bog, continue on Hwy 90 W of Co Rd 28 to Vespra Conc Rds 11 & 12. 3) To enter swamp by canoe (best during spring flood) at Nottawasaga River, continue W to Sunnidale Conc Rd 21–22. In spring, thousands of waterfowl flock to fields along this sdrd; hawks frequent the area in winter.

INFORMATION. MNR; Nottawasaga Valley Conservation Authority.

Georgian Bay Fish Runs

Rainbow Trout can be seen about mid April and sometimes in the fall (late October) in several rivers around Georgian Bay, including the Pretty River in Collingwood (go to Pretty River Parkway southeast of town), the Nottawasaga River at Wasaga Beach and at the Nicolston Dam 3 km east of Alliston on Highway 89, and the Coldwater River in Coldwater and the Copeland Forest. Coho and Chinook Salmon can also be seen at most of these locations in the fall. Around the second and third weeks of April, many Walleye move out of Lake Simcoe and up the Talbot River to spawn (from Gamebridge go 3 km east on Durham Road 50 to Simcoe Road 50 and Talbot River Dam).

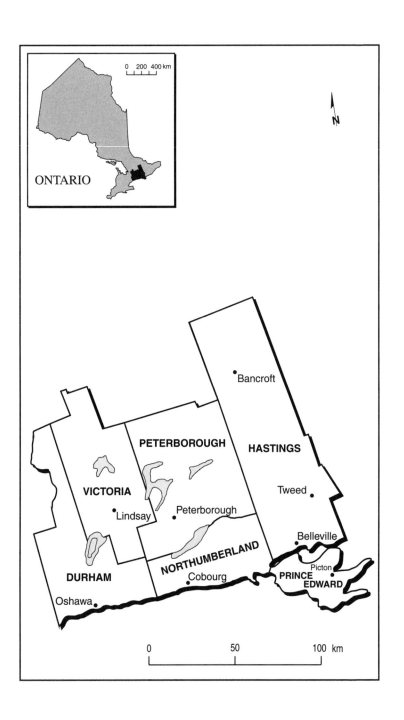

4 North Shore of Lake Ontario

Durham	Northumberland
Victoria	Hastings
Peterborough	Prince Edward

From the Lake Ontario shoreline, relatively narrow lowland sand and clay plains slope upward to the sand-and-gravel-based Oak Ridges moraine. Beyond it, a broad, rolling till plain is dominated by numerous drumlins and eskers. Stony soils, steep slopes, and wet swampy hollows are common in this plain. To the north and east of it lie rough, stony landscapes or limestone plains overlain by shallow soils. The granite rocks of the Canadian Shield form highlands across the northern and northeastern portions of the counties in the region. Along the southern edge of the shield, numerous finger-like lakes and connecting waterways create the Kawartha Lakes system.

The entire area lies within the Great Lakes–St Lawrence Forest Region. Natural woodlands contain a broad mixture of both coniferous and deciduous trees, including White Pine, Eastern Hemlock, Sugar and Red Maples, Red Oak, White Cedar, and Large-toothed Aspen. On the higher elevations of the shield, Eastern Hemlock, White Spruce, and Balsam Fir become more evident in the mixed woodlands. Elements of the Carolinian Forest zone are largely confined to the Lake Ontario shoreline.

The greatest population density of humans is found close to the lakeshore, particularly near Toronto. Farming activity occurs mainly in the southern areas of the region, while the numerous lakes and woodlands farther north support lumbering and tourism.

REGIONAL MUNICIPALITY OF DURHAM

> On the night of the 12th of November, 1833, my father ... was salmon-spearing in a boat in the creek, at its outlet into Lake Ontario, now Port Oshawa ... From out of an intensely dark November night, globes of fire as big as goose eggs began falling all around his boat. These balls continued to fall until my father, becoming frightened, went home ... Happening to glance out of the window [before daybreak next morning], to his intense amazement he saw ... the whole sky filled with shooting stars ... Gradually the fire-balls grew less and less, and, with the day, ceased altogether. (Thomas Conant [1842–1905])

Located east of Toronto and extending from Lake Simcoe south to Lake Ontario, the Regional Municipality of Durham contains four main topographical features. 1) The Lake Ontario slope makes up the southern, most populated portion. 2) Immediately inland lies the Oak Ridges moraine, an undulating sandy ridge that forms a watershed divide. The waterways that drain to the north eventually flow into the Severn or Trent rivers, and those that drain south flow into Lake Ontario. 3) From the moraine, the land dips northward to a flat plain marked by slow-moving creeks bordered by wide wetlands. Most prominent of these are Pefferlaw Brook and Beaverton River, which flow into Lake Simcoe, and Nonquon River, which empties into Lake Scugog. 4) The fourth feature, Lake Scugog, a highly productive area for wildlife, was created by damming in 1832. It is known for its extensive wetlands with distinctly northern characteristics.

The natural wooded areas in Durham are typical of the mature American Beech–Sugar Maple forests of the Great Lakes–St Lawrence Forest Region. Extensive marshes along the Lake Ontario shore are home to many species of water and marsh birds and are important migration stopover sites. The wildlife of Durham is transitional in nature, species that typically occupy more northern habitats, such as Winter Wren and White-throated Sparrow, occurring here along with southerners such as Northern Cardinal and Field Sparrow.

Nonquon Provincial Wildlife Area

White Cedar, Trembling Aspen, and Balsam Poplar dominate the woodlands along the Nonquon River. Marshy wetlands in the valley are home to Yellow-spotted Salamander, Great Blue Heron, American and Least Bitterns, and various species of dabbling ducks. The 1,100-ha site also supports upland species, such as Ruffed Grouse, American Woodcock, Snowshoe Hare, and Eastern Cottontail.

DIRECTIONS. Located NW of Port Perry, SE of jct of Hwys 12/7 & 47. Park on Scugog Conc Rd 11, E of Hwy 12/7.

Lake Scugog Marsh (Osler Tract)

This huge wetland is privately owned and accessible for viewing only along the causeways. South of the west causeway, a large bay and extensive cattail marsh are frequented by staging waterfowl and summering marsh birds, such as Least and American Bitterns, Common Moorhen, and Black Tern. Watch for Osprey and Common Loon. Stands of wild rice are found in the marsh. In sharp contrast, the vegetation along the east causeway consists of a northern-type bog and fen complex. Typical woody plants are Leatherleaf, Sweet Gale, Swamp Birch, and Bog Willow. Pitcher-plants and several orchid species are found. Mink Frog occurs here near the southern edge of its range.

DIRECTIONS. E of Port Perry Hwy 7A passes through large wetlands on both E & W sides of Scugog Island.

Oak Ridges Trail

See entry under Regional Municipality of York.

Durham Regional Forest

The main tract of regional forest is located in Uxbridge Township, where sandy moraine slopes were once heavily eroded. The area was reforested with Red, White, Scots, and Jack Pines beginning in the 1920s. These woodlands are now regenerating to hardwoods and White Pine, providing an excellent example of the transition from conifer plantation back to natural forest. Pockets of original deciduous woods also persist; these host spring wildflower displays of Red and White Trilliums, Large-flowered Bellwort, and other plants. Mammals of the dry, hilly uplands include White-tailed Deer, Northern Flying Squirrel, and Pygmy Shrew. In winter, finches and woodpeckers are evident in the forest. During summer, check open country to the south for Field, Grasshopper, and Clay-colored Sparrows, and for Eastern Bluebirds using roadside nest boxes. The forest and nearby conservation authority lands are traversed by hiking and cross-country ski trails.

DIRECTIONS. From Manchester on Hwy 12, go 10 km W on Reg Rd 21; go S on Conc Rd 7 to parking lot on E side at ranger station. For sparrows, continue S on Conc Rd 7 to just past forest; follow track E to communications tower. Stay on Conc Rd 7 S for bluebirds.

INFORMATION. MNR; Metro Toronto and Region Conservation Authority.

Claremont Conservation Area

Extensive stands of White Cedar grow here along the valley of Duffins Creek, with nearby slopes dominated by Red Oak, Sugar Maple, Black Cherry, and White Ash. Ferns grow in the shaded wetlands, and wildflowers proliferate on deciduous hillsides. The 160-ha site is a good spot to look for winter finches, especially Pine Grosbeak. Bohemian Waxwings are attracted to the hedge of Multiflora Rose just west of the main gate. Pileated Woodpecker and Wild Turkey (introduced) are residents of the area. Trails can be used summer and winter.

DIRECTIONS. On Hwy 7 drive 4 km E from Brougham; go 2 km N on Westney Rd (Reg Rd 31).

INFORMATION. Metro Toronto and Region Conservation Authority.

Herber Down Conservation Area

Herber Down, situated on the former shoreline of glacial Lake Iroquois, offers panoramic views. Particularly noteworthy is the steep Devils Den valley. Nature and cross-country ski trails lead through deciduous and mixed forests and through plantations of Red and Scots Pines. Wildflowers flourish; spring offers the best variety.

DIRECTIONS. 1) From Whitby go 10 km N on Hwy 12 (Exit 410

from Hwy 401); turn left on Hwy 7 & go 3.3 km; turn S on Coronation Rd & go 1 km. 2) From Hwy 12 turn left on Taunton Rd (Reg Rd 4); go 2 km; turn N on country lane & go to S gate.
INFORMATION. Central Lake Ontario Conservation Authority.

Purple Woods Conservation Area

Purple Woods, a mature Maple Sugar woodland on the Oak Ridges moraine, overlooks Lake Ontario to the south and Lake Scugog to the north. The 238-ha property supports a lush show of wildflowers in spring, including Red and White Trilliums, Bloodroot, and Wild Ginger. The fields to the east illustrate scenic moraine topography and provide good habitat for Eastern Bluebirds and Grasshopper Sparrows. Clay-colored Sparrows occur in nearby conifer plantations. Whip-poor-wills call at dusk.
DIRECTIONS. From Oshawa, follow Simcoe St (Reg Rd 2) N for 13 km past Taunton Rd (Reg Rd 4); turn E & follow signs at Oshawa-Scugog Townline.
INFORMATION. Central Lake Ontario Conservation Authority.

Harmony Valley Conservation Area

Located on the shoreline of glacial Lake Iroquois, the 28-ha site contains two large, open areas separated by a wooded creek valley. This is a good spot to look for unusual overwintering birds.
DIRECTIONS. From Exit 419 on Hwy 401 at Oshawa, go N on Harmony Rd (Reg Rd 33) to Taunton Rd (Reg Rd 4); go E to Grandview St & S to parking lot.
INFORMATION. Central Lake Ontario Conservation Authority.

Enniskillen Conservation Area

White Cedars predominate along the bottomlands of Bowmanville Creek. On higher sites open parkland and mixed hardwood and conifer stands occur. Two small cattail ponds provide habitat for herpetofauna. Large numbers of American Crows roost here in winter. The 65-ha area can be visited year-round.
DIRECTIONS. From Bowmanville go N on Reg Rd 57 to Enniskillen; turn left on Reg Rd 3 (Conc Rd 8).
INFORMATION. Central Lake Ontario Conservation Authority.

Long Sault Conservation Area

Long Sault bears the rolling landscape typical of the Oak Ridges moraine. Mature mixed forest, dry open uplands, a White Cedar–Eastern Hemlock swamp, and reforested plantations of Red and Scots Pines are represented within the 286-ha tract. The dry uplands contain interesting southern flora, such as Hoary Vervain, Early Buttercup, and Tall White Cinquefoil. Flora with boreal affinities is also present. Birds summering in the area include Whip-poor-will, Eastern Bluebird, Pine Warbler, and Grasshopper Sparrow. This is one of the few areas in Durham where Eastern Smooth Green Snakes are found. Trails can be used all year.

DIRECTIONS. From Hwy 401 at Bowmanville, take Waverley Rd (Exit 431) to Reg Rd 57, go 13 km N; turn E on Reg Rd 20 (Darlington Conc Rd 9); go 3 & 4 km to 2 entrances on N side.

INFORMATION. Central Lake Ontario Conservation Authority.

Stephens Gulch Conservation Area

Trails meander through gently rolling terrain bordering this relatively undisturbed area along Soper Creek. White Cedar wetlands thrive in the bottomlands. Successional old fields, Scots Pine plantations, and remnants of the natural Sugar Maple–American Beech forest are found in the upland.

DIRECTIONS. From Reg Rd 4 (Taunton Rd) N of Bowmanville go E to the 1st road E of Liberty St (Reg Rd 14); go S to 1st road on left; follow winding road to parking lot.

INFORMATION. Central Lake Ontario Conservation Authority.

North Pickering (Seaton) Hiking Trail

This 13-km-long trail passes through varied topography in the West Duffins Creek valley. Grassy meadows and creekside bluffs complement remnants of natural forest. Here, some ancient Sugar Maple and American Beech trees are 300–400 years old. Stands of Eastern Hemlock and of White Cedar, as well as various ferns, thrive in the valley. Among an abundance of small mammals are Smoky Shrew, Hairy-tailed Mole, Snowshoe Hare, and Porcupine.

DIRECTIONS. 1) From Pickering go N on Brock Rd (Reg Rd 1) to

Rossland Rd (Pickering Conc Rd 3), then W to parking lot on S at end of conc rd; trail is visible over hill. 2) N entrance is on Hwy 7, W of Altona Rd & E of Green River.

Altona Forest

Surrounded by development, the tract is a small natural oasis adjacent to Petticoat Creek. Heavily forested mature woodlands are dominated by White Cedar and Sugar Maple–Eastern Hemlock communities. White Pine, American Beech, Hop-hornbeam, and Black Ash also occur. A range of other habitats includes thickets, cattail marsh, and second-growth woods. The site offers good birding and also harbours a number of uncommon plants, such as Perfoliate Bellwort and Arrow-leaved Aster. Altona Forest is part of a natural corridor that permits movement of wildlife between the valleys of the Rouge River and Duffins Creek. Now under acquisition, the site will remain as undeveloped green space.

DIRECTIONS. From Finch Ave (Reg Rd 37) in Pickering, go 1.3 km S on Altona Rd (Reg Rd 27). Enter via informal trails on E side. Boundaries of public land are poorly marked; avoid trespassing. Roadside parking is limited. Altona Rd is on bus route.

INFORMATION. Metro Toronto and Region Conservation Authority.

Petticoat Creek Conservation Area

This area encompasses 68 ha bordering the lakeshore eastward from the mouth of the Rouge River. Clifftops and semi-open, rolling landscape slope to a small cattail marsh at the mouth of Petticoat Creek. Sheltered woodlands attract spring migrants and frequently induce species such as American Robin and Brown Creeper to overwinter. The pine-bordered creek valley harbours a number of unusual plants. Resident mammals range from Porcupine and Water Shrew to Woodland Jumping Mouse. Map Turtle inhabits the wetlands, while Northern Brown Snake and Redbelly Snake hunt for food in the old fields.

DIRECTIONS. Take Exit 394S from Hwy 401 at Pickering; go 1.5 km S on White's Rd (Reg Rd 38).

INFORMATION. Metro Toronto and Region Conservation Authority.

Corner Marsh

Situated at the mouth of Duffins Creek, Corner Marsh contains extensive stands of cattails as well as a deciduous woodlot, hedgerows, open fields, and lakeshore. This is an excellent place for viewing migratory water birds and many species of shorebirds in late summer and autumn and, to a lesser degree, in spring. Merlins and Peregrine Falcons are occasionally observed chasing shorebirds. Check offshore for loons, grebes (including Red-necked Grebe), and waterfowl in spring and fall. Rarities regularly occur.

DIRECTIONS. S of Pickering village, from Bayly St, go S on Squire's Beach Rd (1 km E of Reg Rd 1) to pollution control plant. Go left on Jodrel Rd & left again at Montgomery Park to parking lot at N end of Frisco Rd.

Lynde Shores Conservation Area
(including Cranberry Marsh)

Trails and observation platforms at Cranberry Marsh provide access to one of the best locations in the region for viewing common and uncommon migratory birds in both spring and autumn. Numerous water birds stage in Cranberry Marsh or immediately offshore in Lake Ontario. The small woodlot south of the parking lot provides very good viewing for migratory and wintering passerines. In May, watch for Brant and, about May 24, for Whimbrel. Cattails dominate the marshes, but also note the presence of bur-reeds and a sedge meadow. The marsh is a good place for observing turtles. Plants such as Common Cocklebur and Sea Rocket colonize the open shoreline. White Pine, Eastern Hemlock, Red Oak, Hop-hornbeam, Sugar Maple, Red Ash, Basswood, and American Beech grow in the woodlots.

DIRECTIONS. From Exit 410 of Hwy 401 at Whitby take Brock St 0.5 km S to Victoria St; go 2.6 km W.

INFORMATION. Central Lake Ontario Conservation Authority.

Whitby Harbour

Among numerous ducks and gulls, check here for Glaucous, Iceland, and Lesser Black-backed Gulls in fall and winter. Hundreds of shorebirds feed on the mudflats near the mouth of Pringle Creek during autumn.

DIRECTIONS. From Hwy 401, take Brock St (Exit 410) S to lake.

Thickson's Woods

Thickson's Woods Heritage Foundation owns and protects this remnant of mature mixed forest bordering Lake Ontario. In addition to Black Cherry, Black Walnut, Butternut, Blue-beech, and Red Oak, the woodlot contains some spectacularly large, 150-year-old White Pines. Among northern species are Mountain Maple, Speckled Alder, Starflower, and Bunchberry. The lakeshore woodlot is an exceptional location for watching migratory passerines and, during fall migration, Monarch butterflies. Check adjacent Corbett Creek Marsh for water birds.

DIRECTIONS. From Exit 412 on Hwy 401 between Oshawa & Whitby, go 1.8 km S on Thickson Rd to waterfront trail; turn left for parking. Access woods just E of gate across trail.

Pumphouse Marsh

A small cattail marsh and adjacent damp meadows here are home to wetland plants such as Marsh Cinquefoil and Great Water Dock. Ducks can be observed migrating along the Lake Ontario shoreline. Sora, Virginia Rail, Black Tern, Green and Great Blue Herons, and Black-crowned Night-Heron summer in the area.

DIRECTIONS. From Hwy 401 at Oshawa take Exit 417S; go W on Bloor St, then follow Park Rd S to lake; turn E on Stone St & go to foot of Cedar St.

Oshawa Second Marsh and McLaughlin Bay Wildlife Reserve

Home to a wealth of wildlife species, the significant wetland at Second Marsh is an important staging area for migratory waterfowl, gulls, shorebirds, and songbirds. The 123-ha site is currently undergoing massive restoration. Trails traverse open cattail marsh, barrier beach, and wooded swampland. In October, check the woods for Northern Saw-whet and Long-eared Owls. Noteworthy beach plants include Sea Rocket, Seaside Spurge, and Strange Cinquefoil.

Immediately to the east, McLaughlin Bay Wildlife Reserve, a project of General Motors of Canada Ltd, protects 41 ha of gently rolling open meadow. Trails provide access to McLaughlin Bay, Lake Ontario, Second Marsh, and Darlington Provincial Park.

DIRECTIONS. From Hwy 401 take Exit 419: 1) if W-bound, go left at 1st stoplight (Bloor); at 2nd stoplight go left on Farewell; 2) if E-bound, take Harmony/Bloor exit S to Farewell. Go S on Farewell, then left on Colonel Sam Dr to: 1) W-side trail (Second Marsh Wildlife Area) just past sewage plant; 2) trail to pond & lookout at small pumping station; 3) E-side trail, observation platform, & trails to MBWR at W parking lot of GM hdqts.
INFORMATION. Friends of Second Marsh, 905-579-0411 ext 26.

Bowmanville Marshes

Port Darlington Marsh and West Marsh are located south of Bowmanville along Lake Ontario. These shallow cattail marshes host a variety of typical marsh birdlife, with concentrations of waterfowl, shorebirds, gulls, and herons during periods of migration. The West Marsh harbours a number of species of herpetofauna, including Blue-spotted Salamander and Bullfrog.
DIRECTIONS. For Port Darlington Marsh: take Liberty St S from Exit 432 on Hwy 401; follow signs to Port Darlington & go W on West Beach Rd. For West Marsh: 1) follow West Beach Rd & Cove Rd W from N end of Port Darlington Marsh; or 2) go S from Waverley Rd (Exit 431) off Hwy 401, then E on Cedar Crest Beach Rd.

VICTORIA COUNTY

> ... reminds me of [a feast] we saw devoured on the ice last spring. John had been observing the motions of an eagle, and, taking the telescope, saw it with its beak break through the ice, which must have been pretty thick, though softish, and afterwards with its talons hook on to a large muskinonge. We watched it for a long time enjoying its meal, whilst another eagle waited patiently to seize upon the remainder, when its companion should be satisfied, the smaller birds hovering round at a more respectful distance. (Sturgeon Lake, Verulam Township, late winter 1842, Anne Langton [1804–93], English settler)

Victoria County stretches from Muskoka and Haliburton in the north to Durham in the south. Peterborough County lies to the east and Simcoe County abuts along the northwest boundary.

At home along woodland waterways, the adaptable Raccoon also thrives in urban and agricultural habitats. (Dr H.G. Hedges)

Rattlesnake Point, an outlier of the Niagara Escarpment, rises 91 metres above the Milton-area countryside. (Michael Patrikeev)

At Websters Falls, near Dundas, Spencer Creek descends from a height of 21 metres over the Niagara Escarpment. (Dr H.G. Hedges)

The Luna Moth inhabits woodlands, where its larvae feed on deciduous trees. (P. Allen Woodliffe)

Active at night, the Eastern Milk Snake preys mainly on mice. (Dr H.G. Hedges)

The population of the Least Bittern, a nesting species in larger marshes, is declining because of habitat loss. (Jim Richards)

The Rouge River valley in Scarborough is regarded by some experts as the eastern edge of Ontario's Carolinian zone. (Doug van Hemessen)

Warm winters allow the Virginia Opossum, North America's only marsupial, to extend its range northward. (Mary E. Gartshore)

Prothonotary Warbler populations have fallen to precariously low levels in southern Ontario's slough forests. (P. Allen Woodliffe)

Open-grown oaks and tallgrass prairie predominate at Sandpits Savanna on Walpole Island. (P. Allen Woodliffe)

Tall Ironweed, a favourite of butterflies, flowers in remnant tallgrass prairies in southwestern Ontario. (P. Allen Woodliffe)

Although most katydids are green, the rare pink morph is encountered occasionally. (P. Allen Woodliffe)

One of Canada's rarest plants, the White Prairie Gentian grows in open savannas. (P. Allen Woodliffe)

Sandy, erosion-prone bluffs near Port Rowan contribute sediments to Long Point's inner bay. (Bill Caulfeild-Browne)

Fish Point forms the southernmost extremity of Pelee Island, where rare plants and animals flourish. (P. Allen Woodliffe)

The Sydenham River descends the Niagara Escarpment at Inglis Falls, just south of Owen Sound. (Dr H.G. Hedges)

Wave action along Flowerpot Island's limestone cliffs has sculpted rocky pillars known as flowerpots. (Bill Caulfeild-Browne)

Rare in Ontario, the Spotted Turtle resides in cool, shallow bodies of water. (Dr H.G. Hedges)

The Red Fox is found throughout Ontario. (P. Allen Woodliffe)

An insect eater, the Eastern Smooth Green Snake becomes almost invisible when it enters grassy habitats. (Michael Patrikeev)

The delicate, nodding flowers of Wild Columbine brighten woodlands in early summer. (P. Allen Woodliffe)

The White-tailed Deer population expanded northward in response to the opening up of the landscape by settlers. (P. Allen Woodliffe)

The fish-eating Osprey, common in the Kawartha Lakes, is making a comeback in Ontario. (Jim Richards)

Presqu'ile Provincial Park is home to an unusual combination of coniferous trees and wet meadows. (Jim Richards)

Duckweed and many grasslike species are abundant in the natural wetland at Oshawa Second Marsh. (Jim Richards)

Lush stands of American Ostrich Ferns border the creek in Peterborough's Jackson Park. (Doug van Hemessen)

The Northern Saw-whet Owl, a relatively common breeder in eastern Ontario, migrates south each fall. (P. Allen Woodliffe)

Ontario's Black Bears are extremely rare south of the Bruce Peninsula and the Canadian Shield. (FON library)

The colourful Wood Duck nests in tree cavities in wooded wetlands.
(P. Allen Woodliffe)

The Mourning Cloak is one of the most common and familiar butterflies
in Ontario. (Dr H.G. Hedges)

The La Cloche Mountains and the North Channel are visible from McLeans Mountain on Manitoulin Island. (Bill Caulfeild-Browne)

In Bunchberry, four white petal-like bracts surround a cluster of tiny flowers. (Doug van Hemessen)

The sombre majesty of Algonquin Park's woodlands is accented by a dusting of snow. (Bill Caulfeild-Browne)

A rocky outcrop of the Canadian Shield showcases the autumn foliage near Rock Lake in Algonquin Park. (Bill Caulfeild-Browne)

Spruce Grouse are found in the Jack Pine and Black Spruce forests of northern Ontario. (Jim Richards)

The landscape near the Shagamu River in Polar Bear Provincial Park typifies the Hudson Bay Lowland. (P. Allen Woodliffe)

The most southerly population of Polar Bears in the world is found in Ontario's far north. (Jim Richards)

Once on Canada's endangered species list, American White Pelicans now thrive on Lake of the Woods. (FON library)

This tiny cove near the mouth of the Pic River lies within Pukaskwa National Park. (Bill Caulfeild-Browne)

The rushing waters of the Englehart River are a focal point of Kap-Kig-Iwan Provincial Park in Timiskaming. (FON library)

Moose inhabit woodlands and associated wetlands from the Canadian Shield north to the treeline. (Joseph Pearce)

Magnolia Warblers breed in mixed and coniferous forests throughout Ontario. (Jim Richards)

White Mountain-avens is found on beaches and stony ridges near Hudson and James bays. (P. Allen Woodliffe)

This Black Spruce and *Sphagnum* bog in Wabakimi Provincial Park is typical of many northern wetlands. (Ric Symmes)

The furry-tongued Arethusa orchid, also known as dragon-mouth, blooms in bogs and fens. (P. Allen Woodliffe)

The Banded Purple butterfly, whose larvae eat poplar and birch, is common in much of Ontario. (Dr H.G. Hedges)

Ontario's largest orchid, the Showy Lady's-slipper blossoms in bogs and wet open woodlands. (Mary E. Gartshore)

Originally a prairie resident, the Coyote now flourishes in open woodlands, farms, and settlements across Ontario. (Richmond Hill Naturalists)

The Bullfrog, the largest frog in Ontario, occupies shorelines along deep, permanent bodies of water. (Bill Caulfeild-Browne)

The cavity-nesting Eastern Bluebird is found primarily near poor or marginal farmland. (Jim Richards)

From south to north the main physiographic features of Victoria County are 1) the Oak Ridges moraine, 2) a clay plain to the north of Lake Scugog, 3) a broad, rolling till plain characterized by numerous drumlins, 4) limestone plains, and 5) the Canadian Shield. The Kawartha Lakes zigzag their way across the central part of the county. The southern part of the county is characterized by scattered, small communities and extensive agricultural undertakings. As one moves towards the central regions, numerous lakes and more heavily forested lands become evident. The north-central areas are reminiscent of shortgrass prairies with scattered limestone outcrops. The extreme northern parts of the county are typical of the heavily forested Canadian Shield.

Victoria County offers many possibilities for canoeing, including the Gull River and Burnt River routes, which lead southward towards the Trent-Severn Waterway.

Road to Ragged Rapids

This area is generally heavily forested with a mixture of White Spruce and Eastern Hemlock, interspersed with stands of White Pine and hardwoods. Several rare or unusual plants grow along the road, and many species of butterflies can be observed in large numbers. This is also a good area for seeing damselflies and dragonflies.

DIRECTIONS. From just E of village of Coopers Falls (Co Rd 6/52) where the District Municipality of Muskoka & Simcoe & Victoria counties meet, take dirt road running E along Black River through Victoria Co to Ragged Rapids or Victoria Bridge.

Kawartha Lakes

See entries under Pigeon Lake and Peterborough County.

Ganaraska Trail

See entry under Simcoe County.

Carden Alvar

Carden alvar, one of the best examples of its type in Ontario, lies within a vast tract of land north of Kirkfield and south of

Sebright and Uphill. The general area is typically composed of slowly rolling hills, small limestone outcrops, and numerous abandoned or marginally farmed fields. In early June roadside fields bloom with Long-plumed Purple Avens and Indian Paintbrush. Here, thin, drought-prone soils support a mix of alvar and prairie plants. Late summer brings a fine display of prairie flowers. Rare and unusual species abound, such as Small Beggar's-ticks, Downy Arrow-wood, Rock Sandwort, and Narrow-leaved New Jersey Tea. More colour and variety are added by Fragrant Sumac, Golden Corydalis, Tall White Cinquefoil, Early Buttercup, Barren Strawberry, False Pennyroyal, Snowberry, and large patches of Long-leaved Bluets. Several species of butterflies have been found, and Upland Sandpiper, Loggerhead Shrike, and other rare birds have been observed.

DIRECTIONS. Alvar is bounded on W & N by Hwy 503 & on E by Hwy 505. Most of land is privately owned & posted; view from roadside only.

– Sedge Marsh. An extensive sedge marsh straddling the road is frequented by Sedge Wren, Yellow Rail, and Black Tern during the summer. Moose, Black Bear, and White-tailed Deer all occur here.

DIRECTIONS. From Kirkfield go 5 km N on Hwy 503; where hwy veers sharply left, go right on dirt road; turn left almost immediately & go 3 km N. View from road.

Altberg Southern Shield Nature Reserve

The west side of this undeveloped 200-ha Federation of Ontario Naturalists' reserve occupies a limestone plain; the remainder is on the Canadian Shield. Mixed forests of Eastern Hemlock, Sugar Maple, White Birch, Red Oak, and Trembling Aspen dominate the shield section. The site also includes old fields, pond, pockets of marsh, White Cedar swamp, and a small limestone escarpment. Such habitat diversity brings forth abundant wildlife, ranging from Pink and Showy Lady's-slippers and Northern Beech Fern to Beaver, Moose, and White-tailed Deer. Golden-winged, Chestnut-sided, Black-throated Blue, and Black-throated Green Warblers are among breeding warblers. Adjacent to the reserve on the east side are extensive conifer plantations of the Victoria County Forest (Sommerville Tract); these contain cross-country ski trails.

DIRECTIONS. From Coboconk on Hwy 35 go N to Norland. Turn E on Hwy 503 & go about 10 km. Reserve is on S side past a cleared farm. Look for limestone outcrop, E of which is gravel drwy & gate. Follow overgrown trail through old fields.

Indian Point Provincial Park

A limestone plain with typical Great Lakes–St Lawrence mixed forest and abandoned farm fields underlies this undeveloped provincial park. There are over 100 species of trees, shrubs, and spring flowers and about 100 species of resident birds. Golden-winged Warbler and Barred Owls nest here, and northern woodpeckers are present in winter.

DIRECTIONS. From Coboconk on Hwy 35, take Grandy Ave 3.1 km W & then 2.5 km S. Turn left at tennis court road; park at court & walk.

Altberg Wetland Nature Reserve

This undeveloped Federation of Ontario Naturalists' reserve is part of a large wetland complex at the southwest corner of South Bay on Balsam Lake. Nestled in a gently rolling plain, the 39-ha property consists almost entirely of swamp forest. Near the road Balsam Poplar, Trembling Aspen, and Red-osier Dogwood dominate, while farther east, Silver Maple, Black and White Ashes, White Spruce, and Balsam Fir also occur.

DIRECTIONS. From Fenelon Falls, go W on Hwy 35A, Hwy 35, & Co Rd 8 to Glenarm. Go 3 km N on Co Rd 35; look for reserve on E side (0.5 km N of 1st road on W side). Access is through gated fields at N & S ends of property.

Pigeon Lake

The lake is noted for its extensive cattail marshes. Osprey, Great Blue Heron, Black and Common Terns, American Bittern, rails, and Marsh Wren all breed in the area.

DIRECTIONS. From Bobcaygeon head S by boat or canoe. Best areas are: 1) 6 km S along W shore, and 2) 5 km farther S past inlet from Buckhorn Lake on E side; Caspian Tern and Double-crested Cormorant are regular here.

Ken Reid Conservation Area

The 110-ha park is typified by open meadow, mixed forest, and extensive marshes. There is a very high density of active Osprey nests here. Boardwalks and all-season trails are provided.
DIRECTIONS. From Lindsay go 5 km N on Hwy 35; turn right on Kenrei Park Rd & go 3 km.
INFORMATION. Kawartha Region Conservation Authority.

Victoria County Forest (Emily Tract)

Mature stands of Red Pine and a mixed forest with a good display of spring wildflowers are found here. A prominent esker rises from surrounding glacial tills. There are about 100 migrant and resident bird species in this 78-ha parcel of land. Trails and streams wind through the area.
DIRECTIONS. From Omemee go 4 km E on Hwy 7 to Co Rd 10; go N to Co Rd 14, then W over Pigeon River 1 km to Emily Tract on S side.

Emily Provincial Park

Here rolling hills, damp White Cedar woodlands, and open meadows border the Pigeon River, part of the Kawartha Lakes system. A boardwalk leads through a cattail marsh onto an island of *Sphagnum* moss. View Osprey, Great Blue Heron, Muskrat, and other marsh species by canoe. Cross-country skiing is popular in winter.
DIRECTIONS. Located 5 km NE of Omemee on Co Rd 10; see prov hwy map.
INFORMATION. Emily Provincial Park, RR 4, Omemee, Ont, K0L 2W0, 705-799-5170.

Pigeon River Headwaters Conservation Area and Vicinity

Extensive coniferous forests border the upper reaches of the Pigeon River. Among the various features of interest, old-growth White Cedar, Eastern Hemlock, Sugar Maple, and Black Cherry trees are notable. The area is best explored by canoe, but trails are available in the 125-ha conservation area.
DIRECTIONS. From Hwy 35, go W on Hwy 7A. For canoeing: drive 1.5 km to where river crosses road. For CA: continue W

for another 1.5 km; turn left on McGill Rd; go 2.5 km to Manvers Conc Rd 7; turn left & go 1 km.
INFORMATION. Kawartha Region Conservation Authority.

Fleetwood Creek Natural Area

This 380-ha property lies in a beautiful bowl of old-growth forest typified by White Cedar, White Pine, and mixed hardwoods. There are extensive willow and alder stands near Fleetwood Creek. Wild Turkey has been successfully released in the area. Each fall the surrounding hills present an impressive display of colourful foliage. Located on a moraine, the site also contains other glacial features, such as kames and eskers.
DIRECTIONS. From Pontypool drive N on Hwy 35; turn right at Manvers Conc Rd 6. Go 4 km along rough road.
INFORMATION. Kawartha Region Conservation Authority.

PETERBOROUGH COUNTY

> A merry party we were that sallied forth that evening into the glorious starlight ... And truly never did I look upon a lovelier sight than the woods presented; there had been a heavy fall of snow the preceding day; owing to the extreme stillness of the air not a particle of it had been shaken from the trees. The evergreens were bending beneath their brilliant burden; every twig, every leaf, and spray was covered, and some of the weak saplings actually bowed down to the earth with the weight of snow, forming the most lovely and fanciful bowers and arcades across our path. (Douro Township, winter 1834, Catharine Parr Trail [1802–99], writer and botanist)

The Canadian Shield, where most of Peterborough County's forests occur, covers the northeastern portion of the county, roughly north of the Kawartha Lakes. Here shallow soils over granitic bedrock tend to be drought-prone, and White and Red Pines and White, Bur, and Red Oaks dominate. In the hollows, where soil has accumulated, drainage is often poor, and swamps, marshes, and other wet pockets are found. Groundcover plants, frequently evergreen, differ markedly from many of the woodland plants to the south. Some rarer plants of this part of the shield are Virginia Meadow-beauty, Three-toothed Cinquefoil, and various orchids.

Bordering the southern edge of the shield, the Dummer moraine dominates the landscape. Middle Ordovician limestone is close to the surface and often forms outcrops. The area is poor for farming but contains a good deal of undeveloped countryside comprising shortgrass fields that were formerly cleared as farmland. Lime-loving plants such as junipers and stonecrops are prominent.

The Kawartha Lakes, with the Trent Canal, extend by way of the Otonabee River system south through the city of Peterborough to Rice Lake, and continue as the Trent River to Trenton. Rice Lake, the southern boundary of the county, contains extensive cattail marshes that support good numbers of water birds.

In the southwestern part of the county between Rice Lake and the Kawartha Lakes, the land is covered with glacially deposited till, which makes it generally suitable for farming. Among the 4,000 egg-shaped hills of the Peterborough drumlin field are wetland areas and numerous woodlots with mixed forest remnants. Several eskers can be traced, notably a long one visible from Highway 7 just west of Norwood that extends eastward as well as southwest to Westwood.

Kawartha Lakes

The Kawartha Lakes, a chain of 14 long finger-like lakes stretching across Peterborough and Victoria counties, include rich cattail marshes that attract waterfowl, marsh birds, and other wetland wildlife. The south ends of Pigeon and Katchewanooka lakes, for instance, contain extensive marshland. Parts of Katchewanooka Lake and most of the Otonabee River north of Peterborough do not freeze so are among the few local places where waterfowl can be observed in winter. Diving ducks, such as Bufflehead, Common Goldeneye, Hooded Merganser, and Greater and Lesser Scaup, can be seen in early spring.

Pigeon Lake

See entry under Victoria County.

Petroglyphs Provincial Park

Petroglyphs Park contains one of the largest single concentrations of prehistoric Indian rock carvings in Canada. Native Canadians still honour the spiritual significance of this area.

Situated on the southern edge of the Canadian Shield, the 1,550-ha park features rugged shield terrain and the extensive vegetative cover of the Great Lakes–St Lawrence Forest Region. Large stands of Red and White Pines are interspersed with pockets of White Spruce, Eastern Hemlock, and mixed hardwoods such as White Birch, Sugar Maple, and Red Oak. Beaver dams have created a number of wetlands. The deep marl-based waters of McGinnis Lake shimmer a rich turquoise-blue in the summer sun. Species of interest include Fringed Polygala, Five-lined Skink, and Northern Water Snake. An extensive trail system traverses wetlands, coniferous and deciduous woodlands, and bare, rocky ridges where pink granite protrudes through softer limestone. In winter, cross-country skiers using the road into the park should watch for Bald and Golden Eagles, as well as Red Crossbills and resident Gray Jays.

DIRECTIONS. NE of Stony Lake, 11 km E of Woodview via Northey's Bay Rd; see prov hwy map.

INFORMATION. MNR.

– Peterborough Crown Game Preserve. Immediately to the west and north of Petroglyphs Park is this 22,000-ha game preserve, where White-tailed Deer are easily seen. Present, but less frequently observed, are their natural predators, Gray Wolves. The preserve is laced by numerous trails, open to both hikers and cross-country skiers.

DIRECTIONS. NE of Stony Lake, 11 km E of Woodview via Northey's Bay Rd; see prov hwy map.

INFORMATION. MNR.

Burleigh Falls Area

Just south of Eels Creek bridge a road-cut shows a sequence of geological events. The basic rock is metamorphic limestone (a form of marble), which is traversed by an intrusive dyke of black rock from deep inside the Earth. At a later date, heaving and cracking of the crust enabled shallower granitic magma to criss-cross this pattern. The 10-km stretch of Eels Creek downstream from Haultain provides a pleasant day's canoeing to Stony Lake (but exercise caution at falls and rapids).

DIRECTIONS. To see geological features, on Hwy 28 go 10.5 km N from Burleigh Falls to Haultain.

Selwyn Conservation Area

Here cross-country skiing and hiking trails lead through White Cedar woods along the shoreline of Chemong Lake. At the north end is a deciduous woodland on a point, where typical hardwood bird species, such as nuthatches, Brown Creeper, and woodpeckers, may be found. The property contains 29 ha.

DIRECTIONS. From Peterborough go 8 km N on Hwy 28, then 8 km N on Hwy 507 to Selwyn. Go 1.5 km W on Smith Conc Rd 12; follow signs.

INFORMATION. Otonabee Region Conservation Authority.

Warsaw Caves Conservation Area

Ten thousand years ago the Indian River spillway drained rushing meltwaters from glacial Lake Algonquin to glacial Lake Iroquois. Underground fissures were created after a massive prehistoric cave-in of undermined slabs of limestone. Today, exploration of the caves is difficult and dirty, and requires a flashlight. Many of them are small, and overhanging rock can make access a problem. Other geological features include an underground stream, fossils, limestone pavement, large potholes (kettles), an impressive river gorge, and a view of the Dummer moraine. Limestone-loving ferns grow in the White Cedar woodlands and relict prairie plants, such as Indian Paintbrush, are found on an alvar. Trails through the 224-ha tract can be used all year.

DIRECTIONS. From Warsaw go 3.5 km N on Co Rd 4.

INFORMATION. Otonabee Region Conservation Authority.

Peterborough and Area

– **Little Lake.** A wide part of the Otonabee River, Little Lake lies in the city south of the central business district. Good views can be had of migrating waterfowl, especially diving ducks and grebes.

DIRECTIONS. For best viewing, from S end of downtown go E along shore to well-treed cemetery.

– **Jackson Park and Lily Lake Area.** Walk along the Jackson Park trail west through the old White Pines (look for Blackburnian Warbler) and across the concrete bridge over Jackson

Creek. Turn left along the old railway right-of-way; follow the creek for several kilometres through varied habitat, or take detours along footpaths. This area can be good for watching birds any time of year; the shorter trail along the southern bank is wilder. The flat rocks in the creekbed hold a good variety of stream life, such as freshwater sponges. About 3 km along the railway track is Lily Lake, a partly hidden marlpit, which can be an excellent birding area. The lake is clearly visible from the small bridge over the creek.

DIRECTIONS. From jct of Parkhill Rd & Water St, go 1.6 km W to Jackson Park gate on right opp Monaghan Rd.

– Mark S. Burnham Provincial Park. This 43-ha old-growth woodland sits on the side of a drumlin. It is noted for its many large specimens of native trees, such as Sugar Maple, American Beech, Red and White Oaks, White Pine, and Eastern Hemlock. There is a fine spring wildflower display. An all-season trail traverses much of the park, but misses the swampy area on the west side.

DIRECTIONS. On Hwy 7 just E of jct with Television Rd (Co Rd 30); see prov hwy map.

INFORMATION. MNR.

– Cavan Swamp. A remnant of a glacial lake, this large swamp supports a wet mixed woodland of Trembling Aspen, Black Ash, White Cedar, and White Birch. Unusual shrubs include Swamp Birch, Mountain Holly, and Highbush Cranberry. The swamp is noted for its numerous orchids and other rare plants. A small northern bog is located in one corner. Muskrat, Beaver, White-tailed Deer, waterfowl, marsh birds, and songbirds are all common. Most of the tract is privately owned; contact ORCA for information on access.

DIRECTIONS. Go W on Sherbrooke St (Co Rd 9) 2 km past jct with Hwy 7A.

INFORMATION. Otonabee Region Conservation Authority.

Serpent Mounds Provincial Park

Stately forests of Red and White Oaks border the shores of Rice Lake here. Great Blue Herons feed in the shallow waters, and waterfowl stop during migration. Two large drumlins occur on the 28-ha site. Located at the tip of a small peninsula, the burial mounds were built 2,000 years ago by Hopewellian Indians. The park provides canoe access to the extensive cattail marshes at the mouth of the Indian River. Trails can be used all year.

DIRECTIONS. On N shore of Rice Lake at S end of Co Rd 34; see prov hwy map.

INFORMATION. Serpent Mounds Provincial Park, RR 3, Keene, Ont, K0L 2G0, 705-295-6879.

NORTHUMBERLAND COUNTY

> I was working in a field close to the woods when I heard something falling repeatedly from a large tree and I crossed the fence to investigate and found that there was a large butternut tree loaded with fruit and the squirrels were up amongst the limbs cutting the nuts off and letting them fall to the ground. I picked up over a bushel and piled them at the base of the tree and went back to my work. After supper, I took a large bag and went back to get my nuts, but behold, they were all gone. At first I thought some person must have stolen them, but I found out later that the squirrels had quietly carried them off. (Seymour Township, late summer 1850, John Macoun [1831–1920], naturalist)

Sandwiched between Lake Ontario to the south and Rice Lake to the north, Northumberland County is characterized by sand and clay plains close to the Lake Ontario shoreline and in the lower Trent River drainage area. The eastern terminus of the Oak Ridges moraine lies south of Rice Lake. Numerous drumlins occur throughout the county. Farming activities and population centres are most prominent near Lake Ontario. Some Carolinian species can be found among the mixed coniferous and deciduous woodlands.

Oak Ridges Trail

See entry under Regional Municipality of York.

Ganaraska Trail

See entry under Simcoe County.

Ganaraska Forest Conservation Area

This 4,500-ha tract on the Oak Ridges moraine results from a reforestation and land reclamation program begun in the 1930s. The intent was to stabilize eroding soils, prevent downstream flooding, and protect the source area of numerous streams, including the Ganaraska River. About half of the forest consists of conifer plantation, predominantly Red Pine. The remainder is a more natural mixed woodland, containing species such as maple, oak, cherry, Eastern Hemlock, and birch. White Cedar grows along stream valleys. Wild Turkeys were reintroduced into the area in the 1980s. A good selection of woodland birds is present, with Clay-colored Sparrows in young pines. Look for Ruffed Grouse, owls, and White-tailed Deer. The forest includes numerous trails (open year-round), several prominent hilltop lookouts, and the Ganaraska Forest Centre. Fall colour peaks between late September and mid October.

DIRECTIONS. To reach Forest Centre: 1) take Exit 436 from Hwy 401 at Newcastle; go N on Hwy 115 to Reg Rd 9 at Kirby; go E to Northumberland-Durham boundary; turn N on paved road & go 3 km; 2) take Exit 461 from Hwy 401 at Port Hope; go N on Hwy 2, then N on Co Rd 10 to Garden Hill; take Co Rd 9 (Ganaraska Rd) W to Northumberland-Durham boundary; turn N on paved road & go 3 km.

INFORMATION. Ganaraska Forest Centre, RR 1, Campbellcroft, Ont, L0A 1B0, 905-797-2721.

Harwood Area

Harwood Marsh is located on the south shore of Rice Lake. South of Harwood, open, rolling fields of former farmland have been reforested as commercial Christmas-tree farms and pine plantations. The area is excellent for viewing Eastern Bluebirds and Clay-colored and Grasshopper Sparrows.

DIRECTIONS. For Clay-colored Sparrows: from jct of Co Rd 9 (Ganaraska Rd) & Co Rd 18 SW of Harwood, go S on Co Rd 18 to Beaver Creek Rd; go E past 2 crossroads. Watch for Christmas trees on left.

Northumberland County Forest

When sandy soils forced the cessation of farming activity many years ago, reforestation followed. Now, even-aged stands of mature Red Pine cover most of this extensive area. A network of trails and fire roads (open for hiking and cross-country skiing) traverses the scenic hills and plantations. Coyotes and White-tailed Deer occur here.

DIRECTIONS. The forest borders Hwy 45 between Baltimore and Fenella, 14–19 km NE of Cobourg.

Peter's Woods Provincial Nature Reserve

This park is situated where the Peterborough drumlin field abuts the Oak Ridges moraine. The most significant feature of the 33-ha reserve is a magnificent old-growth forest of Sugar Maple, American Beech, and White Pine. The uplands slope down to a small stream, bordered by a swamp of White Cedar, Balsam Fir, and Tamarack. Showy Orchis, Wild Sarsaparilla, Narrow-leaved Spring-beauty, Rattlesnake Fern, Maidenhair Fern, Round-lobed Hepatica, Fringed Polygala, and many trillium mutants flourish on the forest floor. Woodlands and grassy meadows are frequented by Eastern Bluebird, Wood Thrush, Indigo Bunting, Northern Oriole, Great Horned Owl, and Northern Harrier. Look for Raccoon, Snowshoe Hare, Red Squirrel, Eastern Chipmunk, and Porcupine. The park is open to foot traffic in winter.

DIRECTIONS. From Exit 487 on Hwy 401 at Grafton, go N on Co Rd 23 to Centreton. Continue N on McDonald Rd exactly 5 km to entrance on E.

INFORMATION. MNR.

Goodrich-Loomis Conservation Area

Much of this large area consists of open old fields with scattered Red Pine plantations. Other habitats represented include aquatic communities, mature American Beech–Sugar Maple forest, and White Cedar lowland. The 208-ha conservation area is rich in its variety of flora and fauna. Prairie Buttercup and Beaver are present. Look for Eastern Bluebird, Rufous-sided Towhee, Black-billed Cuckoo, and Cooper's Hawk. The area is good for hawk viewing during migration. The landscape exhibits features of erosion and deposition moulded by the glaciers. Codrington esker, the most notable of these, forms the northern boundary of the conservation area. Cold Creek, the main water route of the region, passes through the property. The extensive trail system can be used all year.

DIRECTIONS. From Brighton, go 12.6 km N on Hwy 30 to jct with Co Rd 28; turn W on 7th Line of Brighton & go 5.4 km.

INFORMATION. Lower Trent Region Conservation Authority.

Port Hope

– Ganaraska River Fishway. Rainbow and Brown Trout and salmon can be seen here. Salmon spawn in mid April.

DIRECTIONS. Take Hwy 28 N to traffic lights S of Hwy 401; go W on Molson St to river. Fish ladder is at Corbett's Dam, N of bridge.

– Harbour. Look for waterfowl and gulls in winter. Most of the common wintering ducks can be found here. Harlequin Duck is occasional. Snowy Owl and Glaucous and Iceland Gulls are regular winter visitors.

– Lake Street Trail. This walking trail from the east end of Port Hope to the mouth of Gage Creek follows an embankment overlooking a stretch of Lake Ontario shoreline marsh.

DIRECTIONS. From downtown go E on Hwy 2 to Hope St; go S towards lake, then E along lakeshore.

Carr's Marsh Conservation Area

Located on the shores of Lake Ontario, this significant wetland is rich in waterfowl, shorebirds, amphibians, and wetland plants.

DIRECTIONS. From Hwy 2 between Port Hope & Cobourg, go S on Carr's Rd to lake.

INFORMATION. Ganaraska Region Conservation Authority.

Cobourg Harbour

Cobourg Harbour can be good for observing wintering and migrant ducks and gulls; October to April is best. A few migrant shorebirds occur along the west side. From the east pier there is excellent viewing of the harbour, the beach, and the lake to the east. Gulls loiter here and loons occur in migration. Further lake views are possible from the foot of D'Arcy Street, where flat rocks contain fossils of the Ordovician Period. Gulls and waterfowl also loiter here; shorebirds are possible; and Red-necked Grebe may sometimes be seen in early April.

DIRECTIONS. 1) From Exit 474 on Hwy 401, go S on Division St (Hwy 45) to E pier. 2) W side of hbr is accessed by pedestrian walk or from foot of Hibernia St, 3 blocks W of Division. 3) Foot of D'Arcy St is 5 blocks E of Division.

Lakeshore East from Wicklow

The road along Lake Ontario south of Wicklow offers birding possibilities. From Wicklow, turn south on Wicklow Beach Road. Drive to the lake, then eastward along the shore. Loons and grebes stage offshore here during migration. The wet woods of Haldimand Conservation Area to the north attract migrants. Ponds to the east, where the road curves away from the shoreline, attract dabbling ducks and other water birds.

Presqu'ile Provincial Park

This 10-km-long peninsula jutting into Lake Ontario is a 930-ha oasis of exceptional fauna and flora. The varied shore and near-shore habitats contain over 700 species of plants, including numerous rarities. Presqu'ile is highly rated as a birding destination. Like many peninsulas, it serves as a migrant trap for songbirds. Waterfowl, other water birds, and shorebirds migrate through in large numbers. Rarities show up regularly. On occasion, adverse weather causes major groundings, involving species such as Whimbrel, Dunlin, and Gray-cheeked and Swainson's Thrushes. The park also supports a high number of nesting species. The best birding is found at Owen Point, the natural beach area, the lighthouse, Presqu'ile Bay, the Calf Pasture, and the marsh boardwalk.

Among the park's amenities are trails, a boardwalk, a viewing tower, an interpretive program, a visitor centre, a bookstore, and a bird sightings board. Trails are open for cross-country skiing in winter.

Geology. Presqu'ile's bedrock is Middle Ordovician limestone, deposited about 450 million years ago. Fossils are very common, especially snails, but there are also trilobites, cephalopods, brachiopods, and crinoids.

Habitats. An example of a landform known as a tombolo, the peninsula was formed at the end of the last Ice Age when a limestone island became joined to the mainland by a broad sandbar. From west to east, the tombolo consists of a wide sandy beach, a succession of low foredune ridges, a wet panne area, high backdunes, and a series of recurved sandbars extending into a large marsh. This is one of the largest and most complex tombolos on the Great Lakes; its sandy landscapes are dynamic and undergo frequent changes.

Marsh and Bar Complex. The most extensive habitat in the park is a relatively pristine 236-ha marsh. This serves as a major spring staging area for waterfowl; up to 40,000 birds of 25 species, mostly diving ducks, migrate through. Best viewing times are late March and early April. This is a good site for listening on spring evenings for the calls of rails, American and Least Bitterns, Common Snipe, American Woodcock, and various frogs. Herpetofauna are an important element of the wildlife, 23 species having been reported. The recurved sandbars projecting into the marsh support a coniferous forest; here plants with northern affinities, such as One-flowered Pyrola, may be found.

Woodlands. Presqu'ile lies in a transition area between the Carolinian and the Great Lakes–St Lawrence forest regions. Striped Maple, at its southern limit, is a common understorey tree; in fact, the park boasts the largest provincial example, which has a 27-cm diameter. Stands of Yellow Birch, Eastern Hemlock, and Sugar Maple grow in a mature woodlot. Of special note are an abundance of ferns (25 species) and the presence of plants typical of the Atlantic coastal plain, such as Tubercled Orchid.

Islands. Gull and High Bluff islands, located just offshore, supply nesting habitat for colonial water birds. Although the islands are off limits from March 10 to September 10, the birds may be readily viewed from the mainland. By far the most prolific species is the Ring-billed Gull, with about 70,000 nests. Other nesting species include Double-crested Cormorant, Caspian and Common Terns, Black-crowned Night-Heron, and Great Black-backed and Herring Gulls. In November, two rarities may appear: Purple Sandpipers foraging along the shore-line and King Eiders swimming just offshore.

Old Fields. Field wildflowers attract a large variety of butter-flies, particularly Monarchs. In late August and September, these insects concentrate on the peninsula during their fall migration.

Pannes. August and September are a good time to explore the pannes, a low, seasonally flooded area with calcareous soil and specialized plants. Presqu'ile has the best example of panne vegetation on Lake Ontario. Characteristic species include False Dragonhead, Grass-of-Parnassus, Kalm's Lobelia, three species of ladies'-tresses, two species of gentians, a hybrid horsetail, Small-flowered Gerardia, and Low Nut-rush. Paths permit visi-tor access to this highly sensitive habitat.

DIRECTIONS. Located S of Brighton; see prov hwy map.

INFORMATION. Presqu'ile Provincial Park, RR 4, Brighton, Ont, K0K 1H0, 613-475-2204.

HASTINGS COUNTY

> This Oakhill pond is a small, clear, and very deep lake, on the sum-mit of a high hill ... The waters are intensely blue, the back-ground is filled up with groves of dark pine, while the woods in front are composed of the dwarf oaks and firs ... interspersed with low bushes ... [From the Oakhills] you look down upon an immense forest, whose tree-tops, moved by the wind, cause it to undulate like a green ocean ... The last time I gazed from the top of this hill a thunder-storm was frowning over the woods, and the dense black clouds gave an awful grandeur to the noble picture. (Near the vil-lage of Rawdon, 1840s, Susanna Moodie [1803–85], writer)

Hastings is one of three physiographically diverse eastern Ontario counties (the others being Lennox and Addington, and Frontenac) that stretch from Lake Ontario all the way inland to the Madawaska-Algonquin Highlands.

The southern third of the county is underlain by limestone. Near the Bay of Quinte, the soil is shallow and lands formerly cleared for pasture or agriculture are regenerating to Red Cedar. White Cedar is common in lowlands. Northward, where the eastern ends of the Oak Ridges moraine and the Peterborough drumlin field terminate in the county, the land becomes hilly, soils become deeper, and the forested uplands are dominated by Red and White Oaks and Sugar Maple. Farther north, a band of the Dummer moraine crosses the county. Its characteristically stony, shallow soils support extensive mixed forests of Balsam Fir, White Cedar, White Spruce, White Birch, and Trembling Aspen, as well as occasional tracts of hardwoods, dominated by Sugar Maple.

Near Highway 7, the bedrock changes abruptly to the granites of the Canadian Shield. The northern two-thirds of the county are underlain by the shield. Here the vegetation gradually becomes more boreal as one continues northward, primarily in response to the increased elevation.

Lake St Peter Provincial Park

Located in rugged shield country near the northern edge of the county, this 478-ha park lies just south of Algonquin Park. Immature forests of White Birch and White Pine have developed here following logging and fire. Woodland trails lead to a small kettle lake and a lookout. Watch for glacial erratics and a marsh with abundant birdlife.

DIRECTIONS. Located 13 km N of Maynooth on Hwy 127; see prov hwy map.

INFORMATION. MNR.

Bancroft Area Rockhounding

Bancroft and the northern part of Hastings County are popular with rockhounds because of the wide array of semiprecious gems and other minerals that are present in the area. Up to 300 kinds of minerals have been found, at sites ranging from old mining facilities to roadside rock outcrops. The region's woodlands are ablaze with reds and golds in late September and early October.

INFORMATION. Bancroft and District Chamber of Commerce, Box 539, Bancroft, Ont, K0L 1C0, 613-332-1513.

The Gut Conservation Area

At this little-known park, the scenic Crowe River makes a right-angled turn over several small waterfalls and pours through a straight-sided, 15-m-deep gorge. At the far end, it reverses its turn and continues south. Formed by a natural fault in a basalt lava ridge, the gorge is especially worth visiting during spring runoff. Northwoods plants, including Trailing Arbutus, grow in the area, and Common Ravens nest in the gut. The property contains 162 ha.

DIRECTIONS. From jct of Hwy 504 & Co Rd 46 at Lasswade in NE Peterborough Co, go 6.5 km E on gravel road. Watch for signs.

INFORMATION. Crowe Valley Conservation Authority.

Callaghan's Rapids Conservation Area

This conservation area is largely covered by a relatively mature White Spruce–White Birch–Trembling Aspen–White Cedar–Balsam Fir forest which is representative of the shallowly soiled Dummer moraine. The property spans the Crowe River, which flows across flat limestone and drops over two series of rapids. Geological features include karst topography, ranging from shallow grooves and deeply fissured rock to underground streams and caves. Seepage areas along the shoreline support Closed Gentian and Turtlehead. Cooper's Milk-vetch and Climbing Fumitory occur in the forests. Gulls frequent the rapids. Open-water areas in and below the rapids should be checked for waterfowl from late fall through spring. Three small parking areas allow access to the west side of the river; a rough trail follows the shoreline, but at lower water levels it is easier to walk on the dry edge of the riverbed.

DIRECTIONS. From stoplights in Marmora, go 3.8 km W on Hwy 7, then 3 km S on Tiffin Rd to T-jct, then 0.8 km E to entrance.

INFORMATION. Crowe Valley Conservation Authority.

O'Hara Mill Conservation Area

This 34-ha conservation area combines human and natural history. In addition to restored mill buildings and related artifacts, there is a surprising diversity of habitats, including marsh and open-water wetland (in the millpond), mixed lowland forest, and upland Sugar Maple–Basswood–Hop-hornbeam–White Ash forest. A scenic stream flows over limestone bedrock into and out of the millpond. The upland forest has a rich ephemeral

flora in spring. Two trails access the natural parts of the property.
DIRECTIONS. From jct of Hwys 62 & 7 in Madoc, go 1.4 km W to O'Hara Rd, then 1.8 km N, then 1.8 km W to entrance.
INFORMATION. Moira River Conservation Authority.

Price Conservation Area

Here the Skootamatta River falls quickly towards its confluence with the Moira River. Within the falls area, when the water is low, Riverweed can be seen. This rare plant uses fleshy holdfasts to anchor itself tenaciously to rocks in waterfalls and rapids. As Riverweed is highly sensitive to pollution, its presence indicates a healthy aquatic ecosystem.
DIRECTIONS. Located on S side of Hwy 7 just W of jct of Hwy 37 at Actinolite.
INFORMATION. Moira River Conservation Authority.

Colonel Roscoe Vanderwater Conservation Area

With 257 ha of land and over 4 km of frontage on the east shore of the Moira River, this conservation area clearly focuses on the river. River habitats associated with slow-moving water, including bulrush and wild rice beds, Swamp Loosestrife copses, and Silver Maple floodplain forests, as well as those associated with rapids, are represented. Land-based habitats include naturally regenerating old fields, Red Pine and White Spruce plantations, ash-poplar woods, White Cedar stands, and mixed forests. Spring and fall are probably the best seasons for birdwatching but late summer is a good time for observing the diverse shoreline flora. There are a number of trails, usable year-round. Poison-ivy is abundant in some areas.
DIRECTIONS. From Thomasburg, 25 km N of Belleville on Hwy 37, go 2.8 km E on Vanderwater Park Rd (Hungerford Conc Rd 4) to entrance on right, just E of bridge over Moira River.
INFORMATION. Moira River Conservation Authority.

Scuttle Holes

The Scuttle Holes is an area of karst topography on the east shore of the Moira River. The unusual rock formations were created by the collapse of limestone bedrock into underlying caves, which were and continue to be eroded by the river, especially during spring floods. In addition to the spectacular geological formations, a number of interesting plant species can be found here, including Common Hackberry (the dominant tree species) and several uncommon grasses, such as Hairy Wild-rye. Poison-ivy is abundant. There are informal trails but no facilities.

DIRECTIONS. From Exit 544 on Hwy 401 at Belleville, go 15 km N on Hwy 37 to Latta; turn right at main jct & go about 0.5 km to bridge on Moira River; cross bridge, immediately turn left onto Scuttlehole Rd; go 2.4 km (past housing developments) to small, unmarked parking area on left.

Plainfield Conservation Area

Serving as an outdoor education centre, this 138-ha conserva-tion area is also open to the public. Year-round trails lead to a diversity of habitats, including naturally regenerated old fields (mostly Red Cedar savanna), White Cedar forest, Sugar Maple–Large-toothed Aspen forest on a drumlin, and cedar-ash swamp forest. Even more interesting are the less-disturbed habitats associated with the Moira River: Silver Maple floodplain forest, extensive mats of Pickerelweed and Swamp Loosestrife, and submerged vegetation. In summer Wood Ducks and Mallards can be seen, while spring and fall seasons host a greater diver-sity of waterfowl.

DIRECTIONS. From Hwy 401 Exit 544 at Belleville, go 10 km N on Hwy 37 to Thrasher's Corners, then 1.9 km E on Thurlow Conc Rd 6 to small public parking lot on right; CA is on both sides of road.

INFORMATION. Moira River Conservation Authority.

King's Mill Conservation Area

At this site of a former mill on Hoards Creek, the old dam has been replaced by a more modern structure that maintains a wet-land upstream. The wetland contains Common Cattail–Soft-stem Bulrush marsh, open water, and Red Maple swamp forest habitats. Common wetland birds, including Great Blue Heron and Belted Kingfisher, occur. The conservation area offers few facilities.

DIRECTIONS. From Stirling, go 6 km N on Hwy 14, then 3.8 km W on Rawdon Conc Rd 5 to small parking area at dam on right, just before jog in road.
INFORMATION. Lower Trent Region Conservation Authority.

Sager Conservation Area

The Oak Hills, a large upland area underlain by sands and gravels, once formed an island in postglacial Lake Iroquois. The conservation area is located at the western end of the hills, which today mark the eastern limit of the Oak Ridges moraine. A viewing tower provides a tremendous view over the present Trent River valley and the hills of the Oak Ridges moraine to the west. The Oak Hills contain the most easterly known remnants of prairie in Ontario. Although the best sites are not in the conservation area, it is possible to see some prairie grasses, such as Big Bluestem, near the entrance.
DIRECTIONS. From Hwy 401 Exit 543 at Belleville, go 8.1 km N on Hwy 62 to Foxboro, then 4.3 km NW on Hwy 14, then 3.6 km W on Range Rd; turn right onto twp rd to entrance on immediate right.
INFORMATION. Lower Trent Region Conservation Authority.

PRINCE EDWARD COUNTY

> This county is celebrated for ... a curious lake situated near the banks on a high hill, some two hundred feet above the waters of the adjoining lake to the west, which lake on the hill is said to be almost fathomless in depth. How the water can remain so high, and is forced up above the great Lake Ontario, near it, is difficult to conjecture, for we all know water will find its level. It would seem to have some connection with the waters of the Georgian Bay, or some lake inland on the Ottawa. (Lake on the Mountain, Charles Durand [1811–1905], lawyer)

Prince Edward County, an irregularly shaped peninsula, occupies the northeast corner of Lake Ontario. Almost completely separated from the mainland by the Bay of Quinte, it sits on a low limestone plateau overlain by shallow soils. Several deep valleys cut across the plain, indenting the 500 km of shoreline with a number of long bays and inlets. On the western and southern shores, the land is low-lying. Here marshy lagoons have developed in the lee of barrier beaches crowned by sand dunes that rise to 25 m in height. The plain slopes gradually upward to the northeast, where coastal cliffs reach heights of 30 m or more. Elsewhere, 50 to 60 drumlins and one significant esker add variety to the topography of the county.

A good diversity of flora and fauna is supported by varied habitats; these include a number of mixed-farming operations, both deciduous and coniferous woodlots, and over 5,000 ha of significant cattail marshes. A favourable climate enables a number of species of southern affinity to survive here. Some of these are relicts of a prolonged warm period following the last glaciation, when plants of southern and western regions temporarily extended their ranges northward. Because of its location on Lake Ontario, the county is known for its significant bird migration.

Ameliasburgh Inlier

This interesting geological formation consists of a hill of Precambrian granitic rock that projects up through the surrounding limestone. Covering an area of about 5 ha, it protrudes through Palaeozoic deposits to an elevation of 100 m. Such areas are of ecological as well as geological interest because they are essentially islands of acidic-soil habitat. Elsewhere in the county, Precambrian granite is overlain by sedimentary rocks, at least 200 m thick just north of Consecon Lake and about 300 m just south of East Lake. North of the inlier, exposed Precambrian rock is not encountered again for 50 km. Although the inlier is located on private property, the granite knob extends out to the edge of the township road, from which it can be viewed.
DIRECTIONS. From Hwy 2 in Belleville, go 8 km S on Hwy 62; inlier is 0.8 km E of hwy on Centre Rd.

Huffs Island

The island, accessed by a causeway, is almost entirely surrounded by extensive cattail marshes, many of which are privately owned. Best public viewing is from the township road, which crosses over 1 km of Sawguin Marsh. Here, watch for Marsh Wren, Swamp Sparrow, and American and Least Bitterns.
DIRECTIONS. From Hwy 2 in Belleville, go 10 km S on Hwy 62;

turn E on Huffs Island Rd & go 3.5 km. For Sawguin Marsh, turn N. Continue straight for island.

Sandbanks Provincial Park

The park features one of the finest examples of active sand dune formation in southern Ontario. Some dunes here reach an impressive 25 m or more in height. Longshore currents flowing from west to east along Lake Ontario's north shore have created the largest freshwater sand dune and baymouth bar system in the world. Behind the sparsely vegetated and still growing fore-dunes lies a successsion of increasingly mature dune stages. Here can be found the varied vegetation communities associated with pannes, backdunes, and reforested sand ridges. Among the drifting sands of the outer beach and foredunes Sea Rocket, American Beach Grass, Tall Wormwood, Russian-thistle, and Sand Cherry gain a toehold. Sedges and rushes colonize the wet pannes, in concert with more colourful orchids, Purple Gerardia, Kalm's Lobelia, Silverweed, and twayblades. Heathy mats of Creeping Juniper and forests of White Cedar, Eastern Hemlock, Sugar Maple, White Spruce, Balsam Fir, and White, Scots, and Red Pines grow on stabilized dunes.

The diversity of flora at Sandbanks is enhanced by a number of prairie species. Hoary Puccoon, Sand Dropseed, and Butter-fly-weed, among others, are relicts of warmer times. Several Carolinian species occur in the park, including Twinleaf and White Trout-lily. Behind the dunes, marsh and lake habitats support good populations of amphibians, Largemouth and Small-mouth Bass, and other fish. The extensive shorelines and flooded pannes at Sandbanks attract large numbers of migrating shorebirds. Access to the 1,600-ha park is permitted year-round.

DIRECTIONS. Located 14 km SW of Picton; see prov hwy map.
INFORMATION. Sandbanks Provincial Park, RR 1, Picton, Ont, K0K 2T0, 613-393-3319.

Beaver Meadow Conservation Area

Three basic vegetation zones – swamp, deciduous woodlands, and open fields – highlight this 88-ha property. A control weir ensures a maximum of 52 ha of flooded land. The fields have been planted with various shrubs to attract wildlife; these include Caragana, Highbush Cranberry, and Pin Cherry. Trails provide excellent opportunities for seeing Wood Duck, other dabbling ducks, Osprey, and Great Blue Heron. During fall migration various species of shorebirds may be found in the mudflats. Herpetofauna and aquatic insects are abundant.

DIRECTIONS. From Picton go 6 km SW on Co Rd 10 (Lake St). Turn right on Co Rd 11 & drive 1.5 km.

INFORMATION. Prince Edward Region Conservation Authority.

MacAulay Mountain Conservation Area

This 172-ha site features a steep east–west escarpment rising 30–40 m above the local terrain. A woodlot contains many Carolinian species, including Butternut and a mature forest of Sugar Maple, Red Oak, and Shagbark Hickory. Trails, which are open year-round, introduce visitors to a variety of flora and fauna, including Northern Maidenhair Fern, Jack-in-the-pulpit, Ovenbird, Wood Thrush, Red Fox, and White-tailed Deer. A birdhouse display, memorial grove, and museum are adjacent.

DIRECTIONS. From Bridge St (Hwy 33) in Picton, go S on Union St (Co Rd 8); entrance is 0.5 km E of town limits.

INFORMATION. Prince Edward Region Conservation Authority.

Lake on the Mountain Provincial Park

The park's main feature is an unusual spring-fed turquoise lake perched on top of a limestone escarpment 60 m above the nearby waters of Lake Ontario. The lake is 1 km in diameter and occupies a sinkhole created when the roof of a large underground cavity called a doline collapsed. The cavern had originally been created over many centuries as water percolating through the bedrock gradually dissolved the carbonate in the layers of limestone. When the doline became so large that it could no longer support the weight of rock above it, the ceiling caved in and the resulting hole filled with water. The location offers a panoramic view of the Bay of Quinte, Glenora ferry, and the Adolphustown peninsula.

DIRECTIONS. Located 8 km E of Picton on Hwy 33; see prov hwy map.

INFORMATION. Lake on the Mountain Provincial Park, RR 1, Picton, Ont, K0K 2T0, 613-393-3319.

Little Bluff Conservation Area

The spectacular limestone bluff rising to over 18 m presents a sweeping view of Prince Edward Bay, Waupoos Island, and the North Marysburgh shoreline. An adjacent cobblestone beach and small cattail mash attract numerous species of birds, including waterfowl, bitterns, and Marsh Wren. The 28-ha site also contains the century-old ruins of a large grain storage bin and dock along the western shore of the bluff.

DIRECTIONS. Take Co Rd 8, then Co Rd 17 SE from Picton for 8 km; turn left on Co Rd 16; turn right on Co Rd 13, which, at South Bay, becomes Co Rd 9. Continue 5 km to CA.

INFORMATION. Prince Edward Region Conservation Authority.

Prince Edward Point National Wildlife Area (Long Point)

The 8-km-long peninsula is noted for the truly remarkable numbers of birds and variety of species that appear during migration. There is no other location on the Canadian side of Lake Ontario where densities and abundance of migrating songbirds are known to compare with those at Prince Edward Point. During migration, woodlots, hedgerows, and fields are literally hopping with passerines. The lakeshore provides excellent opportunities for sighting several species of gulls, many species of ducks, and skeins of Double-crested Cormorants. Black, Surf, and White-winged Scoters may appear, as well as Red-throated Loon and Horned and Red-necked Grebes. Ontario's first House Finch sighting was made here in 1972. Autumn hawk flights can be spectacular. In October Northern Saw-whet Owls pass through the point in large numbers. The area is noted for its numerous bird rarities.

Cattail marshes along the shore at the tip of the point are bordered by gravel berms pushed by winter ice into ledges on which Silverweed grows. Sea Rocket and Beach Pea inhabit the stonier beaches. The Prince Edward Point lighthouse, once known by Great Lakes mariners as the Red Onion, is located at the tip.

DIRECTIONS. Take Co Rd 8, then Co Rd 17 SE from Picton for 8 km; turn left on Co Rd 16; turn right on Co Rd 13, which, at South Bay, becomes Co Rd 9. Continue 18 km to point.

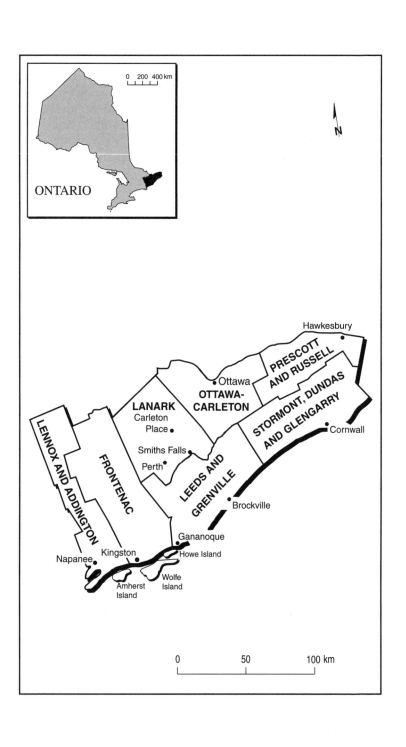

0   200   400 km

ONTARIO

N

Hawkesbury

PRESCOTT AND RUSSELL

Ottawa

OTTAWA-CARLETON

STORMONT, DUNDAS AND GLENGARRY

LANARK

Carleton Place

Cornwall

Smiths Falls

Perth

LEEDS AND GRENVILLE

LENNOX AND ADDINGTON

FRONTENAC

Brockville

Gananoque

Napanee

Kingston

Howe Island

Wolfe Island

Amherst Island

5 St Lawrence and Lower Ottawa River Valleys

Lennox and Addington
Frontenac
Leeds and Grenville
Stormont, Dundas, and Glengarry

Prescott and Russell
Ottawa-Carleton
Lanark

The Canadian Shield and its extension the Frontenac Axis sweep into this region from the northwest. One-billion-year-old Precambrian bedrock covers large portions of Lennox and Addington, Frontenac, and Lanark counties, crossing the St Lawrence River between Gananoque and Brockville in the United Counties of Leeds and Grenville. Typical of shield country in southern Ontario, this area is marked by numerous lakes and rivers and extensive tracts of woodland.

The lands adjacent to the shield in eastern Ontario are part of the Great Lakes–St Lawrence Lowland. South of the shield, the Napanee plain spreads across the southern portions of Lennox and Addington and Frontenac counties. The plain is characterized by shallow soils overlying limestone bedrock of Ordovician origin.

In the large lowland that covers eastern Ontario east of the shield, Ordovician limestone also forms the bedrock. Within it, 450-million-year-old fossil corals, bryozoans, gastropods, and cephalopods are common. Following the last glaciation, eastern Ontario was inundated by the chilly waters of the Champlain Sea, which supported marine animals such as Bowhead Whale, Ringed Seal, Longnose Sucker, and Arctic Saxicave clam. For a time the upper Great Lakes drained eastward into this sea, dropping enormous quantities of sands between the Pembroke area and the town of Alfred. Clays were deposited in the deeper parts of the sea. After the seawater retreated, these extensive deposits of marine clays and sands were left behind in the Ottawa valley. Today, evidence of ancient shorelines and deltas is visible near the inland limits of the former seabed.

The lowland once inundated by seawater now exhibits varying physiographic features. Immediately east of the shield a large, thin-soiled, poorly drained limestone plain extends across large areas of the former or present counties of Leeds, Grenville, Lanark, and Carleton. Bisected by the Rideau River, this area contains extensive patches of mixed coniferous and deciduous forest, wetlands, and marginal farmland. From the St Lawrence shore in eastern Grenville north and east to the Quebec border, undulating sedimentary ridges, glacial till, and clay plains form a divide between the St Lawrence and Ottawa drainage systems. The Ottawa valley is composed of sand plains and clay plains; drumlin fields and outcrops of sedimentary rock are prevalent. Throughout the area farming is mainly practised on the rich deposits of the Champlain Sea.

The area covered in this chapter falls within the Great Lakes–St Lawrence Forest Region. On the shield, Sugar Maple, American Beech, Yellow Birch, Red Maple, Eastern Hemlock, and White and Red Pines are major forest components. On the lowlands, the proportion of coniferous trees decreases. Many plant species reach their northern limits of distribution in the area, the Ottawa and Rideau valleys having served as important postglacial migration corridors.

Except for the major centres of Ottawa, Cornwall, Brockville, and Kingston, the region has a low density of human population and a primarily rural and wild landscape.

LENNOX AND ADDINGTON COUNTY

On the 4th of August [1869] we crossed from Mazinaw to Buckshot Lake. If any one would test his powers of endurance, let him shoulder his pack and try this 'portage,' much of which passes through swamps and beaver-meadow, where the mud and water are knee deep, and the mosquitos make their onset with a ferocity beyond description. (B.J. Harrington [1848–1907], mineralogist)

The long finger-like county of Lennox and Addington stretches inland from the shore of Lake Ontario to the Madawaska Highlands. Most of the county lies on the Canadian Shield, but the southernmost section is a relatively level limestone plain with shallow soils. Two rivers, the Salmon and the Napanee, have cut valleys across this stony plain.

In the southwestern corner of the county significant wetlands are located at Hay Bay on the Bay of Quinte. Here wintering (when there are leads of open water) and migrating waterfowl can be seen from many vantage points along adjoining roads. As one proceeds north of Highway 401, the soil depth becomes shallower, as evidenced by old fields with extensive Red Cedar cover and many areas of essentially alvar terrain where species such as Long-plumed Purple Avens can occasionally be found. Shield topography begins south of Highway 7 with scattered low wetland areas, bare rock, and mixed forest. North of Highway 7 the terrain becomes progressively more rugged and hilly.

Bon Echo Provincial Park

Bon Echo Rock (also called Mazinaw Rock), a spectacular geological feature known as a reverse thrust fault, stretches for approximately 2 km along the east shore of Mazinaw Lake. Here the massive granite-gneiss cliff towers vertically to a height of 125 m, while the waters below reach depths of 100 m. Over 250 native pictographs (rock paintings) adorn the cliff just above the waterline. Rare Prairie Warblers frequent the scrub Common Juniper and Red Oak above the cliff face.

Open year-round, the 6,500-ha park is well traversed by trails and canoe routes. The terrain is rugged and varied, with rock outcrops, scenic lookouts, shallow lakes, wetlands, and erratic boulders left by glaciers. Here at the meeting point of the Canadian Shield proper and its southern spur, the Frontenac Axis, there is a high diversity of flora and fauna and, from mid September to mid October, a fine show of fall colour. Ridges of mature American Beech, Sugar Maple, and Yellow Birch thrive not far from stands of White Pine, second-growth forests of poplar, White Birch, and Red Maple, and boggy lakes bordered by Black Spruce and Tamarack.

Unusual plants are numerous. Lance-leaved Violet and Yellow-eyed Grass grow at Joeperry Lake, while Smooth Cliffbrake clings to the Bon Echo cliff face and Green Alder overhangs the Mazinaw Lake shoreline. Cardinal-flower adds colour beside Bon Echo and other creeks, as do Bog Aster and Horned Bladderwort around bog lakes. Pinesap is found near Bon Echo Rock on the downslope to Kishkebus Lake, and Trailing Arbutus in upland pine-poplar woods. There is also an abundance of Yellow Clintonia, Round-leaved Pyrola, Starflower, and Jack-in-the-pulpit.

Woodland hawks, Turkey Vultures, and many forest songbirds, such as Veery, Wood Thrush, Scarlet Tanager, and Yellow-throated Vireo, occur in the park. Resident animals represent both northern and southern species – White-tailed Deer, Gray Squirrel, Black Bear, Moose, Gray Wolf, Fisher, River Otter, and Five-lined Skink, to name a few.

DIRECTIONS. Located about 30 km N of Kaladar on Hwy 41; see prov hwy map.

INFORMATION. Bon Echo Provincial Park, RR 1, Cloyne, Ont, K0H 1K0, 613-336-2228.

Skootamatta Lake

Walleye spawn April 10–20.

DIRECTIONS. From jct of Hwys 41 & 506 18 km N of Kaladar, continue 3 km N on Hwy 41; turn left & go 1 km; turn left on Sheldrake Lake Rd to causeway.

Kaladar Jack Pine Barrens

Unusual woodland vegetation here includes an essentially pure medium-aged Jack Pine forest on a granite outcrop ridge, far south of the normal range for this boreal species. Accompanying wildflowers, including Bearberry and Bastard Toadflax, are typical of northern Ontario. Among southern plants are Whorled Loosestrife and Shining Sumac. Uncommon elsewhere in the area, Field Sparrow, Rufous-sided Towhee (a southern species), and Yellow-rumped Warbler (a northern species) gravitate to this dry, hot site. At present there are no trails, and interior travel is difficult because of Beaver ponds.

DIRECTIONS. Site lies on S side of Hwy 7, 7 km W of Kaladar.

INFORMATION. MNR.

Sheffield Conservation Area

An interesting area for plants, herpetofauna, and birds, the site is situated on the Kaladar Ridges, a semi-bare undulating terrain of metamorphosed rocks. Lakes, marshes, and rock ridges provide habitat for a number of rare species, such as Five-lined Skink, Shining Sumac, and Indian Grass.

DIRECTIONS. Take Hwy 41 S from Kaladar for 11 km.
INFORMATION. Moira River Conservation Authority.

Camden Lake Provincial Wildlife Area

The shallow lake and marshy wetland attract waterfowl during migration (hunting is permitted in season). A trail, boardwalk, and observation tower overlooking the lake facilitate viewing. This is a pleasant, little-used area.

DIRECTIONS. From Exit 599 on Hwy 401 at Odessa go 22 km N on Co Rd 6 to Moscow; turn left & go 1.5 km; turn right & go 3 km N.
INFORMATION. MNR.

Parrott Bay Conservation Area

A shallow inlet of Lake Ontario, the area boasts wetland, woodland, and field habitats. Watch for Black-backed Woodpecker, Caspian Tern, songbirds in spring, and ducks in migration. Canoe access and good hiking and cross-country ski trails are provided.

DIRECTIONS. From Kingston follow Bath Rd (Hwy 33) W past Co Rd 6 to house number 5000 Bath Rd; park on right & follow trail N.

Amherst Island

The island is relatively flat and mostly used for mixed farming. Tilled fields, pasture, old fields, and small woodlots are characteristic. Excellent birding is possible by car and on foot along the roadsides. One road skirts the shoreline around most of the island; others, both east–west and north–south, offer a variety of habitat. Amherst Island is extensively used by wintering raptors, including Rough-legged and Red-tailed Hawks, American Kestrel, and the following owls: Snowy, Short-eared, Long-eared, and Northern Saw-whet. The numbers and diversity of these raptor species in any given winter are related to the size of the vole population and how accessible it is through snow and ice cover. All of the island is privately owned; please take care to avoid trespassing.

DIRECTIONS. Take ferry (fee) from Hwy 33 (Bath Rd) at Mill-haven.

FRONTENAC COUNTY

> I was amused by observing the various barks of Trees – the most deeply indented & light coloured White Ash, the rugged shag bark Hickory, the regular marked Iron wood, the perpendicular ribbed Cedar, the Bass wood, the varieties of black and White Oak, the Maple, Chestnut etc. the strong lines of the Pine, particularly the Norway, which is of a rich yellow brown & when cut approaches to a bright orange colour, among all this the smooth bark of the Beach looked as naked as a frog & had a very mean appearance amongst the rest of the Trees. (Gananoque to Kingston, February 28, 1795, Elizabeth Simcoe [1762?–1850], wife of lieutenant-governor)

Largely underlain by the rocks of the Canadian Shield, Frontenac County extends from the Madawaska Highlands to Lake Ontario. Within the county, Precambrian bedrock dips southward towards the St Lawrence, and shallow-soiled limestone plains meet the red granite outcroppings of the shield. Close to the river, elements of the oak–Shagbark Hickory forest typical of more southerly regions associate with Sugar and Red Maples, major components of the Great Lakes–St Lawrence mixed woodlands. Most of the Lake Ontario shore consists of limestone rock with low cliffs or pebbly beaches. The flat, open fields and small woodlots of Wolfe, Simcoe, and Howe islands lie on the limestone plain.

Schooner–Fortune Lakes Area

This area at the very northern edge of Frontenac County stretches north and east from Fortune Lake to Skead Creek, Round Schooner Lake, Long Schooner Lake, Pondlily Marsh, and

Camp Lake. The upland forest here is extensive and rugged, and represents one of the wildest parts of eastern Ontario. Dry woodlands of Red Maple, Red Oak, White and Red Pines, and Trembling Aspen grow on outcrop granite knolls and slopes, while Sugar Maple, American Beech, Eastern Hemlock, and Yellow Birch are found in the loamy valleys. An ancient White Cedar on the northeast shore of Fortune Lake is well over 300 years old. A colony of Smooth Cliffbrake grows on a cliff on Long Schooner Lake.

Pondlily Marsh bog complex, one of the larger wetlands in northern Frontenac County, is a fine place for viewing wildlife such as Moose. Northern aquatic species, including Water-marigold, are found along Mackie Creek. Other plants of interest are Cardinal-flower, Hooded Ladies'-tresses, Spiny-spored Quillwort, and a stand of Big Bluestem grass well beyond its usual range.

DIRECTIONS. Best accessed by canoe: from Hwy 506/509, go N on Mountain Rd at E outskirts of Plevna; follow signs about 20 km to Long Schooner Lake & launching area at end of road.

Palmerston Canonto Conservation Area

Here, a trail through an upland hardwood forest leads to the top of a high granitic hill on the north side of Palmerston and Canonto lakes. In season, displaying Red-shouldered Hawks can be seen from this lookout. There is a fine showing of fall colour in the vicinity of the 107-ha conservation area.

DIRECTIONS. From Ompah on Hwy 509, go 2 km E; turn N on Canonto Rd & follow CA signs 3.5 km to parking lot just across bridge.

INFORMATION. Mississippi Valley Conservation Authority.

Bon Echo Provincial Park

See entry under Lennox and Addington County.

Hungry Lake Barrens

This is one of the largest reasonably undisturbed granitic bedrock barrens in southern Ontario. Long, narrow wetlands with forests of Black Spruce, Balsam Fir, and White Cedar wind through the area. Virginia Chain Fern occurs in some of the bogs. The barrens are about half crown land and about half privately owned.

DIRECTIONS. 1) From flashing light on Hwy 7 that marks jct with Arden (S) & Henderson (N) roads, go 3.5 km N to small parking areas at S edge of large bog. 2) From aforementioned jct go 2.5 km N, then about 3 km E on Hungry Lake Rd to stop in midst of large block of public land.

INFORMATION. MNR.

Depot Lakes Conservation Area

Typical Precambrian Shield topography dominates the landscape, with shallow, stony soils and rugged outcrops ground by glaciers. Rocks include granite, gneisses, and schists. Some evidence remains of earlier logging activity and unsuccessful attempts at farming. Second, Third, and Fourth Depot lakes form a reservoir system designed to augment the low summer flow of the Napanee River. The vegetation here contains both hardwood and softwood species, such as poplar, White and Red Oaks, pine, and White Birch. Varied habitats in the 1,000-ha tract include dry woodlands, Beaver ponds, and wetlands. Among species of interest are Red-shouldered Hawk, Yellow-billed and Black-billed Cuckoos, Yellow-throated Vireo, Golden-winged Warbler, Five-lined Skink, and Fisher. There is a network of scenic trails, usable year-round.

DIRECTIONS. Go N on Hwy 38 past Verona; turn left at CA sign at Snider Rd & go to T-jct; turn left & go to Second Depot Lake Dam; park at campground. For Third Depot Lake Dam, continue past campsite; take 1st right turn.

INFORMATION. Napanee Region Conservation Authority.

Holleford Crater

This 500-million-year-old meteorite crater is 1.5–3 km in diameter and has outcrops of limestone with Palaeozoic fossils. In the centre is a swampy depression about 30 m below the rim. Although privately owned, the crater is visible from the road.

DIRECTIONS. From Exit 611 on Hwy 401 at Kingston, go 20.5 km N on Hwy 38 to Hartington; turn right & go 2 km; turn left & go

1.5 km; turn right along S edge of crater towards Crater Farm at next jct. Explanatory sign just E of farm.

Frontenac Provincial Park

This 7,100-ha tract of shield country on the Frontenac Axis offers varied wilderness experiences amidst the rugged terrain of deep lakes, rocky ridges, high cliffs, and scenic gorges. The park contains three distinct habitat zones. 1) Among rolling hills, extensive tracts of mature hardwood forest, largely Sugar Maple and Red Oak, flourish on deep soils. Scattered throughout are occasional ponds and lakes, and fern-filled valleys in which rare plants grow. 2) An area of ridges and valleys contains a younger, more open mixed forest, interrupted by numerous lakes and some successional old fields. 3) Where bare burned-over ridges of exposed rock predominate, scattered bogs, marshes, fens, and Beaver ponds occur in low-lying pockets. The varied topography and the meeting of northern and southern landscapes create a rich diversity of species. Among the specialties are Osprey, Red-shouldered Hawk, Prairie and Pine Warblers, Turkey Vulture, Five-lined Skink, Black Rat Snake, Great-spurred Violet, Hooker's Orchid, and Silvery Glade Fern. The park offers self-guided trails, canoeing, hiking, wilderness camping, and cross-country skiing.

DIRECTIONS. Located N of Sydenham off Co Rd 19; see prov hwy map.

INFORMATION. Frontenac Provincial Park, Box 11, Sydenham, Ont, K0H 2TO, 613-376-3489.

Gould Lake Conservation Area

Here the shield landscape is marked by rugged knolls and intervening swamps and Beaver ponds. Mature hardwood stands are dominated by Sugar Maple and Red Oak, in association with some American Beech, White Birch, and Basswood. Osprey, Red-shouldered and Broad-winged Hawks, and Black Rat Snake occur. Abandoned mines attract rockhounds. Trails through the 583-ha property can be used in all seasons.

DIRECTIONS. From Sydenham on Co Rd 19, follow signs 8 km N.

INFORMATION. Cataraqui Region Conservation Authority.

Birding Sydenham to Fermoy via Canoe Lake

Try this birding route on an early morning in May or June. Eastern Bluebird, Red-shouldered Hawk, Cerulean Warbler, Indigo Bunting, and Louisiana Waterthrush are all possible sightings. At the northern tip of Canoe Lake, listen for the ascending notes of Prairie Warbler across the lake. Pine Warblers can usually be found at Desert Lake cemetery.

DIRECTIONS. From Sydenham go N on Co Rd 19. Include stops at Frontenac Prov Park (turn right 12 km N of Sydenham & go 2 km), Otter Lake (on Co Rd 19, 2 km N of turn to Frontenac Prov Park), and Canoe Lake (where Co Rd 19 veers left 2 km N of Otter Lake, keep straight & go about 13 km). Continue N to Fermoy on Co Rd 8.

Kingston and Area

– **Cataraqui Cemetery.** The good variety of trees here includes Kentucky Coffee Tree and mature White Spruce, White Pine, and Tamarack. The site is an excellent place for observing winter finches, sometimes including crossbills.

DIRECTIONS. From Princess St (Hwy 2) at W edge of Kingston go N on Sydenham Rd. Park N of cemetery 1 km S of Hwy 401.

NOTE. On Hwy 2 just W of Sydenham Rd (opp Walnut Grove Motel) is the largest Black Walnut tree in Ontario, with a circumference of 5.74 m.

– **Lemoine Point Conservation Area.** Trails in this 137-ha site lead through mature hardwoods, across meadows, and along the lakeshore. Red-headed and Pileated Woodpeckers are found. There is an excellent representation of spring wildflowers, including White Trillium, Mayapple, Yellow Trout-lily, and Bloodroot. A large botanical heritage garden has been developed, featuring labelled plants.

DIRECTIONS. From Kingston go W on Front Rd (Co Rd 1) past airport to end of road.

INFORMATION. Cataraqui Region Conservation Authority.

– **Little Cataraqui Creek Marshland Area.** Follow the Rideau Trail leading from King Street West (becomes Front Road) to Squaw Point and Bath Road (Highway 33). Where the trail winds through low bushes and planted White Spruce, watch for kinglets, warblers, sparrows, and thrushes during spring migration. At this season a frog chorus is often heard and Yellow Trout-lily blooms profusely. In mature deciduous woods look for Northern Oriole, Scarlet Tanager, and Northern Cardinal. Eastern Meadowlark and Song Sparrow are found in the meadow. Cross the marshes on a boardwalk, checking for Common Snipe and Blue-winged Teal. Along a rarely used railway line spanning the marshes, Swamp Sparrows chatter and Virginia Rails and Soras hide. American Bittern frequent the marsh near Bath Road.

DIRECTIONS. Enter from parking lot on King St W, 0.6 km W of Country Club Dr. Trails adjoin W limits of golf course property at S end.

INFORMATION. Cataraqui Region Conservation Authority.

– Little Cataraqui Creek Conservation Area. This 400-ha tract includes a reservoir, ponds, mixed woodlands, Sugar Maple bush, and softwood plantings. Beaver, songbirds, ducks, herpetofauna, aquatic invertebrates, and a good representation of plants are found along the trails. The site is of considerable geomorphological interest, containing a system of clay ridges thought to have been formed when floating glacial ice slumped down onto flat-lying clay. The clay assumed the contours of the bottom of the ice sheet. An interpretive centre is located on one of the clay ridges. Hiking and cross-country skiing are among the numerous opportunities offered for outdoor education and recreation.

DIRECTIONS. From Kingston go N on Division St (Perth Rd, Co Rd 10) 1.5 km past Hwy 401; watch for sign on left.

INFORMATION. Cataraqui Region Conservation Authority.

– Cataraqui River. The Cataraqui River in Kingston serves as the southern end of the Rideau Canal. At Kingston Mills, about 7 km upstream from Kingston Harbour, the waterway makes an abrupt descent from the granite uplands of the Frontenac Axis to the lowland plain that here borders the St Lawrence River. The Cataraqui's lower reaches pass through an extensive wetland known as the Cataraqui Marsh. The general area near the mouth of the river is used as a waterfowl staging area during spring and fall migration.

DIRECTIONS. 1) For Woods Landing (located on E shore): take Hwy 15 N from Kingston to Gore Rd traffic light; turn left & go to stop sign; turn left on Pt St Mark Rd; go to stop sign; turn right onto Ken Woods Circle & go to Lilla Burke Park. 2) For Kingston Mills: from Kingston go N on Hwy 15 to 0.2 km N of Hwy 401; turn left at Station Rd; keep left to 1st set of locks of Rideau Canal; walk downstream on W bank. 3) For Belle Isle Park: from downtown Kingston go N on Montreal St past Railway St; turn right on Belle Park Dr; walk to oak woods along shore beyond golf course.

Rideau Trail

Lying somewhat to the north of and roughly paralleling the Rideau Canal and River, this 385-km (including side trails) hiking trail extends from Kingston on Lake Ontario to Chaudière Falls on the Ottawa River at Ottawa. The 30 km north of Kingston and the whole northern half of the route lie on a gently rolling, often poorly drained, limestone plain. Here landscapes range from abandoned scrub to prosperous farms. The central portion of the trail traverses the rugged wilderness of the Canadian Shield, including parts of Frontenac and Murphy's Point provincial parks.

INFORMATION. Rideau Trail Association, Box 15, Kingston, Ont, K7L 4V6, 613-545-0823 (guidebook available).

Wolfe Island

This island is usually the best area in the region for observing wintering raptors. Open mixed farmland characterizes Wolfe Island, the large island in the St Lawrence River visible from the Kingston shoreline. All of the accessible land is privately owned, but birding is excellent from concession roads and roads along the shore. Snowy Owls are usually found in winter, as are Snow Buntings, Lapland Longspurs, and Rough-legged Hawks. Red-tailed Hawks, American Kestrels, and Short-eared and Long-eared Owls are also frequently observed. During migration, large rafts of waterfowl congregate along the island's shores: Redhead, Canvasback, Bufflehead, Common Goldeneye, Common and Red-breasted Mergansers, and huge numbers of Greater Scaup and Canada Geese.

DIRECTIONS. In downtown Kingston, take ferry from Ontario St near foot of Queen St. Good spots for roadside viewing are: 1) head of Reeds Bay (from jct of Hwy 95 at Marysville go 2.5 km W on Hwy 96, then 5 km S); 2) Button Bay–Horne's Ferry area at S end of Hwy 95. Avoid trespassing.

UNITED COUNTIES OF LEEDS AND GRENVILLE

> Many of these islands are scarcely larger than a bateau, and none of them, except such as are situated at the upper and lower extremities of the lake [The Lake of a Thousand Islands], appeared to me to contain more than fifteen English acres each. They are all covered with wood, even to the very smallest. The trees on these last are stunted in their growth, but the larger islands produce as fine timber as is to be found on the main shores ... The shores of all these islands under our notice are rocky; most of them rise very boldly, and some exhibit perpendicular masses of rock towards the water upwards of twenty feet high. (Thousand Islands, September 5, 1796, Isaac Weld [1774–1856], British traveller)

The Frontenac Axis of the Canadian Shield thrusts into the county from the northwest. Near the St Lawrence River the knobby protrusions of granitic rocks are partially buried under a clay plain. Central Leeds and Grenville are covered by an extensive limestone plain, while much of the northeast lies within a poorly drained sand plain. The Thousand Islands in the St Lawrence River consist of Precambrian bedrock granite outcroppings with mixed coniferous and deciduous woods. Bluebird trails have been established throughout the former Leeds County; watch for Eastern Bluebirds along country roads.

Foley Mountain Conservation Area

A geological fault runs along the north shore of Upper Rideau Lake between the Precambrian rocks of the shield and the Palae-ozoic rocks of the Great Lakes–St Lawrence Lowland. Sixty-metre-high granite rock outcrops provide a great view of the landscape to the south. Trails, usable year-round, go through a forest of oak, White Pine, and Red Cedar, where White-tailed Deer and other wildlife typical of the area are found. This is a very good spot for observing breeding warblers. The property contains 240 ha of land.

DIRECTIONS. Go 0.4 km N of Westport on Co Rd 10; follow signs on right.
INFORMATION. Rideau Valley Conservation Authority.

Mill Pond Conservation Area

This park is located on the east side of Big Rideau Lake around a large wetland that once stored water for a mill. The two trails, which are of historical interest (as indicated by their names – Mill Pond and Lime Kiln), take one through a variety of upland habitats (hardwood forests, White Pine–Eastern Hemlock forest, and regenerated old fields) and along diverse wetlands. Although situated on the shield, much of the area is underlain by marble. This is reflected by the number of calcium-loving plants in the vegetation, such as Kalm's Lobelia, which grows abundantly along the shore of the pond. Wildlife typical of the area occurs, including Common Loon and Black Rat Snake. Canoes and small boats can be launched in the Mill Pond. Trails can be toured in all seasons.
DIRECTIONS. From Hwy 15, 18 km S of Smiths Falls, go 5 km W on Co Rd 38 (Briton–Houghton Bay Rd).
INFORMATION. Rideau Valley Conservation Authority.

Rideau Trail

See entry under Frontenac County.

Charleston Lake Provincial Park

This large, 2,400-ha park is located amidst the rugged rocks and gently rolling hills of the Frontenac Axis. Flora and fauna are representative of both the Canadian Shield and the St Lawrence Lowland. Black Spruce bogs more typical of northern Ontario can be found beside more southern trees, such as Pitch Pine. Common Loon and Common Raven, birds of the northwoods, follow the axis south to Charleston Lake, while Black Rat Snake occurs here near the northern limit of its range. Showy Orchis, Long-bracted Orchid, Pitcher-plant, and Shining Sumac add to the rich assemblage of park flora.

Charleston Lake's southern arms provide opportunities for canoeists or hikers to explore the shoreline and surrounding woodlands. The 194-m-high summit of Blue Mountain offers a wonderful view of lake, forest, and farm country. Access is via the 4-km-long Blue Mountain Trail from Huckleberry Hollow, reached by boat or by driving around the lake and hiking in from one of three access points. There are some unusual rock formations which were once used as shelters by prehistoric peoples. An extensive network of hiking trails is available in winter for cross-country skiing and snowshoeing. The park can also be used as a base for a two- or three-day loop canoe route through Charleston Lake, Wiltse Creek, Gananoque River, Red Horse Lake, and back into Charleston Lake. There is a good chance of seeing a Bald Eagle, as well as Osprey and hundreds of Marsh Wrens, along this scenic and diverse route (canoe route brochure available).

DIRECTIONS. Located 20 km N of Lansdowne off Co Rd 3; see prov hwy map.

INFORMATION. Charleston Lake Provincial Park, RR 4, Lansdowne, Ont, K0E 1L0, 613-659-2065.

St Lawrence Islands National Park

Part of the Thousand Islands system that runs from Kingston to Brockville, the park includes a small area of mainland and portions of 26 islands spread over an 80-km stretch of the St Lawrence River. Ranging in size from a few to several hundred hectares, these islands are composed of the granitic bedrock of the Frontenac Axis. Gordon Island managed to retain its caprock of limestone through the glaciation. Grenadier Island has a good cover of till deposited by glacial meltwaters. All other islands have been stripped more or less to bare granite.

Here, at the intersection of the St Lawrence River and the Frontenac Axis, unusually diverse flora and fauna have developed. White Pine, Eastern Hemlock, and various deciduous trees and shrubs grow on the shallow soils. A number of distinctly eastern elements, including Red Spruce and Gray Birch, flourish close to southern species such as Chinquapin Oak, Rue-anemone, Ebony Spleenwort, and Five-lined Skink. The largest islands, Hill and Grenadier, boast an outstanding diversity of plant and animal life. Black Rat Snake and eight other species of snake are found on Hill Island alone, a mere 365 ha in area. Deerberry, Pitch Pine, Round-leaved Tick-trefoil, Hairy and Round-headed Bush-clovers, and other unusual plants thrive in company with uncommon animals, such as Blanding's Turtle. Common Loon, Wild Turkey (introduced), Marsh Wren, Least Bittern, Blue-gray Gnatcatcher, and Cerulean, Pine, and Blackburnian Warblers represent but a fragment of the abundant bird life. Bald Eagles winter along the St Lawrence between Ivy Lea and Brockville. The area boasts a fine display of fall colour.

DIRECTIONS. To reach mainland portion of park at Mallorytown Landing, take Exit 675 from Hwy 401 at Mallorytown; go 3.5 km S. Access to islands is by boat.

INFORMATION. St Lawrence Islands National Park, Box 469, Mallorytown, Ont, K0E 1R0, 613-923-5261.

Jones Creek

This is a large, diverse area sandwiched between Highway 401 and the Thousand Islands Parkway. The creekmouth has cut through the Palaeozoic bedrock to the underlying Precambrian granitic gneisses. The exposed cliffs consist of sandstone and limestone with a layer of conglomerate beneath. Farther up the creek, the bedrock is exclusively Precambrian and forms a series of east–west trending ridges separated by marshy wetlands. The ridges characteristically have oak-dominated forests on the south slopes, Eastern Hemlock on the north slopes, and a variety of pine and oak stands on the summits. Cattails predominate in the extensive marsh along the creek and its tributaries; the wetland provides nesting habitat for marsh birds, and cover and food for mammals, herpetofauna, and fish. The area is a mixture of public and private lands, so have regard for posted and enclosed land. Although best seen by canoe, two other approaches are possible.

DIRECTIONS. 1) By canoe (allow 2–3 hr minimum): from Hwy 401 Exit 685, 12 km W of Brockville, go 3 km W on Thousand Islands Pkwy & launch canoe at bridge over Jones Creek. 2) To see low cliffs & basal conglomerate rock that erodes to form shallow caves: view from Brown's Bay Park campground on Thousand Islands Pkwy 4 km W of Hwy 401 Exit 685 (if campground closed, walk few hundred m in from pkwy). 3) To see

example of dry oak–White Pine ridges: view from picnic area at service centre on S side of Hwy 401 between Exits 675 & 685.
INFORMATION. St Lawrence Parks Commission, RR 1, Morrisburg, Ont, K0C 1X0, 613-543-3704.

Limerick Forest

Limerick Forest is a large and dispersed entity that is partly county forest and partly crown land. It lies on the Smiths Falls limestone plain and has large areas of very shallow soil. There are also extensive peat-bottomed wetlands and sand ridges – remnants of Champlain Sea dunes and beaches. The area described here includes part of the Merrickville Bog (also known as Wolford Bog or Hanlan's Marsh) and adjacent uplands. The upland area is mostly Red Pine plantation on sand, with some Jack Pine plantation on the more shallow soils. There are also some remnants of naturally regenerating farmland. Forest access roads make good trails for hiking and birdwatching. A good trail continues from the end of Craig Road out into the bog, where the usual bog plants, such as cotton grasses, *Sphagnum* mosses, and heath shrubs, are found; in addition, a few species that are largely restricted to eastern Ontario, such as Gray Birch, are common here. There is a well-developed moat, maintained by Beaver, around the bog. While not the most diverse of eastern Ontario bogs, this is one of the more easily accessed.
DIRECTIONS. From Kemptville, take Oxford Mills Rd (Co Rd 18) S; instead of crossing Kemptville Creek bridge into Oxford Mills, continue straight 0.5 km on Co Rd 25; turn left, then immediately right onto Craig Rd. Go W on Craig Rd to very end. Forest access road lies on left & trail into bog straight ahead.
INFORMATION. MNR.

G. Howard Ferguson Forestry Station

Also known as the Kemptville Tree Nursery, over half of the station's roughly 400 ha is forested with a combination of natural forests and Red Pine plantation. Several walking-ski trails and seasonal roads provide year-round access. The topography undulates, with low sand ridges separated by swampy troughs; these features are the result of the area having been

shallowly flooded by the Champlain Sea following deglacia-
tion. There is considerable diversity of habitat. Woodlands
include extensive mixed forest of White Birch, poplar, White
Spruce, and Balsam Fir, as well as hardwood forest of Sugar
Maple, American Beech, and Eastern Hemlock. There are also
pine plantation, lowland Red Maple–ash forest, White Cedar
forest, and extensive marsh, especially near the mouth of
Kemptville Creek. A good diversity of wildlife can be seen,
including Red-shouldered Hawk, Northern Goshawk (in winter), White-tailed Deer, and Mink. Among the more interesting
plants are the eastern acid-loving Painted Trillium in spring
and Nodding Ladies'-tresses, Slender Gerardia, and both
Fringed and Closed Gentians in fall. Mosquitoes are abundant
in season (mid May to mid August).
DIRECTIONS. From Hwy 43 in Kemptville go N on Co Rd 44. Station is on right; 2 parking lots (1.0 & 2.0 km from Hwy 43) provide access to trails; 2nd lot is ploughed in winter.
INFORMATION. G. Howard Ferguson Forestry Station, RR 4,
Kemptville, Ont, K0G 1J0, 613-258-8355.

St Lawrence Parks Commission (Parks of the St Lawrence)

See entry under United Counties of Stormont, Dundas, and
Glengarry.

UNITED COUNTIES OF STORMONT, DUNDAS, AND GLENGARRY

> [At] that part of the [St Lawrence] river called the *Long Sault* ...
> the attention of the traveller must be particularly arrested by the
> immense body of water, and the awful rapidity of its current ...
> In the middle is a long island, whose stately forests intercept the
> sight in many parts of the opposite shore. On each side of this
> island the branches of the river are about half a mile broad, and
> that which is now in view tumbles down with a tremendous
> fury, that makes the surge rise somewhat like the sea in a gale of
> wind. (Mid November 1791, Patrick Campbell [?–1823], Scottish
> traveller)

Situated primarily on rich soil, often artificially drained for agricultural purposes, this area contains some of the most disturbed landscape in eastern Ontario. The northwestern portions of Stormont and Dundas are covered by a low-lying clay plain, broken occasionally by low drumlins. Roughly paralleling the St Lawrence, a gently undulating ridge of stony limestone till and occasional outcrops traverses the length of the combined county and forms the divide between the Ottawa and the St Lawrence rivers. Along the St Lawrence close to the Quebec border is an area of poorly drained clay flats.

Mountain Provincial Wildlife Area

This provincial wildlife area is situated in the former Winchester Bog, a 2,000-ha wetland that once supported extensive bog vegetation. Because of past drainage efforts, the area is now mostly a poplar and willow-alder shrub swamp. While there are no formal walking trails, the wildlife area can be accessed by trails that follow the ditches. Some artificial ponds have been created; these support frogs and Midland Painted Turtles. The usual birds of scrubby wetlands, such as American Woodcock, Swamp Sparrow, Common Yellowthroat, and Yellow Warbler, can be seen. There is a large population of Wood Frogs.

DIRECTIONS. From its jct with Hwy 31 at Winchester, go 7.5 km W on Hwy 43, turn right on Development Rd & go about 4 km to end.

INFORMATION. MNR.

St Lawrence Parks Commission (Parks of the St Lawrence)

The St Lawrence Parks Commission manages many areas of public lands along the St Lawrence River from Adolphustown (west of Kingston) to the Quebec border. These properties often provide the best opportunities for accessing the river for viewing waterfowl and other species, such as shorebirds and gulls. Spring and fall during migration are the best times for a visit. In addition to sites described elsewhere in this guide, areas worth visiting include the Long Sault Parkway (connects Mille Roches Park and a number of islands between Ingleside and Long Sault), Riverside Park (west of Morrisburg), and Charlottenburgh Park (east of Summerstown). Various vantage points along the Thousand Islands Parkway, including Ivy Lea Park near the international bridge, are good places to look for Bald Eagles during the winter and rafts of ducks in the early spring before the ice leaves inland lakes.

– **Upper Canada Migratory Bird Sanctuary.** This is a large area of old fields, forest, and wetlands. Crops are grown to attract wildlife. In addition to harbouring a resident Canada Goose breeding population, the site has become an important stopover for many thousands of migrating geese and other waterfowl that can be viewed from observation towers. An interpretive centre and self-guided trails make the sanctuary worth visiting spring through fall. White-tailed Deer and Red Fox are often seen along the road. From the sanctuary, a short causeway leads to a campground and more second-growth forest and over-grown field habitat on Nairne Island.

DIRECTIONS. From Hwy 401 Exit 758 go 1.5 km S on Upper Canada Rd, then 5.9 km E on Hwy 2 past Upper Canada Village to Migratory Bird Sanctuary Rd; turn right & go 2.5 km to parking lot at interpretive centre; road continues on to Nairne & Morrison islands.

INFORMATION. St Lawrence Parks Commission, RR 1, Morrisburg, Ont, K0C 1X0, 613-543-3704.

Hoople Creek Provincial Wildlife Area

Several isolated ponds and channels have been created along the shore of shallow Hoople Bay. These provide habitat for American Bittern, waterfowl, and shorebirds, including Common Snipe. Most of the upland portion of the wildlife area consists of old fields, thickly overgrown with Reed Canary Grass, Wild Parsnip, and other species of herbs and low shrubs such as dogwoods and willows. Earthen mounds provide elevated viewing sites although trails are badly overgrown. Best viewing is likely during migration but waterfowl are hunted here in fall.

DIRECTIONS. 1) From Hwy 401 Exit 770 go 2 km S on Co Rd 14, then 5.8 km E on Hwy 2 to Wales Rd (Co Rd 12), then 1.2 km N to parking lot on W side of road. 2) From Hwy 401 Exit 778, go S to Long Sault, then 2.4 km W on Hwy 2 to Wales Rd.

INFORMATION. MNR.

Grays Creek Conservation Area

A well-maintained trail leads through a diversity of upland habitats here, including naturally regenerated old fields and hedgerows of hawthorn, apple, and oak. The deciduous forest has a rich ground flora containing species such as False Solomon's-seal, Blue Cohosh, White Trillium, and Early Meadow-rue. The abundance of fruit and nut-bearing trees and shrubs makes the 43-ha conservation area a good site to visit for birdwatching, especially in the fall. Another good time to visit is in spring when woodland flowers are at their peak. In late summer, the uncommon non-native but handsome Hairy Willow-herb blooms in the ditches.

DIRECTIONS. Located on Boundary Rd at E edge of Cornwall between 2nd St & Montreal Rd. 1) Follow Hwy 2 E from downtown Cornwall & watch for signs. 2) Take Hwy 401 Exit 796 & follow Boundary Rd 3.5 km S.

INFORMATION. Raisin Region Conservation Authority.

Cooper Marsh Conservation Area

This large St Lawrence River wetland is managed for waterfowl production. Open year-round, it offers an interpretation centre, viewing towers, several trails following dykes, and a boardwalk. Habitats include marsh, treed and thicket swamp, and areas of open water with abundant Purple Loosestrife and Frog's-bit (both invasive exotic species). Expect to see several species of ducks as well as American Coot, Green and Great Blue Herons, Black Tern, Tree Swallow, Muskrat, and Mink. Over 135 species of birds have been recorded; birdwatching is best between May and October.

DIRECTIONS. From Hwy 401 Exit 814, go 1 km S on Hwy 34 to South Lancaster, then 2.5 km W on Hwy 2.

INFORMATION. Raisin River Conservation Authority.

McIntyre Rapids

Walleye spawn in April.

DIRECTIONS. Go 3 km W of Williamstown on Co Rd 17 along Raisin River.

UNITED COUNTIES OF PRESCOTT AND RUSSELL

The Sun intensely hot today and the water of the Grand, or
Uttowas [Ottawa] river as smooth as glass; the Country on either
side a thick Forest; the trees near the edge of the Water low, &
branching, chiefly Aspen; while those behind were Pine, straight
as Arrows, and growing to an enormous height: everything was
calm & quiet, not a sound to be heard excepting the stroke of the
paddle and the clear mellow voice of our principal vocalist,
Tomma Felix, singing 'La Belle Rosier' and other sweet Voyageurs
airs. (Chute-à-Blondeau upstream to Lièvre River, May 3, 1830,
Frances Simpson [1812–53], wife of Hudson's Bay Company gov-
ernor]

At the close of the last glaciation when the upper Great Lakes
drained eastward through the Ottawa River, the lower portion
of the valley was immersed beneath the Champlain Sea. During
this time huge quantities of sand and silty marine clays were
laid down in eastern Ontario. Today, in Prescott and Russell, a
broad clay plain spreads southward from the Ottawa River. This
is overlain by raised sandy ridges and a large elongated sand
plain that stretches from west to east across the south-central
part of the county. The original forest cover was largely deciduous, dominated by Sugar Maple and American Beech. Much of
the county is now devoted to agriculture.

LaRose Agreement Forest

At 10,800 ha, this is the most extensive tract of forest in extreme
eastern Ontario. It occupies a large sand plain, deposited in the
glacial Champlain Sea. The plain overlies marine clays that
impede drainage and result in much of the area being wet for at
least part of the growing season. Several streams have cut down
through the sands and into the clay, creating steep-sided valleys. In recent years, Beaver have created numerous ponds
along these valleys. Another significant geological feature of the
area is the numerous landslides that occur near steep slopes
when the underlying clays become supersaturated with water.
Both ancient and recent landslide scars can be seen within and
adjacent to the agreement forest.

Much of the sand plain is covered by Red Pine and White Spruce plantations, although there is also a considerable amount of naturally regenerated forest (poplar, Red Maple, and mixed), particularly in the wetter sections. The valleys, ravines, and older landslide areas often support a Sugar Maple-dominated mixed hardwood forest. These forests are particularly rich in ferns, Hay-scented Fern being abundant in many areas. Ditches along the many forest access roads and firebreaks are good places to look for plant species that like wet sands, such as Variegated Scouring-rush, Ragged Fringed Orchid, Field Milkwort, and both Small-flowered and Slender Gerardias. Some of the Red Pine plantations are old enough for species such as Pink Lady's-slipper to have become established. Red Spruce is occasionally found in the natural mixed forest. The forest is large enough to support a population of Moose, considered to be an offshoot of the Alfred Bog population (best seen in spring and fall). The agreement forest also provides habitat for a diversity of birds and is worth visiting for birding year-round. There are numerous trails and access roads, but it is best to drive only on the main roads, thus avoiding the possibility of a long walk to get a tow.

DIRECTIONS. 1) From Exit 79 on Hwy 417, follow Co Rd 5 N through Limoges about 5 km; go past jct with Co Rd 8, follow road as it sweeps 90° to right & continue E; this road goes to heart of agreement forest (about 7 km to centre, from jct of Co Rds 5 & 8). 2) If approaching from Ottawa, take Exit 88 from Hwy 417, & go 6 km E on Co Rd 5/8 to its jct with Co Rd 5, turn left & proceed as above.

INFORMATION. MNR.

Cobbs Lake

Cobbs Lake is a long, narrow marshy pond within Cobbs Creek. The waterway was once the channel of a much larger postglacial river that drained the entire upper Great Lakes. When the flat, clay-bottomed creek valley floods each spring, it becomes a staging area for huge numbers of Canada Geese and other waterfowl, including Northern Pintail, Mallard, and Snow Goose. A nearby salt spring originates in deep underground deposits laid down 10,000 years ago by the salty waters of the

Champlain Sea. The spring supports Walter's Barnyard Grass, a rare southern species, and the salt-loving Seaside Buttercup.
DIRECTIONS. Go 5 km E of Bourget on Co Rd 2 (Bear Brook Rd). Salt-tolerant plants grow in ditch on N side of road 50 m W of lake.

Alfred Bog

Located in a broad, abandoned channel of the Ottawa River, this 4,000-ha wetland is the largest peatland in southern Ontario. A peat layer up to 7 m thick forms a dome on top of flat, poorly drained clays laid down 10,000–12,000 years ago beneath the salty waters of the Champlain Sea. Chiefly characterized by Black Spruce and *Sphagnum* mosses, the bog protects an amazing diversity of both northern and southern plants and animals, including numerous rare species. Among plant rarities are Rhodora, Prickly Bog Sedge, Southern Twayblade, Massachusetts Fern, and Twin-scaped Bladderwort. Moose occur within the bog, and several northern bird species, such as Wilson's and Palm Warblers, Gray Jay, and Black-backed and Three-toed Woodpeckers, may be seen.

Variations in the flow of groundwater through the bog have created a patterned effect in the vegetation, a feature more typical of northern bogs. Sections of open heath are dominated by Leatherleaf, laurels, Labrador Tea, and other low shrubs. Centred around islands of Black Spruce and Tamarack, thickets of taller shrubs have developed containing Wild Raisin, Black Chokeberry, Highbush Blueberry, and Swamp Birch. Dense coniferous bog forest thrives in areas of better drainage. Patches of Red Maple and White Cedar grow where springs well up. Gray Birch flourishes around the edge of the bog where fire has occurred.

About one-third of Alfred Bog is in public ownership. Access is difficult and, except for the boardwalk area, should only be attempted on an organized trip led by knowledgeable leaders.
DIRECTIONS. From Hwy 17 at W outskirts of Alfred, go 5.5 km S on Co Rd 15; where Co Rd 15 swings right, continue straight ahead on gravel twp rd about 1.5 km; turn left at dirt crossroad & go about 1 km to end of road. Boardwalk into bog is on right.

Voyageur (Carillon) Provincial Park

Tucked among marshes and inlets along the Ottawa River, Voyageur sits at the boundary of the fertile St Lawrence Lowland and the Canadian Shield to the north. The park has some interesting geological features, including glacial and interglacial deposits of till, sands, and gravels, as well as a former channel of the Ottawa River. Among the habitats are marshes, Beaver ponds, fern swamps, and hilly hardwood forests. Shorebirds and waterfowl stop during migration. There is a spectacular view of the Laurentian Mountains across the river. Cross-country skiing is available in winter.

DIRECTIONS. Located just W of Quebec border off Hwy 417 & Co Rd 4; see prov hwy map.

INFORMATION. Voyageur Provincial Park, Box 130, Chute-à-Blondeau, Ont, K0B 1B0, 613-674-2825.

REGIONAL MUNICIPALITY OF OTTAWA-CARLETON

[Of the] several waterfalls and many rapids and dangerous precipices ... this Chaudiere fall ... is the most wonderful, dangerous, and terrifying of all ... It has athwart it many little islands, which are merely rugged and inaccessible rocks, partly covered with wretched little trees, and the whole expanse is cut up into holes and precipices made in long course of time by these boiling cataracts ... especially in one particular place where the water dashes so violently upon a rock in the middle of the river that a wide deep basin has been hollowed out in it, so that the water circling round within it makes mighty upheavals, producing great clouds of spray that rise into the air. (Ottawa River, spring 1624, Gabriel Sagard [?–1650], Récollet brother)

The municipality lies within the St Lawrence Lowland, sandwiched between sections of the Canadian Shield not far to the north and southwest. The region is mostly underlain by Palaeozoic limestones and sandstones, topped with marine sediments accumulated during the time that eastern Ontario was flooded by the Champlain Sea. Various physiographic features are visible in the landscape. Lying closest to the Ottawa River are clay plains punctuated by occasional rocky outcrops. Farther south, from west to east, are limestone plains, drumlins, and sand plains.

Ottawa-Carleton sits within the Great Lakes–St Lawrence Forest Region. Although most of the land has now been cleared, White Pine–Sugar Maple–American Beech forest dominated much of the original woodlands of the area. Conifers became locally prominent under specialized conditions such as are found in lowland bogs, some fens, sand deposits, and alvars.

Low-Lying Farmlands

In some parts of the municipality (such as along Regional Road 31 north of Carlsbad Springs, and along Regional Road 49 east of Richmond), extensive areas of low-lying farmland flood in early spring, attracting large flocks of waterfowl, which feed primarily on waste corn. Watch for thousands of Canada Geese, some Snow Geese, many ducks, and the occasional Tundra Swan and Greater White-fronted Goose. Open areas of damp grasslands also draw other birds in season, including Horned Lark, Northern Harrier, American Pipit in migration, and Snowy Owl in winter. View from roads.

Constance Bay Sandhills

This complex of sandhills arose along the Ottawa River following the departure of the Champlain Sea. The site contains some unusual plants and butterflies. The landscape has been greatly altered by cottage development, pine plantations, and the suppression of natural fires. Fortunately some significant species survive along the disturbed edges of fire roads through the dunes. These include Puccoon, Butterfly-weed, and Arrow-leaved Violet.

DIRECTIONS. From Hwy 417 at Kanata take Exit 138 N; follow Reg Rd 49, then Reg Rd 9; turn off to Constance Bay. Walk into publicly owned Torbolton Forest via fire roads.

INFORMATION. MNR.

Shirleys Bay

This quiet backwater bay is one of the best birdwatching spots in the region. Large numbers and species of songbirds, shorebirds, and waterfowl move along the Ottawa River migration corridor. Sewage-enhanced feeding and resting habitats induce a stop at Shirleys Bay. Here, weary migrants take advantage of Northern Wild Rice stands, exposed mudflats, cattail marsh, maple swamp, and upland forests. An earthen berm (causeway) extending northward from the mouth of Watts Creek to Chartrand and Haycock islands provides excellent views. Innis Point to the north of the bay contains a fantastic alvar-shrub prairie with unusual western and northern plants, such as Shrubby St John's-wort. The beach and backshore area east of the boat launch and parking area described in the directions has some prairie species typical of Ottawa River shorelines, including Little Bluestem, Indian Grass, and Tall Cord Grass.

DIRECTIONS. Take Exit 134 from Hwy 417, go 1.5 km N on Moodie Dr (Reg Rd 59), then 2.5 km W on Reg Rd 38 (Carling Ave), then 2 km N on Range Rd to parking area at end. Short walk to W along shore leads to berm. *Most of rest of Shirleys Bay area is owned by Dept of National Defence & is off limits* except for groups with special agreements; contact Ottawa Field Naturalists (613-722-3050) for more information re access. *Do not go W of berm without permission as this area lies downrange of Connaught Rifle Ranges & is a strict safety exclusion zone.*

Andrew Haydon Park (Ottawa Beach)

This area is one of Ottawa's best staging areas for water birds during fall migration. Declining water levels in the Ottawa River in early fall expose extensive sand- and mudflats in the shallow bay. Ducks, geese, herons, and gulls, sometimes in staggering numbers, then congregate. More rarities occur here and along the shoreline to the east than anywhere else in the region.

DIRECTIONS. Located along shore of Britannia Bay. From Ottawa continue W on Carling Ave.

The Burnt Lands

Straddling the boundary between Lanark County and Ottawa-Carleton, the Burnt Lands are dominated by vast broken areas of alvar, one of the easternmost in North America. Wetland coniferous forests and mixed woodlands provide a surrounding buffer. Species having northern, southern, and western affinities are all found here. These include relict boreal and Champlain Sea flora and fauna, such as several species of saw-moths and land snails. For thousands of years, flooding, drought, and natural fires have maintained huge natural meadows on the flat, thin-soiled limestone plateau. A large meadow of Prairie Dropseed is notable. The spectacular spring floral display in the White Cedar glades includes numerous Yellow Lady's-slipper, Seneca Snakeroot, Wood Lily, and Starry False Solomon's-seal. Several rare sedges and grasses are present. These areas are ablaze with colour throughout the year – Balsam Ragwort and Harebell in summer, and goldenrods and asters in the fall. Among uncommon northern and western breeding birds are Hermit Thrush and Clay-colored Sparrow. Adapted to disturbance, primarily fire, these alvars are probably closer to pre-European conditions than almost any other habitat in Ontario.

DIRECTIONS. Of 2 publicly owned sections of Burnt Lands, the easier to access is on S side of Hwy 44, 8.5 km W of Hwy 17 or 5 km E of Almonte.

INFORMATION. MNR.

Carp Hills

An island of Precambrian rocks, the Carp Hills protrude upward through surrounding marine sedimentary deposits. The rolling countryside and sparsely wooded knobby outcrops contrast sharply with adjacent farmlands. There are Beaver ponds where waterfowl nest, wet meadows, groves of oak on rocky knolls, and young Trembling Aspen–White Birch forests. The diversity of habitats harbours many unusual species. Raptors winter in the area.

DIRECTIONS. Hills lie N & W of Carp & Kanata, roughly bounded by Marchurst Rd & Reg Rds 49, 5, & 20 (Kinburn Sdrd). Try Thomas Dolan Pkwy (turn right 5 km N of Carp on Reg Rd 5) for best birding. Most of land is privately owned; view from roads.

South March Highlands

This complex, consisting of sandstone and outcrops of Precambrian bedrock, forms the southern extension of the Carp Hills. Among the extensive bedrock barrens are rich Sugar Maple hardwoods and treed and open wetlands. The rich flora and fauna include northern bird species near the outcrops, and Maidenhair Spleenwort, Goldie's Wood Fern, and Silvery Glade Fern in the mature hardwoods. Habitat is also available for southern species such as Blue-gray Gnatcatcher and Golden-winged Warbler. The spring wildflower display is spectacular. Coyote, White-tailed Deer, Meadow Jumping Mouse, and other mammals typical of large undisturbed tracts are found here. Trails pass through private and public lands.

DIRECTIONS. Highlands are W of Kanata Lake area of Kanata along Terry Fox Dr (Exit 140 N from Hwy 417), Old Carp Rd, & Huntmar Dr.

Stony Swamp Conservation Area

Here a rich mosaic of habitats is situated over both limestone and sandstone bedrock. This enables the 2,000-ha complex to support more than 700 species of plants, including numerous rarities. Poorly drained sites support alvar, bog, marsh, Beaver ponds, and a deciduous swamp that serves as the headwaters area for several local creeks. Elsewhere are regenerating old fields, Jack Pine plantations, and deciduous uplands dominated by Sugar Maple. In spite of heavy year-round recreational use, the numerous trails at Stony Swamp make it the best area in the region for viewing a wealth of habitats, plants, and animals. A large bird-feeder complex on the Jack Pine Trail attracts chicka-dees, nuthatches, woodpeckers, Evening Grosbeaks, and other finches in winter.

DIRECTIONS. Located in W Nepean, S of Bells Corners (from Hwy 417 take Exit 134S). Parking lots for trails are located along various roads, including Richmond Rd (Reg Rd 59) & Moodie Dr (Reg Rd 11).

INFORMATION. National Capital Commission (Greenbelt All Seasons Trail Map available).

Richmond Lagoons

These former sewage lagoons, now a conservation area, are being managed to attract the diversity of waterfowl, shorebirds, and swallows that has made this a popular birding site.

DIRECTIONS. From Hwy 417 Exit 138, go 14 km S on Reg Rd 49

(Eagleson Rd); lagoons are on right (W) side of road S of Reg Rd 10, between Jock River & RR tracks.

Marlborough Forest

This is a vast (7,000 ha), relatively level area of private and public lands. Situated on a thinly buried limestone plain, it consists primarily of extensive wetlands interspersed with wooded uplands. Among the wide diversity of habitats are meadows, fens, swamps, marshes, Beaver ponds, hardwood forests, mixed coniferous and deciduous woodlands, White Cedar forests, alvar, and limestone plains. Flood Road alvar and the Phragmites and Richmond fens are particular highlights. Both fens support rare plants, birds, and butterflies, often with northern affinities.

In summer the alvar openings are dotted with the flowers of species such as Fringed Gentian, Upland White Aster, Foxglove Beardtongue, and Tall White Cinquefoil. More colour and variety are added by Virginia Mountain-mint, Torrey's Rush, False Pennyroyal, and Hairy Beardtongue. Fen areas are home to Sedge Wren, Yellow Rail, and other northern birds. Greenish-flowered Pyrola blooms in the cedar woodlands, and Cardinal-flower colonizes damp sites. Wetlands, woodlands, and scrubby openings provide habitat for Black Tern, Barred Owl, and Clay-colored Sparrow. Midland Chorus Frog, Gray Treefrog, and Mink Frog enliven spring and summer evenings with their calls. Reptiles include Redbelly Snake, Blandings's Turtle, Northern Water Snake, and Eastern Smooth Green Snake.

DIRECTIONS. Located S of Richmond, W of North Gower & N of Burritts Rapids. Access from Roger Stevens Dr (Reg Rd 6) or Dwyer Hill Rd (Reg Rd 3); 2 parking lots on Roger Stevens Dr are 9 km (N side) & 10.5 km (S side) W of stoplights in North Gower. Follow hiking trails or, for specialized sites, join organized tours.

INFORMATION. Planning Dept, Ottawa-Carleton, 222 Queen St, Ottawa, Ont, K1P 5Z3, 613-560-2053; Ottawa Field-Naturalists' Club, 613-722-3050.

Baxter Conservation Area

This 68-ha conservation area, located on the Rideau River, has a variety of forested and wetland habitats. These include open fields, alder thickets, mixed forests, Silver Maple floodplain forest, and marshes along the river. Osprey and herons are regularly observed. There are trails (usable year-round) and an interpretation centre.

DIRECTIONS. About 40 km S of Ottawa on Hwy 16, go 3 km E on Dilworth Rd (Reg Rd 13); entrance is on right at sharp left bend in road.

INFORMATION. Rideau Valley Conservation Authority.

Rideau Trail

See entry under Frontenac County.

Mer Bleue Conservation Area

A 2,500-ha peatland, Mer Bleue is situated over poorly drained clay soils in an abandoned channel of the Ottawa River. Typical of raised northern bogs, it contains large stretches of open heath, and stands of Black Spruce and Tamarack. The area is particularly attractive during the height of cotton-grass bloom in late spring. A cattail marsh has developed in one section. An unusual feature in the middle of the *Sphagnum* mat is isolated islands of sand on which grow poplar and birch. Pools and rivulets maintained by Beaver around the periphery of the bog have created a marshy moat-like wetland known as a lagg. Numerous rare plants and animals have been recorded, including Blanding's Turtle, Twin-scaped Bladderwort, Lincoln's and Clay-colored Sparrows, Palm Warbler, and other boreal nesters. Larger sand ridges, once bars in the postglacial channel, now support regenerating pastureland and a rich mix of deciduous and coniferous forest plants. Among them are relict species from a time when conditions were cooler and harsher. On the lower slopes of the ridges, Red Maple swamps shelter an abundance of ferns as well as rare plants such as Large Purple Fringed Orchid. The rich diversity of habitats and flora at Mer Bleue provides homes for animals such as River Otter, Marten, Coyote, Red Squirrel, and the rare Fletcher's Dragonfly.

DIRECTIONS. From Exit 104 on Hwy 417 E of Ottawa, go N on Reg Rd 27 (Anderson Rd) for: 1) 4 km & turn right on Borthwick

Ridge Rd (boardwalk at end); or 2) 6 km & turn right at Dolman Ridge Rd.

INFORMATION. National Capital Commission.

Green's Creek Conservation Area

The narrow, steep-sided valley supports Silver Maple swamps and mature Eastern Hemlock–Sugar Maple forests. Rich ground flora thrives underneath. Plants of note are Cattail Sedge, Witch-hazel, Pinedrops, and Checkered Rattlesnake-plantain. The heavy clay soils in the 400-ha conservation area are prone to slumping. Rock-hard nodules in the soil contain 10,000-year-old fossils of animals and plants from the Champlain Sea.

DIRECTIONS. Between Ottawa River & Innis Rd (Reg Rd 30) along Green's Creek in NW Gloucester. Enter from Eastern Pkwy, NW corner of NCC nursery off Innis Rd, or NE corner of Pineview Golf Course off Blair Rd. Steep slopes & lack of trails make access difficult.

INFORMATION. National Capital Commission.

Ottawa

Ottawa is bisected by the Rideau River, which drains the gently rolling agricultural lowlands to the south. Encircling the city is a 19,000-ha greenbelt, mostly owned by the National Capital Commission. This 3-km-wide strip of land extends from Lac Deschênes (a wide section of the Ottawa River) in the west, includes Uplands Airport and some Central Experimental Farm land on the south, and continues east and north to rejoin the Ottawa River near Green's Creek.

INFORMATION. National Capital Commission.

– **Britannia Conservation Area.** A variety of habitats sur-rounds Mud Lake, a former embayment of the Ottawa River and one of the best birding areas in the capital. Abundant aquatic flora flourishes in the shallow pond above limestone and sandstone bedrock. A Buttonbush swamp at the south end teems with turtles, including Midland Painted and Com-mon Snapping Turtles. Stands of White Pine, Red Oak, and Sugar and Red Maples grow on upland sites. The woodlands harbour Porcupines, Great Horned Owls, and winter finches in winter and, during warm seasons, a diverse flora with many uncommon species.

Songbirds, regularly including rarities, frequent the tangled shrubbery during migration. Wet areas are heavily used by migratory waterfowl – geese, diving ducks, and dabblers, especially American Wigeon, Blue-winged and Green-winged Teal, Gadwall, and Wood Duck. Black-crowned Night-Herons appear in late summer. Gulls, waterfowl, and Double-crested Cormorant roost on exposed rocks in Deschênes Rapids in the Ottawa River, especially in fall. Look for Brant and Arctic Tern from late May to early June. Best viewing is from the east end of Cassels Street.

DIRECTIONS. From Carling Ave (Hwy 17B) in W Ottawa, go N on Britannia Rd to Cassels St; turn right & go to parking area at end of street near filtration plant.

– Champlain Bridge and Ottawa River. The bridge connects three islands and crosses the Remic Rapids. There is good winter waterfowl viewing from Bate Island; watch for diving ducks, including Common Merganser, and Common and Barrow's Goldeneyes feeding in the open waters of the rapids. Gulls roost here in the fall, among them Little, Laughing (very rarely), Franklin's, Lesser Black-backed, Glaucous, and Iceland Gulls.

DIRECTIONS. From Hwy 17B (Carling Ave), go N on Island Park Dr.

– Rockcliffe Park. Steep, wooded slopes overlooking the Ottawa River at Governor Bay contain a stand of Common Hackberry, some uncommon ferns, and a variety of other interesting plants. Eastern Redback Salamanders inhabit the talus slopes, and migratory songbirds use the area as a stopover. Much of the rest of the park is highly manicured.

DIRECTIONS. From end of Sussex Dr continue E on Rockcliffe Pkwy; there are several parking lots on N side.

– Dows Lake. Although intensively used for aquatic recreation in summer, Dows Lake attracts numbers of migrating gulls in spring and fall. Wintering birds are drawn to the fruit of various trees planted along the lake and adjacent roadways.

DIRECTIONS. Located SW of Carling Ave (Hwy 17B) & Bronson Ave (Hwy 31). Access via Queen Elizabeth Drwy.

– Central Experimental Farm. Here rolling farm fields, flower gardens, an arboretum, and a wildlife garden have created one of the best year-round birding spots within the city. Fruit and seed trees in the arboretum and wildlife garden support wintering species such as Bohemian Waxwing and Pine Grosbeak. Open fields attract gulls and shorebirds (especially Black-bellied Plover and American Golden-Plover) in fall; Gray Partridge, Horned Lark, Gyrfalcon (an infrequent occurrence), and Snowy Owl in winter; and Eastern Meadowlark and Savannah Sparrow in summer. The Fletcher Wildlife Garden demonstrates how landowners can create or improve wildlife habitat on their own properties.

DIRECTIONS. Located SW of Dows Lake bounded by Carling Ave (Hwy 17B), Merivale Rd, Base Line Rd, & Prince of Wales Dr. From traffic circle on Prince of Wales Dr, arboretum is on E side.

– Vincent Massey Park and Hogs Back Park. Mature mixed woods line the high banks of the Rideau River here, while the shoreline offers both marshy and rocky stretches. The floodplain supports plentiful southern flora, especially visible in spring. Birds are easily observed from the trails. At Hogs Back, spectacular faults in the sedimentary rocks can be inspected.

DIRECTIONS. Located on E side of Rideau River across from Experimental Farm. Access off Hwy 16 via bridges on Heron Rd and Hogs Back Rd.

LANARK COUNTY

> We had to encounter ... a very serious evil ..., namely, the musquitoes. This is a very aggravating and distressing circumstance, as they tormented us both by day and night continually. The only remedy left to avoid this serious inconvenience, was the kindling of fires, which tended greatly to keep them away. Whenever they stung, it pierced through the skin. I have had my legs all over pierced with the fangs of these tormenting and mischievous insects, and from the effects of their bites, they seemed as if they had been covered all over with the small pox, and attended with an equal itch. (Early August 1821, John M'Donald, Scottish traveller)

Much of Lanark County lies on the Canadian Shield. Here the terrain is irregular, and hills, valleys, and wetlands are frequent. The remainder of the county, the southeastern portion, is underlain by a limestone plain covered by shallow, stony, often poorly drained soils. Natural woodlands are mostly deciduous, with some representation of conifers. The northeastern edge of the county shares some areas of alvar vegetation with adjacent Ottawa-Carleton. There are a number of bluebird trails in the southern part of the county (e.g., North Burgess Township); watch for Eastern Bluebirds along country roads.

Mill of Kintail Conservation Area

Set in rolling countryside, this mature Sugar Maple woodland is noted for its fine display of fall colour. The uplands also support Eastern Hemlock, White Cedar, Yellow Birch, Bur Oak, Basswood, Green Ash, and a number of southern plants. In damper areas White Cedar swamps and wet thickets are found. The rich hardwoods harbour a great diversity of species, including Scarlet Tanager, Black Maple, and Zigzag Goldenrod. Two-lined Salamanders inhabit the shores of the Indian River, as an extension of populations occurring throughout much of the Mississippi River drainage. Large stands of Cardinal-flower are present. The property encompasses 68 ha in total.

DIRECTIONS. From Almonte go 3 km N on Hwy 15; turn W on Clayton Rd & go 1 km; turn N on Ramsay Conc Rd 8 & go 2 km. INFORMATION. Mississippi Valley Conservation Authority.

The Burnt Lands

Although most of the Burnt Lands alvar is in Lanark County, the most accessible part is in Ottawa-Carleton. See entry under Regional Municipality of Ottawa-Carleton.

Carleton Place Hackberry Stand

Common Hackberry, usually found much farther south, dominates this small, rocky woodlot. Among other southern species found here is Hairy Wild-eye. Wintering ducks frequent the nearby rapids.

DIRECTIONS. Located along Mississippi River in downtown Carleton Place 0.5 km downstream from bridge on Hwy 15 (Bridge St); access via Franklin & Princess Sts.

Purdon Fen Conservation Area

Amidst rolling Precambrian hills, a depression in calcareous marble bedrock creates here a home for a small fen. Many thousands of Showy Lady's-slippers bloom each June, presenting a spectacular scene. The boardwalk is open year-round.
DIRECTIONS. From Perth, go NW on Hwy 511; 4 km past Lanark turn left on Co Rd 8 to Watsons Corners; follow signs.
INFORMATION. Mississippi Valley Conservation Authority.

Rideau Trail

See entry under Frontenac County.

Murphy's Point Provincial Park

A lovely, rugged landscape along the northwest shore of Big Rideau Lake, this is a fine example of the rich Frontenac Axis country of eastern Ontario. Northern elements predominate in a spruce and Balsam Fir forest that contains a wide variety of shield plants and animals. A number of rare species, including Black Rat Snake, are found in or near the park. The point area of the park supports flora typical of the Great Lakes–St Lawrence Forest Region. Large Sugar Maple, American Beech, Basswood, White Ash, and Red Oak trees shelter woodpeckers, Raccoons, hawks, and many songbirds. Hogg Bay, Black Creek, and Round and Loon lakes provide wetter habitats for birds such as herons, ducks, Osprey, and Common Loon; for mammals such as Muskrat, Beaver, and White-tailed Deer; and for amphibians and reptiles such as Common Snapping Turtle, Northern Water Snake, and Blue-spotted Salamander. Forest-edge species occur around successional old fields near abandoned homesteads and mica mines. The 1,240-ha park welcomes winter visitors.
DIRECTIONS. Located 16 km S of Perth on Co Rd 21; see prov hwy map.
INFORMATION. Murphy's Point Provincial Park, RR 5, Perth, Ont, K7H 3C7, 613-267-5060.

Perth Wildlife Reserve

This site has a diversity of natural and managed wildlife habitats, including cattail marsh, ponds, and old fields with a variety of planted wildlife shrubs and trees. Depending upon the season, look for Eastern Bluebirds, migrating Canada Geese, Wood Ducks, and a variety of other marsh birds, as well as Midland Painted Turtles. White-tailed Deer, Red Foxes, and Muskrats are present in most seasons. Interpretation on the trails is largely geared towards ways to improve land for wildlife, but the abundance of wildlife will be of interest to everyone.

DIRECTIONS. Follow main street (Gore St E) in Perth S (becomes Co Rd 1 or Rideau Ferry Rd); 1.5 km S of town limits turn left at reserve sign & go 4.5 km E to end of road.

INFORMATION. Rideau Valley Conservation Authority.

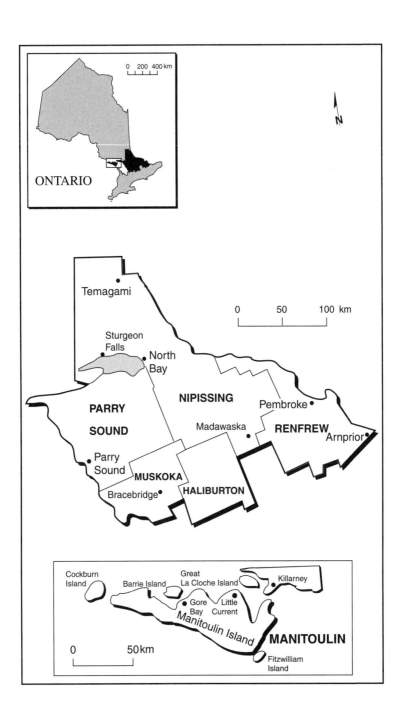

6 Manitoulin Island to Upper Ottawa River

Manitoulin	Nipissing
Parry Sound	(Algonquin Park)
Muskoka	Renfrew
Haliburton	

Except for the Ottawa valley and the limestone-based extension of the Niagara Escarpment that forms Manitoulin Island, this entire area lies on the Precambrian rocks of the Canadian Shield. The Algonquin Highlands dominate the central portion of the region, sloping westward to Georgian Bay and eastward to the lowlands of the Ottawa River valley. In general, thin soils barely cover the gneissic bedrock, and the rugged landscape is dominated by lakes and forests. Logging and recreational tourism are the main activities.

All counties and districts covered in this chapter fall within the Great Lakes–St Lawrence Forest Region, a large transition zone of mixed forest between the boreal forests to the north and the deciduous forests to the south. Conifers and broad-leaved trees are well mixed in the woodlands, although there is a tendency for hardwoods to predominate on better-drained sites and warmer slopes, and for conifers to be more abundant in cooler, low-lying areas and at the highest altitudes.

The French River, Lake Nipissing, and the Mattawa and Ottawa rivers arc across the northern part of the region. These interconnecting waterways lie along a 600-million-year-old fracture in the Earth's crust. Towards the end of the last glaciation, when shrinking ice sheets were retreating northward, their massive weight severely depressed the land in this area. This permitted the upper Great Lakes and a mighty flow of glacial meltwater to drain eastward through the faultline to the upper

Ottawa valley. Here the ancient river encountered the Champlain Sea, a salty embayment of ocean water thrust inland along the St Lawrence River valley by high seawater levels. Later, with the weight of the departing glaciers removed, the land slowly rebounded, eventually forming a watershed divide that diverted drainage from the upper Great Lakes southward through the St Clair River.

DISTRICT OF MANITOULIN

Before sunrise we entered Lake Huron [from the French River] ... We dined on an island celebrated for a stone which, when struck, emits a musical or metallic sound; and about eight in the evening we reached the Company's establishment, taking the name of La Cloche from the natural bell just mentioned. The northern shore of Lake Huron consists of rocky hills, dotted with stunted trees, chiefly pines; and the adjacent waters are closely studded with islands, varying from ten feet in diameter to many miles in length. (Mid May 1841, Sir George Simpson [ca 1787–1860], governor of Hudson's Bay Company)

This district encompasses Manitoulin Island, numerous smaller neighbouring islands, and a portion of the mainland shore north of Georgian Bay, including a large part of Killarney Provincial Park.

Manitoulin Island, the largest freshwater island in the world, is situated in northern Lake Huron. It is separated from the north shore of the lake by the North Channel and the northwestern corner of Georgian Bay. The island, mainly a limestone tableland, is slightly tilted from north to south or southwest, creating nearly perpendicular limestone cliffs overlooking the North Channel. These cliffs form part of the Niagara Escarpment. The tableland slopes gently towards Lake Huron on the south shore. In the northeast, at Sheguiandah, quartzite outcrops, with accompanying distinctive flora, are a dominant feature.

Extensive rock plains, flat and thinly covered with soil, characterize much of Manitoulin Island's topography. As a result of

Pleistocene glaciation, grooves appear on some of the exposed limestone, and glacially deposited boulders are abundant. In certain areas, notably along the south road between Poplar and Burpee, there are postglacial beach terraces well above the present lake level. Second-growth mixed hardwood-conifer forest covers extensive areas. When approaching Manitoulin Island from the north on Highway 6 between Whitefish Falls and Little Current, one notices a rather abrupt transition from Precambrian Shield granite to Palaeozoic limestone.

There is an unusual diversity of plant communities on Manitoulin Island, containing western, prairie, arctic, maritime, and endemic Great Lakes species. Great Lakes endemics, species which are largely restricted in their distribution to the Great Lakes region, are well represented on Manitoulin. Examples are Lakeside Daisy, Dwarf Lake Iris, and Hill's and Pitcher's Thistles. As might be expected, species with prairie affinities, such as Tall White Cinquefoil and Long-plumed Purple Avens, grow on dry, open sites. Alaska Orchid occurs on the island, disjunct from its stronghold in the hills and forests of western North America. Beach Pea, Sea Rocket, and American Dune Grass – species characteristic of the Atlantic coast – thrive on Manitoulin's sandy south-shore beaches. Typically northern or arctic plants, such as Goldthread and Butterwort, inhabit exposed shorelines or other cold sites.

Certain of Manitoulin's varied habitats contain particularly significant assemblages of plants. Limestone cliffs, crevices, and boulders support an abundance of limestone-loving ferns, including Smooth and Slender Cliffbrakes and less common species such as Wall-rue, Walking Fern, Limestone Oak Fern, and Purple-stemmed Cliffbrake. Bur Oak prairie is found on warm, dry sites where thin soils cover limestone bedrock. Sand dune systems, well-drained grassy openings, and areas of drought-prone dolostone pavement on which alvars develop are noted for their colourful and uncommon plants. Watch for Lance-leaved Coreopsis, Cylindric Blazing-star, Eyebright, and various orchids, including coralroots and Slender Ladies'-tresses. A specialty of the island is the rare Lakeside Daisy, a species whose world range is concentrated on Manitoulin Island and the upper Bruce Peninsula.

Manitoulin Island Country Roads

Extensive regions of Manitoulin Island were once cleared for agriculture. Although farming is still practised, much is marginal and there are many abandoned farms. Forestry is an important industry, especially west of Silver Lake. As most of the island is privately owned, it is best to visit publicly owned areas, including roads and their verges. Roads, many still lined by original rail fences, generally are quite well maintained and little travelled, so frequent stops for viewing can be safely made. Road allowances are richly flowered with common but beautiful flowers, and the meadows beyond the fences contain masses of colourful plants. Chicory, Ox-eye Daisy, Indian Paintbrush, Common Tansy, and several species of buttercups are very plentiful. Yellow Lady's-slipper is common in the region. In moist areas Small Purple Fringed Orchid, Swamp Milkweed, and Cardinal-flower can be seen along roadsides. Choke Cherry, Wild Plum, Apple, and hawthorn, which occur in many hedgerows, are dazzling when in blossom and often richly fruited. Bobolink, Eastern Meadowlark, Eastern Kingbird, and Eastern Bluebird frequent the roadside fences, as does the less common Upland Sandpiper. The fall foliage display is best from late September to mid October.

Mississagi Strait Migration Viewing Point

Cockburn Island and western Manitoulin are on a major bird migration route. The Mississagi Lighthouse Park, operated by the Quebec and Ontario Paper Company, is open to the public. The lighthouse and company property farther north on the mainland offer excellent sites for observing migration. The area contains interesting vegetation, including dense stands of White Cedar on poorly drained sites.

DIRECTIONS. Take Hwy 540 almost to Meldrum Bay; turn left at only road (watch for sign) leading to extreme W end of Manitoulin Island; go 10 km to lighthouse. Road passes through beautiful, privately owned deciduous woodlands; avoid trespassing.

Beaver Lake Meadows

Between Meldrum Bay and Silver Water, Highway 540 passes

through a very large area of wet meadow that can be viewed from the road. The site is good for observing wetland birds such as Common Snipe, rails, and sandpipers.

DIRECTIONS. Located on both sides of Hwy 540 about 10 km W of Silver Water & about 12 km E of Meldrum Bay.

Silver Lake Fire Tower

This area is characterized by a very distinctive fractured dolostone-limestone plateau dominated by alvar vegetation. The site is thinly wooded with White Birch, Trembling Aspen, White Spruce, Balsam Fir, and White Cedar together with some White Pine, Red Oak, and Sugar Maple and a well-developed scrub layer of Creeping Juniper, Downy Arrow-wood, and Smooth Sumac. Among numerous uncommon flora are Dwarf Lake Iris, Smooth Cliffbrake, and Oregon Woodsia. The area also includes Niagara Escarpment cliff face and good examples of moist deciduous woods with swampy areas that support such northern species as Painted Trillium, as well as Blue Cohosh and other typically more southern plants.

DIRECTIONS. Head N, then W from village of Silver Water on Hwy 540 past N end of Silver Lake. Hwy gradually dips S, then turns back N. About 2.75 km after your last view of Silver Lake, hwy turns sharply to left to head straight W again. Short trail to Silver Lake ranger station starts behind small cabin on N side of hwy.

Burnt Island Harbour–Christina Bay

This section of the southern shoreline in western Manitoulin Island offers some fine alvar vegetation communities. The area is gently sloping limestone tableland which gradually rises inland. Thin layers of sand over the bedrock are found at Burnt Island Harbour and in localized spots around Christina Bay. The scrub forest of Jack and Red Pines, Balsam Fir, White Cedar, aspen, and birch is interspersed with limestone openings, where several significant plants, including Hill's Thistle, grow. Among other species commonly found are Fringed Gentian, Small-flowered Gerardia, Cut-leaved Anemone, Low Calamint, Linear-leaved Sundew, various coralroots, Grass-pink, and Rose Pogonia.

This area is known as one of the richest sites on the island for butterflies and moths. The shorelines are excellent for viewing shorebirds during migration and waterfowl in spring and summer. Hooded, Common, and Red-breasted Mergansers all summer in the area and Great Blue Heron are abundant. Check the adjacent forest for warblers (especially American Redstart) as well as White-throated Sparrow and Red-breasted Nuthatch.

DIRECTIONS. Take Hwy 540 W to Silver Water. Where hwy bends N continue straight W; turn S at next jct & follow scenic, winding, partly surfaced main road 7 km to Burnt Island Harbour. (In mid June watch for Lance-leaved Coreopsis along roadside.) Just before crossing causeway over wetland to Burnt Island, turn right & follow short, rough car trail over bedrock pavement to water. Park on limestone pavement. For Christina Bay: from previous stop, walk back out to road; turn right; walk down road 100 m to old logging road; turn E to walk through some outstanding alvar areas eventually ending at Christina Bay. Note that this land (E of main road near shore) is owned by Quebec & Ontario Paper Co; *permission must be obtained before access.*

Carroll Wood Bay

A beautiful White Pine forest, through which the dirt road to Walkhouse Point passes, offers good woodland birding. From the roadside watch for warblers (Ovenbird, Blackburnian, Black-and-white, Black-throated Green, Magnolia, and Pine), vireos, Brown Creeper, kinglets, and thrushes.

DIRECTIONS. From Silver Water go 2 km E on Hwy 540; turn S towards Walkhouse Point.

Cooks Bay

Limestone ledges at the base of the small escarpment cliff along the south shore of Cooks Bay support a number of uncommon ferns, including Limestone Oak Fern and Purple-stemmed Cliffbrake. Warblers are abundant in the area. Watch for Sandhill Cranes in wet fields beside the road leading to Cooks Dock.

DIRECTIONS. Take Hwy 540 W from Elizabeth Bay; turn N at sign to Cooks Dock; follow road down escarpment to bay. From dock, a trail runs E along lakeshore.

Misery Bay Provincial Nature Reserve

This park protects a large tract of land (697 ha) extending east from the Robinson-Burpee Townline to Mac's Bay. The site encompasses extensive dolostone pavement replete with fossil pittings and, concentrated at the head of the bay, a series of undulating parallel ridges of sand, cobble, and shingle. This limestone pavement presents an impressive alvar complex interspersed with islands of seasonally wet woodland. The beach strands at the head of the bay form a series of marsh, bog, and calcareous fen communities where Sedge Wrens are found. Small dunes occur west of Misery Point along the shore of Lake Huron. The alvar provides habitat for many plant species having Great Lakes shoreline and western prairie affinities. Merlins frequent the area in summer. The bog and fen complex at the head of the bay offers a rich assortment of orchids, including Tall White Bog Orchid, Rose Pogonia, Grass-pink, and Showy Lady's-slipper, as well as many Great Lakes fen species. Midland Painted Turtles are frequently seen along the beach.

DIRECTIONS. Go 15 km W from Evansville on Hwy 540. At small sign to Little Lake Huron Estates, turn left onto single-track road (very sandy at first, then very rough limestone pavement). Where road splits after climbing onto area of rock pavement, follow little-used left fork; park there & walk to Misery Bay. Avoid private property.

Gore Bay Area

– **Bur Oak Savanna.** On privately owned property along the west side of Highway 540 is an area of very thin soil over limestone pavement. Bur Oaks are scattered across the landscape, while the ground beneath is covered with Long-plumed Purple Avens. Breezes blowing along the ground cause the feathery plumes to give the illusion of prairie smoke, another name for this species.

DIRECTIONS. From Gore Bay go W on Hwy 540 to 3 km S of jct with Hwy 540A. View from road only.

– **Road to Barrie Island.** Along Highway 540A just west of the Gore Bay airport is one of the best places on Manitoulin for seeing Eastern Bluebirds, Upland Sandpipers, and Ospreys.

DIRECTIONS. From Gore Bay go W on Hwys 540 & 540A.

– East Bluff. A small park perched on the 85-m-high bluff offers a great view of Gore Bay and west along the north shore of Manitoulin.
DIRECTIONS. From town of Gore Bay, follow road signs E & N up to East Bluff.

Kagawong

Kagawong is a charming unspoilt village nestled in an escarpment notch looking out onto the North Channel. On the west side of the valley, below where Bridal Veil Falls drops over a limestone ledge, a pleasant trail leads down to the village. The slopes have rushing springs. Owing to its sheltered position, the valley contains unusually lush vegetation and diverse flora.
DIRECTIONS. For Bridal Veil Falls: from Hwy 540 watch for parking area E of Kagawong village before hwy turns W towards Gore Bay.

West Bay

The West Bay First Nation has developed a small system of hiking trails (Mchigeeng Trail) which winds its way through hardwoods and streams to the top of the escarpment. The varied habitats along the route support many species of ferns and woodland wildflowers.
DIRECTIONS. Proceed S in village of West Bay on Hwy 551 to covered picnic shelter on E side of hwy.

Cup and Saucer Trail

Here the north-facing cliffs provide habitat for interesting ferns, such as Smooth Cliffbrake and Rock Polypody. Many wildflowers typical of mixed conifer-hardwood forest are frequently found along the trails. Both loops of the trail end up on top of High Hill, one of the highest bluff outcrops on the Niagara Escarpment. Lake Manitou can be seen to the south and the quartzite hills of the La Cloche Mountains across the North Channel to the north.
DIRECTIONS. Trail begins at parking area 4 km NE of West Bay on Hwy 540.

McLeans Mountain

A short distance south of Little Current is McLeans Mountain, a north-facing shale escarpment. Beach terraces left behind by retreating glacial lakes are visible on the slopes. From the mountain, look across North Channel to the ghostly white hills of the La Cloche Mountains.

DIRECTIONS. Take Hwy 540 out of Little Current; continue straight S when hwy takes sharp bend W & follow winding road up mountain; park on roadside.

A.J. Wagg Memorial Park

Trails through this woodland area lead from the rich hardwoods of the lower land, where Moonseed vines and Lopseed occur, to the wooded escarpment face with its abundance of ferns, including woodsia, Slender Cliffbrake, Maidenhair Spleenwort, and Fragile Fern.

DIRECTIONS. Located in village of Mindemoya on S side of Hwy 542, 0.8 km E of jct with Hwy 551.

Mud Lake

Mud Lake is shallow and surrounded by an extensive fen. The road across one edge provides excellent viewing. Black Terns, Ring-necked Ducks, and Pied-billed Grebes are among species to be expected here.

DIRECTIONS. From jct of Hwys 542 & 551 in Mindemoya, proceed 1 km due S on gravel road.

Fields of Mindemoya Lakeshore

This extensive area of flat agricultural land is favoured by a variety of migrating shorebirds. Sandhill Cranes gather here each autumn. Vast flocks of Horned Larks and American Pipits pass through in fall migration.

DIRECTIONS. Follow Hwy 542 for 5 km W from village of Mindemoya, skirting S shore of Mindemoya Lake, to fields on S side of road just E of bridge over Mindemoya River. Or, follow gravel road 1 km S of & parallel to hwy. View fields from roadsides only.

Providence Bay

Although heavily used for recreation, Providence Bay has representative dune systems and interdunal wet meadows. The best examples occur west of the main village. When visiting the continuous dune and wet meadow community along the shoreline, stay well away from cottage frontages. Minimize damage to the vegetation by staying on boardwalks.
DIRECTIONS. On Hwy 551 on S side of island.

Carter Bay

This is a beautiful spot. Although somewhat disturbed, the dune bluffs here are some of the best in the upper Great Lakes. The primary dunes are covered by American Beach Grass interspersed with such interesting plants as Beach Pea, Sea Rocket, Tall Wormwood, and Heart-leaved Willow. The slacks in between provide habitat for Grass-of-Parnassus, White Camass, Fringed Gentian, Kalm's St John's-wort, Kalm's Lobelia, Linear-leaved Sundew, and Seaside Arrow-grass. Of note is the rare Great Lakes Wheat Grass, endemic to the Great Lakes. The older dunes are forested with White Cedar, Balsam Fir, White Birch, and White Pine, with a rich understorey of club-mosses, lady's-slippers, and twayblades. Visit with care; this delicate ecosystem can tolerate only minimal trampling. Coastal forests to the west of Carter Bay contain spruces draped in *Usnea* lichens, good habitat for Northern Parula.
DIRECTIONS. Take Hwy 6 N from South Baymouth; turn left onto Hwy 542, then Hwy 542A. Continue past Tehkummah towards Providence Bay. Carter Bay entrance is 4 km past turnoff to Michael's Bay, & is marked by stone walls & metal gate. Follow very rough road 4.5 km to dunes; park along access road. Land is privately owned, but public access is permitted.

Michael's Bay Road

Winding through the typical White Spruce and Balsam Fir forest of the south shore, this scenic road follows the Manitou River to the Huron shore at Michael's Bay, where there is a small township park. American Redstart, Black-throated Green Warbler, and Northern Parula occur along the route (view from roadside only). Osprey and Caspian Tern fish in the shallow waters of Michael's Bay. A hiking trail along the Carnarvon and Tehkummah township line runs north from Michael's Bay for several kilometres.

DIRECTIONS. Take Hwy 6 N from South Baymouth; turn left on Hwy 542, then left on Hwy 542A. Go W past Tehkummah for 8 km on gov't road towards Providence Bay; turn left just past Manitou River.

Rogers Creek Area

Sandhill Cranes and other marsh birds frequent the large marsh and river here. Sandhill Cranes nest at several sites on Manitoulin. In October migrant cranes from the north congregate in large numbers, especially on the Spring Bay and Tehkummah farmlands.

DIRECTIONS. From South Baymouth proceed 3 km N on Hwy 6 to Lake Shore Rd; turn right & follow shore of South Bay for 6 km to creek mouth.

Voyageur Trail

See entry under District of Algoma.

Great La Cloche Island

When driving north from Manitoulin Island on Highway 6, after crossing the swing-bridge, notice a broad, open limestone plain. This area supports shortgrass prairie habitats related to those found in western Canada. The dominant grass here is Prairie Dropseed.

Killarney Provincial Park

See entry under District of Sudbury.

DISTRICT OF PARRY SOUND

It is said that there are 3,000 islands on the north shore of this lake [Huron], of different shapes and sizes; most of them are composed of granite, with trees of evergreen growing from the interstices of the rocks, while others are entirely barren ... Some of them, towering far above the rest, are barren and rugged; others beautifully wooded, with the diversified foliage of the cedar, pine, and spruce. When on the lake, you see them stretching in the distance as far as the eye can reach, with swarms of gulls and ducks flying about. (Rev. Peter Jones [1802–56], Ojibway Methodist minister)

Located between Georgian Bay and the Algonquin Highlands, the District of Parry Sound is characterized by low, rounded, rocky hills with numerous lakes and rivers. Mixed stands of Sugar Maple, American Beech, Basswood, Yellow Birch, Eastern Hemlock, White Pine, Red Maple, and White Ash are found on the uplands, while White Spruce grows on sandy sites. The rocky Georgian Bay shore has stunted, wind-blown White Pine and Red Oak growing in the thin soil. The Thirty Thousand Islands consist of myriad small islets that stretch along the coast for 150 km, from Honey Harbour in the south to the French River in the north. This area is famous for its fall colours, which are at their peak from mid September to mid October.

Atlantic coastal plain flora such as Virginia Meadow-beauty, Lesser Waterwort, Stiff Yellow Flax, and Ridged Yellow Flax are of special interest. In Ontario these plants are largely restricted to specialized sites along the former coastlines of glacial Lake Algonquin, which once covered most of the District of Parry Sound.

The District of Parry Sound is home to the threatened Eastern Massasauga, Ontario's only venomous snake. 'Hardwood rattlers,' formally known as Eastern Fox Snakes, occur in the woodlands adjacent to the coast. These harmless snakes get their name from their habit of vibrating their tails when disturbed, making a rattling sound in dried leaves. The Five-lined Skink, Ontario's only lizard, inhabits the Georgian Bay shoreline.

Wasi River

There is a Walleye spawning run from about April 20 to May 10. DIRECTIONS. Go to mouth of river at Callander off Hwys 11 & 654.

Restoule Provincial Park

This park, noted for its beautiful northern scenery, fronts on two lakes which link via canoe routes to the French River. A high granite shoreline bluff towers 60 m to provide a spectacular view. Hobblebush, with its large, round, veiny leaves, is found along woodland paths. Watch for Broad-winged Hawks. The Loring deer yard, where up to 14,000 White-tailed Deer winter, is located southwest of the 1,128-ha park.

DIRECTIONS. Located 45 km W of Powassan on Hwy 534; see prov hwy map.

INFORMATION. Restoule Provincial Park, Restoule, Ont, P0H 2R0, 705-729-2010.

French River Provincial Park

See entry under District of Sudbury.

Pickerel River

The Pickerel River and its close neighbour to the north, the French River, lie in one of the most scenic parts of Ontario, an area which also offers excellent wildlife viewing opportunities. The Pickerel River flows over some of the best exposed bedrock in the province. The barren granite with its windswept pines provides breathtaking scenery. A population of Wapiti released near Burwash in the 1930s has thrived and spread, and bugling stags can now be heard during the rutting season. Black Bears and Gray Wolves are found here, and River Otters frolic in the river. Look for Merlin and Osprey as you canoe along the watercourse. Walleye spawn at the bases of the rapids in the river.

DIRECTIONS. Access via Grundy Lake Provincial Park.

Grundy Lake Provincial Park

Scattered among the park's forests are expanses of rugged granite rock and a network of small lakes and marshes. Woodlands support a mix of coniferous and deciduous trees, predominantly Red and White Pines, Sugar and Red Maples, and Yellow Birch. Trees more typical of forests to the north, such as White Birch, Trembling Aspen, and Jack Pine, also occur. Moose, Beaver, Mink, Blanding's Turtle, and Great Blue Heron frequent the

wetlands. Watch for Osprey, Whip-poor-will, Boreal Chickadee, Warbling Vireo, and Golden-winged Warbler in the 2,500-ha park.
DIRECTIONS. Located at jct of Hwys 69 & 522; see prov hwy map.
INFORMATION. Grundy Lake Provincial Park, RR 1, Britt, Ont, P0G 1A0, 705-383-2369.

Brown and Wilson Townships and Area

These townships are, for the most part, remote and rugged, with numerous lakes, pine-rimmed shores, Beaver-controlled stream systems, and open rock barrens. The area supports an exceptional abundance of wildlife, including several packs of Gray Wolves and other fur-bearers. Osprey are frequently seen and, in winter, Golden Eagles occasionally visit. Purple Bladderwort is common. A wilderness park has been proposed in this area.

– **Magnetawan River.** Although sections of the shoreline are considerably developed for recreation, parts of the Magnetawan River canoe route are bordered with Cardinal-flowers, lush marshes, sheer cliff faces, and immensely beautiful landscapes. Watch for Virginia Meadow-beauty blooming on sandy shores from July to September. Gray Wolves howl along the river, especially near the confluence of the south and north branches. Listen in August for yelping pups and howling adults in the main pack, answered by lone adults in the distance.
DIRECTIONS. 1) Via Harris Lake: from Pointe au Baril Station go 12 km N on Hwy 69 & turn E on road along Harris River to lake. 2) Via Wahwashkesh Lake: from Ahmic Harbour go 5 km W on Hwy 124; turn N on Hwy 520; go 14 km & turn N on road to Wahwashkesh; go 7 km to lake.

Limestone Islands Provincial Nature Reserve

The two most remote of the Thirty Thousand Islands, these islands are located offshore from Snug Harbour. Unlike the barren granitic islands that form most of the coastal archipelago, these low-lying islands are pure limestone, created from the remains of 450-million-year-old sea creatures, such as horn corals, large cephalopods, and trilobites.

The most significant feature of these islands is the colonial nesting birds: Caspian and Common Terns; Double-crested Cormorant; Ring-billed, Herring, and Little Gulls; and Black-crowned Night-Heron. The flora consists of an odd mixture of alien weeds, southern and boreal species, and alvar species such as Early Buttercup, Balsam Ragwort, and Twig-rush. Herbaceous plants grow on the white bedrock among clumps of stunted trees, low shrubby Black Cherry, Red-osier Dogwood, and Poison-ivy. The moderating influence of Georgian Bay allows species such as Porcupine Sedge to extend their ranges northward to this area.

DIRECTIONS. Access is by boat from Snug Harbour. Entry is restricted until after mid July, when nesting season is over.

INFORMATION. MNR.

Killbear Provincial Park

When glacial floods swept the Georgian Bay shoreline clean of sand and till, Killbear was somehow spared. Today a chain of crescent-shaped sand beaches is backed by low, thinly forested dunes. Along the backshore, where outcrops of pink rock protrude through the white sands, look for chattermarks. These rows of parallel arcs were etched on the bedrock when boulders frozen to the undersides of moving glaciers were bounced over the rock surface. Watch for Blanding's and Map Turtles in the wetlands. Listen for Barred Owl and Whip-poor-will in the wooded uplands. Fall colours in the 1,736-ha park peak in late September and early October. Park trails can be used year-round.

DIRECTIONS. Located at mouth of Parry Sound on Hwy 559; see prov hwy map.

INFORMATION. Killbear Provincial Park, RR 1, Nobel, Ont, P0G 1G0, 705-342-5492.

Oastler Lake Provincial Park

Here a scenic peninsula jutting into Oastler Lake is dominated by rolling hills and rocky outcrops. Check for Prairie Warblers in open, scrubby vegetation. Trails can be used for cross-country skiing and snowshoeing in winter.

DIRECTIONS. Located 12 km S of Parry Sound on Hwy 69; see prov hwy map.

INFORMATION. Oastler Lake Provincial Park, RR 2, Parry Sound, Ont, P2A 1S4, 705-378-2401.

Massasauga Provincial Park (Blackstone Harbour)

Massasauga Provincial Park protects almost 12,000 ha of coast in the southwest corner of the District of Parry Sound. The landscape of this remote area features granite rock with windswept pines, *Sphagnum* bogs, alder swamps, and various other types of wetlands. The array of significant plants includes Atlantic coastal plain species such as Virginia Meadow-beauty and Southern Yellow-eyed Grass.

Among mammals of interest are Canada Lynx (here approaching the southern edge of its Ontario distribution), Meadow Jumping Mouse, and Gray Wolf. The herpetofauna is diverse; Eastern Massasauga, Eastern Hognose Snake, Northern Ribbon Snake, Eastern Fox Snake, Map Turtle, and Five-lined Skink are all found in the park. This area has one of the largest populations of Prairie Warblers in the country. Check open, rocky barrens where White Pine, Red Oak, and Common Juniper grow. Watch too for Osprey and Red-shouldered Hawk.

DIRECTIONS. Access is by water only. 1) If travelling by boat from S end of Georgian Bay, park islands are first encountered to N of Twelve Mile Bay. 2) If travelling by car with small boat on trailer, most common route is W off Hwy 69 (via Muskoka Rd 11 N through MacTier, or S from Gordon Bay via Hwy 612), then 16 km W on Healey Lake Rd to marinas at Woods Bay. 3) Most canoeists enter park via Three Legged Lake; to reach parking lot at lake, take James Bay Junction Rd (just S of Oastler Lake Prov Park on Hwy 69), then Blue Lake Rd, then Three Legged Lake Rd.

INFORMATION. MNR; Oastler Lake Provincial Park, RR 2, Parry Sound, Ont, P2A 1S4, 705-378-2401.

Gordon Bay Area

In the area inland from the bay you can sometimes find Red-shouldered Hawk; American Kestrel; Golden-winged, Black-throated Green, and Black-throated Blue Warblers; Common Snipe; American Bittern; Winter Wren; Indigo Bunting; Black-billed Cuckoo; Pileated Woodpecker; and many more species of birds.

DIRECTIONS. On Hwy 69 S of Parry Sound, 8 km S of Hwy 141 jct.

H.N. Crossley Nature Reserve

This Federation of Ontario Naturalists' reserve protects a 12-ha tract featuring an eyed bog and its wooded drainage area. The open waters of Bruce Pond form the eye, which is encircled by a *Sphagnum* mat fringed by a band of shrubs and trees. The bog's outer edge is marked by a lagg, a watery moat-like zone. Look for Pitcher-plant, Spatulate-leaved and Round-leaved Sundews, Grass-pink, Checkered Rattlesnake-plantain, Virginia Meadow-beauty, and Virginia Chain Fern.

DIRECTIONS. 1) From Rosseau go 6 km S on Hwy 632; turn E on 1st road & drive 3 km to entrance sign on S side. 2) Take Muskoka Rd 7 N from Hwy 118 just W of Port Carling.

DISTRICT MUNICIPALITY OF MUSKOKA

It is truly named Fairy Lake, being a most beautiful sheet of water, and having the peculiarity of carrying any ordinary sound from one end to the other with marvellous distinctness. On entering it, the laughing cackle of a couple of loons was heard, and they were supposed to be around a point close at hand, but a little investigation revealed the fact that they were fully four miles distant. On seeing our little fleet, their notes grew louder, and we enjoyed a perfect concert of melody from their clarion throats during our stay. (September 2, 1865, 'Up the Muskoka & Down the Trent,' *Toronto Globe*, October 4, 1865)

Straddling the latitude of 45°N, halfway between the Equator and the North Pole, Muskoka lies along the southern edge of the ancient Precambrian Shield, just north of the Ordovician sedimentary bedrock of the Great Lakes Lowland. The district's location on the east side of Georgian Bay makes it prone to heavy winter snowfall.

Muskoka is a mix of lakes and rivers surrounded by landscapes of tall White Pines growing on gneissic rockland. It contains a rich assemblage of northern and southern species of plants, animals, and birds, many on the edge of their ranges. Mixed woodlands on the uplands support deciduous trees such as Sugar Maple, American Beech, Basswood, and Yellow Birch, as well as conifers, including Eastern Hemlock and White Pine. Scrubby trees grow along the rocky, windswept shores of Georgian Bay, while extensive wooded swamps are found in the southern and western sections of the district. At higher inland elevations, species with boreal affinities begin to appear.

Muskoka is the centre of concentration for Atlantic coastal plain species in Ontario. Such plants are more typically found in the coastal wetlands between Cape Cod and Georgia. The district is renowned for its spectacular fall colours, the scarlets, yellows, and russets being set off by dark green conifers. The best viewing time is between September 20 and October 10. In winter, watch on warmer days for White-tailed Deer on the ice of Muskoka's numerous lakes.

The southern boundary of Muskoka is the Severn River, a part of the Trent-Severn Canal system that serves as a highway for boats from the eastern part of the province to Georgian Bay.

Twelve Mile Bay

Red igneous rock exposures against deep green White Pines and clear blue water create a strikingly beautiful landscape here. There is no park, although sections of Georgian Bay Islands National Park are found along Twelve Mile Bay. A plethora of reptiles and amphibians is present in the area, including Stinkpot and Blanding's, Map, Common Snapping, and Midland Painted Turtles, along with Northern Water Snake, Eastern Garter Snake, Eastern Fox Snake, and Eastern Milk Snake. Muskellunge, Northern Pike, Shorthead Redhorse, and Bowfin inhabit the bay, while Smallmouth Bass frequents the shoals. Double-crested Cormorant, Great Blue Heron, and Prairie Warbler are summer residents. Northern Flying Squirrels are active at night, and Cardinal-flower blooms in August.

DIRECTIONS. From jct of Hwy 169 at Foot's Bay, go 10 km S on Hwy 69; turn W on Dist Rd 12, last half of which parallels bay.

Georgian Bay Islands National Park

Of the approximately 60 islands in the park, some contain areas of bare granite rock while others are well forested with Red Oak, Sugar and Red Maples, American Beech, White Pine, and Eastern Hemlock. Abundant shoreline and wetland provide habitat for rich and varied flora. Prairie Warblers inhabit open areas. One of the park's highlights is its diversity of herpeto-fauna. Midland Chorus Frog, Eastern Hognose Snake, Eastern Massasauga, Stinkpot, Blanding's Turtle, Two-lined Sala-mander, Mudpuppy, and Red-spotted Newt are among the 35 species present.

DIRECTIONS. From Honey Harbour (end of Dist Rd 5, off Hwy 69) take canoe, motor boat, or water taxi. Beausoleil Island is 5 km out from Honey Harbour.

INFORMATION. Georgian Bay Islands National Park, Box 28, Honey Harbour, Ont, P0E 1E0, 705-756-2415.

– Beausoleil Island. Relative to all the other islands, the natural features of Beausoleil Island stand out. Here, two distinctly dif-ferent landscapes meet: the Precambrian Shield and the Great Lakes Lowland. The result is northern mixed hardwoods con-taining species with Carolinian affinities. Trails that ring and criss-cross the 8-km-long island illustrate the diversity.

Huron Trail. Between Beausoleil Point and Cedar Spring the trail passes through a mature Sugar Maple–American Beech–Red Oak forest. Listen for Cerulean Warblers, Scarlet Tanagers, and Pileated Woodpeckers. Look for Squawroot and Beech-drops. A successional field at Cedar Spring is filled with native and alien wildflowers and birds of open fields.

Thumb Point–Bobbie's Trail. This area is a patchwork of mature hardwood, mixed coniferous and deciduous, White Cedar, and Eastern Hemlock forests, as well as several inland and shoreline wetlands. Birds and amphibians are abundant. Among notable plants are Yellow Lady's-slipper, Green-leaved Rattlesnake-plantain, and several ferns, including Bulblet Fern, Marsh Fern, and Spinulose, Crested, Glandular, and Marginal Wood Ferns.

Fairy Lake and Goblin Lake. Circle these lakes using Cam-brian Trail and Fairy Trail. The landscape here is composed of pockets of White Pine, Red Oak (with some White Oak), and Common and Red Junipers set among granite outcrops. Com-monly observed birds are Prairie Warbler and Rufous-sided

Towhee. Present but elusive are Eastern Fox Snake, Eastern Smooth Green Snake, and Northern Ribbon Snake. Plants of interest include Atlantic coastal plain species such as Lesser Waterwort, Southern Yellow-eyed Grass, and Carey's Knotweed. Check protected shorelines for Smith's Bulrush, Grass-leaved Arrowhead, Grass-of-Parnassus, and Spatulate-leaved and Linear-leaved Sundews. Just off Fairy Trail behind Ojibway Bay is a wetland covered with Virginia Chain Fern.

Big Chute Rocklands

This complex of dry, rocky uplands and wetland vegetation has a high concentration of rare plants. Many of these grow along the Severn River on the point west of the power plant. Five-lined Skink and several rare species of birds, including Prairie Warbler, occur in the area.

Among the many plants of note are a number that somewhat resemble grasses. These include Grass-leaved Arrowhead, Long and Field Sedges, and Eaton's and Engelmann's Quillworts; all prefer aquatic habitats or other damp sites. Ebony and Maidenhair Spleenworts, on the other hand, are attracted to the rocky terrain. Showier species also flourish at Big Chute; watch for the nodding white spikes of Lizard's-tail, the clustered pink blossoms of Carolina Crane's-bill, the golden petals of Early Buttercup, and the hairy stems of Tall White Cinquefoil. Other floral specialties of the site include Yellow Pimpernel, Dragonhead, Naked-flowered Tick-trefoil, Whorled Milkwort, Venus' Looking Glass, and Purple Meadow-rue.

At Big Chute, two navigational marine railways, constructed in 1917 and 1979, part of the Trent-Severn Waterway, are now operated by Parks Canada. A museum occupies parts of an Ontario Hydro power plant dating from 1917 but recently replaced.

DIRECTIONS. Follow Hwy 69 N of Port Severn; turn right on Muskoka Rd 34 (White's Falls Rd) & go to marine railway.

Ragged Woods

This area supports a mix of hardwoods and conifers; Red Oak, White Pine, American Beech, White and Yellow Birches, and

Eastern Hemlock all occur. These woodlands near the Ragged Rapids generating station are the best location in Muskoka for observing mushrooms. Interesting plants, including Squawroot and Pinesap, grow here. Large mammals, such as Black Bear and White-tailed Deer, can be seen, and Red-shouldered Hawks frequent the area. The openings along the roadside are good spots for observing several species of butterflies. The Musquash and Moon rivers provide a first-rate canoe route to Georgian Bay.

DIRECTIONS. From Hwy 169 at Bala, go about 6 km W on Dist Rd 38; turn right just past IONA camp & follow road to generating station parking lot. Canoes can be launched above or below hydro plant.

Hardy Lake Provincial Park

The western half of this 765-ha park is overlain by deep ground moraine, whereas the eastern portion consists of barren rock, ridges, and swampy depressions. The 98-ha Hardy Lake is an excellent lake to explore by canoe. At least 14 species of Atlantic coastal plain flora, a number of them rare, grow along its pristine shoreline. Grass-like plants such as Bayonet Rush, Robbins' Spike-rush, and Twig-rush stand half a metre tall along the water's edge. Lesser Waterwort forms small mats on damp shoreline mud, while Cordate Floating Heart anchors offshore. Horned Bladderwort and Spatulate-leaved Sundew supplement their diets with insects. Flowers bloom colourfully beside the lakeshore – yellows in Golden Hedge-hyssop and Southern Yellow-eyed Grass, and pinks in Marsh St John's-wort and Virginia Meadow-beauty. The fen bordering Hardy Lake is also rich in plant life, especially orchids. Butterflies of various species can be found.

DIRECTIONS. Located 6.5 km E of Bala (near Torrance) on Hwy 169.

Torrance Oak Barrens

This area is a large expanse of bedrock barrens, treed with Red Oak, White Pine, and White Ash as well as some White Oak. Triangle Grape Fern, Southern Twayblade, Biculpate Pondweed, and Yellow Bartonia grow in the area. Three-toothed Cinquefoil is at the southernmost limit of its range at this location. This is a good area for observing butterflies, and for finding Eastern Hognose Snake and Five-lined Skink. Several bird species have been noted on the barrens, including Eastern Bluebird and   Yellow-billed Cuckoo.

DIRECTIONS. From Torrance on Hwy 169, go about 5 km S on Dist Rd 13. Park in lot on rock pavement near Highland Pond on NE side of road.

Sparrow Lake

Sparrow Lake on the Severn River is one of the best places in Ontario for studying aquatic plants. Many other interesting and sometimes rare plants also grow here. Sedges and bulrushes flourish; Field Sedge, Low Cyperus, and Slender Bulrush all occur. Grasses are well represented by species such as Kalm's Brome, Switch Grass, Virginia Wild-rye, Tuckerman's Witch Grass, and Rough and Prairie Dropseeds. The varied assemblage of wildflowers includes Wild Garlic, Small Beggar's-ticks, Three-seeded Mercury, Showy Tick-trefoil, Hairy Beardtongue, Small Purple Fringed Orchid, and Tubercled Orchid. Northern Wild Rice colonies support many species of waterfowl during fall migration. Common and Caspian Terns summer in the area.

DIRECTIONS. From Hwy 11 at N edge of Severn Bridge, go 3 km W on Muskoka Rd 13; turn left & go 4 km. Boat access: municipal launch on NE shore, or at Severn River on SE end of lake.

Riley Lake Rocklands

This area consists of a series of Precambrian gneissic ridges and water-filled depressions. Smooth Rock-cress, Carey's Knotweed, and Switch Grass grow here. Five-lined Skink is common on the hot, dry ridges, and Eastern Hognose Snake has been recorded. There is also a good mixture of mammal and bird species.

DIRECTIONS. From Hwy 11 just S of Severn Bridge, go E on Simcoe Rd 52 (becomes Muskoka Rd 6) for 17 km; turn E to lake.

Bracebridge Lagoons

These former sewage treatment cells represent one of the best birding locations in Muskoka. During migration large numbers of warblers and other songbirds are found in the forest adjacent to the lagoons. When water levels are low, the area can be excellent for viewing shorebirds and waterfowl. Northern Shovelers summer in the area. There is an observation platform at the top of the hill overlooking the lagoons. A cross-country ski trail traverses the woods.

DIRECTIONS. From Hwy 11 at Muskoka Falls, go 4.7 km NW on Hwy 118 (Dist Rd 4) to Beaumont Dr (Dist Rd 16); turn left & go 0.8 km to James W. Kerr Park on left. Walk up hill.

Big East River Delta

This area supports plants uncommon in much of Muskoka, including many sedges and rushes. Large stands of Bayonet Rush and Knotty Pondweed grow in the water, and Marsh St John's-wort and Nodding Trillium grow on the delta. The Big East River is a good canoe route for naturalists.

DIRECTIONS. Located at mouth of Big East River on N side of Lake Vernon just W of town of Huntsville. Best access is by boat from end of Kinsman Beach Rd (S from Ravenscliffe Rd [Dist Rd 2], W of Hwy 11). Paddle W to mouth of river.

Arrowhead Provincial Park

Evidence of a former shoreline of glacial Lake Algonquin can be seen in Arrowhead. Below the ancient waterline, sandy soils are found in the park's present-day lowlands. At higher levels a rugged landscape is clothed in hardwood forests. Following the course of a much larger postglacial waterway, the sheltered valley of the Big East River harbours several southern plants, such as Cardinal-flower. Canoeing, hiking, and cross-country skiing are popular park activities. There is a fine show of fall colour.

DIRECTIONS. Located 6 km N of Huntsville on Hwy 11; see prov hwy map.

INFORMATION. Arrowhead Provincial Park, RR 3, Huntsville, Ont, P0A 1K0, 705-789-5105.

Oxtongue River–Ragged Falls Provincial Park

See entry under Haliburton County.

Leslie M. Frost Natural Resource Centre

See entry under Haliburton County.

HALIBURTON COUNTY

> I was sitting alone in the month of March on a high forest hill
> overlooking Red Stone Lake in that township. The ice was still on
> the lake and presently beneath me I saw a band of deer, thirty in
> number, young and old, headed by a great buck, crossing the lake
> to a large island where they would stay until the ice disappeared.
> This band of deer had a wintering place not far distant and lived
> on ground hemlock and buds until the leaves appeared and other
> herbage in the forest. (Guildford Township, 1862, Vernon Wads-
> worth [1843?–1940], surveyor)

Haliburton County, with its numerous lakes, rugged landscape,
and scenic beauty, is located on the Canadian Shield, a region of
typically thin soils and primarily granitic rocks. Grenville limestones occur in strips in the central and southern portions of the
county. Haliburton County is situated on the Algonquin dome,
which attains its greatest height in the part of Algonquin Park
that lies just north of the county border. From Manitou Mountain in the northeast, the county slopes downward to the lowest
point at Gull Lake in the southwestern corner. A 16-km-long
esker stretches east and west of the town of Gooderham.

Haliburton's mixed coniferous and deciduous tree communities are typical of the Great Lakes–St Lawrence Forest Region.
The most common tree is the Sugar Maple, the primary actor in
a spectacular show of autumn colour. White Ash, Basswood,
American Beech, Yellow Birch, Hop-hornbeam, Balsam Fir, Eastern Hemlock, and White Pine are also major components of the
woodlands.

Quillworts and other elements of the Atlantic coastal plain
flora are among the interesting plants present in the county.
Orchids include Blunt-leaved Orchid, Hooded Ladies'-tresses,
Pink Lady's-slipper, Grass-pink, Rose Pogonia, and Ragged
Fringed Orchid. Pink Corydalis brightens rocky openings, and
trilliums bloom in profusion in the woodlands. With more than
600 lakes and numerous streams, Haliburton County has excel-

lent habitat for many species of aquatic vegetation. Twenty-one species of pondweed, six species of milfoil, and eight species of bladderwort, including the rare Twin-scaped Bladderwort, have been recorded.

Significant winter birds include Golden and Bald Eagles, Red and White-winged Crossbills, Pine Grosbeak, and Snowy Owl. In the summer look for Cooper's and Red-shouldered Hawks, Sedge Wren, Golden-winged Warbler, Barred and Northern Saw-whet Owls, and many other species that inhabit the woodlands of the region.

Among mammals of note are Gray Wolf, Black Bear (check the dumps), Marten, Fisher, River Otter, Moose, and Southern Red-backed Vole (which reaches the southern limit of its Ontario distribution in Haliburton County). The Southern Flying Squirrel is near the northern limits of its range in the hardwood forests around Dorset; it prefers woodlands in which maple, beech, oak, and serviceberries are prominent.

Among the significant herpetofauna is the Eastern Hognose Snake, resident on the sandy beaches of the numerous lakes.

Approximately one-half of Ontario's butterfly species have been recorded in Haliburton County, sitting as it does at the southern edge of the Canadian Shield. There is a mixture of northern species, such as Macoun's Arctic, Chryxus Arctic, Hoary Comma, Western Pine Elfin, and Saepiolus Blue, and of southern species, such as Red Spotted Purple, the Buckeye, Snout Butterfly, Early Hairstreak, and Little Sulphur. The height of the butterfly-watching season is in late June and early July.

Haliburton County is known for its cross-country skiing. For ski trail maps contact: Haliburton Highlands Chamber of Commerce, Box 147, Minden, Ont, K0M 2K0, 1-800-461-7677.

Oxtongue River–Ragged Falls Provincial Park

This waterway park lies along a glacial spillway that once carried meltwater southward from glaciers covering the Algonquin Highlands to glacial Lake Algonquin. The river journeys through rugged landscape, and tumbles over rapids and waterfalls, including the spectacular Ragged Falls. Eastern Hemlock and White Cedar occur on ravine slopes and in wet depressions, while mixed forests of Sugar Maple, Eastern Hemlock, and Yellow Birch occupy sandy sites. Where the Oxtongue meanders through lowlands flats, Balsam Fir grades into bog forests of Black Spruce. A number of the park's plants, such as Cardinal-flower, are found close to the edges of their ranges.

DIRECTIONS. Located 2 km NE of Oxtongue Lake village on Hwy 60; see prov hwy map. Trail leads to waterfalls.

Algonquin Provincial Park

See entry under District of Nipissing.

Leslie M. Frost Natural Resources Centre

Located in the rugged Haliburton Highlands, the centre consists of 24,000 ha of rolling hardwood forest and an abundance of lakes. The forests here have a long history of fire and intensive logging. Higher lands in the northeast support a greater proportion of coniferous trees, including Red Pine and Red Spruce, while, to the southeast, deciduous trees such as American Beech, Basswood, and American Elm tend to predominate. Steep cliffs found throughout the area result from faults in the bedrock. A number of northern species are present, such as Moose and Olive-sided Flycatcher, as well as southern species, including Northern Oriole and Warbling Vireo. Several rare aquatic plants belong to the Atlantic coastal plain flora. A series of canoe routes runs through the area, connecting to the Trent-Severn system and Algonquin Park. Most of the larger accessible lakes are ringed with cottages. Trails are available for hiking and skiing. The Frost Centre offers numerous programs and activities related to resource management.

DIRECTIONS. To reach hdqts (with self-guiding trails) at St Nora Lake go 11 km S of Dorset on Hwy 35. Access to other portions of site: 1) off Hwy 35; 2) from hdqts go several km S on Hwy 35 & turn W on Mennill Rd (Margaret Lake Rd); 3) from Hwy 35 N of Dorset, follow Co Rd 8 along S shore of Kawagama Lake; & 4) follow numerous other unpaved roads.

INFORMATION. Leslie M. Frost Natural Resources Centre, RR 2, Minden, Ont, K0M 2K0, 705-766-2451.

Bentshoe Lake

Located on granitic bedrock, this shallow, nutrient-poor lake is surrounded by an early successional woodland of White and Red Pines, Trembling Aspen, White Birch, and Red Maple. The most significant feature of the site is a rich assemblage of aquatic species of Atlantic coastal plain flora. These plants grow in greatest abundance along the peaty shores of the northeastern portion of the main lake.

DIRECTIONS. Access from N side of Hwy 118, 18 km W of Carnarvon.

INFORMATION. MNR.

Buttermilk Falls

An interesting botanical site occurs below the falls, where a wide fan of gravel, silt, and sand marks the entry of the Kennisis River into the north end of nutrient-poor Boshkunk Lake. In late summer the shallow near-shore waters support an abundance of Common Pipewort, Brown-fruited Rush, and quillworts, as well as unusual species such as Aquatic Mustard, American Littorella, and Lesser Waterwort.

DIRECTIONS. Located on S side of Hwy 35, 5.5 km NW of Carnarvon. Narrow strip of public land extends from picnic area along river to lake.

INFORMATION. MNR.

Silent Lake Provincial Park

This relatively undeveloped 1,450-ha park encircles the rocky shoreline and rugged hills surrounding Silent Lake. Much of the landscape is covered in mixed, medium-aged forests of Yellow Birch, Sugar Maple, Eastern Hemlock, and White Pine, a witness to past ravages of logging and fire. Wetlands include Beaver meadows, marshy shorelines, and swampy stands of Black Ash and White Cedar. The marble substrate introduces calcium to the soils and permits pockets of unusual plant associations, some of which are unexpected this far north. The valleys support 25 species of ferns, including the rare Silvery Glade Fern. Associated with *Sphagnum* bogs are Rose Pogonia, Virginia Chain Fern, Twig-rush, Buckbean, and Pitcher-plant. Other species of interest include Four-toed Salamander, Ruby-throated Hummingbird, and Scarlet Tanager. The park is also a good place for viewing wildlife species typical of southern shield country, such as River Otter, Common Loon, and Osprey.

Rockhounding is popular in the area, although collecting is not permitted within the park. There is an extensive network of hiking and cross-country ski trails. Fall colour is excellent.

DIRECTIONS. Located on Hwy 28 in SE corner of county; see prov hwy map.

INFORMATION. Silent Lake Provincial Park, Box 500, Bancroft, Ont, K0L 1C0, 613-339-2807.

DISTRICT OF NIPISSING

> We proceeded to the mouth of the lake [Nipissing], at which is the carrying-place of La Chaudière Française, a name, part of which it has obtained from the holes, in the rock over which we passed; and which holes, being of the kind which is known to be formed by water, with the assistance of pebbles, demonstrate that it has not always been dry, as at present it is, but the phenomenon is not peculiar to this spot, the same being observable, at almost every carrying-place on the Outaouais [Ottawa]. At the height of a hundred feet above the river, I commonly found pebbles, worn into a round form, like those upon the beach below. Everywhere, the water appears to have subsided from its ancient levels. (Outlet of Lake Nipissing, late August 1761, Alexander Henry [1739–1824], fur trader)

A 600-million-year-old fault in the Precambrian bedrock bisects the District of Nipissing along the Mattawa River. The area to the south is dominated by the massive bulk of Algonquin Park, sprawled across the Algonquin Highlands. Here, coarse, shallow soils and glacial features such as drumlins and sand terraces lie atop granitic bedrock in a rough and irregular landscape. There is good representation of both deciduous and coniferous species, with hardwoods tending to predominate on hilltops and warm slopes.

During the final withdrawal of the continental ice sheets from Ontario, the waters of the upper Great Lakes drained eastward across Algonquin Park and later through Lake Nipissing and the Mattawa-Ottawa system. Subsequently, the land rebounded and a height of land arose at North Bay. Now the Mattawa continues to flow eastward, while Lake Nipissing drains westward through the French River to Georgian Bay.

The northern portion of the District of Nipissing slopes southward towards the lowlands adjacent to Lake Nipissing. Pine, usually in association with other tree species, is an important component of upland forests. Sandy soils, numerous rock outcroppings, and a history of fire have traditionally encouraged the growth of White, Red, and Jack Pines. The northern edge of the district lies close to the transition to the Boreal Forest Region, and boreal elements become increasingly noticeable there.

Obabika River Provincial Park

This waterway park straddles the boundaries of the Districts of Sudbury, Nipissing, and Timiskaming. The river is steady and peaceful, with few portages. Boulder fields and glacially polished bedrock outcrops occur. There are wetlands, beaches, and forests, where Red and White Pines predominate. A large area of older-growth forest dominated by Red and White Pines is located at the northern end of Obabika Lake.

DIRECTIONS. For old-growth site: from Sturgeon Falls, go 100 km N on Hwys 64, 539, 539A, & 805, & then bush road to end; canoe to trails at NE corner of lake.

Lake Temagami

Lake Temagami, with its cold waters, pine vistas, and scenic shoreline, is located in the centre of Temagami, an area that has traditionally been noted for its undisturbed old-growth forest. The northern portion of Temagami Island, in the middle of the lake, contains an old upland, mixed forest dominated by mature Red and White Pines. The Temagami area lies at the heart of one of the finest networks of canoe routes in Ontario. There are also numerous cross-country ski trails in the Temagami region.

DIRECTIONS. From Hwy 11, 6.5 km S of town of Temagami, go 18 km W on Central Lake Temagami Access Rd (Temagami Mine Access Rd) to end; take boat; follow trails on island.

Marten River Provincial Park

Bordering a winding river are wide, open fields and second-growth forests of White and Red Pines, White Spruce, and maple. Yellow Birch grows on warm, dry sites and Black Spruce in cool, boggy wetlands. Moose may be seen along the river feeding on the stems and leaves of aquatic plants, such as Water-shield. Watch at dawn or dusk from early June to mid August. Hiking and cross-country ski trails are available in the 400-ha park.

DIRECTIONS. Located 56 km N of North Bay on Hwy 11; see prov hwy map.

INFORMATION. Marten River Provincial Park, Marten River, Ont, P0H 1T0, 705-892-2200.

Mattawa River and Samuel de Champlain Provincial Parks

The 65-km Mattawa River follows a 600-million-year-old fault-line between the Great Lakes and the Ottawa valley. Rugged Canadian Shield landscape features boulder-strewn rapids, sheer cliffs, placid lakes, a stretch of river over 100 m deep, and stands of White and Red Pines, Yellow Birch, and Eastern Hemlock. Known for its huge Lake Sturgeon, this historic fur-trade route offers excellent canoeing. Smooth Wild Rose blooms beside roadsides, Cardinal-flower grows along the river, and cliff plants are found at spectacular Talon Chute and waterfall. Stones swirled by water have gouged potholes in the bedrock at the east end of Lake Talon. Typical wildlife include Moose, Black Bear, Porcupine, Eastern Chipmunk, Common Snapping and Midland Painted Turtles, Common Merganser, and Common Raven. The 2,350-ha Samuel de Champlain Park lies within a White-tailed Deer wintering yard. There are a number of hiking and cross-country ski trails, and the area offers a fine show of fall foliage.

DIRECTIONS. Upper end of waterway can be accessed from Hwy 63 & Lakeside Dr in North Bay; Champlain Park is 52 km E of North Bay on Hwy 17; see prov hwy map.

INFORMATION. Samuel de Champlain & Mattawa River Provincial Parks, Box 147, Mattawa, Ont, P0H 1V0, 705-744-2276.

Algonquin Provincial Park

Approximately 780,000 ha in area, Algonquin Park lies between Georgian Bay and the Ottawa River on a southern extension of the Precambrian Shield. The area is a transition zone between the broad-leaved, deciduous forests of the south and the coniferous forests of the north. Both forest types are found throughout the vast tract of rolling hills and sparkling lakes that makes up the park. The northern coniferous forests predominate, because the park lies on a broad dome known as the Algonquin Highlands, where elevations are typically 200 m above the surrounding country. This creates colder, windier conditions, and favours northern plants and animals. The meeting of north and south in Algonquin is exemplified by the occurrence of such northern birds as Gray Jay, Boreal Chickadee, Common Loon, and Spruce Grouse alongside such southerners as Indigo Bunting, Scarlet Tanager, and Wood Thrush. Enhanced by rugged topography, the diversity of habitats includes Sugar Maple–American Beech forests, Black Spruce bogs, Beaver ponds, lakes, rivers, and cliffs. There are extensive trail systems, canoe routes, and campsites, a spectacular visitor centre, and numerous fine park publications. Fall colours are superb (they peak usually during the last week of September) and the cross-country skiing is excellent.

INFORMATION. Algonquin Provincial Park, Box 219, Whitney, Ont, K0J 2M0, 705-633-5572; Visitor Centre, 613-622-2828; Friends of Algonquin Park, Box 248, Whitney, Ont, K0J 2M0 (trail guides, canoe route maps, natural history publications, etc. available).

– Highway 60 Corridor through Algonquin Park. Forests in the western two-thirds of the park consist largely of Sugar Maple, American Beech, and Yellow Birch. Shoreline edges are fringed with Balsam Fir, Eastern Hemlock, White Cedar, and White and Black Spruces. Most visitors to Algonquin enter on Highway 60, which traverses the southwestern corner of the park. From the West Gate (km 0.0) to the East Gate (km 56.0), there are kilometre markers to assist in locating facilities and points of interest. Moose, White-tailed Deer, Beaver, River Otter, and Red Fox are often seen along this road. Gray Wolves may be heard howling at night, especially in August and September.

Northern birds such as Common Loon, Common Raven, Black-backed Woodpecker, Gray Jay, Boreal Chickadee, and Spruce Grouse all breed here. During winters with large cone crops, winter finches are frequently abundant along the road. There is usually excellent leaf colour in late September.

Park Boundary (5 km W of West Gate). Park or Long Lake parallels the road here. Enter by canoe in spring for waterfowl, and in early summer to see Rose Pogonia, bladderworts, bog plants, and pondweeds in the boggy water and bordering peat mat. Watch in fall for shorebirds on exposed mud.

Western Uplands Hiking Trail (km 3.0). This trail presents an excellent cross-section of the western, hardwood-dominated portion of the park. Check the entrance area near the Oxtongue River for Black-backed Woodpecker, Gray Jay, Boreal Chickadee, and Northern Parula. Listen at night from March to May along the valley for calling Northern Saw-whet Owls.

Whiskey Rapids Trail (km 7.2). Much of this trail runs along the Oxtongue River through Black Spruce–Balsam Fir stands. The Sugar Maple–Yellow Birch forest here is floristically rich. Look for winter finches, Black-backed Woodpecker, Boreal Chickadee, Brown Creeper, and Northern Parula.

Coot Lake (km 10.0). Search the road margin during August and September for Case's and Nodding Ladies'-tresses.

Smoke Creek (km 12.0). During August and September Nodding Ladies'-tresses bloom along the road margin on the south side.

Mizzy Lake Trail (km 15.4). This 11-km loop trail visits nine small lakes and ponds that provide opportunities to see Moose, Beaver, and River Otter. The Wolf Howl Pond and West Rose Lake sections are particularly good spots for seeing Ring-necked Duck, Hooded Merganser, Spruce Grouse, Black-backed Woodpecker, Olive-sided and Yellow-bellied Flycatchers, Boreal Chickadee, Winter Wren, Lincoln's Sparrow, and Rusty Blackbird. Wolf Howl Pond also has a large population of Midland Painted Turtles. The vegetation of floating bog habitat and northern sand plain deposit is well established here and includes rare ferns and related plants such as Mountain Clubmoss.

Hardwood Hill Picnic Area (km 16.7). The hardwood forest features large Sugar Maple, Yellow Birch, American Beech, and

Hop-hornbeam, with such birds as Yellow-bellied Sapsucker, Pileated Woodpecker, Wood Thrush, and Scarlet Tanager. After dark, listen for Barred Owls.

West of Peck Lake Trail (km 18.0). Search the road margin on the south side for Loesel's Twayblade in June and Ragged Fringed Orchid in July.

Found Lake (km 20.0). The nature reserve zone north of the highway here features at least 33 ferns and fern allies, including Silvery Glade Fern, Boott's Wood Fern, Triangle Grape Fern, and Mountain and Bog Clubmosses. Red Spruce and White Trillium (very rare on Algonquin's dome) are also present in this reserve.

Cache Lake (km 23.0). The highway margin displays blooming Ragged Fringed Orchid in July. The nearby cattail marsh often has both Sora and Virginia Rail.

Hemlock Bluff Trail (km 27.2). This trail goes 3.5 km through mixed hardwood and Eastern Hemlock forest, which may yield Barred Owl (after dark), Yellow-bellied Sapsucker, Brown Creeper, Winter Wren, Golden-crowned Kinglet, Swainson's and Hermit Thrushes, Northern Parula, and Black-throated Green and Blackburnian Warblers.

Mew Lake (km 30.0). In spring and fall shallow water here attracts waterfowl, especially Ring-necked and Wood Ducks and Hooded Merganser. The diverse aquatic vegetation of the weedy western bay includes pondweeds, bladderworts such as Purple Bladderwort, quillworts, and a variety of rare sedges.

Old Airfield (km 30.6). Reach this area via Mew Lake campground entrance road. A rare, open space in a vast forested tract, this large field with its shrubby borders can attract unusual birds. Regular migrants include Horned Lark, American Pipit, Lapland Longspur, Snow Bunting, and Eastern Meadowlark. Several interesting butterflies occur.

Lookout Trail (km 39.7). In addition to a magnificent view, this 1.9-km loop trail may offer soaring Broad-winged Hawks and Common Ravens. Hermit Thrush and Dark-eyed Junco nest along the cliff. Several rare plants grow near the trail parking lot, including Northern Adder's-tongue Fern, Loesel's Twayblade, Narrow-leaved Cattail, and Dwarf Grape Fern.

Spruce Bog Boardwalk (km 42.5). A 1.5-km loop trail affords the most accessible birding for boreal species along Highway 60. Search the trail and bordering open Black Spruce and Balsam Fir forest for Spruce Grouse, Yellow-bellied Flycatcher, Gray Jay, Boreal Chickadee, and Hermit Thrush. From the highway just east of the trail, paddle down Sunday Creek to Norway and Fork lakes to reach extensive bog habitat that may produce American Bittern, Northern Harrier, and possibly Sedge Wren or Lincoln's Sparrow.

Visitor Centre (km 43). Don't miss this natural history highlight. Learn more about Algonquin, its excellent interpretive trails and programs, and numerous exploration possibilities.

Opeongo Lake Road (km 46.3). This road runs north for 6.2 km through extensive areas of bog, Black Spruce forest, and cattail marsh to huge Lake Opeongo. The typical boreal habitat is home to American Bittern, Ring-necked Duck, Hooded Merganser, Northern Harrier, Spruce Grouse, Black-backed Woodpecker, Olive-sided and Alder Flycatchers, Gray Jay, Boreal Chickadee, Swainson's Thrush, Lincoln's Sparrow, and Rusty Blackbird.

– Eastern Algonquin Park via Sand Lake Road. The eastern third of Algonquin Park has distinctly different forests from the Highway 60 region. Warmer, drier, rugged ridges with intervening sand plains support stands heavily dominated by aspen, birch, and White, Red, or Jack Pine. Where ridgetops lack pine, scrubby Red Oak often predominates. Black Spruce bogs thrive on poorly drained sites. The east side of the park is much lower in elevation than the west side and includes many species of plants, mammals, and birds found rarely, if at all, on the west side. Sand Lake Road extends into the heart of Algonquin's east side. DIRECTIONS. From Hwy 17, 9 km W of Pembroke & 3.5 km W of Forest Lea Rd, turn S onto Co Rd 26; travel 300 m; turn right at Achray Rd (Co Rd 28) & drive 26 km to Sand Lake Gate. Note kilometre signs along road in park. (Sand Lake Gate is at km 17.5).

Barron Canyon Trail (km 28.9). This 1.5-km loop trail travels along the north rim of the Barron Canyon, a spectacular gorge with 100-m-high gneissic walls. Originally formed along a faultline, the canyon has been broadened by erosion, much of which occurred 10,000 years ago, when drainage from glacial Lake Algonquin carried huge amounts of meltwater through this area to the Champlain Sea.

Calcium in the rock crevices attracts rare plants such as Maidenhair Spleenwort and Bulblet Fern. Other rare species, some of them relics from the chilly postglacial era, include Encrusted Saxifrage, Fragrant Cliff Fern, Smooth Woodsia, Purple-stemmed Cliffbrake, rock-cress, and an unusual form of White Cedar. The rock shore and shallow water of the Barron River support a number of rare plants, among them Slender Naiad and Mountain Woodsia. Barn Swallows and Eastern Phoebes nest on the canyon walls; Common Ravens use the cliff ledges; and Yellow-bellied Flycatchers, Northern Waterthrushes, and Common Yellowthroats breed on the talus slopes.

Achray Road (km 37.8). Turn left here and proceed 4.8 km to Achray campground on Grand Lake. Check the lake for water-fowl and gulls. The campground can be a good place for observing Pine Warbler and Red Crossbill.

Hydro Line Junction (km 50.0). The open-field habitat of this transmission corridor may have Red-tailed Hawk, American Kestrel, Eastern Bluebird, and Field Sparrow.

Lake Travers (km 70.5). The open Jack Pine barrens extending from km 63 to Lake Travers may produce American Kestrel, Merlin, Spruce Grouse, Hermit Thrush, Lincoln's Sparrow, and Dark-eyed Junco. The lake attracts migrants such as Red-necked Grebe, Oldsquaw, scoters, Common Goldeneye, Red-breasted Merganser, and Bonaparte's Gull. Northern Water Snake and Eastern Smooth Green Snake are regularly observed.

– **Algonquin Park Interior.** This is the rugged and essentially undeveloped area of the park away from the Highway 60 and Sand Lake Road corridors. Visitors travel by canoe and foot to experience the wilderness character of the park, even though much of the interior is still logged. Some of the best examples of natural areas are protected within nature reserve and wilderness zones.

Brent Crater (look for observation tower between Gilmour and Tecumseh lakes along road near Brent). This 4-km-wide crater was created 450 million years ago by the impact of a meteorite. Subsequent geological activity added calcium to the substrate. The southern edge of the crater, where this is exposed, now supports a rich plant community, including mosses, liverworts, wildflowers, and the uncommon Bulblet Fern. Two lakes occur within the shallow crater basin.

Nadine Lake Hardwoods (north of Nipissing River, east of Skuce & Osler Lakes). This largest mature deciduous forest in the park has large stands of Sugar Maple, Yellow Birch, American Beech, and occasional White Pine. Look for rare wildflowers in calcium seepage areas. Lowland stands of White Cedar, Balsam Fir, and Black Ash have extremely large specimens of Black Ash. The Two-lined Salamanders here are among the most northerly in Ontario.

Tim River Burn (east of where Trout Creek enters Tim River). Created by fire in 1922, this large open meadow is frequented by Gray Wolves in fall and by Moose and White-tailed Deer year-round. The uncommon Canada Mountain-rice grows here.

Big Crow White Pine Nature Reserve Zone (west of Hillcrest Lake; access from Crow River). Huge ancient White Pines here are over 40 m high and up to 120 cm in diameter.

Hailstorm Creek (near Opeongo Lake, south and east of Bower Lake). One of the largest peatlands in the park, this complex contains large open bogs, shrub bogs, and Black Spruce–Tamarack forest. Open sedge meadows support breeding birds usually found south of this area, such as Bobolink.

Dickson Lake (south of Lake Lavieille). Eastern Hemlocks on the steep slopes of Dickson Lake are over 300 years old. The Red Pines here, at over 340 years of age, are the oldest trees known in the park.

Petawawa Rapids. The land around the Petawawa River Rapids between Lake Travers and McManus Lake has over 400 species of plants, making it the most diverse area for vegetation in the park. Cardinal-flower is abundant. Among rare species are Clinton's Bulrush at the Natch Rapids. Relict northern species live on cliff faces and relict southern species in protected valleys. The rare Wood Turtle is found in the Petawawa River.

Greenleaf Creek Watershed. This entire watershed has been left virtually undisturbed as a nature reserve. It forms a huge wetland that stretches from Loonskin Lake east to Barron, Greenleaf, and Lost lakes.

Dividing Lake Provincial Nature Reserve (southeast of Crown Lake on southwest border of park in Haliburton). This is one of the finest examples of pristine, old-growth White Pine–hardwood forest anywhere. White Pines 35 m high averaging 100 cm in diameter frequently top the ridges and steep lakeshores.

RENFREW COUNTY

> We rested on the shore of a pond, which was rather pleasant, and
> made a fire to drive off the mosquitoes, which tormented us
> greatly ... The next day we ... went by land ... by a harder country
> than we had ever seen, in that the winds had beaten down the
> pines on top of one another, which is no slight obstacle, for it is
> necessary to pass sometimes over and sometimes under these
> trees. In this way we came to a lake [Muskrat Lake] very full of
> fish; and the people of the country about come there to fish. Near
> this lake there is a settlement of [natives] who till the soil and raise
> maize. (June 6, 1615, Samuel de Champlain [ca 1570–1635],
> explorer and governor of New France)

The southern and southwestern portions of Renfrew County lie
on the billion-year-old rocks of the Canadian Shield. The
remainder of the county is contained within the Ottawa River
valley, which is underlain by 450-million-year-old Ordovician
limestone deposits. When melting glaciers withdrew from this
area about 12,000 years ago, ocean waters pushed inland up the
Ottawa valley to create the Champlain Sea. Worn marble shorelines of the ancient sea are visible today in the cliffs of the White
Lake Hills (southwest of Arnprior), where these features can be
viewed from the roadside. A sand plain near Petawawa originated as a delta formed at the edge of this marine embayment.
Downriver, deep silty clays cover the old seabed, interrupted at
intervals by the protruding crests of fault blocks largely composed of billion-year-old Precambrian rock. In places, gravel
deposits and limestone ridges are evident. (See also introduction to Chapter 5.)

Renfrew County is drained by three major river systems and
numerous smaller ones, all of which eventually flow to the
Ottawa. The waters in much of northern Algonquin Park flow
eastward across northern Renfrew through the Petawawa River
or its tributary the Barron. The Bonnechere River also has its
headwaters in Algonquin Park; it follows a diagonal route
across the county before joining the Ottawa near Castleford. The
scenic Madawaska valley lies in the western and southern portions of Renfrew County. The Madawaska River, by times surg-
ing through rocky gorges and turbulent rapids and waterfalls,

descends 224 m from its source in Algonquin Park to its mouth at Arnprior.

The entire county falls within the Great Lakes–St Lawrence Forest Region. Mixed hardwoods dominated by Sugar Maple and American Beech characterize upland forests. Coniferous elements gain some prominence on poorer soils. Lakes and rivers are more prevalent on the higher lands of the Canadian Shield than in the Ottawa valley. Renfrew County is noted for its scenic hills and lakes. Vividly coloured trees stage a spectacular show each autumn.

Greenbough Esker

This 16-km-long esker, the largest in the region, extends from Deux-Rivières to Wendigo Lake. Wooded uplands support Red and White Pines as well as Large-toothed Aspen, White Birch, and White Spruce. The esker gives rise to significant wetland complexes that include kettle lakes. Rare plants such as Small Bur-reed, Virginia Chain Fern, and Swamp Beggar's-ticks grow in peatlands bordering the southern third of the esker.

DIRECTIONS. From Hwy 17, 2 km W of Deux-Rivières go 5 km S on Brent Rd. Road follows esker S.

Ottawa River

The Ottawa River rises in a chain of lakes in Quebec's Laurentian Uplands before flowing southward through Lake Timiskaming. Eventually carrying more water than all the rivers in Britain combined, the Ottawa defines Renfrew County's northern and eastern boundary. The stretch of river between Mattawa and Deep River offers particularly fine scenery. Here massive hills rise steeply to heights of 300 m along the Quebec shore. The upper reaches of the Ottawa River are popular for rafting, kayaking, and whitewater canoeing.

The Ottawa River serves as a major migration corridor for the spring and fall movement of waterfowl. It is used by a host of migrating species, including Lesser and Great Scaup, Bufflehead, Canada Goose, and Common and Barrow's Goldeneyes (at Calumet Island, Pembroke). Red-necked and Horned Grebes and White-winged, Surf, and Black Scoters also stage in the river. Bonaparte's Gulls are regular migrants, and Pomarine and

Parasitic Jaegers are occasionally encountered in the fall. Certain areas, including the mouths of the Muskrat, Bonnechere, and Madawaska rivers, are excellent waterfowl staging areas, particularly from mid April to mid May, and from late September to late October. An excellent location for gulls, including Glaucous and Iceland Gulls in late fall and early spring, is Braeside landfill and sawmill (from the junction of County Roads 1 and 3 at Braeside, go northeast on County Road 3).

Grants Creek

A significant 3-km-long marsh on this creek can be best explored by canoe. Watch for ducks and water birds such as Great Blue Herons and Double-crested Cormorants.
DIRECTIONS. Put in at bridge on Hwy 17 3 km upriver from Stonecliffe. To reach marsh, paddle 3 km up creek (3 portages), passing 2 waterfalls en route.

Petawawa Research Forest

This 10,000-ha tract of federally owned land is used for research in forest science. In addition to plantations and other intensively managed research plots, there are extensive areas of more natural woodland. The countryside is scenic, rolling, and, at times, rugged, especially in the western sections towards Algonquin Park. At intervals, granitic rocks of the underlying Canadian Shield appear as outcrops. To the east, towards the Ottawa River, the land becomes more level. Soils are generally thin, with numerous boulders and a high content of sand and gravel; pockets of deeper loams also occur. Lakes and waterways are numerous.

The woodlands contain a mosaic of coniferous, deciduous, and mixed stands. White Pine and aspens are the most common species encountered. White and Red Pines and Red Oak predominate on the shallow soils, which also harbour White Spruce, White Birch, and Trembling and Large-toothed Aspens. The flats of the Ottawa plain support Trembling and Large-toothed Aspens, as well as White Spruce, White Birch, and some pine. A number of sites within the forest have been set aside as designated natural areas. These protect representative examples of habitat and a variety of significant features, such as White Cedar swamps, Jack Pine flats, and Sugar Maple–Eastern Hemlock stands.

There are numerous roadways and trails that can be used for hiking and cross-country skiing.

DIRECTIONS. Main entry road is 3 km S of Chalk River on Hwy 17.

Petawawa Fish Culture Station

This former fish hatchery property contains significant earth science and biological features. Terraced bluffs lining the Ottawa River were formed by erosion during the time that glacial Lake Algonquin drained down the Ottawa River to the Champlain Sea. Numerous rare plants occur here, including Silky Dogwood, Northern Starwort, and False Pimpernel. Wet meadows and deciduous swamps along the river harbour a diversity of plants, among which are uncommon emergent aquatics; species of note include Field Sedge, Tubercled Orchid, and Lake Cress. Other rare plants grow around cold, clear springs in swampy White Cedar woods below the bluffs of the Ottawa River. Wetlands along the river shoreline serve as feeding areas for migratory waterfowl. Trails through the property can be used for walking in summer and cross-country skiing in winter.

DIRECTIONS. From Co Rd 17, go E on Laurentian Dr (Co Rd 25) to E side of Petawawa, S of Petawawa River.

INFORMATION. Call 613-687-5935.

Bonnechere River Provincial Waterway Park and Valley

Stretching along the Bonnechere River between Bonnechere and Algonquin provincial parks is a series of natural areas linked together by the Bonnechere River Waterway Park. Most are on public land and are readily accessible by canoe, cottage road, and forest access trails. The valley itself is an important migration corridor for White-tailed Deer and Gray Wolves from Algonquin Park. Wolf howls are held in the area in late summer, hosted by staff of Bonnechere Park.

The White Oak stand at Stevenson Lake is the site of one of the province's northernmost populations of this species. Clinging to south-facing slopes and stunted as if at treeline, the White Oak here is a shadow of its more typical stately form. A climb to the hilltop (watch for Poison-ivy) gives a nice view of the lake and river valley stretching northwest towards Algonquin Park.

Farther north, a hike up Squaw Rock provides another fine vista of the river valley, this time overlooking Stringers Lake bog and fen. This wetland is known for its fine stands of the rare Arethusa orchid and includes dry Jack Pine stands juxtaposed with marshes.

The Bonnechere River itself has some rapids but is mostly flatwater. It takes the paddler along natural shores and wetlands such as Greenwood Marsh, which links Curriers Lake with White Mountain Bay. On the west shore of the river is White Mountain, featuring a stand of pine and poplar and topped by an unparalleled view up the river valley. As the river meets the sandflats of the Round Lake basin, it turns into a meandering stream that is actively creating oxbows that continue on into Bonnechere Provincial Park.

DIRECTIONS. 1) From Hwy 62, 2 km E of Bonnechere Park gate, drive 3 km NW to Stevenson Lake & base of hill to N with White Oak stand. Trails are not developed yet, so use care in choosing route up hill. 2) From Hwy 62 just N of Bonnechere Park gate, go NW on Turner's Rd for numerous access points to river along waterway park. Squaw Rock is 22 km from Hwy 62, at Algonquin Park boundary. Again, there are no formal trails, so pick route carefully. Across road, canoes can be put in to explore Stringers Lake area.

INFORMATION. Bonnechere Provincial Park, Box 220, Pembroke, Ont, K8A 6X4, 613-732-3661.

Bonnechere Deer Yard

From late December to mid March White-tailed Deer concentrate here in low-lying stands of White Cedar and other conifers.

DIRECTIONS. In Hagarty & Richards Twps (i.e., twps containing Round Lake Centre, Bonnechere, & Killaloe Station). Drive roads to locate areas used by deer; avoid disturbing animals.

Deacon Escarpment

Rising 100 m above the Bonnechere River flatlands, this forested escarpment supports unusual communities of cliff vegetation and dry, southern oak parkland. Red Cedar and Fragrant Sumac, both relict southern species, grow commonly along the

cliff face. Northern cliff species found here include False Oats. Migrating raptors ride the updrafts along the escarpment.
DIRECTIONS. On E side of Bonnechere River N of Golden Lake near Deacon. Access through county forest along Hwy 60.

Shaw Woods

Few forests in the county harbour tees of such size, age, and stature as Shaw Woods. A trail winds through towering stands of Sugar Maple, Eastern Hemlock, American Beech, Basswood, and Yellow Birch up to 35 m in height. The old trees range from 150 to 200 years in age, evoking images of forests seen by the Ottawa valley's first settlers. Only lightly touched by logging, the site has a healthy supply of old, dead, and fallen tree habitats, and excellent examples of the artistic workings of Pileated Woodpeckers. An ancient White Cedar swamp is located in a glacial spillway in the southwest portion of the property. Dedicated as a nature preserve by the Shaw family, the 78-ha site is open to the public.
DIRECTIONS. Go 13 km N from Eganville on Hwy 41; woods is 1.5 km E of N end of Lake Doré along Co Rd 9. Look for signs to trail entrance on S side of road.
INFORMATION. MNR.

Bonnechere Caves

Located at one of the rapids (Fourth Chute) along the scenic Bonnechere River, the limestone caves are a local tourist attraction. To permit access, water has been diverted from the subterranean caverns, which were originally underground river channels. Tours offered during the tourist season discuss the karst topography and geological history of the cave area, and interpret the fossil remnants that continue to emerge from the cave walls.
DIRECTIONS. From Hwy 41 at Eganville go 8 km E along co rd that follows S side of river. Watch for signs.
INFORMATION. Call 1-800-469-2283.

Westmeath Provincial Park

This 610-ha park is one of the few undeveloped areas left along the Ottawa River. Its flora is exceptional. The dry beach and several wetland and upland communities provide habitat for rare species, including Blue-beech and Silky Dogwood. The park contains lots of pine, and good areas for fall mushroom walks. Watch for Poison-ivy. Check the dry beach on the east shore of the sandspit around Bellows Bay and the marshes on the west side of the bay for unusual landforms, such as relict shorelines and terraces. Bellows Bay is an important staging area for waterfowl in late April and early to mid September. Shorebirds use the beaches along the Ottawa River from late August to October.

DIRECTIONS. Follow Ottawa River 16.5 km E from Pembroke along Hwy 148, then Co Rds 21 & 12.

INFORMATION. Westmeath Provincial Park, Box 220, Pembroke, Ont, K8A 6X4, 613-732-3661.

Pretty's Hill

A terrific vantage point and scenic lookout are found atop Pretty's Hill, a dramatic kame moraine overlooking the Ottawa River south of Westmeath. To the southwest can be seen the large tract of Black Spruce in the Westmeath Bog.

DIRECTIONS. From Co Rd 12 just S of Westmeath go about 3 km SE on Co Rd 31.

Mud Lake

Watch for Black Terns frequenting the area in summer.

DIRECTIONS. On boundary between Stafford & Westmeath twps, just W of Hwy 17, 15 km N of Cobden.

Cobden Marsh and Muskrat Lake

Muskrat Lake lies in a preglacial valley that occupies an old faultline. The western shore of this long, narrow lake abuts a clay plain while, to the east, an escarpment of Precambrian rock rises more than 60 m. A marsh at the south end of the lake supports Sora, Virginia Rail, Marsh Wren, and migrants in season. The south shore of the lake is a very good place for viewing ducks and shorebirds in migration. Also watch for Mussie, the Monster of Muskrat Lake.

DIRECTIONS. Marsh is on E side of Hwy 17 at S end of Cobden; lake stretches 14 km N.

Bonnechere Falls

This spectacular waterfalls, known locally as the First Chute, is the last remaining undammed waterfall along the Bonnechere River. After carving a meandering course through the farmland clays of the area, the river meets erosion-resistant granite, where it is compressed into crevices and cascades down ledges of rock. The falls and its natural setting, the site of a local recreation park, are located just west of the confluence of the Bonnechere and Ottawa rivers.

DIRECTIONS. From Renfrew go 2 km E on Co Rd 6; turn left onto Thompson Rd & go 4.5 km E. A fence opening & trails mark ways to falls.

Lochwinnoch Landslide Scar

Here, a massive slumpage in the infamous leda clays of the area allowed a huge block of land to slip downslope. Leda clays are unstable postglacial deposits of the Champlain Sea, which covered the lower Ottawa valley about 10,000 years ago. When saturated with water they tend to slump. The scar is a prominent scalloped edge of an otherwise gently rolling farm field.

DIRECTIONS. From Renfrew go E on Co Rd 6; turn left onto Thompson Rd. Go 3 km E along Thompson Rd & watch for dirt twp rd on S side. Head S on dirt road. Cross tracks & forested creek valley at toe of slide. Continue uphill. Landform can be seen on both sides of twp rd.

Braeside Alvar

This is the only alvar in Renfrew County. Plants of interest include orchids, Pinedrops, and Canada and Cooper's Milk-vetches.

DIRECTIONS. At Braeside go N from Sand Point on Golf Course Rd to Co Rd 1; alvar is between Co Rds 1 & 3.

Gillies Grove

This is a spectacular stand of pine and old-growth hardwoods within the Arnprior town limits. Watch for Red-shouldered Hawk, Barred Owl, Pileated Woodpecker, and Merlin. Visitors can view the majestic stands from a trail network accessible from all sides of the grove.

DIRECTIONS. From Hwy 17 at Arnprior, go NE on Division St; turn left at first T-jct. Continue past 2 RR tracks and stop sign; then watch for forest on right.

Stewartville Swamp Nature Reserve

This 12.5-ha Federation of Ontario Naturalists' property consists of grassy meadow, pine plantation, and a swampy mixed forest of White Cedar, Yellow Birch, Balsam Fir, White Birch, and Black Ash. Orchids thrive in spectacular abundance and variety in the mossy shadows beneath a small stand of old-growth White Cedars. Among other plants of interest are Indian-pipe, Pinesap, One-flowered Pyrola, and many ferns. Boots are necessary, as is a careful eye, to avoid trampling on the orchids accidentally.

DIRECTIONS. Go 0.5 km S from Arnprior on White Lake Rd (Co Rd 2); take 1st right (W) onto Vanjumar Dr; go 0.5 km to end; turn left (S) onto Flat Rapids Rd (Co Rd 45) & travel 5 km. When road swings right, continue straight for 4.3 km on secondary road to stop sign at Stewartville. Continue straight through on dirt road for 0.7 km; swamp is on right, through cedars.

White Lake Wetlands

A small fen and adjacent wet forest at the north end of this 1,400-ha wetland support interesting plants and insects, including rare mosses, Arethusa, large populations of Tall White Bog Orchid, Grass-pink, and Rose Pogonia. The Hayes Bay section of the lake is important for waterfowl.

DIRECTIONS. From Arnprior take Co Rd 2 for 17 km SW to White Lake; access lake SW of town via canoe.

INFORMATION. MNR.

Constant Creek Swamp and Fen

A mix of public and private property, most of this 850-ha wetland is undisturbed swamp along Constant Creek. The complex geology creates varied plant communities and interesting linear ridges of habitat. A bayou-like Silver Maple swamp borders the river, while wetlands such as large, open fen meadows stretch off to the north. Noted for its great beauty, the creek contains diverse plant life, including Southern Wild Rice in large beds and Water-willow, uncommon this far north.

DIRECTIONS. Public parts of wetland can be reached by canoe via Ferguson Lake. From jct of Hwys 511 & 508 at Calabogie drive 12.5 km W (on road towards Centennial Lake) to Ferguson Lake Rd (en route crossing final rapids of Constant Creek 4 km W of Calabogie). To launch canoe, go N on Ferguson Lake Rd for 6 km to bridge or 7.2 km to set of culverts.

Black Donald Island Provincial Nature Reserve

A great many exceptional plant species are concentrated on Black Donald Island, a haven for marble-loving flora. This was once a hilltop, but became an island with the flooding of Black Donald and Centennial lakes in the late 1960s. A rock exposure on the shore, a cliff on the original Black Donald Lake shoreline, is the only substantial evidence of the former lake's shores. Open, dry barrens and scrub habitats support communities of Purple-stemmed Cliffbrake and Mountain Woodsia, as well as rarities such as Kalm's Brome and New Jersey Tea. There is an essentially pure (and not planted) Red Pine forest on the west side of the island. Rare aquatic plants, such as Long-stemmed Waterwort, grow in shallow waters along the shore.

The island is one parcel of the 530-ha Centennial Lake Provincial Nature Reserve, most of which is located in the watershed of Black Donald Creek to the northeast of the island. Access to the remainder of the reserve is by forest access roads and trails. The island is an important White-tailed Deer yarding area in winter. At the outlet of the lake is Mountain Chute Dam, where Bald Eagles can be seen year-round.

DIRECTIONS. Island is accessible only by boat or canoe. From jct of Hwys 508 & 511 at Calabogie, drive 25 km W along road towards Centennial Lake to public boat launch on N shore of Black Donald Lake 2 km NE of island. Boating facilities, rentals, parking, & maps are available farther up road at White Pines Resort (call 613-752-2884 for info). To reach Mountain Chute

Dam: drive 18 km W from Calabogie on road towards Centennial Lake; turn S onto road towards SE side of Black Donald Lake; go to end; watch for Ontario Hydro signs.
INFORMATION. MNR.

Centennial Lake

This is a spectacular landscape of wild shores, rugged hills, and rare plant communities. Much of the area is publicly owned. Varied and complex forest vegetation on dry sites consists largely of White and Red Pines, Red Oak, and Red Maple. Small grassy clearings, especially along the lakeshore, support abundant plant life, including rare southern species such as New Jersey Tea, Kalm's Brome, Cooper's Milk-vetch, Woodland Sunflower, and Balsam Ragwort. Big Island harbours an extensive and dramatic stand of pine. The lake's aquatic plant communities are of particular significance. Large populations of Grass-leaved Water-plantain grow in north-shore bays, and an extensive Long-stemmed Waterwort community thrives in quiet, shallow bays along the northeast shore.
DIRECTIONS. Lake is best toured by water. From Hwy 41 at Griffith, drive S along W side of Madawaska River towards Matawatchan. Where road goes right to Matawatchan, turn left to Centennial Lake bridge, where canoe or boat can be launched.

Griffith Uplands

A significant natural area on public land just to the north of Griffith, this upland site is a typical representative of dry oak, pine, and other forest types on granite and marble. It is a wild, rugged area, with rocky outcrops and sheltered valleys to explore. The area provides excellent vistas of the Madawaska Highlands landscape.
DIRECTIONS. Located along Hwy 41 in Griffith, on E side of Madawaska River. Go to Pine Valley Restaurant for parking & information about access to the base of uplands, which beckon to the north. Informal trails penetrate portions of site. A steep ascent begins the climb.
INFORMATION. MNR.

Conroys Marsh

This 2,000-ha wetland is a wild, undeveloped riverine marsh that straddles the border of Renfrew and Hastings counties. Conroys Marsh, emptying into Negeek Lake, links the confluence of the York, Little Mississippi, and Madawaska rivers and is an excellent natural area for exploring by canoe or boat. Comprising a diverse assemblage of vegetation types, including fens and flooded swamps, the wetland provides habitat for an array of wetland plants and wildlife. It is a good site for viewing River Otter, Osprey, the occasional Bald Eagle, and waterfowl such as Black and Ring-necked Ducks. Significant plants include Green Water-milfoil.

DIRECTIONS. From Combermere drive 5 km SE on Hwy 515; turn right on McPhees Bay Rd & left to boat launch.

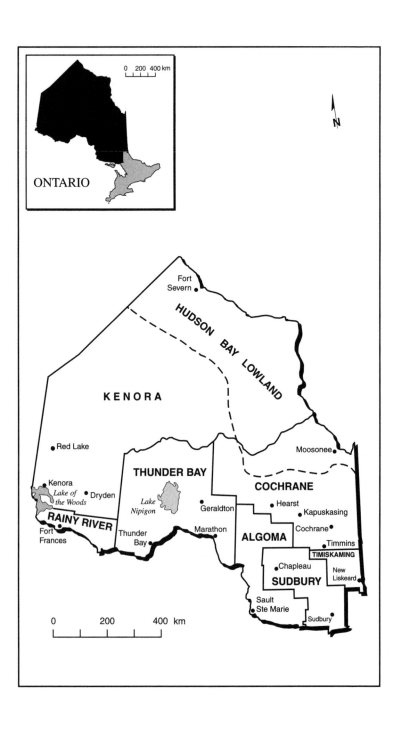

ONTARIO

0   200 400 km

N

Fort
Severn

HUDSON BAY LOWLAND

KENORA

Red Lake

Moosonee

THUNDER BAY

COCHRANE

Kenora
*Lake of
the Woods* Dryden

*Lake
Nipigon*

Geraldton

Hearst

Kapuskasing

RAINY RIVER

Fort
Frances

Thunder
Bay

Marathon

Cochrane

ALGOMA

Timmins

TIMISKAMING

Chapleau

New
Liskeard

SUDBURY

Sault
Ste Marie

Sudbury

0   200   400 km

7 Northern Ontario

Rainy River	Sudbury
Kenora	Timiskaming
Thunder Bay	Cochrane
Algoma	Hudson Bay Lowland

The vast region covered in this chapter stretches from the District of Sudbury and the Quebec border in the east to the Manitoba boundary in the west. The area is bounded on the south by Georgian Bay, Lake Superior, and the United States; northern limits are defined by Hudson and James bays. Except for the Hudson Bay Lowland, the entire region is underlain by the granitic rocks of the Canadian Shield.

The forested landscape undergoes a transition from south to north, with Great Lakes–St Lawrence Forest dominating the southern regions east and west of Lake Superior. To the north, this mixed coniferous-deciduous forest gives way to the expansive Boreal Forest, the eastern portion characterized generally as the wet boreal and the western portion as the dry boreal. The height of land follows a circuitous route across the north, dividing the southerly flowing waters of the Great Lakes watershed from the northerly flowing rivers of the Hudson Bay watershed. Northward and well beyond Cochrane and Hearst, continuous muskeg and innumerable creeks, rivers, and lakes grade into Ontario's only treeless tundra along the Hudson Bay coast. Here marine mammals, arctic vegetation, and expansive breeding grounds for shorebirds and geese bring a distinctive element of diversity to the province.

DISTRICT OF RAINY RIVER

> The wild rice is found ... in water, about two feet deep, where there is a rich muddy bottom. It rises more than eight feet above the water ... It is gathered about the latter end of September, in the following manner. The Natives pass in among it in canoes. Each canoe has in it two persons, one ... in each end, with a long hooked stick, in one hand, and a straight one in the other. With the hooked stick, he brings the heads of the grain over the canoe, and holds it there; while, with the other, he beats it out. When the canoe is thus sufficiently loaded, it is taken to the shore and emptied. (Along the Rainy River, July 5, 1805, Daniel Harmon Williams [1778–1845], fur trader)

Although the entire District of Rainy River lies within the Great Lakes–St Lawrence Forest Region, there is a strong boreal influence, particularly in the area north and east of Fort Frances. The landscape is typical Canadian Shield country with exposed bedrock, numerous lakes, and stands of Jack Pine, Black Spruce, Trembling Aspen, and White Birch. Fall colour peaks in late September, marked by rich greens, yellows, and splashes of red.

West of Fort Frances, where an arm of glacial Lake Agassiz once extended across the southern portion of Lake of the Woods to Rainy Lake, the land becomes flat. Sediments deposited by the ancestral lake form a clay plain on which peatlands have developed in low-lying areas. Today, farming country predominates, with open fields broken by scattered patches of Trembling Aspen woodland. The natural history has a distinctly western flavour.

The Rainy River plain is well known for its birds. Many locally breeding species are not found elsewhere in the province: American White Pelican, Piping Plover, Marbled Godwit, Franklin's Gull, Western Kingbird, and Black-billed Magpie. With a little effort and reasonable luck, all of the following should also be found: Sharp-tailed Grouse, Sandhill Crane, Yellow Rail, Wilson's Phalarope, Connecticut Warbler, Brewer's and Yellow-headed Blackbirds, Western Meadowlark, and Clay-colored and LeConte's Sparrows. Bald Eagle, Osprey, Great Blue Heron, and Common Loon are familiar sights throughout the District of Rainy River.

Mammals include White-tailed Deer, Moose, Black Bear, Red Fox, Coyote, Striped Skunk, and Porcupine. Specialties to be watched for on the Rainy River plain are Franklin's Ground Squirrel and White-tailed Jackrabbit. Mosquitoes, blackflies, deer flies, moose flies, and wood ticks are summertime features.

Unusual plants, many of them western or having an affinity for lime soils, abound on the Rainy River plain. In mid June, roadsides are coloured by Indian Paintbrush, Small and Large Yellow Lady's-slippers, and the spectacular Showy Lady's-slipper. Other intriguing species include Tall White Bog and Round-leaved Orchids, Marsh Arrow-grass, and Hoary Willow.

Town of Rainy River Area

The land bordering the southeastern corner of Lake of the Woods harbours a number of species of western plants and birds. For examples, see district overview (above) and entries for Lake of the Woods Provincial Park (below) and Lake of the Woods (under District of Kenora).

DIRECTIONS: Focus on region N of Hwy 11 & W of Hwy 71, especially Hwy 600 area. Near Hwy 600 & River Rd, look for Clay-colored Sparrow, Western Meadowlark, & Brewer's Blackbird. Scan grassy meadows on Hwy 600 for Sedge Wren, Yellow Rail, & other marsh birds. Avoid private property.

Lake of the Woods

See entry under District of Kenora.

Sable Islands Provincial Nature Reserve

This chain of sand islands (including dunes) off the mouth of Rainy River at the south end of Lake of the Woods protects numerous significant species, such as Common Hackberry. Watch for gulls, waterfowl, and shorebirds as well as American White Pelicans. American Avocet, Black-bellied Plover, Ruddy Turnstone, Marbled Godwit, Caspian and Black Terns, and Franklin's Gull are but a few of the bird species to be seen on the islands or adjacent waters.

DIRECTIONS. Rent boat short distance upstream from mouth of

Rainy River at Budreau's Oak Grove Campground at Oak Point (located 16 km downstream from town of Rainy River; take Hwy 600 & River Rd). Distance by boat from campground to islands is 4 km. Ensure that birds are not disturbed, and avoid privately owned portions of islands.

Lake of the Woods Provincial Park

The park's level sandy terrain originated at the bottom of an ancient lake. Although the area lies within the Great Lakes–St Lawrence Forest Region, many species typical of prairie, southern, and boreal habitats are also evident. Thus Basswood, Manitoba Maple, and Jack Pine can be found in close proximity. A walk along the park's shoreline provides excellent viewing opportunities. Look over the lake for American White Pelican, Double-crested Cormorant, Bald Eagle, and Osprey. Drive along roads at dusk for Long-eared and Short-eared Owls. Palm Warblers occur in bogs. Western species here include Yellow-headed Blackbird and Franklin's Ground Squirrel.

DIRECTIONS. Located N of Rainy River off Hwy 621; see prov hwy map. To access park islands (no facilities) take boat from mainland portion of park.

INFORMATION. Lake of the Woods Provincial Park, RR 1, Sleeman, Ont, P0W 1M0, 807-274-5337.

Rainy River Peatlands

Extensive peatlands scattered across the Rainy River clay plain include fine examples of various features associated with these wetlands: raised bogs, coalescing water tracks, teardrop-shaped tree islands, and patterned peatland. Water tracks – the channels within the peatland complex – exist in both wet and ponded forms within a pattern of ridges and swales. These patterned water tracks are part of a network of pools and ridges oriented perpendicular to the very gentle slope of the peatland and of teardrop-shaped islands of Black Spruce oriented parallel to the slope. When sensitive equilibriums are altered, agents of erosion, such as wind-driven waves, cause deterioration of ridges and allow adjacent water tracks to coalesce into shallow lakes. Raised bogs feature a slightly elevated dome of *Sphagnum* mosses surrounded by more watery conditions. A few sections of the Rainy River peatlands are now protected in provincial parks.

DIRECTIONS. Use maps to locate sites on public property. Walking is arduous; compass required. One public site is on E side of Hwy 600, 13 km N of Rainy River.

Caliper Lake Provincial Park

Open meadows, rocky outcrops, and mature forests of White and Red Pines border the lake. American White Pelicans can be seen from May to September.

DIRECTIONS. Located on Hwy 71 in NW corner of District of Rainy River; see prov hwy map.

Crilly Dam, Seine River

Lake Sturgeon spawn in the Seine River in May.

DIRECTIONS. From Atikokan go 52 km W on Hwy 11; go 1.5 km N on Crilly Rd to dam.

Turtle River–White Otter Lake Provincial Park

See entry under District of Kenora.

Squirrel Falls

Walleye, Northern Pike, Lake Whitefish, Mooneye, and Lake Sturgeon spawn here in April, May, October, and November.

DIRECTIONS. At SE corner of Rainy Lake near US border, between Rainy & Namakan lakes. Boat access on Rainy Lake at Fort Frances or at Bear Pass 35 km E of Fort Frances off Hwy 11.

Steep Rock Formation at Atikokan

The abandoned open-pit iron mines north of Atikokan are of considerable geological interest. Stromatolites (fossils of blue-green algae) are found along the pit walls. The earliest evidence of life in North America, these fossils from the Archaean Eon of the Precambrian are approximately 2.7 billion years old.

DIRECTIONS. From Atikokan, go 6 km N on O'Brien St; turn right just before airport; go to end of pavement at mine site.

Quetico Provincial Park

Quetico is a wilderness park, legendary for exceptionally fine canoeing, extensive networks of rivers and lakes, wild landscapes, and fabulous cliffs. Fall colour is best in late September. Winter camping, snowshoeing, and cross-country skiing are possible in the off-season. Although located in the Great Lakes–St Lawrence Forest Region, the 470,000-ha park lies between the boreal forests to the north and the prairies to the west and thus contains elements of all three vegetation zones.

Geology. Quetico's 3-billion-year-old Precambrian rocks are part of the Canadian Shield, the Earth's original crust. Deep, parallel valleys mark a greenstone belt. The park lies within the Arctic watershed, draining to Hudson Bay via Lake Winnipeg. Soils are shallow (less than 1 m deep) and generally acidic. Between some lakes, deeper soils have developed, on which grow Black Ash, American Elm, and Yellow Birch. Deep soil communities are found on eskers and on Steep Rock moraine between Pickerel Lake and Trousers and Zephira lakes. A few clay soil deposits in the west and southwest of the park support diverse floral communities.

Flora. Decidedly boreal in flavour, Quetico is densely forested with closed-canopy coniferous woodlands. Species such as Jack Pine, Black Spruce, White Birch, and Trembling Aspen cover nearly 90% of the forests. Understorey plants include Smooth Woodsia and Mountain Clubmoss. Varied and colourful lichens grow on trees and exposed bedrock among the Jack Pine ridges and across the moss-coated Black Spruce wetlands. Leatherleaf, Labrador Tea, and Sweet Gale thrive in the numerous bogs. More nutrient-rich bogs harbour Pitcher-plant, sundews, and orchids.

Mixed woodlands of the Great Lakes–St Lawrence type contain Red and White Pines, Red and Silver Maples, Yellow Birch, and American Elm. These cover a shrub and forest floor layer of American Yew, Snowberry, Winterberry, Downy Arrow-wood, Climbing Bittersweet, and Sessile-leaved Bellwort.

Among prairie influences are Bur Oak, Gray-stemmed Prairie Goldenrod, Pin Oak, Trembling Aspen, Alumroot, and Hoary Puccoon. Arctic-alpine plants such as Encrusted Saxifrage grow in cold pockets on cliff faces.

The park's numerous rare plants include Floating Marsh-marigold, Field and Sun-stimulated Sedges, Narrow-leaved Collomia, Limestone Oak Fern, Lake Quillwort, Small Sweet Cicely, New England Blue Violet, Smooth and Oregon Woodsias, Impoverished Panic Grass, and Somewhat Hairy Panic Grass.

Fauna. Among mammals adapted to Quetico's long, cold winters are leggy Moose capable of tromping through thick snow and Snowshoe Hare with their thick, furry snowshoe-like footpads. Watch for Beaver, Mink, and Red Squirrel. Canoeists sometimes see Gray Wolf, Canada Lynx, Marten, and Fisher along stream and lake edges. The park's rarest mammals are Heath and Rock Voles.

Highly diverse bird populations are attributed to Quetico's geographic location. The area is a major nesting ground for Bald Eagle and Osprey. An eagle nest on an island at French Lake on the northeastern side of Quetico is visible from the road. Three-toed Woodpecker and Spruce Grouse breed in Quetico, as do several owls, including Northern Hawk, Great Gray, and Barred Owls.

About 15 species of reptiles and amphibians inhabit the park, the number kept low by the brief summers and hard winters. Lake Trout haunt cool, deep lakes, and Walleye, Northern Pike, and Smallmouth Bass flourish in warm, shallow waters. About 50 species of butterflies are found.

DIRECTIONS. Located E of Atikokan off Hwy 11; see prov hwy map.

INFORMATION. Quetico Provincial Park, Atikokan, Ont, P0T 1C0, 807-597-2735 or 807-929-2571.

– Sites of Interest. Although the best and most interesting natural features in Quetico are accessible only by canoe, there are several short nature trails near the park's main entrance at French Lake.

McNiece Lake. This area has one of the park's best examples of large, old-growth Red and White Pines.

Sark Lake Portage. Look along the creek edge here and on many other park portages for Black Ash, American Elm, Virginia Creeper, and Spikenard.

Beaver Creek. Check out this exceptional marsh with its Northern Wild Rice, Common Reed, rushes, and sedges.

Bearpelt Lake Bog. This *Sphagnum* bog shows all successional stages, with such plants as Spatulate-leaved and Round-leaved Sundews, Rose Pogonia, and Arethusa.

Glacier Lake Fen. Quetico's only known fen has quantities of Brownish Beak-rush and Rose Pogonia.

Agnes Lake Narrows Cliff. The limestone in this cliff supports ferns such as Smooth Cliffbrake, Maidenhair Spleenwort, Limestone Oak Fern, and Oregon Woodsia.

Emerald Lake. Lime is responsible for the giant White Cedars here (1 m in diameter).

Wawiag River Levee. Deep soil deposited by flowing river water on top of the Wawiag River levee nurtures a unique assemblage of Silver Maple, American Elm, Red Ash, Nannyberry, Perfoliate Bellwort, Common Hops, Carrion-flower, Cow Parsnip, American Ostrich Fern, Wild Ginger, and hawthorn.

Iron Lake Shoreline. As the driest and warmest part of Quetico, Iron Lake hosts southern and prairie species, such as Big Bluestem, Tall Cord Grass, Field Sedge, Kalm's Lobelia, and Swamp Milkweed.

Beaver Meadows Nature Trail (2.5 km). Noted for its variety of plant communities, this loop trail starts near the entrance to the Chippewa campground and heads over ridges and along lowlands through boreal forest.

Whiskeyjack Nature Trail (2.5 km). This loop trail leads through Black Spruce bog and along Jack Pine ridges. Access is from Highway 11.

DISTRICT OF KENORA

Reach after reach we now passed with fresh beauties; at times we were land-locked, and no power of divination could imagine how we were to find an outlet; then we opened suddenly upon a little lake, then, perhaps, a narrow river passage with abrupt rocks on either side ... And so it was; when the water was deep and calm, there is a pleasing sound in the full well-measured stroke, which makes the canoe bound, as with a spring, over the surface, like a steed over a level plain. (English River, July 10, 1852, Rev. David Anderson [1814–85], bishop of Rupert's Land)

Bordered on the west by the province of Manitoba, this huge district extends from Lake of the Woods and the District of Rainy River north and east to Hudson Bay and northern James Bay. The northern part of the region contains the extensive sub-arctic open woodlands of the Hudson Bay Lowland and a narrow fringe of tundra hugging the Hudson Bay shoreline.

From the inland edge of the lowland, a largely closed-canopy boreal forest stretches southward across the thin soils, barren bedrock highlands, and countless lakes of the Canadian Shield. This is Black Spruce country, although Jack Pine, Tamarack, White Spruce, Balsam Fir, Trembling Aspen, Balsam Poplar, and White Birch are also important components of the landscape. The occurrence and relative abundance of the various species are influenced by variations in latitude, soil, climate, drainage, incidence of fire, and logging.

Southward from the English River drainage basin, elements of the Great Lakes–St Lawrence Forest appear; these include Red and White Pines and some of the deciduous hardwoods more common to the south. The southwestern corner of the district, which once lay under the waters of glacial Lake Agassiz, shows western and prairie influences in its vegetative cover.

There are excellent wildlife viewing opportunities throughout the District of Kenora, including the southern portion of the district, which can be reached by car. Watch for birds such as Bald Eagle, Osprey, Great Blue Heron, American Bittern, and nesting and migrating ducks. Among frequently seen mammals are Moose, White-tailed Deer, Beaver, and Muskrat. Western Painted Turtle and Red-sided Garter Snake add a western flavour to local herpetofauna. From mid April to mid May observe Walleye and Northern Pike spawning in creeks and other wetlands. Mid to late September offers fine views of fall foliage when golden birch and poplar leaves stand against a backdrop of evergreens. Major service centres for accessing the region include Kenora, Red Lake, Sioux Lookout, Ignace, and Dryden.

Hudson Bay Lowland

See separate section on Hudson Bay Lowland.

Woodland Caribou Provincial Park

Located adjacent to the Manitoba border, this park represents a vast, unspoiled wilderness, with myriad pristine lakes and rivers, bedrock ridges, and boreal forest. The 462,000-ha tract contains thousands of kilometres of superb canoe routes, including the upper portions of the historic Bloodvein and Gammon rivers which drain westward to Lake Winnipeg. Within the web of interconnecting waterways are numerous scenic rapids and waterfalls, some of the best sports fishing in the province, and one of Canada's largest concentrations of pictographs.

Canadian Shield formations in the park include 2.6-billion-year-old Kenoran Rock, among the oldest rocks in Canada. Thin soils, hot and dry summers, large sections of exposed bedrock, and a landscape dominated by conifers combine to create conditions conducive to forest fires. Usually started by lightning, fire is the major factor in determining pattern and diversity of habitats in the area. The park, an undisturbed example (no dams, no logging) of upland boreal forest, is dominated by Jack Pine on dry sites, Black Spruce in damp lowlands, and scattered stands of Balsam Poplar, White Birch, and Trembling Aspen. Reindeer lichen grows under mature Jack Pine forests on sandy soils. After a burn, new life springs forth among charred Jack Pine snags: Velvet-leaf Blueberry, Bicknell's Crane's-bill, Pale Yellow Corydalis, Hook-spurred Violet, Fireweed, Fringed Bindweed, and Jack Pine seedlings.

Protected here are several rare species, as well as one of the largest herds of Woodland Caribou south of the Hudson Bay Lowland. Among other mammals are Moose, Gray Wolf, Canada Lynx, River Otter, Marten, Black Bear, Heath Vole, and Wolverine. Birds include Barred Owl, Turkey Vulture, Canada Goose, Common Loon, Bald Eagle, Double-crested Cormorant, Palm Warbler, Three-toed and Black-backed Woodpeckers, and Great Gray Owl.

A prairie influence is noticeable in species such as Forster's Tern, American White Pelican, Franklin's Ground Squirrel, and Red-sided Garter Snake. There is a surprising diversity of plants exhibiting a strong prairie-boreal influence, including Prairie Crocus, Prairie Rush, Prairie Spikemoss, Parsley Fern, Ten-flowered Showy Goldenrod, and Floating Marsh-marigold.

DIRECTIONS. Located NW of Red Lake; see prov hwy map. Fly in or take canoe. Arrangements must be made in advance.
INFORMATION. MNR.

Ojibway Provincial Park

A rich forest composed mainly of conifers such as Jack Pine and Black and White Spruces blankets the rolling hills south of Vermilion Lake. Scattered Red and White Pines grow here near the northern limits of their ranges. Wild rice flourishes in shallow wetlands. Moose may be seen feeding at Moose Creek from May to October. Beaver are active during the same period. Watch for ducks from May 15 to September 15.
DIRECTIONS. Located SW of Sioux Lookout on Hwy 72; see prov hwy map.
INFORMATION. Ojibway Provincial Park, Sioux Lookout, Ont, P0V 2T0, 807-737-2033.

Lake of the Woods

Waterfowl concentrate here in April and early May. About 120 pairs of Bald Eagles nest on the lake. There are about 50 breeding pairs of Osprey and numerous Great Blue Heron colonies. Marshes in Lake of the Woods provide good birdwatching in breeding season, especially in June. Rock and shield communities at the north end of the lake contrast with prairie habitats in the southern part. Some western highlights in summer are Yellow-headed Blackbird, Black-billed Magpie, Marbled Godwit, Western Kingbird, and Western Meadowlark. Short-eared Owl and Yellow Rail can also be found. The American White Pelican population on the lake is estimated at 12,000–16,000 birds; pelicans can be seen feeding in the shallow bays from late May to late August. In late May look for Marbled and Hudsonian Godwits; an abundance of shorebirds haunts the lakeshore early in August. September is the time for hawks, while late September and early October bring flocks of Sandhill Cranes. Red-necked Grebes and Yellow-headed Blackbirds are visible at a number of locations, such as Sultana Marsh, Haides, and Windy Point.

The area harbours various western plants and mammals found nowhere else in Ontario. Examples are Franklin's Ground

Squirrel, White-tailed Jackrabbit, and the rare Brittle Prickly-pear Cactus. Numerous pictographs and petroglyphs are visible on the lake, and there is a fine show of autumn foliage in the area.

DIRECTIONS. By boat from town of Kenora or from S end of lake.
INFORMATION. MNR.

Lake of the Woods Provincial Park

See entry under District of Rainy River.

Turtle River–White Otter Lake Provincial Park

This waterway park consists of a 160-km stretch of lakes and rivers, largely situated within the long and scenic Turtle River valley. The southern reaches of the river are lined with large marshes and beds of Northern Wild Rice, which provide abundant habitat for Moose and waterfowl. An excellent canoe route, the waterway links with other lakes and rivers, so various loop trips can be made. There are numerous sets of scenic rapids and waterfalls along the way, particularly in the lower reaches. Western Painted Turtles are prevalent in the river, and several pictograph sites occur along the waterways.

Although White Otter Lake is probably best known for the legendary White Otter Castle, it is also recognized for its superb scenery, backcountry camping, and fine Lake Trout angling. The water is cold and crystal clear. Beautiful and rugged shorelines include numerous beaches and rock cliffs. Around the lake are mature stands of Red and White Pines.

Covered with a thin layer of glacial till, the park's bedrock determines vegetation and drainage patterns in the landscape, as is typical of Canadian Shield country. The vegetation is representative of the transitional zone between the Great Lakes–St Lawrence and Boreal forest regions. Boreal species such as White and Black Spruce, Balsam Fir, Jack Pine, Trembling Aspen, and White Birch are found interspersed with Red and White Pines and other species more typical of the mixed woodlands to the south.

DIRECTIONS. Situated between Ignace on Hwy 17 & Mine Centre on Hwy 11; see prov hwy map. Access from either location or from Hwy 622. River flows from Ignace to Mine Centre.

INFORMATION. Box 448, Ignace, Ont, P0T 1T0, 807-934-2233 or 108 Saturn Ave, Atikokan, Ont, P0T 1C0, 807-597-6971.

DISTRICT OF THUNDER BAY

Lake Superior is the largest and most magnificent body of fresh water in the world; it is clear and pellucid, of great depth, and abounding in a great variety of fish, which are the most excellent of their kind ... [The] best of all [is] the Ticamang, or white fish, which weighs from four to sixteen pounds, and is of a superior quality in these waters ... This vast collection of water is often covered with fog, particularly when the wind is from the east, which, driving against the high barren rocks on the north and west shore, dissolves in torrents of rain. (Ca 1790s, Sir Alexander Mackenzie [1764–1820], fur trader and explorer)

The vast District of Thunder Bay arcs northward around Lake Superior from the American border in the southwest to White River and Pukaskwa National Park in the east, and north to the Albany River.

Landforms

The entire District of Thunder Bay lies on the Canadian Shield, where Precambrian bedrock has been shaped by volcanoes, erosion, and glaciation to create a mosaic of granite, sediments, and volcanic features. One billion years ago volcanic activity forced molten rock upward through cracks in the Earth's crust. The flow hardened to form a hard black rock known as diabase. Diabase cliffs, sills, and mesas are a feature of the area from east of Nipigon north to Lake Nipigon, west to Thunder Bay, and then southwest to the United States border, mostly fairly close to Lake Superior. Today's landscape is characterized by rugged terrain, island-studded lakes, and very thin soils. Exposed bedrock frequently controls drainage routes, shapes of lakes, and patterns of vegetation. Moraine ridges, cliffs, beaches, sand dunes shaped by winds, and meandering river channels add to the variety of landforms. Low-lying areas are occupied by bogs and swamps. Soils in the Thunder Bay area consist of clays and sands laid down by glacial Lake Minong. There is some agricultural land west of the city.

Flora

North of Lake Superior the landscape is boreal, with periodic fire a natural feature. Forests of Jack Pine, Black Spruce, White Birch, and Trembling Aspen spread across the worn-down hills. Balsam Fir, White Spruce, Showy Mountain-ash, Tamarack, and White Cedar are also present. Woodland Caribou habitat is found where extensive stands of Black Spruce or Jack Pine, along with *Cladina* lichens, grow on barely covered bedrock or sand.

Among dominant shrubs in the boreal uplands are Mountain Maple, Red-osier Dogwood, Low Sweet Blueberry, Common Juniper, Speckled Alder, Bush Honeysuckle, Labrador Tea, and Squashberry. Ground cover in the boreal environment includes Yellow Clintonia, Bunchberry, pyrolas, Goldthread, Naked Miterwort, Wild Sarsaparilla, Creeping Snowberry, Twinflower, Starflower, Oak Fern, Northern Beech Fern, Rock Polypody, and Spinulose Wood Fern. The rugged shoreline of Lake Superior is noted for its arctic-alpine plants.

Lichens, liverworts, and mosses are prolific in the moist maritime climate of the Lake Superior coast and the damp forest floor of the Canadian Shield. Among the lichens, old man's beard hangs in pale wisps from trees, whereas the upright *Cladina* lichens live on bare, sun-littered soil. Lung Lichen, with its leafy lobes, attaches itself to poplar trunks. Along Lake Superior, map lichen and rock tripe occupy the transition zone between the high-water level and the edge of the boreal forest, while *Xanthoria*, a bright yellow crust-like lichen, grows along rocky shores.

The Great Lakes–St Lawrence Forest Region extends northward from the American border to the city of Thunder Bay. White and Red Pines with a scattering of hardwood species such as Sugar Maple and Yellow Birch are found, along with boreal elements.

Birds

Many of the birds of the district are typical boreal species.

Nesting ducks include Mallard, American Black Duck, Common Goldeneye, Ring-necked Duck, and Red-breasted, Common, and Hooded Mergansers. Common Loon, Double-crested Cormorant, Killdeer, and Spotted Sandpiper frequent the Lake Superior shore in summer. Herring and Ring-billed Gulls, Double-crested Cormorant, and Great Blue Heron nest along the coast and on coastal islands. Bald Eagle and Merlin are common throughout the district.

Among common forest songbirds are Swainson's Thrush, Red-eyed Vireo, Least Flycatcher, White-throated Sparrow, Ovenbird, and Magnolia, Black-throated Green, Nashville, Bay-breasted, and Yellow-rumped Warblers. Red-breasted Nuthatch, Blackburnian Warbler, and Winter Wren are also frequently heard.

Northern Goshawk, Spruce and Ruffed Grouse, Gray Jay, and Three-toed, Black-backed, Hairy, and Downy Woodpeckers are year-round residents. In November, hawks migrate along the Lake Superior coast. Rough-legged Hawks use updrafts created by ridges and thermals to travel around Lake Superior towards the midwest.

Mammals

The typical boreal assemblage of mammals includes Moose, Gray Wolf, Black Bear, Marten, Canada Lynx, Woodland Caribou, Red Fox, weasels, Striped Skunk, squirrels, Beaver, River Otter, Snowshoe Hare, mice, voles, bats, shrews, and moles. White-tailed Deer occur in southern areas.

Wabakimi Provincial Park

Deep in northwestern Ontario, some 300 km north of Thunder Bay, lies Wabakimi, the largest area of protected boreal forest in Ontario. Containing almost 900,000 ha, the park is located in the Ogoki River basin, which connects with the larger wilderness canoeing area known as Ogoki-Albany. Famous for superb canoeing, Wabakimi offers myriad interconnecting waterways, fine whitewater, elongated lakes, relatively short portages, abundant campsites, and good sports fishing.

The landscape shows typical features of the boreal forest and the Canadian Shield, with rugged terrain and island-studded lakes. Forested areas are typified by Jack Pine and Black Spruce, with some poplar and White Birch. Red Pine and Black Ash are at the northern edges of their ranges here. Much of Wabakimi has very thin soils, and bedrock scraped bare by glaciers is a pervasive feature. Landforms such as cliffs, beaches, wind-sculpted sand dunes, and meandering river channels are scattered throughout the park, while bogs and swamps occupy low-lying areas. DeGeer moraine ridges mark successional halts by retreating glaciers. Some of the extensive peatlands exhibit excellent ridge and ponded swale patterns, typical of northern fens.

Mature coniferous woodlands and their accompanying ground cover of *Cladina* lichens provide habitat for one of the largest Woodland Caribou herds south of the Hudson Bay Lowland. Other mammals include Moose, Black Bear, Marten, Canada Lynx, Beaver, River Otter, and Gray Wolf. Numerous pictograph sites, including one at Cliff Lake, are found in the park.

DIRECTIONS. See prov hwy map. Access to park via CN railway, float plane, or bush road N from Armstrong reaching to within a day's paddle of park.

Lake Nipigon Provincial Park

Enjoy here rugged scenery and a clifftop view of Lake Nipigon, at 300,000 ha the largest lake located entirely within the province of Ontario. Black sands line the park's beaches and, along the road approaching from the south, spectacular black diabase cliffs rise 170 m above the surrounding countryside. The 1,200-ha park's second-growth forest is dominated by Trembling Aspen and White Birch. Black Spruce occurs in bogs and along the lakeshore, while Red Pine occupies sunny well-drained sites. Watch for northern orchids along the woodland trails. Fall foliage is best in late September.

DIRECTIONS. Located 55 km N of Nipigon off Hwy 11; see prov hwy map.

INFORMATION. Lake Nipigon Provincial Park, Box 970, Nipigon, Ont, P0T 2J0, 807-885-3181.

Longlac Marshes

From the roadside, scan the extensive cattail marshes for Common Tern, Virginia Rail, Sora, and possibly Yellow-headed Blackbird. Bobolinks, at the northern edge of their breeding range, are found in the fields close to the Indian church.

DIRECTIONS. Located just W of Longlac where Hwy 11 crosses N end of Long Lake.

South and West of Thunder Bay City

– Greenwood Lake White Pines. This magnificent stand of huge White Pine is a fine example of old-growth forest, probably one of the oldest remaining in the province. Summering birds include Pine and Black-throated Blue Warblers and Scarlet Tanager at the northwestern limits of their breeding ranges. At present, access is difficult; road upgrades and a trail are under consideration.

DIRECTIONS. From Thunder Bay drive W on Hwy 11 to 1.9 km past Kashabowie; turn left (S) on Hwy 802. At 5.9 km, take left (gravel) road. At 26.7 km, turn right at T-jct. At 33.3 km, take left fork (Mowe Lake Rd). At 36.9 km, take right fork. At 38.7 km, take right fork. Proceed to pine stand at 43.4 km from Hwy 11. At press time, road is very rough logging road (4WD vehicle recommended).

– Whitefish Lake. This shallow lake of Northern Wild Rice is frequented by Bald Eagle and good numbers of summering Red-necked Grebe. Connecticut Warbler and uncommon orchids are features of the Black Spruce bog at the west end of the lake.

DIRECTIONS. From Thunder Bay, drive 20 km W on Hwy 11/17 to Stanley; turn left onto Hwy 588 & go 54 km to Artesian Wells Resort at W end of lake (5 km past Whitefish store). Rent canoe at resort or scan from shore for grebes.

INFORMATION. Artesian Wells Resort, RR 2, Nolalu, Ont, P0T 2K0, 807-933-5000.

– Middle Falls Provincial Park. This park is located on the American border overlooking the Pigeon River. Once a meltwater channel for glacial Lake Agassiz, the Pigeon is now one of the main tributaries of Lake Superior. Over the millennia the river carved its way through soft sedimentary rocks to create two waterfalls. The 6-m-high Middle Falls is wide and scenic; 1.5 km away at the spectacular Pigeon Falls, sheets of water pour over a 28-m cliff to a gorge below. Bur Oak, Black Ash, and American Elm are among southern species found in the woodlands of the 900-ha park. Steep-sided ridges and mesas of diabase create striking scenery in the rugged local landscape.

DIRECTIONS. Located on Hwy 593 just N of US border; see prov hwy map.

INFORMATION. Box 5000, Thunder Bay, Ont, P7C 5G6, 807-964-2097.

– Kakabeka Falls Provincial Park. As the park's name suggests, the primary feature here is the splendid 39-m-high Kakabeka Falls as it tumbles over cliffs of layered slate. The gorge below was carved out of Precambrian bedrock by glacial meltwaters. At 1.6 billion years, fossils found in the area are among the oldest known. The 500-ha park is open in winter.

DIRECTIONS. Located 32 km W of Thunder Bay on Hwy 11/17; see prov hwy map.

INFORMATION. Box 5000, Thunder Bay, Ont, P7C 5G6, 807-473-9231.

– Stanley. Examples of western mixedgrass prairie and open oak woodland, including many rare prairie species, occur along the Kaministiquia River in the vicinity of Stanley. These rare vegetation communities are believed to have originated about 8,000 years ago when a number of prairie species migrated eastward into the area during a warm period that followed the last glaciation. Today, remnants of these communities persist on hot, dry sites that are subject to periodic burning. The Stanley area prairie and savanna habitats differ from western grasslands in that they exhibit an increased representation of boreal species. Among the plants of interest occurring in the general area are Hoary Puccoon, Rough Fescue, Canada Plum, and Seneca Snakeroot. A vigorous stand of Bur Oak grows on a gravelly terrace along the Kaministiquia River in Stanley.

The fauna found along this stretch of the Kaministiquia River has a somewhat more southerly affinity than is usual in the region. Birds that reach the northern limits of their breeding ranges here include Northern Oriole, Great Crested Flycatcher, Warbling Vireo, and Indigo Bunting.

DIRECTIONS. From Thunder Bay, drive 20 km W on Hwy 11/17 to Hwy 588; turn left & go past arena to Stanley Hotel on Kam River. Walk or drive W along Harstone Rd from hotel to bridge; oaks are closer to bridge.

– Big Thunder Ski Training Centre. The Nor'Westers are a chain of small mountains that fringe the south side of the city of Thunder Bay. Scenic and interesting geologically, these mountains are elements of diabase mesas. Stands of Sugar Maple and Yellow Birch found here are the northernmost in the area. Access to the mountains is through the Big Thunder Ski Training Centre, where numerous cross-country ski trails originate. The trails are also good for hiking in summer and fall.

DIRECTIONS. From jct of Hwys 11/17 & 61 at SW edge of Thunder Bay, go 11.5 km S on Hwy 61; turn left on Little Norway Rd & go to end. Park in lot & follow signs to ski trails.

Thunder Bay City and Area

– Wishart Conservation Area. A pure Black Spruce and Jack Pine stand growing above a carpet of moss brings a northern flavour to this pleasant area along the Current River. Walking and cross-country ski trails explore the rolling topography of the 212-ha conservation area.

DIRECTIONS. Located 11 km N of city. Go N on Balsam St (past Hwy 11/17); turn W on Wardrope Ave, then N on Onion Lake Rd.

INFORMATION. Lakehead Region Conservation Authority.

– Cascades Conservation Area. Here, rock outcrops border the Current River while nature and cross-country ski trails wander across the 156-ha tract of rolling landscape. The woods have a deciduous flavour, including White Birch and Trembling Aspen.

DIRECTIONS. Go N on Balsam St (past Hwy 11/17) to end.

INFORMATION. Lakehead Region Conservation Authority.

– Trowbridge Falls–Centennial Park. In the northern part of the city, the Current River has cut through gently dipping shales of the Gunflint Formation, producing narrow gorges whose walls provide niches for a number of significant fern species.

DIRECTIONS. From jct of Hodder Ave & Thunder Bay Express-way (Hwy 11/17), go 0.5 km N on Copenhagen Rd to entrance to Trowbridge Falls on left. Trails lead along river from parking lot.

– Mission Island Marsh Conservation Area. The most exten-sive remaining marsh on the Thunder Bay waterfront, this place is excellent for observing migrating waterfowl. Dabbling ducks feed in the marsh, while diving ducks are seen farther out. Bald Eagles are often observed. LeConte's Sparrows and Sedge Wrens occur in fields inland from the marsh. Depending on Lake Superior water levels, migrating shorebirds may also be found in good numbers.
DIRECTIONS. From jct of Syndicate Ave & Walsh St in S end of city, go E on Jackknife Bridge & 106th St to parking lot & board-walk on lakeshore.
INFORMATION. Lakehead Region Conservation Authority.

– Chippewa Park and Landfill. This city park and the adjacent dredge-dumping facility are located on the Lake Superior shore at the south edge of the city. The woods of Chippewa Park pro-vide good viewing for warblers during migration, while the coast by the landfill site excels for observing migrating water-fowl. Look for LeConte's Sparrows and Yellow-headed Black-birds summering in the area.
DIRECTIONS. From downtown, drive S on Hwy 61B across Kaministiquia River; turn left on City Rd & follow signs to park-ing areas in park. Paths & roadways go through coniferous woods & path leads N past campground to landfill gate.

– Mills Block Agreement Forest. An old road goes through this Black Spruce bog. Several interesting butterfly species occur here.
DIRECTIONS. From jct with Hwy 102, go 1 km S on Hwy 11/17 (Thunder Bay Expressway) to John St Exit; turn right, then left onto John St Rd; proceed 6 km to parking lot on left.
INFORMATION. Lakehead Region Conservation Authority.

Sleeping Giant (Sibley) Provincial Park

This large peninsula northeast of Thunder Bay extends 40 km southward into Lake Superior. The terrain rises gradually from the eastern shoreline to a massive escarpment towering up to 240 m above Thunder Bay on the west. Between lie rugged cliffs, deeply cut valleys, and fast-flowing streams. At the south end of the park is the Sleeping Giant, a large diabase butte whose sides form the tallest cliffs in Ontario. The formation actually consists of a series of mesas formed from soft sedimentary rocks and capped with erosion-resistant diabase sill. Trails follow the cliffs and coast.

Sleeping Giant's long, narrow shape makes Thunder Cape, at its southern end, a concentration point for migrating birds. Migrants can be seen along the south shore of the peninsula in fall, particularly around the settlement of Silver Islet, just outside the park at the end of the road. Boreal forest warblers abound; 20 species nest in the park and an additional 7 have been seen during migration. At Pickerel Lake, look and listen for Olive-sided Flycatcher and Pine Warbler. Another good birding location is the outlet of Marie Louise Lake. Because the area has not been hunted for many years, large mammals are abundant and relatively easy to observe. White-tailed Deer are especially common.

Sleeping Giant is noted for its diversity of interesting plants, including numerous orchids. Bog Adder's-mouth grows in ravines on the west side, and arctic plants such as Alpine Bistort, Sticky Tofieldia, Butterwort, and Cloudberry can be found on rocky shores at Tee Harbour and elsewhere. The 24,500-ha park offers an interpretive program and an extensive network of hiking and cross-country ski trails. Fall colour peaks during the latter part of September.

DIRECTIONS. Located on Hwy 587; see prov hwy map.

INFORMATION. Sleeping Giant Provincial Park, Pass Lake, Ont, P0T 2M0, 807-933-4332 or 807-977-2526.

– Thunder Cape Bird Observatory. Although the walk to the site is long and, in places, difficult, the southern tip of the Sibley Peninsula is an excellent spot for observing and monitoring bird migration. Day-visitors are welcome unannounced, but volunteers wishing to spend a few days at the observatory should make prior arrangements (address below).

DIRECTIONS. Drive through Sleeping Giant Prov Park to 5 km past entrance to Lake Marie Louise campground; park in trailhead lot on right. Hike or bike Tee Harbour Trail past Tee Harbour to start of Chimney Trail. Leave bike in woods here; proceed on foot along Kabeyun Trail, up over foot of Sleeping Giant. Before descending W side of giant's foot, turn left on Thunder Cape Trail; follow to end. Total distance from trailhead to cape is 13 km, a walk of 3 to 4 hr.

INFORMATION. N.G. Escott, c/o Thunder Bay Field Naturalists, Box 1073, Thunder Bay, Ont, P7C 4X8.

Ouimet Canyon Provincial Nature Reserve

Over the millennia here, erosion by glaciers, frost, and water has turned a crack in the diabase sill bedrock into a spectacular gorge 100 m deep, 150 m across, and 2.4 km long. Lichens have colonized the steep, column-like cliff faces, and subarctic plants such as Arctic Pyrola and Encrusted Saxifrage flourish in the cool conditions at the bottom. A forest of Jack Pine, Balsam Fir, and White Birch grows above the canyon, while a talus slope of stony rubble lies against the foot of the walls. The reserve protects almost 2,000 ha of land.

DIRECTIONS. Located 70 km E of Thunder Bay off Hwy 11/17; see prov hwy map.

INFORMATION. Ouimet Canyon Provincial Park, Box 5000, Thunder Bay, Ont, P7C 5G6, 807-933-4332 or 807-977-2526.

Hurkett Cove Conservation Area

Located on the shores of Black Bay, this 120-ha conservation area abounds with birds in spring and fall. During migration, large numbers of waterfowl can be observed in the marshes. When water levels on Lake Superior are low, exposed sandbars attract migrant shorebirds.

DIRECTIONS. From Thunder Bay, drive 85 km NE on Hwy 11/17 past Dorion; turn E at Wolf River Rd & go 3 km.

INFORMATION. Lakehead Region Conservation Authority.

North Shore of Lake Superior (along Highway 17)

Towns and other clearings tucked among the coniferous trees create breaks in the boreal forest. Here rare birds occasionally show up in September and October and sometimes in the spring. Look for vagrants around such communities as Red Rock, Nipigon, Rossport, Schreiber, Terrace Bay, and Marathon and at the mouth of the Pic River. In late September a generous sprinkling of yellow leaves contrasts with the greens of the coniferous woodlands. The north shore of Lake Superior is noted for its rugged and spectacular scenery.

– Rossport. Fall migrants tend to concentrate around this small community nestled on Lake Superior's shore. A walk through the village along the road and railway tracks can be rewarding. Waterfowl and sometimes shorebirds are found along the shoreline.
DIRECTIONS. Located on Hwy 17, 35 km W of Terrace Bay.

– Prairie River Mouth Provincial Nature Reserve. Where the river flows into Prairie Cove, a raised sand and gravel beach ridge is covered by an extensive open spruce-lichen woodland. This community type, typical of Woodland Caribou habitat, is uncommon in the southern boreal forest. The area is home to Spruce Grouse, Boreal Chickadee, and Gray Jay.
DIRECTIONS. About halfway between Terrace Bay & Neys Prov Park. From jct of Mill Rd & Hwy 17 in Terrace Bay, drive 34.5 km E on Hwy 17 to dirt road leading S. Or, from E, road is 1.7 km W of Prairie River bridge. Drive 0.6 km down dirt road to gate at RR tracks. Park & walk across tracks & down road to gravel pit. From NE corner of pit follow flagging tape & blazes marking narrow trail to dunes. Total walking time less than 30 min each way.

– Neys Provincial Park. The park's location on a peninsula protruding into the chill winds and waves of Lake Superior permits the growth of a number of subarctic plants, such as Black Crowberry and Encrusted Saxifrage. The 3,300-ha park has a truly boreal character, with White Spruce, Balsam Fir, White Birch, and Trembling Aspen found on drier sites and Black Spruce, Tamarack, and White Cedar occupying wetter locales. Migrating birds, including occasional rarities, collect here in spring and fall. Spruce Grouse are present year-round. There are good populations of large mammals. Churning lake waters have carved unusual shapes into shoreline rocks. The park was a favourite haunt of Group of Seven artists.

DIRECTIONS. Located off Hwy 17 between Marathon & Terrace Bay; see prov hwy map.
INFORMATION. PO Bag 3, Terrace Bay, Ont, P0T 2W0, 807-229-1624 or 807-825-3205.

– Marathon (Craig's Bluff). The shoreline woods just east of the town is an excellent location for observing large numbers of late fall migrants, including rare species. Most migrating hawks pass through in September, but there is a strong Rough-legged Hawk movement along the shoreline in the second half of October.
DIRECTIONS. From Hwy 17, drive S on Hwy 626 to Marathon; cross RR tracks & turn left at stop sign. Proceed to public school & park. Walk 3 km down RR track to Craig's Bluff.

– Pic River Mouth. This is one of the largest sand dune complexes on the north shore of Lake Superior. The mouth of the river attracts waterfowl and geese, and migrating Rough-legged Hawks fly over in the second half of October.
DIRECTIONS. From Hwy 17, 7 km E of Marathon, drive S on Hwy 627 through Heron Bay; just before road crosses Pic River, proceed straight down dirt road.

Pukaskwa National Park

Pukaskwa National Park (pronounced puk-a-saw) protects 187,800 ha of Canadian Shield wilderness made up of boreal forest and rugged Lake Superior coastline. Wild-country adventurers such as kayakers, canoeists, and backpackers are attracted by massive headlands, sheltered coves, steep valley slopes, whitewater rivers, forested upland plateaus, varied wetland habitats, and opportunities to see large mammals. Woodland Caribou are found in the park. Birds present are the typical species of boreal habitats.

Geology. Most of the rock in the park consists of a granitic batholith, produced when masses of magma cooled deep beneath the Earth's surface. The resulting complex of gneissic rock includes Tip Top Mountain; at 640 m above sea level, this is Ontario's third-highest point of land. Near the northern and southern ends of the park are small greenstone belts. Glaciers have modified Pukaskwa's Precambrian bedrock, and the landscape now displays terraces, waterfalls, dissected uplands, fast-flowing rivers, steep-sided valleys, and rolling and undulating topography. At Hattie Cove there are numerous opportunities to view faults, pillow lavas, schisting, greenstones, diabase dykes, and glacial features (go to end of Highway 627 and follow trails).

Vascular Plants. Periodic fires sweep Pukaskwa's boreal landscape, where Black Spruce, Jack Pine, and White Birch are dominant. Near the southern edge of the park, there are elements of the transition zone between the Boreal and Great Lakes–St Lawrence forest regions. Here, stands of Red and Sugar Maples, Yellow Birch, and White and Red Pines grow in sheltered sites.

The harsh climate along exposed headlands creates habitat for arctic-alpine species such as Encrusted Saxifrage, Butterwort, Knotted Pearlwort, Bird's-eye Primrose, Black Crowberry, Smooth Woodsia, and Alpine Bilberry. Other northern species, including American Dune Grass, Northern Twayblade, and Sparrow's-egg Lady's-slipper, grow tucked in among dunes and beaches along the coast. Pitcher's Thistle, a more southerly species endemic to the Great Lakes, colonizes dune and beach washouts which are devoid of other plant life.

DIRECTIONS. Located E of Marathon with access via Hwy 627; see prov hwy map.

INFORMATION. Pukaskwa National Park, Heron Bay, Ont, P0T 1R0, 807-229-0801.

Voyageur Trail

See entry under District of Algoma.

DISTRICT OF ALGOMA

For Breakfast we had the famous White Fish. All that I had heard of its excellent Quality and Taste fell far short of its real Excellence ... It is the most delicate tasted Fish I ever eat ... The Rapid [at Sault Ste Marie] falls over a Ridge of Rocks about 23 Feet over a space of half a mile. There are ten beautiful Islands in the middle covered with the most magnificent trees and the Banks on each side of the River [St Mary] have equally this Attraction. The dark Foliage and the beautiful Verdure of the long Grass form a fine contrast with the snowy Whiteness and bright Foam of the Cataract. (June 25, 1821, Nicholas Garry [ca 1782–1856], deputy governor of Hudson's Bay Company)

This district extends inland for varying distances from the eastern shore of Lake Superior and the north shore of Lake Huron. With the exception of limestone-based St Josephs Island in northern Lake Huron, the entire jurisdiction sits on the Canadian Shield. Ancient rocks of the Superior province underlie almost all of the mainland portion of the district, but the bedrock adjacent to Lake Huron belongs to the somewhat younger Southern province. Great Lakes–St Lawrence Forest predominates in the southern part of Algoma, while Boreal Forest blankets the portion north of Lake Superior Provincial Park.

Nagagamisis Provincial Park

Here, majestic old-growth boreal woodlands border a large lake with numerous back bays. Forests of Balsam Fir, Balsam Poplar, White Birch, Jack Pine, and White and Black Spruces predominate on the hilly, well-drained uplands. Bunchberry, Yellow Clintonia, and Large-leaved Aster grow on dry sites, while Tamarack, Speckled Alder, *Sphagnum*, and Labrador Tea are found in the boggy lowlands. Watch for Moose in the wetlands at dusk. The challenging canoe routes of the Nagagami and Shekak rivers connect with the 8,131-ha park.
DIRECTIONS. Located 135 km N of White River on Hwy 631; see prov hwy map.
INFORMATION. MNR.

Kakakiwibik Esker-Fen Complex

A number of glacial ice-contact features are evident at this large complex. Kettle-trough lakes, fed by springs, parallel the esker. There is a Jack Pine woodland with ground cover of reindeer lichen. Where canopy openings have been created by storms, low shrubs grow.
DIRECTIONS. From White River go 10 km SE on Hwy 17 to CPR underpass near O'Brien Siding. Park in gravel pit; follow rough trail.

Chapleau Crown Game Preserve

At 722,500 ha this is the largest game preserve in the world. Located north and west of Chapleau, the reserve encompasses the southern portion of Missinaibi River Provincial Park. Chapleau-Nemegosenda Provincial Waterway Park lies along its eastern boundary. The preserve, in which hunting and trapping are prohibited, is noted for its scenic wilderness character and an abundance and diversity of animal species. The area offers excellent opportunities for wildlife viewing. Mammals include Moose, Black Bear, Canada Lynx, Marten, Fisher, and Gray Wolf. DIRECTIONS. Access at Missanabie via Hwy 651, or from Hwy 519 at Dubreuilville; see prov hwy map.

Missinaibi River Provincial Park

See entry under District of Cochrane.

Lake Superior Provincial Park

Lake Superior, at 155,000 ha one of the province's largest parks, is located at the meeting point of two forest regions – the Boreal and the Great Lakes–St Lawrence. Rounded Precambrian hills, high shoreline cliffs, and panoramic vistas create stunning beauty. Rugged shield landscape, chilling onshore winds, and varied soils and drainage patterns contribute to habitat diversity. Logging within the park is under a temporary moratorium. Fall colour peaks during the third week of September. In winter, deep snow creates opportunities for cross-country skiing.

Geology. Worn-down remnants of ancient mountain ranges dominate the park's landscape. Granites and gneisses are the most common rocks, but there are also examples of lava from long-dead volcanoes, diabase dykes along the shore, and much younger Cambrian sandstones that formed a mere half-billion years ago. Geological faults result in breathtaking scenery at Agawa Canyon, Agawa Rock, and Old Woman Bay.

Vegetation Communities. The park is a good place for viewing a particularly abrupt transition between northern and southern forest types. This can be observed best in fall when the contrast between dark evergreen forests and brilliantly coloured deciduous woodlands is most pronounced.

Great Lakes–St Lawrence Forest. The hills of the southern part of the park are dominated by stands of Sugar Maple, with Yellow Birch and White and Red Pines also present. Among plants of interest are Triangle Grape Fern, Marginal Wood Fern, Braun's Holly Fern, and Northern Panic Grass. Exceptionally large hardwoods can be seen in the Agawa Valley Nature Reserve.

Boreal Forest. Trembling Aspen and coniferous trees such as Black and White Spruces and Balsam Fir fill the third of the park north of Old Woman Bay. Fingers of boreal vegetation reach farther south, especially in the lowlands. The uncommon Golden Corydalis is noteworthy.

Lake Superior Coast. Bedrock outcrops, sheer cliffs, and sand, shingle, and cobble beaches are found along the coast. The cold waters and winds of Lake Superior create arctic conditions, enabling arctic-alpine plants, relicts of postglacial times, to survive on cliffs, headlands, and beaches. Boreal plants hug the coast with mats of herbs. Rare plants include Slender Cliffbrake, Sticky Tofieldia, Encrusted Saxifrage, and Butterwort.

Wetlands. Most of the park's wetlands are acidic; those that are less so support a diverse flora. Among rarities are Sticky Tofieldia, Northern Adder's-tongue Fern, Yellow-eyed Grass, Arethusa, Heart-leaved Twayblade, Rose Pogonia, Red-stemmed Gentian, and Kalm's Lobelia.

Disturbed Land. Where logging occurs and along the highway, weedy species thrive. Watch for Live-forever.

Fauna. Habitat diversity leads to excellent birding, especially when vagrants, usually from the west, regularly drift in across Lake Superior. There is a notable fall hawk migration. Nesting species include Black-backed Woodpecker, Spruce Grouse, and Pine Siskin as well as various warblers, vireos, and shorebirds. Woodland Caribou have been reintroduced at Montreal Island and around Gargantua. Look for their tracks on sand beaches at Gargantua and Warp Bay; the print of dewclaws and much rounder curves distinguish them from those of Moose, which are also common in the park. From Agawa Bay scenic lookout, use a telescope to scan for caribou on the sandspit at the east end of Montreal Island. Gray Wolf, Canada Lynx, and Marten are park residents, as are Northern Leopard Frog, Mink Frog, and Redbelly Snake. Brook Trout and Lake Trout occur throughout streams and lakes.

DIRECTIONS. On Hwy 17 (see prov hwy map) or enter on E side of park from Algoma Central Railway.

INFORMATION. Lake Superior Provincial Park, Box 267, Wawa, Ont, P0S 1K0, 705-856-2284.

– Sites of Interest. Lake Superior Provincial Park offers excellent hiking, backpacking, canoeing, and kayaking opportunities, as well as numerous significant landscape and natural history features.

Coastal Trail (55 km). This jagged and exacting route traces the superbly beautiful Lake Superior coastline along cliffs, sand beaches, cobble beaches, and sculpted black rocks. At Gargantua Harbour there are boulders the size of melons. Deep-blue lobelias poke up in the spaces among the rocks. Butterwort and Encrusted Saxifrage are sprinkled along the coast on outcrops of rock. Look for Bald Eagle and Double-crested Cormorant, especially between the Sand and Agawa Rivers. The whole trail takes 5–7 days; many days-trips are also possible.

Nokomis Trail (5-km loop). Enjoy an interesting patch of boreal forest and spectacular views of Lake Superior. At the first lookout, notice the imprint of an old woman's face in the cliff to the west at Old Woman Bay.

Peat Mountain Trail (11-km loop). From the top of the mountain, ridges shaped by glaciers are visible.

Trapper's Trail (1.5-km loop). Moose are often seen from the bog lake boardwalk at dawn or dusk. Watch for River Otter, Marten, flycatchers, and Black-backed Woodpecker.

South Old Woman River Trail (2.5-km loop). The moist forest here nurtures a good diversity of ferns and wildflowers.

Orphan Lake Trail (8-km loop). This trail traverses many habitats, including lake and river shore. The shift from southern Great Lakes–St Lawrence Forest to northern Boreal Forest is well illustrated. In the hardwoods, look for a flood of spring wildflowers and listen for Black-throated Blue Warbler and Scarlet Tanager. On the way down, watch for Bay-breasted and Cape May Warblers among the spruce. You may see Northern Parula.

Agawa Rock Indian Pictographs Trail (0.4 km). Abrupt cliffs and chasms line the trail to the rock paintings on a 30-m-high shoreline bluff. Black diabase rock fills cracks in the pink granite.

Awausee Trail (10-km loop). This trail climbs the hills around the Agawa Valley Nature Reserve. Raptors hover over the high points and Black-throated Blue Warbler is found at the summit.

Towab Trail (24 km return). Set in the valley floor by the Agawa River, this route leads to Agawa Falls, the park's highest waterfall.

Mirimoki Wetlands. Open water interlaced with large stretches of *Sphagnum* creates opportunities for canoeists to view wetland wildlife: Moose, River Otter, Osprey, Solitary Sandpiper, Sandhill Crane, waterfowl, marsh birds such as American Bittern and songbirds such as Cape May and Bay-breasted Warblers. Look for Buckbean, Arethusa, Rose Pogonia, Pitcher-plant, and Pale Laurel. The wetlands are located on the Old Woman Lake canoe route between Mijinemungshing and Mirimoki lakes.

Sand River Canoe Route. This route traverses a good cross-section of the park. Moose walk downriver in June and July to cool off and feed. Muskrats cruise the sedges, and River Otters fish or slide down steep banks. Watch for Sandhill Cranes. Access the canoe route from Highway 17.

Old Woman Bay. Coastal arctic-alpine plants grow on the cliff faces here; these include Encrusted Saxifrage, Butterwort, and Black Crowberry. Watch for Whimbrel and other migrating shorebirds from mid August on.

Agawa Bay Campground. Look for Merlin and, in the Red Pine groves, Pine Warbler. Visit the meadows north of the campground for sand-loving plants such as Beach Pea, Sand Cherry, evening-primrose, Beach Heath, Prickly Wild Rose, and earth-star fungus.

Agawa River Bridge. Cliff, Bank, and Barn Swallows nest underneath the bridge.

Montreal River Provincial Nature Reserve

Fronted by the steep bluff of glacial Lake Nipissing, this series of raised cobble beaches graphically presents the story of the rise and fall of the ancient lakes that in succession occupied the Superior basin. These boulder beaches may have originated as offshore bars or as storm beach ridges. The cobbles support an extensive array of fragile lichens and scattered patches of Bear-berry.

DIRECTIONS. Halfway down steep hill on Hwy 17, 1–2 km S of Montreal River Harbour.

Mamainse Point

Between Mamainse Point and Flour Bay, conglomerates and dipping flows of basalt lava form a series of low ridges that project into the lake as finger-like headlands. This distinctive coastline harbours an assemblage of arctic-alpine plants, including Fragrant Cliff Fern, Glaucous Blue Grass, Bird's-eye Primrose, and False Oats.

DIRECTIONS. On Hwy 17 about 1.5 hr N of Sault Ste Marie.

Batchawana Bay Provincial Park and Vicinity

This small lineal park is noted for its long sandy beach and beautiful setting. Across Highway 17, use a compass to hike straight north to a raised beach and fen swale complex containing a number of significant plants, such as Oregon Woodsia, Western Fescue, and Northern Holly Fern. There are up to 100 successive beach strands between the highway and the bedrock uplands.

DIRECTIONS. Located 65 km NW of Sault Ste Marie on Hwy 17; see prov hwy map.

INFORMATION. Batchawana Bay Provincial Park, Box 130, Sault Ste Marie, Ont, P6A 5L5, 705-882-2209.

Goulais River

A high-quality delta complex located at the mouth of the Goulais River contains a number of interesting features. Among these are meander channels, an oxbow lake in the process of being formed, old channel scars, offshore underwater bars, a subdelta off a secondary distribution channel, recurved spits, levees, and an assemblage of marsh and swamp wetland communities. Access to these areas is best by boat or canoe. Straddling the entire valley mouth from north to south and from the Lake Superior shoreline, east of Highway 17, is a curving raised beach ridge and swale complex. Fen, bog, and swamp communities are present. Uniflora Muhly Grass and other plants typical of boreal wetlands and peatlands grow in the area.

DIRECTIONS. From Sault Ste Marie go 27 km NW on Hwy 17; take Pineshores Rd to Goulais village.

Hiawatha Highlands Conservation Area

Here excellent trails through mixed woods lead to high water-falls cutting through moist, deep granite gorges. Ferns, wild-flowers, and birds abound. Trails are open for cross-country skiing in winter.

DIRECTIONS. From Sault Ste Marie go N on Hwy 17 (Great Northern Rd); turn right on 5th Line E.

INFORMATION. Sault Ste Marie Region Conservation Authority.

Gros Cap Conservation Area

This high, rocky promontory north of the road offers an excellent view of Lake Superior. Look offshore for Gros Cap Reefs, an important feature in the evolution of the various lakes that have occupied the Lake Superior basin since the last Ice Age. Along the road, watch for old glacial beaches. Hooker's Orchid, False Mermaid, and Encrusted Saxifrage are among the interesting rare plants that grow at Gros Cap. This is a good place for observing spring hawk and loon migrations; watch for Broad-winged Hawk and both Common and Red-throated Loons.

DIRECTIONS. From Sault Ste Marie, go W on 2nd Line (Hwy 550) for 19 km to end at Lake Superior; walk trails to hilltop.

INFORMATION. Sault Ste Marie Region Conservation Authority.

Voyageur Trail

When completed, this long-distance hiking trail is expected to extend 1,000 km from Manitoulin Island, along the northern shores of Lakes Huron and Superior, to Thunder Bay. About half of the planned total length of the route is now open to hikers.

INFORMATION. Voyageur Trail Association, Box 20040, Sault Ste Marie, Ont, P6A 6W3, 705-759-2480 (guidebook available).

Echo Bay Flats

This broad expanse of marsh affords a good chance to see Sand-hill Cranes in the hundreds, and scaup in the thousands, during migration. Black Terns frequent area marshes in summer.

DIRECTIONS. From Sault Ste Marie, go 24 km E on Hwy 17 to Echo Bay; turn left on Hwy 638 & go 100 m to Lake St; go left to marsh.

Ripple Rocks

Rock cuts here, especially on the north side of the road, show excellent examples of fossil ripple marks preserved in the severely tilted rocks of the Archaean quartzite formations. Watch elsewhere in the area for smaller occurrences through various quartzites.

DIRECTIONS. Go 43 km E of Sault Ste Marie on Hwy 17; watch for sign on N side.

St Josephs Island

This limestone island (45 km long by 24 km wide) is a continuation of the Manitoulin chain. There are several accessible rock outcrops, with good fossils. Puddingstone, a jasper-bearing conglomerate, can be found in gravel pits and along the shores of Rock Lake. Sand dunes, old shorelines, and old shorecliffs provide evidence of the glacial lakes that preceded today's Great Lakes. Scan the shoreline marshes for water birds. There is a bird sanctuary at the south end of the island near the old fort. Deciduous woodlands are ablaze with colour each fall.

DIRECTIONS. From Sault Ste Marie go 40 km E on Hwy 17; take bridge to island.

– St Josephs Island Nature Reserve. This 40-ha Federation of Ontario Naturalists' reserve is dominated by a very wet White Cedar swamp. Other habitats on the property include shrub fen, treed fen, abandoned fields, a wooded knoll, and swampy thickets of alder and dogwood. Of note are a number of orchids, such as Green Adder's-mouth and Green-leaved Rattlesnake-plantain. Among northern birds present are Black-throated Green Warbler, and, in winter, Gray Jay. Beaver, Muskrat, Mink, and White-tailed Deer inhabit the site.

DIRECTIONS. Located on W side of Hwy 548, S of Hilton Beach.

INFORMATION. Sault Naturalists Club (Box 21035, RPO 292 Northern Ave, Sault Ste Marie, Ont, P6B 6H3) holds regular field trips to area; contact it before visiting.

Little Rapids

Watch for Sandhill Cranes in fields southwest of the village from mid August to early September. Pink Salmon spawning runs occur below the dam on the Bridgeland River from late August to early September.

DIRECTIONS. From Thessalon on Hwy 17, go 2 km N on Hwy 129.

Blind River Swift Roost

Up to 2,000 Chimney Swifts gather to roost at the Palace Theatre chimney in Blind River. Best viewing is in August at dawn or dusk.

DIRECTIONS. At jct of Hwy 17 & Hanes St in town of Blind River.

Spanish River Mouth (Spanish Marsh)

At the mouth of the Spanish River, extensive wetlands have developed on the numerous islands and bars created by river-borne sediments, and in the intervening distributary channels and offshore shallows. Vegetation typical of grassy meadows, and of shallow and deep emergent marshes, occurs. Wild rice grows here, and Sedge Wrens are abundant. The islands are used by waterfowl for nesting and migratory stopovers. Turkey Vultures haunt the area or perch on trees along the adjacent mainland shoreline.

DIRECTIONS. Use boat or canoe to access river mouth; boat launch & rentals available at town of Spanish on Hwy 17.

Mississagi Provincial Park

Hiking and cross-country ski trails traverse rolling hills and valleys here, while canoe routes penetrate the numerous lakes and streams. Located in the transition zone between the Boreal Forest to the north and the more mixed woodlands of the Great Lakes–St Lawrence Forest to the south, the 4,720-ha park contains elements of both. White Pine grows within forests dominated by Sugar Maple, Yellow Birch, and Eastern Hemlock. White Birch, Trembling Aspen, White Spruce, and Balsam Fir are also common. From the Helenbar Lake lookout one can look north to boreal forest. In a rare exposure, 2-billion-year-old fossil ripple marks show where waves once lapped against a sandy shore.

DIRECTIONS. Located 25 km N of Elliot Lake on Hwy 108/639; see prov hwy map.

INFORMATION. MNR.

Mississagi River Provincial Park

See entry under District of Sudbury.

DISTRICT OF SUDBURY

> And the River has its moods, like any living thing, and no one stretch of it is like to any other. In some of its reaches a dark sullen flood, powerful and deep, flowing swiftly and smoothly with a high, forbidding precipice on either side ..., on emerging will spring to sudden fury and become a raging, irresistible torrent ..., to break quite suddenly into a rabble of chattering wavelets, clattering amongst the gravel of a shallows. Often it runs docilely along, carefree and singing, or murmuring and sleepy ... until its current is quite gone and it broadens peacefully out into tranquil, island-studded lakes. (Mississagi River, 1914 and later, Archibald Belaney, also known as Grey Owl [1888–1938], conservationist and writer)

From a relatively short coastline on the north shore of Georgian Bay, the District of Sudbury (surrounding Sudbury Regional Municipality) extends north and west across the Canadian Shield to beyond Chapleau. The northern portion falls within the Boreal Forest Region, while the south is characterized by the mixed coniferous and deciduous woodlands of the Great Lakes–St Lawrence Forest Region.

Chapleau Crown Game Preserve

See entry under District of Algoma.

Missinaibi River Provincial Park

See entry under District of Cochrane.

The Shoals Provincial Park

Deposited by streams of glacial meltwater, the sandy shoals in Little Wawa Lake are part of an unusual esker-delta complex shaped like a bird's foot. Extensive canoe routes wind through the park's 10,600 ha of conifer-dominated woodlands.

DIRECTIONS. Located 45 km W of Chapleau on Hwy 101; see prov hwy map.

Ivanhoe Lake Provincial Park

Although this 1,500-ha park is largely covered by second-growth boreal forest, several plant associations of note are found within its borders. These include a quaking bog formed by a mat of vegetation floating on top of the semifluid substrate around the edges of a kettle lake. On an old lake bottom that floods each spring, a panne community occupies an area of lime-rich but nutrient-poor soil. Such interesting plants as Seaside Arrow-grass grow here. A pleasant paddle on the crystal-clear waters of Saw Lake allows exploration of shoreline habitats. Eskers are a major feature in the park.

DIRECTIONS. Located 13 km SW of Foleyet off Hwy 101; see prov hwy map.

INFORMATION. Ivanhoe Lake Provincial Park, 190 Cherry St, Chapleau, Ont, P0M 1K0, 705-899-2644.

Mississagi River Provincial Park

The canoe route along the upper Mississagi River offers lake paddling at both ends and a section of challenging river in between. At Bardney Lake a portage bridges the height of land between the Hudson Bay and Great Lakes watersheds. Varied habitats along the way include mixed second-growth forests, pine stands, marshes, and barren rocky uplands. Hellsgate Falls and the sheer rock face at Aubrey Falls are scenic highlights. Watch for Moose and listen for Gray Wolves.

DIRECTIONS. From Biscotasing (via Hwy 667 or 144) to Aubrey Falls (Hwy 129) takes 7–10 days.

INFORMATION. MNR.

Upper Spanish River

Known for its wild beauty, the upper Spanish River and its border of second-growth woodlands between Duke and Agnew lakes are protected by the Ministry of Natural Resources as a 'Special Area.' From boreal forests of spruce and Balsam Fir in the north, the river passes through a transition zone to a mixed forest of Silver Maple, Black Ash, and White Birch in the south. The northern range limit for White Trillium occurs just above Agnew Lake. Abundant wildlife populations include Black Bear, Moose, and Osprey. This sparkling whitewater river is easily accessible and canoeable by non-experts all summer long.
DIRECTIONS. For 2–3-day canoe trip to Agnew Lake on E branch, from Sudbury go W on Hwy 17, then N on Hwy 144; turn left on road along N boundary of Windy Lake Prov Park leading to Fox Lake & the Elbow on Spanish River. Just a few km down from the Elbow, portage around Graveyard Rapids (obtain 1:50,000 map sheets for info on rapids). For a longer trip, access Pogamasing (4-day) or West Branch on Biscotasi Lake (7-day) via CPR Bud Car from Sudbury with take-out at Agnew Lake.
INFORMATION. MNR

Halfway Lake Provincial Park

Straddling Highway 144 at the very southern edge of the boreal forest, this 4,700-ha park contains rolling hills, vast boreal woodlands, and more than 20 lakes. Glacial features abound, including eskers, kames, and moraines.

Moose Ridge Trail (4 km). Look for Moose, particularly near Raven Lake. Listen for packs of Gray Wolves howling.

Echo Pond Trail (10 km). Check the Beaver pond for wetland wildlife. In winter, Moose feed on Mountain Maple and Beaked Hazel. Look for Canada Lynx tracks and watch for Moose and River Otters in the water.

Hawk Ridge Trail (25 km). This trail traverses Jack Pine stands, grassy meadows, and granite cliffs. Moose and Black Bear travel the White Birch and Trembling Aspen ridges in summer. Rivers and streams are frequented by River Otter and Mink.
DIRECTIONS. On Hwy 144, about 90 km NW of Sudbury; see prov hwy map.
INFORMATION. MNR.

Fairbank Provincial Park

This small, 105-ha park is located on the Sudbury Nickel Irruptive, noted for its high concentrations of nickel and copper ore. This unusual geological formation resulted from the impact of a huge meteorite that hit the planet millions of years ago. Fairbank also includes a geological fault – a fracture in the Earth's crust. Deciduous woodlands contain Yellow Birch and Sugar Maple bordering the lakeshore. The clear spring-fed waters of Fairbank Lake make it a good place for snorkelling. In winter, visitors on foot are welcome.

DIRECTIONS. Located 13 km N of Worthington on Reg Rd 4; see prov hwy map.

INFORMATION. MNR.

Vermilion River Delta Wetlands

The meandering Vermilion River enters Vermilion Lake in a diverse array of abandoned channels, levees, and swamp, marsh, and fen communities. Willow and Speckled Alder thicket swamps occupy transitional areas between the wetter marsh and peripheral Silver Maple swamps. Silver Maple dominates drier ridges, which also support Bur Oak; both species are close to their northern range limits here. The site is an important waterfowl nesting and migratory stopover area.

DIRECTIONS. Turn W from Hwy 144 at Larchwood (jct with Reg Rd 12 near Dowling).

Windy Lake Provincial Park

Amid jagged rock outcrops, boreal forest cloaks the rugged hills here. A high sand bluff a short distance inland from the lakeshore is a legacy of retreating glaciers. There are fine beaches and nature and cross-country ski trails in the 140-ha park.

DIRECTIONS. Located 40 km NW of Sudbury on Hwy 144; see prov hwy map.

INFORMATION. MNR.

Sandcherry Creek Ice-Contact Delta

Climb the delta face or walk up the road to reach the top surface of this glacial landform. Known as a hanging or perched delta, the feature was formed at the edge of a melting ice sheet when the valley below was filled with water. The feature is now exposed on the side of the valley.

DIRECTIONS. Leave Hwy 144 at Chelmsford; head N & cross Vermilion River; turn right & follow road to Sandcherry Creek. Park in woods beside stream.

INFORMATION. MNR.

Sudbury

INFORMATION (Sudbury & area natural history & geology). Science North, 100 Ramsey Lake Rd, Sudbury, Ont, P3E 5S9, 705-522-3701.

– Lily Creek Marsh. A boardwalk traverses 10 ha of cattail marsh in the heart of Sudbury. Watch for Common Snapping and Midland Painted Turtles, Great Blue Heron, Virginia Rail, Green-winged Teal, Beaver, and an active Muskrat population.

DIRECTIONS. Follow Science North signs; marsh is at jct of Paris St & Ramsey Lake Rd.

– Lake Laurentian Conservation Area. A good cross-section of northern Ontario habitats is protected here, from lake to marshes to hardwood stands. There is good birding. Northern Pike spawning can be seen in late April and early May. Wetlands, flatwater, and small-lake canoeing is possible. Trails are open in winter.

DIRECTIONS. From Paris St (Reg Rd 80) go E on Ramsey Lake Rd; turn right on South Bay Rd & go to end.

INFORMATION. Nickel District Conservation Authority.

– Kelly Lake. Great rafts of waterfowl congregate at this privately owned lake in spring and early fall. The east end of the lake is best for ducks and shorebirds.

DIRECTIONS. From downtown, drive W on Hwy 17; turn S onto Kelly Lake Rd (Reg Rd 37), then W on Southview Dr; view from road only.

Sudbury Area Geological Features

Sudbury Basin. A huge elliptical crater was created by a meteorite crashing into the Earth. Watch for evidence at the north end of Sudbury.

Shatter Cones. These rock formations were produced by shockwaves from the impact of meteorites. Examples are visible in the Science North entrance tunnel along Ramsey Lake Road.

Kettleholes. Located on an esker and kame feature, this series of deep holes was formed when sand and gravel were washed away from the glacial ice front and deposited around and over large blocks of ice. When the ice melted, kettles resulted. Watch for kettles on both sides of Regional Road 86 just north of the Sudbury airport.

INFORMATION. Science North (tours & map), address under Sudbury above.

Voyageur Trail

See entry under District of Algoma.

Killarney Provincial Park

This 48,500-ha wilderness park, containing myriad lakes and hills, is noted for its clear turquoise lakewaters and the ivory-white La Cloche Mountains, a folded quartzite formation that covers three-quarters of the park. Precipitous fiords arc into Georgian Bay; canoeing and hiking are excellent; and Sugar Maples offer a spectacular display of fall colour. The extensive trail system follows white quartzite and pink granite ridges, and both day and overnight trips are possible. The route goes along slopes and into valleys through pine and ancient hardwood forests, passes young mixed woods by roadsides, and crosses scattered wetlands where orchids and ferns grow in profusion. The park can be visited year-round.

Birds of note include Connecticut Warbler and Warbling Vireo. Updrafts above shore ridges draw Common Raven, Turkey Vulture, and Osprey. Among resident mammals are Gray Wolf, Black Bear, Snowshoe Hare, Moose, Muskrat, and Bobcat. Because of acidification, fish are scarce in park lakes.

Killarney Lake. River Otters sometimes frequent strips of floating bog at the west end of the lake. A remarkably dense forest of Eastern Hemlock grows nearby. To see steep talus slopes, paddle to a small bay east of campsite 16.

George Lake. By canoe, look for River Otter at the outlet to Chikanishing, and Tree Swallows and Eastern Kingbirds flitting among drowned White Cedars. Showy Lady's-slippers, American Beech, and Black Cherry grow around the rim of the lake.

Baie Fine Hiking Trail. A beautiful old-growth hardwood forest contains Sugar Maple and Red Oak, with some White Pine and Eastern Hemlock. Look for Ruffed Grouse, Yellow-bellied Sapsucker, Barred Owl, Red and White Trilliums, and Dutchman's Breeches. The hardwoods can be accessed from the northwest end of George Lake; hike 2.5 km to the main trail, turn right, and go 0.5 km.

La Cloche Mountains. Numerous perched bogs are found on top of this range. Watch for Virginia Chain Fern in the Hawk Ridge area. Stunted Red Oak, Red Maple, and Jack Pine forests here are stressed by periodic fires and forest tent caterpillar and budworm cycles.

La Cloche Silhouette Trail (100 km, 7-day). This trail circles the park through a roadless area; a spur leads to Killarney's highest point, Silver Peak.

Cranberry Bog Trail (4 km). Watch for American Bittern in the cattail marsh, and Leatherleaf, sundews, Pitcher-plant, and cranberry on the floating *Sphagnum* mat.

Grenville Front. Here the pink granite ridge south of the park meets the white quartzite mountains to the north. View at the start of Cranberry Bog Trail. South of George Lake watch for ripples in the rock created by massive moving plates.

Granite Ridge Trail (2 km). Enjoy great views of the La Cloche Mountains to the north, and Collins Inlet and islands in Georgian Bay to the south.

DIRECTIONS. Located off Hwy 637; see prov hwy map.

INFORMATION. Killarney Provincial Park, Killarney, Ont, P0M 2A0, 705-287-2900 (trail guides & maps).

French River Provincial Park

The French River runs 110 km in a straight course from Lake Nipissing to Georgian Bay, forming the boundary between the Districts of Sudbury and Parry Sound. The river is noted for its complex geology. Evidence of faulting along the Grenville Front, where two ancient continents collided, can be seen in the high, rock-walled preglacial gorge at the Highway 69 crossing. Of historic significance as a fur-trade route and designated as a

'Canadian Heritage River,' the French River is best appreciated by canoe or boat. The waterway park contains 51,000 ha.

A population of Wapiti introduced a half-century ago to the Burwash area south of Sudbury can now be found along the Wanapitei and French river systems. These elusive elk can be heard bugling during the rutting season. Gray Wolves and Black Bears occur in the area, and River Otters play in the waterways. The most important sport fish is the Walleye, which spawns at the base of rapids. Watch overhead for Osprey and Merlin.

The mouth of the French River broadens into an array of channels, with thousands of smooth, bare, water-washed rock islets known as whalebacks. This area contains a spectacular series of sculpted erosional features called S-forms. These extensive grooves in the bedrock above Rainbow Tramway on the west shore of Bass Lake were made by powerful flows of turbulent meltwater beneath glacial ice. Virginia Chain Fern is found in pockets of bog north of the Dalles Rapids. Look for the chain-like spore pattern under the fronds.

DIRECTIONS. Nominal fees for access from marinas. 1) For upper river: North Bay Chief Commander. 2) For central river: from Monetville on Hwy 64 go E to Dokis village & Chaudière Dam; or go E on Hwy 528A to Wolseley Bay; or at supply post off Hwy 69. 3) For delta: from Bigwood go W on Hartley Bay Rd. INFORMATION. MNR.

Obabika River Provincial Park

See entry under District of Nipissing.

DISTRICT OF TIMISKAMING

[The fire] burned into the woods with great fierceness, pushed along by a very strong wind ... Whirlwinds of flame swept the length of the portage ... We were obliged to run with all our strength, while the fire pressed so closely that the sleeve of my shirt was burned by the shower of sparks and burning cinders ... We hurriedly climbed into two canoes ... and moved to the centre of the lake, which at that spot was only thirty feet wide. The fire then became so furious that the flames swept like a torrent over our heads, and set fire to the bush on the other side of the lake.

(North of Lake Timiskaming, May 30, 1686, Pierre de Troyes [?–1688], military officer)

The southern and eastern sections of the District of Timiskaming mark the extreme northern limits of the Great Lakes–St Lawrence Forest Region. White Pine is often the dominant tree along lake and river shores. White Birch, White Spruce, Balsam Fir, Trembling and Large-toothed Aspens, and Red and Jack Pines are well represented. Black Spruce, Tamarack, and White Cedar grow in low-lying areas. Tolerant hardwoods such as Yellow Birch and Sugar Maple are found here at their northern range limits. The northwestern portion of Timiskaming falls within the Boreal Forest Region. Here, White and Red Pines have largely disappeared, and the predominant woodland mix frequently consists of Black Spruce, Trembling Aspen, Balsam Fir, and White Birch with scattered White Spruce. Large stands of pure Jack Pine can also be seen.

The 90-km-long Lake Timiskaming lies in a geological fault which, at its northern end, broadens into a gently rolling, glacial lake plain known as the Little Claybelt, where agricultural land-use is dominant. The northern end of the lake is marked by a limestone escarpment, the only such exposure between Lake Huron and James Bay. This feature is best viewed from a boat; launches are available at New Liskeard and Haileybury. Timiskaming's rivers contribute to three major watersheds: the Ottawa River (probably more than 90%), James Bay, and Lake Nipissing (a small amount). A height of land is located north of Kirkland Lake at the northern edge of the district.

Kap-Kig-Iwan Provincial Park

Located at the northern edge of the Little Claybelt, this 325-ha park has as its most prominent feature the Englehart River, noted for its spectacular waterfalls, whitewater rapids, rugged rock outcrops, and deep ravines. The forests here contain a mix of boreal and more southern trees, such as Trembling Aspen, White Birch, Red and White Pines, and even American Elm and Black Ash. Cross-country skiing is available in winter.

DIRECTIONS. Located 2 km from Englehart off Hwy 11; see prov hwy map.

INFORMATION. MNR.

Hilliardton Marsh

This large marsh and wetland complex was constructed in 1993–4 along the Blanche River. Three cells were created to provide habitat for nesting and migrating waterfowl as well as other wetland species.
DIRECTIONS. From New Liskeard go 14 km N on Hwy 11; continue 14 km N on Hwy 569; go less than 1 km W on Hilliard-Ingram Boundary Rd.

Casey Township Marsh

The marshes and farmland at the north end of Lake Timiskaming (Blanche River wetlands and Casey Marsh) are a staging area for waterfowl during spring and fall migrations. Redhead, Northern Pintail, Black Duck, Mallard, American Wigeon, Northern Shoveler, Gadwall, Blue-winged and Green-winged Teal, Ring-necked Duck, scaup, Common Goldeneye, Bufflehead, and Canada Goose congregate for a short period just after spring melt and during fall migration. Brant are seen in the area in mid to late May.
DIRECTIONS. From New Liskeard, go about 11 km E & N on Hwy 65; take Harris Conc Rd 5/6 E; follow road N & E about 5 km to marsh.

Lady Evelyn–Smoothwater Provincial Park

This park lies within an area of moderately broken meta-sedimentary rock of the Canadian Shield. It contains 80–100 km of freshwater streams bordered by fen wetlands. Grays and North and South Lady Evelyn rivers and some park lakes are representative of the shield. Rising close to the height of land, park waterways flow southward via the Montreal River to the Ottawa. Lake habitat within the park supports Northern Pike.
DIRECTIONS. Only road access is S of Elk Lake (jct Hwys 65 & 560) on Beauty Lake Rd; N & S Lady Evelyn & Grays rivers (combined length of 90 km) are the travelways through park.
INFORMATION. MNR.

   Ishpatina Ridge. This massive and remote ridge lies to the west of the Lady Evelyn River and includes the highest point of land in Ontario. To reach the ridge, fly in from Sudbury, Temagami, or Elk Lake to Scarecrow Lake. If driving, approach from the north via Highway 560 or from the south via Highway 545. Then travel by canoe (including long portages) to the trail that leads to the top (topographical map required).

Lady Evelyn Lake and Maple Mountain. Along the south-central shoreline of Lady Evelyn Lake is a maze of partially submerged forested sand dunes. This extensive complex of dune-fields developed through postglacial wind action. The conical-shaped Maple Mountain is the fourth-highest elevation in the province. Sugar Maple occurs here at the northern limit of its continuous range. In the spring Painted Trillium can be seen in the forest within 100 m of the shore of Tupper Lake. Lady Evelyn rivers, water-sculpted shorelines, and numerous rapids and falls gave rise to imaginative place-names, such as Stonehenge, Shangrila, and Twin Sisters Falls.

Obabika River Provincial Park

See entry under District of Nipissing.

Montreal River

Upstream from Latchford, the slow-moving waters of the Montreal River form a large marsh and swamp complex frequented by waterfowl. Near its outflow, the lower Montreal River becomes a reservoir. Here, upstream flooding of steep-sided, former stream channels has created backwaters where Beaver lodges and slides of River Otter are numerous. Shallower sites are used by waterfowl, and slumping sand banks on the main reservoir are home to Bank Swallows.

DIRECTIONS. Access by boat at Latchford on Hwy 11 & at S end of Hwy 567.

DISTRICT OF COCHRANE

[A local trapper] told us that Martin, Fisher and Lynx were very common in the vicinity [of Kapuskasing] but with the reduction of the rabbits a few seasons ago they have become much scarcer, especially the latter ... He told me that on the muskegs to the south there was a very small weasel with a white tipped tail that was so common as to be a pest to the trapper springing the traps set for more valuable game. This is evidently the Least weasel ... Moose are said to be abundant and there are reported to be a few deer in the neighborhood. (Summer 1919, Percy Taverner [1875–1947], ornithologist)

The District of Cochrane stretches from Iroquois Falls and Timmins in the southeast to beyond Hearst in the northwest and to the Albany River and the James Bay shoreline in the north. The northern part of the district lies within the Hudson Bay Lowland, a poorly drained, open landscape dominated by stunted Black Spruce and Tamarack. Stretching in a band across the southern portion of the District of Cochrane is northern Ontario's Claybelt, a level till plain inherited from glacial Lake Ojibway. Although some farming is carried on, most of the area is covered by the expansive tracts of Black Spruce that characterize the boreal forest. Barren bedrock outcrops and ponds, lakes, and streams are numerous. Habitats range from open *Sphagnum* bog and sedge-fen communities through to drier upland forests of Black and White Spruces, Jack Pine, Balsam Poplar, and White Birch. The landscape is typified by the long, northward-flowing river systems that form the Moose River basin in the James Bay watershed, such as the Abitibi, Mattagami, Groundhog, and Missinaibi.

Moose Factory, Moosonee, Polar Bear Provincial Park, etc.

See section on Hudson Bay Lowland.

Hearst Area

– Nagagami Canyon. Here, an impressive 45-m rock wall canyon is located on the Nagagami River.
DIRECTIONS. Located 75 km W of Hearst, 5 km S of Hwy 11. Launch canoe or boat above 1st rapids behind Ministry of Transportation yard on hwy; travel upriver to base of Jackpine Rapids. Take portage on W side of river to bypass canyon; explore from there.

– Fushimi Lake Provincial Park. Balsam Fir, White and Black Spruces, Balsam Poplar, and White Birch dominate the woodlands in this 5,300-ha park. White Cedars rim the lake and, at Valentine River, there is a stand of exceptionally large Tamaracks. Lilypad Bay is noted for its natural and scenic features.
DIRECTIONS. Located 41 km NW of Hearst off Hwy 11; see prov hwy map.
INFORMATION. Fushimi Lake Provincial Park, Box 670, Hearst, Ont, P0L 1N0, 705-362-4346.

– Mattawishkwia Marsh. This extensive marsh complex offers good duck habitat for spring viewing.
DIRECTIONS. From Hwy 11 at Hearst, go 3 km N on Hwy 583 to Golf Course Conc Rd, then 3 km E to landing. Launch boat or canoe & travel 5 km downriver to beginning of marsh complex.

– Sandhill Crane Hotspots. The Hearst area provides good Sandhill Crane breeding habitat. Farm fields 5–10 km east of Hearst on Highway 11 are known dancing grounds for cranes in spring and summer. View from roadside only, and avoid disturbing birds. Fall staging occurs in open farm fields in the Hearst area, 24 km east along Highway 11, and in the Copell and Mead areas about 30 km south on Highway 583.

Mattice Area

– Missinaibi River Provincial Park. The 500-km-long Missinaibi is the longest free-flowing and readily accessible wilderness river in Ontario. From its headwaters at Little Missinaibi Lake on the Canadian Shield just 60 km northeast of Lake Superior, the river flows north across the shield and through the Claybelt to Thunder House Falls, where it descends onto the Hudson Bay Lowland and eventually empties into the Moose River and James Bay. Unscarred by dams, the lakes and rivers that comprise the 100,000-ha park are renowned for their scenic beauty, high rock walls, numerous rapids and waterfalls, massive granite outcrops, Indian pictographs, varied natural history features, and historic importance as a major fur-trading route. A good diversity of plants has been recorded in the park, including such orchids as Calypso and Yellow and Pink Lady's-slippers. Bald Eagle, Osprey, and Great Blue Heron, as well as many other birds, occur in the park. Sandhill Cranes feed along the shoreline in the lowlands.

DIRECTIONS. Accesses: 1) by road at Mattice (halfway along river on Hwy 11; segments above & below each require 8–10 days to paddle); 2) by road at Missinaibi Lake 88 km N of Hwy 101 (Chapleau); 3) by train at Peterbell N of Hwy 101, Moose River Crossing, and Moosonee.

INFORMATION. MNR.

Kapuskasing Area

– Spawning Lake Sturgeon. The remote Pot (a hole of deep water) on the Kapuskasing River offers unique fish-viewing opportunities. From May 1 to July 15 Lake Sturgeon congregate in this fish sanctuary following spawning. During morning and evening hours, up to 30 or 40 sturgeon, weighing about 25 kg each, clear the water.

DIRECTIONS. Take Gurney Rd, then Fred Flat Rd 40 km N from Kapuskasing to bridge by marsh; boat down Kapuskasing River & up Groundhog River (total of 60 km, takes 3–4 hr).

INFORMATION. MNR.

– René Brunelle Provincial Park. Forests of Black Spruce, Balsam Fir, Trembling Aspen, White Birch, and Tamarack grow on the fertile soils of the Claybelt here. Canada Lynx and Bonaparte's Gull also occur. The 2,900-ha park is open for winter use.

DIRECTIONS. Located 32 km E of Kapuskasing on Hwy 581 N of Hwy 11; see prov hwy map.

INFORMATION. René Brunelle Provincial Park, 6 Government Rd, Kapuskasing, Ont, P5N 2W4, 705-367-2692.

Fraserdale Area

Sharp-tailed Grouse establish a lek here from late April to mid May for the performance of their breeding displays. (Ensure that birds are not disturbed.) There is good northern birding around the Fraserdale area and at the nearby Abitibi Canyon. Check the Abitibi hydro dam for boreal birds and possible out-of-range migrants.

DIRECTIONS. From Hwy 11 at Smooth Rock Falls go 76 km N on

Hwy 634 to jct of 2 logging roads at Fraserdale & Abitibi Canyon.

Cochrane Area

– **Greenwater Provincial Park.** Trails here explore the varied, second-growth forest habitats that have developed following fire, logging, and the abandonment of farmland. The range of warblers includes Black-throated Blue, Black-and-white, Blackburnian, Bay-breasted, Nashville, and Tennessee Warblers, among many others. Watch for ducks along Sunset Trail. Examples of resident mammals are Canada Lynx, Marten, Fisher, River Otter, Mink, and Muskrat. Fall colours are painted in shades of gold and green. The 5,350-ha park includes a 60-m-high esker complex.
DIRECTIONS. Located 30 km NW of Cochrane on Hwy 668 off Hwy 11; see prov hwy map.
INFORMATION. Greenwater Provincial Park, Box 730, Cochrane, Ont, P0L 1C0; MNR, Cochrane, 705-272-4365.

– **Nahma Bog.** This 186-ha peatland is a good example of a basin fen with a centre-wet raised bog. Lagg swamps, or moats, surround the bog. Sandhill Cranes summer in the area, as do northern warblers, such as Connecticut and Palm Warblers.
DIRECTIONS. From 5 km S of Cochrane on Hwy 11, go 5 km E on Nahma Rd to sdrd at Nahma hamlet. Turn N & go 100 m to rail line. Walk 2 km NW on rail line to bog on left. Aerial photo advised for serious exploration.

– **Drury Park Campground.** This municipally run campground offers a broad array of habitats within a small area, including mixed White and Black Spruce–Balsam Poplar forest, open parkland, abandoned field with alder overgrowth, White Cedar shorelines on small pothole lakes, and an extensive marsh complex. Look for various warblers, ducks, Pied-billed Grebe, American Bittern, Merlin, and other birds.
DIRECTIONS. From 3rd Ave (main entrance to Cochrane), turn E at Ontario Prov Police office & go 2 km.

– **Lillabelle Lake and Area.** Lillabelle Lake, one of the most nutrient-rich lakes in the area, hosts good numbers of ducks in spring and fall. Species include Ring-necked, Wood, and Black

Ducks, Northern Shoveler, Mallard, Northern Pintail, American Wigeon, and scaup. Bonaparte's Gulls are common and Red-necked Grebes summer here. In spring and fall Sandhill Cranes are common, staging in groups of 10 to as many as 500 birds in open farm fields around the lake. Watch for Rough-legged Hawk, Snowy Owl, Short-eared Owl, and migrant shorebirds. At a small lagoon, look for Wood Ducks, teal, Red-necked Phalarope, Greater and Lesser Yellowlegs, and, in the surrounding Black Spruce forest, various songbirds. Marsh birds such as Pied-billed Grebe, Sora, and American Bittern can be found at Dump Marsh.

DIRECTIONS. From Cochrane, go 2 or 3 km N on Genier Rd towards airport; drive sdrds around lake. For sewage lagoons go N on Genier Rd, then right on Conc Rd 2/3; go 0.25 km to lagoons on right; Dump Marsh is on Golf Club Rd.

– Wally Creek. This area is part of a long-term experiment by the Ministry of Natural Resources to study the effects of drainage on the growth rate of Black Spruce. A trail goes into the heart of a dense spruce forest with a lush ground cover of *Sphagnum* moss, Small Cranberry, Bearberry, Starflower, Spearmint, and other flora typical of the habitat. Spruce Grouse are common. Watch for Great Gray Owl.

DIRECTIONS. From Cochrane go 20 km E on Hwy 652 to small parking lot & sign on N side of road.

Timmins Area

Founded in 1911 as a gold-mining town, Timmins now has under its jurisdiction more than 500 lakes and hundreds of kilometres of rivers and streams. Numerous natural areas within this boreal landscape are accessible to the public.

– Mountjoy Township. Farming country just west of the city supports a variety of open-country birds. Sandhill Cranes stage here during migration in late April and late August and early September.

DIRECTIONS. Go W from Timmins on Hwy 101 past shopping plaza; go N on Conc Rds 2 & 3; watch for cranes in fields.

– Timmins Recreation Trail System. A 25-km-long, year-round, non-motorized trail network stretches across the city, encompassing many natural, scenic, and historic features. At the north end of Toke Street, excellent mixed habitat for thrushes and warblers is found.

DIRECTIONS. Accessible in several locations.

INFORMATION. Mattagami Region Conservation Authority.

– Gillies Lake Conservation Area. Marsh habitat here attracts a variety of birds, including several types of waterfowl, Red-necked Grebe, Bonaparte's Gull, and Black Tern.

DIRECTIONS. Just E of Timmins on Hwy 655, just N of Hwy 101 jct.

INFORMATION. Mattagami Region Conservation Authority.

– Hersey Lake Conservation Area. This 178-ha park can be explored along hiking trails.

DIRECTIONS. From Hwy 101 just E of Timmins go 5 km N on Hwy 655.

INFORMATION. Mattagami Region Conservation Authority.

– Pearl Lake. Birds here include grebes, bitterns, migrating and nesting ducks, and migrating shorebirds and rails. Common Tern and Bonaparte's Gull are present during spring and fall.

DIRECTIONS. At Schumacher (1.5 km E of Timmins on Hwy 101), go N to McIntyre Porcupine Mines property.

– Shaw Township. Open fields here serve as a good spring and fall staging area for Sandhill Cranes.

DIRECTIONS. From South Porcupine (12 km E of Timmins on Hwy 101), go 25 km S on Stringer Rd.

– Night Hawk Lake. One of the larger lakes in the area, Night Hawk Lake contains numerous small islands which are home to colonies of Common Tern and Great Blue Heron. (Avoid approaching or disturbing colonies during the breeding season.) During spring and fall, waterfowl stage along the shoreline of the lake.

DIRECTIONS. From Timmins go 30 km E on Hwy 101; go 5 km S on Hwy 803 to explore shorelines of North Peninsula.

– Kettle Lakes Provincial Park. Within this 1,300-ha park, the range of habitats includes 20 glacially formed kettle lakes; stands of Jack Pine, Trembling Aspen, and White Birch on dry, fire-prone sites; and Black Spruce, Tamarack, and *Sphagnum* in the low-

lands. Pink Lady's-slipper, Bush Honeysuckle, Yellow Clintonia, and Pitcher-plant are characteristic flora of the area. Trails are open for hiking, cross-country skiing, and snowshoeing.
DIRECTIONS. Located 40 km NE of Timmins on Hwy 67; see prov hwy map.
INFORMATION. Kettle Lakes Provincial Park, 896 Riverside Dr, Timmins, Ont, P4N 3W2, 705-363-3511.

Lake Abitibi

With an average depth of 3.5 m and a surface area of 80,000 ha, Ontario's fifth-largest lake is noted for its shallowness. Formed following the retreat of the glaciers and the draining of glacial Lake Barlow-Ojibway about 6,000 years ago, Lake Abitibi has a fetch of 37 km and contains more than 630 islands. Because windy weather easily churns up rolling waves, water travel on the murky brown, silt-rich lake can be risky. Bonaparte's Gull, Black and Common Terns, and many ducks are found on the lake, and colonies of Great Blue Heron and Double-crested Cormorant on the islands. Teddy Bear Marsh on the southeast shore offers excellent waterfowl viewing opportunities. Long Point Peninsula, part of Abitibi de Troyes Provincial Park, contains diverse habitat.
DIRECTIONS. 1) From Twin Falls access point just E of Iroquois Falls, canoe or boat Abitibi River 40 km to big lake & Long Point Peninsula. 2) Canoe or boat from Ghost River access point road, 60 km E of Matheson on Hwy 101.

Esker Lakes Provincial Park

Within this park's 3,200 ha are glacial features such as sand dunes, eskers (including Ontario's largest), and 29 small, clear, kettle lakes connected by short portages. Jack Pine and White Birch thrive in burnt-over areas, while bogs support Black Spruce and Tamarack. Northern warblers haunt the woodlands. There is an extensive trail network. The height of land separating the Hudson Bay and Ottawa River watersheds passes through the park.
DIRECTIONS. Located 37 km NE of Kirkland Lake off Hwy 672; see prov hwy map.
INFORMATION. MNR, Kirkland Lake.

HUDSON BAY LOWLAND (northern portions of Districts of Kenora and Cochrane)

> About noon [the thick fog] cleared, and we saw land ... When we anchored in six fathom, about a mile from shore, we hoisted out the boat ... and went ashore ... On looking around, we saw a great many deer [caribou] and set to stalking them with all the skill we had. We even set the dogs on them, but to no avail, for the deer ran away from them at their pleasure ... Nor could we get close enough to shoot them, although I saw about a dozen – old and young – that were very goodly beasts. By wading into the pools, we took half a dozen young geese. (Cape Henrietta Maria, July 22, 1632, Captain Thomas James [1593–1635], English explorer)

The Hudson Bay Lowland is the most northern and one of the largest landforms in the province of Ontario. Located adjacent to the marine waters of Hudson and James bays, this land represents approximately 25% of Ontario's land-base. Extending from 100 to 200 km inland from the coast, the lowland rises on average only 1 m per km, resulting in a massive, flat, swampy plain dominated by peatlands and overlain by innumerable pools. At the boundary between the Hudson Bay Lowland and the Precambrian Shield to the south, the elevation is a mere 152 m above sea level. Across the lowland, muskegs and patterned fens support an open woodland of Black Spruce and Tamarack in a subarctic landscape that is one of the largest wetlands in the world.

Over 6,500 Cree Indians live in Ontario's Hudson Bay Lowland. Many families, especially those living north of Moosonee, are dependent on the fur industry, waterfowl hunts, and a variety of wild food and fuel-wood resources obtained from along the major river systems and coastal areas.

Climate

The region is influenced by a modified continental climate, with long, cold winters and warm, pleasant, but rather short summers. This climate and the presence of vast wetlands have generally restricted soil development to organic peats, which in turn have reduced the diversity of plants and animals. Mean minimum daily January temperatures range from –27°C in the south to –29°C in the north, and the mean maximum daily July temperatures approach 23°C and 21°C for the southern and northern sections of the lowland respectively.

Geology and Topography

Surface deposits such as peat, clay, and sand extensively cover Palaeozoic sedimentary rocks of limestone, sandstone, shale, dolostone, and gypsum. Underlying bedrock geology is Precambrian in origin, and, in the southeastern corner of the lowland, granites and basalt rocks are represented. Diabase and argillite rocks are clearly exposed within the Hawley and Sutton lakes area along the Sutton Ridges (southwest of Cape Henrietta Maria). These ridges, which reach an elevation of 275 m above sea level, are the only major topographical relief within the lowland. Freed from the weight of the glaciers, the lowland has been gradually rising through isostatic rebound, as evidenced by numerous parallel, raised beach ridges near and for some distance inland from marine coastlines.

Flora

Like the climate and the topography of the lowland, the vegetation found in this portion of Ontario is unique to the province.

Tundra. True tundra flora exists within a strip of land extending from the Ontario-Manitoba border eastward along the Hudson Bay coast to the James Bay coast just south of where the two marine bays meet at Cape Henrietta Maria. This area of continuous, year-round permafrost is dominated by lichens, grasses, sedges, and low shrubs that create a tundra landscape where the vegetation is often only a few centimetres high. Within this coastal tundra zone, ponds, small lakes, and mudflats of grass and sedge meadows fill in the space between bay waters and coastal beach ridges. Recently formed beach ridges still influenced by tidal action are sparsely vegetated; however, farther inland older ridges support White and Black Spruces, and eventually lichen woodlands in which both trees and lichens predominate.

Hudson Bay Lowland Forest (Northern Boreal Forest). South of the 'forest' tundra the land is dominated by a mosaic of northern boreal forest, bogs, and fens. An area of discontinuous permafrost stretches from the permafrost region south to between the Albany and Moose rivers; no permafrost regions occur in the southern portion of the lowland. Black Spruce, *Sphagnum* mosses, and ground lichens are typical of bogs, whereas fen areas contain sedges, Dwarf Birch, and Tamarack. Cutting across the northern boreal landscape are the large rivers that drain the lowland. These support White Spruce, Balsam Fir, Trembling Aspen, Balsam Poplar, and White Birch on well-drained riverbanks.

Fauna

Compared to animal communities farther south, the lowland's faunal complement is rich in arctic species; many of these are nearing the southern limits of their ranges. Arctic elements are most prevalent within the tidal coastal zone, where peat wetlands give way to mudflats and bay waters. Here a mix of northern species and ones more familiar to residents of southern Ontario share habitat. During the short summer months Woodland Caribou, Snow and Canada Geese, numerous species of shorebirds, Polar Bear, and other marine mammals can be found where the lowland meets the sea.

Marine Mammals. Besides Polar Bears, other marine mammals that frequent the coast during generally ice-free periods include Walrus, Harbor, Ringed, and Bearded Seals, and Beluga. Bearded and Ringed Seals can be seen in the early spring after ice break-up or early fall within the large river estuaries of the Moose, Albany, Attawapiskat, Winisk, and Severn rivers. Boat docks, gravel bars, and shorelines are often used as 'haul-out' sites. Belugas (or white whales) are common within the lowland's large river estuaries. Pods of 100–150 animals can be seen during the summer months. These toothed whales frequent the large river mouths, possibly because it is easier for young calves to maintain their body temperatures in the warmer, shallow, estuarine waters, or in order to remove old, unwanted skin by rubbing against the bottom, or so that pods can feed on sea-run Lake Whitefish.

Birds. The Hudson Bay Lowland contains a variety of habitats that attract numerous migratory and resident birds. Over 225 species have been recorded in the lowland, including nesting Willow Ptarmigan, Parasitic Jaeger, Arctic Tern, Blackpoll Warbler, White-crowned Sparrow, and Common Redpoll. Major waterfowl and shorebird nesting and staging areas are located along both marine coastlines. Between break-up and freeze-up, over four million geese of five species use the lowland for staging, nesting, and/or moulting. Canada and Snow Geese are the most abundant species. Fall migrations of waterfowl are spectacular, birds from the high Arctic joining local birds to form huge numbers of flocks, all heading south. Shorebirds and other migratory species also pass through in high numbers. Migrants funnel down the west and east coasts of James Bay through a narrow area of land at the base of the bay, which is within easy access from Moosonee and Moose Factory.

Woodland Caribou. A large land mammal not often seen by Ontario residents is the Woodland Caribou. These animals tend to use specific habitats, depending on the season. The lowland contains some of the best year-round caribou range in Ontario. Caribou use the coastal areas during spring calving and summer concentration periods, and move farther inland during the winter months. The coastal summer range provides summer foods such as sedges, grasses, and deciduous shrubs. Nearly continuous breezes along the coast reduce the effects of flies and warm temperatures on the herds. The banks of large rivers and lake shorelines are also frequented by caribou in the summer. The winter range is inland, where abundant lichens are available for food, and Black Spruce forests provide shelter from winter winds and a refuge from deep snow.

Fish. Freshwater species are restricted to the major river systems, coastal streams, and a few inland lakes north of Moosonee and south of Polar Bear Provincial Park. Northern Pike, Walleye, Lake Whitefish, and sucker species are widespread in the larger lakes and rivers. Lake Sturgeon are found in the larger rivers, such as the Moose, Albany, Attawapiskat, Winisk, and Severn, while most of the coastal streams and rivers contain sea-run (unique within Ontario) and resident Brook Trout. Lake Trout, not widespread in the lowland, are known to be present in only four lakes near the Sutton Ridges.

Other Fauna. Other mammals include Moose, Black Bear,

Beaver, Snowshoe Hare, River Otter, Gray Wolf, Red Fox, and Marten; these inhabit muskeg and boreal woodlands, while the Arctic Fox frequents the coast. The rare Wolverine can be found west of the Severn River. Few herpetofaunal species exist within the lowland. Eastern Garter Snake is the only reptile represented. Amphibians present are American Toad, Wood Frog, Boreal Chorus Frog, Spring Peeper, Northern Leopard Frog, and Blue-spotted Salamander. The most conspicuous insects are blackflies and mosquitoes and other fly species. Butterflies of interest include Melissa Arctic, found along the tundra shores of Hudson Bay, and Pelidne Sulphur, in Ontario only recorded within the Hudson Bay Lowland.

Natural Heritage Areas

The Ontario Hudson Bay Lowland contains five provincial parks: Polar Bear, Tidewater, Kesagami Lake, Winisk River, and Missinaibi River. Of these, only Tidewater Provincial Park has camping and picnicking facilities readily accessible to the public. The other four parks offer backcountry, wilderness experiences.

– Polar Bear Provincial Park. Polar Bear Provincial Park, Ontario's largest park (some 2,400,000 ha), stretches along 450 km of marine coastline from the northwest shores of James Bay north to Cape Henrietta Maria and west along the southern coast of Hudson Bay to just west of the Shagamu River. Flying north from Moosonee towards Polar Bear Provincial Park, the visitor is struck by the shear size of the lowland, for here lies a vast land of pothole lakes, ribbon-like rivers, and endless skies. Once within the boundaries of the park, visitors will encounter flora and fauna that are influenced by and adapted to the bedrock, soils, and climate of this arctic wilderness.

Flora. The park contains the most northerly extension of the Northern Boreal Forest as well as a significant portion of Ontario's tundra. The Northern Boreal Forest supports such species as Black and White Spruces, Tamarack, Balsam Poplar, Dwarf Birch, and many species of willows. The larger trees are restricted to the better-drained sites along rivers, while watery bogs produce stunted trees or no trees at all.

The major rivers, with their well-drained, more mature soils, are bordered by a ribbon of White Spruce with an understorey, especially in clearings, of heath plants such as Black Crowberry, Mountain Cranberry, and ground lichens. Wetter sites away from the riverbanks produce Black Spruce–heath–*Sphagnum* bogs. On drier interior sites Tamarack fens form a richer floral mosaic.

The Northern Boreal Forest's spruce, willow, and Tamarack become progressively smaller in size with increasing latitude. Lichens grow profusely on the trees and form the major ground cover, especially on drier sites. The northern border of this transition forest forms the treeline. The distance of the treeline from the coast ranges from 32 km southwest of Cape Henrietta Maria to within 1 km in the western portion of the park.

Ontario's only tundra can be easily observed in Polar Bear Provincial Park. Within this southern arctic tundra area White Spruce exists in a stunted candelabra form with a number of trees often clumped together, the result of branches from the parent tree taking root and producing new plants. Wet areas contain Sheathed Cotton-grass and Dwarf Birch, while Lapland Rosebay, Black Crowberry, Alpine Bilberry, and Mountain Cranberry grow on drier sites. Summer temperatures bring forth a variety of arctic tundra colour from White Mountain-avens, louseworts, saxifrages, and other plants. Old beach ridges support a variety of reindeer 'mosses' of the lichen genus *Cladina*. On the more recently created beach ridges, gravel, sand, and exposed soil form the substrate for such species as Oysterleaf, Seabeach Sandwort, and American Dune Grass. Along the coast, salt marshes, shallow inter-ridge lakes, and marine lagoons support sedges, cotton-grasses, and Goosegrass.

Fauna. The park's fauna is very diverse and includes such animal groups as waterfowl, shorebirds, marine mammals, fish, and fur-bearers, as well as large mammals such as Woodland Caribou, Moose, and Black Bear. The park received its name from the Polar Bears that frequent the coastal shores each summer. It is this animal, above all others, that captures the imagination of most park visitors.

The major Polar Bear concentrations are located along the marine coastline between Hook Point on James Bay west towards the Sutton River within Polar Bear Provincial Park and west of the park from Fort Severn to the Ontario-Manitoba border, including offshore islands. The southernmost area of regular occurrence is found in James Bay, on the northern and eastern shores of Akimiski Island, Northwest Territories. Some 100–200 bears occupy the entire coast at any given time from late July, when sea ice begins to break up, to late November and early December, when ice re-forms on the bays.

Pregnant females remain inland over the winter and den from the eastern portion of Polar Bear Provincial Park westward towards the Manitoba border. One, two and, on occasion, three cubs are born in midwinter. The family group leaves the den in February, March, or early April to travel onto the pack ice in search of seals. Adult females weigh up to 360 kg and mature males 550 kg. Feeding mainly on seals, the Polar Bear population at times reaches 1,000–1,200 animals in southern Hudson Bay and western James Bay.

ACCESS BY AIR. Coastal aircraft may access designated locations in Shagamu, Sutton, & Brant rivers; inland aircraft access via beach ridge at old Mid-Canada radar station, site 415; flights available from companies in Moosonee, Cochrane, Timmins, & Hearst.

WATER ACCESS. Feasible only on major rivers, such as Winisk, Sutton, Brant, & Shagamu; a competent local guide is essential for travel on Hudson & James bays; however, any bay travel is not recommended.

INFORMATION. MNR.

– Winisk River Provincial Park. From a core area around Winisk Lake on the Canadian Shield, this 160,000-ha park follows the Winisk River 350 km northward across the Hudson Bay Lowland to the tidewaters of Hudson Bay. The river offers plenty of whitewater and passes through Polar Bear denning country.

INFORMATION. MNR.

– Missinaibi River Provincial Park. See entry under District of Cochrane.

– Kesagami Lake Provincial Park. Located just south of James Bay, this park is noted for its potential for backcountry and wilderness experiences. From Kesagami Lake in the Abitibi Uplands of the Canadian Shield, the 54,000-ha park continues downstream via the swift, shallow, boulder-filled Kesagami River through the Hudson Bay Lowland to the coast.

INFORMATION. MNR.

– **Tidewater Provincial Park.** Located on islands in the Moose River, a few kilometres from Moosonee, the park shows the influences of tides, spring ice, and river dynamics on vegetative succession and shoreline erosion. Tree species include Tamarack, Black and White Spruces, Balsam Poplar, and Trembling Aspen. Labrador Tea, Pale Laurel, and Nodding Trillium grow here. Wood warblers, Red Squirrel, and Muskrat are the major faunal species present. Camping is available in the park.
ACCESS. Via water taxi from boat docks in Moosonee & Moose Factory.
INFORMATION. MNR.

Additional Hudson Bay Lowland Canoe Routes

INFORMATION. For overview information on routes of interest to naturalists, see *Canoeing Ontario's Rivers* (by Ron Reid & Janet Grand) & *Canoe Routes of Ontario* (available from any MNR office).

Moosonee

Situated near the mouth of the Moose River, Moosonee offers a summer interpretive centre located in the Ministry of Natural Resources building, a historical museum, nature trails, occasional boat trips to Ship Sands Island, the waterfront, the Ontario Northland Railway (ONR) line, and the quarry road south of Store Creek. Spring and fall migrations are equally good. October may produce unexpected bird vagrants.
ACCESS. Train from Cochrane to Moosonee. Passengers & freight via ONR's Polar Bear Express, which runs daily except Friday from June 20 to Labour Day weekend. Air services by charter or Air Creebec. Summer accommodations limited; make reservations before arrival.

Moose Factory

Moose Factory Island is located approximately 3 km from the townsite of Moosonee and is situated on islands in the Moose River. Birding areas for the island include town bird feeders, sewage lagoons, open fields, tidal pools on the east shore, and nature trails which circumscribe the perimeter of the island.

Interpretive facilities to date generally include local historic sites.

ACCESS. Access to Moose Factory & other river islands via water taxi from boat docks in Moosonee & Moose Factory.

Ship Sands Island

Ship Sands Island, located at the mouth of the Moose River 19 km downriver from Moosonee–Moose Factory, contains marine marshlands, willow meadows, and expansive tidewater- and mudflats. Near the coast and along freshwater streams Marsh Ragwort and Seaside Plantain grow.

Ship Sands attracts many shorebird species from late May to August, with a minor lull in late June. Whimbrel, Hudsonian Godwit, and Red Knot appear in good numbers, especially during the spring and fall migration. Western species such as Wilson's Phalarope and Marbled Godwit nest along the shores of southwestern James Bay. Look for Sandhill Crane, Peregrine Falcon, and Northern Harrier in flight over the marshlands and mudflats. Good numbers of Peregrine Falcon pass through from August to October; Gyrfalcon is present in October and early November. Migrating Northern Goshawk and Rough-legged Hawk are seen in October.

Ship Sands Island forms part of the federal migratory bird sanctuary at the mouth of the Moose River. In September, thousands of Snow Geese (both blue and white phases) flock to the southern shores of James Bay and are visible at Ship Sands Island on their way south. Canada Geese and a good variety of duck species also frequent the sanctuary area in spring and fall.

Large marine mammals, such as Bearded Seal and Beluga, can sometimes be seen, especially in early spring and fall, within the Moose River delta area and along shorelines near Moosonee and Moose Factory.

ACCESS. Water taxi service to river islands available at boat docks in Moosonee & Moose Factory. Because of tides it is important that coastal travel in this area be undertaken only with scheduled tour companies or competent local guides. Travelling on southern James Bay is not recommended.

Addresses

Ministry of Natural Resources, Box 190, Moosonee, Ont, P0L 1Y0, 705-336-2987 (provincial parks, list of tourist outfitters, & canoe routes)

James Bay Frontier Travel Association, Box 920, Schumacher, Ont, P0N 1G0, 705-264-9589 (tourism information & travel plans)

Ontario Northland Railway, Box 203, Moosonee, Ont, P0L 1Y0, 416-965-4268 or 1-800-268-9281 (train schedules, accommodation, & tourism information)

Air Creebec, RR 2, Timmins, Ont, P4N 7C3, 705-264-9521 (flight schedules)

Bushland Airways, Moosonee, Ont, 705-336-2966 (short air excursions to remote rivers & lakes & southern James Bay)

Glossary

Agassiz, glacial Lake – A huge, shallow meltwater lake covering large portions of northwestern Ontario, Manitoba, and adjacent areas during the last retreat of the glaciers.

Algonquin, glacial Lake – Precursor of Lake Huron, a meltwater lake occupying the basins of Lakes Michigan and Huron and adjacent lands following the withdrawal of the glaciers.

alvar – An area of flat limestone bedrock overlain by very thin soil; usually meadow-like and scrubby; supports a characteristic and sparse plant community (including prairie species) adapted to periodic fires, frequent extremes of heat and drought in summer, extreme cold in winter, periodic flooding caused by poor drainage (in spring and fall and during summer rains), low nutrient levels, and high concentrations of calcium resulting from excessive evaporation.

aquatic – Living in or on the surface of water.

arch – In geology, an up-bowing in the Earth's crust to form a dome.

Atlantic coastal plain – A narrow strip of low-lying land, characterized by extensive wetlands, between the Appalachian Mountains and the Atlantic Ocean, and extending from Cape Cod to Georgia. A number of species of plants (known as Atlantic coastal plain flora) typical of the plain occur as disjunct or isolated populations in the Districts of Muskoka and Parry Sound and Haliburton County. They migrated to Ontario about 10,000 years ago along the corridor established when the lower Great Lakes drained south to the Atlantic through the Mohawk valley in New York. In Ontario, they are mostly found between the shorelines of Georgian Bay and glacial Lake Algonquin.

They occupy wave-washed sand and gravel shorelines where water levels fluctuate every few years, thereby reducing nutrient levels and suppressing competition from shrubby species.

basalt – A fine-grained, dark-coloured rock; the most common type of volcanic rock; it forms when liquid rock cools rapidly at the Earth's surface, sometimes occurs in columns, and is common on ocean floors.

batholith – A very large mass of igneous rock, usually granite; often forms the base of mountain ranges; uncovered only by erosion.

bayou – A backwater or marshy inlet or outlet to a lake, river, etc.

beach, barrier – A beach of sand or gravel built across the entrance of a bay and attached to the mainland at both ends.

beach, raised – A former shoreline of a glacial lake or sea that has been raised by isostatic rebound (uplifting of land) following the withdrawal of the weight of the glaciers; also called raised beach ridge.

bedrock – Any solid rock, either exposed or lying beneath the soil and other unconsolidated materials at the surface of the Earth.

bluff – A high, perpendicular broad-faced cliff.

bog – An acidic, nutrient-poor, stagnant, waterlogged wetland under-lain by peat and dominated by a thick layer of *Sphagnum* mosses. Bogs occur where drainage is blocked, as happens in a natural depression or above hardpan. Lack of oxygen in waterlogged soils prevents dead plant material from decaying and allows it to accumulate as peat, thereby locking up most of the nutrients in the bog. Peat and acid-loving *Sphagnum* produce humic acid, which further increases acidity. Bogs are most common in cold, wet climates; more prevalent in northern Ontario, they occur rarely in the south, in cooler microhabitats such as hollows to which cool air drains at night. Rainfall provides water and small quantities of nutrients. Water loss occurs through evaporation from the bog surface or through the leaves of plants. Cool climate, shortage of nutrients and oxygen, waterlogged conditions, and high acidity dictate that only very specialized plants can survive in bogs. *Sphagnum*, sedges, and heath plants are characteristic. All bog plants are perennial, as growth is very slow under such adverse conditions. Most have developed ways to conserve water in their tissues because free water in the bog is too acidic for regular use. Extensive roots and rhizomes are required to hold bog plants upright in the unstable semifluid bog surface. All bog plants supplement their nutrient supply, some by ingenious methods of capturing insects and others through associations with bacteria or fungi that facilitate nutrient uptake.

bog, raised – A raised bog has a slightly elevated dome of *Sphagnum* in the centre (supported by capillary activity) and a watery moat-like zone around the edge (where conditions are less favourable for *Sphagnum* growth). A raised bog forms where *Sphagnum* and other bog vegetation have gradually closed in a round or oval-shaped lake, beginning at the edges and working towards the centre. If there is still a doughnut hole of open water in the middle, the bog is known as an **eyed bog**.

boreal forest – A type of northern hemisphere forest (also called coniferous) that is dominated by conifers and extends between the tundra to the north and a mixed forest of conifers and deciduous trees to the south.

Boreal Forest Region – In Ontario, the coniferous woodlands that cover the northern portion of the Canadian Shield; also called Coniferous Forest Region; sometimes also includes Hudson Bay Lowland (Northern Boreal) Forest.

bottomland – Low-lying land through which a river flows, which is prone to flooding and often rich in water-borne deposits; a floodplain.

brachiopod – Any of a group of small, soft-bodied sea animals having two shells and two fringed arms, one on each side of the mouth; they thrived during the Palaeozoic Era but are still present today; also called lampshells.

calcareous – Containing calcium, as in limestone.

Canadian Shield – *See* Shield, Canadian.

Carolinian Forest Region – The forest zone found in the most southerly parts of Ontario (immediately north of Lake Erie). It lies on the Great Lakes Lowland, is characterized by deciduous trees, and harbours many species at or close to their northern distributional limits. Also called Deciduous Forest, especially in the United States.

cave, solution – A cave formed by dripping water which dissolves the limestone bedrock.

cave, wave-cut – A cave in the side of a cliff sculpted by waves when the water level remained at a particular height for a relatively long period of time; a sea cave.

cephalopod – An animal of the mollusk group with a distinctive head bearing muscular tentacles about the mouth; e.g., octopus and squid.

Champlain Sea – An arm of the Atlantic Ocean that flooded inland through the St Lawrence valley to cover eastern Ontario at the end of the last glaciation.

channel, meltwater – A channel created by meltwater from retreating glaciers.

Churchill province – One of four geological provinces in Ontario, also called Trans-Hudson Orogen, which is intermediate in age between Superior and Grenville provinces; primarily found from northern Manitoba north and west, in Ontario it surfaces in the Hudson Bay Lowland southwest of Cape Henrietta Maria.

Claybelt – A level till plain stretching across northern Ontario from Hearst through Kapuskasing and Cochrane to Timmins, and containing deposits inherited from glacial Lake Ojibway. The **Little Claybelt** is an area of clay deposits north of Lake Timiskaming.

Committee on the Status of Endangered Wildlife in Canada (COSEWIC) – A committee composed of federal, provincial, and territorial wildlife officials and representatives from conservation organizations, which considers the best available information and assigns status to species at risk in categories of 'extinct,' 'extirpated,' 'endangered,' 'threatened,' and 'vulnerable.'

conglomerate (rock) – A sedimentary rock composed of rounded pebbles or larger rock fragments cemented together in a mass of hardened sand; also known as puddingstone.

conifer – Any of the cone-bearing trees and shrubs, mostly evergreens, such as pine, spruce, fir, and cedar.

conservation area – A natural area or recreation area operated by a conservation authority.

conservation authority – In Ontario, a body funded by provincial and municipal governments, organized on a watershed basis, with responsibilities for water quality, erosion, flood control, and conservation of natural resources; involved in reforestation, operation of dams, and recreational facilities, etc.

crinoid – A sea lily, a flower-like marine animal with frond-like arms, anchored by a long, flexible stalk; prominent during the Palaeozoic Era.

crust – The outermost rocky layer of the Earth, characterized by thicker, usually granitic, continental crust and thinner, usually basaltic, oceanic crust.

cuesta – The rim at the top of an escarpment.

deciduous – Referring to trees or other plants whose leaves fall when mature or at the end of the growing season.

Deciduous Forest – The forest zone dominated by deciduous trees that occurs throughout much of northeastern United States and extends into the southernmost parts of Ontario; also called Carolinian Forest.

diabase – A dark-coloured, fine-grained, basaltic volcanic rock made up largely of feldspars and pyroxenes.

disjunct – Refers to a population of plants or animals that is geographically isolated from the main range of the species.

dolostone – A sedimentary rock consisting mostly of dolomite. This hard limestone rock weathers into small potholes (about 2.5 cm in diameter) which fill with water and debris.

drift – All unconsolidated and unsorted mineral material lying above the bedrock; **glacial drift** refers to all materials transported and deposited by glaciers or their meltwaters.

drumlin – An elongated, oval-shaped whaleback ridge or hill of glacial till with smoothly rounded contours, moulded by moving ice and oriented in the direction of ice flow, with the steeper end pointing towards the direction from which the ice advanced; all drumlins in one drumlin field are oriented in the same direction.

dune – A rounded hill or ridge of loose sand piled by the wind; the dune ridge closest to the shore is the **foredune**.

dyke (intrusive) – A hardened slab-like mass of igneous rock that has been forced (intruded) while in a melted state into a fissure between layers of older rock.

emergent (vegetation) – Refers to plants whose roots are found temporarily or permanently under water but whose upper parts (where photosynthesis takes place) are found on or above the surface of the water (e.g., water lily, cattail, bulrush).

endangered – As defined by the Committee on the Status of Endangered Wildlife in Canada, any indigenous species of flora or fauna that is threatened with imminent extirpation or extinction throughout all or a significant portion of its range in Canada (*see* threatened *and* vulnerable). Ontario employs a similar definition for species at risk in the province.

endemic – Native to and often restricted to a particular region. A group of plants referred to as **Great Lakes endemics** is particularly well represented along the Lake Huron shoreline.

ephemeral (spring) – Usually any of a number of short-lived wildflowers of deciduous forests that flower and produce leaves early in the spring before the tree leaf canopy has developed, then die down before the full onset of summer.

erratic (glacial) – A boulder that has been transported a considerable distance from its place of origin by a glacier and deposited at random when the ice melted.

escarpment – A steep slope or cliff, often formed by a fault in the bedrock or by differing rates of erosion on adjacent rock formations.

esker – A steep-sided, winding ridge of sorted gravel and sand, typically 10–45 m high and a few kilometres long (but can be much longer), formed by the debris laid down on the bed of a meltwater stream flowing through crevasses or tunnels within or under a glacier; when the glacier melted the streambed deposits dropped to the ground immediately below the route of the glacial stream.

extinct – Refers to a species which no longer has any living members anywhere.

extirpated – Refers to a species in which members have been eliminated from a given part of its range but which still exists elsewhere in the world.

fault, geological – A break or fracture in the Earth's crust which causes a section of bedrock to shift position relative to adjacent blocks of bedrock on the other side of the **faultline**. Movements along faultlines are often associated with earthquakes.

fault, reverse thrust – A fault or break that occurs in the Earth's crust at a slight angle to the vertical. Rocks on the upper side of the slanted faultline rise relative to those on the lower side. This results in the upper block overhanging the lower one at an angle, although weathering may eventually produce a vertical cliff face.

fen – A peatland that has water slowly flowing through it, bringing in nutrients and flushing out acids. Grasses and sedges are often dominant. Fens develop in lowlands in which the impeded drainage produces waterlogged soils and poor aeration, but where conditions are less stagnant, nutrient poor, and acidic than in bogs. A **patterned fen** consists of alternating water-filled hollows and parallel low ridges of peat that support grasses, sedges, and rushes. These features, which develop over permafrost or where thin soil layers overlie bedrock, are oriented perpendicular to the very gentle slope of the landscape. Although often referred to as bogs, patterned fens are the most common type of peatland in the north, blanketing huge areas of the Hudson Bay Lowland.

floodplain – A flat, low-lying plain adjacent to a stream, formed by deposition of stream sediments during regular flooding.

flowerpot – A shoreline feature created when wave action sculpts sedimentary rock into asymmetrical pillars or sea stacks; the shape and thickness of the column depend on the hardness of individual rock layers and on how long water levels remained stationary at a particular height. Along the Bruce Peninsula soft limestone is eroded from under the harder dolostone caprock to form an arch; when this collapses a flowerpot remains.

forest, mixed – *See* Great Lakes–St Lawrence Forest Region.

forest region – A major geographic belt or zone dominated by a distinctive assemblage of tree species; there are four forest regions in Ontario (five if the treeless Tundra Region is included).

fossil – Any hardened remains or other evidence of life during a previous geological period preserved in rocks, such as impressions, tracks, trails, hard parts, and skeletons.

Frontenac Axis (Arch) – An ancient bridge of Precambrian rock that connects the Canadian Shield with the Adirondack Uplands in New York state.

gastropod – A mollusk having a one-piece spiral shell (e.g., snail).

glacier – A large mass of ice formed from accumulated layers of packed snow; it moves slowly downslope under its own weight.

gneiss – A coarse-grained metamorphic rock resembling granite but with smaller crystals; may be formed from granite or sedimentary rock; contains distinct layers or bands of minerals such as feldspar, quartz, mica, and hornblende; forms up to 80% of the Canadian Shield.

graben – An escarpment-bordered valley created when a large linear block of bedrock downdrops between two parallel faults in the Earth's crust.

granite – The most common igneous rock, usually light grey or pink in colour; consists of feldspar, quartz, and usually some mica.

Great Lakes Lowland – In Ontario, the land lying to the south of the Canadian Shield and bordered by Lakes Ontario, Erie, and Huron.

Great Lakes–St Lawrence Forest Region – The band of mixed coniferous and deciduous trees found between the Boreal Forest to the north and the Carolinian Forest to the south, also called mixed forest; in Ontario this forest type lies partly on the Canadian Shield and partly on the Great Lakes–St Lawrence Lowland.

Great Lakes–St Lawrence Lowland – In southern and eastern Ontario, the land lying to the south or east of the Canadian Shield.

greenbelt – An area in which development is restricted, and which is often used for parkland or agriculture.

greenstone – Any of various fine-grained, dark green weakly meta-morphosed volcanic rocks, the most common being basalt; **greenstone belts** contain deposits of gold, silver, platinum, zinc, and copper.

Grenville province – The youngest of four structural rock formations in Ontario, which underlies much of eastern Ontario, composed of metamorphic rocks of late Precambrian origin; the northwestern edge of the Grenville province is called the **Grenville Front**.

herpetofauna – Reptiles and amphibians.

Hudson Bay Lowland – In northern Ontario, the land lying to the north of the Canadian Shield.

Hudson Bay Lowland Forest Region – In northern Ontario, the stunted coniferous forest lying to the north of the Canadian Shield and south of the tundra; sometimes also called Northern Boreal Forest.

Ice Age – In North America, the last 1.5 million years (Pleistocene Epoch), during which glaciers covered the northern part of the continent four times; any one of the four glaciations.

ice sheet – A large mass of glacial ice that covers extensive portions of the Earth's surface.

ice-contact features – Landscape features created by moving glaciers.

igneous rock – Rock that formed deep within the Earth from molten magma; may form a slab-like intrusion within layers of other types of rock or, through upward migration and erosion, may reach the Earth's surface as an outcrop.

indigenous – Native to a particular area.

inlier – An older rock formation which forms an outcrop through surrounding younger rock.

intrusive – A hard slab of igneous rock formed from molten rock which crystallized and cooled within the Earth's crust after flowing between layers of another pre-existing type of rock.

Iroquois, glacial Lake – Precursor to Lake Ontario, formed by meltwaters from the retreating glaciers.

isostatic rebound – The process by which the Earth's surface gradually rises to achieve equilibrium after being pressed down by large masses, such as ice sheets or huge temporary lakes.

kame – A steep-sided, cone-shaped hill deposited at the base of a waterfall either at the edge of a glacier or in crevices within it; formed from accumulated debris carried over the lip of the ice; contains sorted layers of gravel and sand; associated with glacial meltwater streams and hence with esker ridges. A **kame delta** resulted when the debris fell into a glacial lake at the foot of a glacier. A **kame terrace** developed where a stream flowed between the edge of a glacier and the slope of a valley wall. A **kame moraine** may occur as an extended ridge composed mainly of kames and outwash.

karst – A type of topography created by the extensive chemical weathering of limestones as water dissolves the carbonate-rich bedrock. Karst features include tall rock pillars, escarpments, circular sinkholes, underground drainage, caves, caverns, and limestone pavement that exhibits a peculiar pock-marked surface characterized by numerous cracks and irregular holes.

kettle – A round stone concretion or structure formed from accumulated mineral deposits and enclosed within another type of rock. If the outer rock erodes away, as occurs at Kettle Point, large round kettles of rock are left.

kettle – A steep-sided circular depression found in glacial drift, formed when a large block of glacial ice became buried and later melted, allowing the covering sediments to collapse into the hole. Kettle lakes (ponds) or kettle bogs now occupy many such sites. They are kept filled by rainwater and underground springs, and usually have no inlets or outlets. Kettle formations are often associated with moraines.

kettle – A rounded hollow in rock, formed when a harder rock was caught by an eddy in a river and whirled about and ground into the softer bedrock; also called a pothole.

lagg – A moat-like zone of more or less open water around the outer edge of a raised bog. It is especially likely to develop if the bog is surrounded by hills. Adjacent slopes allow the amount of water and the degree of acidity around the edges of the bog to fluctuate with varying amounts of runoff from rainfall, etc., thereby reducing stability and making conditions less suitable for the growth of *Sphagnum* mosses.

lake, meromictic – A lake having the unusual characteristic of no exchange of water between the warm oxygen-rich upper waters and the cold, deep oxygen-poor lower waters; upper and lower layers also separated by chemical differences; lack of circulation the result of small surface area relative to depth of lake. No turnover of water means bottom sediments are preserved in an undisturbed state and therefore significant for palaeoecological research.

lava – Rock formed when liquid magma erupts onto the Earth's surface (as during a volcanic eruption), then cools. Bun-shaped globules of **pillow lava** form when basaltic magma is released into water and rapidly chilled, as occurs during eruptions on the ocean floor.

levee – An elevated mound forming a border along a riverbank, created from silt deposits laid down during annual spring floods.

lichen – Any of an unusual group of primitive plants formed by a combination of algae and fungi; they live mostly on rocks, bark, or soil; e.g., map lichen, rock tripe, old man's beard, and reindeer lichen.

limestone – A sedimentary rock consisting mainly of the carbonate mineral calcite; becomes marble when crystallized by heat and pressure.

magma – Molten rock deep in the Earth which hardens to form igneous rock.

marble – A hard, crystalline or granular rock metamorphosed from limestone and dolomitic limestone.

marl – A soft, crumbly, whitish-coloured soil consisting mainly of clay, sand, and calcium carbonate; accumulates on lake and pond bottoms by precipitation from lime-rich waters; marl deposits may also be found under marshes, swamps, and bogs formed over former glacial lakes. **Marl lakes** are shallow water bodies overlying limestone basins; because of the stagnant and highly calcareous water, aquatic flora is poor but rich fens often form around these lakes. **Marl precipitate** is the white mucky ooze deposited at the bottom of a marl lake.

marsh – A nutrient-rich treeless wetland in which the predominant vegetation consists of grasses, sedges, and rushes.

meander – A semicircular bend in a slow-flowing stream, with erosion occuring along the outer bank and deposition along the inner one; often found on a floodplain.

melanism – The abnormal development of black pigments in skin, hair, or feathers giving an animal or bird a black colour.

mesa – A large, broad, steep-sided flat-topped rock formation capped by erosion-resistant rock; stands above surrounding countryside.

metamorphic rock – New rock created from existing igneous, metamorphic, volcanic, or sedimentary rock through the application of pressure and heat below the melting point of the original rock; the process reorganizes the crystalline structure and mineral types of the rock while it remains solid.

meteorite – A fragment of metal or stone that has fallen to the Earth from outer space.

moraine – An accumulation of unsorted glacial till containing sand, gravel, stones, and boulders carried and finally deposited by a glacier; usually a much larger formation than an esker; may be hundreds of kilometres long and up to 250 m high. A **ground moraine** is created when a glacier melts to leave a blanket of gently rolling till deposited across the landscape. As a glacier advances it bulldozes materials in front of it and, when it stops, materials continue to be added by meltwater carrying rubble from within or under the ice. A **terminal moraine** is the ridge that marks the greatest advance of a glacier. As the glacier recedes, it may pause at a certain location long enough to allow a new ridge called an **end moraine** to form along its front edge. End moraines formed in sequence along the path of the retreating ice mass are **recessional moraines. Lateral moraines** form along the sides of glaciers in contact with valley walls. Materials carried by running water in association with glaciers can produce **kame moraine** features, such as deltas in ponded meltwater, terraces flanking the ice mass, and conical hills of rubble at the foot of glacial waterfalls. When two advancing glacial lobes converge, the rubble shoved together between them creates an **interlobate moraine.** Moraines formed along a glacier when deep water is ponded against the edge of the ice are known as **DeGeer moraines.**

muskeg – Vast boreal peatland dominated by *Sphagnum* mosses and sparsely forested with Black Spruce; forms a semidry mosaic of bogs and fens.

Ojibway, glacial Lake – The meltwater lake centred around Lake Abitibi following glacial withdrawal.

outcrop – An exposure of bedrock above the surface of the ground.

outlier – An isolated rock formation found some distance away from the main formation as a result of the erosion of similar rock in the interval between.

outwash, glacial – A broad, gently sloping plain of sorted silt, sand, and gravel deposited by meltwater immediately below a glacier; the surface may be characterized by terraced (braided) streams, broad fans of water draining away from the glacier, and a somewhat undulating topography; serves as the distribution area for rubble outwashed from the glacier.

overburden – Soft unconsolidated till overlying the bedrock.

oxbow – The semicircular wanderings of a stream as it meanders across its floodplain. If the river changes course, an abandoned U-shaped loop of former channel, now cut off from the main stream, may fill with water to form an **oxbow lake.**

panne – A flat, low-lying seasonally flooded area between foredunes and backdunes, characterized by soils rich in lime but low in other nutrients; supports a specialized wet-meadow community.

park, provincial – A park operated by a provincial government. In Ontario, categories include: **nature reserve park** (often undeveloped, protects unusual landforms or associations of species), **wilderness park** (a huge wilderness area with access by foot or canoe), **natural environment park** (emphasis on protection but some recreational facilities), **waterway park** (a linear corridor consisting of a watercourse and adjacent lands, for canoeists), and **recreation park** (recreational emphasis).

pavement, boulder – A boulder-strewn surface on a former lakeshore or streambed.

pavement, limestone (dolostone) – An area of exposed limestone bedrock characterized by extremes of temperature and moisture and sparsely inhabited by specialized plants often having prairie affinities.

peat – An organic soil material consisting of undecomposed or partially decomposed vegetation (largely *Sphagnum* mosses); develops where decomposition is impeded by waterlogged conditions and lack of oxygen. Peat is formed when remains accumulate and become compressed. In fens and, more especially, bogs most of the nutrients are tied up in peat.

petroglyph – A rock carving, especially a prehistoric one made by Indians.

pictograph – A rock painting of ancient or historic origin, often featuring symbolic figures.

plate – One section or subdivision of the Earth's crust which moves about relative to other sections.

population – All of the individuals of one species which live within a defined area.

pothole – A round hole gouged in bedrock by stones swirled about by water; a kettle.

prairie – A large area of level or slightly rolling grassland with deep fertile soils; **tallgrass prairie** (typical of eastern prairies) is characterized by moister climate and 2-m-tall grasses, **shortgrass prairie** (typical of western prairies) occurs on drier sites and supports shorter species, and **mixedgrass prairie** contains elements of both.

Precambrian Shield – *See* Shield, Precambrian.

rare – As defined by the province of Ontario, any indigenous species of fauna or flora that is represented in the province by small but relatively stable populations, and/or that occurs sporadically or in a very restricted area of Ontario or at the fringe of its range, and that should be monitored periodically for evidence of a possible decline.

re-entrant valley – A valley or notch that extends into a geological formation; e.g., any of the large steep-sided valleys that cut deeply into the interior of the Niagara Escarpment and terminate at its face.

relict – A plant or animal species that colonized a particular area during an earlier period when conditions were more favourable, and continues to survive there by occupying the now very restricted amount of suitable habitat; geological evidence of primitive life.

rock cycle – The very slow but continuous process through which the particles in all rocks are gradually recycled from one type of rock to another by means of sedimentation, melting, or metamorphosis.

St Lawrence Lowland – In eastern Ontario, the land lying to the east of the Canadian Shield and bordered by the St Lawrence and Ottawa rivers; sometimes also called Ottawa–St Lawrence Lowland.

sandbar – A narrow shoal of sand deposited in a river or along a coast by currents or tides.

sandspit – A long, narrow ridge of sand or dunes attached to the mainland at one end; may partially close the entrance to a bay.

sandstone – A sedimentary rock composed of sand grains that have been cemented together.

savanna – A grassland with trees scattered across it.

sedimentary rock – Rock formed at low temperatures and pressures on the Earth's surface; consists of accumulated fragments of rocks and minerals most often originally deposited as layers in the bottom of a water body; e.g., mud becomes shale and sand becomes sandstone.

seepage slope – A wet area on the side or foot of a hill or slope where groundwater seeps to the surface.

shale – A kind of fine-grained sedimentary rock composed mainly of clays; splits easily into thin layers.

shield – Any part of the Earth's continental crust that has become stabilized; forms platforms on which sedimentary rocks can be laid down; most shield rocks are Precambrian in origin; within Canada, shield refers to Canadian Shield.

Shield, Canadian – The ancient worn-down Precambrian rocks exposed above the surface in Canada; in Ontario made up of four distinct structural provinces: Superior, Southern, Churchill, and Grenville.

Shield, Precambrian – A hard crust of rock formed when the primitive Earth cooled from its molten state; serves as the geological foundation of North America. The Precambrian Shield is now largely buried beneath later rock deposits but where it is exposed in a broad swath arcing across much of Canada it is called the Canadian Shield.

shorecliff – A wave-cut cliff (i.e., created by wave action), often with a terrace of boulders at its base.

sill – A slab-like intrusion of igneous rock between layers of enclosing rock.

sinkhole – A large circular depression caused by the collapse of the roof of an underground cavern; found on limestone and dolostone plains where percolating water creates karst topography.

slate – A hard, fine-grained metamorphic rock which naturally splits into thin, smooth bluish-grey layers, created from shale.

slough – A wet area such as a swamp, bog, or marsh, usually part of an inlet or backwater.

Southern province – One of four geological provinces in Ontario, intermediate in age between Superior and Grenville provinces; in Ontario found near Thunder Bay–Lake Nipigon, north of Lake Huron, and in a band between Superior and Grenville provinces; consists largely of volcanic and intrusive rocks.

Sphagnum – Any of a number of moss species growing in wet acidic sites, such as bogs; accumulated remains when compacted with other plant debris form peat.

spillway, glacial – A channel (often a broad valley) carrying glacial meltwater, now abandoned or carrying only a very small stream.

spit – A long point of land, often a ridge of sand (sandspit), that is attached to the mainland at one end and projects into a body of water; formed by currents and longshore drift that transport sediments along a coast until they are slowed and settling occurs.

staging area – An area where large numbers of birds, especially waterfowl, gather to feed and rest at intervals along a migration route; e.g., the marshes at Long Point.

stream, braided – A shallow stream whose channel is choked with sand and gravel bars through which water threads its way.

stromatolites – Fossils of blue-green algae laid down on platforms of carbonate rock in shallow seas; formed when respiration by the algae caused lime muds to precipitate out of the water and be deposited as layers around the tissues of the algae; common from middle Precambrian on.

substrate – A substance, material, etc. that forms a foundation on which another is supported; e.g., rocks and tree bark are substrates used by lichens.

succession – The sequence through which a landscape is recolonized by plants following a disruption such as fire, logging, or farming, until the vegetation type appropriate for that site achieves maturity; e.g., from farmland to meadow, shrub meadow, poplar and birch woodland, and finally maple-dominated forest.

Superior province – One of four geological provinces in Ontario, found in much of northern Ontario north and west of Sudbury except in the Hudson Bay Lowland; forms the basement complex to which all other rocks in Ontario were added; contains the oldest rocks of the Precambrian Shield, mainly consisting of igneous but also of volcanic, metamorphosed, and sedimentary rocks.

swamp – A wooded wetland on mucky soil where a small amount of peat may accumulate owing to waterlogging, poor aeration, and stagnation.

talus – A loose pile of angular weathered rock fragments carried by gravity to the foot of a steep hill or cliff. A **talus slope** is the inclined accumulation or apron of such debris lying at the base of the cliff.

terrace, beach – A raised terrace of sand along a beach.

terrace, river – Beds of gravel and sand deposited by a stream.

terrace, wave-cut – A strip of level land at the foot of a shorecliff.

thermal – A huge bubble of daytime air which rises through surrounding cooler air; produced when the sun warms the ground and the air just above it, causing the heated air mass to expand and rise. At 800 m or so, moisture in the thermal condenses to droplets to create small cumulus clouds, which saps the heat of the thermal. As a thermal rises, it is used by migrating hawks (as a means of conserving energy) to gain altitude; from the top of one they glide downward seeking the next thermal.

threatened – As defined by the Committee on the Status of Endangered Wildlife in Canada, any indigenous species of flora or fauna that is likely to become endangered in Canada if the factors affecting its vulnerability do not become reversed (*see* endangered *and* vulnerable). Ontario employs a similar definition for species at risk in the province.

tidal zone – The area of shoreline covered and exposed daily by rising and falling tides.

till (glacial) – The unsorted mix of clay, sand, pebbles, and boulders laid down by a glacier when it melts.

trilobite – A member of a large group of extinct arthropods with bodies divided into three lobes, found in fossils in Palaeozoic rocks; modern-day relatives include spiders, insects, and scorpions.

tundra – An area of low treeless vegetation found at high latitudes and high altitudes; characterized by lichens, sedges, and dwarf shrubs.

Tundra Forest Region – In Ontario, a vegetation zone bordering the shore of Hudson Bay characterized by low vegetation.

understorey – Intermediate-sized plants growing under the canopy of the tallest layer of trees in a woodland; e.g., tall shrubs and small trees.

vascular plants – Plants (i.e., all higher plants, as in ferns , conifers, and flowering plants) having a vascular system (conducting tissues for the transport of water and nutrients), usually with true roots, stems, and leaves.

volcanic rock – Rock formed when lava cooled rapidly at the Earth's surface.

vulnerable – As defined by the Committee on the Status of Endangered Wildlife in Canada, any indigenous species of flora or fauna that is particularly at risk because of low or declining numbers, occurrences at the fringe of its range or in restricted areas, or for some other reason, but is not a threatened species (*see* threatened *and* endangered).

Warren, glacial Lake – The meltwater lake in the Lake Erie basin following the last glaciation.

weathering – Breakdown of rock into smaller fragments or particles by physical or chemical means (e.g., wind, rain, changes in temperature).

Wisconsin Glaciation – The last great Ice Age in North America, 115,000–10,000 years ago.

yard, deer (wintering yard) – An area where deer congregate in winter to obtain shelter and food; often located in swampy woodlands.

Reference Materials

BIRDS

General

Austen, M.J.W., M.D. Cadman, and R.D. James. 1994. *Ontario Birds at Risk: Status and Conservation Needs*. Federation of Ontario Naturalists and Long Point Bird Observatory

Cadman, M.D., P.F.J. Eagles, and F.M. Helleiner. 1987. *Atlas of the Breeding Birds of Ontario*. Waterloo: University of Waterloo Press

Godfrey, Earl W. 1986. *The Birds of Canada*. Ottawa: National Museums of Canada

Goodwin, Clive E. 1995. *A Bird-Finding Guide to Ontario*. Toronto: University of Toronto Press

James, Ross D. 1991. *Annotated Checklist of the Birds of Ontario*. 2nd ed. Toronto: Royal Ontario Museum

McNicholl, M.K., and J.L. Cranmer-Byng. 1994. *Ornithology in Ontario*. Ontario Field Ornithologists Special Publication No. 1. Whitby: Hawk Owl Publishing

Peck, George, and Ross James. 1983. *Breeding Birds of Ontario: Nidiology and Distribution*. Vols. 1–2. Toronto: Royal Ontario Museum

Speirs, J. Murray. 1985. *Birds of Ontario*. Vols. 1–2. Toronto: Natural Heritage/Natural History

Field Identification Guides

Bull, John, and John Farrand, Jr. 1977. *The Audubon Society Field Guide to North American Birds*. New York: Knopf

National Geographic Society. 1987. *Field Guide to the Birds of North America*. Rev. 2nd ed. Washington: National Geographic Society

Peterson, Roger Tory. 1980. *A Field Guide to the Birds East of the Rockies*. 4th ed. Peterson Field Guide. Boston: Houghton Mifflin

Robbins, Chandler S., Bertel Bruun, and Herbert S. Zim. 1983. *Birds of North America*. Golden Guide. New York: Golden Press

Regional Bird Guides

Many naturalists' clubs have put out local bird checklists and guides. If visiting a region contact the local club for information (address available from FON).

MAMMALS

Banfield, A.W.F. 1974. *Mammals of Canada*. Toronto: University of Toronto Press

Dobbyn, J.S. 1994. *Atlas of the Mammals of Ontario*. Federation of Ontario Naturalists

Van Zyll de Jong, C.G. 1983. *Handbook of Canadian Mammals*. Vols. 1–2. Ottawa: National Museum of Natural Sciences

Field Guides

Burt, William H., and Richard P. Grossenheider. 1980. *A Field Guide to the Mammals*. 3rd ed. Peterson Field Guide. Boston: Houghton Mifflin

Murie, Olaus J. 1974. *A Field Guide to Animal Tracks*. 2nd ed. Peterson Field Guide. Boston: Houghton Mifflin

Whitaker, J.O. 1980. *The Audubon Society Field Guide to North American Mammals*. New York: Knopf

REPTILES AND AMPHIBIANS

Conant, Roger. 1991. *A Field Guide to Reptiles and Amphibians: Eastern and Central North America*. Peterson Field Guide. Boston: Houghton Mifflin

Cook, Francis R. 1984. *An Introduction to Canadian Amphibians and Reptiles*. Ottawa: National Museum of Natural Sciences

Johnson, Bob. 1989. *Familiar Reptiles and Amphibians of Ontario*. Toronto: Natural Heritage/Natural History

King, Wayne, and John Behler. 1979. *The Audubon Society Field Guide to Northern Reptiles and Amphibians*. New York: Knopf

FISH

Mandrak, N.E., and E.J. Crossman. 1992. *A Checklist of Ontario Freshwater Fishes*. Toronto: Royal Ontario Museum

Scott, W.B. 1967. *Freshwater Fishes of Eastern Canada*. 2nd ed. Toronto: University of Toronto Press

Scott, W.B., and E.J. Crossman. 1973. *Freshwater Fishes of Canada*. Ottawa: Fisheries Research Board of Canada

INSECTS

Borror, Donald J., and Richard E. White. 1970. *A Field Guide to the Insects of America North of Mexico*. Peterson Field Guide. Boston: Houghton Mifflin

Covell, Charles V. 1984. *A Field Guide to the Moths of Eastern North America*. Peterson Field Guide. Boston: Houghton Mifflin

Holmes, A.M., Q.F. Hess, R.R. Tasker, and A.J. Hanks. 1991. *The Ontario Butterfly Atlas*. Toronto: Toronto Entomologists' Association

Mitchell, Robert T., and Herbert S. Zim. 1987. *Butterflies and Moths*. Golden Field Guide. New York: Golden Press

Opler, Paul A., and Vichai Malikul. 1992. *A Field Guide to Eastern Butterflies*. Peterson Field Guide. Boston: Houghton Mifflin

Pyle, Robert M. 1981. *The Audubon Society Field Guide to North American Butterflies*. New York: Knopf

White, Richard E. 1983. *A Field Guide to the Beetles of North America*. Peterson Field Guide. Boston: Houghton Mifflin

PLANTS

Field Guides and Other Popular Works

Brockman, C. Frank. 1968. *Trees of North America*. Golden Field Guide. New York: Golden Press

Brown, Lauren. 1979. *Grasses: An Identification Guide*. Peterson Nature Library. Boston: Houghton Mifflin

Cobb, Boughton. 1963. *A Field Guide to Ferns*. Peterson Field Guide. Boston: Houghton Mifflin

Cody, W.J., and D.M. Britton. 1989. *Ferns and Fern Allies of Canada*. Ottawa: Agriculture Canada

Dore, William G., and J. McNeill. 1980. *Grasses of Ontario*. Ottawa: Agriculture Canada

Farrar, John Laird. 1995. *Trees in Canada*. Markham: Fitzhenry and Whiteside

Groves, J. Walton. 1962. *Edible and Poisonous Mushrooms of Canada*. Ottawa: Agriculture Canada

Hosie, R.C. 1979. *Native Trees of Canada*. 8th ed. Toronto: Fitzhenry and Whiteside

Johnson, Karen L. 1987. *Wildflowers of Churchill and the Hudson Bay Region*. Winnipeg: Manitoba Museum of Man and Nature

Lauriault, Jean. 1989. *Identification Guide to the Trees of Canada*. Markham: Fitzhenry and Whiteside

Little, Elbert L., Jr. 1980. *The Audubon Society Field Guide to North American Trees (Eastern)*. New York: Knopf

McKay, Sheila, and Paul Catling. 1979. *Trees, Shrubs, and Flowers to Know in Ontario*. Toronto: J.M. Dent and Sons

McKnight, Kent, and Verna McKnight. 1987. *A Field Guide to Mushrooms: North America*. Peterson Field Guide. Boston: Houghton Mifflin

Newcomb, Lawrence. 1977. *Newcomb's Wildflower Guide*. Boston: Little, Brown and Co

Niering, William A., and Nancy C. Olmstead. 1979. *The Audubon Society Field Guide to North American Wildflowers (Eastern)*. New York: Knopf

Peterson, Roger Tory, and Margaret McKenny. 1968. *A Field Guide to Wildflowers of Northeastern and North-central North America*. Boston: Houghton Mifflin

Soper, James H., and Margaret L. Heimburger. 1982. *Shrubs of Ontario*. Toronto: Royal Ontario Museum

Vance, F.R., J.R. Jowsey, and J.S. McLean. 1984. *Wildflowers across the Prairies*. Saskatoon: Western Producer Prairie Books

Technical Identification Keys

Fernald, M.L. 1970. *Gray's Manual of Botany*. New York: Van Nostrand

Gleason, Henry A. 1952. *The New Britton and Brown Illustrated Flora of the Northeastern United States and Adjacent Canada*. Vols 1–3. New York: Botanical Garden

Gleason, Henry A., and Arthur Cronquist. 1963. *Manual of Vascular Plants of Northeastern United States and Adjacent Canada*. New York: Van Nostrand

Marie-Victorin, Frère. 1964. *Flore laurentienne.* Montreal: Les Presses de l'Université de Montréal

Scoggan, Homer. 1979. *The Flora of Canada.* Vols 1–4. Ottawa: National Museum of Natural Sciences

Regional Flora and Checklists (mostly lists or of a technical nature)

Argus, G.W., K.M. Pryer, D.J. White, and C.J. Keddy, eds. 1982–7. *Atlas of the Rare Vascular Plants of Ontario.* Parts 1–4. Ottawa: National Museum of Natural Sciences

Gillet, John M., and David J. White. 1978. *Checklist of Vascular Plants of the Ottawa-Hull Region.* Ottawa: National Museum of Natural Sciences

Morton, J.K., and Joan M. Venn. 1982. *The Flora of Manitoulin Island.* 2nd ed. Waterloo: University of Waterloo

– 1987. *The Flora of the Tobermory Islands.* Waterloo: University of Waterloo

– 1990. *A Checklist of the Flora of Ontario: Vascular Plants.* Waterloo: University of Waterloo

Skeleton, Eleanor, and Emerson Skeleton. 1991. *Haliburton Flora.* Toronto: Royal Ontario Museum

Soper, J.H., C.E. Garton, and D.R. Given. 1989. *Flora of the North Shore of Lake Superior.* Ottawa: National Museums

Walshe, Shan. 1980. *Plants of Quetico and the Ontario Shield.* Toronto: University of Toronto Press

Whiting, R.E., and P.M. Catling. 1986. *Orchids of Ontario.* Ottawa: Cana-Coll Foundation

GEOLOGY

Baird, D.M. 1968. *Guide to the Geology and Scenery of the National Capital Area.* Geological Survey of Canada

Chapman, L.J., and D.F. Putnam. 1984. *The Physiography of Southern Ontario.* 3rd ed. Toronto: University of Toronto Press

Chesterman, Charles W. 1978. *The Audubon Society Field Guide to North American Rocks and Minerals.* New York: Knopf

Ludvigsen, Rolf. 1979. *Fossils of Ontario.* Parts 1–3. Toronto: Royal Ontario Museum

Ontario Ministry of Northern Development and Mines. 1994. *ROCK ONtario.* Toronto: Queen's Printer

Thurston, P.C., H.R. Williams, R.H. Sutcliffe, and G.M. Stott, eds. 1991–2. *Geology of Ontario.* Vols 1–2. Ontario Geological Survey

Tovell, W.M. 1992. *Guide to the Geology of the Niagara Escarpment, with Field Trips* (available from Niagara Escarpment Commission)

Trenhaille, A. 1991. *The Geomorphology of Canada: An Introduction.* Oxford University Press

Note also Geological Guidebook Series, Ministry of Northern Development and Mines, Ontario, which includes following titles:

Debicki, R.L. 1982. 6. *Geology and Scenery, Killarney Provincial Park*

Hewitt, Donald F. 1969. 3. *Geology and Scenery; Peterborough, Bancroft, and Madoc Area*

Pye, E.G. 1968. 1. *Geology and Scenery; Rainy Lake and East to Lake Superior*

– 1969. 2. *Geology and Scenery; North Shore of Lake Superior*

Robertson, J.A., and K.D. Card. 1972. 4. *Geology and Scenery; North Shore of Lake Huron Region*

REGIONAL AND SPECIALTY GUIDES

Brunton, D.F. 1988. *Nature and Natural Areas in Canada's Capital.* The Ottawa *Citizen* in cooperation with the Ottawa Field-Naturalists' Club

Lewis, John Cameron. 1992. *Guide to the Natural History of the Niagara Region.* St Catharines: J.C. Lewis

Lorimer, Shirley, ed. 1996. *Guide to the Natural Areas of London and Vicinity.* 2nd ed. London: McIlwraith Field Naturalists

Peterborough Field Naturalists. 1992. *Kawarthas Nature.* Erin, Ont: Boston Mills Press

Runtz, Michael. 1993. *The Explorer's Guide to Algonquin Park.* Don Mills: Stoddart

For additional titles of regional guides, contact local naturalists' clubs (addresses available from FON).

Hiking

Bruce Trail Association. 1994. *Bruce Trail Association Trail Reference: Trail Guide and Maps.* 19th ed

Rideau Trail Association. 1993. *The Rideau Trail Guidebook.* 3rd ed. Kingston

Teasdale, Shirley. 1993. *Hiking Ontario's Heartland*. Toronto: Whitecap
  Books

Contact Hike Ontario (see address elsewhere) for additional titles.

Canoeing

Ministry of Natural Resources. 1991. *Canoe Routes of Ontario*. Toronto:
  McClelland and Stewart
Reid, Ron, and Janet Grand. 1985. *Canoeing Ontario's Rivers*. Vancou-
  ver/Toronto: Douglas and McIntyre

For maps and guidebooks for canoeing individual river systems, consult nearby Ministry of Natural Resources offices.

GENERAL

Kricher, John C., and Gordon Morrison. 1988. *A Field Guide to Eastern
  Forests*. Peterson Field Guide. Boston: Houghton Mifflin
Labatt, Lori, and Bruce Litteljohn, eds. 1992. *Islands of Hope: Ontario's
  Parks and Wilderness*. Willowdale: Firefly Books
Rowe, J.S. 1972. *Forest Regions of Canada*. Ottawa: Canadian Forestry
  Service
Sutton, Ann, and Myron Sutton. 1985. *The Audubon Society Field Guide to
  Eastern Forests*. New York: Knopf
Theberge, John, ed. 1989. *Legacy: The Natural History of Ontario*. Toronto:
  McClelland and Stewart

Peterson and Audubon field guides are available on a wide variety of
topics relating to natural history.

NATURE RECORDINGS

Brigham, Monty. *Birds of Canada*. 1993. Vols 1–3. Holborne (available
  Box 1061, Manotick, Ont, K4M 1A9)
Cornell Laboratory of Ornithology. *Guide to Bird Sounds*
Cornell Laboratory of Ornithology with Federation of Ontario Natural-
  ists. *Songs of the Warblers of North America*. Vols 1–3
Elliott, Lang. 1992. *The Calls of Frogs and Toads: Eastern and Central North
  America*. Ithaca, New York: NatureSound Studio
Federation of Ontario Naturalists. *Sounds of Nature Recordings*. Vol. 1:
  Sounds of Spring; Vol. 6: *Finches;* Vol. 8: *Thrushes, Wrens, and Mocking-
  birds*

Walton, Richard K., and Robert W. Lawson. 1989. *Birding by Ear: Eastern*. Peterson Field Guide. Boston: Houghton Mifflin

MAGAZINES

Birder's Journal
Birds of the Wild
The Canadian Field-Naturalist   The Ottawa Field-Naturalists' Club
Nature Canada   Canadian Nature Federation
Ontario Birds   Ontario Field Ornithologists
Seasons   Federation of Ontario Naturalists
Wildflower   Canadian Wildflower Society

FIELD CHECKLISTS

Provincial field checklists of birds (1994), mammals (1993), and reptiles and amphibians (1988) can be obtained from the Federation of Ontario Naturalists. Many naturalists' clubs across the province also produce local bird checklists.

NATURALISTS' CLUBS

Contact FON for an up-to-date listing of clubs and addresses.

SOURCES OF MAPS

Ontario Official Road Map. Ministry of Transportation local offices (see blue pages in phone book); or General Distribution Services, 34 Lesmill Rd, Don Mills, Ont, M3B 2T6, 1-800-387-0141; or Ministry of Citizenship, Culture, and Recreation in Toronto (1-800-ONTARIO)
Ontario Transportation Map Series. Nos 1–8 (covers Thessalon, Sudbury, and North Bay southward). Ministry of Transportation local offices or General Distribution Services (see above)
Topographic Maps. Ministry of Natural Resources Information Centre, Toronto, or Canada Map Office, Ottawa (see address listings)
Geological Maps. See sources for topographic maps.
Geological Highway Maps (northern and southern Ontario). Ministry of Northern Development and Mines (see address listing under Mines and Minerals Information Centre)

FEDERATION OF ONTARIO NATURALISTS' PUBLICATIONS

The FON produces numerous publications – books, pamphlets, check-lists, posters, education kits, videos, nature recordings, etc. – relating to natural history and conservation. Themes covered range from water-way parks and wetlands to nature reserves and naturalizing your back-yard. Contact FON for a catalogue.

FIELD TRIPS

The Federation of Ontario Naturalists organizes numerous field out-ings throughout the year, ranging from butterfly walks to canoe trips in northern Ontario to an annual camp on the Bruce Peninsula. Dozens of FON federated naturalists' clubs across the province offer extensive programs of field trips. Contact FON for trip listings and addresses of local clubs. National, provincial, and municipal parks, conservation authorities, and other agencies may also offer guided nature walks.

BIRDING LINES

For up-to-date information on birds to be seen locally, call the follow-ing:

Ontario Rare Bird Alert (Toronto) 416-350-3000 ext 2293 (touch tone
    only)
Hamilton (Hamilton Field Naturalists) 905-648-9537
London (McIlwraith Field Naturalists) 519-473-5853
Oshawa (Durham Region Field Naturalists) 905-576-2738
Ottawa (Ottawa Field-Naturalists' Club) 613-825-7444
Point Pelee (Point Pelee National Park) 519-322-2371
Sault Ste Marie (Sault Naturalists of Ontario and Michigan)
    705-256-2790
Windsor (Essex County Field Naturalists) 519-252-2473

Useful Addresses

Association of Conservation Authorities of Ontario, Box 11, 120 Bayview Pkwy, Newmarket, Ont, L3Y 4W3, 905-895-0716

Bruce Trail Association, Box 857, Hamilton, Ont, L8N 3N9, 905-529-6821

Canada Map Office, 130 Bentley Ave, Nepean, Ont, K2E 6G9, 1-800-465-6277

Canadian Recreational Canoeing Association, Box 398, 446 Main St W, Merrickville, Ont, K0G 1N0, 613-269-2910

Canadian Wildlife Service, Place Vincent Massey, 351 St Joseph Blvd, Hull, Que, K1A OH3

Federation of Ontario Naturalists, 355 Lesmill Rd, Don Mills, Ont, M3B 2W8, 416-444-8419 or 1-800-440-2366, FAX 416-444-9866

Hike Ontario, 1185 Eglinton Ave E, Suite 411, North York, Ont, M3C 3C6, 1-800-422-0552

Mines and Minerals Information Centre (Ministry of Northern Development and Mines), M2-17 Macdonald Block, 900 Bay St, Toronto, Ont, M7A 1C3, 416-314-3800

Ministry of Natural Resources Information Centre, M1-73 Macdonald Block, 900 Bay St, Toronto, Ont, M7A 2C1, 416-314-2000

National Capital Commission, 161 Laurier St, Ottawa, Ont, K1P 6J6, 613-239-5000 (visitor centre) or 613-239-5595 (conservation section)

Niagara Escarpment Commission, 232 Guelph St, Georgetown, Ont, L7G 4B1, 905-877-5191

Ontario Natural Heritage Information Centre, Box 7000, Peterborough, Ont, K9J 8M5, 705-745-6767

Parks Canada, Jules Leger Building, 10th floor, 25 Eddy St, Hull, Que,
K1A 0M5
World Wildlife Fund Canada, 90 Eglinton Ave E, Toronto, Ont,
M4P 2Z7

MINISTRY OF NATURAL RESOURCES

MNR offices across the province are able to provide the public with
information on forestry, wildlife, provincial parks, nature reserves, etc.
Check the blue pages of the phone book for local office locations.

CONSERVATION AUTHORITIES

Ausable-Bayfield Conservation Authority, RR 3, Exeter, Ont,
N0M 1S5, 519-235-2610
Cataraqui Region Conservation Authority, Box 160, 1641 Perth Rd,
Glenburnie, Ont, K0H 1S0, 613-546-4228
Catfish Creek Conservation Authority, RR 5, Aylmer, Ont, N5H 2R4,
519-773-9037
Central Lake Ontario Conservation Authority, 100 Whiting Ave,
Oshawa, Ont, L1H 3T3, 905-579-0411
Credit Valley Conservation Authority, 1255 Derry Rd W, Meadowvale,
Ont, L5N 6R4, 905-670-1615
Crowe Valley Conservation Authority, Box 416, Marmora, Ont,
K0K 2M0, 613-472-3137
Essex Region Conservation Authority, 360 Fairview Ave W, Essex,
Ont, N8M 1Y6, 519-776-5209
Ganaraska Region Conservation Authority, Box 328, Port Hope, Ont,
L1A 3W4, 905-885-8173
Grand River Conservation Authority, 400 Clyde Rd, Box 729, Cam-
bridge, Ont, N1R 5W6, 519-621-2761
Grey Sauble Conservation Authority, RR 4, Inglis Falls Rd, Owen
Sound, Ont, N4K 5N6, 519-376-3076
Halton Region Conservation Authority, 2596 Britannia Rd W, RR 2,
Milton, Ont, L9T 2X6, 905-336-1158
Hamilton Region Conservation Authority, 838 Mineral Springs Rd,
Box 7099, Ancaster, Ont, L9G 3L3, 905-525-2181
Kawartha Region Conservation Authority, Kenrei Park Rd, RR 1,
Lindsay, Ont, K9V 4R1, 705-328-2271

Kettle Creek Conservation Authority, RR 8, St Thomas, Ont, N5P 3T3, 519-631-1270

Lake Simcoe Region Conservation Authority, 120 Bayview Ave, Box 282, Newmarket, Ont, L3Y 4X1, 905-895-1281

Lakehead Region Conservation Authority, 130 Concession Rd, Box 3476, Thunder Bay, Ont, P7B 5J9, 807-344-5857

Long Point Region Conservation Authority, RR 3, Simcoe, Ont, N3Y 4K2, 519-428-4623

Lower Thames Valley Conservation Authority, 100 Thames St, Chatham, Ont, N7L 2Y8, 519-354-7310

Lower Trent Region Conservation Authority, 441 Front St, Trenton, Ont, K8V 6C1, 613-394-4829

Maitland Valley Conservation Authority, Marietta St, Box 127, Wroxeter, Ont, N0G 2X0, 519-335-3557

Mattagami Region Conservation Authority, 100 Lakeshore Rd, Timmins, Ont, P4N 8R5, 705-264-5309

Metro Toronto and Region Conservation Authority, 5 Shoreham Dr, North York, Ont, M3N 1S4, 416-661-6600

Mississippi Valley Conservation Authority, Box 268, Lanark, Ont, K0G 1K0, 613-259-2421

Moira River Conservation Authority, Box 698, Belleville, Ont, K8N 5B3, 613-968-3434

Napanee Region Conservation Authority, c/o Box 698, Belleville, Ont, K8N 5B3, 613-354-3312 or 613-968-3434

Niagara Peninsula Conservation Authority, 2358 Centre St, Allanburg, Ont, L0S 1A0, 905-227-1013

Nickel District Conservation Authority, 200 Brady St, Sudbury, Ont, P3E 5K3, 705-674-5249

North Bay–Mattawa Conservation Authority, RR 5, Site 12, Comp 5, 233 Birchs Rd, North Bay, Ont, P1B 8Z4, 705-474-5420

Nottawasaga Valley Conservation Authority, RR 1, Angus, Ont, L0M 1B0, 705-424-1479

Otonabee Region Conservation Authority, Suite 200, Time Square, 380 Armour Rd, Peterborough, Ont, K9H 7L7, 705-745-5791

Prince Edward Region Conservation Authority, c/o Box 698, Belleville, Ont, K8N 5B3, 613-476-7408 or 613-968-3434

Raisin Region Conservation Authority, Box 429, 6589 Boundary Rd, Cornwall, Ont, K6H 5T2, 613-938-3611

Rideau Valley Conservation Authority, Box 599, Manotick, Ont, K4M 1A5, 613-692-3571

St Clair Region Conservation Authority, 205 Mill Pond Cresc, Strath-
roy, Ont, N7G 3P9, 519-245-3710

Saugeen Valley Conservation Authority, RR 1, Hanover, Ont, N4N
3B8, 519-364-1255

Sault Ste Marie Region Conservation Authority, 1100 Fifth Line East,
RR 2, Sault Ste Marie, Ont, P6A 5K7, 705-946-8530

South Nation River Conservation Authority, 15 Union St, Box 69,
Berwick, Ont, K0C 1G0, 613-984-2948

Upper Thames River Conservation Authority, 1424 Clarke Rd, London, Ont, N5V 5B9, 519-451-2800

Common and Scientific Name Equivalents for Species Cited

Flora

Adder's-mouth, Bog *Malaxis paludosa*

Adder's-mouth, Green *Malaxis unifolia*

Adder's-mouth, White *Malaxis monophyllos* ssp. *brachypoda*

Adder's-tongue Fern, Northern *Ophioglossum pusillum*

Agrimony, Hairy *Agrimonia pubescens*

Alder, Green *Alnus viridis* ssp. *crispa*

Alder, Speckled *Alnus incana* ssp. *rugosa*

Alexanders, Golden *Zizia aurea*

Alumroot *Heuchera americana*

Ammannia, Scarlet *Ammannia robusta*

Anemone, Cut-leaved *Anemone multifida*

Anemone, Wood *Anemone quinquefolia*

Apple *Malus pumila*

Arbutus, Trailing *Epigaea repens*

Arethusa *Arethusa bulbosa*

Arrow-grass, Marsh *Triglochin palustre*

Arrow-grass, Seaside *Triglochin maritimum*

Arrowhead, Grass-leaved *Sagittaria graminea*

Arrow-wood, Downy *Viburnum rafinesquianum*

Arrow-wood, Southern *Viburnum recognitum*

Ash, Black *Fraxinus nigra*

Ash, Blue *Fraxinus quadrangulata*

Ash, Green *Fraxinus pennsylvanica* var. *subintegerrima*

Ash, Red *Fraxinus pennsylvanica* var. *pennsylvanica*

Ash, White *Fraxinus americana*

Aspen, Large-toothed *Populus grandidentata*

Aspen, Trembling *Populus tremuloides*

Aster, Arrow-leaved *Aster urophyllus*
Aster, Azure *Aster oolentangiensis*
Aster, Bog *Aster nemoralis*
Aster, Bushy *Aster dumosus*
Aster, Large-leaved *Aster macrophyllus*
Aster, Pringle's *Aster pilosus* var. *pringlei*
Aster, Rush *Aster borealis*
Aster, Upland White *Solidago ptarmicoides*
Avens, Cut-leaved *Geum laciniatum*
Avens, Long-plumed Purple *Geum triflorum*
Avens, Water *Geum rivale*

Barnyard Grass, Walter's *Echinochloa walteri*
Bartonia, Yellow *Bartonia virginica*
Basswood *Tilia americana*
Bayberry *Myrica pensylvanica*
Beach Grass, American *Ammophila breviligulata*
Beak-rush, Brownish *Rhynchospora fusca*
Beak-rush, White *Rhynchospora alba*
Bearberry *Arctostaphylos uva-ursi*
Bearberry, Alpine *Arctostaphylos alpina*
Beardtongue, Foxglove *Penstemon digitalis*
Beardtongue, Hairy *Penstemon hirsutus*
Bedstraw, Northern *Galium boreale*

Beech, American *Fagus grandifolia*
Beech Fern, Northern *Phegopteris connectilis*
Beech Fern, Southern *Phegopteris hexagonoptera*
Beechdrops *Epifagus virginiana*
Beggar's-ticks, Small *Bidens discoidea*
Beggar's-ticks, Swamp *Bidens tripartita*
Bellflower, Marsh *Campanula aparinoides*
Bellflower, Tall *Campanula americana*
Bellwort, Large-flowered *Uvularia grandiflora*
Bellwort, Perfoliate *Uvularia perfoliata*
Bellwort, Sessile-leaved *Uvularia sessilifolia*
Bergamot, Wild *Monarda fistulosa*
Bilberry, Alpine *Vaccinium uliginosum*
Bindweed, Fringed *Polygonum cilinode*
Birch, Dwarf *Betula glandulosa*
Birch, Gray *Betula populifolia*
Birch, Swamp *Betula pumila*
Birch, White *Betula papyrifera*
Birch, Yellow *Betula alleghaniensis*
Bistort, Alpine *Polygonum viviparum*
Bittersweet, Climbing *Celastrus scandens*
Black-eyed Susan *Rudbeckia hirta*
Bladdernut *Staphylea trifolia*
Bladderwort, Horned *Utricularia cornuta*
Bladderwort, Purple *Utricularia purpurea*

Bladderwort, Small *Utricularia minor*

Bladderwort, Twin-scaped *Utricularia geminiscapa*

Blazing-star, Cylindric *Liatris cylindracea*

Blazing-star, Rough *Liatris aspera*

Blazing-star, Spiked *Liatris spicata*

Bloodroot *Sanguinaria canadensis*

Blue Grass, Glaucous *Poa glauca*

Blue-beech *Carpinus caroliniana*

Blueberry, Dryland *Vaccinium pallidum*

Blueberry, Highbush *Vaccinium corymbosum*

Blueberry, Low Sweet *Vaccinium angustifolium*

Blueberry, Velvet-leaf *Vaccinium myrtilloides*

Blue-eyed Grass, White *Sisyrinchium albidum*

Blue-hearts *Buchnera americana*

Blue-joint, Canada *Calamagrostis canadensis*

Bluestem, Big *Andropogon gerardii*

Bluestem, Little *Schizachyrium scoparium*

Bluets, Long-leaved *Hedyotis longifolia*

Brome, Kalm's *Bromus kalmii*

Buckbean *Menyanthes trifoliata*

Buckeye, Ohio *Aesculus glabra*

Buckthorn, Alder-leaved *Rhamnus alnifolia*

Bugloss, Viper's *Echium vulgare*

Bulblet Fern *Cystopteris bulbifera*

Bulrush, Clinton's *Scirpus clintonii*

Bulrush, Hudsonian *Scirpus hudsonianus*

Bulrush, Shy *Scirpus verecundus*

Bulrush, Slender *Scirpus heterochaetus*

Bulrush, Smith's *Scirpus smithii*

Bulrush, Soft-stem *Scirpus validus*

Bunchberry *Cornus canadensis*

Burning Bush *Euonymus atropurpurea*

Bur-reed, Small *Sparganium natans*

Bush-clover, Hairy *Lespedeza hirta*

Bush-clover, Round-headed *Lespedeza capitata*

Bush-clover, Wandlike *Lespedeza intermedia*

Buttercup, Early *Ranunculus fascicularis*

Buttercup, Hispid *Ranunculus hispidus*

Buttercup, Prairie *Ranunculus rhomboideus*

Buttercup, Seaside *Ranunculus cymbalaria*

Buttercup, Yellow Water *Ranunculus flabellaris*

Butterfly-weed *Asclepias tuberosa*

Butternut *Juglans cinerea*

Butterwort *Pinguicula vulgaris*

Buttonbush *Cephalanthus occidentalis*

Cactus, Brittle Prickly-pear *Opuntia fragilis*

Cactus, Prickly-pear *Opuntia humifusa*

Calamint, Low *Calamintha arkansana*

Calypso *Calypso bulbosa*

Camass, White *Zigadenus elegans*

Campion, Bladder *Silene vulgaris*

Canary Grass, Reed *Phalaris arundinacea*

Caragana *Caragana arborescens*

Cardinal-flower *Lobelia cardinalis*

Carex sedge *Carex* sp.

Carrion-flower *Smilax herbacea*

Carrot, Wild *Daucus carota*

Cattail, Common *Typha latifolia*

Cattail, Narrow-leaved *Typha angustifolia*

Cedar, Red *Juniperus virginiana*

Cedar, White *Thuja occidentalis*

Chain Fern, Virginia *Woodwardia virginica*

Cherry, Black *Prunus serotina*

Cherry, Choke *Prunus virginiana*

Cherry, Pin *Prunus pensylvanica*

Cherry, Sand *Prunus pumila*

Chervil, Creeping *Chaerophyllum procumbens*

Chestnut, American *Castanea dentata*

Chicory *Cichorium intybus*

Chokeberry, Black *Aronia melanocarpa*

Christmas Fern *Polystichum acrostichoides*

Cinnamon Fern *Osmunda cinnamomea*

Cinquefoil, Marsh *Potentilla palustris*

Cinquefoil, Shrubby *Potentilla fruticosa*

Cinquefoil, Strange *Potentilla paradoxa*

Cinquefoil, Tall White *Potentilla arguta*

Cinquefoil, Three-toothed *Potentilla tridentata*

Clammyweed *Polanisia dodecandra*

Clearweed *Pilea pumila*

Clearweed, Spring *Pilea fontana*

Cliffbrake, Purple-stemmed *Pellaea atropurpurea*

Cliffbrake, Slender *Cryptogramma stelleri*

Cliffbrake, Smooth *Pellaea glabella*

Clintonia, Yellow *Clintonia borealis*

Cloudberry *Rubus chamaemorus*

Clubmoss, Bog *Lycopodium inundatum*

Clubmoss, Mountain *Lycopodium selago*

Cocklebur, Common *Xanthium strumarium*

Coffee Tree, Kentucky *Gymnocladus dioicus*

Cohosh, Black *Cimicifuga racemosa*

Cohosh, Blue *Caulophyllum thalictroides*

Colicroot *Aletris farinosa*

Collomia, Narrow-leaved *Collomia linearis*

Columbine, Wild *Aquilegia canadensis*

Columbo, American *Frasera caroliniensis*

Coneflower, Gray-headed *Ratibida pinnata*

Coralroot, Late *Corallorhiza odontorhiza*

Coralroot, Spotted *Corallorhiza maculata*

Coralroot, Striped *Corallorhiza striata*

Cord Grass, Tall *Spartina pectinata*

Coreopsis, Lance-leaved *Coreopsis lanceolata*

Coreopsis, Tall *Coreopsis tripteris*

Corydalis, Golden *Corydalis aurea*

Corydalis, Pale Yellow *Corydalis flavula*

Corydalis, Pink *Corydalis sempervirens*

Cotton-grass, Sheathed *Eriophorum vaginatum*

Cottonwood *Populus deltoides*

Cowslip, Virginia *Mertensia virginica*

Crabapple, Wild *Malus coronaria*

Cranberry, Highbush *Viburnum trilobum*

Cranberry, Mountain *Vaccinium vitis-idaea*

Cranberry, Small *Vaccinium oxycoccos*

Crane's-bill, Bicknell's *Geranium bicknellii*

Crane's-bill, Carolina *Geranium carolinianum*

Cress, Lake *Armoracia lacustris*

Cress, Purple Spring *Cardamine douglassii*

Crocus, Prairie *Pulsatilla patens*

Crowberry, Black *Empetrum nigrum*

Cucumber, Bur *Sicyos angulatus*

Cucumber-root, Indian *Medeola virginiana*

Cucumber-tree *Magnolia acuminata*

Culver's-root *Veronicastrum virginicum*

Cup-plant *Silphium perfoliatum*

Currant, Bristly Black *Ribes lacustre*

Cyperus, Houghton's *Cyperus houghtonii*

Cyperus, Low *Cyperus diandrus*

Cyperus, Schweinitz's *Cyperus schweinitzii*

Cyperus, Yellow *Cyperus flavescens*

Daisy, Lakeside *Hymenoxys acaulis*

Daisy, Ox-eye *Chrysanthemum leucanthemum*

Dame's Rocket *Hesperis matronalis*

Dandelion, Common *Taraxacum officinale*

Deerberry *Vaccinium stamineum*

Dewberry, Swamp *Rubus hispidus*

Dewdrop *Dalibarda repens*

Dock, Great Water *Rumex orbiculatus*

Dock, Prairie *Silphium terebinthinaceum*

Dogwood, Alternate-leaved *Cornus alternifolia*

Dogwood, Flowering *Cornus florida*

Dogwood, Red-osier *Cornus stolonifera*

Dogwood, Rough-leaved *Cornus drummondii*

Dogwood, Silky *Cornus amomum*

Dragonhead *Dracocephalum parviflorum*

Dragonhead, False *Physostegia virginiana*

Dropseed, Ensheathed *Sporobolus vaginiflorus*

Dropseed, Prairie *Sporobolus heterolepis*

Dropseed, Rough *Sporobolus asper*

Dropseed, Sand *Sporobolus cryptandrus*

duckweed *Lemna* sp.

Dune Grass, American *Leymus mollis*

Dutchman's Breeches *Dicentra cucullaria*

Elder, Red-berried *Sambucus racemosa*

Elm, American *Ulmus americana*

Elm, Rock *Ulmus thomasii*

Elm, Slippery *Ulmus rubra*

Evening-primrose, Oakes' *Oenothera oakesiana*

Eyebright *Euphrasia nemorosa*

False Foxglove, Downy *Aureolaria virginica*

False Foxglove, Fern-leaved *Aureolaria pedicularia*

False Mermaid *Floerkea proserpinacoides*

Fescue, Rough *Festuca hallii*

Fescue, Western *Festuca occidentalis*

Feverwort *Triosteum perfoliatum*

Fir, Balsam *Abies balsamea*

Fireweed *Epilobium angustifolium*

Flax, Ridged Yellow *Linum striatum*

Flax, Stiff Yellow *Linum medium*

Flax, Virginia Yellow *Linum virginianum*

Floating Heart, Cordate *Nymphoides cordata*

Flowering-rush *Butomus umbellatus*

Fragile Fern *Cystopteris fragilis*

Fragrant Cliff Fern *Dryopteris fragrans*

Frog's-bit *Hydrocharis morsus-ranae*

Frostweed *Helianthemum canadense*

Fumitory, Climbing *Adlumia fungosa*

Garlic, Wild *Allium canadense*

Gaura, Biennial *Gaura biennis*

Gentian, Closed *Gentiana andrewsii*

Gentian, Fringed *Gentianopsis crinita*

Gentian, Red-stemmed *Gentiana rubricaulis*

Gentian, Smaller Fringed *Gentianopsis virgata*

Gentian, Stiff *Gentianella quinquefolia*

Gentian, White Prairie *Gentiana flavida*

Geranium, Wild *Geranium maculatum*

Gerardia, Purple *Agalinis purpurea*

Gerardia, Slender *Agalinis tenuifolia*

Gerardia, Small-flowered *Agalinis paupercula*

Ginger, Wild *Asarum canadense*

Glade Fern, Silvery *Athyrium thelypterioides*

Goat's-rue *Tephrosia virginiana*

Goldenrod, Alpine *Solidago multiradiata*

Goldenrod, Bog *Solidago uliginosa*

Goldenrod, Elm-leaved *Solidago ulmifolia*

Goldenrod, Gray-stemmed Prairie *Solidago missouriensis*

Goldenrod, Ohio *Solidago ohioensis*

Goldenrod, Riddell's *Solidago riddellii*

Goldenrod, Rough-leaved *Solidago patula*

Goldenrod, Sharp-leaved *Solidago arguta*

Goldenrod, Showy *Solidago speciosa*

Goldenrod, Stiff-leaved *Solidago rigida*

Goldenrod, Ten-flowered Showy *Solidago nemoralis* ssp. *decemflora*

Goldenrod, Zigzag *Solidago flexicaulis*

Goldthread *Coptis trifolia*

Goosegrass *Puccinellia phryganodes*

Grape, Riverbank *Vitis riparia*

Grape, Summer *Vitis aestivalis*

Grape Fern, Blunt-lobed *Botrychium oneidense*

Grape Fern, Daisy-leaved *Botrychium matricariaefolium*

Grape Fern, Dwarf *Botrychium simplex*

Grape Fern, Triangle *Botrychium lanceolatum*

Grass-of-Parnassus *Parnassia glauca*

Grass-pink *Calopogon tuberosus*

Green Dragon *Arisaema dracontium*

Greenbrier, Bristly *Smilax hispida*

Gromwell, False *Onosmodium molle*

Groundnut *Apios americana*

Gum, Black *Nyssa sylvatica*

Hackberry, Common *Celtis occidentalis*

Hackberry, Dwarf *Celtis tenuifolia*

Harbinger-of-spring *Erigenia bulbosa*

Harebell *Campanula rotundifolia*

Hart's-tongue Fern *Phyllitis scolopendrium*

Hawkweed, Hairy *Hieracium gronovii*

Hawkweed, Orange *Hieracium aurantiacum*

Hawkweed, Panicled *Hieracium paniculatum*

hawthorn *Crataegus* sp.

Hay-scented Fern *Dennstaedtia punctilobula*

Hazel, American *Corylus americana*

Hazel, Beaked *Corylus cornuta*

Heath, Beach *Hudsonia tomentosa*

Hedge-hyssop, Golden *Gratiola aurea*

Helleborine *Epipactis helleborine*

Hemlock, Eastern *Tsuga canadensis*

Hepatica, Round-lobed *Hepatica americana*

Hepatica, Sharp-lobed *Hepatica acutiloba*

Hickory, Big Shellbark *Carya laciniosa*

Hickory, Bitternut *Carya cordiformis*

Hickory, Pignut *Carya glabra*

Hickory, Shagbark *Carya ovata*

Hobblebush *Viburnum lantanoides*

Hog Peanut *Amphicarpaea bracteata*

Holly, Mountain *Nemopanthus mucronatus*

Holly Fern, Braun's *Polystichum braunii*

Holly Fern, Northern *Polystichum lonchitis*

Honeysuckle, Bush *Diervilla lonicera*

Honeysuckle, Fly *Lonicera canadensis*

Honeysuckle, Hairy *Lonicera hirsuta*

Honeysuckle, Morrow's *Lonicera morrowii*

Honeysuckle, Mountain Fly *Lonicera villosa*

Honeysuckle, Swamp Fly *Lonicera oblongifolia*

Honeysuckle, Tartarian *Lonicera tatarica*

Hop-hornbeam *Ostrya virginiana*

Hops, Common *Humulus lupulus*

Hop-tree *Ptelea trifoliata*

Horsebalm *Collinsonia canadensis*

Horsetail, Marsh *Equisetum palustre*

Horsetail, Meadow *Equisetum pratense*

Huckleberry, Black *Gaylussacia baccata*

Hyacinth, Wild *Camassia scilloides*

Hyssop, Yellow Giant *Agastache nepetoides*

Indian Grass *Sorghastrum nutans*

Indian-pipe *Monotropa uniflora*

Indian-plantain, Tuberous *Cacalia plantaginea*

Indigo, Wild *Baptisia tinctoria*

Interrupted Fern *Osmunda claytoniana*

Iris, Dwarf Lake *Iris lacustris*

Ironweed, Tall *Vernonia gigantea*

Jack-in-the-pulpit *Arisaema triphyllum*

Joe-Pye-weed, Sweet *Eupatorium purpureum*

Juniper, Common *Juniperus communis*

Juniper, Creeping *Juniperus horizontalis*

Knotweed, Carey's *Polygonum careyi*

Knotweed, Virginia *Polygonum virginianum*

Labrador Tea *Ledum groenlandicum*

Ladies'-tresses, Case's *Spiranthes casei*

Ladies'-tresses, Great Plains *Spiranthes magnicamporum*

Ladies'-tresses, Hooded *Spiranthes romanzoffiana*

Ladies'-tresses, Nodding *Spiranthes cernua*

Ladies'-tresses, Northern Slender *Spiranthes lacera* var. *lacera*

Ladies'-tresses, Shining *Spiranthes lucida*

Ladies'-tresses, Slender *Spiranthes lacera*

Ladies'-tresses, Southern Slender *Spiranthes lacera* var. *gracilis*

Lady Fern, Northeastern *Athyrium filix-femina*

Lady's-slipper, Large Yellow *Cypripedium calceolus* var. *pubescens*

Lady's-slipper, Pink *Cypripedium acaule*

Lady's-slipper, Ram's-head *Cypripedium arietinum*

Lady's-slipper, Showy *Cypripedium reginae*

Lady's-slipper, Small Yellow *Cypripedium calceolus* var. *parviflorum*

Lady's-slipper, Sparrow's-egg *Cypripedium passerinum*

Lady's-slipper, Yellow *Cypripedium calceolus*

Laurel, Pale *Kalmia polifolia*

Laurel, Sheep *Kalmia angustifolia*

Leafcup, Small-flowered *Polymnia canadensis*

Leatherleaf *Chamaedaphne calyculata*

Leatherwood *Dirca palustris*

Leek, Wild *Allium tricoccum*

Licorice, Wild *Glycyrrhiza lepidota*

Lily, Michigan *Lilium michiganense*

Lily, Wood *Lilium philadelphicum*

Lily-of-the-valley, Wild *Maianthemum canadense*

Littorella, American *Littorella americana*

Live-forever *Sedum telephium*

Lizard's-tail *Saururus cernuus*

Lobelia, Great *Lobelia siphilitica*

Lobelia, Kalm's *Lobelia kalmii*

Lobelia, Pale-spiked *Lobelia spicata*

Locust, Honey *Gleditsia triacanthos*

Loosestrife, Prairie *Lysimachia quadriflora*

Loosestrife, Purple *Lythrum salicaria*

Loosestrife, Swamp *Decodon verticillatus*

Loosestrife, Whorled *Lysimachia quadrifolia*

Loosestrife, Winged *Lythrum alatum*

Lopseed *Phryma leptostachya*

Lotus, American *Nelumbo lutea*

Lousewort, Swamp *Pedicularis lanceolata*

Lupine, Wild *Lupinus perennis*

Maidenhair Fern, Northern *Adiantum pedatum*

Male Fern *Dryopteris filix-mas*

Mallow, Virginia *Sida hermaphrodita*

Mandarin, Yellow *Disporum lanuginosum*

Manna Grass, Long *Glyceria melicaria*

Maple, Black *Acer saccharum* ssp. *nigrum*

Maple, Manitoba *Acer negundo*

Maple, Mountain *Acer spicatum*

Maple, Red *Acer rubrum*

Maple, Silver *Acer saccharinum*

Maple, Striped *Acer pensylvanicum*

Maple, Sugar *Acer saccharum*

Mare's-tail *Hippuris vulgaris*

Marsh Fern *Thelypteris palustris*

Marsh-marigold *Caltha palustris*

Marsh-marigold, Floating *Caltha natans*

Massachusetts Fern *Thelypteris simulata*

Mayapple *Podophyllum peltatum*

Meadow-beauty, Virginia *Rhexia virginica*

Meadow-rue, Early *Thalictrum dioicum*

Meadow-rue, Purple *Thalictrum dasycarpum*

Meadow-rue, Waxy *Thalictrum revolutum*

Melic Grass, Smith's *Melica smithii*

Mercury, Three-sided *Acalypha virginica*

Miami-mist *Phacelia purshii*

Milk-vetch, Canada *Astragalus canadensis*

Milk-vetch, Cooper's *Astragalus neglectus*

Milkweed, Common *Asclepias syriaca*

Milkweed, Green *Asclepias viridiflora*

Milkweed, Poke *Asclepias exaltata*

Milkweed, Purple *Asclepias purpurascens*

Milkweed, Sullivant's *Asclepias sullivantii*

Milkweed, Swamp *Asclepias incarnata*

Milkweed, Whorled *Asclepias verticillata*

Milkwort, Field *Polygala sanguinea*

Milkwort, Pink *Polygala incarnata*

Milkwort, Whorled *Polygala verticillata*

Miterwort, Naked *Mitella nuda*

Monkey-flower, Winged *Mimulus alatus*

Moonseed *Menispermum canadense*

Moonwort *Botrychium lunaria*

Moss-pink *Phlox subulata*

Mountain-ash, Showy *Sorbus decora*

Mountain-avens, White *Dryas integrifolia*

Mountain-mint, Virginia *Pycnanthemum virginianum*

Mountain-rice, Canada *Oryzopsis canadensis*

Muhly Grass, Uniflora *Muhlenbergia uniflora*

Mulberry, Red *Morus rubra*

Mullein, Common *Verbascum thapsus*

Mustard, Aquatic *Subularia aquatica* ssp. *americana*

Mustard, Garlic *Alliaria petiolata*

Naiad, Bushy *Najas flexilis*

Naiad, Slender *Najas gracillima*

Nannyberry *Viburnum lentago*

New Jersey Tea *Ceanothus americanus*

New Jersey Tea, Narrow-leaved *Ceanothus herbaceus*

New York Fern *Thelypteris noveboracensis*

Ninebark *Physocarpus opulifolius*

Nut-rush, Low *Scleria verticillata*

Oak, Black *Quercus velutina*

Oak, Bur *Quercus macrocarpa*

Oak, Chinquapin *Quercus muehlenbergii*

Oak, Dwarf Chinquapin *Quercus prinoides*

Oak, Hill's *Quercus ellipsoidalis*

Oak, Pin *Quercus palustris*

Oak, Red *Quercus rubra*

Oak, Swamp White *Quercus bicolor*

Oak, White *Quercus alba*

Oak Fern *Gymnocarpium dryopteris*

Oak Fern, Limestone *Gymnocarpium robertianum*

Oats, False *Trisetum spicatum*

Onion, Nodding Wild *Allium cernuum*

Orchid, Alaska *Piperia unalascensis*

Orchid, Blunt-leaved *Platanthera obtusata*

Orchid, Hooker's *Platanthera hookeri*

Orchid, Large Purple Fringed *Platanthera grandiflora*

Orchid, Long-bracted *Coeloglossum viride*

Orchid, Northern Green *Platanthera hyperborea*

Orchid, Prairie White Fringed *Platanthera leucophaea*

Orchid, Ragged Fringed *Platanthera lacera*

Orchid, Round-leaved *Platanthera orbiculata*

Orchid, Small Purple Fringed *Platanthera psycodes*

Orchid, Tall White Bog *Platanthera dilatata*

Orchid, Three-birds *Triphora trianthophora*

Orchid, Tubercled *Platanthera flava*

Orchis, Showy *Galearis spectabilis*

Ostrich Fern, American *Matteuccia struthiopteris*

Oswego Tea *Monarda didyma*

Ox-eye *Heliopsis helianthoides*

Oysterleaf *Mertensia maritima*

Paintbrush, Indian *Castilleja coccinea*

Panic Grass, Forked *Panicum dichotomum*

Panic Grass, Impoverished *Panicum depauperatum*

Panic Grass, Northern *Panicum boreale*

Panic Grass, Somewhat Hairy *Panicum subvillosum*

Parsley Fern *Cryptogramma crispa*

Parsnip, Cow *Heracleum lanatum*

Parsnip, Wild *Pastinaca sativa*

Pawpaw *Asimina triloba*

Pea, Beach *Lathyrus japonicus*

Pearlwort, Knotted *Sagina nodosa*

Pennyroyal, False *Trichostema brachiatum*

Pickerelweed *Pontederia cordata*

Pilewort *Erechtites hieracifolia*

Pimpernel, False *Lindernia dubia*

Pimpernel, Yellow *Taenidia integerrima*

Pine, Jack *Pinus banksiana*

Pine, Pitch *Pinus rigida*

Pine, Red *Pinus resinosa*

Pine, Scots *Pinus sylvestris*

Pine, White *Pinus strobus*

Pinedrops *Pterospora andromedea*

Pinesap *Monotropa hypopithys*

Pipewort, Common *Eriocaulon aquaticum*

Pitcher-plant *Sarracenia purpurea*

Plantain, Seaside *Plantago maritima*

Plum, Canada *Prunus nigra*

Plum, Wild *Prunus americana*

Pogonia, Rose *Pogonia ophioglossoides*

Pogonia, Smaller Whorled *Isotria medeoloides*

Poison-ivy *Rhus radicans*

Polygala, Fringed *Polygala paucifolia*

Polypody, Rock *Polypodium virginianum*

Pond-lily, Yellow *Nuphar advenum*

Pondweed, Bicupulate *Potamogeton bicupulatus*

Pondweed, Blunt-leaved *Potamogeton obtusifolius*

Pondweed, Knotty *Potamogeton nodosus*

Poplar, Balsam *Populus balsamifera*

Poppy, Wood *Stylophorum diphyllum*

Porcupine Grass *Stipa spartea*

Potato-vine, Wild *Ipomoea pandurata*

Prickly-ash *Zanthoxylum americanum*

Primrose, Bird's-eye *Primula mistassinica*

Puccoon *Lithospermum caroliniense*

Puccoon, Hoary *Lithospermum canescens*

Puccoon, Incised *Lithospermum incisum*

Puttyroot *Aplectrum hyemale*

Pyrola, Arctic *Pyrola grandiflora*

Pyrola, Greenish-flowered *Pyrola chlorantha*

Pyrola, One-flowered *Moneses uniflora*

Pyrola, Pink *Pyrola asarifolia*

Pyrola, Round-leaved *Pyrola americana*

Quillwort, Eaton's *Isoetes eatonii*

Quillwort, Engelmann's *Isoetes engelmannii*

Quillwort, Lake *Isoetes lacustris*

Quillwort, Spiny-spored *Isoetes echinospora*

Ragwort, Balsam *Senecio pauperculus*

Ragwort, Marsh *Senecio congestus*

Raisin, Wild *Viburnum cassinoides*

Raspberry, Northern Dwarf *Rubus acaulis*

Raspberry, Purple-flowering *Rubus odoratus*

Rattlesnake Fern *Botrychium virginianum*

Rattlesnake-plantain, Checkered *Goodyera tesselata*

Rattlesnake-plantain, Downy *Goodyera pubescens*

Rattlesnake-plantain, Green-leaved *Goodyera oblongifolia*

Reed, Common *Phragmites australis*

Reedgrass, Stout Wood *Cinna arundinacea*

Rhodora *Rhododendron canadense*

Riverweed *Podostemum ceratophyllum*

Rock-cress, Hairy *Arabis hirsuta*

Rock-cress, Smooth *Arabis laevigata*

Rose, Multiflora *Rosa multiflora*

Rose, Pasture *Rosa carolina*

Rose, Prairie *Rosa setigera*

Rose, Prickly Wild *Rosa acicularis*

Rose, Smooth Wild *Rosa blanda*

Rose, Swamp *Rosa palustris*

Rosebay, Lapland *Rhododendron lapponicum*

Rose-mallow, Swamp *Hibiscus moscheutos*

Rosemary, Bog *Andromeda glaucophylla*

Royal Fern *Osmunda regalis*

Rue-anemone *Anemonella thalictroides*

Rush, Bayonet *Juncus militaris*

Rush, Brown-fruited *Juncus pelocarpus*

Rush, Prairie *Juncus interior*

Rush, Torrey's *Juncus torreyi*

Rush, Two-flowered *Juncus biflorus*

Russian-thistle *Salsola kali*

St John's-wort, Great *Hypericum ascyron*

St John's-wort, Kalm's *Hypericum kalmianum*

St John's-wort, Marsh *Triadenum virginicum*

St John's-wort, Shrubby *Hypericum prolificum*

Sand Grass, Purple *Triplasis purpurea*

Sandbur, Long-spined *Cenchrus longispinus*

Sandwort, Rock *Minuartia michauxii*

Sandwort, Seabeach *Honkenya peploides*

Sarsaparilla, Wild *Aralia nudicaulis*

Saskatoon-berry *Amelanchier alnifolia*

Sassafras *Sassafras albidum*

Satin Grass *Muhlenbergia mexicana*

Saxifrage, Early *Saxifraga virginiensis*

Saxifrage, Encrusted *Saxifraga paniculata*

Scouring-rush, Variegated *Equisetum variegatum*

Sea Rocket *Cakile edentula*

Sedge, Beaked *Carex utriculata*

Sedge, Black-edged *Carex nigromarginata*

Sedge, Broad-winged *Carex alata*

Sedge, Cattail *Carex typhina*

Sedge, Drooping *Carex prasina*

Sedge, Field *Carex conoidea*

Sedge, Gracilescens *Carex gracilescens*

Sedge, Hairy-fruited *Carex trichocarpa*

Sedge, Long *Carex folliculata*

Sedge, Pale *Carex pallescens*

Sedge, Porcupine *Carex hystericina*

Sedge, Prickly Bog *Carex atlantica*

Sedge, Sun-stimulated *Carex heleonastes*

Sedge, Tussock *Carex stricta*

Shinleaf *Pyrola elliptica*

Sicklepod *Arabis canadensis*

Silverrod *Solidago bicolor*

Silverweed *Potentilla anserina*

Skullcap, Marsh *Scutellaria galericulata*

Skunk-cabbage *Symplocarpus foetidus*

Snakeroot, Canada *Sanicula canadensis*

Snakeroot, Long-fruited *Sanicula trifoliata*

Snakeroot, Seneca *Polygala senega*

Sneezeweed *Helenium autumnale*

Snowberry *Symphoricarpos albus*

Snowberry, Creeping *Gaultheria hispidula*

Soapberry *Shepherdia canadensis*

Solomon's-seal, False *Maianthemum racemosum*

Solomon's-seal, Smooth *Polygonatum biflorum*

Solomon's-seal, Starry False *Maianthemum stellatum*

Spearmint *Mentha spicata*

Speedwell, Water *Veronica anagallis-aquatica*

Spicebush *Lindera benzoin*

Spiderwort, Ohio *Tradescantia ohiensis*

Spikemoss, Fen *Selaginella selaginoides*

Spikemoss, Prairie *Selaginella densa*

Spikenard *Aralia racemosa*

Spike-rush, Beaked *Eleocharis rostellata*

Spike-rush, Capitate *Eleocharis caribaea*

Spike-rush, Four-angled *Eleocharis quadrangulata*

Spike-rush, Horsetail *Eleocharis equisetoides*

Spike-rush, Robbins' *Eleocharis robbinsii*

Spleenwort, Ebony *Asplenium platyneuron*

Spleenwort, Green *Asplenium trichomanes-ramosum*

Spleenwort, Maidenhair *Asplenium trichomanes*

Spring-beauty, Carolina *Claytonia caroliniana*

Spring-beauty, Narrow-leaved *Claytonia virginica*

Spruce, Black *Picea mariana*

Spruce, Red *Picea rubens*

Spruce, White *Picea glauca*

Spurge, Flowering *Euphorbia corollata*

Spurge, Seaside *Chamaesyce polygonifolia*

Squashberry *Viburnum edule*

Squawroot *Conopholis americana*

Squirrel-corn *Dicentra canadensis*

Starflower *Trientalis borealis*

Stargrass, Water *Heteranthera dubia*

Stargrass, Yellow *Hypoxis hirsuta*

Starwort, Northern *Stellaria borealis*

stonecrop *Sedum* sp.

Strawberry, Barren *Waldsteinia fragarioides*

Strawberry-bush, Running *Euonymus obovata*

Sumac, Fragrant *Rhus aromatica*

Sumac, Poison *Rhus vernix*

Sumac, Shining *Rhus copallina*

Sumac, Smooth *Rhus glabra*

Sumac, Staghorn *Rhus typhina*

Sundew, Linear-leaved *Drosera linearis*

Sundew, Round-leaved *Drosera rotundifolia*

Sundew, Spatulate-leaved *Drosera intermedia*

Sundrops, Meadow *Oenothera pilosella*

Sunflower, Pale-leaved *Helianthus strumosus*

Sunflower, Tall *Helianthus giganteus*

Sunflower, Woodland *Helianthus divaricatus*

Swamp Candles *Lysimachia terrestris*

Sweet Cicely, Small *Osmorhiza depauperata*

Sweet Cicely, Soft *Osmorhiza claytonii*

Sweet Gale *Myrica gale*

Sweet-fern *Comptonia peregrina*

Switch Grass *Panicum virgatum*

Sycamore *Platanus occidentalis*

Tamarack *Larix laricina*

Tansy, Common *Tanacetum vulgare*

Tapegrass *Vallisneria americana*

Tearthumb, Halberd-leaved *Polygonum arifolium*

Thistle, Hill's *Cirsium hillii*

Thistle, Nodding *Carduus nutans*

Thistle, Pitcher's *Cirsium pitcheri*

Three-awned Grass, Purple *Aristida purpurascens*

Thrift *Armeria maritima*

Tick-trefoil, Large-bracted *Desmodium cuspidatum*

Tick-trefoil, Naked-flowered *Desmodium nudiflorum*

Tick-trefoil, Round-leaved *Desmodium rotundifolium*

Tick-trefoil, Showy *Desmodium canadense*

Toadflax, Bastard *Comandra umbellata*

Tofieldia, Sticky *Tofieldia glutinosa*

Toothwort, Cut-leaved *Cardamine concatenata*

Touch-me-not, Pale *Impatiens pallida*

Touch-me-not, Spotted *Impatiens capensis*

Trillium, Nodding *Trillium cernuum*

Trillium, Painted *Trillium undulatum*

Trillium, Red *Trillium erectum*

Trillium, Variegated *Trillium grandiflorum* f. *striatum*

Trillium, White *Trillium grandiflorum*

Trout-lily, White *Erythronium albidum*

Trout-lily, Yellow *Erythronium americanum*

Trumpet Creeper *Campsis radicans*

Tulip-tree *Liriodendron tulipifera*

Turtlehead *Chelone glabra*

Twayblade, Broad-lipped *Listera convallarioides*

Twayblade, Heart-leaved *Listera cordata*

Twayblade, Large *Liparis liliifolia*

Twayblade, Loesel's *Liparis loeselii*

Twayblade, Northern *Listera borealis*

Twayblade, Southern *Listera australis*

Twig-rush *Cladium mariscoides*

Twinflower *Linnaea borealis*

Twinleaf *Jeffersonia diphylla*

Twisted-stalk, Rose *Streptopus roseus*

Valerian, Swamp *Valeriana sitchensis*

Venus' Looking Glass *Triodanis perfoliata*

Vervain, Hoary *Verbena stricta*

Vervain, White *Verbena urticifolia*

Vetchling, Pale *Lathyrus ochroleucus*

Viburnum, Maple-leaved *Viburnum acerifolium*

Violet, Arrow-leaved *Viola sagittata*

Violet, Birdfoot *Viola pedata*

Violet, Canada *Viola canadensis*

Violet, Early Blue *Viola palmata*

Violet, Great-spurred *Viola selkirkii*

Violet, Green *Hybanthus concolor*

Voilet, Hook-spurred *Viola adunca*

Violet, Lance-leaved *Viola lanceolata*

Violet, New England Blue *Viola novae-angliae*

Violet, Northern White *Viola macloskeyi* ssp. *pallens*

Violet, Sweet White *Viola blanda*

Virginia Creeper *Parthenocissus quinquefolia*

Virgin's-bower, Purple *Clematis occidentalis*

Walking Fern *Asplenium rhizophyllum*

Wall-rue *Asplenium ruta-muraria*

Walnut, Black *Juglans nigra*

Water-hemp *Amaranthus tuberculatus*

Water-horehound, Stalked *Lycopus rubellus*

Water-horehound, Virginia *Lycopus virginicus*

Waterleaf, Appendaged *Hydrophyllum appendiculatum*

Waterleaf, Broad-leaved *Hydrophyllum canadense*

Waterleaf, Virginia *Hydrophyllum virginianum*

water-lily *Nymphaea* sp.

Water-marigold *Megalodonta beckii*

Water-milfoil, Green *Myriophyllum verticillatum*

Water-milfoil, Northern *Myriophyllum sibiricum*

Water-pennywort *Hydrocotyle americana*

Water-plantain, Grass-leaved *Alisma gramineum*

Water-shield *Brasenia schreberi*

Water-willow *Justicia americana*

Waterwort, Lesser *Elatine minima*

Waterwort, Long-stemmed *Elatine triandra*

Wedge Grass, Shining *Sphenopholis nitida*

Wheat Grass, Great Lakes *Elymus lanceolatus* ssp. *psammophilus*

Wild Rice, Northern *Zizania palustris*

Wild Rice, Southern *Zizania aquatica*

Wild-rye, Hairy *Elymus villosus*
Wild-rye, Virginia *Elymus virginicus*
Willow, Arctic *Salix arctica*
Willow, Bog *Salix pedicellaris*
Willow, Heart-leaved *Salix cordata*
Willow, Hoary *Salix candida*
Willow, Labrador *Salix arctophila*
Willow, Weeping *Salix babylonica*
Willow-herb, Downy *Epilobium strictum*
Willow-herb, Hairy *Epilobium hirsutum*
Wingstem *Verbesina alternifolia*
Winterberry *Ilex verticillata*
Wintergreen *Gaultheria procumbens*
Witch Grass, Tuckerman's *Panicum tuckermanii*
Witch-hazel *Hamamelis virginiana*
Wood Fern, Boott's *Dryopteris* x *boottii*
Wood Fern, Clinton's *Dryopteris clintoniana*
Wood Fern, Crested *Dryopteris cristata*
Wood Fern, Glandular *Dryopteris intermedia*
Wood Fern, Goldie's *Dryopteris goldiana*
Wood Fern, Marginal *Dryopteris marginalis*
Wood Fern, Spinulose *Dryopteris carthusiana*
Woodsia, Mountain *Woodsia scopulina*
Woodsia, Oregon *Woodsia oregana*
Woodsia, Smooth *Woodsia glabella*

Wormwood, Tall *Artemisia campestris*

Yam, Wild *Dioscorea quaternata*
Yellow-eyed Grass *Xyris montana*
Yellow-eyed Grass, Southern *Xyris difformis*
Yew, American *Taxus canadensis*

Non-vascular Plants

Cladina (lichen) *Cladina* spp.
earthstar *Geastrum* sp.
lichen, reindeer *Cladina rangifera* and other *Cladina* spp.
liverwort *Cololejeunea biddlecomiae*
liverwort *Conocephalum conicum*
liverwort *Lejeunea cavifolia*
liverwort *Plagiochila asplenioides*
Lung Lichen *Lobaria pulmonaria*
map lichen *Rhizocarpon* spp.
moss *Fissidens grandifrons*
moss *Gymnostomum aeruginosum*
moss *Gymnostomum recurvirostrum*
moss *Tortella tortuosa*
old man's beard (lichen) *Usnea* spp.
rock tripe (lichen) *Umbilicaria* spp.
Sphagnum (moss) *Sphagnum* spp.
Usnea (lichen) *Usnea* spp.
Xanthoria (lichen) *Xanthoria* spp.

Mammals

Badger *Taxidea taxus*
Bat, Eastern Small-footed *Myotis leibii*

Bear, Black *Ursus americanus*
Bear, Polar *Ursus maritimus*
Beaver *Castor canadensis*
Beluga *Delphinapterus leucas*
Bobcat *Lynx rufus*
Caribou *Rangifer tarandus*
Chipmunk, Eastern *Tamias striatus*
Chipmunk, Least *Tamias minimus*
Cottontail, Eastern *Sylvilagus floridanus*
Cougar *Felis concolor*
Coyote *Canis latrans*
Deer, White-tailed *Odocoileus virginianus*
Ermine *Mustela erminea*
Fisher *Martes pennanti*
Fox, Arctic *Alopex lagopus*
Fox, Gray *Urocyon cinereoargenteus*
Fox, Red *Vulpes vulpes*
Hare, European *Lepus europaeus*
Hare, Snowshoe *Lepus americanus*
Jackrabbit, White-tailed *Lepus townsendii*
Lemming, Northern Bog *Synaptomys borealis*
Lemming, Southern Bog *Synaptomys cooperi*
Lynx, Canada *Lynx canadensis*
Marten *Martes americana*
Mink *Mustela vison*
Mole, Eastern *Scalopus aquaticus*
Mole, Hairy-tailed *Parascalops breweri*
Mole, Star-nosed *Condylura cristata*
Moose *Alces alces*
Mouse, Baird's Deer *Peromyscus maniculatus bairdii*

Mouse, House *Mus musculus*
Mouse, Meadow Jumping *Zapus hudsonius*
Mouse, White-footed *Peromyscus leucopus*
Mouse, Woodland Jumping *Napaeozapus insignis*
Muskrat *Ondatra zibethicus*
Opossum, Virginia *Didelphis virginiana*
Otter, River *Lontra canadensis*
Porcupine *Erethizon dorsatum*
Raccoon *Procyon lotor*
Rat, Norway *Rattus norvegicus*
Seal, Bearded *Erignathus barbatus*
Seal, Harbor *Phoca vitulina*
Seal, Ringed *Phoca hispida*
Shrew, Black-backed *Sorex arcticus*
Shrew, Least *Cryptotis parva*
Shrew, Northern Short-tailed *Blarina brevicauda*
Shrew, Pygmy *Sorex hoyi*
Shrew, Smoky *Sorex fumeus*
Shrew, Water *Sorex palustris*
Skunk, Striped *Mephitis mephitis*
Squirrel, Franklin's Ground *Spermophilus franklinii*
Squirrel, Gray *Sciurus carolinensis*
Squirrel, Northern Flying *Glaucomys sabrinus*
Squirrel, Red *Tamiasciurus hudsonicus*
Squirrel, Southern Flying *Glaucomys volans*
Vole, Heath *Phenacomys intermedius*
Vole, Rock *Microtus chrotorrhinus*

Vole, Southern Red-backed *Clethrionomys gapperi*

Vole, Woodland *Pitymys pinetorum*

Walrus *Odobenus rosmarus*

Wapiti *Cervus elaphus*

Weasel, Long-tailed *Mustela frenata*

Whale, Bowhead *Balaena mysticetus*

Wolf, Gray *Canis lupus*

Wolverine *Gulo gulo*

Herpetofauna

Blanding's Turtle *Emydoidea blandingi*

Blue Racer *Coluber constrictor foxi*

Brown Snake, Northern *Storeria dekayi*

Bullfrog *Rana catesbeiana*

Chorus Frog, Boreal *Pseudacris triseriata maculata*

Chorus Frog, Midland *Pseudacris triseriata triseriata*

Cricket Frog, Blanchard's *Acris crepitans blanchardi*

Fox Snake, Eastern *Elaphe vulpina gloydi*

Garter Snake, Butler's *Thamnophis butleri*

Garter Snake, Eastern *Thamnophis sirtalis sirtalis*

Garter Snake, Red-sided *Thamnophis sirtalis parietalis*

Green Frog *Rana clamitans*

Hognose Snake, Eastern *Heterodon platyrhinos*

Leopard Frog, Northern *Rana pipiens*

Map Turtle *Graptemys geographica*

Massasauga, Eastern *Sistrurus catenatus catenatus*

Milk Snake, Eastern *Lampropeltis triangulum*

Mink Frog *Rana septentrionalis*

Mudpuppy *Necturus maculosus*

Newt, Central *Notophthalmus viridescens louisianensis*

Newt, Red-spotted *Notophthalmus viridescens viridescens*

Painted Turtle, Midland *Chrysemys picta marginata*

Painted Turtle, Western *Chrysemys picta belli*

Pickerel Frog *Rana palustris*

Queen Snake *Regina septemvittata*

Rat Snake, Black *Elaphe obsoleta obsoleta*

Rattlesnake, Timber *Crotalus horridus*

Redbelly Snake *Storeria occipitomaculata*

Ribbon Snake, Northern *Thamnophis sauritus septentrionalis*

Ringneck Snake, Northern *Diadophis punctatus edwardsi*

Salamander, Blue-spotted *Ambystoma laterale*

Salamander, Eastern Redback *Plethodon cinereus*

Salamander, Four-toed *Hemidactylium scutatum*

Salamander, Two-lined *Eurycea bislineata*

Salamander, Yellow-spotted *Ambystoma maculatum*

Salamander complex, Jefferson *Ambystoma* spp.

Skink, Five-lined *Eumeces fasciatus*

Smooth Green Snake, Eastern *Opheodrys vernalis vernalis*

Snapping Turtle, Common *Chelydra serpentina*

Spiny Softshell *Trionyx spiniferus*

Spotted Turtle *Clemmys guttata*

Spring Peeper *Hyla crucifer*

Stinkpot *Sternotherus odoratus*

Toad, American *Bufo americanus*

Toad, Fowler's *Bufo woodhousei fowleri*

Treefrog, Gray *Hyla versicolor*

Water Snake, Lake Erie *Nerodia sipedon insularum*

Water Snake, Northern *Nerodia sipedon sipedon*

Wood Frog *Rana sylvatica*

Wood Turtle *Clemmys insculpta*

Fish

Bass, Largemouth *Micropterus salmoides*

Bass, Smallmouth *Micropterus dolomieu*

Bowfin *Amia calva*

Bullhead, Brown *Ameirus nebulosus*

Carp *Cyprinus carpio*

Char, Arctic *Salvelinus alpinus*

Chub, River *Nocomis micropogon*

Chub, Silver *Macrhybopsis storeriana*

Chubsucker, Lake *Erimyzon sucetta*

Cisco *Coregonus artedi*

Cisco, Blackfin *Coregonus nigripinnis*

Dace, Finescale *Phoxinus neogaeus*

Dace, Redside *Clinostomus elongatus*

Darter, Blackside *Percina maculata*

Darter, Eastern Sand *Ammocrypta pellucida*

Darter, Fantail *Etheostoma flabellare*

Darter, Least *Etheostoma microperca*

Darter, River *Percina shumardi*

Gar, Spotted *Lepisosteus oculatus*

Goldeye *Hiodon alosoides*

Killifish, Banded *Fundulus diaphanus*

Lamprey, American Brook *Lampetra appendix*

Lamprey, Sea *Petromyzon marinus*

Madtom, Brindled *Noturus miurus*

Minnow, Pugnose *Opsopoeodus emiliae*

Mooneye *Hiodon tergisus*

Mudminnow, Central *Umbra limi*

Muskellunge *Esox masquinongy*

Perch, Yellow *Perca flavescens*

Pickerel, Grass *Esox americanus vermiculatus*

Pike, Northern *Esox lucius*

Pumpkinseed *Lepomis gibbosus*

Redhorse, Black *Moxostoma duquesnei*

Redhorse, Greater *Moxostoma valenciennesi*

Redhorse, Shorthead *Moxostoma macrolepidotum*

Salmon, Atlantic *Salmo salar*

Salmon, Chinook *Oncorhynchus tshawytscha*

Salmon, Coho *Oncorhynchus kisutch*

Salmon, Pink *Oncorhynchus gorbuscha*

Shiner, Emerald *Notropis atherinoides*

Shiner, Golden *Notemigonus crysoleucas*

Shiner, Pugnose *Notropis anogenus*

Stickleback, Brook *Culaea inconstans*

Stickleback, Ninespine *Pungitius pungitius*

Sturgeon, Lake *Acipenser fulvescens*

Sucker, Longnose *Catostomus catostomus*

Sucker, White *Catostomus commersoni*

Sunfish, Orange-spotted *Lepomis humilis*

Trout, Brook *Salvelinus fontinalis*

Trout, Brown *Salmo trutta*

Trout, Lake *Salvelinus namaycush*

Trout, Rainbow *Oncorhynchus mykiss*

Walleye *Stizostedion vitreum vitreum*

Whitefish, Lake *Coregonus clupeaformis*

Insects

Admiral, Red *Vanessa atalanta*

Angle Wing, Satyr *Polygonia satyrus*

Arctic, Chryxus *Oeneis chryxus*

Arctic, Macoun's *Oeneis macounii*

Arctic, Melissa *Oeneis melissa*

Baltimore, The *Euphydryas phaeton*

Blue, Arctic *Agriades rustica*

Blue, Karner *Lycaeides melissa samuelis*

Blue, Saepiolus *Plebejus saepiolus*

Blue, Silvery *Glaucopsyche lygdamus*

Buckeye, The *Junonia coenia*

Budworm, Spruce *Choristoneura fumiferana*

Checkerspot, Silvery *Charidryas nycteis*

Comma, Hoary *Polygonia gracilis*

Copper, Purplish *Epidemia helloides*

Dragonfly, Fletcher's *Williamsonia fletcheri*

Dusky Wing, Horace's *Erynnis horatius*

Dusky Wing, Mottled *Erynnis martialis*

Dusky Wing, Persius *Erynnis persius*

Dusky Wing, Wild Indigo *Erynnis baptisiae*

Elfin, Western Pine *Incisalia eryphon*

Fritillary, Bog *Clossiana eunomia*

Fritillary, Great Spangled *Speyeria cybele*

Glassy Wing, Little *Pompeius verna*

Hackberry Butterfly *Asterocampa celtis*

Hairstreak, Early *Erora laeta*

Harvester, The *Feniseca tarquinius*

Katydid, Angular-winged *Microcentrum retinerve*

Katydid, Northern True
  Pterophylla camellifolia
Marblewing, Olympia *Euchloe
  olympia*
Monarch *Danaus plexippus*
Moth, Cecropia *Hyalophora cecro-
  pia*
Moth, Gypsy *Lymantria dispar*
Moth, Luna *Actias luna*
Mulberry Wing *Poanes massasoit*
painted lady *Vanessa* sp.
Mourning Cloak *Nymphalis
  antiopa*
Purple, Banded *Basilarchia arthe-
  mis arthemis*
Purple, Red Spotted *Basilarchia
  arthemis astyanax*
Skipper, Delaware *Atrytone
  logan*
Skipper, Dusted *Atrytonopsis
  hianna*
Skipper, Fiery *Hylephila phyleus*
Skipper, Leonardus *Hesperia
  leonardus*
Skipper, Pepper and Salt *Ambly-
  scirtes hegon*
Skipper, Two Spotted *Euphyes
  bimacula*
Snout Butterfly *Libytheana bach-
  manii*
Sulphur, Common *Colias philodice*
Sulphur, Giant *Colias gigantea*
Sulphur, Little *Eurema lisa*
Sulphur, Pelidne *Colias pelidne*
Sulphur, Pink Edged *Colias inte-
  rior*
Swallowtail, Black *Papilio poly-
  xenes*
Swallowtail, Giant *Heraclides
  cresphontes*

Swallowtail, Old World *Papilio
  machaon*
Swallowtail, Pipe Vine *Battus
  philenor*
Swallowtail, Spicebush *Pterourus
  troilus*
Swallowtail, Tiger *Pterourus glau-
  cus*

Other Invertebrates

Crayfish, Meadow *Cambarus dio-
  genes*
Mussel, Zebra *Dreissena polymor-
  pha*
Saxicave, Arctic (clam) *Hiatella
  arctica*

Birds

Avocet, American *Recurvirostra
  americana*

Bittern, American *Botaurus lenti-
  ginosus*
Bittern, Least *Ixobrychus exilus*
Blackbird, Brewer's *Euphagus
  cyanocephalus*
Blackbird, Red-winged *Agelaius
  phoeniceus*
Blackbird, Rusty *Euphagus
  carolinus*
Blackbird, Yellow-headed *Xan-
  thocephalus xanthocephalus*
Bluebird, Eastern *Sialia sialis*
Bobolink *Dolichonyx oryzivorus*
Bobwhite, Northern *Colinus
  virginianus*
Brant *Branta bernicla*
Bufflehead *Bucephala albeola*

Bunting, Indigo *Passerina cyanea*

Bunting, Snow *Plectrophenax nivalis*

Canvasback *Aythya valisineria*

Cardinal, Northern *Cardinalis cardinalis*

Chat, Yellow-breasted *Icteria virens*

Chickadee, Boreal *Parus hudsonicus*

Chuck-will's-widow *Caprimulgus carolinensis*

Coot, American *Fulica americana*

Cormorant, Double-crested *Phalacrocorax auritus*

Cowbird, Brown-headed *Molothrus ater*

Crane, Sandhill *Grus canadensis*

Creeper, Brown *Certhia americana*

Crossbill, Red *Loxia curvirostra*

Crossbill, White-winged *Loxia leucoptera*

Crow, American *Corvus brachyrhynchos*

Cuckoo, Black-billed *Coccyzus erythropthalmus*

Cuckoo, Yellow-billed *Coccyzus americanus*

Duck, American Black *Anas rubripes*

Duck, Harlequin *Histrionicus histrionicus*

Duck, Ring-necked *Aythya collaris*

Duck, Ruddy *Oxyura jamaicensis*

Duck, Wood *Aix sponsa*

Dunlin *Calidris alpina*

Eagle, Bald *Haliaeetus leucocephalus*

Eagle, Golden *Aquila chrysaetos*

Egret, Great *Casmerodius albus*

Eider, Common *Somateria mollissima*

Eider, King *Somateria spectabilis*

Falcon, Peregrine *Falco peregrinus*

Finch, House *Carpodacus mexicanus*

Finch, Purple *Carpodacus purpureus*

Flycatcher, Acadian *Empidonax virescens*

Flycatcher, Alder *Empidonax alnorum*

Flycatcher, Great Crested *Myiarchus crinitus*

Flycatcher, Least *Empidonax minimus*

Flycatcher, Olive-sided *Contopus borealis*

Flycatcher, Willow *Empidonax traillii*

Flycatcher, Yellow-bellied *Empidonax flaviventris*

Gadwall *Anas strepera*

Gnatcatcher, Blue-gray *Polioptila caerulea*

Godwit, Hudsonian *Limosa haemastica*

Godwit, Marbled *Limosa fedoa*

Golden-Plover, American *Pluvialis dominica*

Goldeneye, Barrow's *Bucephala islandica*

Goldeneye, Common *Bucephala clangula*

Goldfinch, American *Carduelis tristis*

Goose, Canada *Branta canadensis*

Goose, Greater White-fronted *Anser albifrons*

Goose, Snow *Chen caerulescens*

Goshawk, Northern *Accipiter gentilis*

Grebe, Horned *Podiceps auritus*

Grebe, Pied-billed *Podilymbus podiceps*

Grebe, Red-necked *Podiceps grisegena*

Grosbeak, Evening *Coccothraustes vespertinus*

Grosbeak, Pine *Pinicola enucleator*

Grosbeak, Rose-breasted *Pheucticus ludovicianus*

Grouse, Ruffed *Bonasa umbellus*

Grouse, Sharp-tailed *Tympanuchus phasianellus*

Grouse, Spruce *Dendragapus canadensis*

Guillemot, Black *Cepphus grylle*

Gull, Bonaparte's *Larus philadelphia*

Gull, Common Black-headed *Larus ridibundus*

Gull, Franklin's *Larus pipixcan*

Gull, Glaucous *Larus hyperboreus*

Gull, Great Black-backed *Larus marinus*

Gull, Herring *Larus argentatus*

Gull, Iceland *Larus glaucoides*

Gull, Laughing *Larus atricilla*

Gull, Lesser Black-backed *Larus fuscus*

Gull, Little *Larus minutus*

Gull, Ring-billed *Larus delawarensis*

Gull, Sabine's *Xema sabina*

Gull, Thayer's *Larus thayeri*

Gyrfalcon *Falco rusticolus*

Harrier, Northern *Circus cyaneus*

Hawk, Broad-winged *Buteo platypterus*

Hawk, Cooper's *Accipiter cooperii*

Hawk, Red-shouldered *Buteo lineatus*

Hawk, Red-tailed *Buteo jamaicensis*

Hawk, Rough-legged *Buteo lagopus*

Hawk, Sharp-shinned *Accipiter striatus*

Heron, Great Blue *Ardea herodias*

Heron, Green *Butorides striatus*

Hummingbird, Ruby-throated *Archilochus colubris*

Jaeger, Parasitic *Stercorarius parasiticus*

Jaeger, Pomarine *Stercorarius pomarinus*

Jay, Blue *Cyanocitta cristata*

Jay, Gray *Perisoreus canadensis*

Junco, Dark-eyed *Junco hyemalis*

Kestrel, American *Falco sparverius*

Killdeer *Charadrius vociferus*

Kingbird, Eastern *Tyrannus tyrannus*

Kingbird, Western *Tyrannus verticalis*

Kingfisher, Belted *Ceryle alcyon*

Kinglet, Golden-crowned *Regulus satrapa*

Kinglet, Ruby-crowned *Regulus calendula*
Kittiwake, Black-legged *Rissa tridactyla*
Knot, Red *Calidris canutus*

Lark, Horned *Eremophila alpestris*
Longspur, Lapland *Calcarius lapponicus*
Longspur, Smith's *Calcarius pictus*
Loon, Common *Gavia immer*
Loon, Pacific *Gavia pacifica*
Loon, Red-throated *Gavia stellata*

Magpie, Black-billed *Pica pica*
Mallard *Anas platyrhynchos*
Meadowlark, Eastern *Sturnella magna*
Meadowlark, Western *Sturnella neglecta*
Merganser, Common *Mergus merganser*
Merganser, Hooded *Lophodytes cucullatus*
Merganser, Red-breasted *Mergus serrator*
Merlin *Falco columbarius*
Mockingbird, Northern *Mimus polyglottos*
Moorhen, Common *Gallinula chloropus*

Night-Heron, Black-crowned *Nycticorax nycticorax*
Nuthatch, Red-breasted *Sitta canadensis*
Nuthatch, White-breasted *Sitta carolinensis*

Oldsquaw *Clangula hyemalis*
Oriole, Northern *Icterus galbula*
Oriole, Orchard *Icterus spurius*
Osprey *Pandion haliaetus*
Ovenbird *Seiurus aurocapillus*
Owl, Barred *Strix varia*
Owl, Great Gray *Strix nebulosa*
Owl, Great Horned *Bubo virginianus*
Owl, Long-eared *Asio otus*
Owl, Northern Hawk *Surnia ulula*
Owl, Northern Saw-whet *Aegolius acadicus*
Owl, Short-eared *Asio flammeus*
Owl, Snowy *Nyctea scandiaca*

Partridge, Gray *Perdix perdix*
Parula, Northern *Parula americana*
Pelican, American White *Pelecanus erythrorhynchos*
Phalarope, Red *Phalaropus fulicaria*
Phalarope, Red-necked *Phalaropus lobatus*
Phalarope, Wilson's *Phalaropus tricolor*
Pheasant, Ring-necked *Phasianus colchicus*
Phoebe, Eastern *Sayornis phoebe*
Pigeon, Passenger *Ectopistes migratorius*
Pintail, Northern *Anas acuta*
Pipit, American *Anthus rubescens*
Plover, Black-bellied *Pluvialis squatarola*
Plover, Piping *Charadrius melodus*
Ptarmigan, Willow *Lagopus lagopus*

Rail, King *Rallus elegans*
Rail, Virginia *Rallus limicola*
Rail, Yellow *Coturnicops noveboracensis*
Raven, Common *Corvus corax*
Redhead *Aythya americana*
Redpoll, Common *Carduelis flammea*
Redstart, American *Setophaga ruticilla*
Robin, American *Turdus migratorius*

Sandpiper, Buff-breasted *Tryngites subruficollis*
Sandpiper, Purple *Calidris maritima*
Sandpiper, Solitary *Tringa solitaria*
Sandpiper, Spotted *Actitis macularia*
Sandpiper, Stilt *Calidris himantopus*
Sandpiper, Upland *Bartramia longicauda*
Sapsucker, Yellow-bellied *Sphyrapicus varius*
Scaup, Greater *Aythya marila*
Scaup, Lesser *Aythya affinis*
Scoter, Black *Melanitta nigra*
Scoter, Surf *Melanitta perspicillata*
Scoter, White-winged *Melanitta fusca*
Screech-Owl, Eastern *Otus asio*
Shoveler, Northern *Anas clypeata*
Shrike, Loggerhead *Lanius ludovicianus*
Shrike, Northern *Lanius excubitor*
Siskin, Pine *Carduelis pinus*

Snipe, Common *Gallinago gallinago*
Sora *Porzana carolina*
Sparrow, Clay-colored *Spizella pallida*
Sparrow, Field *Spizella pusilla*
Sparrow, Grasshopper *Ammodramus savannarum*
Sparrow, LeConte's *Ammodramus leconteii*
Sparrow, Lincoln's *Melospiza lincolnii*
Sparrow, Savannah *Passerculus sandwichensis*
Sparrow, Song *Melospiza melodia*
Sparrow, Swamp *Melospiza georgiana*
Sparrow, Vesper *Pooecetes gramineus*
Sparrow, White-crowned *Zonotrichia leucophyrs*
Sparrow, White-throated *Zonotrichia albicollis*
Starling, European *Sturnus vulgaris*
Swallow, Bank *Riparia riparia*
Swallow, Barn *Hirundo rustica*
Swallow, Cliff *Hirundo pyrrhonota*
Swallow, Northern Rough-winged *Stelgidopteryx serripennis*
Swallow, Tree *Tachycineta bicolor*
Swan, Trumpeter *Cygnus buccinator*
Swan, Tundra *Cygnus columbianus*
Swift, Chimney *Chaetura pelagica*

Tanager, Scarlet *Piranga olivacea*
Teal, Blue-winged *Anas discors*

Teal, Green-winged *Anas* crecca
Tern, Arctic *Sterna paradisaea*
Tern, Black *Chlidonias niger*
Tern, Caspian *Sterna caspia*
Tern, Common *Sterna hirundo*
Tern, Forster's *Sterna forsteri*
Thrasher, Brown *Toxostoma rufum*
Thrush, Gray-cheeked *Catharus minimus*
Thrush, Hermit *Catharus guttatus*
Thrush, Swainson's *Catharus ustulatus*
Thrush, Wood *Hylocichla mustelina*
Titmouse, Tufted *Parus bicolor*
Towhee, Rufous-sided *Pipilo erythrophthalmus*
Turkey, Wild *Meleagris gallopavo*
Turnstone, Ruddy *Arenaria interpres*

Veery *Catharus fuscescens*
Vireo, Red-eyed *Vireo olivaceus*
Vireo, Solitary *Vireo solitarius*
Vireo, Warbling *Vireo gilvus*
Vireo, White-eyed *Vireo griseus*
Vireo, Yellow-throated *Vireo flavifrons*
Vulture, Turkey *Cathartes aura*

Warbler, Bay-breasted *Dendroica castanea*
Warbler, Black-and-white *Mniotilta varia*
Warbler, Blackburnian *Dendroica fusca*
Warbler, Blackpoll *Dendroica striata*
Warbler, Black-throated Blue *Dendroica caerulescens*

Warbler, Black-throated Green *Dendroica virens*
Warbler, Blue-winged *Vermivora pinus*
Warbler, Canada *Wilsonia canadensis*
Warbler, Cape May *Dendroica tigrina*
Warbler, Cerulean *Dendroica cerulea*
Warbler, Chestnut-sided *Dendroica pensylvanica*
Warbler, Connecticut *Oporornis agilis*
Warbler, Golden-winged *Vermivora chrysoptera*
Warbler, Hooded *Wilsonia citrina*
Warbler, Magnolia *Dendroica magnolia*
Warbler, Mourning *Oporornis philadephia*
Warbler, Nashville *Vermivora ruficapilla*
Warbler, Palm *Dendroica palmarum*
Warbler, Pine *Dendroica pinus*
Warbler, Prairie *Dendroica discolor*
Warbler, Prothonotary *Protonotaria citrea*
Warbler, Tennessee *Vermivora peregrina*
Warbler, Wilson's *Wilsonia pusilla*
Warbler, Yellow *Dendroica petechia*
Warbler, Yellow-rumped *Dendroica coronata*
Waterthrush, Louisiana *Seiurus motacilla*
Waterthrush, Northern *Seiurus noveboracensis*

Waxwing, Bohemian *Bombycilla garrulus*

Waxwing, Cedar *Bombycilla cedrorum*

Whimbrel *Numenius phaeopus*

Whip-poor-will *Caprimulgus vociferus*

Wigeon, American *Anas americana*

Wigeon, Eurasian *Anas penelope*

Woodcock, American *Scolopax minor*

Woodpecker, Black-backed *Picoides arcticus*

Woodpecker, Downy *Picoides pubescens*

Woodpecker, Hairy *Picoides villosus*

Woodpecker, Pileated *Dryocopus pileatus*

Woodpecker, Red-bellied *Melanerpes carolinus*

Woodpecker, Red-headed *Melanerpes erythrocephalus*

Woodpecker, Three-toed *Picoides tridactylus*

Wood-Pewee, Eastern *Contopus virens*

Wren, Carolina *Thryothorus ludovicianus*

Wren, Marsh *Cistothorus palustris*

Wren, Sedge *Cistothorus platensis*

Wren, Winter *Troglodytes troglodytes*

Yellowlegs, Greater *Tringa melanoleuca*

Yellowlegs, Lesser *Tringa flavipes*

Yellowthroat, Common *Geothlypis trichas*

Index of Sites